Industrial Policy of Japan

D1261982

Industrial Policy of Japan

Edited by

Ryutaro Komiya

Masahiro Okuno   Kotaro Suzumura

Faculty of Economics
University of Tokyo
Bunkyo-ku
Tokyo, Japan

Institute of Economic Research
Hitotsubashi University
Kunitachi
Tokyo, Japan

Translated under the supervision of Kazuo Sato

ACADEMIC PRESS, INC.
Harcourt Brace Jovanovich, Publishers
Tokyo   San Diego   New York   Berkeley
Boston   London   Sydney   Toronto

ACADEMIC PRESS JAPAN, INC.
Ichibancho Central Building, 22-1 Ichibancho
Chiyoda-ku, Tokyo 102, Japan

United States Edition published by
ACADEMIC PRESS, INC.
1250 Sixth Avenue, San Diego, California 92101

United Kingdom Edition published by
ACADEMIC PRESS INC. (LONDON) LTD.
24-28 Oval Road, London NW1 7DX

Library of Congress Cataloging-in-Publication Data

Industrial policy of Japan.

Includes index.
1. Industry and state—Japan.   I. Komiya, Ryūtarō,
Date.
HD3616.J331816   1987   338.952   87-1409
ISBN 0-12-418650-5   (U.S.: alk. paper))
ISBN 0-12-418651-3   (paperback)

PRINTED IN THE UNITED STATES OF AMERICA
88 89 90 91   9 8 7 6 5 4 3 2 1

Contents

    Policies   299
V. Conclusion   302

12. The Automotive Industry
    Hiromichi Mutoh

    I. Introduction   307
    II. The Development of Auto Industry Policies   310
    III. The Evaluation of the Government's Performance   320
    IV. Conclusion   327

13. The Computer Industry
    Koji Shinjo

    I. Introduction   333
    II. The Development and Current Status of the Computer
        Industry   335
    III. The Computer Industry: Protection and Promotion
        Policies   341
    IV. Evaluation of Promotion Policies for the Computer
        Industry   354

PART V. INDUSTRIAL ADJUSTMENT POLICY

14. Trade and Adjustment Assistance
    Sueo Sekiguchi and Toshihiro Horiuchi

    I. Introduction   369
    II. The Content of Adjustment Assistance Policy   370
    III. The Japanese Adjustment Assistance Policies   372
    IV. Conclusion   388

15. The Textile Industry
    Ippei Yamazawa

    I. Introduction   395
    II. The Japanese Textile Industry—An Overview   397
    III. Export Controls and Domestic Adjustment Assistance   403
    IV. Import Policy and Competitive Pressures   412
    V. Conclusion   419

Preface

This volume is the result of a joint research project undertaken over a two-year period to investigate and analyze Japanese industrial policy from an economic perspective and to provide a comprehensive, quantitative evaluation of its significance and impact. The project was initiated in response to a paucity of scholarly economic research on Japanese industrial policy and a belief that collaboration on such a topic, bringing together researchers from a variety of related disciplines, would be productive.

For a number of reasons, Japanese industrial policy has captured the attention of scholars and policy-makers in Western countries. Sluggish productivity, large current account imbalances with Japan in advanced industrialized economies, and economic interventionist policies that have arisen as a result of these factors have contributed to this interest. Past research on the topic by non-Japanese scholars, however, has been conducted predominantly from a political or historical perspective. Serious economic studies of Japan's industrial policy are almost nonexistent. Japan is also regarded by developing countries, especially Asian countries, as a source of valuable data on the role of industrial policy in connection with Japan's rapid economic growth in the pre- as well as postwar period. As such, it has received widespread attention from these countries. In view of this existing lack of economic research on industrial policy in postwar Japan, we felt that providing a standard framework for the economic analysis of industrial policy is an important task for Japanese economists. With this situation as the backdrop, this project was organized with the following four objectives. The first objective was to formulate a standard "economic–theoretical" framework for the analysis of industrial policy by making use of recent developments in applied microeconomics and econometrics. Previous work in the area has consisted mainly of historical and descriptive presentations. This objective called for bringing together researchers, from the field of industrial organization, who traditionally have studied industrial policy, and those from the fields of applied microeconomic theory, international economics, welfare economics, and public economics.

The second objective was to examine the changing features of industrial policy over time by dividing the postwar period into three phases corresponding to the decades of the 1950s, the 1960s, and the 1970s and thereafter.

The third objective was to analyze and evaluate policy interventions in each of those sectors which was considered as a priority sector in one period or another from the point of view of Japan's industrial policy, such as basic industrial materials, high technology industries, and declining industries.

The fourth objective of this research was to analyze and evaluate various policies that tried to intervene in industrial organization of various sectors.

The papers presented in this volume were revised and coordinated by incorporating criticisms and advice from discussants and other participants in three conferences held during the joint research project. A special program committee coordinated the original manuscripts for consistency. Although the authors have final responsibility for their respective chapters, the results are consistent with the original plan of producing a standard reference on Japanese industrial policy under a joint research program.

The introductory chapter presents the concept of "industrial policy" and its economic significance, throws light on the doctrine underlying policies followed during respective time periods, surveys theories, and explains the process involved in making and implementing policy decisions. Part I analyzes and evaluates the objectives of Japanese industrial policy, the major policy measures, and the relevant industries in each of the three phases of the postwar Japanese economy. Part II then provides a historical overview and quantitative evaluation of the major tools of the industrial policy: trade (tariffs and quotas) and direct investment policies, taxation system and fiscal investments and loans policy, and technology policy (research and development policy and technology import policy). Part III develops an analysis of industrial policy from the vantage point of economic theory and identifies the impact of industrial policies on national economic welfare, the conditions under which economic welfare improves, and the policy measures that would be most effective.

In Parts IV through VI, various industrial policies are analyzed by classifying them into three major groups according to their objectives and adopted measures. Case studies provide the relevant data for each group. In Part IV the content and impact of industrial policies to promote development of a particular industry are analyzed in the case of the iron and steel, automobile, and computer industries, the most representative priority industries where such policies for industrial development were adopted in postwar Japan. Part V focuses attention on the adjustment assistance policies undertaken in industries that began to decline as a result of the shifting international trade environment, and investigates the significance of policy interventions and the propriety of the policy measures adopted. The textile, shipbuilding, and aluminum refining industries, which were the major areas for adjustment assistance policies in postwar Japan, are examined in detail as case studies. Part VI discusses the policy interventions related to the organization of individual industries, another major aspect of industrial policy, and investigates the economic impact of direct intervention by the policy authorities in pricing, production, investment, mergers, and industrial restructuring. Part VI also discusses policies directed at small- and medium-sized enterprises, and those related to subcontracting. The last chapter of the volume includes general comments presented at the final conference and a summary of the major findings.

This joint research project was conducted as part of the research activities of the Tokyo Center for Economic Research (TCER) and was funded by the Kikawada Foundation. The TCER has been conducting its annual conference series in which researchers from both within and without the Center participate. The first such conference was held in January 1963. This conference series is known as the "Zushi Conference" as it is held in Zushi city in Kanagawa prefecture. In 1982 plans were initiated to hold these conferences on unified themes and publish the proceedings. The theme of the present book, "Japanese Industrial Policy," was the first selected topic.

As pointed out earlier, this joint research project developed a unified and deeper understanding of Japanese industrial policy by holding discussions and taking note of critical comments from practitioners and researchers having a keen interest in industrial policy. Information and ideas on the progress of the research were exchanged at three conferences (the 21st Zushi Conference, held April 10–12, 1983, a mini-conference held on August 11–12, 1983, and the 22nd Zushi Conference, held on January 6–8, 1984). We take this opportunity to thank all the Conference participants for their incisive comments and generous advice.

Acknowledgments

This book is the result of an interuniversity project sponsored by the Tokyo Center for Economic Research and funded by the Kikawada Foundation. The Foundation's financial assistance was extremely important in the facilitation of this project, which incorporated the work of many researchers over a fairly long period of time. We express our deepest gratitude to the foundation for its generosity and understanding.

In preparing the original Japanese edition, which was published by the University of Tokyo Press in December 1984, Motoshige Itoh, Masu Uekusa, and Naoyuki Yoshino not only contributed greatly to implementing the project's conference plans, but also improved this volume by acting as editors for some of the papers. Kazuharu Kiyono was an enormous help in preparing the proceedings and index of the Japanese volume. The editors are deeply indebted to these people.

Finally, the editors wish to thank Shumpei Takemori and Yasuto Enomoto for taking minutes of the conferences, Nanae Imai and Yoko Maiwa for sorting out the voluminous manuscripts and preparing the index, and Reiko Ohse and Hiroshi Sakumoto of the University of Tokyo Press for a meticulous job in preparing this book.

Michael Smitka of Yale University and Anil Khosla of Hitotsubashi University, graduate students in economics, undertook the arduous task of translating the Japanese edition into English. Chapter assignments were: Smitka—1, 2, 3, 4, 9, 10, 11, 12, 13, 18, 20, and 21; Khosla—Preface, 5, 6, 7, 8, 14, 15, 16, 17, and 19. Hideki Konishi, Yosuke Okada, Shinsuke Kanbe, Etsuro Shioji, and Susumu Imai (graduate students at the University of Tokyo), and Ms. Nanae Imai kindly helped in preparing the index for the English edition. Translations were supervised by Kazuo Sato, the principal editor of the English edition. The translation project was financially supported by a grant generously provided by the Kikawada Foundation, to which the editors express their deep gratitude.

CHAPTER 1

Introduction

Faculty of Economics
University of Tokyo
Tokyo, Japan

I. Overview

It is well known that since World War II, and particularly during the 1950s and 1960s, the Japanese government devised a complicated system of policies to promote industrial development and cooperated closely for this purpose with private firms. It is not generally well understood, however, exactly how Japanese industrial policy was carried out or through what process policy decisions were made. While a great number of fragmentary reports appeared at the time in newspapers and elsewhere, an overall picture of the system of industrial policy was seldom clearly presented to the public. In the late 1970s, a fair number of perceptive and informative books and studies on the economic effects of Japanese industrial policy were published.[1] But it is difficult to say that to date there has been adequate economic analysis of the overall structure of these policies or of their impact on or implications for the Japanese economy as a whole.[2]

From the mid-1970s, with the remarkable success of Japanese industry, the content of industrial policy has changed greatly, while at the same time interest abroad in Japanese industrial policy has heightened. From the United States and Europe to the developing countries (especially in East Asia, including China), there is strong interest in the lessons to be learned from postwar Japanese industrial policy. Until now, however, studies by foreign scholars have been limited to either a description of policy measures or have focused more on political aspects than on economic analysis. In addition, there has been a general trend

INDUSTRIAL POLICY OF JAPAN   **1**

© Copyright 1988 by Academic Press Japan, Inc.
All rights of reproduction in any form reserved.

abroad to overestimate the extent and effectiveness of Japanese industrial policy.

In light of the above, Japanese economists are under a heavy responsibility to set forth a theoretical framework for the economic analysis of industrial policy in general, and to then apply this framework to elucidate the content, effectiveness, and overall impact of industrial policy on the Japanese economy. Toward this end, in 1982, we organized a two-year project to study Japanese industrial policy. This book is an outgrowth of that study. The way in which the project was organized is set forth in the Preface, so in this chapter a number of problems will be taken up that are general to industrial policy or to the studies in the remainder of the book. In subsequent sections I will treat (1) the definition of industrial policy, (2) the relevance of industrial policy from an economic perspective, (3) the leitmotiv, or dominant policy stances, and their tie to actual industrial policy during various postwar periods, (4) the concept of excess competition, which has been a common theme in looking at the organization of a particular industry among both government officials and business managers throughout the period, and (5) the process of formulating industrial policy.

II. What Is Industrial Policy?

The term "industrial policy" was until recently seldom used in English, and while found somewhat more often in Continental Europe, was not overly familiar even there. It is safe to say that the term is also of relatively recent vintage in Japan. There is today an Industrial Policy Bureau within the Ministry of International Trade and Industry (MITI), but even within MITI the term was not widely used until around 1970.[3] Prior to that time, various facets of industrial policy were discussed in terms of industrial rationalization, the rationalization of firms, industrial structure and its modernization, a new industrial system, industrial reorganization, and the like.

In the past I defined industrial policy as

> government policies such that, if they had not been adopted, there would have been a different allocation of resources among industries or a different level of some aspect of economic activity of the constituent firms of an industry. In other words, industrial policy increases production, investment, research and development, modernization or restructuring in some industry or industries, and decreases them in other industries. Protective tariffs and excise taxes on luxuries are "classical" examples of policies under this definition.[4]

I now feel that this definition needs to be broadened and amplified.

When examined logically from the standpoint of economic theory, several points can be made concerning what is labeled in the press and in government circles as industrial policy. First, the "industry" of industrial policy is in most cases assumed to be manufacturing and hence does not include agriculture, construction, services,[5] or transportation. Electric power and other energy-related sectors are under the purview of MITI, however, and thus are commonly included as objects of industrial policy. It is normally unclear whether mining is to be considered a targeted industry.[6] Next, if we look at the "policies" of industrial policy, we can group their content as (1) policies that affect the allocation of resources to industry, including (a) items that affect the infrastructure of industry in general, such as the provision of industrial sites, roads and ports, industrial water supplies, and electric power,[7] and (b) items that affect interindustry resource allocation; or (2) policies that affect industrial organization, including (a) items aimed at regulating the internal organization of particular industries, such as industrial restructuring, consolidation of firms, output restrictions, and the adjustment of output and investment, and (b) items affecting crossindustry organization, such as small and medium enterprise measures. Of these groupings, (1b) is what would be thought of as industrial policy in the narrow sense of my original definition, while the guiding principle of (2a) in postwar Japan was the prevention and elimination of "excess" competition (leaving aside for the time being what is implied by this term). I cannot find a clear guiding principle behind small and medium enterprise policy, but my strong impression is that it consists of *ad hoc* measures of varying content adopted under the political pressures faced in a parliamentary democracy, without any apparent ideal or theoretical basis.[8]

III. The Theoretical Case for Industrial Policy

Current industrial policies are directed toward various goals, many of which are noneconomic. The classification of what constitutes economic and what constitutes noneconomic is inevitably in part subjective. The term "economic" will be used in a narrow sense henceforth. Thus it will be held that, for example, local industrial-promotion measures aimed at regional development, measures to restrain the consumption of alcohol and luxury goods, and measures designed to increase the self-sufficiency of certain goods for national security reasons are all noneconomic. Such noneconomic policies are obviously quite wide ranging. The focus of this book will be on policies undertaken for narrowly economic reasons. In addition to the above noneconomic policies, policies aimed at redistributing income or shifting population among regions will not be directly examined.[9]

In the following subsections, I will briefly discuss the theoretical underpinnings of industrial policy and examine postwar debates and practices, limiting myself to policies that are undertaken for reasons specific to conditions in particular industries. I thus will concentrate on policies designed to affect the allocation of resources among industries.

A. Theoretical Basis

If we confine our attention to those policies aimed at intervening in interindustry resource allocation, from the standpoint of economic theory, we can define the content of industrial policy to be those policies that fall under areas (1a) and (1b) above, which are interventions to cope with failures in the market, or price system, that affect resource allocation. Subject to certain conditions, the market, that is, the price mechanism, has proven capable of playing a very substantial role in the allocation of resources; nevertheless, it fails under certain conditions or in the face of certain types of problems, leading to a less-than-optimal allocation of resources. I believe the central function of industrial policy (narrowly defined) is to prevent possible market failures or to compensate for them once they occur.[10]

While it may be necessary to use industrial policy in the face of such market failures, four problems must be considered.

1. What sort of conditions will be recognized as constituting market failures?

2. What sort of policy measures are appropriate in response to the various types of market failure?

3. While it is true that markets may fail, it also is true that policy measures may fail. How are policy failures to be dealt with?

4. In most cases, industrial policy measures incur costs, including budgetary outlays, and are also accompanied by side effects. These cannot in practice be ignored, thus the policy benefits and the various costs must be weighed. How is this to be done? It certainly cannot be said that the government should always intervene whenever there is a market failure!

All of these are difficult problems, and there is much room for divergence of opinion on each of these points, even among informed and disinterested observers. In spite of the problems involved, discussing industrial policy from the perspective of market failures enables the use of terms familiar to economic analysis, such as the presence of economies of scale and externalities, the elimination of monopoly, the criteria for promoting infant industries, the promotion of research and development and technical change, the building of infrastructure, the handling of uncertainties in the course of economic development, and the regulation or limitation of pollution.

In the postwar period, however, the officials who were responsible for industrial policy in Japan, along with a group of academic economists who were close to them, did not accept the basic approach to industrial policy outlined above, at least in public pronouncements. Thus they refused to examine industrial policy in terms of the concepts of economics. Instead they argued that Japan, as a country with little land, few natural resources, and a large population, obviously had to have an industrial policy, or similarly, that to catch up with the industrialized nations or to improve the international competitiveness of domestic industry required industrial policy.

In contrast, from the perspective of economic theory, differing resource endowments or being a latecomer or undergoing reconstruction from war does not in itself constitute a market failure; witness the case of post-WWII West Germany in this regard. As is clear from the cases of Hong Kong and Singapore, with little land and dense populations it may be better to rely on the operation of the price mechanism, which may in fact lead to faster industrialization. I therefore do not think that such items in themselves provide a case for policy intervention.

In any event, until about the mid-1970s, it was hard to have a dialogue among scholars and policymakers about industrial policy, while even among academics and economic writers it took a long time for the common analytic base given here to be accepted. There was little in common between the arguments of those who worked from the standpoint of economic theory and those of the older generation who operated in the "prehistoric" period.[11]

B. Policy versus Practice

While there may have been a big gap between economic theory and the leitmotiv of industrial policy (or the ideology of the policymakers), at the same time there also was a large gap between the ideology of the policymakers and the slogans they used and the policies they actually implemented. To illustrate this, let me briefly summarize the rationale and practice of industrial policy, dividing the postwar era into three subperiods.

C. Reconstruction Era

During the period immediately after the war, the main tasks for industrial policy were held to be reconstruction and achieving economic independence. The leitmotiv of this era included (1) the priority production system, (2) the promotion of basic industries,[12] (3) the supplying of critical raw materials at low and stable prices, and (4) the encouragement of exports. These themes reflect the dregs of prewar and wartime economic thinking with its emphasis on wartime economic controls and planning, such as the materials mobilization program. The influence of the Soviet Gosplan model on prewar and wartime "progressive" bureaucrats and scholars seems to have been carried over into this period. There is room to doubt, however, the theoretical appropriateness of these policies or the way of thinking that they reflected, even given the economic chaos that then prevailed.[13] It would be an interesting project to investigate this question more deeply.

In any event, for a considerable period after the end of the war, even as late as 1962, examples of prewar and wartime economic thinking can be found. One such example is the Petroleum Industry Law with its presumption of pervasive direct government controls for the purpose of "providing for a stable and inexpensive supply of oil." Such a law reflected the strong influence of wartime government materials planning, though another contribution was the memory of the oil embargo placed on Japan by the United States and other countries, one of the causes of Japan's entry into World War II. There was no likelihood, however, of any particular market failures for petroleum products in the 1960s, and I do not believe there was any necessity for government intervention and controls.[14]

I do not think there was much of a gap between the ideology of industrial policy and the policies that were actually carried out during the early postwar period. In a system that incorporated more or less direct controls, industries thought "important" or "basic" were provided with subsidies and low-interest finance and were given priority in import allocations. The authority of the responsible government departments was strong at the time, and not a few businessmen were heard to mutter that they could not manage to get even simple things settled without trekking daily to the Ministry of International Trade and Industry.[15]

D. High-Growth Era

During the period of rapid economic growth, the ideology of the formulators of industrial policy was symbolized by the slogans "building heavy and chemical industry" and "improving the industrial structure." Within manufacturing, a "vision" was drawn up that proposed actively fostering industries that met the dual criteria of experiencing a rapid increase in productivity and producing goods with a high income elasticity of demand.[16] It is exactly this type of thinking that typified the prehistoric era I characterized above, for if goods are produced by an industry in which rapid productivity increases are occurring and for which the income elasticity of demand is high, then the industry will grow on its own. Hence there is no reason why, due to these two criteria, such an industry should be made a particular object for promotion.

It was during this period that a considerable gap developed between the policies that were actually implemented and the ideology or guiding principles (or at any rate the catch phrases) of the formulators of industrial policy. For example, government officials had no intention of promoting industries such as tourism, supermarkets, and fast-food restaurants, even though these industries satisfied their criteria.

I believe rather that in general industrial policy in Japan aimed to develop industries that government officials—with the backing of public opinion— felt Japan should have; criteria for what comprised an appropriate industrial structure were *ex post facto* rationalizations. After the war, the initial industries that policymakers or the general public felt Japan should have were iron and steel, shipbuilding, a merchant marine, machine industries in general, heavy electrical equipment, and chemicals. Later on they added the automotive industry, petrochemicals, nuclear power, and the like, and recently industries such as computers and semiconductors have been added. One might inquire why people wanted these industries in particular, but policymakers had to attach some sort of rationale, and often this was not easy to do. In sum, I believe that the government promoted exactly those industries that most Japanese felt the country had to have. Of such industries, about the only one to date that has not been firmly established in Japan is the aircraft industry.

To give a specific example, for the protection of shipping and shipbuilding, planned shipbuilding has been continued over many years for such stated reasons as rebuilding the merchant fleet, expanding fleet capacity, saving foreign exchange, improving the invisible trade account balance, and so on. In the late 1960s, I was pressed by those related to the shipping industry for an appropriate rationalization for planned shipbuilding at a time when the balance of payments was no longer in deficit but was instead showing running surpluses. Like the policymakers, these individuals were working on the assumption that such policies would be continued, and they were only concerned that it was proving difficult to come up with a rationale for the policies that would obtain public acceptance.

On the other hand, during the period of rapid growth and into the next period, quite a few new industries developed, many of which achieved remarkable success in exporting. Early on were the industries that produced such goods as sewing machines, cameras, bicycles, motorcycles, pianos, zippers, and transistor radios. From the middle of the 1960s on, the list included the manufacturers of color televisions, tape recorders, magnetic recording tape, audio equipment, fishing gear, watches and clocks, calculators, electric wire, machine tools, numerically controlled machine tools, textile machinery, agricultural machinery, insulators, communications equipment, ceramics, and robots. These industries developed without any dependence on industrial protection and promotion policies. The majority of the firms in these growth industries started from nothing after the war or at most were very small firms. They developed under their own power without any particular benefits from industrial policy measures. It would undoubtedly be the executives of these firms who would disagree with the most vehemence to the statement that industrial policy in Japan was extremely strong, systematic, and comprehensive. Given a chance to speak, they would proclaim that they had succeeded on their own, through tremendous labor in the face of great difficulties, and not because of government favors that in fact seldom came their way.

What, then, were the sort of industries that policymakers and public opinion believed were essential for Japan? This is a very difficult question, but my impression is that the industries that those who formulated policy wanted Japan very much to have and to which they devoted much effort in protecting and fostering were those that involved an element of national prestige. It seems that the desired industries were those that met the following two general requirements.

First, they had to be the industries, symbolic of industrial might, that had already been pursued by countries more advanced than Japan (modern states in the Meiji period to the early post-WWII years, advanced nations in the period of rapid growth, and technologically leading nations from the 1970s on.) The industries themselves were seen as ones that Japan could develop with a greater or lesser amount of effort (meaning protection and promotion). Second, these industries had to have a certain size, so that the theme of their development could garner people's attention, that is they had to have "news value" both domestically and internationally. Industries that met these two criteria gained the attention of policymakers as candidates worthy of protection and promotion policies.[17]

One could think of the following industries as meeting these two criteria: iron and steel, machinery, electric equipment, ocean transport, shipbuilding, air transport, petrochemicals, nuclear power, aircraft manufacturing, computers, integrated circuits, and the like. In contrast, many of the export industries listed above, which showed amazing development after the war, did not meet either of these requirements, regardless of whether they fulfilled the requirements of high income elasticity and rapid productivity growth (which are in themselves dubious as standards). The camera, bicycle, watch, tape recorder, and magnetic tape industries are good examples in that they did not have much attractiveness as objects for promotion and protection in terms of public appeal and consequently did not receive much emphasis.

During the period right after the war policymakers possessed a fair amount of leverage over industries and private firms through their power of approval of import licenses, foreign capital inflows, and technology import licenses; the use of Japan Development Bank loans; and the designation of special tax measures. During the rapid growth era the leverage of the government disappeared bit by bit, or at least its importance declined drastically, with the liberalization of trade and capital movements—direct investment, joint ventures with foreign firms, and technology imports. Thus despite wide coverage in the press and the pervasiveness of various catch phrases, throughout this period the reality of industrial policy was that intervention declined in importance and the price mechanism and the autonomous decisions of enterprises in the face of competition came to play the central role in allocating resources.

E. Since the Oil Crisis

As the 1970s unfolded, the interventionist and direct control coloration of the thinking of the formulators of industrial policy began to recede, and gradually a critical attitude toward policy excesses and a more positive view of the price mechanism became apparent. In this period, trade and direct foreign investment were liberalized, tariff and nontariff trade barriers were lowered, and the economies of the advanced nations became more tightly integrated. With this development, foreign criticism of the artificial protective policies of the Japanese government heightened. I thus feel that the gap between economic theory and bureaucratic ideology rapidly lessened.

But it still remains unclear what the thinking is behind the concept of rising knowledge-intensity put forth by the Industrial Structure Council. Will such knowledge-intensive and high-technology industries develop by themselves, or is policy intervention in the form of artificial protection really crucial? And if protection and promotion are required, through what policy tools can this actually be accomplished? Furthermore, fashion design, information-processing software, the advertising industry, and management consulting are knowledge-intensive industries, but it does not seem that the government feels it should be promoting them. They are not the kind of industries that either policymakers or the public think of as requiring artificial promotion.

In addition, during this period more and more industries have been turning to the government for "adjustment" aid. These industries are not limited to agriculture and mining, but include manufacturing industries in decline or suffering under comparative disadvantage in the face of high wage and energy costs or depressed markets for their goods on a worldwide basis. Examples include all types of textiles, nonferrous metal refining, and shipbuilding. In terms of the fiscal burden of industrial restructuring and protection from import competition, the relative weight of declining and internationally uncompetitive industries in industrial policy has been increasing since the high-growth period. The most prominent examples of industries in decline are coal mining, textiles, ocean transport and shipbuilding, nonferrous metals, and petrochemicals. I believe that the direct and indirect cost of backward-looking policies to support such industries has, since the high-growth era, exceeded the cost of resources devoted in a forward-looking sense to the development of new industries.[18]

IV. Excess Competition

In Japan, from the end of the war through today, one guiding principle for the formulators of industrial policy with respect to intraindustry organization has been the prevention of excess competition. Even now one finds in newspapers countless times the statement that a given measure is being used, or should be used, to prevent excess competition. But in terms of economic theory, most of the arguments put forward in debates on excess competition are unclear on the damage done and on the necessity for government intervention to prevent it. Hardly any participants in these debates have bothered to explain with any degree of clarity what they mean by excess competition. One of the few attempts to define excess competition is that of Yoshihiko Morozumi, who was a representative member of the excess competition group. According to Morozumi, " 'excess' competition [is competition] such that the losses to the national economy exceed the gains that arise from that competition."[19] But the use of "excess" is tautological and the meaning of "loss" or "gain" to the "national economy" is vague, so it cannot be said that this definition has much content.

It is sometimes claimed by economists who are critical of the idea that the "excessive" competition of J. S. Bain [1968] is relatively close to the bureaucrats' use of "excess" competition.[20] Briefly, Bain's use of the term refers to a condition in which, in an unconcentrated industry in which the majority of firms show very little profit or even operate at a loss, the transfer of productive resources (principally labor) to other uses and exit by constituent firms is not rapid, so that low profitability or losses continue for a long time.

This industrial organization concept differs, however, in two important aspects from the excess competition of Japanese practitioners. First, the Japanese term literally means "more than appropriate," and as symbolized by Morozumi's discussion of gains to the national economy, the normative sense of the term is dominant and reflects the user's value judgment that the condition referred to is not desirable. In contrast, Bain's excessive competition refers to an objective phenomenon for purposes of analysis, and does not reflect a value judgment. Furthermore, in spite of the strong value judgment reflected in the Japanese use of excess competition, the basis on which the judgment is based is never made clear. The lack of content of phrases such as "gains or losses to the national economy" is a characteristic trait of debates over excess competition.

Second, the term "excessive competition" in Bain's sense refers to a competitive, unconcentrated industry with a large number of firms, such as the numerous small coal mines of West Virginia in the United States or the "moonlighting" weaving sheds run as a self-employment sideline by many farmers in Japan. In Japan, however, the term "excess competition" has been used in conjunction with demands for the lessening of competition in all sorts of industries, not only in unconcentrated industries. Such industries include competitive oligopolies, concentrated tight oligopolies, industries in which market prices are unregulated, and publicly regulated industries, which in addition are virtual monopolies (such as domestic scheduled passenger airline service).

There is much dispute among academic economists on how to deal with the phenomenon of excess competition, and that includes the authors of the various chapters in this book. But it is safe to say that in general economists, especially those specializing in industrial organization, feel this concept has no analytic value. They thus tend to be dubious of, or hostile to, the demands that accompany the use of this term by government or business.

A. The *Genkyoku* System

In Japan there is a strong tendency for a *genkyoku*, the ministerial bureau, division, or section under whose jurisdiction a given industry falls, to want its industry to be orderly and organized and for there to be no disruptions of any kind.[21] I think that excess competition is tied to the Confucian concept of appropriate elder/younger relations. In other words, there seems to be a tendency for the government officials in charge of an industry to feel that the ideal situation is one in which an industry is composed of only a few firms whose market shares are stable and whose rankings in terms of sales, profits, and number of employees are unchanging. The reason why should be fairly clear. When there is strong competition, firms go bankrupt or at any rate clear losers appear, and they and third parties who suffer losses go running to the government to ask for aid and succor. It is the bureaucrats who then suffer in trying to clear up the mess. In such situations, bureaucrats may have to answer questions from the Diet or face the examining eye of the press about what is going on and how they could have permitted such a situation to arise in their domain. Thus government officials have no desire to see excess competition, or for that matter, competition in any form, arise in their bailiwick and would much prefer for a stable order to be maintained in which all firms make a reasonable profit and in which "junior" firms respect their "elders." Thus officials have tried to see to it that, whenever possible, measures are instituted that assure that none of their firms get into trouble, that their firms remain profitable, and that their industry is not faced with the specter of import competition or the entry of foreign firms.

In order to exclude excess competition, the officials in the *genkyoku* for an industry have come to think it desirable, when possible, to reorganize an industry or to consolidate firms. Countless examples from many industries can be given in which the *genkyoku* has raised the banner of reorganization and consolidation, and for which it has provided incentives in varying degrees. Likewise during recessions, when prices tend to decline and firms to run in the red, officials come to think it desirable for prices to be maintained as much as possible so that no firm will go bankrupt. Thus, in line with necessity, there is a need to implement some sort of pricing agreement, recession cartel, output restriction, production controls, orderly investment program, or the like—or at least so it is often claimed. Thus it is not surprising that there are policies for which it is almost impossible to find any positive benefit from an economic perspective, yet about which the responsible bureaucrats are enthusiastic and raise a fanfare. One example of this is the reorganizing of industry through large-scale mergers, such as that of Fuji Steel and Yahata Steel (to form Nippon Steel) or of the Dai-ichi and Kangyo Banks (to form Daiichi Kangin Bank).

Even the Ministry of Finance, which is generally liberally oriented with regard to economic policy, tends in its capacity as a genkyoku to be intent on restraining price competition. For example, the Ministry controls the retail prices of alcoholic beverages under the provisions of the Liquor Tax Law and has continued to regulate bank deposit interest rates, insurance premium rates, issuing terms for bonds, and fees for securities transactions, *de facto* or *de jure*.

This preference for the existing Confucian order, the striving to maintain and extend authority over industry, the xenophobic tendency to exclude foreigners, is not limited to MITI (though recently MITI has changed). It also can be found in the Ministry of Finance, the Ministry of Health and Welfare (pharmaceuticals), the Ministry of Transport (shipbuilding, ocean

transport, airlines, and all types of surface transport), the Ministry of Agriculture (food processing, along with all types of agriculture, forestry,
and fisheries), and elsewhere.

Among these ministries, MITI was the first to pay heed to the emphasis
of academic economists, switching to policies that place more emphasis
on the workings of the price mechanism and the role of interfirm competition. MITI's policies also reflect a change in thinking that emphasizes
international economic ties rather than an orientation toward a closed
economy, viewing favorably the implications of freer trade and foreign
direct investment in Japan. Thus the statement that "industrial policy
consists of the policies formulated and implemented by MITI"[22] is ad-
mirably put, but not quite accurate. Rather, it should be phrased that "in
postwar Japan, industrial policy consists of the policies of the various
genkyoku of the government."

B. Industrial Policy and Antitrust Policy

The predilection of the *genkyoku* bureaucrats for limiting competition
and restructuring—that is, for encouraging mergers, vertical and horizontal
firm groupings, and interfirm operating agreements—is fundamentally at
odds with antitrust policy. Thus the various ministries, and in particular
MITI, have from time to time come into direct conflict with the Fair Trade
Commission (FTC), which is responsible for antitrust policy. Antitrust
policy was initially imported from the United States during the postwar
Occupation, in conjunction with the dissolution of the *zaibatsu*. This did
not fit well with the Japanese tradition of emphasis on the status quo, the
harmony of the Confucian order. Instead, beginning in the pre-World War
II era and continuing throughout the war, the government had been guiding
the formation of cartels. Thus it was not surprising that in the Japanese
situation attempts to implement policies to foster competition did not take
root, representing as they did a 180-degree turn in excluding cartels and
cooperation. From the 1950s through the mid-1960s, during the heyday
of industrial policy, antitrust policy on occasion collided head-on with the
predominant Japanese approach, and in general, antitrust policy (the FTC)
was the loser. Since then antitrust policy has gradually begun to gain better
acceptance, but it is not possible to say that it is as yet firmly rooted and
able to fulfill its appointed role.

C. Effectiveness of Restrictions of Competition

Based on the record, if one asks whether in seeking the prevention of
excess competition and the restructuring of industry the relevant bureau-
cracies have had effective policies and great success, the answer has to

be more no than yes. An oft-used example is that of the automobile industry, which at first MITI sought to limit to one firm, and failing that two, with the final target set at "at most" three firms. They were unable to do this, and at present there are no less than seven "independent" passenger car manufacturers (not including firms formally affiliated with one of these). There was in fact vigorous competition in most industries in postwar Japan, and as a result of widespread competition, there was growth and decline and birth and death among firms. This lively competition was in fact an important source of vitality for the Japanese economy.

What, then, was the source of this vigorous competition, which implies that in spite of weak antitrust policy and the strong inclination of the government ministry responsible for an industry to suppress competition, policies seeking to maintain the "proper" order did not generally succeed? My opinion is that while in general the government and the leading firms in an industry, together with the leaders of the official industry policy councils and advisory committees, favored the limitation of competition and the restructuring of industry, the rank-and-file firms in an industry, new entrants, and the banks and related industries that were pushing these latter firms did not favor restructuring or policy intervention by the government. Rank-and-file firms were always seeking opportunities to eat into the market shares of the top firms, while purchasers of an industry's products desired competition within the industry. Perhaps economists who argued for the fostering of competition and the antitrust policies of the FTC had some influence as well. From the beginning of the 1960s, when extremely rapid economic growth and the transition to an open economy commenced, it came to be thought natural that in the midst of vigorous competition, firms brimming with innovative ideas should grow, leaving behind stagnant firms clinging to the old order.

Furthermore, restructuring, especially mergers and takeovers, seldom went smoothly. One reason is that, in the presence of lifetime employment practices, firm mergers—as with the removal of a feudal lord during the Tokugawa era—often were accompanied by tragedy. Not only the managers of a firm, but the employees as well, would be willing to undergo hardship for a considerable length of time when their firm ran into difficulties, fighting for their independence, and seeking new avenues of development to preserve their firm's existence.

V. Industrial Policy Formation

Through what process were decisions relating to industrial policy made in Japan? There are almost no empirical studies of this question based on questionnaire surveys or other data. I had previously attempted to describe this decision process, based on my own limited observations, scattered interviews, press reports, and the like.[23] The reaction of those involved in policy circles was that as a description of the decision-making process through the 1960s it was on the whole on target. Below I will summarize the situation in the 1960s, based on my earlier work, and will try to indicate ways in which things changed in the 1970s.

A. Through the End of the 1960s

During this period the Diet played almost no role in setting industrial policy. The opposition parties might proclaim that the government was ignoring national welfare in the interest of production, or decry that policies favorable to big business and monopoly capital were being implemented, but they showed almost no concern with the detailed contents of proposed industrial policy measures. Almost all laws were drafted by the bureaucracy, and those that the government sought to have passed in general went through successfully, without amendment.

Those groups whose influence was substantial in the formulation of industrial policy on the government side were the *genkyoku*—the bureaus, divisions, and sections within the various ministries and agencies responsible for particular industries—and the bureaus and divisions that mediated between different parts of a ministry and different ministries. On the private side there were the various industry associations, and in an intermediate role were the various industry councils and advisory committees that formally are part of the government. In addition, two more groups had perhaps some influence, the *zaikai*, a group of corporate executives,[24] and the banks and financial institutions that supplied funds to industry. It was in general quite unusual for only one of the above groups to have a predominant influence regarding a given decision. Thus the decision-making game of setting industrial policy consisted of the above players trying to convince each other as to the proper policy position, to realign their respective goals, or even at times to strongarm their opponents. The fighters in these battles will be described in greater detail below.

1. The Genkyoku and the Mediating Bureaus

The actor that played the predominant role in the formation of industrial policy in Japan was the *genkyoku*, the section of the bureaucracy within the government that had the primary responsibility for developing and supervising policies for a given industry. Then, as now, each industry had one associated *genkyoku*. This system is rather similar to the organization of the industrial bureaucracy in socialist countries and seems to have no direct counterpart in the other advanced Western countries.

Overall MITI is the single most important *genkyoku* ministry within the

Japanese government. In 1970, among its nine bureaus, five acted as *genkyoku:* the Heavy Industries Bureau, the Chemical Industries Bureau, the Textile and Light Industries Bureau, the Coal and Mining Bureau, and the Public Utilities Bureau. Internally a bureau is subdivided into divisions and then into sections, the majority of which are in turn responsible for one or another part of the relevant industry; these can be termed the *genkyoku* divisions or sections. For example, within the Heavy Industries Bureau could be found, among others, sections for iron and steel, industrial machinery, electronics and electrical machinery, automobiles, aircraft, and rolling stock.

Sometimes *genkyoku* bureaus are called vertical because each specializes in an industry or industries, but within MITI there also are four horizontal bureaus that specialize in problems that cut across industries. In 1970, these were the International Trade Bureau, the Trade Promotion Bureau, the Enterprise Bureau, and the Safety and Environmental Protection Bureau. These, together with the Ministerial Secretariat, occasionally had ideas of their own and took the lead in formulating policy, but they also played coordinating roles within MITI and among *genkyoku*.

It should be remembered that even within manufacturing, MITI was not the only *genkyoku* ministry. As noted previously, the Ministry of Agriculture, Forestry, and Fisheries had responsibility for the various food processing industries, such as soft drinks, along with the industries obvious from its name. Pharmaceuticals were overseen by the Ministry of Health and Welfare, while shipbuilding was the bailiwick of the Ministry of Transport. And last, not only were banking, insurance, and securities part of the domain of the Ministry of Finance, but so were beer, sake, and other alcoholic beverages.

Each *genkyoku* was responsible for drawing up policy relating to its industry or industries. For example, the *genkyoku* bureaus and sections of MITI were first responsible for drawing up and implementing various industry laws, such as the Petroleum Industry Law (1962), the Machine Industries Law (1956),[25] and the Electronics Industry Law (1957).[26] Second, the *genkyoku* drew up proposals for (1) making available special tax provisions for a given industry (that is, tax incentives), (2) changing tariff rates, (3) measures to free up imports, and (4) measures to permit direct investment in the industry by foreign firms. Third, in terms of transactions between foreign and domestic firms, each *genkyoku* was responsible, prior to the liberalization of capital transactions, for approving (5) patent and technology agreements and (6) joint ventures. Each *genkyoku* bureau or section was also (7) the authority for the issuing of licenses for industries such as petroleum refining, shipbuilding, and electric utilities, where new capacity was regulated. Finally, the *genkyoku* at the section or bureau, or sometimes the ministerial, level had a deciding voice in the allocation of Japan Development Bank and other government financial institution funds.

The proposals drawn up by the *genkyoku* bureau or section for items (1) through (6) were first considered and coordinated with other policies at the ministerial level. They were then passed on to the Ministry of Finance (MOF). In the case of (1), they would go to the Tax Bureau; for (2) and (3), to the Customs and Tariff Bureau; and for (4) through (6), to the International Finance Bureau. These MOF bureaus had within the government the overall responsibility for coordinating policy, while legal details would be overseen by the Cabinet Legislation Bureau. Without some overriding reason, however, it was very hard to change proposals at the Ministry of Finance or cabinet levels that had been decided on or formally requested by another ministry. Finally, the Fair Trade Commission, which was responsible for antitrust policy, was another prominent agency in the formation of industrial policy. Its existence was largely ignored in the 1950s, but throughout the 1960s its relative status within the bureaucracy was increasing, albeit slowly.

2. Industry Associations

As counterparts to each of the various *genkyoku* were major industry associations, which numbered in the hundreds, such as the Japan Iron and Steel Federation, the Japan Automobile Manufacturers Association, and the Shipbuilders Association of Japan, as well as numerous minor associations at the narrower industry level. In general they worked in close cooperation with the relevant *genkyoku*, but the nature of the relationship varied in each case. From the standpoint of the industry or its major firms, whose presidents served as chairmen of the association on a rotating basis, the main purpose of an association was to work with the *genkyoku* to see that the government adopted policies favorable to their industry or at least toward the major firms. At times there were confrontations between the associations and the *genkyoku*, and at times the associations themselves were divided internally. In addition, in industries dominated by smaller enterprises, firms were often unable to effectively organize themselves and so relied on the *genkyoku* for assistance.

Immediately after the war, the government took the leading role in the interaction of the *genkyoku* and the associations, with there being a strong tendency for the government to propose policies that it felt desirable and then try to pull the industry into line. As time passed, the balance of power shifted toward the industry groups, so that the *genkyoku* ministry or agency came to play more of a mediating role. Later on the *genkyoku* took into consideration the express interests of the industry (or at least its leading firms), organizing these interests and interacting on the basis of them with other sections, bureaus, and ministries on the industry's behalf. As to the industry associations themselves, many of them consisted of nothing more than friendly gatherings or forums for exchanging information with others in the industry. While they might engage in a little lobbying, the majority of the associations probably had relatively little influence on either outsiders (the government and politicians) or insiders (individual, especially dissident, firms).

3. *Policy Councils* (Shingikai)

A system of using *Shingikai* on major policy matters has gradually come into use in postwar Japan. These are consultative bodies whose deliberations are referred to in the process of policy formation, and whose principal members are private individuals, including former bureaucrats. In the case of MITI there were in 1970, for example, 27 different councils and advisory committees *(chosakai),* of which 15 were for industrial policy issues, serving formally to advise the Minister on each of their respective areas. The Industrial Structure Council advised on industrial policy in general, and there also were councils, among others, for machinery, petroleum extraction, coal mining, and promoting electronic data processing, aircraft, and energy. The members of these councils are formally nominated by the Minister of MITI and therefore tend to include those individuals thought useful by MITI bureaucrats. The majority thus consist of industry leaders, *zaikai* members, and former bureaucrats, with there being in addition very small numbers of scholars (academics), journalists (from newspapers), and others.

These councils tend to be criticized as being captive to the ministry, and certainly the bureaucrats work to see that deliberations come out to reflect their opinions. In practice, however, it is not the case that only things desired by the ministry are reflected in the groups' reports, for on issues that directly affect the interests of firms, industry representatives do speak out strongly. In fact, on such issues, the councils take on the coloration of a forum in which parties can adjust proposals to reflect their joint interests. Thus proposals that are passed through these councils, that is, that have been negotiated to reflect vested interests, can be afterwards implemented relatively smoothly, at least in terms of the industries represented on the relevant councils. In this sense the *Shingikai* process is one explicitly democratic development in postwar Japanese government.

One point that needs to be emphasized regarding such councils is their role in the exchange of information and obtaining consensus on policy

matters. I have previously expressed an opinion to the effect that, whatever
the defects in the postwar Japanese approach to industrial policy, forums
such as these have been a very effective means for the collection, exchange, and dissemination of information on industry and as such have
contributed greatly to postwar economic growth.[27] My view remains unchanged.

B. Post-1970 Developments

The above description applies to policymaking during the heyday of
Japanese industrial policy, but there appears to have been some developments since then.[28] The first trend has been the increasing importance
of the horizontal bureaus within MITI (in 1983, these were the International
Trade Policy, International Trade Administration, Industrial Policy, Industrial Location and Environmental Protection Bureaus, and the Secretariat of MITI) relative to the vertical bureaus (in 1983, the Basic Industries, Machinery and Information Industries, Consumer Goods
Industries Bureaus, and the Agency of Natural Resources and Energy).
Cases in which the horizontal bureaus took the initiative in proposing
policies increased greatly relative to those in which the movers were the
vertical bureaus.

Second, this reflects the *genkyoku* having less of a role in formulating
policies for their industries' benefit; the major policy issues are ones that
cut across many industries or across industrial policy or economic policy
as a whole.[29] For MITI, examples of such issues would be responding to
trade friction, pollution and energy problems, dealing with industrial relocation and structural adjustment in declining industries, and promoting
high-technology industries. Those concerned refer to this as a change of
MITI from an "industries" to an "issues" ministry. There has thus been
a gradual transition in the character of industrial policy from its initial
emphasis on infant-industry protection and the promotion of particular
industries to a developed country standpoint in which industrial policy is
one facet of general economic policy. It is this sort of transformation that
is reflected in the rise of the horizontal bureaus. Here MITI has been the
first to change among those ministries that had a *genkyoku* role. It would
probably not be an exaggeration to say that MITI has undergone such a
change 5 to 10 years ahead of the Ministry of Agriculture, the Ministry
of Health and Welfare, the Ministry of Transport, and the *genkyoku* parts
of the Ministry of Finance.

Third, the influence of the ruling Liberal Democratic Party and its
members over industrial policy has increased somewhat. The number of
ruling-party politicians with detailed knowledge of industrial policy, the

tax system, and budget making has increased, as has the importance of geographically concentrated small- and medium-scale manufacturing industries as a source of votes, including textiles and other stagnant industries that are crying out for protection. This trend is probably not unconnected with the prevailing atmosphere of political conservatism. In the face of these trends and the demands for fiscal reform, the role of the Ministry of Finance as a mediating agency has declined and has been supplemented by the Policy Committee of the party in power, with its growing number of members who have experience in ministerial or vice-ministerial posts.

Fourth, the number of Shingikai associated with MITI has increased slightly to 32, and they have come to play an ever greater role as forums for the exchange of information. But overall, apart from the content of industrial policy itself, there has not really been that much change in the process of policy formation.

VI. Afterthoughts

The preceding has surveyed a number of important topics relating to postwar Japanese industrial policy as a whole, but my interpretations do not always coincide with those of the contributors to this book as set out in their chapters. An attempt was made rather to present a comprehensive overview of Japanese industrial policy, including a general framework for the economic analysis of industrial policy, the theoretical basis for industrial policy, the general features of industrial policy during the postwar period, and the policy formation process. To do this I have taken and summarized the opinions of many economists, including the participants in this project, and have added my own personal thoughts as well. Most of the topics I have touched on are covered in greater depth in the chapters that follow, and I urge readers to go through and evaluate the detailed arguments of the other authors and come to their own conclusions.

Notes

1. These include Ueno [1978], Kosai [1981], Tsuruta [1982], and Tsusho Sangyo Gyosei Kenkyukai [1983].
2. I made the same point in 1973 (Komiya [1975a], pp. 307–8), and the situation has not changed much in the intervening period.
3. On this point, I am told that the Vice-Minister of MITI in 1970 gave a talk entitled "Japanese Industrial Policy" before the OECD (Organization for Economic Cooperation and Development) Industry Committee. Subsequently the Secretariat of the OECD published *Industrial Policy of Japan* (OECD [1972]).

4. Komiya [1975a], p. 308.
5. Among service industries, however, those that are closely linked to the development of a manufacturing industry, such as computer software or telecommunications, may well be considered as objects of industrial policy, as may the distribution systems for certain manufactured goods.
6. In English the word "industry" can refer to broad groups of firms producing similar items, as in primary, secondary, and tertiary industries, as well as specifically to manufacturing. In the latter usage, it is not always clear whether construction, electric power, and mining are included.
7. It is probably necessary to include the formulation and implementation of the Japan Industrial Standards (JIS) codes, safety guidelines, and other standards here.
8. The following argument may be worth considering. A strong and diversified small enterprise sector is important as one base for a political or economic democracy. In addition, small firms that are full of creativity are an important element for the advancement of industry. Therefore, it is beneficial to somewhat protect or encourage small enterprises. There have been, however, few discussions that introduced this point of view in advancing theoretical arguments for the protection and promotion of small enterprises. Very recently, a considerable amount of attention has been paid to the more promising of what are thought of as "venture businesses" and of policies to promote such firms. It would thus make sense to carry out economic analyses of the impact and success of promoting "leading" smaller enterprises, such as have been carried out to date by the Investment Development Corporations operated by the Tokyo and other prefectural governments.
9. For actual industrial policy, however, the goals are not always clear. Publicly stated goals may be ambiguous, and it is not uncommon for there to be a gap between purported and actual goals. Furthermore, policy measures and programs that are actually implemented represent the compromises over many years in adjusting the interests of losers and gainers, so that their policy aims become hard to discern. Thus the decision to limit the analysis to industrial policies undertaken for narrowly economic goals represents a fairly severe limitation of the economic approach.
10. Another possible role for industrial policy is to improve a country's terms of trade internationally. This, however, is disadvantageous to trading partners, and except in cases such as that of a monopolistic market, such policies impose a burden on resource allocation from the standpoint of the world as a whole.
11. The majority of the people who were active in the Industrial Structure Council belonged to the "prehistoric" period, including the three giants of the era, Hiromi Arisawa, Ichiro Nakayama, and Miyohei Shinohara. The essays of Yoshihiko Morozumi [1973] and Nobuyoshi Namiki [1973] also belong to the era. Much as their opinions may diverge on the four key issues raised above, the younger generation has come to use a common vocabulary based on economic theory in their analyses. For example, the majority of the younger generation has taken a critical stance toward the strong control aspects of the current Petroleum Industry Law and to the permit system for shipbuilding, which requires a government license for each new ship to be built.
12. There was no clear attempt made to define what sort of industry was a basic industry, but in the immediate postwar period it came to refer to industries such as coal mining, electric power, iron and steel, and ocean transport, as well as shipbuilding.
13. For example, as was the case with West Germany, if the exchange rate had been set at a level that would have permitted maintaining a favorable balance of payments without engaging in other measures, one would not expect it to have been necessary to undertake policies to stimulate exports or to lower and stabilize the prices of important raw material inputs of export goods. Again, as production takes place to eventually

meet final consumption demand, there seems to be little rationality of in general favoring the production of investment goods and intermediate inputs over that of consumer goods.

14. See also Imai [1969].
15. A story that illustrates this point is that of the firm Toyo Rayon, which introduced the then-revolutionary new product of nylon into Japan. Demand far exceeded supply, and many businessmen hoping to purchase a supply were observed going daily to the firm's headquarters in the Muromachi district of Tokyo. Toyo Rayon thereby earned the nickname "the MITI of Muromachi."
16. In the subsequent period, two additional criteria were added: (1) that there be a strong linkage effect to other industries and (2) that there be employment generation. The economic basis for these additional criteria, however, is not clear. Suppose that industries are ranked according to their total labor intensity by using input–output analysis to attribute total costs to labor and other primary inputs. Does the employment generation criterion then imply that the industries that are more labor-intensive should be promoted over those that are less so? What about those industries that satisfied only two or three of these four criteria? Should they be considered candidates for favorable treatment under "industrial structure" policies? There was no clear answer.
17. One other point of view was that, in an industry that was internationally close to a monopoly or a collusive oligopoly and whose firms thereby earned high profits, Japan should have nurtured new firms strong enough to lower the monopoly price or to share in the monopoly profits. Color film, automobiles, heavy electrical equipment, and large-scale computers may be examples of such industries.
18. See Chapter 5 of this book for more detail on these points.
19. Morozumi [1973], as per note 11.
20. For a review and analysis of the debate on excess competition, see Chapter 9, Section V of this book. For my own thinking on this subject, see Imai et al. [1972], pp. 248–256, and Komiya [1975a], pp. 214–215.
21. See Section V, A of this chapter for a full discussion of the *genkyoku*.
22. Kaizuka [1973], p. 167.
23. Komiya [1975a], pp. 308–311.
24. It is not clear who belongs to the *zaikai*, but it refers in general to those top corporate executives who are well informed about economic or policy affairs. They are constantly conferring with one another in various forums, and they play the role of spokespersons for major companies. In general, those thought of as members have prominent positions in the associations that represent big business interests. They do not, however, have the power attributed to them by the press or in popular thinking, and I believe that as time progressed their influence has lessened.
25. Officially, the Law on Temporary Measures for the Promotion of the Machinery Industry.
26. Officially, the Law on Temporary Measures for the Promotion of the Electronics Industry.
27. Komiya [1975a], p. 324.
28. Here I would like to thank Hiroaki Ishii of MITI for his many observations on the topic.
29. Note that from the start there was little criticism of MITI, in contrast to the Ministry of Finance, as being only a conglomeration of independent bureaus and not a "ministry" (though this criticism is overexaggerated).

PART I

Historical Overview 1

CHAPTER 2

The Reconstruction Period

YUTAKA KOSAI

Japan Economic Research Center
Tokyo, Japan

I. The Japanese Economy, 1945–1960

The general environment in which industrial policy needs to be placed in the era 1945–1960 can be summarized by three main trends (Table I). First, this was a period of change, from reconstruction to the onset of rapid growth. Recovering from the collapse at the end of the war, a growth rate averaging nearly 10% per annum was maintained, with demand initially stemming from private consumption and later from private capital formation. At first the capital stock inherited from the war era was utilized, with high growth realized despite a low savings rate. Eventually the pattern shifted to that of growth based on high investment and high saving. Throughout this era there was an excess supply of labor and a very severe debt ceiling imposed by the balance of payments.

Second, during this era there was a gradual shift in the economy from being closed and isolated from world markets to being more open. The collapse of Japan's wartime economy was brought on by the Allied interdiction of raw material and food imports, and due to worldwide shortages, the economy remained closed for a while even after the beginning of the Occupation. But with the fixing of the exchange rate at ¥360 to the dollar and other measures taken in 1949, Japan's participation in world markets progressively increased, and the country's dependence on trade began rising even though foreign exchange licensing and controls on foreign investment and on technology imports continued. Around 1960, demands for the freeing of trade arose in earnest.

Third, the framework of industrial organization changed from govern-

TABLE I
Growth Patterns during the Reconstruction Period

	1946–51	1951–55	1955–60
Rates of change (% per annum)			
GNP	10.0	8.2[c]	8.7[c]
Mining and manufacturing production	29.1	11.3	16.3
Wholesale price index	83.6	0.0	0.5
Fixed capital formation (annual average, as % of GNP)	8.3[b]	11.4[c]	16.5[c]
Trade dependence (%)[a]	12.3[b]	23.8[c]	23.4[c]
Balance of trade (annual average, $ millions)	−189	−393	+ 94
Unemployed (annual average, thousands)	330	660	880
Industrial concentration index[d] (1937 = 100)	58.7	80.1	78.4

Sources: Keizai Kikakucho [1976b], except for:
[a](Exports & Imports)/GNP
[b]Keizai Kikakucho [1958].
[c]Keizai Kikakucho [1976a].
[d]Uekusa [1982], p. 29. The index refers, respectively, to 1950, 1955 and 1960.

ment controls to market competition. Economic controls were a legacy of the wartime era, but the system of regulating and allocating material flows, financing, and prices was dismantled, starting with the adoption of the Dodge Line policies in 1949. To some extent these controls were replaced by other interventions in the form of special fiscal measures, the allocation of foreign exchange, the control of direct investment and technology imports, and lending by government financial institutions.

Some remnants of the earlier controls, such as industry associations, financial groups, and vertical groupings (keiretsu), in fact, developed more fully during this period. In contrast, one facet of Occupation policy was the dissolution of the zaibatsu and the institution of anticoncentration measures such as the Antimonopoly Law. This laid a foundation for vigorous competition, and it goes without saying that greater ties to world markets provided a further spur. Throughout this period one finds the contrasting strands of controls, interventionist policies, and firm groupings in opposition to competition and deconcentration. With reconstruction and the opening of the economy, controls were bound to gradually disappear, but it must be stressed that relative to later periods intervention of the government in industry was great.

II. Framework, Goals, and Tools of Industrial Policy

Accepting the above depiction of the economy, we must ask how these trends were related to industrial policy during the period. Our task is to examine the continuity and effectiveness of industrial policy during these transitions. We will therefore look in greater detail at industrial policy.

A. The Framework of Industrial Policy

The framework of industrial policy during this era—among other items the relationship of the government to firms, the policy formation process, and the ideology regarding policy—was greatly influenced by contemporary economic developments, the heritage of the war, and democratization policies. The postwar economy began to function under the legacy of wartime controls. Firms were very weak due to, among other reasons, the combined impact of the immediate postwar restructuring, the inflation of the early years, and anticoncentration policies. Government–business relationships during this period can be summarized by the phrase "strong government and weak enterprises," and under the guidance of the bureaucracy, industrial policy was carried out with a very interventionist flavor.

The above can be thought of as a general summary of conditions during the period, but the following reservations must be noted. First, the basic production units of the economy were private firms, and this was true even at the time when postwar controls were at their strongest. The proposal to nationalize coal mining under the Katayama Cabinet [May 1947 to March 1948] was gutted because it threatened managerial autonomy in the firms in the industry. Even under price controls, the profit incentive could not be ignored, and in order to guarantee the willingness of firms to increase production, it clearly proved necessary from time to time to change regulated prices.[1] Second, with the imposition of the Dodge Line in 1949, direct controls began to be removed, thus government intervention shifted to indirect means. Third, the carrying out of deconcentration policies and the dissolution of the *zaibatsu* under the Occupation, while weakening large firms and tending to make them more dependent on the government, also served to bring on lively interfirm competition. As a result, the degree of industrial concentration decreased markedly relative to the prewar period. Interfirm competition received a further boost as ties to international markets were rebuilt, and this was backed up by the bountiful opportunities to introduce foreign technology. With the lessening of the burden of military expenditures and a plentiful supply of labor, firms faced a frontier of opportunities providing for rapid growth. Thus, even though industrial policy during this period had a strong bureaucratic coloration, there also was room for the display of the entrepreneurial spirit.

Even though industrial policy was under the guidance of bureaucrats, during the early period businessmen were also active, serving as advisors to government leaders or becoming high-level bureaucrats themselves. It also seems that the advisory council *(shingikai)* system took root during this period as a means of arriving at a consensus. The main arm of industrial policy was at first the Ministry of Commerce and Industry (together with the Economic Stabilization Board) and later its successor, the Ministry of International Trade and Industry (MITI); their authority was great, even within the government proper. For example, MITI was able to outmaneuver the Fair Trade Commission on matters relating to the Antimonopoly Law through its use of administrative guidance for the restriction of output.

MITI was also able to see that overall economic policy reflected its industrial policy concerns by placing its officials in powerful posts (including that of administrative vice-minister) in the Economic Stabilization Board (which later became the Economic Deliberation Agency and is now the Economic Planning Agency). There were, however, limits placed on its power by the Ministry of Finance, one of the most powerful ministries, which had to be convinced by MITI of the necessity of subsidies, tax incentives, government loans and investment, and controls on foreign exchange and foreign investment. Thus there are examples of MITI proposals that the Ministry of Finance would not approve for budgetary or other reasons.

The "ideology" of industrial policy during this period was not based on neoclassical economics or Keynesian thinking, but was rather neomercantilist in lineage.[2] Thus, with the goal of improving national welfare, it was thought appropriate for the government to intervene in the economy to protect and promote industry so as to be able to face foreign competition. Industrial policy also was distinctly influenced by Marxism, in that it was thought inevitable that industrial structure would advance toward the stage of monopoly. Nationalism also was an element. At the same time it was clearly realized that, with Japan's endowment of human and natural resources, economic advancement would be impossible without exports, that is, competitiveness in world markets. But in choosing international exchange over autarky there were inevitably restrictions on the government's ability to protect and to intervene. In other words, there was a reluctant determination, with numerous vicissitudes, that an economic order based on free competition was essential at home as well.

Evidencing this was the policy debate in the early 1950s over trade dependence versus autarkic development, which was won by the pro-trade group.[3] As a proponent of the former position, Ichiro Nakayama and others argued that, with excess population and few natural resources, it was appropriate for Japan to follow an industrialization strategy oriented toward the export of goods processed from imported materials in seeking to increase the population's standard of living. In contrast, Hiromi Arisawa, Shigeto Tsuru, and others argued that world markets were fragmented and unstable and that government planning to systematically exploit coal, hydroelectric power, and other potential domestic resources was best. In terms of economic theory, the superiority of a pro-trade stance appears obvious, but with the chaos of the world economy at that time, and the attraction that planning in the socialist tradition still held for intellectuals, there also was support to be found for autarkic resource development. Considering the decline in production and the standard of living brought about by autarky during the war, it is not surprising that in the end the pro-trade position won out.

B. Goals and Tools of Industrial Policy

In looking at the goals and tools of industrial policy, it is convenient to divide the 1945 to 1960 era into subperiods of roughly five years. In the first five years after the end of the war, reconstruction—the recovery from the tremendous decline in output and the standard of living—was the general task of all economic policy, and the goal of industrial policy was the resumption of production. This goal was pursued in an economy that had been closed since the onset of the war. After the war, economic controls were resurrected as the means for achieving recovery. The specific focus of policy was the resumption of production in industries where recovery was thought to be especially difficult, such as coal and steel. Along with other industries, such as ammonium sulfate and electric power, coal and steel were emphasized in what was known as the "priority production" system. Specific tools utilized in trying to carry out this policy were (1) materials rationing; (2) price controls, including price maintenance subsidies; (3) Reconstruction Finance Corporation loans; and (4) miscellaneous measures. In the following discussion, we will try to reinterpret the priority production system as an import substitution policy forced by the fact that the economy was closed internationally.

The 1949 Dodge Line policies, along with bringing the postwar inflation to a close, eliminated or substantially weakened many policy tools, such as rationing, price controls, price supports, the multitiered exchange rate (and the subsidies implicit therein), and Reconstruction Finance Corporation loans. Furthermore, by imposing a unified exchange rate, the road was paved to renewed participation of Japanese industry in international trade. The chance outbreak of the Korean War in 1951 led to a rapid increase in mining and manufacturing output, but when the boom had run its course, the weakness of the balance of payments (which had been covered up by dollar receipts from United Nations Forces "Special Procurements") became evident; thus economic independence became an issue.[4]

The central goal of industrial policy during this second period was the rationalization of industry, and in particular a solution to the problem of high coal and steel prices, which were affecting the competitiveness of exports. The reorganization of firms as part of the clearing up of war debts and the Occupation deconcentration efforts had come to a close, and firms, freed from controls, were energetic. This transformation coincided with an industrial policy highlighted by various rationalization plans, all of which started in the early 1950s. The First Steel Rationalization Plan, the Coal Mining Rationalization Plan, the Five-Year Electric Power Development Plan, and Planned Shipbuilding are major examples of such policies. For these, the government tried to back up its goal of rationalization through special tax measures, the provision of government finance (Japan Export–Import and Development Bank loans), and interest rate subsidies for shipping, along with the allocation of foreign exchange and the regulation of technology imports. These policies can be interpreted as having been successful in fostering decreasing-cost industries and as having failed in protecting increasing-cost industries. This theme will be taken up in detail in the next section. There are also examples of attempts during this period to encourage new industries, such as synthetic fibers. In addition, there were cases of controls within an industry, through measures such as the restricting of output and the allocation of imported raw materials. The use of recession cartels also began after 1953, when the Antimonopoly Law was revised.

The third period covers the latter half of the 1950s, when the Japanese economy began its rapid growth. The goal of overall economic policy was to raise the growth rate and the standard of living and to achieve full employment. It was understood that the achievement of full employment would lead to the elimination of the dual structure and to the modernization of the economy. The intermediate goals through which this was to be achieved were the promotion of exports and heavy industry.

In terms of industrial development, the modernization of steel and other industries progressed during this period and the mass production system was brought into use for passenger cars and other durable consumer goods. The attempt to rationalize coal mining, however, ended in failure. Instead, an energy revolution occurred based on the utilization of imported crude oil. In this environment, industrial policy sought to build an industrial infrastructure through the provision of sites, water supplies, and transportation. Other themes of industrial policy were the encouragement of new industries such as machinery parts and petrochemicals, intraindustry adjustment through orderly investment and other policies, and the protection and rationalization of declining industries.

The expansion of infrastructure became crucial as the energy revolution and the rise of the durable consumer goods industries drastically changed locational needs. These new industries required sites accessible to ocean transport or near consumer markets rather than locations in the proximity of coal fields. These efforts sped up the transition to new industries and adjustment in old industries.

Tax incentives and government financing remained the main tools of industrial policy, but there were measures such as the 1956 Machinery Industry Promotion Temporary Measures Law for the fostering of new industries and the 1955 Coal Mining Industry Rationalization Temporary Measures Law (together with a tariff on heavy oil and restrictions on the introduction of oil-burning boilers) for declining industries. Adjustments within a given industry were attempted through the use of administrative guidance. Policy measures enacted during this period to foster and promote new and growth industries will be discussed in the next section.

III. Industrial Policy: Content and Evaluation

This section will attempt to outline and evaluate the core of industrial policy used during the three subperiods of the 1945–1960 era. The topics to be taken up are the priority production system of 1946–1948, industry rationalization during the early 1950s, and the promotion of new and growth industries that began from about the middle of the 1950s. An attempt will be made to present something of a cross between a chronology of the measures adopted during these subperiods and case studies of specific measures. The topics to be examined can be considered representative of overall industrial policy during these three periods. In asking why these policies were adopted, an effort will be made to contrast the policies to conceivable alternatives and to examine the dominant thinking of the time. These policies will then be evaluated from the standpoints of economic growth and stability, resource allocation, and equity.

A. Reconstruction Policies: The Priority Production System

The priority production system sought to increase mining and manufacturing output through the joint expansion of the two key sectors of coal and steel. Coal output would be expanded, and the steel industry would have priority in the coal's allocation. The coal industry, in turn, would have priority in obtaining the steel it needed. This policy was adopted by the Yoshida Cabinet in 1946 and stayed in effect throughout 1947 and 1948. Its adoption was signaled by the December 27, 1946, Cabinet Resolution, "Adoption of and Policy Guidelines for the Fiscal 1946 Fourth Quarter Basic Materials Supply and Demand Plan."[5] The policy had been developed and advocated by a brain trust centering around Hiromi Arisawa and comprised largely of members of the Planning Section of the Ministry of Commerce and Industry. The brain trust and the Economic Stabilization Board were the main implementing organizations.[6]

The priority production system brought into full play the direct controls that were then available: materials rationing, reconstruction financing, price controls, price support subsidies, and import allocations (an "invisible" subsidy that was under the multiple exchange rate system). Allocations of coal to the steel industry increased in fiscal 1947 by 62% over the previous year, and at a time when steel output was only able to meet 26% of total demand, the coal mines were able to procure 61% of mill production.[7] In the same year, Reconstruction Finance Corporation (RFC) loans were ¥53.4 billion, about the same amount as the combined loans of all private banks (at ¥56.8 billion). Fully 30% of RFC loans went to the coal industry, providing 70% of the industry's borrowings. Price supports comprised 17.9% of the General Account budget in that year, and rose to 23.8% of the budget in 1948. The largest recipient of these monies was the steel industry.

The purpose of the priority production system was clearly the recovery of production levels from the war-end collapse, or the "restart" of production, as it was termed. This renewal of the economy was essential in order to raise the national livelihood from the point of starvation. Next, let us examine other policies that were devised and implemented at the time.

In macroeconomic policy there was an alternation between attempting the repression of inflation as *the* pressing issue (e.g., the Emergency Financial Measures Ordinance of February 1946) and an activist stance (the Ishibashi fiscal policy) that accepted deficit financing and a rapid increase in the money supply as necessary evils in carrying out the task of restarting production. Macroeconomic policy by itself was, however, held to be insufficient to overcome bottlenecks in production, and hence sector-specific policies were also adopted.

Among sector-specific policies there were those that placed emphasis on an increase in the production of consumer goods (the February 15, 1946, Cabinet Resolution, "Basic Postwar Price Policy Outline") and those that focused on the development of an orderly distribution system (the June 10, 1946 Cabinet Resolution, "Emergency Economic Policies"). In opposition to these, Hiromi Arisawa, the formulator of the priority production concept, foresaw a crisis involving the outstripping of production by consumption, which would give rise to a vicious circle of contracting production. To get around this, he advocated policy intervention to increase intermediate-good production. In Arisawa's thinking, direct measures to stimulate production of final consumption goods would not lead to the resumption of the output of intermediate goods. Furthermore, measures dealing with orderly distribution were not a positive industrial policy and were criticized as something that had come in through the back door.[8]

The logic of the priority production system resembles the Ricardo effect of the Austrian school. This is the situation described by von Hayek of "a people of an isolated island" who find all their free capital exhausted "after having partially constructed an enormous machine which was to provide them all necessities."[9] A closed economy is a basic premise for implementing such policies. At the time, this was an appropriate characterization of the Japanese economy, and the importance of this premise was understood by the proponents of priority production.[10] In spite of its possession of a labor force and capital stock, Japan's wartime economy had collapsed because of the interdiction of natural resource imports, and this situation still continued after the close of the war. Priority production was an attempt to deal with the stoppage of natural resource imports through the substitution of domestic resources, a "forced" import substitution policy.

Even in a closed economy, however, if final consumption demand induces a demand for producer goods, the production of producer goods can be expected to be in the end stimulated. In this case, there is no justification for the government to intervene to encourage the production of producer goods—that is, to implement priority production. What sort of conditions could prevent a demand for consumer goods from inducing a demand for producer goods, thereby making priority production necessary? The problem at that time seems to have been that increases in actual production and prices obtained for intermediate producer goods lagged behind increases in consumer goods production and prices. While the logic is not always clear, along with this lag there were other reasons given for why final demand did not stimulate intermediate goods production. These reasons included the continued impact of the economic controls that were still in place, the problems of financially restructuring firms at the war's end, designations of facilities for reparation, inflation, the near-impossibility of obtaining private financing, and the generally poor working of the market in the confused social conditions of the time. In particular, labor unrest was acute in the coal mines; while this explains the lag in production, it does not explain why relative prices should be so low. Military stockpiles, released to the private sector, were being depleted; while this may have held back price increases, with the expected March 1946 crisis of wartime inventories finally being drawn down, one would have expected prices to rebound. With the drastic reduction in living standards, "starvation" demand was so great there was a remarkable rise in the propensity to consume, which could also serve as a partial explanation.[11] In any event, priority production can only be justified under the extraordinary conditions that prevailed immediately after the war.

In fiscal 1947, while priority production was being implemented, output of ordinary steel increased to 740,000 tons and that of coal to 29.34 million tons, and mining and manufacturing production overall was up by 22.7%. Because of this outcome, priority production was considered a success. Apart from producers' efforts at home, however, improved availability of raw materials and fuels from overseas had a large impact on increased output. Foreign materials and fuels were more readily obtained in 1948, and mining and manufacturing production increased by 33.3%. This backs up the above contention that priority production was an *ad hoc* attempt to deal with the cutoff of foreign raw material and fuel supplies.

The implementing of the priority production system gave a boost to inflation as the budget ballooned with price support payments and as the Bank of Japan discounted the bonds of the Reconstruction Finance Corporation to provide it with funds. In reaction to this, government policy came to focus on the lowering of inflation. This change was reinforced by scandals relating to the provision of reconstruction loans and criticisms of lax standards in the determination of price support payments.[12] The anti-inflationary policy was finally set in place by changes in American policy toward Japan. Industrial policy thus became subject to macroeconomic policy, and when conflicts arose with macro policy goals, industrial policy was forced to change.

In terms of resource allocation, there has been an interpretation that the priority production system paved the way for the growth of heavy industry. This, however, overstates the case. Priority production, it is true, sought to restart production in heavy industry, but its ultimate purpose was to secure inputs for producing consumption goods. The recovery of heavy industry obtained through priority production was small in comparison to that achieved in the course of overall economic growth later on. Furthermore, reliance on coal, the main focus of priority production, was no longer held desirable by the 1950s, and it can probably be said that the emphasis on increasing the quantity of output brought on the problems of high coal prices faced in the subsequent period. Priority production was thus no more than a response to the extraordinary conditions of the time. One might argue that the priority production system acted to convey the legacy of the war-time concern with heavy industry to the subsequent period.

B. Industrial Rationalization: The First Steel Plan

With the adoption of the Dodge Line as a turning point, direct controls were removed and, with the exchange rate set at $1.00 = ¥360, firms came to face direct international competition. After the end of the Korean War, there was tremendous concern about the decline of revenue from the Special Procurements, which had helped to maintain equilibrium in the balance of payments, and about the high cost of Japanese industrial goods made apparent with the removal of subsidies (the high coal and high steel price issues). These came to be thought of as barriers to economic independence. In the early 1950s, many industries began to invest for the purpose of rationalization, and the government adopted a system for supporting these efforts. These industries included steel, coal, ocean transport, electric power, synthetic fibers, and chemical fertilizers. Some of the associated government efforts are documented in the August 18, 1950, Cabinet Resolution "Measures for Rationalizing the Steel and Coal Mining Industries,"[13] the February 23, 1951, Industrial Rationalization Council Report "Methods for Rationalizing Our Industries," and the March 1953 Industrial Rationalization Promotion Law.

The policy tools used to foster rationalization were quite different from those utilized under priority production. The main tools were fiscal incentives and loans by government financial institutions. Among fiscal measures, those that were particularly relevant to industrial policy were accelerated depreciation for "important" and "rationalization" machinery, exemptions from import and other taxes for important raw materials, and tariff exemptions for important types of machinery. These exemptions totaled ¥43 billion during the fiscal 1950–1955 period and 5.7% of corporate tax receipts in fiscal 1955. Alongside these exemptions, there were also exemptions of "modernization facilities" from property taxes. The range of items eligible for these benefits were narrowly specified, and so utilization of these measures was quite concentrated.

The other major element, government financing, came to 28.3% of total lending to industry over the fiscal 1952–1955 period (37.2% for shipping, electric power, coal, and steel). Other financing routes that should not be ignored were Bank of Japan foreign currency lending and World Bank loans. As to subsidies, interest subsidies for the shipping industry, in effect from the sixth through the thirteenth shipbuilding plans (fiscal 1953–1957), were large, coming to ¥10.3 billion. Proposals to use subsidies to deal with the problem of high coal and steel prices were also put forward, but none of these plans were adopted.[14] The system of reciprocal trade and the practice of linking import licenses to export performances were put into effect, however.[15]

Rationalization policy generally presumed an open economy and strove for cost reductions under that premise. Hence, direct interventions—a denial of the market mechanism—were avoided. Both fiscal measures and government lending programs were based on the assumption that firms must earn profits through their regular operations. Rationalization also often called for the importation of machinery and of technology, and in this foreign exchange controls and restrictions on foreign investment in Japan played a major role. One must show caution, however, in assuming that the actual use of these restrictions served the purpose of furthering rationalization efforts.[16]

While industrial rationalization during this period assumed the presence of foreign competition, as should be clear from above, there was also the appearance that the government was targeting "important" industries and adopting a system for intervening in industry. This is one of the phenomena that can be thought of as having given rise to the "Japan, Inc." view. In other words, Japan, Inc. reflects a generalization of the image left by industrial policy during this period. Government–business ties, however, were constantly evolving over time as the economy was opened up and as economic growth was sustained. Even during this period, there were many limitations placed on the use of industrial policy, and it was certainly not omnipotent, as will be seen in more detail below. Nevertheless, it should be remembered that it was these industrial rationalization policies that gave support to the Japan, Inc. interpretation.

The goal of industrial rationalization was economic independence, which in practical terms meant balance of payments equilibrium. This goal could also be pursued through macroeconomic policies such as contractionary fiscal policy and the devaluation of the yen. In reality, however, there was a basic assumption that the exchange rate should be maintained, and it was during the period when there were adequate foreign exchange reserves due to Special Procurement receipts and other factors (and *only* during this period) that industrial rationalization was pursued. When this leeway disappeared in 1954 and there was a return to contractionary policies (the "one trillion yen" budget), it became evident that maintenance of the exchange rate took precedence, and industrial policy gave way. It is thus evident that macroeconomic restrictions were binding and that industrial policy had to be pursued within the limitations placed on it by the balance of payments.

When industrial policy was formulated, there was consideration of Japan's comparative advantage in trade. Hence limits were placed on which industries would be promoted (such as the debate on whether a domestic passenger car industry was desirable).[17] The development of domestic natural resources was also considered important as a means of import substitution. Areas of development included domestic food production, the development of hydroelectric power, and the production of synthetic fibers for which carbide was a raw material to be processed with electricity thus developed.[18] The industrial rationalization policies had from a more-or-less mercantilist standpoint placed emphasis on the so-called basic industries such as coal and steel, but the choice of industries was by no means exclusive, and a rather wide variety of industries were given support. This was perhaps due in part to bureaucratic sectionalism, but it presumably also was due in many cases to the government acknowledging *ex post facto* the autonomous efforts of private firms to rationalize. During that period, in fact, many private companies, having survived postwar reorganization, the Occupation deconcentration policies, and other upheavals and having recovered their profitability during the Korean War, were eager to rationalize. One can find many examples of firms that vigorously pursued rationalization without the receipt of much government assistance. Toyota Motors, for instance, enacted a five-year production facility modernization plan for 1951–1956. In part due to the long hiatus imposed by the war, there were many cases in which rationalization investments improved efficiency markedly (see Table II).

If this were the case, however, one must wonder why in the first place the government had to intervene to encourage industrial rationalization.

TABLE II
Effects of Rationalization Investments

Industry	Percentage Cost Reduction	Improvements
Pig iron	4	Preprocessing of raw materials
Steel	10	Oxygen-process steel production and mass-production-sized open-hearth furnaces
Steel sheets	27	Continuous process rolling mills compared to old-style facilities
Steel pipe	30	Flettsmunn process compared to old seamless pipe facilities
Oil refining	15	Newly built refineries compared to old-fashioned ones
Rayon fibers	25	Continuous process compared to prior method
Ammonium sulfate	21	Simultaneous production of urea

Sources: Tsusansho [1957], Nihon Tekko Remmei [1959].

One conceivable explanation is that the financial, market, and techno-logical risks of such investment were great, and government assistance served to lower these risks. Facilities in the heavy and chemical industries were for the most part of ancient vintage, having been carried through the war; high costs made profits low, and firms were not able to accumulate enough funds internally to finance essential new investment. If capital markets were perfect, this would not be a barrier to raising investment funds, but capital markets at the time could by no means be considered perfect.[19] In addition, the emphasis in industrial rationalization on the elimination of high coal and steel prices was due to the fact that with the industrial structure of the time, their share in total costs was high, and the repercussions of rationalization in these industries were thought to be great.[20]

A peak in investment for industrial rationalization was reached in 1953, and this investment boom brought on a balance of payments deficit and contractionary fiscal policy. With the deflationary policies that took effect from 1954, industrial rationalization policies were temporarily brought to a standstill. But the original purpose of these policies was economic in-dependence (balance of payments equilibrium), and toward that end, the strengthening of the international competitive position of Japanese in-dustry. In looking at the course of events after 1955, these policies can perhaps be said to have shown some results. This contention is based on the successful rationalization of firms under the fixed exchange rate regime. It is only to the extent that industrial rationalization policies significantly supported these rationalization efforts that they can be said to have had any effect.[21]

Even if industrial rationalization policies can be said to have been suc-cessful in their overall direction, it is not the case that all of the policies advanced at the time were effective. While steel grew to become an export industry after the conclusion of the First Steel Rationalization Plan, efforts to rationalize the coal industry were not in the end successful. Through the course of the steel rationalization plan dependence on foreign ore and coal increased, and contemporary observers credited the switch to using heavy oil as having been very important.[22] Attempts to increase electric generating capacity by relying on hydroelectric power ran into the problem of limited sites, and development came to rely more on thermal generation. Industrial policy was not a panacea, as some adherents of the Japan, Inc. view would have one believe. Whatever the intent of industrial ration-alization policies, during the course of their use, it was industries with declining costs that were successfully promoted, while the policies were a failure for increasing-cost industries.[23] To the extent that industrial ra-tionalization policies represented an attempt to come to terms with an open economy, this was a natural outcome. And to the extent that competitiveness on world markets became a basis for making policy judgments, one can also see that it became difficult to advance policies whose success was difficult to envisage.

C. Industrial Promotion Policies: The Machinery Industry Law

During the latter part of the 1950s the Japanese economy began to set out on the path to rapid growth, and technological innovations were introduced in earnest. Notable changes included a shift in the basic energy sources used by the economy, the utilization of new materials and the introduction of mass production methods in producing consumer durables, and the beginnings of a technological revolution. Along with the continuation of industrial rationalization policies, the building of industrial infrastructure,[24] the fostering and promotion of new and growth industries, and the protection and adjustment of declining industries came to be part of a many-faceted industrial policy. Promotion policies for new and growth industries will be examined here.

An early target of promotion policies was synthetic fibers (the April 1953 Synthetic Fiber Five-Year Development Plan); other examples of the promotion of new and growth industries include petrochemicals (Petrochemicals Promotion Measures, July 1955), machinery parts and general machinery (Machinery Industry Promotion Temporary Measures Law, May 1956), and electronics (Electronic Industry Promotion Temporary Measures Law, June 1957). Acetate fibers, carbide, tar, synthetic rubbers, plastics, aircraft, and nuclear power have also been targets of infant industry policies. Among these are ones for which promotion policies were limited in scope almost from the start due to the scarcity of natural resources or other problems.

The principal measures for promoting petrochemicals included the sale to the private sector of former military fuel storage facilities, loans from the Japan Development Bank and other government banks, accelerated depreciation, reductions in corporate income taxes and tariffs on imported machinery, and the approval of imports of foreign technology. For the machinery industries, under the Machinery Industry Law, provision was made for the drawing up of industry-by-industry rationalization programs, the supplying of government funds, the designation of rationalization cartels, and the drawing up of industry standards to aid in advancing production techniques. Most of the rest of the industry promotion programs consisted of some combination of the measures used in these two cases, but there were also examples of direct government investment (for example, synthetic rubber).

In addition to the policies used in promoting the industries outlined above, the use of import restrictions to protect domestic manufacturers should perhaps be mentioned. In the case of petrochemicals, the domestic market had been opened to imports, and domestic firms were in effect new entrants into the market. Domestic output surpassed imports for the first time in 1964, by which time foreign exchange savings from domestic production were placed at US$82 million. Domestic manufacturers in industries such as automobiles and heavy electrical equipment were protected through import restrictions. But even in these cases, the aim was not to protect firms for the sake of protection; there was a mechanism that brought the pressure of foreign competition to bear upon them. In the case of heavy electrical equipment, for instance, the first generator was imported and the second was domestically produced, thereby forcing the domestic producers to step up their efforts at catching up in technology. The specialization of Japanese auto companies in the production of compact cars was also a response to the offensive of foreign car imports,[25] and the importation of foreign manufacturing technology in the industry was readily approved. On the other hand, there was relatively little assistance in the form of tax incentives and government lending to these industries, and even such as was given was largely eliminated by the late 1950s.[26] This was because by that time the electrical and automotive industries had advanced to the point where they were highly profitable.

In the tax reform of 1957, excise tax exemptions for important materials were limited to new industries, which for the most part meant petrochemical products. For machinery parts, basic machinery, and electronic equipment, temporary promotion laws were drawn up. The reason given to justify the special treatment of these industries was the claim that they were infant industries. It is most interesting that it was also about this time that there was a policy debate to justify government intervention where industrial organization was a policy concern, that is, where small and medium enterprises were prevalent and where there was excess competition such that large-scale production was not sufficiently profitable.

Petrochemicals, for example, are an archetype for industries where large-scale facilities are the core, where returns-to-scale are high and the minimum scale of investment is large, and where flexibility in production is not great. Nevertheless there were many firms that sought to enter the industry, such as the old *zaibatsu* chemical companies, carbide producers, and petroleum companies, so that excess competition became a concern. In promoting petrochemicals, "orderly" investment was thought to be necessary, and notable efforts were made by MITI to regulate the industry.

MITI appeared to have levers that it could use for this purpose in the sale of former military fuel facilities and its monopoly on the approval of foreign technology licenses. Such controls were even thought to make MITI almighty. In practice, such tools do not seem to have been used very selectively: firms that sought to enter the industry were, in the end, able to do so. Even with the tremendous powers MITI had, it was not able to prevent excess competition. Rather, it seems that because of this vigorous competition, the petrochemical industry was able to expand.

In contrast to the petrochemical industry, which was comprised of large-scale firms, machine parts and basic machinery were assembly industries composed of small-scale firms. Their promotion was the object of the Machinery Industry Promotion Temporary Measures Law. Government intervention in these industries was justified from the perspective of the theory of industrial organization, seeking to rectify a situation in which firms were so small that their productivity was necessarily low. But because the machinery industries were for the most part composed of small firms, policies under the Machinery Industry Law had facets relatively different from those of industrial policy aimed at the other industries that have been so far discussed. First, industrial policy up to that time had focused on basic industries and hence was directly involved in the support of large firms. The Machinery Industry Law dealt with a host of smaller firms, though the rationalization of smaller firms producing parts and basic machinery would of course be beneficial to the automotive and other large firms. At any rate, the view that "all industries that MITI judged to be either strategic or growth industries were large-scale 'facility' industries"[27] is too simplistic. Second, in line with this, the industries that were the object of the Machinery Industry Law were held to be labor-intensive and to be ones in which Japan had traditionally had a comparative advantage.[28] These policies were also held to contribute to the goal of full employment, which had been part of economic policy (alongside that of economic independence) since 1955.

The holding up of full employment as a goal of industrial policy calls for special comment, as it is normally thought of as a macroeconomic problem. In the mid-1950s, full employment was used to mean the elimination of the dual structure. In a dualistic structure in which the economy was divided between a handful of large firms and a host of very small firms, the object of the Machinery Industry Law can be seen as fostering medium-scale, specialized manufacturers. While the Machinery Industry Law had small and medium enterprises as its focus, this was not being done by MITI "as an element of social policy, but as an active participant in developing manufacturing systems."[29] The concern was that where there was too great a gap between a final assembler and its parts subcontractors, there is a tendency for the parent firm to adopt a self-contained manufacturing structure, integrated back even into parts, and an irrational structure results in which each of the parent firms maintains poorly utilized productive facilities . . . [while] subcontractors have to survive at a low technical level by relying on low-wage labor, and are reduced to the status of serving as safety valves through which the parent adjusts to the business cycle, a dependent status from which they are unable to escape.[30]

In other words, the Machinery Industry Law sought to bring about an ideal social division of labor, that is, it was an industrial organization policy. It incorporated a refined "vision" that did not simply view larger as better or, in terms of the make-or-buy decision, did not see in-house production as unconditionally superior.[31] It was because of this that rationalization cartels were held to be an important policy instrument under the Machinery Industry Law.

How should the impact of the mid-1950s policies for promoting new and growth industries be evaluated? From the latter 1950s the Japanese economy maintained rapid growth centered on the development of these new and growth industries. At the least this indicates that there were no critical failures in industrial policy during this period. But there were many factors other than industrial policy that contributed to the growth and development of the economy during this period; thus it cannot be concluded that because of the evident economic growth, industrial policy was successful.

In the presence of imperfect capital markets, the tax system and government lending seemed to have resulted in a freer flow of funds into new and growth industries. Certainly in the case of the small and medium enterprises that were the targets of the Machinery Industry Law, it is recognized that government finance paved the way for better access to other funding, and the possibility of loans spurred firms to improve their accounting practices and, while markets were yet narrow, provided the push to carry out investment for rationalization. According to the Japan Development Bank, during 1956–1960, dependence on government funding was 41% for engineering works that qualified for Special Machinery loans.[32] Initially the record was not very impressive, but rationalization cartels were recognized as having been beneficial for, among other things, imposing uniform standards on certain product areas.[33] But if one asked what the basic reasons were for the growth and development of parts and basic machinery manufacturing, the answer was that it was the expansion of the market and the introduction of new technologies.[34] For example, in the case of auto parts manufacturers, even though subcontractors were dependent on a single car company for the bulk of their sales, the amount purchased from them increased sufficiently to permit productivity improvement through specialization.

Among industrial promotion measures, there was much attention paid to the use of licensing of foreign capital (including foreign borrowing), of purchases of foreign technology, and of imports of foreign machinery. It must first be noted that, if there had not been restrictions on these, such policies would not have been thought of as promotion tools. It may be argued that without import restrictions, many other goods would have been imported, resulting in contractionary fiscal policy, so that in order to equilibrate the balance of payments, imports needed by the new industries would have been crowded out. But countering this it can be argued that in the absence of restrictions, the market would have operated with sufficient foresight. When imports in an industry increased, the capital and labor resources deployed therein would have shifted toward alternative uses; this presumably would have represented a favorable situation for new industries that were competitive. For heavy electrical equipment, it must be recognized that the policy of permitting initial but not subsequent items to be imported was beneficial to the development of the domestic industry, but this policy does not serve to explain how the domestic industry was able to improve technically so as to be able to actually produce the "second" machine.

In sum, industrial promotion policies had some small impact in supplementing the direction that the market gave to industry, thereby reducing friction. Industrial policy could not by itself bring forth a new industry, however; nor were appropriate industries always chosen for promotion.

IV. Conclusion

In reflecting on Japanese industrial policy over the period 1945–1960, the unusual initial conditions must first be noted. The Japanese economy was isolated from world markets, and wartime direct controls were being continued. Under the Allied Occupation the *zaibatsu* were broken up, and together with anticoncentration measures this served to weaken the ability of firms to recover at that time. In such a situation, that government interventions in and influence on industry were very substantial could not be helped. The priority production system, for example, was carried out through the use of direct controls over prices and materials backed up by subsidies and government lending programs. In the case of industrial rationalization policies, the government often took the initiative in designating industries and applying appropriate policy instruments (with the assumption that there would be foreign competition), even though policy shifted to the provision of incentives to the private sector through special tax measures and low-cost finance, as opposed to direct intervention.

Throughout the period there was an evolution of the Japanese economy, as it proceeded from being closed to open and as industry moved from facing controls to facing the market. The goals and tools of industrial policy could not help but reflect these changes. In addition, especially after the imposition of the Dodge Line, industrial policy was not free from limitations placed on it by overall macroeconomic policy, such as the desire to hold the exchange rate fixed or to balance the budget; policymakers were not wholly unified. In terms of policy effectiveness, there are examples where the expected benefits did not arise and cases where bureaucratic controls were a barrier. Policy was certainly not all-powerful. In fact, during this period, examples are not uncommon where the entrepreneurial spirit at play in the private sector took the lead in showing the direction in which the economy would develop.[35]

In sum, this period was one of transition from extraordinary initial conditions to a time of normalcy, and industrial policy served both to supplement the workings of the market and at times to interfere with its operations. If there was something in industrial policy that had an enduring impact on the development of Japanese industry, it must be found in the speeding up of the adaptation of firms to the market system. A new phase in industrial policy began after 1960, with the economy in the midst of rapid growth and the freeing of trade.

Notes

1. This was often referred to explicitly in government documents; e.g., "to further the desire of coal mine operators to increase output, producer prices should be raised as soon as possible" (Okurasho, Zaiseishi Shitsu [1981], p. 324. See also pp. 305 and 306.) In terms of the effectiveness of guidelines for financial institution lending, Nihon Kogyo Ginko (Industrial Bank of Japan) [1957], p. 680, claims that in spite of the investment priorities set forth by the government, funds in fact flowed into industries that were highly profitable.
2. Johnson [1982], pp. 17 ff, Ueno [1978], pp. 12–14.
3. Nakayama [1953], Arisawa [1953]. Tsusansho Kigyo Kyoku (MITI Enterprises Bureau [1952], p. 9) states that "the position which we choose is in the main mercantilist."
4. For the use of the term "economic independence" see Tsusansho Kigyo Kyoku (MITI Enterprises Bureau [1952], p. 2) and Hayashi, Yujiro [1957], p. 99.
5. "The entirety of domestic policy is focused on increasing the output of coal. Because of this the industry has the absolute top priority in obtaining the raw materials necessary to increase production." (Okurasho Zaiseishi Shitsu [1981], p. 317.)
6. For example, Arisawa [1957], p. 210.
7. Nihon Tekko Remmei [1959], pp. 23 and 485.
8. Arisawa [1957], pp. 223 and 226–227, Arisawa [1948], p. 87.
9. Hayek [1931], p. 94. Hayek (p. 103) draws attention to Bresciani-Turroni's [1937] analysis of the German inflation, which Arisawa had studied closely.

10. Arisawa ([1948], pp. 32 and 192) observed that post-WWII Japan, in contrast to post-WWI Germany, "was an isolated economy, almost totally closed off to the outside."

11. Let us assume there is slack in the capital stock. Production (O) is restricted by the availability of one basic input (labor L) and an intermediate input (M). Output is divided between K and final consumption (C). Let w be the real wage and c the propensity to consume. Then $O = C + K$ (allocation of output); $O = AL^a M^{1-a}$ (production function); $C = ckL = caO = caA^{1/a}L(1 - ca)^{(1 - a)/a.}$ The propensity to consume c, which maximizes consumption, must satisfy $dC/dc = 0$ and $d^2C/dc^2 < 0$. Hence c is equal to one, as with the well-known Golden Rule of neoclassical growth theory. A propensity to consume in excess of unity, which comes from living beyond one's means, fails to maximize consumption.

12. On the determination of amounts due under price support subsidies, see Nihon Tokei Kenkyusho [1956], pp. 61–62 and 106–113, and Nihon Tekko Remmei [1959], p. 41.

13. Okurasho Zaiseishi Shitsu ([1981], pp. 350–352) states: "Domestic coal prices, especially the prices of special coals such as those usable for coking, were very high relative to international prices. This presented a barrier to the independence of steel and other heavy industries, and it was extremely difficult to export profitably once price support payments had been reduced or eliminated. In consideration of this, a goal was set of achieving by 1953 the rationalization of the steel industry as the most important export and basic industry, and at the same time carrying out various policies for the rationalization of the coal industry so as to obtain a reduction in coal prices. Through the joint efforts of these two industries in line with the above target date, a foundation would be laid for the independence of Japanese industry."

14. On the progress of this debate, see Nihon Tekko Remmei [1959], pp. 154–157.

15. On the linking system, see footnote 3 in Chapter 5.

16. The promotion of new industries will be discussed later in this chapter.

17. At the time Governor Ichimada of the Bank of Japan opposed the idea of a domestic passenger car industry and was held to have said that the Kawasaki Steel Chiba Plant would be abandoned to the weeds (Tsuruta [1982], p. 39). Ichimada claims that he made no such statement (Nakamura, Takafusa [1970]). For more on the Bank of Japan and the automotive industry, see Toyota Jidosha [1958], pp. 544–545.

18. Hayashi [1957], pp. 179–185, and Keizai Kikakucho [1953], pp. 38–40.

19. It is not easy to adequately verify these assertions. Note, however, the sign reversal in the coefficient of government funds between 1947–1955 and 1956–1965 in the private fixed business investment function as estimated below by the present author:

Private Fixed Business Investment Function

Period	Constant	Corporate Saving	GNP Increment	Interest Rate	Government Funds	Private Funds
1947– 1955	1129	0.477 (7.30)	−0.076 (−1.06)	−0.036 (−1.39)	1.257 (3.21)	—
1947– 1955	1020	0.460 (6.52)	—	−0.024 (−0.69)	1.095 (2.59)	0.033 (0.31)
1956– 1965	29,792	0.929 (3.79)	0.100 (0.57)	−4229 (0.46)	−0.210 (−0.06)	—

20. According to the input–output tables for 1951, 1955, 1960, and 1965 (Uno [1983]), 10% reductions of mining and steel product prices have the following impact on the price index for mining and manufacturing. This indicates an especially strong impact (percent reduction) from correcting the high coal and steel prices in 1951.

Reduction (%) in Mining and Manufacturing Price Index in Response to a 10% Reduction in Mining and Steel Prices

Year	Mining	Steel
1951	3.07	1.01
1955	2.98	0.81
1960	2.28	1.00
1965	2.13	0.77

21. One test of whether the selection of the targets of government policy consisted of industries that later actually grew rapidly can be made by looking at the industries that were made eligible for accelerated depreciation in Article 6 of the Industry Rationalization Promotion Law. Limiting the comparison to industries for which there were corresponding categories in the Census of Manufactures, and comparing the growth rate of value added relative to that of manufacturing as a whole, there is a significant difference in the rates of growth of the two groups for the period 1955–1960.

Growth in Value Added for Industries Designated Under Article 6 of the Industry Rationalization Promotion Law

	1950–55	1955–60
All manufacturing[a]	287%	230%
Designated industries[b]	302%	257%
(Initially designated industries)	288%	267%

Source: Census of Manufactures (Tsusho Tokei Kyokai [1982]).

[a]Nondesignated industries are at the 3-digit level; if a designated industry is at the 4-digit level, that industry is excluded from the 3-digit industry to which it belongs.

[b]Includes only those industries for which a comparable classification exists in the Census (25 of the 26 industries designated initially and 11 of the 18 industries designated subsequently).

Analysis of Variance (1955–60)[a]

	Sum of Squares	Degrees of Freedom	Variance	F-Ratio
Between groups	16.38	1	16.38	4.16
Within groups	544.04	138	3.94	—

Source: Census of Manufactures (Tsusho Tokei Kyokai [1982]).

[a]The averages used for the analysis are unweighted averages of industries.

22. Nihon Tekko Remmei [1959], pp. 373–376.
23. For evidence that coal mining was an increasing-cost industry, see Tsusansho Kigyo Kyoku (MITI Enterprises Bureau) [1952], pp. 405–406, and Keizai Kikakucho Chosakyoku (Economic Planning Agency Research Bureau) [1972], p. 71. As shown below, the production function for mining estimated for 1949–1960 exhibits low returns to scale and negative technical progress.

$$\log O = -4.75 + 0.723 \log K + 0.235 \log L - 0.031t \quad R = 0.978$$
$$ (2.88) \qquad (1.30) \qquad (-1.23)$$

$$\log O = -7.44 + 0.749 \log K + 0.375 \log hL - 0.032t \quad R = 0.982$$
$$ (3.48) \qquad (1.96) \qquad (-1.49)$$

where O = mining production index (Tsusansho); K = mining capital stock (Keizai Kikakucho Kenkyusho [1962]); L = mining employment index (Monthly Labor Statistics); h = index of hours worked in mining (Monthly Labor Statistics); t = time (t-ratios in parentheses).
24. The construction of industrial infrastructure was recommended in the 1951 Industrial Structure Council report, but the building up of social overhead capital related to industry was not begun in earnest until the latter part of the 1950s, when after the contractionary "One Trillion Yen" budget there began a trend of growth in government expenditure. At that time, the provision of an industrial base appeared in the 1957 New Long-Term Economic Plan as a major element in macroeconomic planning.
25. Toyota Jidosha Kogyo [1958], pp. 371–373.
26. Tsusansho [1957], p. 367, and Nihon Kaihatsu Ginko [1963], pp. 291–292.
27. Ueno [1978], p. 10.
28. Tsusansho Jukogyo Kyoku [1956], p. 9.
29. Ibid, p. 56.
30. Ibid, pp. 55–56.
31. See Odaka [1978].
32. Nihon Kaihatsu Ginko [1963], p. 298.
33. The number of rationalization cartels under the law were as follows:

Rationalization Cartels Approved Under the Machinery Promotion and Electrical Industry Promotion Laws, 1956–1970

	1956	57	58	59	60	61	62	63	64	65	66	67	68	69	70
Machinery	0	0	0	1	1	5	6	14	14	9	6	8	17	16	17
Electric	—	0	0	0	0	0	0	0	1	1	1	0	0	1	2

Source: Kosei Torihiki Iinkai [1977], p. 767.

34. See Miwa [1959].
35. Let me here touch on a few common misconceptions about Japanese industrial policy. First, as has been commented on above, the Japan, Inc. interpretation had as its model the industrial rationalization policies discussed in this chapter. Even so, the view reflects an excessive simplification even of those policies. Second, Katzenstein [1978] claims that rapid growth was sought in Japan through "a formidable set of policy instruments which directly influence[d] individual industries and firms" (p. 20), but in Japan the

maintenance of the yen exchange rate was important as was the defense by the United Kingdom of the Pound Sterling (ibid., p. 107), and under contractionary policies industrial policy was restricted. Third, Murakami [1982] sees the role of industrial policy as having been to limit competition through restricting entry, but this ignores the fact that industrial concentration in Japan followed a strictly declining trend.

CHAPTER 3

The Rapid Growth Era[1]

TOSHIMASA TSURUTA

Department of Economics
Senshu University
Tokyo, Japan

I. The Japanese Economy in the 1960s

To facilitate an objective assessment of industrial policy during the rapid growth era, let us first examine an overview of the Japanese economy during the 1960s.[2] Both positive and negative aspects of economic performance can be discerned. Three positive facets of the economy are apparent. First, during this period the economy grew at a historically unprecedented rate (see Table I). During the 1950s the economy also grew quite rapidly, but this growth accelerated in the 1960s, and the last five years of the period were distinguished by an average growth rate of over 10%. With the incremental capital-output ratio remaining at a low level, the source of this growth lay in the marked increase in the investment rate. As a result of rapid growth, in 1968 Japan became the second largest economy in the free world (after the United States), joining the ranks of the major economic powers. This period also marked the transition to a full-employment economy.

Beginning in the 1950s and continuing throughout the 1960s, rapid growth was realized under the ideal conditions of a balanced budget and stable wholesale prices. From about 1960 there was an onset of a creeping inflation, with overall inflation (as measured by the GNP deflator) increasing to an annual rate of 5%, but during the first half of the period wholesale prices remained virtually constant and rose on average at a low 2.5% p.a. during the second half. This was the result of technological advances in many industries, which facilitated the expansion of supply and resulted in increases in productivity. Fiscal balance was achieved through a sub-

TABLE I
Japanese Principal Economic Indicators

Economic indicators	1950–55	1955–60	1960–65	1965–70	1970–75	1975–80
Real growth rate[1], %	10.90	8.7	9.7	12.2	5.1	5.6
Investment/GNP ratio (A)[1], %	7.9	11.4	14.8	18.1	18.2	17.1
Investment/GNP ratio (B)[1], %	10.8	16.5	18.5	18.5	17.8	14.7
Incremental capital-output ratio[1]	0.7	1.3	1.5	1.5	3.6	3.1
Productivity growth[2], %	8.2	6.5	8.0	10.4	4.7	4.4
Change in total employment, %	2.7	2.2	1.7	1.8	0.4	1.2
Change in index of mining and manufacturing production, %	15.5	20.3	11.3	15.5	2.0	6.7
Change in GNP deflator, %	4.1[3]	3.3	5.0	5.1	10.7	4.4
Change in wholesale price index, %	+0.0[4]	0.5	0.4	2.5	9.4	5.6
Change in consumer price index, %	3.9[4]	2.0	6.2	5.4	11.3	6.4
Current account surplus ($ million)	—	534	Δ1,058	7,133	6,910	11,632
Foreign reserves ($ million)[5]	738	1,824	2,017	4,399	12,815	25,232

[1]Adapted from Kosai [1981], p. 4. Investment in (A) is in nominal terms and in (B) is in real terms.
[2]Mining and manufacturing.
[3]1952–55.
[4]1951–55.
[5]Balance at the end of period.

stantial natural increase in revenue each year, which was the result of a consistent underestimation of the growth rate by the government.

Second, there was progress in industrialization and greater diversification in industry. The rapid pace of industrialization can be clearly seen in changes in the sectoral composition of employment (see Table II). Employment dropped rapidly in the primary sector and increased in the secondary and tertiary sectors, a clear confirmation of the Petty–Clark Law. Within manufacturing, heavy industry—with its high income elasticity of demand—continued to grow rapidly, so that the share of heavy industry in manufacturing reached more than 62% in 1970 (see Table III). Fur-

TABLE II
Sectoral Distribution of Employment

	Total Employment (thousands)	Primary Sector (%)	Secondary Sector (%)	Tertiary Sector (%)
1930	29,649	49.7	20.3	29.8
1950	36,025	48.5	21.8	29.6
1960	43,961	32.6	29.2	38.2
1970	52,468	19.4	33.9	46.7
1975	53,140	13.9	34.1	51.7

Source: Sorifu [Prime Minister's Office], Kokusei Chosa [Population Census].

thermore, during the 1960s the economy's dual structure began to disappear. Diversification in the economy can be seen in the increased role of "mainstay" firms,[3] the rapid expansion of supermarkets in retailing, and the general increase in the number of business establishments.[4]

Third, throughout the 1960s, exports expanded rapidly, and from around 1965–1968, under the fixed exchange rate system, the country began running a chronic current account surplus. The quantity index of exports rose

TABLE III
Composition and Growth of Manufacturing

	Manufacturing Output	Heavy Industry				Light Industry			
		Chemicals	Metals	Machinery	Sub-total	Foods	Textiles	Other	Sub-total
	(¥ billion)	Composition (%)							
1950	2,276	14.9	12.6	14.1	41.6	14.0	24.0	20.4	58.4
1955	6,780	12.9	16.8	15.0	44.6	17.9	17.4	20.0	55.4
1960	15,579	11.8	18.8	25.8	56.4	12.4	12.3	18.9	43.6
1965	29,497	12.3	17.7	26.6	56.6	12.5	10.3	20.6	43.4
1970	69,035	10.6	19.3	32.3	62.3	10.4	7.7	19.6	37.7
1975	127,521	14.1	17.1	29.8	61.0	11.9	6.8	20.3	39.0
	Average Annual Growth Rate (%)								
1955/50	24.4	20.9	31.7	25.9	26.2	30.7	16.7	23.9	23.1
1960/55	18.1	16.0	20.9	31.6	23.7	9.7	10.2	13.9	12.6
1965/60	13.6	14.6	12.3	14.3	13.7	13.9	9.6	15.5	13.5
1970/65	18.5	15.1	20.6	23.3	20.8	14.1	11.9	17.4	15.3
1975/70	13.0	19.7	10.3	11.3	12.6	16.2	10.1	13.8	13.8

Source: Sangyo Kenkyu Jo [1979].

at an annual average rate of 17.9% during the first half of the period and at 15.1% during the second half, approximately double the rate of increase of world imports. At the industry level, chemicals, steel, and machinery (broadly defined) were particularly important; on a customs-clearance basis, the growth of exports in these industries accounted for over 75% of the overall growth of exports. In contrast, traditional export goods, such as processed foods, textiles, and nonmetalic mineral products, declined in relative importance, reflecting a shift in the leading export products. Under rapid growth, the comparative advantage of the former industries increased, and the comparative disadvantage of the latter became obvious (see Table IV).

During the 1960s, Japan came to share many of the salient characteristics of a developed economy. Some obvious items were (1) the achievement of full employment, (2) modernization of the industrial structure, (3) the eclipse of the dual economy, (4) the importance of heavy industry exports and the chronic current account surplus, and (5) institutionally, the liberalization of trade and foreign direct investment in Japan. The first four of these had been the main objectives of economic policy from the 1950s, and rapid growth can be said to have speeded the achievement of these goals. The fifth item, the transition to an open economy, was in line with the terms set earlier under which Japan joined the IMF and GATT and hence was something that Japan was obligated to do, whatever the actual intentions of the government.

On the other hand, during the 1960s, negative aspects could be seen in (1) the onset of creeping inflation from about 1960, (2) increasingly severe problems with pollution and citizen's movements concerned with it, and (3) problems with the oligopolist dominance of markets in industry and the rise of a consumers' movement. Creeping inflation was regarded as a malaise endemic to developed market economies, and it made its appearance in Japan as the economy approached full employment and the dual structure gave way. The problems with pollution became acute because of the single-minded pursuit of economies of scale in industrial policy and the tardiness in trying to regulate negative externalities. Problems with the oligopolistic dominance of markets arose because of the failure of antitrust policy to gain widespread support in Japan and was evidenced in events such as the illegal price maintenance activities of Matsushita and Sony, the two-tiered pricing of color TVs, and the creation of Nippon Steel through the merger of Fuji Steel and Yahata Steel. The awareness of problems with pollution and oligopolistic markets in the 1960s foreshadowed the more prominent role of regulatory policies in the 1970s.

TABLE IV
Principal Exports

	Total Exports	Foods	Textiles	Chemicals	Mineral Products	Metals and Metal Products		Machinery		Other
	($ million)					Total %	Steel	Total %	Autos	
				Share of Total Exports (Customs Base), %						
1950	298	6.0	48.3	2.0	3.7	18.1	8.7	10.1	—	12.1
1955	2,010	6.3	37.3	5.1	4.6	19.3	12.9	12.4	0.3	15.1
1960	4,005	6.3	30.2	4.5	4.2	14.0	9.6	22.9	1.9	9.6
1965	8,452	4.1	18.7	6.5	3.1	20.3	15.3	35.2	2.8	12.1
1970	19,318	3.3	12.5	6.4	1.9	19.7	14.7	46.3	6.9	9.9
1975	55,753	1.4	6.7	7.0	1.3	22.5	18.3	53.8	11.1	7.4
1980	129,807	1.2	4.9	5.2	1.4	16.4	11.9	63.8	17.9	8.1
				Average Annual Growth Rate, Export Volume Index (Customs Base), %						
1955/50	18.2	21.9	11.8	44.2	20.4	15.1	—	28.7	—	24.4
1960/55	14.1	14.7	10.3	17.7	11.9	6.6	4.8	24.4	99.4	19.1
1965/60	17.9	2.6	5.7	28.1	6.3	28.3	31.6	31.7	38.0	10.8
1970/65	15.1	6.8	7.1	22.9	2.6	13.3	12.7	21.4	41.1	13.1
1975/70	9.9	Δ7.8	0.9	6.4	Δ0.3	8.9	10.8	15.0	19.8	0.7
1980/75	9.2	4.3	0.4	1.7	9.9	4.1	0.2	12.7	17.4	10.9

Source: Nihon Kanzei Kyokai.

II. The Framework of Industrial Policy

In trying to objectively evaluate industrial policy during the rapid growth era, Section II examines the framework of industrial policy: changes in institutional elements, changes in government–business relations, and changes in the policymaking environment, such as changes in political ideology, the policy formation process, and the objectives of government policy. In the remainder of the chapter it will be shown that the 1960s was a transitional period during which the free enterprise system model came to dominate the conception of industrial policy.[5] To illustrate this point, Section III will take up a few of the central industrial policies of the 1960s and attempt to evaluate them from the perspective of the leverage of the government over the private sector. Section IV will conclude by giving some reflections on industrial policy during the rapid growth era.

A. Changes in the Institutional Environment

Resource allocation in the Japanese economy in the 1950s took place through the price system but within the context of protective government policy that allocated imports and regulated direct foreign investment. But in June 1960, the government announced a trade and foreign exchange liberalization plan for the transition from protectionism to a free trade system. After 1964, when Japan joined the OECD, the liberalization of direct foreign investment (capital liberalization) became another important policy issue.

Trade liberalization proceeded in stages from 1961, with trade more than 90% free by 1964. Japan also became an Article VIII IMF member, liberalizing foreign exchange transactions in April 1964. Trade liberalization progressed in stages through the latter half of the 1960s and the early 1970s, including even agricultural commodities, so that by December 1975 import restrictions remained for only 27 classes of goods (see Table V). The liberalization of capital transactions commenced with the First Stage Capital Liberalization of 1967 and was completed with the Fifth Stage of 1973.

Trade liberalization meant that the government lost its power to allocate imports, while capital liberalization resulted in the loss of the power to approve technology imports, joint ventures with foreign firms, and new plant construction, which was a consequence of the control of technology imports. Government intervention in industry gradually declined from the late 1940s through the start of the 1950s, with the transition from a con-

TABLE V
Import Liberalization

Year	Month	Restrictions Removed	Restrictions Remaining		
			Total Number	Manufactured Goods	Agricultural Commodities
1962	4	8	466	—	—
	10	230	232	—	—
	11	8	224	—	—
1963	4	25	197	—	—
	6	2	195	—	—
	8	35	155	87	68
1964	1	3	152	84	68
	2	7	145	77	68
	4	8	136	69	67
	10	12	123	56	67
1965	10	1	122	55	67
1966	4	2	120	54	66
	5	—	126*	57	69
	10	1	124	56	68
1968	4	2	122	54	68
	10	1	121	53	68
1969	4	1	120	52	68
	10	2	118	50	68
1970	2	9	109	45	64
	4	11	98	39	59
	9	8	90	35	55
1971	1	10	80	31	49
	6	20	60	20	40
	10	20	40	12	28
1972	4	6	33	9	24
1973	4	1	32	8	24
	11	1	31	8	23
1974	10	1	30	8	22
	12	1	29	7	22
1975	12	2	27	5	22

Source: Nihon Boeki Kyokai.
*Increased due to a revision of the tariff schedule.

trolled to a free market economy, but the government still was able to intervene in industrial activity through the licensing of technology imports and direct foreign investment and the allocation of imports. Liberalization eliminated the leverage of the government for intervening in industrial activity, and resource allocation by means of the price system was extended even to trade and direct foreign investment.

B. Government–Business Relations

The Japanese economy in the 1960s was on the whole based on the free enterprise system; although it was within the framework of a protectionist trade policy, free enterprise had already become the base for the economy by the 1950s. With the exception of agriculture and an extremely small number of other industries, firms were able to make independent decisions. Except as firms bear risk and provide quality goods and services at reasonable prices, it was very difficult for them to prosper.

From the 1950s, firms were able to follow a path of rapid growth through Schumpeterian innovation: new product development, the implementation of thorough quality control methods, and the improvement of production processes. They were able to do this because by that time the price system in Japan was already functioning relatively smoothly. The world of the Penrosian firm[6] was realized in Japan at that time, where the accumulation of human capital was the limiting factor in firm growth. Since the oil crisis, the performance of the Japanese economy has garnered much attention, both at home and abroad, but the foundation for this performance was being laid throughout the 1950s and 1960s.

During the 1960s, the capital-output ratio remained at a low level, without doubt the result of technical change. Features such as rapid growth, the modernization of industry, the expansion of exports, and the maintenance of a current account surplus were certainly not the result of constant government intervention to bring about economic change, but were rather due to a smoothly functioning price system and the development of a competitive market environment. The Japan, Inc. model, which insists that these achievements were due to the guiding hand of the government, is simply incapable of explaining the Japanese economy in the 1960s.

Nevertheless, the government was not able to correctly discern the pattern of growth of the Japanese economy and tried through its interventions to give direction to industrial activity. The economic variables that in fact had the deciding impact on the tenor of industrial policy were the institutional changes such as trade and capital liberalization. In the postwar period, many Japanese industries developed very rapidly, but they did this without facing the market test of foreign competition. Thus, the government did not always have complete confidence in the ability of firms to adapt to the changing institutional environment. The idea that the government should take a guiding hand in the modernization of industry had its origins in this lack of confidence.

Even though the government sought to guide the modernization of industry, it is important to note that at that time the role of the government in the private sector was extremely limited. Insofar as Japan opted for an economic system in which firms were free to make their own decisions, it could not be expected that government intentions could be realized in full when they went against the grain of the direction in which the economy was developing. The government, though, was able to contribute to macroeconomic balance through indirect policy tools such as fiscal and monetary policy and can be commended for maintaining such balance throughout the 1960s.

Government intervention in industry was not carried out without guiding principles. Intervention could be divided between institutionalized intervention backed by specific laws and "administrative guidance" not backed by specific laws. To the extent that the basic political system in Japan was a parliamentary democracy with a tripartite division of powers, there was no assurance that the government (that is, the bureaucracy) could enact the laws it desired. There was, for example, the ultimate failure (discussed later in more detail) to enact the Special Industries Law,[7] considered as potentially the most important law in the area of industrial policy in the postwar era. There were in fact many such laws that supported government intervention in agriculture, transportation, communications, finance, and services, but there were not that many in manufacturing, which formed the backbone of the economy.[8]

Opinion is divided on the extent to which the government could effectively intervene through the use of administrative guidance; to the extent that such guidance was not backed by law, government goals in the end could only be achieved through the persuasion of and acquiescence by firms. One must be dubious of claims that government guidance was effective in decisively influencing industrial development, given its particularistic and limited nature.

C. The Policy Environment and Ideology

In Japan in the 1960s, the government and the private sector did not have as much faith as they do in the effectiveness of the price mechanism in allocating resources. In comparison with previous plans, the long-term economic plan announced by the government in December 1960 (the Income Doubling Plan) had a wide variety of novel features, among which was an emphasis on the allocation of resources through the price mechanism and reliance on a free enterprise system in which firms were free to make their own choices. This was the first plan in which the government set forth a clear vision of the utilization of the free enterprise system.[9]

Even in the Income Doubling Plan, however, a number of policy concerns (intermediate targets) were set forth as essential conditions for economic growth. These areas of concern were (1) the modernization of agriculture, (2) the correction of "differentials" through the modernization of small- and medium-scale enterprises and the elimination of the dual structure, and (3) the need to form a new industrial order to cope with liberalization.[10] In the area of agriculture, the direction of policy, which aimed for the removal of direct controls, the fostering of independent family farms through the reform of the agricultural landholding system, and the increasing of productivity, was appropriate. In areas (2) and (3), a common theme was the achievement of economies of scale. The Income Doubling Plan argued for government intervention in industry by claiming that, for the new industrial order, there was a need to achieve an "appropriate scale" of activity. This was to be done through the concentration (merger or formal tie-up) of firms, the development of firm-level product specialization, and the modernization of small-scale industry.

If one claims to believe in the effectiveness of resource allocation through the price system, there is no room for this sort of policy approach. Government intervention is limited to cases of market failure, and government has an important role to play, not in bringing about industrial restructuring, that is, greater concentration, but rather in the maintenance of the competitive base of the economy through procompetition policies. In understanding the political thinking of the time, it is necessary to remember that there was not the recognition that there is today of the importance of antimonopoly policy in delimiting the rules of competition.[11] The Antimonopoly Law had been imported into Japan in 1947, but in the process of postwar industrialization it took a subordinate role to industrial policy, and there was virtually no debate about the importance of antimonopoly policy from the standpoint of economic welfare. This was because of the underlying doubt about the effectiveness of the price mechanism in allocating resources.

D. The Policy Formation Process

The policy council system took root during this period. In this system, all important policies were first discussed in a policy council, with a formal report sent to the responsible minister—in some cases to be made into law. At the start of the 1960s, industrial policy was for the most part dealt with in the Industrial Structure Advisory Committee,[12] and from 1964 in the Industrial Structure Council (ISC).[13] The Coordination Committee of the ISC was at the top, and under it were committees for the debate of industrial policy toward specific industries.[14] Alongside the ISC, there were also the Electronics Industry Council, the Textile Industry Council, and other councils set up under the terms of specific laws.

In general, the ISC was made up of former bureaucrats, journalists, and representatives of private firms. The ISC was a forum for the formation

of a consensus about industrial policies, the exchange of information between the government and the private sector, and concerted appeals by
the private sector to the government. The ISC released a great variety of
reports during the 1960s,[15] and at first glance, these reports tend to give
the impression that the government was effective in its direct interventions
in industrial activity and its guidance and coordination of industry.

There are many problems in these reports from the standpoint of the
equity of these policies and the standard for allocating resources, but in
thinking about the role of these councils what was really important was
that in fact a great many industry representatives took part. Because of
their participation in the councils, it can be expected that they would react
against any government proposals that would severely restrict the ability
of their firms to act independently. The recommendations of the councils
thus could not help being little more than abstract statements of the stance
of industry, with its presumption of the independence of firms, and at the
level of implementation, it was in fact difficult for the *genkyoku*[16] to act
outside of this framework. The councils can thus be evaluated as having
put a brake on industrial policy that sought to change the organization of
industry through direct intervention. In fact, a great many of the council
reports did not provide backing for the implementation of the industrial
policies, originally sought by the government, which included interventions
in industry.

E. The Goals of Industrial Policy

Industrial policy during the 1960s sought, on the one hand, to carry out
in a progressive fashion trade and capital liberalization, at the same time
taking care to see that liberalization did not cause decisive damage to
various industries. On the other hand, industrial policy sought an industrial
system that could survive liberalization. The latter took the form of concern
with strengthening international competitiveness. From this standpoint,
fiscal and government lending policies can be favorably evaluated as having
contributed to the maintenance of the industrial base.

The government attitude toward liberalization was one of extreme caution. During the progressive liberalization of trade, when there were
thought to be problems with the quality of goods or the competitive
strength of strategic industries, such as the automotive and computer industries, liberalization was delayed until it was certain that the industries
would be competitive with those of foreign countries. The government
also revised the tariff system, raising some tariffs and changing others
from a value to a quantity basis, introducing an emergency tariff system,
a tariff-quota system, a mixed tariff system, and other protectionist tariff

measures as a response to liberalization.[17] While Japan joined the OECD in 1964, it did not begin to liberalize capital transactions until 1967, and it did not complete liberalization until 1973. With 1960 as the starting point, Japan's transition to an open economy required 13 years.

In the transition to an open economic system, the government paid tremendous attention to the creation of a new industrial order capable of facing these changes. The theme of building a new industrial order was centered on the problem of modernizing Japanese industry overall, from large corporations to small-scale enterprises. The creation of a new industrial order was seen as involving items such as (1) a redefining of government–industry relations, which meant a broadening of the power of the government to intervene in industry, (2) a rethinking of the appropriate competitive order, and (3) an increase in the scale of firms through industrial restructuring.

The theme of redefining government–industry relations was a call for replacing the price system with a system of "cooperation" by the private sector with government in artificially coordinating resource allocation (*kanmin kyocho hoshiki,* hereafter the Kanmin System). This bore with it the possibility of a collision with the path development was taking and with the free enterprise system in Japan. The rethinking of the competitive order and the policy concern with increasing the scale of firms were at odds with the rational choices of firms in a market system. The government's conception of industry peculiarities, the need to merge firms in line with presumed economies of scale, the divvying up of products among different makers, the coordination of facilities investment, tie-ups among firms—all these were playing with plans on paper. They could not help but be quite different from the production system chosen by firms in the face of the severe restrictions placed on them by reality.

III. Principal Policies: An Evaluation

In this section, a number of industrial policies representative of the 1960s will be examined in an effort to determine how effective they were in affecting resource allocation and the forms industrial organization took in the Japanese economy. In this effort, an important criterion for evaluating the effectiveness of industrial policy is the interrelationship among policy goals, the available tools, and achievements. Our standpoint is a refutation of the Japan, Inc. interpretation. Those who truly believe in the Japan, Inc. model may think of the 1960s as being the golden age of industrial policy, but our position is that industrial policy during this period was not effective in changing the macroeconomic performance of the economy or in influencing the allocation of resources by industry.

During the 1960s industrial policy was in fact extremely variegated.[18] First, as a response to trade and capital liberalization, there was the attempt to construct a new industrial order. The main policy debates were over the new industrial order (in response to trade liberalization) and over industrial restructuring (in response to capital liberalization). The new industrial order debate ended in the (unsuccessful) attempt to pass the Special Industries Law designed to implement the Kanmin System in which the bureaucracy would have powers to intervene in private decision making. The industrial restructuring debate eventually took the form in the latter 1960s of a policy of encouraging large-scale mergers. The merchant marine reorganization policies and the proposal to combine the firms in the automotive industry into three groups can be thought of as part of this debate.[19]

Second, there was the attempt to guide investment patterns. In the 1960s firms expected the growth rate to be high, and so most firms were very optimistic in their fixed investment behavior. In the government, the ambitious investment behavior of firms gave rise to the judgment that it would be difficult in the near future to avoid excess capacity. The origin of this view was a pessimistic evaluation of the allocative ability of the price system. Thus throughout the 1960s there was government intervention in the investment in new facilities of the steel, synthetic fibers, petroleum refining, petrochemicals, paper and pulp, and other industries. It was through the Kanmin System that MITI sought to guide investment in capital equipment.

Third, where there were many suppliers, where market concentration was low, an attempt was made at policy intervention to coordinate the division of products among firms, to foster a system of specialized producers, and to develop cooperation in production. The interventions undertaken to establish specialized machine tool producers are a classic example of this approach. Again, in the 1963 Small and Medium Enterprises Modernization Law, there was intervention aimed at bringing about an "appropriate scale" and coordinated production among small- and medium-sized firms.

Fourth, there was the attempt to develop an overall energy policy. The Petroleum Industry Law of 1962, the Electric Utilities Law of 1964, the General Energy Advisory Council Law of 1965, the Power Generation and Nuclear Fuel Development Agency Law of 1967, the Coal Mining Industry Reorganization Temporary Measures Law of 1967, and other measures were enacted. These laws sought to achieve many policy goals, including (1) obtaining a stable supply of energy, (2) maintaining domestic ownership (the Petroleum Industry Law), (3) the smoothing of adjustment in the coal mining industry as the primary energy source shifted from coal to oil, and (4) the fostering of the nuclear power industry as a new source of energy (the Nuclear Fuel Development Law).

Fifth, there was the attempt to foster specific industries. Industrial promotion was the object in the 1960s of the Machine Industry Law,[20] the Electronic Industry Promotion Law, and the Aircraft Industry Promotion Law, all of which were carried over from the 1950s. For the computer industry, the Japan Electronic Computer Corporation, a private company, was established in 1961 with the support of the government as a joint venture of the six domestic computer firms to serve as a conduit for government procurement of domestic computers.

In considering the effectiveness of industrial policy, our discussion will center around three of the major industrial policies of the 1960s. First, the attempt to develop a new industrial order as a response to trade liberalization will be evaluated. Second, the coordination of investment and the effectiveness of government intervention will be discussed. Third, the attempt to set up a production system composed of specialized producers will be evaluated. In doing this, the first of the above three topics are taken up as being representative of the 1960s. The fourth and fifth topics are covered elsewhere in the book and thus will not be discussed here.

The reasons for considering these three topics as representative are as follows. First, the response to trade liberalization by promoting the new industrial order through the attempt to legislate special laws in the Diet was symbolic of the thinking toward industrial policy in the early 1960s. The debate over industrial restructuring as a response to capital liberalization arose because policymakers had blind faith in mergers and greater firm concentration leading to economies of scale.[21] Second, the attempt to coordinate investment provides an example of how policymakers at that time saw as irrational the portfolio choices of firms under the price system. In particular, the attempt to coordinate investment through the Kanmin System provides an appropriate case for testing the effectiveness of government policy in changing the otherwise endogenous, market-based investment decisions of firms. Third, examining the attempt to foster a specialized production system in industries in which concentration was low, including small- and medium-scale enterprises, is important in understanding the limits of policy intervention. The theme of fostering a specialized production system as a response to trade and capital liberalization had the machinery industries as its main focus. The policy rational for forming cooperatives for small- and medium-scale firms and the achievement of appropriate scale was the same.

A. The Attempt and Failure to Form a New Industrial Order

The standards for evaluating policy intervention are the system of checks and balances for such policies, the impact on resource allocation, and equity considerations. In the following discussion, particular attention will be paid to the system of checks on government action. Industrial policy in the 1960s reflected the government's strong proclivity to intervene in industrial activities, so that the evaluation of this point is critical to our overall assessment of industrial policy. The Japan, Inc. model is based on a judgment that checks on government policy intervention were weak.

1. The New Industrial Order Debate

The New Industrial Order debate was over the proper form for the industrial system and industrial organization in an era of trade liberalization and of the appropriate pattern for government–business relations, the role within the economic system for antitrust policy, and other topics.[22] There were basically two proposals. One was to encourage the concentration of production—through tie-ups or mergers of firms—so as to change the competitive structure from one of excessive to one of workable competition. The second was to change the nature of government–business relations in order to create an industrial order in which the government could intervene to affect prices, investment, output quantities, and other variables better determined endogenously in the market.

The two topics of achieving an "appropriate" firm size and of maintaining the market order were covered in the above discussion. Achieving an appropriate scale meant the use of mergers and similar means and was based on a blind faith in the myth of economies of scale. Maintaining the market order meant an exclusion of excess competition and the creation of workable competition. These two judgments were interrelated. The source of "insufficient" scale was seen to lie in excess competition, and excess competition arose when the scale of firms was too small. Policies to merge firms or concentrate production sought therefore to simultaneously eliminate these two perceived defects.

Next, the basis for declaring that scale was insufficient was that the leading firms in an industry were still smaller in terms of total sales, total assets, net profits, and employment than comparable firms in the United States and Europe, and hence that they had not yet reached the scale of production where they were at the minimum optimal scale in terms of the long-run average cost curve. Competition was judged excess when there was strong sales competition through price cutting and the offering of promotional gifts and when firms in an industry were encroaching into the production of products already made by others, so that interfirm rivalry increased. Competition was also considered excess when firms were active in building new plant or introducing up-to-date machinery, and as a result of this investment competition, there was the possibility in the near future of extreme excess capacity with utilization rates below 50%. Finally, competition was considered excess when, in cases where competition through model changes and the introduction of new technology was vigorous, innovation in products or production methods lessened the interest of firms in developing new technology themselves, resulting in a sharp jump in royalty payments for technology and other unnecessary expenses.

Third, it was argued that the unusual features in Japanese industrial organization of insufficient scale and excess competition were related to the form in which funds were provided to industry, namely, indirect financing. Under the "one set" development pattern,[23] major banks competed in lending to their *keiretsu,* and the constituent firms were thereby induced to invest more. Consequently, these firms had to depend on their banks. This vicious circle produced excess competition. It was this understanding that gave rise to an insistence on the need for a new system of industrial finance in place of the *keiretsu* financing system.

Finally, there was the proposal for a new pattern for relations between government and business, the Kanmin System, which would overcome the defects of Japanese industrial organization and the industrial finance system. There were three elements to it. First, in place of adjustments governed by the price system, a forum would be created in which representatives of government, industry, finance, and academe would get together to artificially coordinate industrial activity. Second, the bulk of the financing for this system would come from the Japan Development Bank, which would actively use its ability to guide financial flows to the crucial area of facilities investment as a way to bring about firm mergers and more concentrated production and to bring about the use of mass production. Third, with the Japan Development Bank at the core, the cooperation of private financial institutions would be mobilized.

The Kanmin System sought to reform the system of government–business relations. It denied the effectiveness of the price system in coordinating industrial activity, and through the lending of government financial institutions, sought to guide financial flows into priority areas, that is, particular industries. In doing so it was hoped international competitiveness would be strengthened.

2. Weak Points in the New Industrial Order Concept: Excess Competition

The concept of excess competition appeared not only in the debate over the New Industrial Order, but was also a term used frequently in a variety of forums. Despite this, few terms were as vague in meaning. Using J. S. Bain's discussion of excessive (cut-throat) competition in an unconcentrated industry as a model, the following four points were held relevant.[24] These were that in such industries, (1) the manufacturer's price of the product falls below average cost, (2) firms are able to earn only meager profits so that the returns earned on the productive factors employed in the industry are chronically below the normal rate of return, (3) while in principle firms are free to exit and labor is free to move to other uses, they shift to other industries only very slowly, and (4) the industry is insensitive to business cycles.

Bain's discussion of excessive competition was in terms of an unconcentrated industry. The four symptoms referred to by Bain, however, can also be found when an industry is oligopolistic. Each of the following situations could lead to these symptoms:[25] The first of these is that for some reason the realized rate of growth of an industry is below the expected long-term growth rate, and in this dynamic setting excess capacity arises (this excludes the development of excess capacity due to short-term cyclical changes in economic conditions). One example of the development of relatively long-term excess capacity is when the product cycle evolves from the growth stage into the mature stage. During the growth stage, excess capacity can be eliminated fairly quickly. In the mature stage the extent to which excess capacity develops depends on the difference between the expected and the actual growth rates. A sudden external shock, such as the oil crisis, is liable to increase this difference. The time and expense needed to adjust the capital stock likewise increases, as in the case of the petrochemical industry after the oil crisis. The emergence of excess capacity, however, need not immediately lead to excessive competition. The outcome hinges on whether the market structure is competitive or collusive (as in the case of steel blast furnaces).

The second case is when there is a continuous shift in demand due to the development of strong competitive or substitute products. Where the average cost structure of the industries producing such products is substantially lower than the industry of concern, case (1) of Bain occurs. In order for the industry to survive, one of three things can be done. First, the government can provide subsidies. Second, when there are multiple plants, production can be concentrated in the most efficient ones and old, inefficient plants can be closed, thereby reducing the average costs of the industry as a whole. Third, there can be an introduction of a revolutionary technical innovation. In general, only the second of these courses of action can be relied on for long-term adjustment. In the 1960s coal, which had to compete with oil, and cotton textiles, which had to compete with synthetics, adopted this second course of action. Competition stemming from imported goods can also be included here; for example, in the 1980s many firms exited from aluminum refining.

The third case is when export markets are lost because of the use by trading partners of tariffs or nontariff import restrictions, or through the competition of producers from other countries, or through movements in exchange rates. Even when this happens, the imbalance is only temporary when the industry is in the growth stage of the product cycle or when productive inputs can be shifted to other uses or sales can be shifted to the domestic market. When these conditions do not hold, case (1) of Bain can again arise.

Finally, there is the case in which there are institutional or artificial barriers to exit, restricting the reallocation of resources. In such a situation Bain's case (3) can readily occur. Milk provides a recent example of such a situation. Government subsidies keep marginal dairy farms in business, while at the distribution stage, an oligopolistic structure and tied retailers means that old-style milk stores are still found; competition from high-volume retailers means that there is also the possibility of Bain's case (2) arising. Again, since the oil crisis, the lengthy duration of the adjustment process in oil refining may not have been unrelated to the presence of barriers to exit in the Petroleum Industry Law.

In terms of the above four conditions, however, while they might on occasion have been observed, they were not found in any of the major industries in the 1960s. This was because it was a period of rapid growth—with the rate of growth consistently surpassing expectations—and also because most industries were in the growth period of their product cycle. The following evaluation can thus be made.

First, the new industrial order debate held competitive price reductions to be a symptom of an unhealthy organization of industry. In fact, rather than indicating an unhealthy situation, this was instead an indication that, through the development of the industry, economies of scale were being realized and average costs lowered. Price declines were then simply a reflection of competitive conditions. If one looks strictly at the short run, there may be industries where the demand curve may be nearly vertical because of product differentiation and the like. But in the long run, through new entry and the development of new products that are close substitutes, a firm's ability to control prices becomes relatively weak, and the slope of the long-run demand curve becomes much closer to horizontal. This suggests that the workable competition hypothesis of J. M. Clark held true in Japan at that time.[26]

Second, there was new entry in most industries. This reflected the expectations by firms of high growth and their accumulation of management resources, so that they sought out ways to grow, entering new markets whenever possible. As a result of new entry in most industries, market concentration was on a declining trend throughout the 1950s and early 1960s. Wholesale prices remained flexible across business cycles and stable over the long run, indicating that at that time an environment of workable competition had developed.

Third, competitive investment in new facilities does not necessarily indicate an unhealthy organization of industry. In a society in which industry is becoming more oligopolistic, where output and capacity are regulated, competition for market share will not arise. Under the conditions of rapid economic growth, and the impetus this gives to investment for the expansion of facilities, it is instead an expression of the dynamism of the market system when firms choose an aggressive investment strategy in attempting to increase their own market share.

Finally, at that time, most firms had in fact jumped on the bandwagon of rationalization and modernization. They were constantly adjusting their input mix and eagerly sought to introduce new technology and new production methods. The competitive introduction of new technology was nothing more than a reflection of the desire of firms to grow. Most firms were exerting themselves through the development of new products to meet the demands of the market. These features were all evidence that the source of firm growth lay in a broad process of Schumpeterian innovation.

3. Weak Points in the New Industrial Order Concept: Insufficient Scale

There is no economic meaning in comparing the size of firms in one country with those in another. The size of firms is the outcome of the interplay of market features and the progress of the social division of labor. If the expansion of scale is sought without regard to market characteristics, then the result can be instead the appearance of diseconomies of scale of large firms. As a response to trade liberalization, the government encouraged the merger and concentration of firms based on the judgment that firms were too small in most Japanese industries, and thus were not yet at the minimum optimal scale in terms of the long-run cost curve. MITI had in mind expansion in firm scale to reach the minimum optimal scale in the shortest time possible through mergers and the concentration of production, which would result in product specialization by firms and thus higher output levels of any given item.

Lying behind this sort of thinking on MITI's part was the assumption that industries in Japan and in the United States and Europe lay on the same cost curve. When one takes into consideration the time lag in the industrialization of Japan relative to the United States and Europe, productive capabilities were obviously different among them. In fact, as a late developer, Japan was in a better position to take advantage of the results of technical progress in other countries and was able to base its facilities on the very latest technology. Thus one can presume the long-run cost curve of a later developing nation to be below those of the developed countries, as there will be a gap in the technology embodied in machinery and facilities. In such a case, even though the scale of production may be relatively small, it cannot therefore be presumed that this represents a competitive disadvantage; during this period the steel industry provides a good example of this.

There are also varying responses in the internal organization of firms in coping with X-inefficiencies. Even if the production system embodies the same technology, efforts to improve productive efficiency will vary across countries and firms, just as there will be many ways of allocating technicians and workers within a firm. Customs and traditions and the social environment of countries differ, so that even in the same industry, similar yet different systems of production may develop. Labor relations in different nations vary, and the interest of workers in participating in management can be totally different, depending on whether relations are cooperative or not. The fact that within the automobile industry there can be found both the "Toyota Production System"[27] and the "Volvo System"[28] is one example of this; it should furthermore be noted that the Toyota Production System was developed in the early 1960s.

Even if these sorts of cross-national differences are ignored, and industries in Japan and in the United States and Europe are assumed to lie on the same cost curve, the presumption of MITI that most Japanese industries had not achieved the minimum optimal scale still does not mean that Japanese industry suffered from structural weakness. The Japanese economy at that time was growing over twice as fast as the Western economies, and so it was extremely easy to overcome any time lag. This was not a problem that can be said to have required paying the costs of artificial intervention instead of relying on the market.[29]

Finally, in response to capital liberalization in the latter half of the 1960s, the government sought policies to reorganize industry, encouraging firm mergers and the concentration of production. The presupposition of these policies was that there was a positive relationship between firm size and the capacity to innovate, and between size and overall management and marketing and fundraising abilities. This is a testable hypothesis, and at that time no empirical evidence was given to prove this to be true.[30]

4. The Special Industries Law: Background of the Debate

Industry, favoring an autonomous adjustment mechanism, opposed the government and its proposal for the Kanmin System.[31] By an autonomous adjustment mechanism is meant the development of the new industrial order through the autonomous (or joint) activities of the firms in an industry. Lying behind this insistence by industry on an autonomous system was the fear that the Kanmin System would be a forerunner to direct government controls, and that such a system would tend to value economic efficiency lightly in decisions affecting the allocation of resources.

The autonomous system and the Kanmin System, however, had the following elements in common: (1) the view that the organization of industry was distinguished by the presence of excess competition and insufficient scale, (2) the feeling that it was necessary in coping with international competition to merge firms and concentrate production so as to expand firm size, and (3) that the Antimonopoly Law should be gutted so as to give freedom in principle to form cartels and to arrange mergers. The main difference was that the autonomous system relied on the efforts of industry itself to bring about industrial concentration, without turning to the government. The Kanmin System had the same goals, but looked to the government for leadership in bringing these about.

5. The Special Industries Law: Introduction to and Failure in the Diet

The Special Industries Law was submitted to the Diet in 1963, following in general the recommendations of the Industrial Structure Advisory Committee for the adoption of a Kanmin System. The law provided for the designation of industries that needed strengthening in their international competitiveness, and by providing tax incentives and preferential financing, would encourage mergers and coordinated activity for the purposes of rationalization. The three industries designated in the law were automobiles, specialty steels, and petrochemicals, all of which were thought at the time to have problems in terms of international competitiveness.

Industry, however, was against the Special Industries Law, and the ruling Liberal Democratic Party was reluctant to pass the bill, while the opposition parties took the stand that the proposed law was an evil one that would make an empty shell of the Antimonopoly Law. With opposition

from beginning to end, debate was halted and the bill killed.[32] The bill
was resubmitted on two other occasions, but even within MITI interest
in it gradually declined, and so neither time did the bill see the light of
day. But as will be discussed later, the concept of the Kanmin System
was preserved and used in coordinating investment in petrochemicals and
synthetic fibers.

6. The Special Industries Law: Evaluation

The advisory council system took root in postwar Japan and was used
in a wide variety of cases for policy formation. Because of this, when
industry opposed a plan, one cannot find many examples where the government drew up and tried to have implemented a bill affecting industrial
policy. The Special Industries Law is one of these exceptions.

There are many problems from the perspective of social equity in having
businesspeople sit on the advisory councils. They may use the advisory
councils as forums for industry to make concerted appeals to the government, thereby exerting undue influence on policy formation. This,
however, is not always a weakness; because of the participation of many
businesspeople on the advisory councils, it could be expected that the
councils would put an end to proposals for government intervention in
industrial activity that go against the direction in which the market is moving. In fact, one can state that this was the major function of the advisory
councils during the 1960s.

The Industrial System Committee of the Industrial Structure Advisory
Committee was thus exceptional in its drawing up of the Special Industries
Law. Its seven members included former bureaucrats, but no one who
was at that time involved in private industry.[33] It was because of this that
a plan could be drawn up that was so strongly linked to bureaucratic controls and that was opposed by industry. But during the 1960s, parliamentary
democracy had already taken root in Japan, and the Diet functioned in
placing a check on policies based on a narrow ideology. Finally, that a
law that would be hard for industry to accept was drawn up in such a
forced way is perhaps not unrelated to the bureaucracy, as a consequence
of liberalization policies, losing its legal basis for intervention in industry.

B. Guiding Investment: The Kanmin System in Practice

The Kanmin System was a resource allocation policy in which the government tried to guide private investment in line with its expectations of
economic growth by intervening in the investment activities of the firms
in an industry. This approach was inextricably linked to the perception
of excess competition as a special feature of Japanese industry. The guid-

ance of private investment was based on the judgment of the government that prior action was needed in the face of possible excess capacity in the near future.

This policy of coordinating investment had in mind such raw material processing industries as steel, petroleum refining, synthetic textiles, paper, and pulp; machining and assembly manufacturing were excluded from consideration. Outside of the Petroleum Industry Law, there was no legal basis for this guidance of investment; having no such backing, such industrial policy was thus unofficial. The tool of this policy was administrative guidance, and opinions differ over whether this tool was in fact effective in guiding investment.[34] The difference of opinion centers around whether there was anything that could secure the effectiveness of government policy.

When it became difficult to avoid the liberalization of capital transactions in the latter 1960s, the idea of the Kanmin System was made concrete by the establishment of the Kanmin Coordination Consultative Groups; the Chemical Fibers Consultative Group was set up in October 1964 and the Petrochemical Consultative Group in December 1964. The Kanmin System differed from coordination of an industry by the members themselves in that the government sought to have its policy targets reflected in industry decisions. For this purpose, the government had to have some sort of power to intervene, as an essential prerequisite for guaranteeing effectiveness.

In the case of petrochemicals, the government's power for intervention lay in the Foreign Capital Law. Until the liberalization of capital transactions, the Foreign Capital Council had approval powers over the importation of foreign technology. The petrochemical industry was with few exceptions dependent on foreign technology, so that in order for there to be new entry into the industry or the formation of a joint venture or an expansion or the setting up of new facilities, a government license was necessary. This licensing system continued until 1972, when capital transactions in the petrochemical industry were liberalized. The setting up of the Kanmin System for synthetic textiles was also because foreign technology was not unimportant in the industry.

1. Patterns in Government Intervention

For petrochemicals, government intervention was important from the very start of the industry.[35] In the first period (1955–1958) of the Petrochemical Industry Plan, four complexes were approved, those of Mitsui Petrochemical, Sumitomo Chemical, Japan Petrochemical, and Mitsubishi Petrochemical. During the second period of the Plan (1959–1964), expansion of the existing complexes was approved along with the establishment of five new complexes, those of Tonen Petrochemical, Dai Kyowa Petrochemical, Maruzen Petrochemical, Idemitsu Petrochemical, and Kasei Mizushima. The two goals of the government were the effective utilization of olefins and the building of larger scale facilities, with a capacity for ethylene production of 40,000 tons per plant per year. At the conclusion of the Plan, the industry was to be covered as one of the designated industries of the Special Industries Law—which did not pass the Diet.

In 1964–1965, ethylene production reached 300,000 tons per year, and the Petrochemical Industry Plan entered its third and fourth periods. With the rapid increase in the scale of facilities, the Kanmin Consultative Group was established; and in line with government guidance, the minimum suggested scale of new facilities was at once substantially increased. In January 1965, the Kanmin Consultative Group set guidelines for new naphtha facilities, and the goal of the technology license approval guidelines became ethylene production of 100,000 tons per year, with the added condition that there be the potential for future expansion to 200,000 tons or more per year.

These guidelines were almost immediately revised, providing for a substantially larger scale, as in other countries the trend had become one of plants with a capacity of 300,000 tons or more per year. As a result, in 1967 a capacity standard of 300,000 tons per year was set for new ethylene facilities. This 300,000 ton capacity standard was set with the trends in foreign technology in mind, but it was also thought of as a way to discourage new entry.[36] During the second period of the Plan, the government in fact approved the applications of all firms seeking to enter the industry, so that it expanded from four firms to nine firms, increasing interfirm competition but at the same time causing displeasure among the original entrants.

Despite the desire of MITI and existing producers to prevent new entry, there continued to be firms that met the standards for technology, market development, and financing ability. MITI went on to approve the establishment of complexes by three new entrants: a joint venture by Showa Electrical Industries and Yahata Chemicals, a joint venture by Asahi Chemicals and Nippon Mining, and a venture by Osaka Petrochemical. In addition, plans for new complexes of the original four entrants and one later entrant were approved, making for a total of eight new complexes. All of these complexes were completed just after the first oil crisis.

2. Evaluation of Policies

a. Their Legal Basis. A clear statement of the direction in which the government was seeking to build up the petrochemical industry is found in the failed Special Industries Law. In order to improve international competitiveness, the law had as its goal "improvement in the efficiency of industrial activity through the achievement of an appropriate scale of operations in production or management." The methods for promoting an industry set forth in the law included "the setting of standards, the specialization of production, appropriate capital investment programs, tie-ups and mergers."[37] As revealed in the debate on the new industrial order, it is clear that the main goal of the Special Industries Law was to encourage interfirm ties through merger and to foster a mass production system composed of a small number of large firms.

Petrochemicals were one of the industries designated in the law. The law makes very plain the direction in which industrial policy at that time was aimed, in terms of building up the industry. The results obtained through the Kanmin System, however, were the exact opposite of the goal of the original policy. This is clear in the successive entry in two waves of eight more firms. The government had powers based on the Foreign Capital Law, but even though the government in this case had licensing powers over the industry, in the face of the rapid economic growth during this era, the bureaucracy was in fact limited in the decisions it could make. This point is also important in looking at the effectiveness of policy in coordinating investment in other industries. It also demonstrates the flexibility of the bureaucratic system, with its policy divisions responding in an *ad hoc* fashion by limited approval to unlimited approval of licenses, effectively changing policy.

b. Their Equity. The setting of the minimum capacity for new plants at 300,000 tons a year limited firms in their choice of technology, unless firms were able to develop their own technology. A more positive feature of this objective standard, however, was that the bureaucracy was not given discretion to favor particular firms. If a firm had the resources to meet the technical, financial, and marketing requirements, and was willing to bear the risk, it was free to enter. Whatever the original intent of policy, as judged by the results, government intervention certainly did not serve as a barrier to new entry.

c. Their Impact on Resource Allocation. Due to the operation of the "0.6 rule,"[38] it was particularly important for process industries to seek economies of scale. Prices rapidly declined in petrochemicals under the multiple impact of the formation of a competitive market through new entry, the increase in the scale of plants, and the new ability to use olefins. Ethylene fell in price from ¥83–¥75 per kilogram in 1960 to ¥27–¥30 per kilogram in 1971–1972. The decrease in price resulted in the devel-

opment of new markets and a larger total market. This positive feedback
stimulated further growth in petrochemicals and the achievement of further
economies of scale; the setting of the 300,000 ton per year standard served
to accelerate this virtuous circle.

With the increased minimum plant capacity and with firms beginning
the construction of large-scale plants all at the same time, there was the
possibility that a gap would develop between the expected and the actual
growth rates, with overcapacity giving rise to excess competition and a
squeezing of firms' profitability, especially in a business downswing,
though for only a short time. As compared to the case in which the choice
of the scale of facilities is left up to the individual firms, the depth of the
cyclical swings in the industry may have been made worse. In the case
of the 300,000 ton capacity plants, they all began operating at the same
time, unfortunately just when the first oil crisis occurred. In consequence
of this unforeseen external shock, the relative price of petroleum rose,
and the growth era for petrochemicals came to an end. One can thus suspect that government intervention in the industry expanded its overcapacity.

In general, when firms operating in a free market carry out investment,
each firm does so on the basis of its own judgment, so that even were the
plans for investment all to be drawn up at the same time, one would not
expect firms to carry out their investment on the same scale and with the
same timing. When firms make their investment decisions, they are all
facing many types of uncertainties; the future trends of the growth of the
market are unclear, changes due to the business cycle are unpredictable.
As expectations of firms vary, there are both "bears" and "bulls" among
them.

The management capabilities that firms have developed also vary; investments would be in line with these varying abilities. Even if a firm is
bullish, it does not follow that its investment plan can immediately be
realized. The actions of rival firms also exert an influence. When competitors have ambitious investment plans, a firm may delay its own investment, or when rivals are cautious, a firm may be made bolder in carrying out its own investment. Because of such varied determinants at the
firm level of investment activity in a free market, it is normal that at the
industry level the timing of investment is dispersed.[39]

When, however, the government intervenes with some means of compulsion, the natural pattern of investment to which the market structure
gives rise can be destroyed, and firms may each carry out similar amounts
of investment at the same time. This can take place even though it strains
the individual firms' financial or marketing capabilities, as it is critical for
each firm to obtain a license in order to leave room for future growth. In

other words, firms act to procure the rents that accrue to existing producers, shifting their investment strategies. In Japan, *keiretsu* financing may have accelerated this process. In the case of petrochemicals, with the setting of the new 300,000 ton capacity standard, it was difficult to avoid investing the same amount as other firms. This may have made government intervention responsible for excess capacity over and above what would have resulted from the investment of firms in a free market. This assertion is, however, difficult to verify.

C. Dividing Up the Market: Failure in Fostering Specialized Producers

1. The Goal of Product Specialization in Manufacturing

The approaches that industrial policy actively supported in order to achieve economies of scale and to strengthen international competitiveness were the fostering of specialized manufacturers through the concentration of production and through advocating cooperatives and tie-ups among firms. These two approaches were chosen to deal with the "weak points" of Japanese industrial organization, an overabundance of producers, their small size, and excess competition. These approaches were adopted for the machinery industries, and for small and medium enterprises,[40] where most firms were supplying a wide range of goods and services. The extent to which such industrial policies could be effective will be discussed below in the case of the machine tool industry and the plan for reforming the structure of the industry and for developing specialized producers therein.

2. Market Structure and Policy Issues in the Industry

The machine tool industry has the following distinctive characteristics.[41] First, the term *machine tool* encompasses a wide variety of items. The Japan Machine-Tool Builder's Association classification, for example, uses 76 different categories, and as there are items that could not be classified, the variation is in fact larger. Second, there are a multitude of producers, reflecting the variety of products; this is true of the industry worldwide and not just in Japan. For example, according to the Industrial Structure Advisory Committee, there were 318 producers in West Germany, 165 in the U.K., 95 in Japan, and 125 in France—and these numbers would be higher if "outsiders," who are not members of industry associations, were included. In each of these countries, industry members vary widely in scale, from small firms to giant enterprises, and include specialized producers along with firms for which machine tools are only one of several product lines. Third, there is a horizontal division of production. Because of the wide variety of machine tools, in each of the major producing countries there are firms that hold a comparative advantage in producing particular types of tools, thus there is a division of production internationally. This can be verified by noting that the ratios of both imports and exports to domestic production are high (Table VI). In each country the industry has its own peculiarities, and the machine types in which countries have a comparative advantage presumably reflect this. Note that Japan stands out for its low ratio of exports to total production.

The Industrial Structure Advisory Committee made the following diagnosis of the industry's status, raising certain policy issues and suggesting policy initiatives. The first was the scale of firms. On average, the size of machine tool producers was about the same in Japan as in other developed economies, but this was because for most types of machine tools market concentration in Japan was high, and the leading firms had a large scale of operations. Middle- and lower-ranked producers and outsiders remained small in international terms. Policies to change this were held necessary. Second, the level of technology in the industry had improved rapidly following policies during 1953–1957 that encouraged research and new product development by providing subsidies for the development of prototypes. The government also encouraged the importing of technology, so that small- and medium-sized machines were soon on a par with those made in the United States and Europe. Considerable efforts still needed to be devoted to the production of large-sized, precision, and high performance machine tools. Third, a large variety of domestic items were considerably above international levels in price. This was due to low labor

TABLE VI
Production, Exports, and Imports of Machine Tools, 1960

	U.S.	WGer	U.K.	France	Switz.	Italy	Japan
Employment (1,000)	128.1	110.0	50.0	24.4	17.8	12.0	24.0[a]
A. Production (¥ billion)	280.0	199.8	94.8	57.6	39.3	39.1	45.2
B. Exports (¥ billion)	56.6	91.9	38.2	12.5	27.6	12.9	1.6
C. Imports (¥ billion)	—	26.4	22.5	22.8	8.3	14.1	19.7
D. Domestic demand $(A - B + C)$ (¥ billion)	—	134.3	79.1	67.9	20.0	40.3	63.3
E. Share of exports $(B/A, \%)$	20.2	46.0	29.8	21.7	72.0	33.0	3.6
F. Share of imports $(C/D, \%)$	—	19.7	28.4	33.6	41.5	35.0	31.1

Source: Adapted from Sangyo Kozo Chosa Kai [1964], vol. 4, p. 101, tables 1–2.
[a]An estimate.

productivity, the distorting effect of a large number of workers in non-production jobs, outdated designs, and high interest payments accompanying a deterioration in debt/equity ratios. It was thus seen as essential to reduce prices so as to enable import substitution and export promotion. Finally, the target of policy was to "coordinate" the choice of products, to encourage basic research and product development, and to set uniform industry standards. The "coordination" of product choice (involving the reorganization of output across firms, including the shifting of product lines among firms) was to bring about specialization and mass production. To encourage cooperatives, tie-ups, and mergers, it was recommended that the government use measures such as the provision of tax incentives and access to government finance. Targets were to be met by the year 1967.

3. Policy Implementation and Results

a. Legal Basis of Policy Tools. The ability of the government to have its policy goals reflected in the decisions of industry, that is, the extent to which the government is able to wield influence, depends on whether the government has legally binding powers to intervene and the extent to which such intervention is backed up by law. For postwar industrial policy, the archetypical case in which the government was able to meet its policy goals by exerting a quite strong influence over the actions of industry was the intervention in petroleum refining based on the Petroleum Industry Law.

The Petroleum Industry Law gave the government quite comprehensive authority, including the power to authorize new entry and expansion of production facilities, the requirement to file crude oil import and refinery production plans with the government, the ability to recommend changes in production plans in line with changes in demand and supply, and the power to set standard retail prices of petroleum products. When the government holds such comprehensive ability to affect industry decisions, the government can exert substantial influence over the development of the organization of the industry.[42]

In the machine tool industry, policy interventions were based on the 1956 Machine Industry Law. Government authority was limited to areas such as formulating and promulgating "Basic Rationalization" plans and suggesting that the cooperation needed to achieve the rationalization targets should be undertaken. There was furthermore the restriction that, in drawing up rationalization plans and plans for their implementation, the opinions of the Machine Industry Council had to be respected. While it can be claimed that there was specific legal backing for policy, in the case of machine tools, government policy in fact had to take a back seat to industry, as in the petroleum industry.

b. The Agreement on the Concentration of Production. The coordination of product specialization was to be handled through an industry association, the Product Specialization Committee of the Japan Machine-Tool Builder's Association, formed in August 1957.[43] At the time, the committee was active in collecting and exchanging information on the status of different product areas, production by machine type, imports by machine type and size, and similar items. In March 1960, in response to MITI policy, the committee drew up an "Agreement on the Concentration of Production," which was to become effective in November. The Agreement included the following provisions:

1. Firms will not add as new products machines that might be presumed to upset the existing pattern of product specialization in the industry.

2. Firms will work toward concentrating production, among the machine tools that they produce, by emphasizing only a few representative types.

3. Firms will work actively to develop types of machines not yet domestically produced.

4. Priority will be given to production of machines that, under interfirm technical or operating agreements, have been traded among or given to other firms, to the extent that this contributes to the development of the industry, is beneficial to member firms, and does not upset the pattern of product specialization in the industry.

5. To the extent that it does not upset the pattern of product specialization in the industry, firms will be encouraged to undertake the production of machine tools under foreign license where this is thought to contribute to improving domestic technology.

6. Member firms will notify the Japan Machine-Tool Builder's Association when they decide to undertake the production of new types of machine tools, including when this is done under (1), (3), (4), and (5) above.

c. Effectiveness of the Agreement. It is perfectly clear that there were no compulsory elements in the Agreement through which effectiveness in adjusting product specialization could be obtained. While Clause (1) would seem to restrict entry into the manufacturing of machine tools that were currently being produced, under Clause (6), member firms were permitted to begin producing new types of machine tools merely by giving prior notification. Even when such machine tools were made in very small quantities, firms were free to enter into their production. This was true as well for items being made under technical licenses as per Clauses (3) and (5). Even the emphasis on producing a few representative types of machine tools, through which a more concentrated productive structure was sought, was left entirely up to the autonomous decisions of each firm. Finally, no penalties were provided for firms that went against the agreement, and no requirement was placed on firms to revise or drop their secondary product lines. There were thus no elements in the Agreement that bound firms in their decision making.

d. The Basic Promotion Plan. In July 1968, MITI promulgated the Basic Machine Tool Industry Promotion Plan under the Machine Industry Law as a policy response to capital liberalization. The plan for improving the structure of the industry included (1) the fixing of an "appropriate" scale of production for 12 classes of general purpose machine tools, such as standard metal lathes, (2) the creation of a specialized production system in which firms produced at least this minimum amount, and (3) the cessation of production of any of such machine tools by a firm when they had less than a 5% market share for that type and when output of the item was less than 20% of the firm's sales, except when the item did not compete with the products of other firms.[44]

Considering this guidance of MITI for the cessation of small-scale production of machine tools as being more thoroughgoing than its own Agreement, the Japan Machine-Tool Builder's Association decided to revise the Agreement to make it clear that it was based on the Promotion Plan. The New Agreement, which went into effect April 1969, was as follows:

1. Products covered: as per (1) and (2) of the MITI Plan.
2. Products to be dropped: as per (3) of the MITI Plan. However, specialized machine tools are to be excluded from the list, such as programmable and numerically controlled machine tools and other advanced types, very large and ultra small machine tools, and other types for which competition is weak.
3. Production rights: other than the types under Clause (1) of the MITI plan, a firm maintains the right to produce any machine tool type that it has produced at some time during the previous six years.
4. Excluded types: as a general rule, even when a firm has no prior production experience, it will be permitted to manufacture machining centers, numerically controlled and other programmable machine tools.
5. Changing product mixes: when it is difficult for each member firm to achieve the relevant scale of production, the product mix will be coordinated among the firms of a group[45] or affiliated firms.
6. Notification and deliberation: when for special reasons a firm wishes to undertake the production of an item that it has not previously developed

or otherwise produced, the firm will notify the Association and the notification will enter into the deliberations of the Special Committee on Product Mixes, which will report on such notifications to the Trustees.

As can be seen, neither the New Agreement nor the original Agreement placed any bounds on the decisions of member firms. This is highlighted by the Operating Summary, which was approved by the Board of Trustees in July 1969:[46]

1. Of products to be dropped: there were 13 cases in which production ceased, and 13 in which it continued.

2. Of products for which production rights are reserved: there were 92 cases in which products were dropped, and 102 in which they were maintained.

3. Of excluded types: there were 20 cases in which production was continued.

As a result, there were 110 firms that added new product areas, for a total of 570 types of machine tools on a cumulative basis. Furthermore, of the 56 cases in which there was notification to the Association of the intent to enter a new product area (including existing product types), all notices were accepted except for the two cases in which the ''reason for commencing production'' could not be verified. The operation of the Agreement in fact respected the individual choices of constituent firms.[47]

e. Policy Evaluation.   The goal of government policy was to bring about a concentration of production and the formation of an industrial structure of specialized manufacturers. This was done with the aim of improving international competitiveness in advance of the opening of the economy, but one cannot say that the policy was successful.[48] This was because MITI did not have any power strong enough to influence the decisions of the industry association. The authority given by the Machine Industries Law was extremely limited. In the case of machine tools, the work of coordinating product mixes among firms was left up to independent action by the industry association.

The industry association of course could not undertake activities or make decisions that were unfavorable to members of the association. This is because, when there are no restrictions on outsiders, firms are free to leave the association.[49] Thus, even though production of certain types of machine tools was to cease, according to MITI instructions, the industry in fact approved continued production; there was no choice but for the association to honor the independent actions of firms.

The policy goal of import substitution and export promotion was reached in the 1970s. While imports of metal-working machinery (machine tools, presses, and the like) increased only slightly from $188 million in 1962 to $234 million in 1980, exports increased by a factor of 39, from $45 million to $1.743 billion, shifting Japan from being a net importer to a net exporter. This was not a result of industrial policies during the 1960s, however, but rather occurred because government intervention in industrial activity was unsuccessful, that is, it was the result of adjustments brought about by the price mechanism.

Finally, the policy approach of MITI was not constant during the 1960s; thinking on industrial policy shifted around 1968.[50] The Structural Reform Plan for the machine tool industry was promulgated in July 1968, but within it, proposals for adjusting production of advanced types of machine tools such as programmable NC machines were dropped. The reason for this seems to be that, for advanced technology items, firms staked their future on one or another product. Attempts by the government or the industry association to interfere with this brought on stout resistance, and by this time period such intervention had become quite impossible.

IV. Conclusion

Reflecting on industrial policy during the era of rapid growth, there remains the strong impression of an overreaction in trying to create a new industrial order, with the government disinclined to further trade and capital liberalization and other measures designed to create an open economy. As a result of the government's cautious attitude toward trade liberalization, firms were only gradually exposed to the trial of market competition, and one can claim that they thereby had time to garner their strength. Nevertheless, one must wonder why the government was so concerned about creating a new industrial order. Here four possible reasons will be discussed.

First, in liberalizing trade and capital movements, the government was giving up its power to allocate import licenses and to authorize or grant licenses for technology imports and joint ventures, and hence to approve new investment in facilities that utilized foreign technology. In the course of postwar industrialization, the government used these powers to guide the course of industrialization and was proud of what it felt it had achieved. It is clear that the bureaucracy was aware of its need to develop new policy tools to maintain its influence, to keep its ability to gradually redirect firms in response to changing conditions. The efforts that it made to have the Special Industries Law passed were a clear example of this.

Second, during this period neither the government nor the public had

the faith in the ability of the price mechanism to facilitate adjustments
that they have in the 1980s. As a result they did not trust in the ability
of firms to adequately respond to changes in the economic environment.
Liberalization meant that the price mechanism would extend to the governing of trade and even foreign investment, but because Japan had
adopted protectionist policies throughout the postwar period of industrialization, there had been few opportunities to compete directly against
foreign firms. The lack of faith in the price mechanism and the limited
opportunities for passing the test of market competition reinforced each
other and were the source of the blind faith in the myth of economies of
scale.

Third, there was a strong nationalistic tendency, and only a weak in-
ternationalist strand. After the war, the countries of Western Europe, like
Japan, had adopted protectionist policies and had imposed restrictions on
imports from the U.S. dollar currency bloc, but they differed from Japan
in that from the start they had placed no restrictions on foreign direct
investment. Foreign investment was thought to expand employment and
income-earning opportunities through the international transmission of
managerial resources, with beneficial effects for industrialization; it was
thus natural that in Europe there should be no restrictions.

Japan, however, was reluctant to permit foreign direct investment in
industries, and for a long time Japan not only regulated such investment,
but as a response to policies liberalizing capital transactions, sought to
concentrate industry through mergers and tie-ups among firms. One mo-
tivation for this was a nationalistic desire to protect domestic capital.
Expressions of this approach can be found in the interventions by the
government in petroleum refining through the Petroleum Industry Law[51]
and in the interference by the government in capital tie-ups of local automotive firms with foreign producers.[52]

Finally, the growth potential of the Japanese economy had in general
been underestimated.[53] The National Income Doubling Plan was the first
official statement of rapid growth policies, but even so the government
growth projections were substantially below the actual growth rate. The
government response to private investment activities was to intervene in
an attempt to forestall excess competition, but at the same time such intervention represented an attempt by the government to guide investment
to levels in line with its own growth projections. In fact, it was this very
underestimation of the growth potential of the economy that, in the face
of vigorous private investment activity, gave rise to the fear that in the
near future it would be hard to avoid the emergence of excess capacity.

The willingness of the government to intervene in industrial activity
was at its strongest in the 1960s. The conclusion must be, however, that

the rapid growth of the 1960s, the modernization of the industrial structure, and the strengthening of export competitiveness were the result not of industrial policy, but rather of the relatively smooth operation of the price mechanism and the ability of firms through their own decisions to adapt. The initial objectives of industrial policy could not be realized, and they remained empty plans because of the Japanese policy formation and implementation process and the interaction of market mechanism.

In evaluating industrial policy in the 1960s, it is important to remember that the government had forgotten the necessity for intervention in the face of market failures. The government did not begin responding to pollution and other negative externalities in an appropriate fashion until 1971–1973, when judgments were rendered in four important pollution-related court cases. Again, there was little attempt to bring antitrust policy to bear on the problem of market domination by oligopolistic firms, and it was not until the 1970s that antitrust policy came to have its rightful position in the arena of economic policy. The 1960s are best thought of as a period of transition during which the model of freely competing firms gained acceptance.

Notes

1. Tsuruta [1982] is a study of the formation of and changes in industrial policy over the postwar era. This chapter draws heavily on Chapters 4 through 6 of that book, which may be referred to for more details.
2. If one looks at only the growth rate of the economy, then the rapid growth era must be said to have begun in the 1950s. The reason for limiting the period to the 1960s is that the government began consciously to pursue "rapid growth" policies from 1960, and at the same time, Japan's transition to an open economy began in that year, which meant a change in the government's conception of industrial policy.
3. See S. Nakamura [1964]. "Mainstay" firms are small- and medium-sized firms that, unlike the bulk of such enterprises, are in the process of growing.
4. Over the 12-year period of 1959–1971, the number of incorporated and unincorporated enterprises increased by 2,830,000. See S. Nakamura et al. [1981], p. 187.
5. The free enterprise system is a model of an economic system consisting of a market economy under a parliamentary democracy. In this system, government intervention in economic activity is limited to the minimum amount necessary to deal with cases of market failure and other problems. There is of course always a gap between such idealizations and reality. In terms of this chapter, the transition is not one of achieving the ideal, but rather one in which the implementation of policy became closer to this ideal.
6. See Penrose [1959].
7. The law is officially titled the Law on Extraordinary Measures for the Promotion of Specified Manufacturing Industries. Herein it will be referred to as the Special Industries Law.

8. See Ueno [1978].
9. Okita ([1961], pp. 1–22) states that the Five-Year Economic Recovery Plan (1956) and the New Long-Term Economic Plan (1957) were plans that maintained a strong direct economic control orientation toward industry. The National Income Doubling Plan (1960), on the other hand, limited actual planning to government investment and foresaw a limited role for the government in regard to activities of the private sector. The figures given in the Income Doubling Plan were more in the way of projections and guides than of "plans."
10. See Keizai Kikakucho [1961], pp. 46–64.
11. See Tsuruta [1982], pp. 82–154.
12. The Industrial Structure Advisory Committee began functioning in April 1961; the Industrial Structure Research Section was established at the same time as part of the Secretariat of MITI. See Tsusansho [1975], p. 182.
13. The Industrial Structure Council, which began functioning in May 1964, was a union and expansion of the Industrial Structure Advisory Committee and the Industrial Rationalization Council, which began functioning in 1949.
14. Among others, the following committees were successively set up in the 1960s: the Energy, International Economic, Industrial Finance, Heavy Industry, Industrial Technology, Steel, Chemical Industry, Industrial Siting, Industrial Pollution, Miscellaneous Goods and Construction Materials, Consumer Economy, Information Industry, Distribution, Industrial Labor, and Management Committees. See Tsusansho [1975], pp. 194–216.
15. See Tsusansho [1975], pp. 194–216.
16. See Chapter 1, Section V, A.
17. The government carried out an overhaul of the tariff system in 1961. The postwar tariff system had been substantially overhauled in 1951, but in a period when import quotas were being used, tariffs did not serve as an effective tool of economic policy. In addition, the 1951 overhaul had inherited the original tariff system of 1910 and maintained some important defects of the original system. The number of classifications in the tariff schedule remained extremely small—928 classes in comparison to over 3,000 for the United States, Germany, and the United Kingdom, and 5,170 for France—and there were also an inordinate number of catch-all categories. The purpose of the 1961 reform was to rectify these defects, and new tariff rates were set for 2,233 categories. While the reform put into place a modern tariff system, it was also a response to trade liberalization. Among the new tariff rates, the old rate was continued for 1,596 classes, lowered for 386 classes, and raised for 251 classes. There were 77 specific tariffs. Though more tariffs were lowered than raised, the former were all minor items. Hence, overall, the reform resulted in a raising of the level of tariffs. Many internationally high tariff rates were maintained unchanged. As a response to trade liberalization, a new special tariff system was established. The 1961 system strengthened the protectionist coloration of trade policy. See Oka [1964], pp. 237–317. Tariff rates were uniformly lowered later on, during the Kennedy Round negotiations; and in view of the strengthened international competitiveness of Japan in the 1970s, the government progressively lowered tariff rates. As a result, even before the Tokyo Round commenced, in comparison to the average tariff rate of 6.0% for the United States and 6.4% for the EEC, the average Japanese tariff rate of 3.7% was the lowest among the industrialized nations. See Tsusansho [1982], p. 266.
18. See for example Tsusansho [1975], and Tsuruta [1982].
19. MITI aired its proposal to consolidate the automotive industry in June 1961. This consolidation policy was made public by the Industrial Finance Committee of the Industrial

Rationalization Council. The core of the proposal was the reorganization of the industry into a "mass production" group, a luxury passenger car group, and a minicar group. MITI, however, had no tools through which it could implement this policy, and in the end it was a failure.

20. The law is officially titled the Law on Temporary Measures for the Promotion of the Machine Industry. Herein it will be referred to as the Machine Industries Law.

21. This refers to the belief that the larger the firm size, the better the competitive position relative to foreign firms. At the time, this sort of thinking was found not only in Japan but also in Western Europe, where there was direct competition with U.S.-based firms. See Layton [1968].

22. Public statements by the government for the necessity of building a new industrial order may be found in Arisawa and Inaba [1966] and Sangyo Kozo Chosa Kai (Industrial Structure Advisory Committee) [1964], the latter being the most systematic explication, published after two years of debate by the Industrial Structure Advisory Committee. Similar statements by Yoshihiko Morozumi, who at the time was the Section Chief of the First Enterprises Section of the Enterprises Bureau of MITI and later Administrative Vice-Minister of MITI, can be found in Morozumi, Chigusa, et al. [1963], pp. 3–74, and Morozumi [1966]. What follows draws on the former.

23. Representative of this view is Miyazaki [1966], pp. 31–92. [Translator's note: By "one-set" was meant the presumed desire of a *keiretsu* group to have a member in each industry, so that each group had "one set" of firms.]

24. Bain [1968].

25. Bain emphasized historical factors as important conditions for the appearance of "excessive" competition. He gives as examples (1) the transition of an economy from wartime to peacetime conditions, (2) the development of products that are close substitutes or the loss of export markets, (3) an increase in the productivity of existing facilities, and (4) changes in the geographical locus of production.

26. See Clark [1940], pp. 241–256.

27. See Ohno [1978].

28. See Gyllenhammar [1977].

29. See Takafusa Nakamura [1970], p. 166.

30. See Mansfield [1968], Gruber and Marquis [1969], and Nelson et al. [1967] for studies of increasing firm size as a barrier to technical innovation. For the reorganization of industry as a response to capital liberalization, see Hayashi [1967] and Inaba and Sakane [1967], pp. 61–87. For an influential argument against industrial reorganization see Komiya [1967] and Komiya [1975b], pp. 195–223.

31. See Morozumi et al. [1963], pp. 107–134.

32. One can infer that the Liberal Democratic Party, the party in power, was disinclined to press forward the debate on the Special Industries Law because financial circles, as well as industry, were against it. At the time, Miyazaki [1966] hypothesized a "one-set" principle for the lending of the city banks to their associated financial groups *(keiretsu)*. Miyazaki framed this in carrying out a largely negative analysis of the group of firms centered around a "main" bank. Koyama [1966] argues against his views, so the hypothesis cannot be said to have been totally accepted, but at any rate Miyazaki's view reflects something of the realities of the time. The petrochemical industry, to be discussed later, can be considered an example of this principle. Thus, one line of thinking saw the MITI proposal for the restructuring of industries, in which Japan Development Bank financing played a central role, as an attempt to break up the city bank–*keiretsu* financing system, thereby increasing the influence of MITI. The lobbying over the Special Industries Law also had the nature of a power struggle between MITI

and "financial" capital, and this contributed to the strength of the opposition of the private sector.

33. The 7 members of the committee were the chairman, Hiromi Arisawa (Professor Emeritus, University of Tokyo), a former Ministry of Agriculture bureaucrat, the governor of the Japan Development Bank, a member of the editorial staff of the *Asahi Shimbun* (Japan's leading newspaper), the chairman of the Keidanren (The Federation of Economic Organizations), the chairman of a private economic think tank, and a former vice-minister of MITI. None were active industry representatives. See C. Johnson [1982].

34. For outstanding analyses of government coordination of private investment, see Imai [1976], pp. 127–181, and Miwa [1977], which present different evaluations of the effectiveness of such policies.

35. See Tsuruta [1982], pp. 174–198, or Kanoo [1979].

36. The Chairman of the Petrochemical Industry Association, Iwao Iwanaga, former president of Mitsui Petrochemical, stated that "with a scale of 300,000 tons per year, construction costs rise and the amount of land needed increases, so that with these various considerations there was the expectation that some firms would give up plans for entry." See Economict [1977], pp. 98–108.

37. See Arisawa and Inaba [1966], p. 402.

38. The construction costs for facilities in process industries do not rise in proportion to the increase in productive capacity. If construction costs are C (a proxy for fixed costs) and capacity is O (the normal level of output), then the relation between the two is of the form $C = \alpha O^\beta$. The value of β is typically less than 1.0, and in practice is often about 0.6, hence the "0.6 rule." See Imai et al. [1972], pp. 128–129.

39. An empirical study of how government intervention relating to investment can disrupt the normal rhythm of investment in a free market can be found in Imai [1976], pp. 127–181.

40. Here I have in mind items such as the structural reform policies developed under the Small and Medium Enterprises Modernization Law.

41. See Sangyo Kozo Chosa Kai (Industrial Structure Advisory Committee) [1963], pp. 95–180.

42. See Kosei Torihiki Iinkai (Fair Trade Commission) [1983] for Tokyo High Court decisions relating to the petroleum industry cartel.

43. See the newsletter of the Japan Machine-Tool Builder's Association, *Kosaku Kikai News* (Machine Tool News) No. 58 (1968), p. 8.

44. *Kosaku Kikai News* No. 65 (1969), pp. 9–14.

45. At the time, the Association was composed of 10 groups of firms. These groups were not organized on the basis of capital, technical, operating, or other ties, but were solely informal groupings made for policy purposes. See *Kosaku Kikai News* No. 75 (1971), pp. 26–27.

46. See *Kosaku Kikai News* No. 75 (1971), pp. 21–25.

47. The Agreement framework was dropped in 1970 as a result of an unfavorable ruling by the Fair Trade Commission.

48. Neither can the policy to bring about cooperatives and tie-ups among small- and medium-scale enterprises under the Small and Medium Enterprises Modernization Law be called successful. According to S. Nakamura et al. [1981], pp. 193–199, most joint operations were limited to areas peripheral to the main activities of the firms involved, such as the joint provision of sewage and waste disposal, the operation of a joint parking lot, and the like. Such activities did not restrict the freedom of the firms involved and did not result in the achievement of an "appropriate" firm scale, which was the objective of the policy.

49. Even where there are restrictions on outsiders, there are many cases in which conflicts on policy have arisen among members of "the club," leading to the internal breakdown of a cartel. See Tsuruta [1978–79].
50. See Tsuruta [1982], pp. 201–229.
51. See Tanaka [1980], Tsuruta [1982], pp. 196–198 and Imai [1976], pp. 61–106.
52. See Chapter 12 by Mutoh.
53. The first attempt to discuss the possibilities for rapid growth in Japan using the Harrod–Domar model was made by Shimomura [1971], pp. 231–258. During the 1950s and 1960s those who took his stance were in the minority, limited to a very small group of non-Marxist economists.

CHAPTER 4

The Oil Crisis and After

MASU UEKUSA

Faculty of Economics
University of Tokyo
Tokyo, Japan

I. The Japanese Economy After the Oil Crisis

Before surveying and trying to evaluate the main elements of industrial policy since the first oil crisis of 1973, let us set forth the background of the era by examining macroeconomic indicators for this period (Table I). As discussed in Chapter 3, during the 1970s, the Japanese economy came to display more strongly the features of a developed economy. In particular, the public consensus began to shift from the single-minded pursuit of economic growth to a demand for a solution to the problems that accompanied growth, especially pollution, destruction of the environment, overcrowded urban areas and a depopulated countryside, insufficient overhead capital, creeping inflation, and the like. During 1969–1971, the growing surplus in Japan's balance of payments gave rise to trade friction with the United States over textiles, steel, and other products, and led to demands by the United States and other countries that the yen be revalued. Based on this change in public opinion, at the beginning of the 1970s the main focus of economic policy came to be improvement in socioeconomic performance and correction of the disequilibrium in the balance of payments.

The government responded quite positively in the first case, paying attention in particular to the issues of pollution and environmental deterioration in the drawing up of legislation and through the establishment of the Environment Agency. In contrast, the attempt to deal with the balance of payments surplus led to a series of failures. For example, when in 1970–

TABLE I
Main Economic Indicators, FY1971–FY1982[a] (%)

	1971	1972	1973	1974	1975	1976	1977	1978	1979	1980	1981	1982
Aggregate output:												
Nominal GNP	10.2	16.6	21.0	18.4	10.0	12.2	10.9	9.5	7.4	8.4	5.5	5.2
Real GNP	5.3	9.7	5.3	-0.2	3.6	5.1	5.3	5.1	5.3	4.5	3.3	3.3
Real domestic demand	3.9	10.5	7.5	-2.8	2.0	3.6	4.2	6.9	4.8	1.3	1.6	3.0
Production:												
Mining and manufacturing production	1.9	10.3	12.5	-9.7	-4.4	10.8	3.2	7.0	8.2	2.2	2.0	-0.6
Mining and manufacturing shipments	3.1	8.6	12.0	-9.4	-1.7	9.8	3.3	6.2	7.1	0.4	1.5	-1.1
Real consumption/investment:												
Private final consumption	6.2	10.5	6.3	0.8	3.4	3.7	3.7	5.5	4.7	0.8	1.1	4.7
Private fixed investment	-3.7	6.7	14.4	-8.5	-3.6	1.8	2.3	9.7	10.3	7.7	4.4	1.2
Public fixed capital formation	23.7	14.4	-6.3	-1.0	3.8	0.0	15.8	14.4	-0.9	-0.2	2.9	1.7
New housing starts	2.8	21.1	-5.0	-28.5	13.2	7.2	0.1	-2.2	-0.8	-18.3	-5.9	1.3
Money and prices:												
Wholesale price index	-0.8	3.3	22.6	23.5	2.0	5.5	0.4	-2.3	13.0	12.8	1.3	1.0
Consumer price index	5.6	5.3	16.1	21.8	10.4	9.4	6.7	3.4	4.8	7.8	4.0	2.4
Land price index	16.5	12.4	30.9	32.4	-0.9	0.5	1.5	2.5	5.2	10.0	9.6	
Money supply (M2 + CDs)[b]	24.0	25.1	15.1	11.3	15.4	12.8	10.5	12.9	9.7	6.9	10.8	7.6
Balance of payments (US$ 100 million):[c]												
Overall balance	80	29	-134	-33	-17	32	121	-22	-189	-3	-78	-19
Current account	63	61	-39	-23	1	46	139	118	-138	-70	59	91
Balance of trade	84	83	7	39	58	111	203	205	-24	67	203	201
with U.S.	28	27	-4	0	7	40	88	89	59	75	144	122
with Western Europe	15	23	20	39	40	65	73	65	68	120	119	122
Labor:												
Nominal wages	13.7	16.5	21.9	29.1	12.4	11.8	8.1	5.9	6.1	6.0	5.1	4.7
Unemployment rate[d]	1.3	1.3	1.3	1.5	1.9	2.0	2.1	2.2	2.0	2.1	2.2	2.5

Sources: Keizai Kikakucho [Economic Planning Agency], Keizai Yoran [Handbook on Economic Statistics] and Nihon Keizai Shihyo [Japanese Economic Indicators], Okurasho [Ministry of Finance], Shuyo Keizai Shihyo [Major Economic Indicators].
[a]Except for the land price index, which is on a calendar year basis, and unemployment, all percentages are the change from the previous fiscal year.
[b]As of the end of the fiscal year.
[c]IMF basis.
[d]Actual rate.

1971 there was an increasing imbalance in the current account,[1] it was essential to let the yen appreciate, but the government response to the balance of payments surplus, as reflected in its June 1971 Cabinet Resolution, "Eight Measures for the Yen," included an attempt to maintain the exchange rate at ¥360 to the U.S. dollar. While the measures included in the resolution—such as tariff reductions and the elimination of nontariff trade barriers—can be effective in the long run in helping to eliminate the payments surplus, they have little short-term impact. The government should have been able to properly discern the export competitiveness of Japanese manufacturing and the stature of Japan in the world economy, along with the stagnation of the American economy in the 1960s and the strain which that placed on the Bretton Woods system, and to carry out an adjustment of the exchange rate.[2] But as there was no recognition of these items, the Japanese government was thrown into disarray by the surprise announcement in August 1971 of President Nixon's New Economic Policy and in the end was forced at the Smithsonian Conference in December to agree to a substantial appreciation of the yen, to ¥308 to the dollar.[3]

The surplus in the balance of payments during 1969–1972 also resulted, through the supply of high-powered money, in an unusual growth in the money supply. By the fall of 1972 this had produced a strong inflationary trend. This was compounded at the end of 1971 by the adoption of an expansionary budget. Then in 1972 the Tanaka Cabinet took office with its plan to "rebuild the archipelago" and to strengthen welfare policies, and the resulting large budget added further fuel to inflation.[4]

By 1973 the Japanese economy was in an abnormal state, consequent to the failures in the exchange rate and monetary and fiscal policy. The economy was then affected by a series of international events that heightened problems. First, in February 1973 came the collapse of the Bretton Woods system, with the shift to a floating foreign exchange rate regime by Japan and other major countries. Second, with the outbreak of the fourth Middle East conflict in October, the oil producing countries adopted restrictions and embargoes on petroleum exports. This resulted in the first oil crisis, with oil prices soon quadrupling. Furthermore, the growth in the world economy was declining from a peak in 1973, and on a volume basis Japanese exports were declining from April. During 1973–1974 the Japanese economy went through a severe inflation, a sharp drop in its rate of growth, and a shift to a large balance of payments deficit. Among the developed countries, these problems were severest in Japan because of this confluence at the start of the 1970s of domestic policy failures with shocks in the international economy.[5]

The recovery of the Japanese economy from disequilibrium at the time of the first oil crisis took roughly three years,[6] so that by 1976–1978, inflation had been reduced to the level that preceded the oil crisis, and economic growth had recovered. However, with the second oil crisis following on the Iranian Revolution of April 1979, the Japanese economy was again faced by a severe inflation and a deterioration in its balance of payments during 1979–1980. Growth, however, did not decline nearly as much as it had following the first oil crisis. The reason for this was that domestic demand (particularly private investment), strong in 1978, continued to be strong throughout 1979, while exports increased rapidly during 1980.[7] Recovery from the second oil crisis took roughly two years, and from 1980 the economy was growing steadily (albeit at a low rate) and prices were stable.

There have been many analyses of how the Japanese economy was able to recover comparatively rapidly after the two oil crises.[8] Macroeconomic policy was of course an essential element, but that was not the whole story. Firms were quite successful in their rationalization efforts, starting with their conservation of energy, and workers also agreed to limit wage increases, even to the point of accepting reductions in real wages.

Accompanying the changes in the economic environment were unprecedented changes in the structure of the economy, changes that followed from the shift to the floating exchange rate regime and the first and second oil crises of 1973 and 1979. The first of these changes was the decline in the rate of growth. During the high growth era, the real growth rate was around 10%, but in the adjustment after the first oil crisis, the rate fell to 5% (during 1976–1978), and it fell further—to 3% (from 1980)—after the second oil crisis. Part of this was due to a change in the features that supported rapid growth in the postwar period, such as the sharp rise in the cost of energy with the price increases that followed the two oil crises. If one looks at the impact on the supply side of the economy, the sharp rise in energy prices shifted the production frontier of the economy inward, resulting in a lowering of the marginal productivity of labor (real wages) and of the marginal productivity of capital (profits per unit of capital).[9] The reduction in real wages decreased private final consumption, while the reduction in profits decreased private fixed investment, both of which worked to lower the rate of growth.

The second change was in the unequal development of basic materials industries and assembly industries. As can be seen in Figure 4.1, output increased in tandem in these two sectors through 1975, but in contrast to the relatively flat trend in the basic materials industries that followed, output in the assembly industries increased greatly from 1975, and a substantial gap developed between the two sectors. For the basic materials

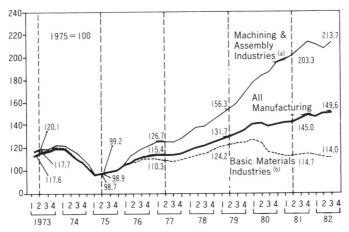

Fig. 4.1. Output indices. (a) Average of general machinery, electrical equipment, transport equipment and precision instruments; (b) average of steel, nonferrous metals, cement, plate glass, stone and clay products, chemicals (excluding pharmaceuticals and cosmetics), pulp and paper, synthetic textiles, and wood and wood products. From Tanabe (ed.) [1983], p. 7, based on MITI, *Kokogyo Shisu Nempo* [Mining and Manufacturing Production Index Annual].

industries, which are heavy users of energy, the tremendous increase in energy costs led to price increases, which shifted demand to substitute and other competitive products and to imported products. When this was combined with the downward shift in demand with the slowdown of growth in the economy as a whole, the result was long-term stagnation in output. On the other hand, in the assembly industries, which use relatively little energy, the increase in energy costs had little effect on total costs. At the same time, the introduction of robots and NC machine tools increased productivity, while quality and design continued to improve, increasing both domestic and foreign demand.[10]

The third change was the emergence of large trade surpluses in 1976–1978 and since 1981, following the adjustment to the two oil crises (see Table I). This change is related to the extreme dependence of the Japanese economy on imported oil,[11] as the yen tends to a lower rate under a floating exchange regime, thereby favoring exports.[12] When this factor is combined with the strengthened export competitiveness of the assembly industries stemming from the above factors, the result is an increase in the balance of trade surplus. The imbalance of trade during this period was thus due not only to the international competitive supremacy of Japanese industry, but also to the structure of trade under the floating rate system.

Important policy issues included not only short-term adjustment to the oil crises, but also the response to the three structural shifts noted above and the related topic of conserving energy and shifting to a structure less dependent on petroleum. The responses to the three structural shifts were as follows: First, there was the need for adjustment in industries such as aluminum and other basic materials industries, which had lost their international competitiveness with the rise in energy costs, or shipbuilding and textiles, which suffered from severe excess capacity with the stagnation in domestic and foreign demand and new competition from developing countries. Second, there was the need to respond to the trade friction that had arisen with the large bilateral trade imbalances with the United States and the EEC. Third, there remained a potential for growth through research and development in high technology industries, and as a response to the lowering of growth, the government looked to this as a way to revitalize the economy, while firms looked at it as a way to grow. The development of high technology has thus been an important topic for both the government and firms from the late 1970s and into the 1980s.

II. Industrial Policy Following the Oil Crisis

As mentioned above, the three principal problems faced by the Japanese economy following the oil crisis were (1) responding to the problems generated by growth, in continuation from the 1960s, (2) short-term adjustment to the disequilibrium engendered by the oil crisis, and (3) responding to the structural changes in the economy brought about by the oil crisis and the shift to a floating exchange rate regime. The latter included the need to deal with declining industries domestically, to handle trade friction internationally, and to develop high technology industry, including alternate energy sources. Industrial policy was not the only means of responding to these issues; fiscal and monetary policy and other macroeconomic policies also had an important role to play.[13] Broadly speaking, the relation between the two is that macroeconomic policy deals with the demand side of the economy, while industrial policy deals with the supply side. In an economy such as that of Japan, which consists of a market system, policy cannot be based on commands issued by planners in the central government. Instead, such policies must be formed as part of a cooperative game among government and the various industries.[14] After the oil crisis, both the government and business changed their positions greatly as they responded to the changes in the Japanese economy; the cooperative game thus was considerably altered.

A. Changes in Government–Business Relations

In comparison to the high growth era, the government, by which I mean
the ministry or agency that was responsible for policy, became much more
passive. In other words, during the high growth period, the government
was on the one hand seeking to bring about rapid growth through industrialization and a strengthening of international competitiveness, while on
the other hand it was preparing for the transition to an open economy
required by Japan's status under GATT and the goal of membership in
the OECD; positive, activist policies were central. After the oil crisis,
however, negative and passive policies became more central. Since near
the end of the high growth era there had been a need to deal with pollution
and the other costs of growth, to respond to the oil and foreign exchange
market crises, and to adjust domestically and internationally to the resulting crisis in the world economy. This all certainly reflects the changes
in the policy environment that affected industrial policy.

Furthermore, from the beginning of the 1970s there was also a shift in
the institutional framework that affected the implementation of industrial
policy. First, during 1971–1973 there were the court decisions on four
important pollution cases. According to Tsuruta, "with these decisions,
the limitations on industrialization changed drastically, from the environment coming second, to a primary emphasis on the preservation of the
natural environment."[15] Second, in response to the large number of cartels
that were formed after the first oil crisis, the Antimonopoly Act was revised
and strengthened in 1977.[16] In addition, in the case brought against the
petroleum cartel by the Fair Trade Commission at this time, the Tokyo
High Court in its 1980 judgment ruled clearly that administrative guidance
by the government, which served to restrain competition, was not permissible, severely restricting the use of industrial policies that restrained
competition or encouraged anticompetitive behavior.[17] Third, in the early
1970s, protectionism gradually reared its head in the main Western countries, and during this period in which the GATT rules were being weakened, Japan took the position that the GATT system should be strictly
adhered to. It thus became impossible to arbitrarily adopt policies to protect or develop domestic industry. Thus the government had to implement
industrial policies during this period that adhered to domestic and international laws relating to problems such as pollution, monopoly, and trade
friction.

There were also changes on the side of industry. Already by the late
1960s industries and firms that had increased their international competitiveness came to disagree with government policies that, in the name of
rationalizing industry and strengthening international competitiveness, in-

tervened even in their basic strategic decisions. Many Japanese industries and firms also revolutionized their way of thinking after going through the international currency and oil crises.[18] In other words, as positive steps needed to survive in the developing domestic and international economy and society, firms had to (1) improve their productivity by using the optimal mix of their basic inputs, including conserving energy and improving labor productivity, (2) follow through with their quality control efforts, (3) develop new products and redesign existing ones to better meet a variety of needs, (4) respond to changes in the structure of industry through diversification and entry into high technology fields, and (5) in order to do the above, increase their expenditures on research and development. In fact, many firms were successful in this, increasing their internal accumulation of capital, human, and technological resources. As a result, rather than government-initiated industrial policy, Japanese industry (with the exception of a number of the declining sectors) has taken the lead in asking the government to provide information on changes in the industrial structure and on developments in high technology.

In view of the above situation of government and industry, the points of agreement in the cooperative policy game are for "soft" options, in which firms are induced to change chiefly through the provision of information, rather than through "hard" measures such as subsidies, low-interest finance, and tax benefits. As a result, the provision of information on long-term trends in industrial structure and the international economy now forms the core of industrial policy.

B. The Goals of Policy

Reflecting the changes in the policy environment described above, such as the changes in the state of the Japanese economy and in government–business relations, the goals of industrial policy changed substantially following the oil crisis. These changes had already been foreshadowed in the report of the Industrial Structure Council of May 1970, *MITI Policy in the 1970's,* known generally as the *Vision for the 1970's.*[19] The viewpoint expressed in that report has governed the carrying out of industrial policy through today. This "Vision" set forth the following three goals for industrial policy in the 1970s.

First, there was a shift from economic policy undertaken in pursuit of growth to economic policy that took advantage of growth. Such policies thus sought "to use the ability of the Japanese economy to grow to (1) improve the labor environment, (2) build up social capital, (3) create a healthy environment, (4) strengthen education, (5) increase investment in research and development, and (6) increase foreign aid."[20] This policy statement can be seen as a response to the problems the Japanese economy faced in improving its socioeconomic performance. Second was the theme of using the market mechanism to the fullest possible extent. In other words, "excess policy intervention and measures which excessively protect industry should be strictly prohibited,"[21] with the market mechanism to be utilized to the fullest extent possible for purposes of resource allocation, and industrial policy to be limited to areas of market failure, such as dealing with pollution, the risk that accompanies the development of technology and natural resources, the supply of social capital and public services, and the promotion of infant industries and helping declining industries to adjust. In this can be seen the recognition (as discussed in Chapter 3 of this book) that the foundation had been built on which the price mechanism could be relied on for resource allocation and which would permit the Japanese economy to continue to develop. In this there was a major shift in the operating principles of industrial policy. Finally, it was suggested that henceforth the industrial structure would shift from being centered around capital-intensive heavy industries to being built around knowledge-intensive machining and assembly industries. In this the core of industrial policy was to be redirected to building up a knowledge-intensive industrial structure. This approach is the archetype of Vision policies,[22] reflecting as well the government–business relationship referred to above.

Several industrial policy Visions were subsequently issued, with the *Long-Term Vision of the Industrial Structure* (the *1975 Vision*) drawn up as a revision to the *Vision for the 1970's,* followed in 1980 by the *MITI Policy Vision for the 1980's,* known generally as the *Vision for the 1980's.* These expanded the *Vision for the 1970's,* adding as time passed and the environment changed energy policy and policy for developing high technology. The *Vision for the 1980's* called for developing an industrial structure with high technology as its core, which it referred to as a "creative, knowledge-intensive industrial structure."

Actual industrial policies were formulated in line with the above basic policy directions. Policy, of course, was decided on in accordance with the economic environment at the time. Thus, in chronological order,[23] there were pricing policies in the adjustment period following the first oil crisis (in particular, the Law for Adjusting Petroleum Supply and Demand and the Law on Temporary Measures for Normalizing the National Life) and emergency measures to procure reliable energy supplies. Continuing from the late 1960s, important policy foci included environmental protection measures (the enactment of laws relating to environmental protection during 1971–1973 and administrative guidance relating to antipollution regulations), the plan to rebuild the Japanese archipelago (the 1973

Law on Measures to Promote Industrial Relocation), and measures to help small business. Next, during the period of stable growth of 1976–1978, there arose as central themes of industrial policy the need for adjustment internationally in the face of growing problems with trade friction, and for adjustment in declining industries (seen particularly in the 1978 Law on Temporary Measures for Stabilization of Specified Depressed Industries). In line with the vision of a knowledge-intensive industrial structure, there was a strengthening of promotion measures for the integrated circuit, computer, and aircraft industries through the enactment of the 1978 Law on Temporary Measures for the Promotion of Specified Machinery and Information Industries. Finally, with the onset of the second oil crisis in 1979–1980, energy policy again became a central focus. After the period of adjustment that followed the second oil crisis, from 1981 through to the present, the main policies have been those for developing high technology, for responding to trade friction, and for facilitating adjustment in secularly depressed industries.

As can be seen, industrial policy following the oil crisis reflected the "turbulent '70s", with the main thrust consisting of *ad hoc* responses to the domestic and international economic events that occurred one after another. It is important to stress that, with the exclusion of policies for promoting a limited number of industries, such as the computer, integrated circuit, and aircraft industries, policy was passive or reactive in the face of environmental problems and the need for adjustment in declining industries or in the need to respond to trade friction.

C. Changes in Policy Tools

There are a variety of instruments of industrial policy, including fiscal, tax, financial, and trade measures. Following the oil crisis, the use of these various policy instruments in all cases changed, and this was particularly true of the use of trade policy. During the 1950s and the first half of the 1960s, Japanese industrial policy sought to concentrate resources in key industries. For that purpose, selective or preferential fiscal, tax, and financial policies were implemented, and domestic firms in these industries were protected from foreign competition by setting up tariff and nontariff trade barriers (such as quotas) and by restricting imports and foreign direct investment.[24] Starting from the late 1960s, these sorts of protective trade policies were lessened as a consequence of trade and capital liberalization policies. This was especially the case during the three periods of 1969–1971, 1976–1978, and 1981 to the present, when protective trade policies were substantially dismantled in the face of increasing trade imbalances and numerous cases of trade friction. Protective trade policies have therefore been eliminated, at least in the case of manufacturing. Ironically, this occurred as the specter of protectionism was being raised in the leading Western nations, with Japan implementing "voluntary" export restraints.

For policy tools other than trade measures, the use of various fiscal, tax, and financial measures aimed at concentrating resources into basic industries declined in the 1970s relative to the 1960s. Instead, the focus was shifted to the encouragement of technological development in areas of high technology (including technologies to lessen dependence on petroleum as an energy source). For this purpose subsidies were granted, along with favorable tax status and access to government financing, which were provided for under the Machinery and Information Industries Promotion Law. In addition, the tax and financial advantages provided for small business, which had been in existence prior to the 1970s, were continued and are still in effect today. By looking at the budget of MITI over 1975–1979, broken down by policies (Table II), it is clear that outlays for small business have increased by significant amounts, while expenditures for energy and high technology policies have expanded very rapidly. With the exception of small business measures, however, the fiscal, tax, and financial provisions for particular industries have declined significantly in comparison to the 1960s. Furthermore, with the slowdown in economic growth since the oil crisis, government deficits have expanded, and the provision of subsidies for industry and the granting of tax reductions has been restricted. This is a prime cause of the decline in importance of favorable fiscal and tax provisions.

As is well known, the use of administrative guidance is a distinctive feature of Japanese industrial policy. This administrative guidance, which is based on a cooperative relationship between the ministry in charge and leading firms or associations in an industry, continues today as an important tool of industrial policy. It must be noted, however, that the sort of guidance used frequently in the 1950s and 1960s to restrain competition (such as cartels set up through administrative guidance) has become difficult to carry out today, with the revision and strengthening of the Antitrust Law in 1977 and the 1980 judgment in the petroleum cartel case.

Beginning in the 1970s, the drawing up of a Vision has increased in importance as a tool of industrial policy. It has been previously noted that the Vision has been used as a method for the government to provide information to private firms on the direction in which the industrial structure and international relations are moving. In addition, the policy goals set forth in the Vision provide guidelines for the behavior of firms, such as the concept of developing a knowledge-intensive industrial structure, and thus play a role in inducing firms to move in that direction. Because

TABLE II
The MITI Budget by Policy Areas, 1975–1979 (¥ million)

Area	1975	1976	1977	1978	1979
1. For drawing up the "MITI Policy Vision for the 1980s"	0	0	0	0	31
2. For promoting harmonious foreign economic ties and contributing to the world economy	16,787	17,966	18,291	18,962	19,520
(1) For developing smooth foreign economic ties	11,810	10,337	10,640	10,970	10,751
(2) For international economic cooperation	4,977	7,629	7,651	7,992	8,769
3. For completing the economic recovery and furthering industrial policy	359	311	388	290	255
(1) For furthering policies toward structurally depressed industries and aiding firms to change their industry	217	172	256	210	179
(2) For promoting industrial organization policies	39	61	66	32	26
(3) For promoting communication between business and the public	103	78	51	47	45
(4) For pilot studies for an International Technology Exposition	0	0	0	0	5
4. In support of small business policies	102,226	120,254	134,418	153,322	172,762
(1) For stable management of small businesses	4,400	5,600	6,000	8,747	10,623
(2) For promoting development by small business	16,021	68,116	76,849	89,869	105,157
(3) For promoting measures for very small firms	34,980	44,502	49,857	49,006	52,423
(4) For measures for small retail and service firms	(145)	(153)	(183)	(237)	(614)
(5) Other items	1,825	2,036	1,712	5,700	4,560
5. For strengthening overall energy policies	26,030	28,822	30,588	158,139	179,494
(1) For petroleum-related power	49	44	55	58	69
(2) For nuclear power	385	529	738	823	1,020
(3) For electric power	1,093	1,410	703	727	868
(4) For energy conservation	128	130	134	319	343
(5) For obtaining natural resources	22,037	24,970	27,395	24,930	24,456
(6) For inclusion in special funds for coal and petroleum	0	0	0	129,500	150,900
(7) Other items	2,338	1,739	1,563	1,782	1,837

TABLE II (Continued)

Area	1975	1976	1977	1978	1979
6. For promoting "industries of the future" and industrial technology	59,214	67,129	76,855	82,827	106,098
(1) For promoting industries of the future	3,531	5,470	11,868	13,712	16,583
(2) For improving the base for research and development	50,357	55,108	57,398	60,552	78,610
(3) For the "Sunshine" project, the development of new energy technologies	3,704	4,626	4,888	5,502	7,059
(4) For the "Moonlight" project, the development of energy conservation technologies	437	500	1,016	1,978	2,771
(5) For developing systems and technologies to improve social welfare	1,185	1,425	1,686	1,083	1,075
7. Environment and industrial location policies and measures for consumers	21,210	23,000	20,835	21,235	20,955
(1) For environmental protection and the use and recycling of waste	4,829	5,027	5,366	5,674	6,299
(2) For responding to earthquakes and other natural disasters and for industrial safety	421	461	481	496	566
(3) For industrial siting	12,061	11,977	11,297	11,299	8,569
(4) For improving consumers' welfare	3,899	5,535	3,691	3,766	5,532
8. Other items	63,466	47,051	36,124	39,321	42,127
TOTAL	289,292	304,533	317,499	474,096	541,242

Source: Tsusho Sangyo Gyosei Kenkyukai [1983], vol. I, pp. 57–58.

of this, the Vision has a role as a tool of industrial policy. The role of the Vision is strongest when the policy goals it sets forth provide a comprehensive framework for other policy measures.

III. An Evaluation of Post-Oil Crisis Industrial Policy

I believe the above discussion gives the framework of industrial policy during this period, and next I want to evaluate industrial policy for this period. To summarize, I consider the main policies during this period to be (1) the Vision and the policies based on that overall framework, of which specific elements are (2) adjustment in depressed industries, (3) international adjustment in response to trade friction, (4) overall energy policy, including obtaining a stable supply of petroleum, energy conservation, and the development and use of substitutes for petroleum, (5) subsidies for research and development in and the promotion of high technology fields, (6) environmental regulation, and (7) measures for small business. I want to evaluate (1), (2), and (3) as being of particular importance for industrial policy in this period. The development of technology in item (4) is covered in part in Chapters 7 through 9 of this book, as is item (5), while (6) is covered in Chapter 12 and (7) in Chapter 20.

A. The Concept of a Knowledge-Intensive Industrial Structure

The "knowledge-intensive industrial structure" envisaged in the *Vision for the 1970s* was expanded to the "creative, knowledge-intensive industrial structure" of the *Vision for the 1980s*. This remains today the basis for industrial policy, especially for policies to protect or promote specific industries. This concept of achieving a knowledge-intensive industrial structure reflects the desire to concentrate resources in such industries, in place of the previous focus on heavy and chemical industries. The background for the introduction of this new concept is as follows.

First, among the heavy and chemical industries that grew rapidly in the 1960s, the growth of steel, nonferrous metals, and chemicals slowed due to reaching the limits of economies of scale and because of their energy requirements. On the other hand, the assembly-type machinery industries expanded rapidly, including general machinery, electronic and electrical equipment, transport equipment, and precision instruments. Distinctive features of these industries were heavy investment in research and development and high input of knowledge-intensive labor. Noting this, such industries came to be referred to as knowledge-intensive industries, and a strategy of using industrial policy to develop these industries was followed. Thus the origins of this concept were empirically rooted.[25] In addition, the knowledge-intensive industry ideas of Machlup [1962], which were widely discussed at the time, were utilized, and the information, information equipment, and education industries were added to the list of knowledge-intensive industries. Second, at the beginning of the 1970s, there was a call for improvement in socioeconomic performance through environmental regulation and other steps. Attention was thus focused on the knowledge-intensive industries as being nonpolluting and low in their demands on the environment.

In either case, the concept of knowledge-intensive industries is highly subjective and is based on arbitrary, convenient assumptions. Because of this, some sort of theoretical rationale for the label of "knowledge-intensive industry" became necessary. Four criteria were given in the *Vision for the 1970s,* the first two drawing from those used for the heavy and chemical industrialization policies of the 1960s. These were the standards of (1) having a high income elasticity of demand, so that it would be expected that as national income grew, demand in the industry would grow rapidly, and (2) having a rapid rate of increase in productivity, with rising physical and value productivity leading to the industry exhibiting a comparative advantage internationally. To these two criteria were added (3) siting and environmental considerations, so that they would help to solve land availability and pollution problems and contribute to the efficient use of energy, and (4) the quality of the work environment, so that the industry would provide many "good" work places.

In the following sense, though, the concept of a knowledge-intensive industrial structure is superior to its precursor. In the past, when changes in the industrial structure were analyzed from the input side, the comparison concentrated on the relative labor inputs required by different industries. Now, however, labor is disaggregated into knowledge-intensive and simple labor, and an attempt is made to compare total factor inputs including capital and natural resources across different industries.[26] Thus, in input–output analysis, the knowledge-intensive industries are those in which the share of knowledge-intensive labor inputs in total factor inputs is relatively great, and those of capital and energy relatively small. In specific, the knowledge-intensive industries are held to be (1) what are now referred to as high technology industries, such as integrated circuits, computers, robotics, fine chemicals, and new alloys, (2) advanced assembly industries, such as aircraft and numerically controlled machine tools, (3) the fashion and design industries, and (4) information processing and distributing industries.

Without a doubt, almost all of these industries have grown relatively quickly from the 1970s on. From Figure 4.1, it can be clearly seen that the assembly industries, which include almost all of the industries in (1) to (4) above, have grown rapidly since 1975. In Figure 4-2, the same trend is clear from looking at the changes in the composition of exports by industry. Among the machining and assembly industries, however, in only a few cases did industrial policy have an impact on the rate of growth. In other words, under the concept of knowledge-intensive industries, industrial promotion policies were only implemented for a very small group of industries, such as computers, integrated circuits, and aircraft, along with energy, information processing, and other tertiary industries.[27] These industries are dealt with in Chapters 7 through 9 of this book, to which

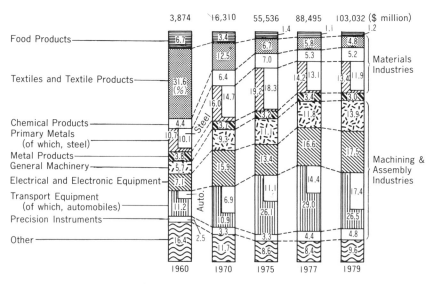

Fig. 4.2. Changes in the composition of Japanese exports (%). From Tsusho Sangyo Gyosei Kenkyukai [1983], pg. 31, based on Okurasho, *Gaikoku Boeki Gaikyo* [Trade of Japan].

the reader is referred; the aircraft industry is not treated, but promotion efforts in it have not born much fruit to date. Rather than a result of industrial policy, the growth of the assembly industries was based on interfirm competition, where firms introduced robots and numerically controlled machine tools to reduce labor costs and improve labor productivity, and which also resulted in stable prices (see Table III) and improvements in quality.

Why were not more industries designated as ones important for promotion, in line with the concept of a knowledge-intensive industrial structure? The reason was above all the changes in government–business relationships indicated above. In short, the leading firms in Japan, which had been able to accumulate substantial capital and managerial resources, disliked government intervention in industry and wanted to be able to develop independently. Furthermore, MITI, which through the 1960s had favored steel, chemicals, and other capital-intensive, energy-consuming basic materials industries, adopted a stance of restricting benefits to those industries. But by MITI's own analysis (see the tables and figures provided for reference in the *Vision for the 1970s*), they were not low in knowledge-intensity, and these industries were repulsed by MITI's stance. This development constrained the management of knowledge-intensive industrial policies throughout the 1970s; only toward the end of the decade

TABLE III
Changes in Labor Productivity, Labor Cost, and Prices by Industry

Average Annual Increase, 1974–1981 (%)	Increases in Labor Productivity	Increases in Labor Costs	1981 Wholesale Price Index (1975 = 100)
1. Food Products	0.5	7.9	129.3
2. Textiles and Apparel	3.4	4.7	121.9
3. Wood and Wood Products	3.7	3.7	132.9
4. Pulp and Paper	3.6	3.1	129.3
5. Chemicals	5.9	2.2	129.4
6. Petroleum Products	− 0.0	9.3	215.6
7. Ceramics and Stone Products	2.7	5.3	149.6
8. Steel	3.2	4.6	131.2
9. Nonferrous Metals	4.8	3.1	129.4
10. Metal Products	2.4	6.0	124.3
11. Machinery, General	6.2	2.3	107.8[a]
12. Electrical and Electronic Equipment	10.7	− 1.1	99.5
13. Transport Equipment	6.0	2.8	104.4
14. Precision Instruments	19.8	− 9.3	
Basic Materials Industries[b]	4.0	3.7	133.6
Machining and Assembly Industries[c]	10.7	− 1.3	103.9

Sources: Keizai Kikakucho [1982], p. 630, for labor productivity and costs, and Nihon Ginko, *Bukka Shisu Nempo* (Price Index Annual), 1981, pp. 2–7 for the WPI.

[a]Includes precision instruments.

[b]Consists of (3) to (5) and (7) to (9).

[c]Consists of (11) to (14).

were industrial promotion policies centered on the information machinery industries implemented. For the above reasons, only a very small number of industries benefited from MITI's policy of allocating resources preferentially to knowledge-intensive industries. Instead, the market mechanism was the main means of resource allocation. In this, the change in industrial policy in the 1970s is to be favorably evaluated.

The concept of an increasingly "creative, knowledge-intensive" economy of the *Vision for the 1980s* holds knowledge-intensive industries, especially high-technology industries, to be the leading sector of the economy. It also seeks to increase knowledge-intensity in all areas of production, including both products and production processes, as an overall way to revitalize the economy. Aware of the conflicts that arose in the treatment of the basic materials industries in the *Vision for the 1970s*, the new concept was distinctive in promoting knowledge-intensity in all areas of industry. Actual policy efforts, however, were concentrated in advanced high-technology areas, such as biotechnology (especially bio-reactors, cell fusion, and gene recombination), new materials (such as new function devices, composite materials, amorphous ceramics, and new alloys), and new energy technologies (solar heating and solar and fusion power) all with the aim of developing technologies for the "industries of the future." The Fifth Generation Computer Project was part of the thrust for an "advanced information society."[28] Another distinction is that recently industrial policy has been expanded to include service industries, and not just (as in the past) manufacturing.[29] This is because, with the progress of the revolution in telecommunications, the communications processing (VAN, value-added networks) and information processing industries have grown rapidly. A reexamination of the service industries is also under way from the perspective of employment policies, reflecting the rise of the "service economy," with the weight of the tertiary sector increasing along with employment in services in the primary and secondary sectors.[30]

It is difficult to evaluate the specific industrial policies being adopted under the concept of an increasingly creative, knowledge-intensive economy, because they have only just begun. To the extent, however, that they concentrate on subsidizing the highly risky research and development for "future" technologies, it is theoretically sound (see Part II of this book). Furthermore, as the economy becomes more service oriented, it is appropriate for MITI, in cooperation with the Ministry of Labor, to implement policies that seek to improve labor mobility (such as labor training and setting up a system of internships). The subsidies that have been so far provided to the integrated circuit and computer industries have lowered both firms' costs and risks, encouraging investment. Research cooperatives and the JECC (Japan Electronic Computer Co.) have also served to protect and promote domestic manufacturers (as discussed in more detail in Chapter 8 of this book). Such policies for protecting and promoting specific industries are a legacy of industrial policy of the 1960s, but henceforth the role in industrial policy for those that consist of "picking the winner" needs to be considered more critically.

B. Adjustment Policies in the Depressed Industries

As noted above, with the onset of the 1970s, the Japanese economy was affected by a variety of occurrences in the international economy and encountered a deceleration in growth and secular depression centered around the basic materials industries. Excess capacity became apparent, particularly in industries such as aluminum, with capacity utilization declining sharply. The government referred to industries that needed to be restructured or in which capacity needed to be disposed of as "structurally depressed industries,"[31] and in May 1978 the Law on Temporary Measures for Stabilizing Specified Depressed Industries (hereafter the Industry Stabilization Law) was enacted, implementing adjustment policies for the structurally depressed industries.

The industries designated as structurally depressed initially were (1) open-hearth and electric-arc furnaces, (2) aluminum refining, and (3) synthetic fibers under MITI, and (4) shipbuilding, under the Ministry of Transport. Later (5) chemical fertilizers, (6) cotton and synthetic textiles, and (7) cardboard were added, all of which fell under MITI's jurisdiction. These industries were depressed for a variety of reasons. Aluminum refining was hit by a sharp jump in the cost of electric power, raising production costs so that the industry lost its competitiveness against low-cost foreign producers. Synthetic fibers were affected by the rise in the price of naphtha, a prime raw material, and appreciation of the yen, so that the industry became less competitive in export markets, while domestic demand remained low. Shipbuilding was hit by the total failure of worldwide tanker demand to expand, causing orders to decline precipitously. Textiles were hurt as developing countries overtook Japan; fertilizers were squeezed by an increase in capacity internationally, the rise in raw material costs, and greater self-sufficiency in developing countries; while steel and cardboard were hurt by stagnant domestic demand caused by the decline in the growth rate following the oil crisis.[32] Among these various causes, the need for industries in Japan to adjust in the face of the increasing industrialization of the developing countries was a situation common to all the advanced countries. In this parallel, adjustment in structurally depressed industries represented a new phase of Japanese industrial policy.

The key features of the Industry Stabilization Law provided for (1) joint action to deal with excess capacity, including scrapping, mothballing, and the cessation of operations, and the transfer of facilities, (2) the drawing up of "Basic Stabilization Plans" and the designation of joint action for dealing with excess capacity, (3) the establishment of common funds to provide the necessary financing to deal with excess capacity, and (4) the designation of special laws to deal with unemployment and regional economies, such as the Law on Temporary Measures for Those Unemployed in Specified Depressed Industries and the Law on Temporary Measures for Those Unemployed in Specified Depressed Regions. These provisions are discussed in more detail in Chapter 14 of this book.

The Industry Stabilization Law can be evaluated favorably on a number of points. Within the time frame of the Basic Stabilization Plan, on average,

95% of the capacity adjustment goals were achieved,[33] and in a number of industries an equilibrium of supply with demand was again reached without the accompaniment of protective adjustment policies such as import restrictions or government subsidies. For shipbuilding in particular, most firms were able to reduce their capacity without going bankrupt, and the policies were effective in stimulating diversification by the largest firms in the industry (see Chapters 14 and 16 of this book). However, this positive evaluation conceals many problems. First, a number of industries, although they carried out capacity adjustments, saw excess capacity increase in the wake of the second oil crisis. Most capacity reduction occurred through mothballing and the cessation of operations, so that in reality capacity was not eliminated or switched to other industries. Furthermore, there were many cases in which firms in an industry were themselves already eliminating capacity before the government's Basic Stabilization Plan was implemented, so that doubts are cast overall, not only on the effectiveness, but also on the relevance of government intervention for the adjustment of capacity. Second, there are criticisms raised from the standpoint of antitrust policy. Capacity adjustment under the Industry Stabilization Law consisted in reality of joint action to eliminate capacity, that is, it consisted of a cartel. For electric-arc steel furnaces and shipbuilding there were also output cartels, while for fertilizers there were cartels for fixing prices and allocating exports. In this way, the approval of a cartel for one purpose brought on the formation of cartels for other purposes, serving not only as a barrier to effective adjustment in an industry, but also by protecting marginal firms, also interfered with rationalization within the industry.[34]

With the above criticisms being directed at industrial adjustment policies under the Industry Stabilization Law, in June 1978 the OECD Ministerial Council approved the "General Policy Guidelines toward Positive Adjustment Policies." This statement urged the adoption of "positive adjustment policies" by the OECD member nations toward industries that had become relatively uncompetitive following the first oil crisis, instead of the competition-restricting, protective "negative adjustment policies" that had in many cases been adopted. Positive adjustment policies had as their basic element reliance on the market mechanism for industrial adjustment, and the following guidelines were set forth to be observed when government intervention to assist a structurally weak industry was necessary. These were (1) that policies should have a definite termination date, and ideally should be gradually removed as that date approaches, and (2) that policies should provide for the gradual elimination of outdated facilities, in accordance with a plan for the restructuring of firms' finances, but prices should not be raised to the point where efficient producers earn more than some appropriate level of profits. In addition, (3) the social costs necessary for adjustment should be made clear to the public, and the sources and uses of funds should be "transparent," (4) public subsidies should be combined with private financing and should serve to improve business performance, and (5) provision should be made for adequate domestic and international comptetion. Finally, positve adjustment policies toward a region should be part of general policy toward the region and (7) policies "for domestic protection" should be used as seldom as possible.[35] This adoption of positive adjustment policies by the OECD came to influence Japanese industrial policy as well.

The Law on Temporary Measures for Structural Improvement of Specified Industries (henceforth the Structural Improvement Law) was enacted in May 1983 to provide new policy measures for adjustment in industries where the Industry Stabilization Law proved inadequate. These industries were aluminum, synthetic fibers, chemical fertilizers, and alloyed steels, which were affected by the onset of the second oil crisis, and paper and cardboard and petrochemicals, which were hurt by the deepening recession that followed the second oil crisis. The first key provision of this law (1) provided for joint reduction of excess capacity, as in the Industry Stabilization Law. The new provisions in the bill were (2) for tie-ups among firms, including joint production and mergers, (3) for the concentration of operations through specialization in a narrower range of products, and (4) for promoting increased productivity through the development of new technology and investment in facilities. The law thus provided not only for the reduction of excess capacity, but also extolled reform of the market structure and the development of an efficient productive structure in an industry through the development of new technology. Put another way, the bill sought at one and the same time to bring about exit from and revitalization of an industry. Another feature of the law is that it requires obtaining the acquiescence of the Fair Trade Commission for implementing measures that restrict competition, such as the designation of cartels for capacity reduction, interfirm tie-ups, and the concentration of operations. Furthermore, the provisions of the law called for the gradual reduction of measures, with their elimination within a set time limit; the avoidance of measures that restrain imports; and policy "transparency."

Industrial adjustment policies under the Structural Improvement Law have only just begun, thus it is difficult to evaluate them. The law does, however, take into account domestic antitrust legislation and the Positive Adjustment Policy guidelines adopted by the OECD, and it should be evaluated very favorably in practice for not implementing policies, including import restraints, that unfairly limit competition. If, by following such policies, depressed industries shrink in size or shift to other products, then this sort of industrial adjustment policy should be evaluated quite favorably.

C. Trade Friction and Trade Policy

It has already been mentioned that Japan was running a large surplus in its balance of payments and had a large imbalance in its trade with the United States at the time of the Nixon shock of August 1971, which led to a substantial appreciation of the yen after the Smithsonian Conference. Currency realignment falls within the area of monetary policy, which is largely the responsibility of the Ministry of Finance, but the response to trade friction between the United States and Japan, which arose during a time of trade imbalances, fell within the area of industrial policy.

As exports to the United States rose rapidly and industries within the United States called for import restraints, the Japanese government instituted export restraints; by the 1950s Japan had already adopted "voluntary" export restraints for textiles and sundries. From the end of the 1960s through the early 1970s, however, the Japanese trade imbalance with the United States continued to increase, and the number of cases in which import relief was filed for and for which restrictions on imports from Japan were imposed increased in the United States. United States demands also increased for Japan to adopt voluntary export restraints, to sign agreements limiting exports, or to adhere to "orderly marketing agreements."[36] The United States was also led to call on Japan to revalue the yen and to eliminate or reduce tariff and nontariff trade barriers. All such occurrences are referred to herein as trade friction. There have been three periods when there were a large number of cases of trade friction between Japan and the United States: during 1969–1972, during 1976–1978, and from 1981 through the present. All of these were periods during which the trade imbalance of Japan with the United States increased, and during the latest period there has also been much trade friction with the EEC.

The response of the Japanese government to trade friction fell into two main areas, not including currency realignments. The first of these responses was the elimination or reduction of tariff and nontariff trade barriers, and the second was the use of measures to restrain exports or encourage imports in individual industries. Tariffs were lowered and quantitative import restrictions reduced during the course of various international negotiations, such as the Kennedy Round (1964–1972) and the Tokyo Round (1972–1979) trade talks. Tariffs were reduced sharply from the latter 1960s through the early 1970s, with Japan's overall tariff burden averaging 3.1% in 1979, lower than the 3.9% levels of the United States and the EEC (see Figure 4.3). The number of categories that remained on the import restriction list was also drastically reduced, to 164 in 1968, to 90 in 1970, and to 27 in 1979.[37] In addition, Japanese customs procedures were simplified and import specifications were revised.

In spite of such measures, the trade imbalance of Japan with the United States and the EEC did not improve, and the Americans made an issue of the "closed" Japanese market, claiming that industrial, agricultural, and research and development policies comprised nontariff trade barriers. The Europeans complained that the distinctive features of Japanese industrial organization constituted nontariff barriers, including features such as firm groups, the subcontracting system, *keiretsu* in the distribution system, strong manufacturers associations, close ties between financial and nonfinancial firms, and industrial policy that provided benefits to particular industries. It is very difficult in both theory and in practice to make a judgment about whether or not such features constitute nontariff barriers, and it is very likely that such debates only add fuel to the fire.[38]

The industries affected by trade friction were textiles, steel, and color televisions in the first period of friction with the United States (1967–1972). During the second period (1976–1978), friction escalated to include steel, color televisions, automobiles, and semiconductors, and there was pressure for Japan to increase imports of beef, citrus fruits, and leaf tobacco, and for NTT, the telephone monopoly, to open its procurements

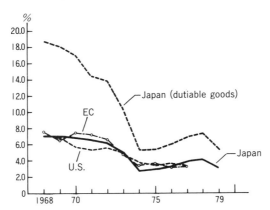

Fig. 4.3. Changes in the tariff burden in Japan, U. S., and EEC. The tariff burden is tariff receipts divided by total imports. For dutiable goods, the burden is tariff receipts divided by total imports of dutiable goods. The rates are calculated for Japan for the period April 1 to March 31; for the U.S., for the period July 1 to June 30; and for the EEC, for the period January 1 through December 31. For the EEC the figure is for the original six members and includes only trade with countries outside the EEC. From Keizai Kikakucho [1982], p. 390.

bidding to U.S. firms. During the third period, as in the second period, the principal import items and the items on which import restrictions remained again became issues, and with the EEC, color televisions, video tape recorders, and other goods became problems. In almost all cases other than those involving agricultural products, the Japanese government responded, for the particular goods over which there was trade friction, by negotiating on a bilateral basis import allocations (in the case of textiles), a trigger price mechanism (in the case of steel), voluntary export restraints (for automobiles and briefly for steel), or measures to increase Japanese imports (overseas procurements by NTT).

The response of the Japanese government to trade friction, whether it was through exchange rate adjustments, voluntary export restraints, or market openings, always took place at a snail's pace and was never undertaken voluntarily, but when a longer-term perspective is taken, there is still much to be said for these policies. For example, (1) Japan has made great efforts to reduce or eliminate tariff and nontariff trade barriers, while (2) protective policies incorporating import restrictions have not been used for declining industries domestically.[39] Also, (3) there has been no artificial manipulation of the yen, at least since the adoption of floating exchange rates, (4) Japan has resisted any weakening of the GATT framework (such as a relaxation of the safeguards of GATT Article 19) as protectionism in the West has increased, and (5) Japan has insisted that payments imbalances should be approached on a global and not a bilateral basis.

Many problems, however, remain even while Japan is waving the flag of free trade and maintenance of the GATT framework. First, restrictions on imports and foreign direct investment in agriculture, financial markets, and the communications and information industries need to be eliminated, perhaps in stages. This should be done not only because of international pressure, but also as a necessary domestic reform in these industries. Second, steps need to be taken to encourage direct foreign investment by Japanese firms, especially in industries where there is great potential for employment generation. Third, foreign aid must be increased, including technical assistance to developing countries. Without undertaking policies such as these in a real way, an insistence, only by Japan, in favor of free trade will be ineffective.

IV. Conclusion

Here I would like to undertake an overall evaluation of industrial policy since the oil crisis. Entering into the 1970s, Japanese industrial policy shifted direction sharply. This change had already begun in the mid-1960s with trade liberalization, particularly under the Kennedy Round negotiations, and the direction was made explicit in the *Vision for the 1970s,* published in 1970, and proceeded in stages with the subsequent shifts in the international economic environment, including changes in the international payments mechanism, the oil crises, and trade friction.

This shift is above all apparent when the principal industrial policies, implemented after the oil crisis, are viewed as part of an overall framework. Such policies can be divided between those that were aimed at specific industries ("vertical" policies) and those that affected a range of industries ("horizontal" policies). The former can be subdivided into targeted industry policies that focused on structural change by the protection, fostering, or strengthening of key industries and those that sought adjustment in depressed and declining industries. The latter horizontal policies included environmental, industrial siting, small business, international relations, natural resources and energy, and pro-consumer policies. Unlike during the rapid growth era, after the oil crisis, targeted industry policies were applied to a very limited number of industries and comprised an extremely small part of overall industrial policy. In contrast, industrial adjustment policies and horizontal policies (especially environmental, international relations, and energy and natural resource policies) played the largest role. All of this was in response to changes in the domestic and international environment that affected industrial policy. The most distinctive feature of industrial policy following the oil crisis was thus the decline in the role of targeted industry policies and the increase in the role of a variety of other policies, such as industrial adjustment and horizontal policies.

The second distinctive feature of industrial policy following the oil crisis was a stress on using the market mechanism to the greatest possible extent. This is readily seen in the decline in targeted industry policies, the lessened role of policy measures that protected, fostered, or strengthened industries, and the introduction of regulatory policies based on straightforward rules. The third feature, the emphasis on using a Vision, a shift in policy that reflected the change in government–business relations, also should not be overlooked.

It should be pointed out that the above changes in industrial policy following the oil crisis generally were *not* something actively sought after by policymakers, but rather had a strong reactive element to them in that they were part of an *ad hoc* response to successive domestic and international incidents. These included domestically the antipollution and environmental protection movements, the consumers' movement, and the Fair Trade Commission judgment against the petroleum cartel. Internationally they included the collapse of the Bretton Woods system, the oil crises, and the multiple cases of trade friction.

My overall evaluation of industrial policy following the oil crisis is that it should be judged favorably, above all because targeted industry policies were limited to a very small number of industries and in addition because the focus has recently been on subsidizing research and development. From the perspective of countries that do not utilize such policies, it is clearly viewed as inequitable for a government, through fiscal, tax, financial, and trade measures, to use its power to accelerate the flow of resources into specific industries with the goal of improving their international competitive ability and increasing exports. Furthermore, while undertaken to strengthen international competitive strength, industrial policies that heightened industrial concentration and brought about combinations with related industries, when looked at from a domestic perspective, served to increase oligopolistic behavior and to increase the horizontal and vertical economic power of particular large firms, distorting the efficient allocation of resources. As they had these severe defects, the eclipse following the oil crisis of targeted industry policies must be considered very favorably.

On the other hand, as is discussed in Part II of this book, regulating pollution, policies extending assistance to help declining industries adjust, developing high technology, conserving energy, and developing alternatives to oil as an energy source are all policies that are appropriate, even when looked at from the standpoint of economic theory. Policies undertaken in response to trade friction to open up domestic markets through the lowering or elimination of tariff and nontariff trade barriers also must be evaluated as appropriate. Furthermore, as long as they did not go against the spirit of GATT, there was no ready way to avoid using policies that restricted exports, such as voluntary export restraints—though it is held by some that the steel and automobile voluntary export restraints do go against the general GATT principle of multilateral trade.[40]

Considering all of the above, it can be said that industrial policy following the oil crisis, while valuing the market mechanism, did have some beneficial effect on the growth, stability, and progress of the Japanese economy by intervening in areas of the economy in which the market mechanism could not be relied on fully. I want to make it unmistakably clear, however, that the Japan, Inc. view that industrial policy plays a central role in the development of the Japanese economy is today inappropriate. The Japan, Inc. model had already become difficult to apply even during the rapid growth era, as discussed in Chapter 3 of this book. Following the oil crisis, when targeted industry policies had largely been dropped, it is totally missing the mark to look at the Japanese economy through the lens of the Japan, Inc. model. Even though the role of bureaucrats may be favorably regarded, when analyzed with the focus on the Japanese political and policy systems, as in C. Johnson [1982], this certainly does not therefore mean that the macro and microeconomic impact of industrial policy should be regarded as positive.

The sources of the postwar development of the Japanese economy are to be sought on the one hand in the antitrust policies of the Occupation, which helped to form and maintain a relatively competitive market mechanism through the dissolution of the *zaibatsu,* the breaking up of firms, and the disbanding of cartel organizations.[41] This formed the basis for the vigorous investment activity of private firms and their efforts to increase productivity and improve quality. On the other hand, these activities were supported by the high propensity to save of the populace and by Japanese-style management, which treated labor and management as a unity. This framework can be applied in the case of the oil crisis as well, while following the oil crisis, the concern of Japanese firms with improving productivity and improving quality became yet stronger. Furthermore, there was a declining trend in industrial concentration in the assembly industries, as there was much new entry by firms into these industries because of the rapid growth in domestic and international demand.[42] The competitive market mechanism that stemmed from this decline in industrial concentration served to further spur improvements in productivity and quality. It was this dynamic shift in industrial organization that was the foundation for the macroeconomic development of the Japanese economy, with industrial policy playing only a supporting role. In other words, industrial policy lent only some support from the sideline to the dynamic development of the economy, which had the market mechanism as its foundation. Many American scholars have also supported this interpretation, such as Wheeler et al. [1982], Trezise [1983], Hadley [1983], and Patrick [1983]. The importance of industrial policy to the growth, stability, and progress of the Japanese economy, and the extent to which it served as a barrier to these, is something that is best approached by going through the book as a whole. To briefly give my own opinion, I believe that the postwar growth of the Japanese economy suggests that in a system comprised of private firms, once development has reached a certain stage and firms a certain scale, the central aspect of supply-side economic policies is to promote and uphold a competitive market mechanism in which workable competition can develop.

Notes

1. See Tsuruta [1982], pp. 222–223.
2. At the time, many studies recommended appreciation of the yen, such as Yasuba [1970].
3. For a more detailed analysis, see Komiya and Suda [1983], Part I.

4. See Chapter 12 of Kosai [1981] and Chapter 8 of Tsuruta [1982] for analyses of the inflation of this period.
5. See Wheeler et al. [1982], pp. 31–36 for an analysis and international comparison of Japan after the first oil crisis.
6. See Yoshitomi [1977] and [1981] for a detailed analysis of the development of and course of adjustment to economic problems after the first oil crisis.
7. For more detail, see Komiya and Yasui [1983].
8. In particular, see Yoshitomi [1981], Komiya and Yasui [1983], and Murakami [1984].
9. This argument draws from Bruno and Sachs [1981], Lipton [1981], and Sachs and Lipton [1981].
10. For more detail, see Tsuruta [1982], Chapter 8.
11. In 1979, Japan depended on imports for 85.7% of its primary energy consumption and for 99.8% of its petroleum. See Tsusho Sangyo Gyosei Kenkyukai [1983], Volume II, p. 152.
12. See Lipton [1981], Sachs [1981] and Murakami [1984] for a discussion of this mechanism.
13. See Komiya and Yasui [1983] for a description and analysis of macroeconomic policy following the oil crisis.
14. To be more precise, this is not simply a two-person game between the part of the government that is responsible for policy and the industry that is its target. It is rather an n-person game in which both management and workers take part, and in which at times banks and other financial institutions become involved alongside business and the government. As a result, industrial policy formation takes place through cooperation and consensus among the government and firms—which in general means the leading firms or an industry association—together with labor unions and financial institutions.
15. Tsuruta [1982], p. 278.
16. For more detail see Kosei Torihiki Iinkai [1977], pp. 275–276.
17. Kosei Torihiki Iinkai [1983], p. 278. The final decision and other documents in the petroleum cartel case are an extremely important source of information for those interested in the details of how administrative guidance operated in reality.
18. Yanagida [1981] is an extremely interesting documentary on this change.
19. The term *Vision* is a Japanese word that has a somewhat different meaning from the English word *vision*. In reference to industrial structure, the term refers to changes that might arise in the near future, that is, the direction of change, with the addition that, from the policy standpoint, change in that direction is a desirable occurrence.
20. Tsusansho Sangyo Kozo Shingikai [1971], p. 15.
21. Ibid.
22. As should be clear from the discussion of the term *Vision* above, Vision policies are policies in which the government tries to induce firms to act in a given fashion by providing information to industry, through reports and advisory councils, as to the direction of change of the industrial structure.
23. See Tsusansho [1979], pp. 7–13 and Tsusho Sangyo Gyosei Kenkyukai [1983], Volume I.
24. See Ueno [1978], p. 11.
25. Shinohara [1976], Chapter 2.
26. Tsusansho Sangyo Kozo Shingikai [1971], pp. 31 and 176–186.
27. Tsusho Sangyo Gyosei Kenkyukai [1983], Volume I, Chapter 10.
28. For more detail, see Tsusho Sangyo Gyosei Kenkyukai [1983], Volume II, Part 5, as well as Chapters 7 and 8 of this book.
29. Here "service industries" do not refer to the service industries narrowly defined, but rather refer to the entire tertiary sector. Included in this sector are public utilities

(electricity, gas, and water), transport, communications, finance, and insurance. These industries are affected by direct government regulation, with the government having power to decide prices, entry and exit, output levels, and the like. Such direct regulatory policies of the government are strictly distinguished from industrial policy *per se*. In other words, industrial policy for our purposes does not consist of policies in which the government intervenes directly to set prices or quantities, but refers rather to policies that, through the provision of pecuniary or other incentives, try to improve the allocation of resources in case in which the market mechanism is inadequate to the task. Obeying the spirit of the antitrust laws, actual price and quantity decisions are left to the market mechanism. A number of areas that previously have been the object of direct government regulation have recently moved into the domain of industrial policy, largely in the area of telecommunications and in particular in information processing, where there is a competitive market mechanism without direct regulatory intervention.

30. For more detail see, for example, Tsusansho Service Sangyo Kenkyukai [1979] and Baba [1983].
31. The definition of the term *structurally depressed* is very vague. It is not clear, for example, whether it refers to declining industries or to industries that are depressed due to relatively long-term cyclical movements. This has also been pointed out by Miwa [1979] and Wheeler et al. [1982], p. 161. The term appears in various laws and is used only for that reason.
32. Tsusansho Sangyo Seisaku Kyoku [1978], p. 3.
33. Keizai Kikakucho [1982], pp. 412–414.
34. Kosei Torihiki Iinkai Keizai Chosa Kenkyukai [1982]. Readers who have gone through this chapter must have noticed that industrial policy seems to have conflicted from time to time with antitrust policy, which seeks to promote or maintain competition. In principle, industrial policy takes into account antitrust policy, as mentioned in note 28, but it has in fact on occasion conflicted with the Antitrust Law, as it sought to concentrate resources in an industry or to encourage the flow of resources out of an industry (see Chapter 11 and Part VI of this book for more detail). However, these conflicts, as mentioned above, gradually disappeared with the onset of the 1970s.
35. Keizai Kikakucho [1982], pp. 395–396.
36. For more detail see Komiya [1983].
37. Keizai Kikakucho [1982], p. 390.
38. See Uekusa (ed.) [1983], pp. 3–5.
39. For more detail, see Part V of this book.
40. See Komiya [1983], p. 105.
41. For more detail see Uekusa [1982], Chapter 8, Section 1, and Chapter 2, Section 2.
42. For changes in the output concentration index by industry from 1970 on see Senoo [1983], pp. 106–122.

PART II

Historical Overview II

CHAPTER 5

The Tax System and the Fiscal Investment and Loan Program[1]

SEIRITSU OGURA

Faculty of Liberal Arts
Saitama University
Urawa-shi, Japan

NAOYUKI YOSHINO

Graduate School for Policy Science
Saitama University
Urawa-shi, Japan

I. The Role of the Government

The changes in major policy objectives in the postwar Japanese economy can be best understood within the framework of the following periodization:

1. The decade of economic reconstruction beginning in 1945;
2. The decade of 'catching up' with the advanced economies through heavy and chemical industrialization, beginning in 1955;
3. The decade of social development beginning in 1965;
4. The decade of building up a welfare state beginning in 1975.

Needless to say, the periodization is highly simplistic and intended merely to provide a broad frame of reference for a complex system of policies actually implemented.

Given such policy goals, it is natural that the government would administer its fiscal spending as well as its fiscal investments and loans in a manner most conducive to the achievement of these objectives. In many cases, however, changes in economic structure, reflected in the shifts in policy objectives, are bound to have differential impact on various segments within the economy and it becomes imperative for the government to adopt proper compensatory measures to mitigate the impact of such changes on adversely affected groups.

This duality in the form of promotional and compensatory roles of the government can be clearly visualized in the functioning of public finance in Japan since 1955. During the period of rapid economic growth, the government promoted industrial development by (1) devoting a large proportion of its annual expenditures for consolidation of industrial infrastructure; (2) raising investment incentives for industries such as iron and steel, automobiles, and shipbuilding through adoption of specially designed depreciation schemes; and (3) reducing joint costs by channeling low-interest loans aimed specially at industries such as electric power, sea transport, and railways. Public finance, since around 1965, has also made direct contributions to projects for technological development, especially large-scale industrial technology, basic technology, next generation industrial infrastructure technology, computer technology, and the like. As against this, a system of liberal assistance and heavy protection for agriculture, huge compensations to the coal mining industry, which had lost its competitive power, and protection and subsidization of structurally depressed industries such as textiles and sea transport reveal the compensatory role of public finance.

A balanced evaluation of the government policy in the context of development of heavy and chemical industries in postwar Japan requires a proper grasp of the duality mentioned above. Table I reveals that agriculture, forestry, and fisheries accounted for over 80% of total subsidies provided to private industry out of the national treasury. Of the subsidies provided to nonagricultural industries, roughly one-half went to competitively weak sectors such as smaller business, textiles, and sake breweries. The contribution to the development of high technology, on the other hand, reached a peak of 4% in 1974 and has again declined to slightly over 1% in recent years.

What follows is our attempt to quantify the dual roles of public finance to the extent that officially published data permit. Our analysis is confined principally to manufacturing industries, though industries such as coal mining, electric power, and sea transport are also referred to as need arises. Agriculture, however, is excluded from the scope of this analysis.

II. Consolidation of Industrial Infrastructure

The Japanese economy recovered and surpassed its prewar level around 1953 and continued into the late 1950s with a high rate of growth primarily propelled by private business investment. However, the development of industrial infrastructure—the setting up of a network of roads and railways, the development of ports, and the securing of land and water resources—received less-than-adequate attention during this period, with the result that shortages in such social overheads gradually came to the fore. The

TABLE I
Sectoral Disbursement of Subsidies (billion yen, % of total in parentheses)[a]

Year	Sea Transport	Coal Mining	Small Business Textiles, etc.[b]	High Technology[c]	Agriculture, Forestry, and Fisheries	Total Subsidies
1955	3.5(5.0)	0 (0)	0.5 (0.6)	0.5(0.7)	65.7(93.4)	70.3
1956	3.2(4.9)	0 (0)	0.7 (1.1)	0.5(0.7)	59.4(93.0)	63.8
1957	0.05(0)	0 (0)	1.9 (2.8)	0.4(0.6)	64.2(96.3)	66.7
1958	0.04(0)	0 (0)	3.1 (4.2)	0.6(0.7)	70.3(94.8)	74.1
1959	0.5(0.6)	0 (0)	2.2 (2.6)	0.5(0.6)	81.9(96.0)	85.3
1960	1.7(1.7)	5.8 (6.0)	2.6 (2.6)	0.5(0.5)	86.1(89.0)	96.7
1961	1.5(1.3)	5.8 (5.3)	4.6 (4.2)	0.6(0.5)	95.2(88.2)	107.9
1962	1.6(1.0)	10.8 (7.2)	9.1 (6.1)	0.7(0.4)	126.2(84.8)	148.8
1963	2.1(1.1)	18.0(10.0)	11.8 (6.6)	0.8(0.4)	146.0(81.5)	179.0
1964	10.1(4.7)	18.3 (8.5)	16.6 (7.7)	0.9(0.4)	167.5(78.3)	713.8
1965	13.6(5.5)	20.1 (8.1)	21.8 (8.8)	0.8(0.3)	190.1(76.9)	246.9
1966	14.5(4.5)	24.0 (7.5)	29.8 (9.4)	1.9(0.5)	246.0(77.6)	316.7
1967	15.4(4.1)	37.7(10.1)	36.2 (9.7)	4.2(1.1)	277.0(74.5)	371.6
1968	15.7(3.7)	42.3(10.0)	39.3 (9.3)	5.5(1.3)	318.6(75.3)	422.6
1969	15.2(3.1)	69.9(14.3)	43.6 (8.9)	6.4(1.3)	351.4(72.0)	487.8
1970	15.4(2.3)	78.8(11.8)	51.6 (7.7)	7.7(1.1)	510.7(76.7)	665.2
1971	15.6(1.9)	68.0 (8.3)	59.2 (7.2)	8.2(1.0)	664.5(81.3)	816.6
1972	16.1(1.6)	58.7 (5.9)	90.8 (9.1)	20.0(2.0)	806.0(81.2)	992.1
1973	16.1(1.4)	63.9 (5.5)	85.4 (7.4)	31.9(2.7)	952.5(82.7)	1,151.0
1974	15.6(1.2)	55.2 (4.5)	103.7 (8.5)	44.5(3.6)	996.6(81.9)	1,216.8
1975	15.0(1.1)	61.1 (4.5)	129.4 (9.5)	43.3(3.2)	1,102.3(81.5)	1,352.2
1976	13.6(0.8)	58.7 (3.7)	166.4(10.7)	36.3(2.3)	1,268.8(82.1)	1,545.0
1977	11.5(0.6)	57.6 (3.2)	173.6 (9.7)	31.3(1.7)	1,514.6(84.6)	1,789.7
1978	9.5(0.4)	59.5 (2.5)	206.8 (8.9)	31.4(1.3)	1,992.3(86.5)	2,300.7
1979	5.5(0.2)	52.2 (1.9)	232.6 (8.7)	34.1(1.2)	2,345.6(87.8)	2,671.4
1980	9.5(0.3)	48.8 (1.7)	243.7 (8.6)	34.6(1.2)	2,473.8(87.9)	2,811.8
1981	10.5(0.3)	44.4 (1.5)	249.9 (8.6)	36.3(1.2)	2,552.7(88.1)	2,895.1
1982	11.0(0.3)	48.1 (1.5)	251.0 (8.2)	37.2(1.2)	2,695.1(88.5)	3,043.7

Source: Okurasho, Kuni no Yosan (National Budget).
[a]General A/c budget. For coal mining, special A/c allocations are also included.
[b]The total of subsidies to small businesses, textiles, and sake breweries.
[c]The total of subsidies to large scale industrial technology, basic technology, next generation industrial infrastructure technology, computer technology, transport machinery, medical equipment, etc.

government set about the task of improving industrial infrastructure in earnest from 1957 onward, formulating a number of medium-term improvement programs. In order to meet this need, a major proportion of the national budget for road development was brought under special accounts and its size expanded from ¥45.9 billion in 1957 to ¥164 billion two years later, a four-fold increase. The national railways system also saw its investments double during the same period. Finally, port development allocations were also brought into the fold of special accounts in 1959, and improvement of ports with a long-term perspective got under way (see Table II).

The Income Doubling Plan (December 1960), visualizing the shortages in social overhead capital as a bottleneck for rapid growth, also aimed at

TABLE II
Investments in Social Overheads and Industrial Infrastructure (billion yen)

Year	Gross Investment in Social Overheads	Share of Industrial Infrastructure	Roads[a]	Ports	Waste Treatment Facilities	Water for Industrial Use	Railways
					of Which		
1955	148.7	79.9	23.0	4.4	0	0	52.5
1956	158.1	89.8	26.4	4.4	0	0.2	58.7
1957	230.6	151.2	45.9	6.8	0.3	0.3	98.7
1958	292.3	229.3	133.6	8.2	0.3	0.5	87.3
1959	398.6	293.7	164.0	20.8	0.4	0.9	107.6
1960	501.0	339.3	197.6	23.5	0.6	1.3	116.4
1961	741.3	554.0	311.8	46.5	0.7	2.5	192.5
1962	850.9	686.4	420.6	57.4	1.1	3.8	203.5
1963	1122.8	856.7	488.0	69.7	2.2	5.4	291.4
1964	1248.4	931.3	580.3	80.4	4.3	7.0	259.3
1965	1457.6	1136.0	704.7	87.2	4.6	8.3	331.2
1966	1645.0	1348.5	876.2	111.0	3.2	8.2	350.0
1967	1858.6	1512.1	1001.1	124.0	2.7	6.2	378.0
1968	1965.5	1608.5	1081.0	121.6	3.0	6.6	396.3
1969	2217.4	1278.8	1254.1	154.2	3.3	7.4	399.8
1970	2565.1	1875.5	1275.3	185.1	3.6	10.1	401.5
1971	3010.4	2354.7	1688.1	220.0	4.4	13.4	428.8
1972	3714.7	2908.9	2055.1	267.3	8.4	18.8	559.3
1973	4747.5	3593.7	2439.5	326.8	16.3	23.3	787.8
1974	4831.3	3624.5	2464.6	328.0	18.6	23.1	790.1
1975	4758.7	3627.6	2507.6	316.2	23.3	21.4	759.0
1976	5522.9	3980.7	2730.2	361.2	28.0	24.3	837.1
1977	6572.3	4904.7	3399.7	412.8	34.6	26.3	1031.2
1978	8320.0	5730.0	4048.7	487.5	48.3	25.0	1120.4
1979	9967.0	6370.7	4386.8	583.4	63.5	23.9	1313.1
1980	9896.1	6683.8	4756.2	579.9	66.2	22.6	1258.9
1981	9850.5	6600.8	4789.4	585.9	67.1	21.0	1137.5
1982	9883.2	6770.4	4982.5	591.1	66.5	19.6	1110.7

Source: Okurasho, *Kuni no Yosan,* (National Budget).

[a]Based on Ministerial Secretariat, Ministry of Home Affairs', *Gyosei Toshi Jisseki* (Performance of Administrative Investments), provided to us by professor Susumu Yamaguchi of Saitama University. Including streets before 1969.

rapid development with the result that investments in industrial infrastructure (roads, ports, railways, waste treatment facilities, water for industrial use) rose from 1% of GNP in 1956 to 3.5% in 1964. Even though a major proportion of this investment, amounting to ¥580.3 billion in 1964, went for the development of roads, the national railways system also invested to the tune of ¥260 billion in ambitious schemes of its own like the building up of the Tokaido Bullet-Train Line. A significant proportion of this huge investment in national railways (¥150 billion in 1964 alone) came out of the funds for the Fiscal Loan and Investment Program.

By the late sixties, the problem of shortage in social overhead capital had been compounded by the so-called "strains" of rapid economic growth in the form of pollution, urban congestion and rural depopulation, and so on, forcing a diversification in policy goals. Despite the shift in transport demand from railways to roads during this period, which resulted from popularization of automobiles and consolidation of a national network of roads, large investments continued to be made in railways. Between 1965 and 1975, on average, ¥500 billion per year was invested in railways. Since 1975, this figure has grown to ¥1 trillion per year. From 1965 to 1975, investment in roads also grew parallel with the growth in GNP at a level of about 2.5% of GNP, although the growth slowed in the subsequent period to 1.8% of GNP. Moreover, two-thirds of the budget for roads was being directed toward sparsely populated areas with low transport demand and the inefficient overinvestment in national railways is revealed in the system's ¥2 trillion-a-year deficit.

III. The Tax System

A. Corporate Taxes

Changes in the corporate income tax rate, covering both national and local levies, are depicted in Figure 5.1. Following the recommendations of the Shoup Mission, the national tax rate on corporate income was set at 35% in 1950 but was raised to 42% in the following year, as corporate income soared with the beginning of the Korean War. In exchange for this tax hike, firms were allowed to treat reserves for covering price changes and reserves for employees' retirement allowances as business expenses and the coverage of special depreciation (to be discussed later) was also broadened. In 1954, with the objective of building up internal revenue sources for local governments, a corporate income tax of 12% and an inhabitant tax surcharge equivalent to 12.5% of the corporate income tax were levied, thus raising the marginal tax rate close to 60%.

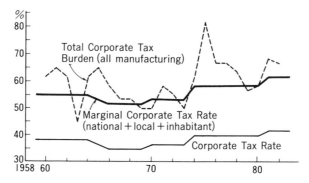

Fig. 5.1. Taxes levied on corporations.

In view of declining corporate earnings with the passing of the Korean war boom, as well as in order to increase corporate savings, the corporate tax was reduced by 2% in 1955. Lower tax rates for smaller businesses were also adopted at the same time. The natural rise in fiscal resources concomitant to economic growth led to a further fall in the corporate tax rate by 2%, bringing it down to 38%. A system of lower tax rates on paid-out dividends was adopted in 1961. With a recession in 1965, the tax rate was reduced by 1%, with a further reduction of 2% in 1966 bringing it back to the initial level of 35%.

The economy turned around in 1966 and stayed buoyant for the next four years. With the fiscal spending growing without any respite during this period there was no room for a reduction in revenues to provide personal income tax cuts. To implement the personal income tax cuts, finally, the corporate tax rate was raised by 1.75% in 1970, reversing the downward trend observed since 1955. Another large-scale reduction in personal income taxes in 1974 was matched by a sharp increase in the corporate tax rate, bringing it up to 40%. Finally, the corporate tax rose by another 2% in 1981 to attain its present level of 42%. (A temporary surcharge of 1.3% was placed for three years during 1984–1986 period.)

In addition to the above-mentioned taxes on corporate income, firms have to bear the burden of taxes on their fixed assets, stamp duties, and other charges. Figure 5.1 presents, for all manufacturing corporations, the tax burden, including all taxes and public charges as percent of current income.[2]

The tax burden reveals a cyclical pattern with a decline or a rise depending on whether business was good or bad. This pattern arises because current profits shoot up under favorable business conditions, but tax obligations do not keep pace due to, first, the existence of certain taxes, like those on fixed assets, totally unrelated to changes in business conditions and, second, lower tax rates on paid-out dividends, as well as firms' manipulation of business accounts for tax saving, such as the carrying over of losses and building up of tax-exempt reserves. Under unfavorable business conditions, not only do these factors work in the reverse direction but also firms that incur losses reduce the size of aggregate profit but not the tax liability, causing a rise in the tax burden. The corporate tax burden peaked in 1961, 1965, 1971, 1975, and 1981, all recession years.

Besides the above mentioned cyclical pattern, one can also discern a U-shaped trend in the tax burden closely conforming to the pattern depicted by the marginal tax rate (Fig. 5.1). The trend was downward from 1960 to 1975 in all manufacturing as well as in major industries, but shifted upward after the first oil shock by about 10 percentage points to 60%. This upward shift was due to (1) the above-mentioned rise in the marginal tax rate, (2) heavier taxes achieved through a large-scale elimination of tax-exempt reserves, and (3) an inflation-induced rise in fixed-asset taxes while business assets were earning less.

B. The Depreciation System

In computing corporate income, corporations are allowed to deduct the acquisition cost of machinery and equipment from their annual incomes over a number of years depending on the stipulated life of the asset. This system, designed to spread the acquisition cost over a certain period of time, does not take into account interest cost and inflation over the relevant period. The longer the stipulated life of an asset, the larger is the spread of corporate tax savings arising out of depreciation schemes and hence the lower the present value of such savings. The corporate tax burden with respect to investment goods can, thus, be reduced through the shortening of stipulated asset lives, even with no change in tax rates.

The first major postwar overhaul of the depreciation system was carried out in 1951[3] and this system remained in operation until 1961 when the next revision was introduced. In 1951, prior to this overhaul, a system of accelerated depreciation for important machinery was adopted, allowing an additional 50% write-off over and above the normal depreciation for three years in the case of certain types of machinery and equipment specially designated by the tax authorities. This measure was intended to stimulate replacement of worn-out machinery and equipment due to overuse during and after the war in order to help firms to improve international competitiveness.

In 1952, this system of accelerated depreciation was expanded to cover machinery acquired for "rationalization" (50% of the purchase price in the first year) and experimental equipment (these were especially quick write-offs, with 50% in the first year and 20% each in the second and third years). With the passage of time, the system became increasingly more specific and more complicated, finally forcing the government's Tax System Council to lament in 1960, thus:

> the special depreciation scheme allowing 50% writeoff in the first year applies to 500 types of machinery and the 3-year 50% accelerated depreciation scheme to 1300 types of machinery. These are specified to such minute details that it becomes extremely difficult to determine the applicability of special depreciation provisions unless one is a specialist. [Nov. 1960, quoted in Komiya (1975)]

The three-year 50% accelerated depreciation system (for important machinery, and so on) was abandoned in 1961. The items covered under the scheme were incorporated into the general depreciation system, which was revised so as to shorten the stipulated asset lives of machinery and equipment by 20% on average. The first-year depreciation allowed on "rationalization machinery" was reduced to one-third of the acquisition cost. A further 15% reduction in the stipulated asset lives was adopted in 1964 and the first-year depreciation on "rationalization machinery" was cut down to one-fourth of the purchase price. Buildings were left out of these two reforms, but their average useful life was reduced by 15% in 1966 with a corresponding restructuring of the provisions of special depreciation schemes.

The special depreciation schemes that prospered in the 1956–1960 period were thus gradually absorbed into the normal depreciation system through a shortening of stipulated asset lives and finally lost their importance. In a sort of reversal of this trend, the coverage of rationalization machinery was once again expanded in 1970 with the view to improving the strength of firms, and in 1971, special depreciation schemes were extended or newly instituted for vessels and large-sized aircraft. This, however, did not last long, and in 1973, it was decided that the former was to be phased out gradually in three years and the latter was to be narrowed in scope.

C. Export-Based Special Depreciation

This system, which was adopted in 1961, permitted a firm with rising exports to claim a special depreciation equal to the product of the increase in its export/sales ratio and the amount of normal depreciation. The multiplier was reduced in 1964 to 80% of the increase in the export/sales ratio but was reverted in 1966 to the full amount. In order to stem the worsening foreign exchange position through expansion of exports, a scheme of 30% and 60% special increases in depreciation, depending on the type of product, was introduced in 1968. This special-increase system was withdrawn in 1971 in face of severe international criticism resulting from huge surplus in Japan's trade balance and the multiplier was reduced to 80% of the increase in the export/sales ratio. The system was finally abandoned in 1972, but a large part of it was allegedly absorbed into the special depreciation schemes for rationalization machinery discussed earlier.

D. Special Depreciation Schemes and Investment Costs

The available data do not lend themselves to an easy interpretation of changes in the depreciation system discussed above.[4] First, as the firms normally do not avail themselves fully of normal depreciation allowances during the periods of subnormal profits, the realized depreciation amounts in effect become dependent on profit levels. Second, in order to utilize special depreciation for designated machinery, investment in such machinery has to be made, thereby making depreciation amounts a function of gross investment. Finally, in the case of export-based special depreciation schemes, the export/sales ratios would naturally affect the amount of depreciation.

1. Special Depreciation Schemes Prior to 1961

Data regarding special depreciation schemes for designated machinery are very scanty prior to 1961. The only continuous time-series data by industry during this period are from the MITI's *Wagakuni Kigyo no Keiei Bunseki* (Financial Statements of the Japanese Enterprises) available for 131 large corporations from 1955 onward. Despite severe limitations, these data can tell us which industries were benefited by special depreciation schemes before 1961.

Figure 5.2 presents the share of special depreciation allowances in the total depreciation amount for major industries. Prior to 1961, the industries can be clearly divided into three groups: (1) industries receiving exceptionally large benefits (iron and steel and automobiles); (2) industries receiving no more than average benefits (shipbuilding, general machinery, and electrical machinery); (3) industries receiving less than average benefits (chemicals, as well as textiles and petroleum refining, which are not shown in Fig. 5.2). For the iron and steel industry, this period happened to coincide with its second rationalization program under which integrated steel mills like Yahata in Tobata, Nippon Kokan in Mizushima, Sumitomo Metal in Fukuyama, and Kobe Steel in Nadahama were established in the new coastal belt. As for the automobile industry, this period coincided with the period of accelerating investment as the full-scale production of passenger cars took root with the release of indigenous models like Datsun and Crown. Another reason for high special depreciation in these industries was their high rates of profits.

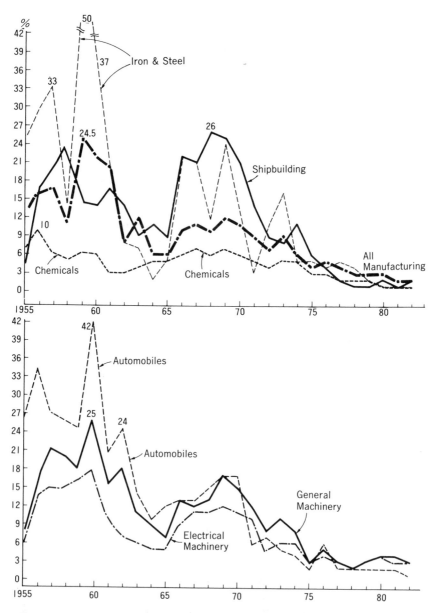

Fig. 5.2. Proportion of special depreciation to total by industry. The figures for All Manufacturing, Iron and Steel, Shipbuilding, and Chemicals are from *Shuyo Kigyo Keiei Bunseki* (Financial Statements of Principal Enterprises) for the period before 1959 and from *Hojin Kigyo Tokei* (Corporate Enterprise Statistics) thereafter. For Automobiles, General Machinery, and Electrical Machinery Industries, *Shuyu Kigyo Keiei Bunseki* figures are used prior to 1961 and *Hojin Kigyo Tokei* thereafter.

2. Trends Since 1962

From 1962 onward, the ratio of special depreciation allowances to total depreciation is calculated by industry from the Ministry of Finance's *Hojin Kigyo Tokei* (Corporate Enterprise Statistics). Figure 5.2 presents results for the industries discussed above. These data reveal the following:

First, as compared to the 1962–1973 average of 8% for all manufacturing, the ratio was above average in shipbuilding (15%), automobiles (13%), iron and steel (12%), general machinery (12%), and textiles (10%), equal to the average in electrical machinery (8%), and was less than the average in chemicals (5%).

Second, within the period of high growth delineated above, one can discern intervals when the ratio of special depreciation allowances was consistently high. In the iron and steel industry, for example, this ratio hovered around 20% during the 1966–1969 period when plants with annual production capacity of 10 million tons like Nippon Kokan's Fukuyama and Nippon Steel's Kimitsu were completed one after another. Construction of extra-large sized docks during the same period raised the ratio for the shipbuilding industry to above 20%. In the sea transport industry, in the wake of a heavy inflow of subsidies following the shipping reorganization policy beginning in 1963, this ratio climbed to the 20% level.

Third, the degree to which various industries benefited from the export-based special depreciation scheme can be estimated indirectly to a certain extent by analyzing the relationship between the export/sales ratio and the ratio of special depreciation to total depreciation for the 1963–1970 period and by the changes in the latter after 1971 when the special increases scheme was abandoned. Based on these criteria, the automobile industry seems to have reaped large benefits from this scheme (1968–1970) and the shipbuilding industry also seems to have used it to its advantage as revealed by a sharp fall in the proportion of special depreciation allowances during 1971–1972. The iron and steel industry also seems to have taken advantage of the system in the 1966–1969 period when the proportion of special depreciation allowances was high.

How far did the special depreciation schemes raise corporate profits? Taking 1970 as a reference point, we find that the total amount of special depreciation allowances availed of during the year was ¥300 billion. With the marginal tax rate at 52%, it helped to save ¥156 billion in taxes. The use of these special depreciation schemes, however, implies an automatic decrease in future depreciation allowances by ¥300 billion, and hence a rise in the future tax burden of the corporations by ¥156 billion. The term *future* in this context is equivalent to the stipulated asset life. Given the average useful life of equipment in manufacturing at 6.7 years in 1970, the interest cost on a loan of ¥156 billion with the maturity period of 6.7

years is the profits accruing on special depreciation. The average effective rate of interest for manufacturing industries (cf. footnote 9) being 10.3% in 1970, total interest cost on the average balance of ¥78 billion amounts to ¥53.8 billion. As current profits in all manufacturing in this year were ¥3.6 trillion, special depreciation schemes accounted for about 1.5% of total profits. During the period of high growth, these gains show a high of ¥66 billion and a low of ¥12.8 billion.

A similar calculation by industry puts the amount of benefits at a maximum of ¥20 billion and a minimum of ¥0.5 billion for the iron and steel industry, less than ¥3 billion a year for the automobile industry and between ¥1 to ¥3 billion for the shipbuilding industry. Figure 5.3 depicts the proportion of gains from special depreciation schemes to investment expenditure. The average for all manufacturing is seen to hover around the 1% level, while that for iron and steel is seen to attain the 2% level in almost every other year. The average for the automobile industry during the period of high growth is slightly less than 1.5%, while the shipbuilding industry shows an exceptionally high proportion during the 1966–1970 period.

IV. The Fiscal Investment and Loan Program

The national government runs the Fiscal Investment and Loan Program (FILP), making use mainly of the surplus funds of postal savings and social security funds (welfare annuities and national annuities),[5] In addition to financing the investment activities of national public organizations like the National Railways (JNR) and the Nippon Telegraph and Telephone Corporation (NTT) or local public entities, these surplus funds, centralized in the Trust Fund Bureau of the Ministry of Finance, are used to provide funds for private-sector investments through public financial institutions like the Housing Loan Corporation, Japan Development Bank, Export-Import Bank, and the Small Business Finance Corporation. The issuing of government guaranteed debt, which some of the institutions are permitted to do in order to supplement their finances,[6] is also included within the FILP.

Figure 5.4 presents time-series data on the ratio of the total FILP funds supplied by postal savings, social security funds, and government guaranteed debt to the increase in financial assets held by households as recorded in the flow of funds tables to indicate the extent to which the FILP absorbed funds in the domestic capital market. The figure reveals a rising share of the FILP in the capital market funds from 20% in 1955–1964 to 30% in 1965–1974 and to 40% since 1975. Within this, the share of postal

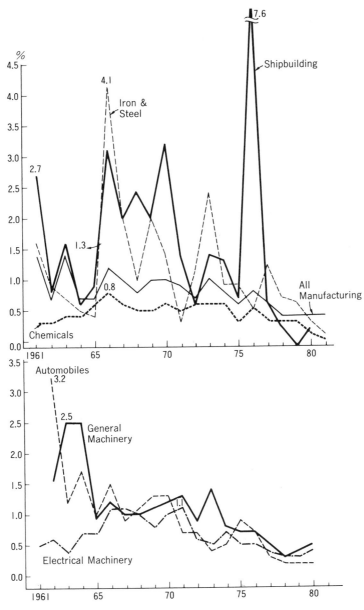

Fig. 5.3. Ratio of benefits from special depreciation schemes to investment expenditures. From the sources listed in Figure 5.2.

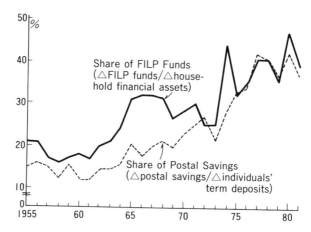

Fig. 5.4. Fund absorption by FILP and share of postal savings. From Nihon Ginko, *Keizai Tokei Nenpo* [Economic Statistics Annual], Flow of Funds tables.

savings rose steadily from 15% in 1955–1964 to 40% in 1975–1980. In contrast, surplus funds from the social security funds rose rapidly until the 1960s but leveled off thereafter, even in absolute terms, due to the scaling up of the annuities and a rise in the number of recipients. At the end of 1982, of the ¥127 trillion in the hands of the Trust Fund Bureau, 60% was accounted for by postal savings and 30% by social security funds.

Table III allows us to follow the changing importance of the user sectors in the FILP by showing us the proportions of the total funds going to these sectors on five yearly basis. The share of the basic industries, such as electric power, sea transport, coal mining, and iron and steel, that was targeted for funding through the Japan Development Bank was well below 25% even in 1953–1955, immediately after the introduction of the FILP, and continued to fall steadily, finally reaching 2.9% in 1976–1981. In contrast, the financing of trade and economic cooperation, through the Export-Import Bank, targeted at the export of vessels and plants, rose till 1970, with a slight fall thereafter.

The overall share of funds going to agriculture and the small-scale sector (modernization of the low productivity sector in Table III) is seen to be stable at around 20% throughout the period, though the share of the small-scale sector, within this category, has increased gradually. The funding related to railways, roads, and communications (building up of the industrial infrastructure) maintained a share of over 20% during the 1965–1975 period, but has fallen off since 1976. Finally, the share of funds going to housing, education, and welfare under the "improvement of living stan-

TABLE III
Composition of Fiscal Investment and Loans Program by Use (%)

	1953–55	1956–60	1961–65	1966–70	1971–75	1976–81
Strengthening of key industries	23.6	16.6	9.9	6.3	3.7	2.9
Trade and economic cooperation	2.8	4.3	7.9	10.4	8.8	6.4
Area development	5.7	9.0	7.5	4.6	3.7	2.6
Equipping the industrial infrastructure	26.4	21.6	26.1	24.3	23.2	18.1
Modernization of low-productivity sectors (small and medium industries)	18.6	20.9 (13.7)	19.0 (12.9)	20.1 (15.6)	19.6 (15.2)	22.6 (17.7)
Improvement of living standards	22.9	27.6	29.6	34.3	41.0	47.4
Total amount of FILP loans (¥100 million)	9,218	23,360	61,958	137,716	340,736	925,471

Source: Okurasho, Zaisei Kinyu Tokei Geppo (Monthly Fiscal and Financial Statistics).

dards'' category revealed a continuous rise, attaining the level of almost 50% since 1976.

It is clear from the above discussion that the weight of the industrial policy related to financing was not exceptionally high in the Fiscal Investment and Loan Program.[7]

A. Role of the Development and Export-Import Banks

For a time after the Second World War, the deployment of postal savings, under the direction of the GHQ, was restricted to national level organizations like the JNR and the NTT and the local public entities. As the inflationary pressures abated around 1950, however, the postal savings began a steep climb. Meanwhile, the beginning of the Korean hostilities in June 1950 boosted the demand for investment funds and the business community made a strong plea that long-term funds for fixed investment be supplied from the postal savings. It was against this background that the Export Bank of Japan was established as a governmental financial institution at the end of 1950 to supply long-term funds for the export of equipment, followed by the establishment of the Japan Development Bank in 1951 for the purposes of supplying long-term investment funds to industry.

1. The Japan Development Bank

For some time after its inception, the Japan Development Bank (JDB) concentrated its attention on the electric power and sea transport industries, followed by coal mining, iron and steel, fertilizers, and machinery in that order. Such emphasis underscored the policy objectives of the time, namely, closing the supply gap in the electric power industry, improving the balance-of-payments positions, and increasing self-sufficiency in food and so on. The enforcement of the financial tightening measures in 1954–1955, however, choked the supply of new funds to the JDB forcing it to specialize in only three industries—electric power, sea transport, and coal mining—until 1960.

The financing of the electric power industry was necessary on the following three counts: (1) The equipment investment in the electric power industry formed approximately 20% of the total equipment investment in all industries at that time; (2) as the electric power charges were held down at low levels throughout, the industry had to depend heavily on external funds; and, (3) low-interest loans with maturities as long as 20 years, which were needed by this industry as public utilities, made this industry relatively unattractive to private financial institutions.

The supply of long-term, low-interest funds to the sea transport industry through the JDB was considered necessary by the government in order to increase the shipping tonnage held, through a planned building of ships, without being affected by short-term fluctuations in firms' earnings. Private financial institutions were wary of financing this industry because of the extreme instability in its earnings record and the long loan maturity in excess of 15 years.

The JDB loans to the coal mining industry reflected the high proportion of such loans in the Reconstruction Finance Corporation (RFC) loans that were inherited by the JDB and the financing of the equipment investment being actively undertaken for cost saving by this industry under the government's rationalization program.

The iron and steel industry, in contrast, rapidly reduced its dependency on the JDB loans during this period. The share of the JDB in the funds raised to implement the first phase of the first rationalization plan for this industry (1951–1953) was as high as 15%. With the enforcement of the financial stringency measures mentioned above, the flow of the JDB funds to this industry dried up almost completely and the Industrial Bank of Japan and the Long-Term Credit Bank of Japan came to occupy the place of central importance in the financing of this industry. After the second rationalization plan (1956–1960), the iron and steel industry depended exclusively on the open market funds for its requirement of funds in the domestic markets.

The decade beginning in 1965 was characterized by rapid growth in the Japanese economy. The electric power suppliers, who had been cornering almost 40% of the JDB loans until then, began depending on the open markets for their fund requirements because of their increased earnings and ability to raise funds on the bond markets. The sea transport industry thereby replaced the electric power industry as the largest recipient of JDB loans. It was only because of the shipping reorganization policy and heavy subsidization that the sea transport industry was able to ride out the shipping depression during the first half of this period. The steep rise in Japanese trade during the latter half of the decade helped the industry engage in the mass production of ships and it absorbed, in the process, over 30% of the JDB loans.

It was during this period that the coal mining industry lost its competitive edge decisively to the petroleum industry. With fund raising in the open markets becoming increasingly difficult, the coal mining industry turned to the JDB, which came to supply 50% of the finances needed by this industry. As the profit position of the industry kept on deteriorating, however, the government took over ¥200 billion of the industry's debt. The financing of equipment investment in this industry also shifted from the JDB to interest-free loans from the Coal Mining Industry Reorganization Corporation.

Anticipating the capital market liberalization, the JDB also began directing its efforts toward strengthening the international competitiveness of Japanese industry by encouraging the petrochemical and the automobile industries to enlarge their scales of production and by promoting improvement of technological standards in industries like auto parts, machine tools, and electronics. The financing of technological development and marketing of indigenous electronic computers rose rapidly over 1966–1970. Though the total finances going into such activities accounted for 20% of the total financing by the JDB, the share of the individual industries, barring the financing of computer marketing (JDB's share 20%), did not exceed a few percentage points, as this type of financing was targeted at a very broad cross section of industries.

Income differentials widened between the industrially developed regions and the rest of the country in the process of rapid growth, and overpopulation of the developed and depopulation of the underdeveloped areas surfaced as a major social problem. The JDB began diverting over 20% of its funds for dispersion of industry to the lagging regions and the improvement of transport facilities in large cities.

The Nixon shock of 1971 and the oil shock of 1973 brought Japan's rapid growth era to an end, but the financing by the JDB expanded into areas as diverse as pollution control investments such as the desulphurization of petroleum, the control of gaseous emissions, and the treatment of polluted water. The trend reversed itself after peaking in 1975, as the financing of the electric power industry resurged. At present, 40% of the total loans by the JDB are concentrated in energy-related fields (of which electric power accounts for 70%). This has been the result of a studied fostering of thermal and hydroelectric power stations for the diversification of energy sources, as well as the increased dependence of the electric power suppliers on JDB funds for the huge construction costs of atomic power stations (Table IV).

2. The Export-Import Bank of Japan

The Export-Import Bank of Japan (EIBJ) was first established toward the end of 1950 as the Export Bank of Japan. The bank had the express purpose of supplying long-term funds for financing plant exports that could not be fully accommodated within the system of preferential treatment being given to short-term export financing by the Bank of Japan (BOJ). At the time, however, the products of light industries, such as textiles, formed the core of Japanese exports and, in the case of machinery products, only ships, rolling stock, and textile machinery showed some degree of competitiveness in the export markets. Consequently, in the scale of lending operations, the Export Bank was only about one-half as large as the Development Bank.

The shipbuilding industry strengthened its competitive power gradually by making full use of the government's export promotion policy. The industry's export of ships was aided further by the "Suez Boom" after 1955. The Export Bank's financing of the shipbuilding industry, especially in view of the effects that it could have on the demand for steel and other related industries, rose rapidly, and despite the highly fluctuating shipping markets, about 50% of the loans issued by the EIBJ went to finance this industry during the decade beginning in 1955.

The financing of exports of various types of machinery also rose gradually from 1960 onward. A large proportion of these loans could be categorized as economic cooperation loans to less-developed countries who were suffering from severe foreign exchange problems in the process of their economic development. These loans were intended to promote the export of Japanese heavy electrical equipment, which lacked international competitiveness. This reflected the importance attached to the policy of promoting machinery exports in the Long-Term Economic Plan of 1957. Because most of the customers of Japanese exports were underdeveloped countries, the existence of a deferred payment clause attached to the low-interest loans from the EIBJ was instrumental in clinching the agreements, even for other products.

TABLE IV

Composition of Loans by the Japan Development Bank (%)

	1951–55	1956–60	1961–65	1966–70	1971–75	1976–80	1981–82
Energy	45.3	58.7	25.8	15.0	7.7	24.4	41.1
Electric power	(38.8)	(39.0)	(16.6)	(7.4)	(—)	(17.7)	(28.6)
Coal	(6.5)	(9.7)	(8.5)	(3.4)	(—)	(—)	(—)
Transport							
Sea transport	25.3	27.3	30.3	35.5	17.7	7.7	11.7
Strengthening of international competitiveness	—	12.1	14.6	8.4	—	—	—
Improvement of the balance of payments position	—	—	4.4	2.5	—	—	—
Area development	—	2.6	21.5	27.5	30.9	30.5	25.8
Anti-pollution measures	—	—	—	0.6	19.1	21.3	8.5
Promotion of technology	—	—	—	8.3	10.6	11.1	9.2
Total JDB loans (¥ 100 million)	2,744	3,027	6,726	13,632	28,275	45,355	22,390

Source: Nihon Kaihatsu Ginko (The Japan Development Bank). [1976], [1982, 1983, 1984].

The Japanese shipbuilding industry, aided by its greater competitive power arising out of the technological superiority and pricing policy, captured 50% of the world market by 1965 and was able to reap rich rewards during the shipping boom beginning 1965. It was against this background that the EIBJ expanded its loans to the shipbuilding industry during 1966–1970.

Japanese exports of plant-related machinery (excluding unitary machines like automobiles and ships) were one-fourth of that of the United States or West Germany, and the government adopted a policy to promote plant exports in 1969. In step with this, the EIBJ also increased its financing of the export of plants. The exports of ships declined steeply following the oil shock of 1973, whereas the export of complete plants, especially to the Middle-East countries, grew rapidly. In terms of loans from the EIBJ, plant exports displaced the shipbuilding industry in 1974 and the gap has been widening ever since.

The expansion in the financing of plant exports resulted in a shifting pattern of disbursement of EIBJ funds during 1971–1975, with the weight of trading companies in total loans to exporters shooting up and the share of intergovernment loans to the countries importing from Japan, like those in the communist camp and the developing countries, rising to over 20% of the total funding by the EIBJ. The increased surplus in the Japanese balance of payments during this period became the target of vehement international criticism resulting in an increase in the financing of imports and overseas investment, each of which has been accounting for nearly 20% of the total funding by the EIBJ in recent years (Table V).

B. The Role of the Fiscal Investment and Loan Program

This section presents a quantitative analysis of the role of government financial intermediaries in lowering the cost of funds within the framework of postwar Japanese industrial policy. Furthermore, a comparison by industry of the role played by the funds supplied by public financial institutions closely related to the industrial policy, such as the JDB, the EIBJ, and the Hokkaido and Tohoku Development Corporation, as well as institutions such as the Small Business Finance Corporation and the People's Finance Corporation, which cater mainly to the needs of small business enterprises, and the role played by funds supplied by private financial intermediaries (ordinary banks, mutual banks, trust banks, and the Central Cooperative Bank for Commerce and Industry) is also undertaken. To achieve this purpose, the effective rate of interest on market borrowings was estimated by industry and was then used to quantify the reduction in the interest burden resulting from the supply of low-interest loans from

TABLE V
Amount of Loans Sanctioned by Export–Import Bank of Japan (100 million yen, %)

	1950–55	1956–60	1961–65	1966–70	1971–75	1976–80
Exports (total)	1,334 (99)	2,821 (85)	6,638 (77)	13,825 (76)	17,196 (44)	22,514 (44)
Ships	886 (66)	1,844 (56)	4,196 (48)	8,225 (45)	7,273 (19)	5,355 (11)
Plants	448 (33)	977 (30)	2,442 (28)	5,600 (31)	9,924 (25)	17,159 (34)
Imports	1 (0)	28 (1)	65 (1)	600 (3)	6,852 (18)	11,045 (22)
Investments	12 (1)	262 (8)	449 (5)	1,437 (8)	6,392 (16)	6,502 (13)
Direct loans	0 (0)	196 (6)	1,514 (17)	2,238 (12)	8,651 (22)	10,925 (21)
Total	1,347(100)	3,306(100)	8,665(100)	18,099(100)	39,090(100)	50,987(100)

Source: Nihon Kikai Yushutsu Kumiai [1982], p 64.

the public financial institutions to these industries. Finally, the weight of such reductions in the total investment expenditure (including land)[8] was calculated to bring out the interest lowering effect of public loans.

Figure 5.5 summarizes the yearly reduction in the interest burden (estimated) as a proportion of investment expenditure (including land) by industry. The figures reveal that the proportion was highest for the sea transport industry, at 20% on the average for the period 1962–1975, followed by transport equipment (mainly shipbuilding during 1960–1966), electric power (including gas and water, but the share of these was very small), and mining. The proportion, in contrast, was below the 5% level in wholesale and retail trade and iron and steel.

The following discussion traces, historically, the changes in policy finance and its interest lowering effect in the context of industries such sea transport, electric power, shipbuilding, automobiles, machinery, iron and steel, coal mining, and petroleum refining, which have been important from the point of view of the postwar Japanese industrial policy.[9]

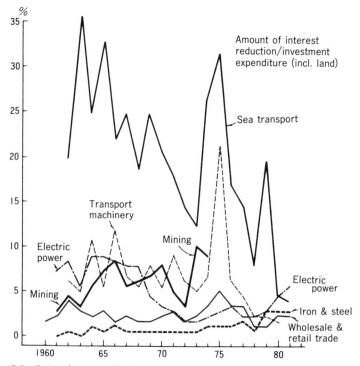

Fig. 5.5   Ratio of estimated reduction in interest burden to investment expenditure.

1. The Sea Transport Industry

The sea transport industry had lost almost the whole of its fleet of ocean going ships during the Second World War and, with the postwar suspension of compensations to this industry, it lacked sufficient financial resources to acquire new ships on its own. The industry did not show any signs of revival in the immediate postwar period. The shipbuilding industry was also at pains to restart production. To pull the industry out of such a tight spot, the government adopted a program of planned building of ships by inducing the sea transport industry to acquire ships by supplying funds through the Reconstruction Finance Corporation (RFC) in 1947.[10] The source of funds needed for acquisition of ships by this industry shifted, for a short time, to the special accounts of the counterpart funds of U.S. aid to Japan as the RFC ceased its activities, and from 1953 on to the JDB.

The terms and conditions governing loans in 1953 included (1) subsidies in the form of interest payments on the JDB loans, and (2) government subsidies in the form of interest payments to the private sector financial intermediaries in order to bring down the market rate of interest. The JDB loan amounted to 70% of the ship's price (freighters) at that time.

The shipping markets prospered with the Suez Boom of 1956 and the interest subsidies were withdrawn in 1957. The shipping firms greatly increased their acquisition of new tonnage, leaning basically on funds from open markets. The industry, however, found itself faced with a recession in the shipping markets as early as 1958, causing the payments to shipyards to fall into arrears to the extent of ¥11.4 billion. Eventually, it had to be rescued with government help. The private financial institutions developed a very conservative attitude toward the financing of the sea transport industry after this event, and the further expansion of the industry came to depend on the JDB funds. As the market continued to deteriorate, the underdepreciation of the industry as a whole in 1962 amounted to ¥66 billion, and loans amounting to ¥96 billion had fallen into arrears. Despite this, the Income Doubling Plan adopted in December 1960 visualized a doubling of the snipping tonnage held within a decade. For this purpose, the Shipping Reconstruction and Reorganization Act (Law on Refurbishing and Consolidating Ocean Transport) was adopted in 1963. The act aimed at the consolidation of the industry by providing incentives in the form of exemption from interest payment on the loans contracted from the JDB before 1961 under the provisions of the program of planned building of ships for a period of five years and reduction in the interest burden for acquirers of ships. This resulted in the consolidation of a hundred companies into six groups. The market for shipping revived in 1965 and the problems of underdepreciation and arrears on loan repayments were finally resolved.

After the reconstruction was over in 1968, the government was able to extricate itself from its overwhelming preoccupation with the subsidization of the firms. While the proportion of financing through the JDB, as well as the proportion of interest subsidies, was reduced in 1969, the ocean going ships were allowed, for the first time, to avail of a 10% special depreciation under the tax system in order to help the firms assert their financial independence. A surge in the transport demand emerging from the iron and steel and the petroleum industries kept the acquisitions of shipping tonnage by the sea transport industry at a high level during 1970–1971. As the Nixon Shock raised the value of the yen sharply upward in 1971 and the first oil shock steeply reduced the world petroleum demand in 1973 and thereafter, the industry was forced into a persistent stagnation. The interest subsidies were also withdrawn in 1975.

The ratio of reduction in the interest burden (estimated) arising from the low-interest loans provided by the JDB to the total investment expenditure of the shipping industry maintained a high level of 20% on the average during 1962–1975 period (Fig. 5.5), a level much higher than in any other industry.

2. The Electric Power Industry

The electric power industry suffered much smaller war damages than other industries and therefore was in a position to contribute to the rehabilitation of the Japanese economy in the postwar period. The government policy of low electricity charges kept this industry perpetually in the red, holding down new investment. Thus, the sudden surge in domestic productive activity as the Korean hostilities began (1950) threw the demand–supply balance into a disarray and load-shedding became a regular phenomenon.

The system of centralized supply of electric power, adopted during the war, was replaced in 1951 by the present decentralized nine-region structure, with one firm to each region. At the same time, the electric power charges were increased by 30% in order to induce an increase in the supply capacity of the industry by stabilizing the business position of the firms. The electricity charges were raised again in 1952 and 1954. An Electric Power Development Company was established, pursuant to the Electric Power Development Promotion Law, which was enacted with the help of government funds aimed at developing large-scale hydroelectric power sources that could not be easily developed by individual electric power companies. By 1955, a number of large-scale hydroelectric power stations had been completed using a huge amount of the FILP resources.

The JDB, which had just been established at that time, gave a high priority to the financing of electric power supply companies for the development of electric power resources and financed about 20% of their fixed investment. Thermal power had become more economical by 1955, resulting in a shift of focus from hydroelectric power to the development of thermal power. The shortage of electric power supply was brought to an end by 1960. The requirement of funds by the electric power companies doubled during this period of high pitched growth in supply capacity and even though these companies continued to get the most-favored customer treatment from the JDB, the JDB loans became less and less important in the total funds as the companies were able to raise funds through new issues of corporate bonds.

The Japanese economy embarked on the process of rapid growth in 1961 and the development of the heavy and chemical industries steeply raised the electricity demand. The exploitation of economies of large scale and the falling prices of crude oil increased the earnings in this industry to the extent that it was able to meet almost 50% of the growth in its demand for investment funds out of retained earnings. The increased fund-raising capacity of the electric supply companies as their securities were made eligible for open market operations by the BOJ in 1962 when it adopted new credit control measures deserves a special mention in this context. From 1964 on, therefore, the JDB shifted its attention from financing the industry's ordinary fixed investment, which was now taken over by private bond financing, to "policy financing," namely, financing projects directed toward specific policy objectives, such as deferred payments on heavy electrical machinery to protect and promote the makers of such equipment, providing incentives for the development of coal-based thermal power in order to maintain coal demand, and the like.[11]

The most important of these projects financed by the JDB was related to the "indigenization of the production of nuclear power generation equipment," a special measure in force since 1966. This project rose in importance from 1970 onward, and its financing now occupies a prominent position in the JDB financing of the electric power industry. With the financing of projects related to the pollution control and joint sewerage works in 1971, as environmental pollution became a social problem, the nature of the JDB financing of this industry diversified. The loans for the development of hydroelectric power rose in importance once again and development of geothermal power sources was also brought within this framework as development of domestic sources of power became imperative with the setting in of the energy crisis in 1973, thereby raising the share of energy-related financing in the total lendings by the public financial institutions (specially the JDB).

The proportion of reductions in the interest burden resulting from the supply of low-interest loans by public financial institutions, led by the JDB, to the investment expenditure (including land) for this industry was perceptibly high at 7.9% on the average for the period 1961–1968, surpassed by sea transport and shipping industries only. The recent resurgence in this proportion is another special feature.

3. The Shipbuilding Industry (Transport Machinery)[12]

The financing of the shipbuilding industry by public financial institutions, led by EIBJ, accounted for nearly 20% of the total loans outstanding against the transport machinery industry in 1955. The shipping markets slipped in the wake of the reopening of the Suez Canal in April 1957 and the demand for new ships fell off. As a result, the proportion of the EIBJ loans to this industry hovered around a low level of 10% in 1960.

The reduction in freight cost toward the end of 1962 and the introduction of large-scale specialized containerships suddenly pulled up the demand for new ships in what was to become the second export boom for the industry. This raised the share of the EIBJ finances to about the 15% level once again. However, the setback suffered by the international economy following the first oil shock and the resulting shift in the oil policy of various countries, led by the United States, drastically cut back the demand for ships, especially large tankers, bringing down the share of the EIBJ finances.

The ratio of reductions in interest burden (estimated) to the investment expenditure (including land) for this industry was surpassed only by the sea transport industry (Fig. 5.5).

4. The Automobile Industry (Transport Machinery)

The contribution of the institutions of policy finance such as the JDB in financing the makers of completed vehicles was almost negligible. In order to ensure international competitiveness through mass production in face of the imminent liberalization of trade and capital in 1965, the government directed its efforts at consolidation of the industry through mergers and groupings. The JDB also contributed in this direction by providing incentives for such consolidation in the form of financing the reorganization setup. These efforts bore fruit only during 1966–1968 and a mere ¥11.9 billion worth of loans were provided for the business tie-ups between Nissan and Prince, Toyota and Hino, Toyota and Daihatsu, and Nissan and Fuji Heavy Industries. The share of the JDB loans, including the above, in the total investment expenditure of the makers of completed vehicles was no more than 0.9% on the average for the period 1966–1971. In the context of auto-parts makers, the JDB and the Small Business Finance

Corporation provided loans under the Law on Temporary Measures for the Promotion of Specified Manufacturing Industries to be discussed below.

5. The Machinery Industry

The machinery industry in 1955 was composed of makers of finished products, dominated by large firms, and materials and component makers, dominated by medium- and small-scale firms. The government, visualizing the latter as a bottleneck for the future development of heavy and chemical industries, attributed their low productivity to small-scale production of a large variety of products with obsolete equipment and enacted the Law on Temporary Measures for the Promotion of Specified Manufacturing Industries in 1956 and the Law on Temporary Measures for the Promotion of the Electronics Industry the following year. Both of these laws aimed at providing low-interest loans (at a yearly rate of 6.5%) through the JDB for modernization of equipment and upgrading of technology in those industries designated by MITI to be basic but underdeveloped. Machine tools, auto parts, and implements were designated as such, but the total amount of public loans to these industries, with basic machinery (machine tools and implements) as the major recipient, did not exceed ¥10.6 billion in five years. Loans to the electronics industry, aimed mainly at consumer-oriented electronics equipment, amounted to only ¥2.2 billion in seven years.

The first of the two laws was revised and extended twice in 1961 and in 1966, in an attempt to strengthen the international competitiveness of the machine industry following the trade and capital liberalization, respectively. The Small Business Finance Corporation joined the JDB in financing this industry, and the funds supplied to this industry amounted to ¥53.8 billion in 1961–1965 (five years) and ¥48.9 billion in 1966–1970 (five years). Especially rapidly increases in these loans were those to auto-parts makers.

The second of the two laws was revised in 1964 and was extended with the main focus shifting to industrial electronic machinery. Loans, with electronic components cornering a major proportion, amounted to ¥12.1 billion.

With the expiration of the two laws in 1971, and in view of the fact that these two industries were being integrated, the government took the opportunity to club these two laws into one and enacted the Law on Temporary Measures for the Promotion of Specified Electronics Industries and Specified Machinery Industries. Financing under this law, directed mainly toward auto-parts and integrated circuit manufacturers, amounted to ¥70.6 billion in a seven year period, with the electronics industry cornering 20% of these funds. Finally, in 1978 when the law expired, it was succeeded by the Law on Temporary Measures for the Promotion of Specified Machinery and Information Industries in order to promote the integration of the electronics, machinery, and information processing industries. The JDB and Small Business Finance Corporation supplied ¥11 billion a year worth of loans, of which nearly 80% were accounted for by the electronics industry.

The share of public funds going to the machinery industry in the total financing was very low, with the share of the JDB loans for specified machinery[13] forming 1.3% to 5% (1956–1974) and that of the Small Business Finance Corporation forming 0.07% to 2.8% (1961–1979). As a result, the reduction in interest burden for general machinery, electrical machinery, and precision instruments was very low.

6. The Iron and Steel Industry

The lagging production of iron and steel after World War II caused a shortage of steel input indispensable for increasing coal production and thereby acted as an impediment to reviving production in other industries. In 1947, the government adopted a "priority production plan" with special emphasis on coal and steel, and the RFC began extending loans to the iron and steel industry. The industry underwent three rationalization programs and the proportion of self-financing rose appreciably. The supply of public funds for rationalization purposes was no longer considered to be necessary for this industry by the JDB, whose loans from 1961 onward were thus restricted mainly to the financing of pollution control and development of indigenous technology.

The proportion of reduction in the interest burden resulting from the low-interest loans, mainly through the JDB, to investment expenditure (including land) was as low as 0.99% on the average during 1961–1981. The benefits arising out of the public loans were also small as compared to other industries (Fig. 5.5).

7. The Coal Mining Industry

The coal mining industry received preferential treatment in terms of resource allocation under the priority production plan adopted in 1947, and 50% of the RFC financing was directed at this industry at its peak. The system of subsidies was abandoned in 1949 when the fiscal policy was tightened on the advice of Mr. Dodge, public-finance advisor to General MacArthur. As the excess demand for coal dwindled with the depression, the industry was put into a serious predicament. The two-year Korean War boom gave the industry a breathing space, but the lifting of controls on crude oil in 1952 produced a shift in demand in favor of liquid energy, throwing the coal mining industry into a protracted depression.

A Law on Temporary Measures for Coal Mining Industry Rationalization was adopted in 1955, and the Coal Mining Industry Council was set up as an inquiry committee of MITI for formulating a rationalization plan. Besides this, a Coal Mining Industry Reorganization Corporation (renamed as Rationalization Corporation in 1960) was established to buy up inefficient mines, and the opening of new pits was brought under a licensing system. The industry got a short reprieval during the Jimmu boom of 1956–1957 but the situation took a turn for the worse in 1958, forcing severe personnel cuts by the firms, which resulted in labor disputes like the one at Miike, thereby turning the problem of the decline of the coal mining industry into a social problem.

Under these circumstances, the government tried to save the coal mining industry by raising labor productivity through an active investment program. The JDB increased its lendings to this industry by a large amount in support of the "build mines" program from 1958 onward. A fall in the petroleum prices beyond expectations during this period, however, brought down the coal prices as well and the earnings in the coal industry continued to decline despite a rise in productivity. The government tried to improve the earnings position of the coal mining firms by supporting the prices of coal used for electric power generation in 1965 and by providing interest subsidies to reduce the interest on borrowings. The earnings of the coal mining firms continued to deteriorate despite these measures, and the government disbursed, besides supplying ¥100 billion out of the tariff proceeds on petroleum and crude for the repayment of principal and interest (the first subrogation), subsidies for adopting safety measures proportionate to production levels in order to make the firms managerially secure. A continued downward shift in demand and an unabated rise in the wages led to the accumulation of deficits once again, and the government disbursed ¥85 billion in grants to the firms in 1969 (the second subrogation). Meanwhile, the main source of investment funds in this industry shifted to the interest-free loans from the Coal Mining Industry Rationalization Corporation, with the JDB in a supplementary role in providing loans only to the firms with a long-run earnings prospect. Finally, in 1973, the government took over the debt of the industry contracted up to June 3, 1972 (third subrogation) and the curtain fell on the coal policy of the government.

The JDB accounted for the highest share in the total funds supplied by the public financial institutions to the mining industry (10% to 20%) until the early 1970s when the curtain fell on the coal policy. The financing of the coal mining industry was an important part of the government finances, as is revealed by the relatively high proportion of reductions in interest burden (estimated) to the investment expenditure (including land) in this industry.

8. The Petroleum Refining Industry

The restrictions on the import of petroleum, which was prohibited by the GHQ after the war, were only lifted in 1950. As soon as the importation began, the Japanese petroleum interests joined the fold of international petroleum capital in order to secure the supplies of crude oil and import of technology. The imports of crude and petroleum products before the liberalization of 1962 were limited by the availability of foreign exchange rationed under the "foreign exchange control system." During this period, the government effectively utilized the rationing measures for nurturing the domestically owned companies, making adjustments with the coal mining industry, building up refining capacity, and promoting the petrochemical industries.

With the liberalization of import of crude in 1962, a Petroleum Industry Law was formulated and the demand–supply adjustment role that was being played by the foreign exchange controls came to be played by the administrative guidance of MITI. Despite this, competition stiffened and the product market collapsed, putting the domestically owned medium and small petroleum firms into dire business difficulties. The government pursued a policy of consolidation and promotion of these firms through vertically integrating the stages of crude production, refining, and sales to bring the industry to a scale comparable to that of international petroleum majors. JDB loans were immediately granted to the Kyodo Petroleum group set up in 1965. The financing of the sales facilities and refining equipment of the Kyodo group has been accounting for 3% to 4% of the total JDB loans since 1965. The problem of atmospheric pollution arising out of the emission of sulphurous acid gas worsened by 1966, and the financing of pollution control measures like that for the equipment for the desulphurization of crude began rising from 1967. The Hokkaido and Tohoku Development Corporation also funded the establishment of new petroleum refining plants in the Tomakomai and Sendai port districts, but its financing was a mere 10% of that provided by the JDB.

Development of overseas crude sources and the stockpiling of petroleum became major policy issues after the first oil shock in 1973 in order to secure stable oil supplies, and the JDB and the Japan Petroleum Development Corporation increased their financing in these areas. The JDB loans to the petroleum refining industry formed only 10% of the total financing of this industry by the financial intermediaries during 1975–1979, but the proportion of reduction in interest burden (estimated) to the total investment expenditure in this industry has been rising since 1979.[14]

V. Conclusion

We round off our discussion in this chapter by looking at the cost-reduction effect of the special depreciation schemes and the FILP taken together. Table VI presents the simple average of the proportion of cost reduction to the total investment expenditures separately for the period of rapid economic growth (1961–1973) and the period of relatively stable growth (1974–1980).

TABLE VI
A Comparison of Benefits Arising out of Reduction in Interest Burden and Special Depreciation Schemes (%)

		Manufacturing				
	Total	Transport Machinery	Iron and Steel	Machinery	Sea Transport	Electric Power
1961–1973						
1. *Reduction in interest burden (est.)* Investment expenditure (incl. land)	1.0 (52)	6.9(85)	0.5(27)	3.6(72)	22.3(76)	5.9(94)
2. *Benefits from spl. dep. schemes* Investment expenditure (incl. land)	0.95(48)	1.3(15)	1.4(73)	1.4(28)	7.2(24)	0.36(6)
Total	1.95	8.2	1.9	4.9	29.5	6.26
1974–1980						
1. *Reduction in interest burden (est.)* Investment expenditure (incl. land)	1.6 (73)	6.4(94)	1.6(70)	2.6(84)	17.0(81)	2.8(77)
2. *Benefits from spl. dep. schemes* Investment expenditure (incl. land)	0.57(27)	0.4 (6)	0.7(30)	0.5(16)	4.1(19)	0.9(24)
Total	2.1	6.8	2.3	3.1	21.1	3.7

Composition (%) within parentheses. May not add up to 100% because of rounding.

The amount of cost reductions in all manufacturing formed approximately 2% of the total investment expenditure in both the periods, but a glance at the sources of these reductions reveals that whereas the special depreciation schemes and the FILP contributed equally in the first period, FILP accounts for almost three-quarters in the second period. The high proportion of 7% to 8% reduction in costs revealed by the transport machinery industry within the manufacturing industries is due to the FILP, mainly in form of the Export-Import Bank loans for deferred payments on ships. The iron and steel industry shows a low proportion of 2% in both the periods, although relatively more was contributed by special depreciations in the first period and by FILP in the second period.

Among the nonmanufacturing industries, the sea transport industry stands out both in special depreciations and in FILP. The total benefits accounted for nearly 30% of its investment expenditure during the rapid growth phase and 20% during the phase of stable growth. The important role played by the JDB in this industry under the planned shipbuilding program is quite obvious. The electric power industry also reaped above-average benefits, mainly due to the JDB finances. Even though the proportion of benefits is seen to decline from 6% to 3% over the two periods, the trend could be reversing itself in the recent years as the dependency of this industry on the JDB funds is growing in the wake of the construction of high-cost nuclear power plants.

With this, we close our discussion of the cost-reduction effect of the special depreciation schemes and the FILP. We intend to take up the discussion of the impact of such cost-reduction on investment in another place.[15]

NOTES

1. The present research is a part of our project funded by the Kikawada Foundation. The authors have benefited from valuable comments received from Yutaka Kosai, Michihiro Oyama, Koji Shinjo, Kazuo Ueda, and many other participants at the Zushi conference. Keimei Kaizuka, Akiyoshi Horiuchi, Masaaki Homma, Juro Teranishi, Toshihiro Ihori, Michiko Yamashita of the EPA, Setsuo Uchihori, Hisashi Yaginuma, Yoshitaka Kurosawa, Kazushi Suzuki, and Tatsuo Takahashi, all of the JDB, were also generous with their comments. Our thanks are also due to Isao Maeda of the Export-Import Bank of Japan, Tatsuo Takahashi and Masahiro Kawata of the JDB, Shigeru Kobayashi and Kazuo Watanabe of the Hokkaido and Tohoku Development Corporation, Hiroshi Karakawa of the Small Business Finance Corporation, Masanobu Kobayashi and Koichi Takesue of the People's Finance Corporation, and Masahiko Yoshida of the Finance Corporation of Local Public Enterprise for insights into institutional aspects and collection of data. Katsuto Masubuchi and Masayuki Kako of Saitama Bank and Ryo Nishimoto, Kazuaki Oshima, and Michiko Hayashi of Saitama University helped out with computational work.

2. More precisely, the tax burden is the ratio of corporate income tax plus other taxes and public charges (which are treated as business cost) to current income (before tax) plus other taxes and public charges. This may not be the best indicator of the tax burden, inasmuch as corporate income tax as well as other taxes and public charges are fraught with problems of incidence of tax burden, but should suffice for following the changes in the tax burden over time.

3. Although the first change in depreciation law came about in 1947, it went no further than bringing the exceptionally short stipulated asset lives back to normal.

4. *Hojin Kigyo Tokei* (Corporate Enterprise Statistics) provides depreciation data by industry, although without breakdown by depreciation scheme. Estimates of the Tax System Council, on the other hand, give aggregate data by depreciation scheme without giving breakdown by industry. Furthermore, these estimates differ significantly, as pointed out in Komiya (1975), from estimates compiled from micro data in *Hojin Kigyo Tokei* and *Wagakuni Kigyo no Keiei Bunseki*.

5. For a discussion of the makeup of the Fiscal Investment and Loan Program, see Kumon, Okamoto, and Taniguchi [1983], and Tachi et al. [1983].

6. The public financial intermediaries issuing government guaranteed debt are the Finance Corporation of Local Public Enterprise, Hokkaido and Tohoku Development Corporation, and Small Business Finance Corporation.

7. The share of basic industries and exports in the total FILP funds, if it can be considered as industrial policy-related finance (defined in a narrow sense), fell from about 25% during 1953–1955, to 20% during 1956–1970 and further from 15% to 10% during 1971–1980.

8. Investment here is the total of net changes in fixed capital including land, normal depreciation, and special depreciation.

9. For detailed data, methodology, and the impact on investment, see Ogura and Yoshino [1985]. Reductions in the interest burden (estimated) have been calculated as follows: Interest and discounts paid to the public financial intermediaries for each of the industries were deducted from the total interest payments and discounts as presented in the *Corporate Enterprise Statistics* and the resulting figure was divided by the borrowings from private financial institutions by industry to get a figure for the nominal rate of interest charged by these organizations. This was then converted into the effective rate of interest by adjusting for bank deposits by industry from the *Corporate Enterprise Statistics*. The excess of the effective rate and the interest rate charged by the public financial institutions was then multiplied by the average borrowings of the industry from such institutions to arrive at the reductions in the interest burden.

10. The Reconstruction Finance Corporation supplied the funds needed for acquiring ships to the Maritime Credit Corporation, which held the newly acquired ships jointly with the ship owners who were in turn allowed to buy up the Maritime Credit Corporation's ownership within a ten-year period.

11. During this period, the share of the JDB loans to the electric power industry fell below that of all banks.

12. For detailed historical discussions of the shipbuilding, automobile, and the iron and steel industries, see Chapters 11, 12, and 13 of this book.

13. The Japan Development Bank differs in behavior from the private financial institutions in that it can only lend to firms in those legally designated industries.

14. Since the data for the petroleum refining industry became available only after 1975, this is not shown in Figure 5.5.

15. Cf. Ogura and Yoshino [1985].

CHAPTER 6

Foreign Trade and Direct Investment

MOTOSHIGE ITOH

Faculty of Economics
University of Tokyo
Tokyo, Japan

KAZUHARU KIYONO

Department of Economics
Gakushuin University
Tokyo, Japan

I. Introduction

Japan, a resource-poor country, cannot afford to miss any opportunity for foreign trade if it is to develop economically and to maintain high standards of living. Policies related to trade and foreign direct investment therefore have occupied a prominent position in the process of economic development in postwar Japan. This chapter evaluates the contribution of these policies to the performance of the Japanese economy.

It is not the high rate of growth *per se,* but the rapid shift to an advanced industrial structure that should merit attention in the process of postwar Japanese economic development. Although a detailed discussion of the concept of an advanced industrial structure and the extent to which it can be accommodated within the framework of accepted economic theory is left for Chapter 10, it can be construed to imply a process whereby industries whose products formed a high proportion in expenditures got progressively integrated into the Japanese industrial structure. The Japanese government, aware of the intricate relationship between industrial structure and gains from trade, had been in pursuit of such an advanced industrial structure for quite some time.

For better or worse, trade policies have contributed extensively to the rapid growth achieved by Japan. Broadly speaking, these policies were initially intended to deal with the foreign exchange constraint in the immediate postwar period but gradually came to serve as instruments for the protection of indigenous industry. The formulation of these policies during the 1970s was influenced to a large extent by the measures taken by Japan in order to stem the aggravating trade friction with its trade partners.

Figure 6.1 shows percentage shares of major industries in total manufacturing production and exports in order to depict postwar changes in Japan's production and export structures. We can easily discern that heavy and chemical industries, particularly machinery industries, increased shares rapidly.

The magnitude of gains from trade accruing to a country is intricately related to its industrial structure. The higher the proportion of goods with high overseas demand entering the Japanese export menu and the higher the propensity in foreign countries to import these goods, the higher would be the levels of income and welfare in Japan. In order to be able to offer such an export menu, a matching industrial structure is a necessity. The advancement of the industrial structure in postwar Japan can be therefore interpreted, in a long-term perspective, as the process of change that en-

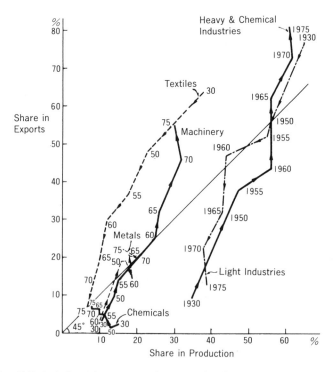

Fig. 6.1. Shifts in industrial structure and pattern of trade. From *Nenji Keizai Hokokusho* (Annual Economic Report), Fiscal 1978.

abled Japan to acquire an industrial structure conducive to such exports. Conversely, one may argue that it is these shifts in the industrial structure that have been responsible for the high rate of growth in the postwar Japanese economy.

Table I, presenting trade data for the major industrial nations, reveals a high income elasticity of world demand for Japanese exports and a low income elasticity of demand for its imports. These figures clearly reflect the advanced nature of the Japanese industrial structure, showing the extent of Japan's reliance on income-elastic commodities for its exports. A graph plotted with the rate of growth of GNP on the vertical axis and the difference between the income elasticities of exports and imports on the horizontal axis clearly reveals a positive correlation, capturing the implied relationship between the industrial structure, the trade pattern, and the rate of economic growth.

Two criteria for determining the optimal industrial structure were provided in early Trade White Papers.[1] According to these papers, an industrial structure is considered desirable when it is based on industries (a) producing commodities with high income elasticity of demand and (b) having a high rate of productivity growth. Although the above criteria cannot be taken at their face value, these are theoretically justifiable to

TABLE I

An International Comparison of Growth Rates in GNP, Exports, and Imports and Income Elasticity of Exports and Imports (1956/57 av. ~ 1964/65)

	Rate of Growth			Income Elasticity		
	Real GNP (A)	Exports (B)	Imports (C)	Exports (D)	Imports (E)	(D) − (E)
Japan	9.8	14.2	11.5	3.55	1.23	2.32
West Germany	6.2	7.0	10.7	2.08	1.80	0.28
Italy	5.5	14.7	12.8	2.95	2.19	0.76
Denmark	5.2	7.7	9.6	1.69	1.31	0.38
France	5.1	7.9	6.3	1.53	1.66	−0.13
Netherlands	4.7	8.4	8.5	1.88	1.89	−0.01
Sweden	4.4	6.8	7.1	1.76	1.42	0.34
Norway	4.2	7.6	7.2	1.59	1.40	0.19
Belgium	3.9	7.2	7.2	1.83	1.94	−0.11
United States	3.6	4.9	5.2	0.99	1.51	−0.52
United Kingdom	3.3	3.3	4.2	0.86	1.66	−0.8

Sources and Notes: (A)–(C) calculated from Keizai Kikakucho Chosakyoku [1972], p. 331. For Japan, 1956/57 ~ 65/66. (B) exports of goods and services; (C) imports of goods and services. (D) and (E) from Houthakker and Magee [1969]; Belgium is for Belgium and Luxembourg. For (D) income is world income.

a certain extent, as discussed in Chapter 10. Just as a firm cannot depend eternally on its existing markets for its growth and has to actively seek new markets, a country like Japan, which is heavily dependent on foreign sources of supply for its raw materials and fuel requirements, must keep on shuffling its industrial structure in order to open up and expand its export markets.

Sections II to IV below present a general picture of the Japanese policies related to import restrictions, regulation of the inflow of foreign direct investment, and export promotion in the high growth period and then examine the impact of these policies on economic development, with special emphasis on the process through which Japan acquired its advanced industrial structure. Finally, in Section V we turn our attention to the economic friction, especially the trade friction arising out of the Japanese exports in the 1970s, and the policy measures undertaken to mitigate this friction.

II. Import Restrictions and Trade Liberalization

The initial import control measures in Japan consisted of a series of foreign exchange allocations and other quantitative restrictions.[2] Faced with severe foreign exchange shortages, the Japanese government placed restrictions on the type and amount of imports as well as the number of importers over a wide range of commodities from raw materials to finished products. Imports of raw materials, capital goods, and advanced technology required for expanding production in the existing foreign-exchange-earning export industries[3] and for the growth and development of the strategic industries targeted for development as future export industries were given preferential treatment in terms of allocation of the meager foreign exchange resources. Allocation of foreign exchange for imports competing with the products of the infant industries in their development throes as well as for luxury goods were severely restricted. This system of foreign exchange allocations proved to be an effective tool in the policy kit aimed at protection and promotion of indigenous industry.

Import quotas formed the core of the protection policy until the early 1960s (Figure 6.2). The quantitative barriers came down sharply beginning in 1960, on the heels of Japan's entry into the IMF (1952) and GATT (1955), raising the relative importance of tariffs, the pecuniary import control measures. This is also revealed in the heavier tariff burdens in Japan as compared to the United States and EEC countries in the 1960s and the

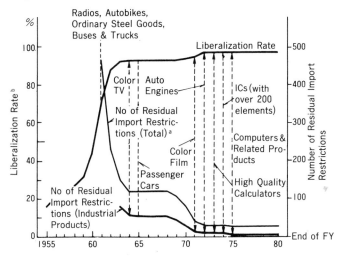

Fig. 6.2. Trade liberalization in Japan. From Tsusansho, (1980), p. 55; Naikai, (1961), p. 37. Joined IMF and WB (1952), GATT (1955); Trade and Exchange Liberalization Guidelines (1960); Inclusion into Article 8 Countries of the IMF (1964); Kennedy Round (1967).[a] Figures for 1961 are those for April, 1962.[b] Calculation discontinued now.

first half of the 1970s in contrast to those in the 1950s (Figure 6.3). There was a built-in tariff escalation system imposing higher tariffs on imports on more processed goods. Further, the effective rates of protection (ERP)[4] were above the nominal tariff rates. In other words, the actual protection enjoyed by the industries at higher levels of processing was thus much higher than nominal figures.[5] As shown in Table II, this trend continued, though in a weaker form, into 1968, the first year after the Kennedy Round (1967).[6]

To grasp salient features of the import control policy as a measure to protect and promote the indigenous industry, it is necessary to examine the role it played in specific industries.

Trade liberalization in terms of the removal of quantitative restrictions proceeded at a fast pace for a short period during the early 1960s, just before Japan's entry into the ranks of Article 8 countries of the IMF (1964), followed by a period of sluggishness, whereafter the program began dragging its feet (Figure 6.2). The international criticism of Japan arising out of its rising trade surplus and the development of trade friction with the United States over textiles, color television, and iron and steel forced

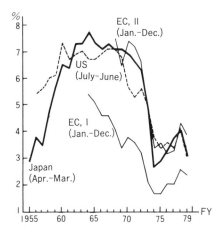

Fig. 6.3. Tariff burden in major countries. From Nihon Keizai Kenkyu Senta (1979); Tsu-sansho (1982). The EC figures up to 1977 include six old EC member countries viz. W. Germany, France, Italy, Netherlands, Belgium, and Luxembourg. For 1978 and 1979, UK, Denmark, and Ireland have also been included. Tariff burden in case of EC includes agricultural surcharges. EC I represents the tariff burden on total imports including intraregional imports. EC II gives the tariff burden on imports from outside the EC.

Japan to proceed with trade liberalization at a faster pace during the late 1960s and early 1970s.[7] The items affected by the trade liberalization were buses and trucks (1961), color televisions (1964), and passenger cars (1965) during the 1960s and color film (1971), high quality electronic calculators and cash registers (1973), integrated circuits (with over 200 elements) (1974), and electronic computers and related equipment (1975) during the 1970s. It, however, took considerable time for trade in these items to be liberalized after the initiation of promotory measures for these industries taken by the Japanese government, especially MITI. For example, the government's intent to promote the automobile industry was translated into protection policy in 1952 and MITI came up with "People's Car Promotion Guidelines" in 1955.[8] As for the machinery and electronics industries, the protection policy was formalized in the Laws on Temporary Measures for the Promotion of the Machinery Industry (1956) and the Electronics Industry (1957), respectively. The indigenous industries on the way to growth were thus protected for quite a long period of time.

What was the extent of protection enjoyed by the indigenous industries? A look at Table II reveals a steep fall in the ERP for the textile industry up to the early 1970s, rising thereafter to considerably high levels. This resulted from the stagnation of the Japanese textile industry as it lost its

TABLE II
Effective Rates of Protection[a] in Japan (%)
(A) By Type of Goods

	1963		1968		ERP–NRP	
	NRP	ERP	NRP	ERP	1963	1968
Raw materials	3.1	0.8	3.9	0.9	−2.3	−3.0
Producer goods	13.7	29.6	15.2	22.3	15.9	7.1
Intermediate producer goods	12.3	28.0	14.1	21.7	15.7	7.6
Final producer goods	15.9	32.3	16.9	23.2	15.4	6.3
Consumer goods	21.6	44.6	23.6	35.8	23.0	12.2

Source: Muto, [1971], Table 14.

(B): By Industry[b]

	1963	1968	1973	1975	1978
Manufacturing	32.3	24.2	14.4	25.3	22.0
Textiles	54.3	28.2	18.6	38.6	38.3
Spinning	27.1	12.5	15.0	15.2	20.4
Weaving	44.6	30.5	15.5	61.6	61.8
Products	72.8	32.8	22.4	30.5	27.7
Wood products	14.0	25.6	16.1	22.2	18.1
Paper and pulp	9.7	18.0	11.0	17.3	9.4
Printing and publishing	−16.7	1.0	−0.9	−8.3	−0.6
Leather and rubber products	30.9	21.8	12.3	16.9	14.1
Chemicals	33.4	17.7	8.8	15.4	11.6
Petroleum and coal products	19.5	14.5	7.1	12.6	19.2
Ceramics and stone products	22.2	15.7	8.1	11.6	8.4
Iron and steel	30.1	30.0	17.1	52.3	19.5
Nonferrous metals	30.4	34.1	22.1	30.3	20.8
Metal products	13.8	19.9	9.9	10.3	6.5
Machinery	36.7	20.0	7.7	8.8	5.7
General machinery	23.0	14.5	8.7	8.7	6.2
Electrical machinery	30.9	16.5	5.4	10.2	7.4
Transport equipment	61.5	31.0	9.2	7.1	2.8
Precision instruments	34.9	22.9	10.4	8.6	6.2

Source: Shouda, [1982].
[a]NRP = Nominal Rate of Protection; ERP = Effective Rate of Protection.
[b]ERP based on simple averages of tariff rates.

competitive edge in the international markets following a catch up by the developing countries.[9] On the other hand, the ERP in industries such as chemicals, petroleum and coal products, iron and steel, nonferrous metals, metal products, and machinery, which were targeted for development in order to achieve an advanced industrial structure, steadily fell in the 1960s through the 1980s, except for the petroleum and coal products and non-ferrous metals that bore the brunt of the oil crises. This trend was exceptionally pronounced in the machinery industry, especially transport equipment.

The machinery industry received special attention within the policy framework of the two plans referred to above for the promotion of the indigenous industry since the late 1950s. This policy continued into the 1960s as revealed by the high ERP for this industry. The low ERP during the 1970s for this industry, however, reflects the increased competitive power of the Japanese machinery industry resulting from the success of the policy to protect and promote the indigenous industry. The tariffs on major machinery imports were relaxed only after this sector became internationally competitive and its export/production ratio rose, a fact vividly brought out in Figure 6.4.

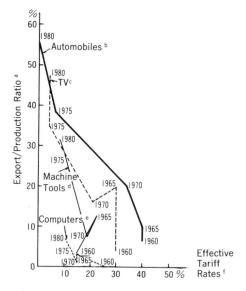

Fig. 6.4. Export/production ratios and effective tariffs. [a]Export/Production Ratio = Amt. of Expts./Prodn. × 100. In case of automobiles, number of units is used. [b]Automobiles include passenger cars, buses, trucks, and three wheelers. [c]Television includes black-and-white and color TVs. Effective tariffs refer to color TVs only. [d]Including NC and others. Effective tariff rate pertains to NC machine tools only after 1970. [e]Includes analog type. Effective rate of tariff is for digital type only. Computers include not only the main-frame but accessories and other related equipment as well. Tariffs are applied in the following order: (1) Preferential Tariffs, (2) GATT rates, (3) Temporary rates, and (4) Basic rates. The one that is actually applied is called effective tariff rate. (2) is used only if it is lower than (3) or (4). Since we are concerned with effective tariffs on trade with developed countries only, (1) has been ignored.

The import restrictions thus played an indispensable role in the development of Japanese industries. The economic rationale underlying the adoption of such a policy and its significance from the point of view of economic welfare are discussed in Chapters 9 and 10 of this book.

III. Regulating Inflow of Direct Foreign Investment and Capital Liberalization

Besides the cautious and heavy protection from trade discussed above, it was necessary for the policy authorities to protect the developing infant industries from the competition of foreign firms in the product markets. The discussion in this section covers the policy regarding regulation of foreign capital inflows.

The basic guidelines regulating the inflow of foreign direct investment were determined by the Law Concerning Foreign Capital (Foreign Capital Law in subsequent discussions) enacted in 1950. Under this law, the approval or rejection of foreign direct investment in Japan was governed by the following general criteria:

*The Approval Criteria (Article 8, Section 1 of the Foreign Capital Law)

1. It (foreign investment) should contribute directly or indirectly to the improvement of international balance of payments.
2. It should be directly or indirectly conducive to the development of the key industries or public utilities.

*The Disapproval Criterion (Section 2 of the above article)

3. If it was considered to have an adverse effect on the reconstruction of the Japanese economy.

The regulation of foreign capital inflows based on such criteria was proposed as a necessary measure by the policy authorities after a careful weighing of its costs and benefits. The postwar Japanese economy lagged behind the United States and the European countries in terms of capital stock and technology and lacked foreign exchange sufficient to import the necessary raw materials and capital goods.[10] The import of foreign capital could have broken these fetters on the early reconstruction and development in one stroke, but a direct entry of foreign (especially American) firms with ample managerial resources into the Japanese markets could have proved detrimental to the development and growth of the domestic industry and indigenous technology.[11] Tie-ups, mergers, and absorption of Japanese firms in "the industrial fields having strong linkages

TABLE III
Liberalization of Foreign Direct Investment in Japan

Date of Liberalization (Day/Month/Year)	Industries Liberalized for Foreign Participation in Case of New Entry		Liberalization of Equity for Foreign Capital Participation in Preexisting Firms (Automatic Approval)		
	Industries where 50% Foreign Capital Equity Participation Was Automatically Approved	Industries where 100% Foreign Capital Equity Participation Was Automatically Approved	Proportion of Equity Held by Foreign Investors (per Investor) (%)	Proportion of Equity Held by all Foreign Investors (Foreign Capital Participation Ratio)	
				Unrestricted Industries (%)	Restricted Industries (%)
Before 1/7/67				up to 15%	up to 10%
1/7/67 (First)	33	17	up to 5%	up to 20%	up to 15%
1/3/69 (Second)	(Cum. Total) 160	(Cum. Total) 44	up to 7%	up to 20%	up to 15%
1/9/70 (Third)	(Cum. Total) 447	(Cum. Total) 77	up to 7%	< 25%	up to 15%
1/4/71 (Auto)	(Cum. Total) 445	(Cum. Total) 77	up to 7%	< 25%	up to 15%

			<10%	<25%	up to 15%
4/8/71 (100% in Principle)	50% Liberalization in Principle	(Cum. Total) 228	<10%	<25%	up to 15%
1/5/73 (Fourth)	100% Liberalization in Principle		<10%	<25%	up to 15%
	In case of consent by a firm, however, 100% Liberalization in Principle.				
1/12/80 (Revision of Foreign Exchange Law)	All except Agriculture, Forestry and Fishing, Mining (Foreign Capital participation rate liberalized up to 50%), Petroleum, Leather and Leather Products				

Major Industries Liberalized After 1973

Name of Industry	Date when	Notes
Integrated circuits	1/12/1974	50% liberalization till then.
Pharmaceuticals and agricultural chemicals	1/5/1975	-do-
Electronic precision instruments (for medical and electrical measurements)	1/5/1975	-do-
Manufacture, sale, and leasing of electronic computers and control systems	1/12/1975	Case by case up to 3/8/74, later 50% liberalization
Information processing	1/4/1976	Case by case till 11/30/74, later 50% liberalized.
Photosensitive materials	1/5/1976	50% liberalization till then

Source: Japan Tariff Association, *Boeki Nenkan* (Trade Yearbook), 1983, pp. 190–191.

with related industries and the still developing infant industries" with foreign firms was feared to the extent that opinions "questioning the advisability of leaving the decisions regarding management rights (participation shares, etc.) completely to the firms' autonomy" in such industries came to the fore.[12] Such fears strengthened in the backdrop of the anxiety shown by the EEC countries about the control of European firms by American capital in the 1960s.[13]

Under these circumstances, the implementation of the policy regulations on the inflow of foreign direct investment, although conforming to the above mentioned criteria in principle, left ample room for discretion in the hands of the policy authorities in terms of its applicability since the details of the approval criteria were never made public. This enabled the authorities to enforce the regulation with extreme strictness.[14] The major multinationals functioning in Japan today used the partial relaxation on foreign capital inflows under the "system of free purchase of yen-dominated stock"[15] in force during 1956–1963 preceding Japan's entry into the Article 8 countries of the IMF to make inroads into the Japanese economy. Otherwise, as is revealed by the figures presented in Table III, the capital liberalization program proceeded at an extremely slow pace and a 100% liberalization had to wait until 1973.

As can be easily discerned from Table III, classified by industry, the capital liberalization lagged behind the trade liberalization, all coming in the 1970s: automobiles (1971), integrated circuits (1974), electronic computers (1975), and information processing (1976). In the presence of the fears mentioned above, the policy authorities opposed the adoption of the alternative development strategy inviting foreign firms through liberal inflows of foreign investment.

Table IV reveals the consequences of adopting such controls. The ratio of foreign direct investment and hence the proportion of manufacturing production held by foreign firms in Japan was far lower than in other developed countries throughout the 1960s and the 1970s. The high returns on foreign investment relative to its share in investment and production reflected the strict control exercised by the policy authorities. The so-called "TI incident" following the entry of Texas Instruments Inc. into the Japanese semiconductor market is still fresh in Japan's memory.[16] Japan preferred a closed development strategy with strictly regulated foreign investment and strictly supervised import of technology in respect of its content, royalty, and so on to the pursuit of a more open development strategy based on a free inflow of foreign investments.[17] There is doubt as to whether this strategy was the only option available to Japan at that time. The traditional theory of international trade points to the possibility

TABLE IV

International Comparison of Trends in Foreign Direct Investment

	Direct Investment Outflow (%)[a]			Direct Investment Inflow (%)[a]			Return on Investments[b,c] 1970 ~ 78		Proportion of Mfg. Prodn. Held by Foreign Affiliate Firms	
	1961–67	1968–73	1974–79	1961–67	1968–73	1974–78	Receipts (%)	Payments (%)	Participation Ratio (%)	Proportion (%, Year)
Canada	2.3	4.5	6.2	16.2	12.1	3.2	2.8	12.3	$\geqslant 50$	56.6(1977)
United States	61.1	45.8	29.3	2.6	11.1	26.7	50.6	34.6	n.a.	n.a.
Japan	2.4	6.7	13.0	2.0	1.7	1.2	5.9	8.5	$\geqslant 25$	4.2(1978)[5]
Australia	0.7	1.4	1.6[1]	15.6	12.9	9.5[1]	n.a.	n.a.	$\geqslant 25$	36.2(1972/73)
Belgium	0.3[2]	1.4	2.5	4.5[2]	6.1	9.4	n.a.	n.a.	n.a.	n.a.
France	6.9	5.2	7.8	8.2	8.2	15.2	8.2	10.0	$\geqslant 20$	27.8(1975)
West Germany	7.2	12.5	17.0	21.3	16.4	14.7	9.7	12.7	$\geqslant 25$	21.7(1976)[6]
Italy	3.6	3.3	2.0	11.5	8.3	5.0	n.a.	n.a.	> 50	23.8(1977)[6]
Netherlands	4.4	6.8	9.6[3]	4.7	8.5	6.0[3]	5.6	7.6	n.a.	n.a.
Sweden	2.0	2.4	3.7[4]	2.4	1.7	0.5[4]	n.a.	n.a.	$\geqslant 20$	10.8(1976)
United Kingdom	8.7	9.1	9.2	9.7	7.4	6.1	13.0	13.6	$\geqslant 50$	21.2(1977)
Spain	0	0.3	0.6	2.7	3.7	3.7	n.a.	n.a.	> 50	11.2(1971)
Norway	0	0.3	0.9	0.8	1.4	4.1	n.a.	n.a.	$\geqslant 20$	18.7(1977)

Source: Miyazaki et al. [1981]; OECD, [1981].

[a] Proportion among 13 countries.

[b] Returns on direct investment, equity, and other investments abroad (including reinvestment). (Service incomes such as royalties, management fees, etc. are not included.)

[c] Proportion among seven countries.

[1] 1974 ~ 76.

[2] 1965 ~ 67.

[3] 1974 ~ 78.

[4] 1974 ~ 77.

[5] Sales.

[6] Transactions.

of using foreign investment as a means to develop domestic industry rather than foster domestic industry through its control.

A foreign firm is not merely an aggregation of capital but also brings together a wide spectrum of managerial resources. The inflow of foreign capital, therefore, could be favored on the following counts:[18]

1. Increased efficiency in resource allocation through international capital movements and the resulting increase in real income in the recipient country;
2. Promotion of capital accumulation in the receiving country;
3. Improvement in the balance of payments in favor of the recipient country through inflow of capital;
4. External economies for the host country (e.g., the spread of new technology, new management techniques, etc., to the domestic firms) generated by the richness of the managerial resources of the foreign firms.

Combined with the problems of foreign exchange shortages, lagging technology, and the lack of capital stock faced by Japan for quite some time in the immediate postwar period, inviting foreign capital could have been an easier way out for Japan. Why, then, did Japan not avail itself of this alternative? It is possible to enumerate sufficient reasons justifying regulation of foreign capital inflows.

First, the available international data do not give a clear idea as to the extent of benefits from the four positive elements mentioned above in the context of inflow of foreign investment.[19] For example, the improvement in international payments, mentioned under (3) above, has been a short-term phenomenon and the repatriation of profits can even result in the worsening of the balance-of-payments in the long run.

Second, if the actual foreign investors are the "monopolistically superior" international oligopolies, it may result in an outflow of monopoly rents generated through the foreign firms' control over pricing in the domestic markets. Although a detailed discussion of the problem of transfer of monopoly rents is left for Chapter 9, it can be easily visualized that such a drain of resources would invariably result in an international income distribution unfavorable to the recipient country. Liberalization of foreign investment inflows facilitates transfer of monopoly rents to a foreign country by enabling direct penetration of the domestic markets by the foreign oligopolies.[20] Japanese markets would have been much more oligopolistic than they in fact are had Japan opted for developing its industries, such as automobiles and computers, with the help of foreign investment.[21] This could have resulted in an outflow of sizable amounts in the form of monopoly rents (this outflow takes the form of, for example, appropriation of a large proportion of the receipts of the subsidiaries as return on investment or payments to the parent company).

Third, the subsidiaries of foreign firms established through direct investment may not be as vigorous in technological and product development as the domestic industries, since such technological and product development in the case of subsidiaries is directed by the parent company abroad. To the extent this happens, the role of foreign subsidiaries in improving Japanese industrial structure would be minimized.

IV. Foreign Exchange Shortages and Export Promotion Policy

The postwar Japanese trade policies have been invariably guided by the considerations about solving the problem of foreign exchange shortages. The constraint that the available foreign exchange reserves imposed on economic reconstruction and development of postwar Japan, which was faced with the "vicious circle of foreign exchange shortages," namely, "raw material shortages→stagnating production→stagnating exports→foreign exchange shortages→difficulty in expanding raw material imports→raw material shortages," formed the raison d'etre for such a course of action.[22] An analysis of the trends in international balance of payments may be helpful for a better understanding of this point.

Table V shows a falling trend in Japanese foreign exchange reserves after the War up to the early 1960s. Had it not been for the surplus in transfer payments in the form of U.S. aid to Japan in the late 1940s and nontrade surplus arising out of the Special Procurements of the UN Forces as the Korean hostilities began in the early 1950s, the Japanese foreign exchange reserves would have been greatly depleted. This foreign exchange shortage continued to restrain the rate of growth even after the trade balance turned favorable in the 1960s.[23] In order to break this vicious circle, not only were exchange and import restrictions adopted in an effort to cut down the spending of scarce foreign exchange, as described earlier, but a series of export promotion measures, discussed below, were also undertaken to enhance accumulation of foreign exchange.

A system of priority financing of exports, an export promoting tax system, and an export insurance system were some of the tools in the authorities' policy kit for promoting exports.

The priority financing of exports (1946–1972) facilitated exports by advancing loans for production and processing of exportables during the period between signing of an export contract to cargo loading and for collection of cargo as well as export usance financing required after the

TABLE V

International Balance-of-Payments in Postwar Japan (annual average, million $)

	1946–52	1953–57	1958–64	1965–70	1971–72	1973–75	1976–79
Trade balance	Δ233	Δ 360	151	2,588	8,379	3,410	13,455
Exports	661	2,041	4,480	12,601	25,799	48,522	85,547
Imports	894	2,401	4,329	10,013	17,470	45,111	72,091
Invisible trade balance	100	211	Δ 304	Δ 1,239	Δ 1,810	Δ 4,927	Δ 7,202
Transfers	316	12	Δ 64	Δ 160	Δ 358	Δ 319	Δ 631
Current A/c balance	183	Δ 137	Δ 217	1,189	6,210	1,830	5,622
Long-term capital balance	Δ 8	23	116	Δ 670	Δ 2,784	Δ 4,639	Δ 7,384
Basic balance	175	Δ 114	Δ 101	519	3,426	6,476	Δ 1,762
Short-run capital balance	17	33	85	303	2,783	Δ 54	1,750
Overall balance	192	Δ 81	Δ 16	822	6,209	6,530	Δ 11
Changes in foreign exchange reserves	143	Δ 58	Δ 211	400	6,983	Δ 1,850	1,878
Financial balance	49	Δ 23	Δ 227	443	Δ 774	Δ 4,680	Δ 1,889

Sources: Keizai Kikakucho Chosakyoku [1972] and *Keizai Hakusho* (Economic White Paper), various years.

shipment of goods was made. To do this, the Bank of Japan rediscounted export bills at low rates of interest or provided loans to foreign exchange banks on the security of export bills. The rate of interest applied for discounting these bills was 1% to 2% lower (annually) than that applicable to general trade bills,[24] and the BOJ diverted 10% of its loans for export financing, which formed about 50% of the total export related bank lendings.[25]

The export promoting tax system provided direct incentives mainly in the form of deductions on export earnings (1953–1963), accelerated depreciation allowances for exports (1964–1971), and a system of deductions on incomes related to foreign transactions like technology (1959–), and indirect incentives in the form of reserves for development of foreign markets (1964–1972), and so on. These, however, lost their importance both qualitatively and quantitatively after 1972.

The export insurance system (1950–) contributed toward insulating exporters from risks involved in export transactions that could not be covered by the private sector and insurance companies.

Besides the policy measures discussed above, the Japan External Trade Organization (JETRO), established in 1954, has also been contributing to the export promotion activity by disseminating information necessary for the development of foreign markets. The tax system was perhaps the most effectively used instrument for promoting exports in the 1950s and 1960s, the period of rapid economic and export growth. Table VI presents figures on the reduction in gross tax receipts as a measure of the size of incentives provided by four major tax schemes designed to promote exports.[26] Even though the policy authorities were actively involved in export promotion, the figures reveal the incentives that were actually availed of to be no more than 1% of the total value of exports. The export subsidies in Korea, which was experiencing a high rate of economic growth in the postwar period based on a rapid expansion of exports, are also provided in the same table. A comparison with these figures leads us to a conclusion that achievements of the Japanese export policy were far from the initial expectations of the policy authorities.

If the effect of the export promotion policy is in fact so questionable, then how can one look for an explanation for the high rate of export growth in postwar Japan. This explanation can perhaps be found, though paradoxically, in the rapid expansion of domestic markets.

A rising share of heavy and chemical industries in domestic production during the process of industrialization in Japan seems to have been gradually translated into a rising share of exports, as is seen in Figure 6.1. A similar process, though not discussed here, can also be observed for individual products.[27]

TABLE VI
Effect of Export Promoting Tax System (million $, %)

Year	Revenues Lost on Account of Export Promoting Tax System (A)[a]	Revenues Lost Due to Special Tax Measures (B)	A/B	Amount of Exports (C)	A/C	Rate of Export Subsidies in Korea[b]
1953	13.1	162.5	8.0	1,275	1.0	—
54	11.1	191.7	5.8	1,629	0.7	—
55	9.7	259.4	3.7	2,011	0.5	—
56	12.5	264.7	4.7	2,501	0.5	—
57	20.8	204.2	10.2	2,858	0.7	—
58	34.7	197.5	17.6	2,877	1.2	2.3
59	27.8	229.7	12.1	3,456	0.8	2.5
60	31.9	280.8	11.4	4,055	0.8	1.9
61	30.6	284.7	10.4	4,236	0.7	6.6
62	59.7	349.4	17.1	4,916	1.2	16.5
63	65.3	471.1	13.9	5,452	1.2	15.1
64	66.1	596.7	11.1	6,673	1.0	12.8
65	68.3	613.3	11.1	8,452	0.8	14.8
66	72.5	650.3	11.1	9.776	0.7	19.0
67	71.6	635.8	11.3	10,442	0.7	23.0
68	104.2	720.8	14.5	12,972	0.8	28.1
69	139.7	879.2	15.6	15,990	0.9	26.1
70	210.8	1,040.8	20.3	19,318	1.1	27.8

Sources: Zeisei Chosakai (Tax System Council), [1972], p. 187; Keizai Kikakucho, *Keizai Yoran* (Handbook of Economic Statistics), various issues; C. R. Frank et al. [1975], pp. 70–71.

[a]Includes accelerated depreciation for exports, special deductions on overseas incomes, and reserves for opening up of overseas markets.

[b]Total export subsidies/total exports. Export subsidies include direct subsidies, domestic tax concessions, tax rebates on exports, and interest subsidies.

Industrial development leveraged on an expansion of domestic markets was made possible by the availability of a large internal market aided by government protection through import restrictions and regulation of foreign investment. A large internal market enabling accumulation of the learning effect, as discussed in Chapter 9, is necessary for the import control policies to be effective in fostering the indigenous industry. Japan satisfied these conditions, and the growth and development of such industries as automobiles, household electric appliances, pianos, and integrated circuits were sustained by domestic demand, and the products that developed in the process largely reflected the demand of Japanese consumers.[28]

The import control policy was sufficient to protect indigenous industry in Japan blessed with a large potential market. Linder (1961) and Vernon

(1966) pointed out that an intimate knowledge of consumer needs through a constant interaction with consumers is indispensable for effective product development and improvement. If it is so, domestically generated industrial development could be more effective, *ceteris paribus*, than the export-led industrialization.[29]

If the Japanese industrialization was domestically generated, was the export promotion policy meaningless? It is well known, as a corollary to Lerner's symmetry theorem, that a uniform rate of tariff on all imports accompanied by export subsidies at the same rate to all exports cancel each other out leading, in effect, to a free trade situation (Lerner [1936]). A wide range of commodities have been receiving export subsidies through the export bills acceptance system and the like in Japan. These, however, are considered to be of no policy value, as they diluted the effect of import restrictions.

But an evaluation of export promotion policy on the above lines is fraught with problems. In Lerner's symmetry theorem formulated in the context of a simple two-commodity world with one exportable and one importable good, export subsidies could not affect the pattern of trade. The only changes were in the volume of trade. But an export promotion policy does not affect just the quantity of exports but can also result in converting an importable or nontraded good into an exportable. If the policy of developing an industry with potentially competitive power into an export industry through subsidization and promotion can be encompassed into the fold of an export promotion policy, its effect can be important.

Itoh and Kiyono (1983) have shown that an export promotion policy conducive to shifts in trade pattern raises economic welfare in the exporter's own country. Furthermore, such an export promotion policy results in the same effect on the domestic economy as that of an import control policy. Our result differs from the standard trade theory on account of the shifts in trade pattern induced by export promotion policy. While analyzing the Japanese export promotion policy, it is important to take this effect into account. It would be difficult, under these circumstances, to ignore the effect of export promotion policy.[30]

To put it in a more concrete fashion, the shift in trade pattern mentioned above resulting from the export promotion policy in the form of a diversified export menu is intricately related to the development of heavy and chemical industries or the advancement of industrial structure discussed in Section 6.1. As pointed out there, the diversification of the Japanese export menu speeded up Japanese economic development, and if export promotion policy also worked in this direction, the economic welfare in the domestic economy could have risen.

V. Trade Friction and the Japanese Policy Response[31]

Trade friction has perhaps been the most urgent problem of the Japanese trade policy since the mid-1970s. This problem has been getting increasingly complicated, and the policy responses spelled out to deal with it have determined the main course of the Japanese trade policy in the 1970s. Since it is practically impossible to analyze the nature of trade friction fully within a limited space, we restrict ourselves to an investigation of the mechanism through which the problem arose, along with an evaluation of the Japanese policy response it has called forth mainly in the context of industrial goods.

While analyzing the structure of Japanese trade, one cannot fail to recognize that advancement in the Japanese industrial structure was one of the important factors in generating trade friction. Table VII presents figures on major commodities entering Japan-U.S. trade, and it can be easily seen that various Japanese industries made quick inroads into the American markets with the advancement in the Japanese industrial structure. This advancement in the industrial structure was also responsible, to a large extent, in making the distribution of trade gains favorable to Japan, as discussed in Chapter 9. This naturally implied usurpation of the U.S. and other countries' shares. It is difficult to substantiate this point quantitatively, but Itoh (1984) has shown that a diversification of the export menu accompanying the advancement in industrial structure in a large economy results in a contraction of the trading partner's share of gains from trade.

The advancement in the Japanese industrial structure and the resultant shift in the shares of various countries in the economic pie cannot be explained simply in terms of Japan's usurpation of other countries' shares. The relative economic prosperity of the United States in the 1950s up to the mid-1960s in contrast to other countries was due to the decisive superiority of American technology in industries whose products enjoyed a higher proportion in expenditure (automobiles, iron and steel, household electrical appliances, etc.). The exceptionally high level of income in the United States relative to other countries was consequent on the existence of such a huge technology gap (Krugman [1979]). The advancement in the Japanese industrial structure narrowed this gap and eroded the advantage held by the United States in industrial structure and technology.

The Japanese share of the gains from trade rose as its industrial structure advanced, but at the same time it became a source of trade friction with other countries, especially the United States. Generally, it is a sudden rise in exports within a short span of time rather than a gradual shift in the industrial and trade structure that kindles trade friction. A sudden jump in exports of a country, according to Haberler (1950) and others,

TABLE VII
Composition of Japan–U.S. Trade (thousand $)

Exports to the U.S.	1960		1970		1979		1979/60
Automobiles		2,164		536,039		8,245,727	3,810.4
Watches		584		22,124		188,814	323.3
Televisions	(1961)	1,721		264,838		232,025	134.8
Tape recorders		6,068		256,171		763,375	125.8
Desk-top electronic calculators		—	(1967)	2,561	(1978)	242,827	94.8
Motorcycles		9,928		280,076		888,104	89.5
Scientific and engineering equipment		18,923		—		1,327,093	70.1
Metal products		68,624		323,834		910,775	57.4
Synthetic fiber products	(1962)	3,542		135,447		152,444	43.0
Iron and steel		71,684		899,037		2,739,243	38.2

Imports from the U.S.	1960		1970	1979	1979/60
Wood products		18,337	517,791	2,297,108	125.3
Corn		11,190	75,006	1,018,537	91.0
Iron ore		12,760	48,859	254,059	19.9
Aircraft		40,904	245,174	716,189	17.5
Office equipment (including electronic computers)		30,597	—	530,131	17.3
Sorghum	(1962)	18,566	133,514	259,086	14.0
Soybeans		102,997	329,610	1,169,288	11.4
Coal		91,561	623,012	1,021,376	11.2
Wheat		62,982	173,698	612,599	9.7
Pulp	(1961)	27,779	64,197	224,082	8.1

Source: Nihon Kogyo Ginko [1981], *Kogin Chosa* (Industrial Bank Survey), No. 207.

seriously affects the economy of the trading partner, by causing structural unemployment as factor prices, especially wages, are sticky downward. A sudden rise in imports is detrimental not only for the industry concerned but also for the welfare of the economy as a whole. A case in point is the widespread structural unemployment in the American automobile-related industries resulting in part from a steep rise in the Japanese exports of passenger cars in the late 1970s and early 1980s, abetted by a shift in the domestic demand toward small cars.

Difficulties in industrial adjustment and consequent emergence of structural unemployment can provide sufficient justification for a policy to restrict sudden export spurts within a short period. The voluntary export restraints used a number of times by Japan can be justified under the following circumstances. It has been shown by Itoh and Ono (1982, 1984) that under oligopolistic conditions, voluntary export restraints or import quotas, as against tariffs, bestow price leadership to the producers in the importing country in a Stackelberg sense raising the price level above what would prevail under tariffs or other related measures.[32] The export-cartel effect of such restraints can be easily read from Table VIII, which presents figures on auto prices in the U.S. market while voluntary export restraints on Japanese auto exports were in force.

The rise in domestic prices concomitant on voluntary export restraints by the exporting country could have a redeeming feature for the importing nation as rise provides a respite from the factors resulting in structural unemployment (voluntary export restraints by the trading partner could have an overall favorable effect in the importing country if the social costs of structural unemployment overwhelm the benefits from lower import price to the consumers). For the exporting country also, the effect of such restraints may not be necessarily negative. A large export-cartel effect may also enable the producers in the exporting nation to partake in the profits arising out of export restraints. (Itoh and Ono [1982, 1984] show the profits of the exporters to be exceptionally large under oligopolistic conditions.) Thus, voluntary export restraints have sufficient justification as a second best solution in the short run when trade friction arises out of structural unemployment. With a slight difference, one could expect similar results from the minimum price maintenance policy as under the "trigger price mechanism" if the minimum price is set at an appropriate level.

TABLE VIII
Passenger Car Prices in the United States (Industry Survey) ($)

	Model	1980	1981	1982	1983	1984	Rate of Increase in Prices (%) 1980–83
Toyota	Corolla	4,698	5,458	6,138	6,138	6,498	30.7
	Crusader (Mk.II)	6,429	6,979	8,159	8,599	8,799	47.5
Nissan	Sunny	4,619	5,219	5,319	5,999	—	29.9
	Maxima (Blue Bird)	8,129	9,979	10,549	10,869	11,399	40.2
GM	Century (Compact)	5,446	7,094	7,141	9,002	—	65.3
	Citation (Subcompact)	5,153	6,282	6,399	6,934	7,046	34.6

Source: Asahi Shimbun (Asahi Daily News), October 19, 1983. (Evening Edition).

Besides the export (import) control measures discussed above, a subsidy policy facilitating factor movements among industries can also achieve industrial adjustment. Even though such direct policy intervention might become necessary at some stage of industrial adjustment process, the effectiveness of such a policy in mitigating structural unemployment without recourse to short-run trade restraints is suspect.[33] Trade control measures, such as voluntary export restraints, on the other hand, must be short-run measures only and a switch to an active industrial adjustment policy becomes necessary. Furthermore, politically distributed export quotas under voluntary export restraints could result in inefficiency and if these restraints are in force for a long time, this inefficiency may accumulate and cause the industry to lose vitality.

The Japanese trade pattern, which is quite different from that of other countries, is perhaps another reason for the aggravating Japan–U.S. and Japan–EEC trade friction. The ratio of finished product imports to total imports is seen to be far lower in Japan than in other developed countries as depicted in Table IX. It reflects Japan's high dependence on foreign sources for the supply of natural resources. Sharp rises in the share of oil imports to the total following the two oil shocks in the 1970s have also been responsible for keeping the ratio of imports of finished products to the total at a low level.

This feature of the Japanese import structure has resulted in an export surplus with developed countries and an import surplus with resource-rich countries. A trade pattern based on the zero bilateral balances is basically inefficient and more so in the case of a specialized economy like Japan. Too much concern with bilateral balances is unwarranted, but the

TABLE IX
Ratio of Finished Products in Total Imports by Country

	Year	U.S.	Total	EEC Intraregional	EEC Interregional	Japan
Product Import Ratio A[a]	1970	67.0	61.2	75.5	46.0	31.7
	75	54.3	56.5	72.8	39.9	19.4
	80	51.8	57.5	71.8	42.8	21.7
Product Import Ratio B[b]	1970	73.2	67.9	79.1	54.4	39.9
	75	75.7	70.1	77.4	59.5	37.1
	80	80.5	74.6	79.8	67.1	44.9

Source: Nomura Sogo Kenkyujo, [1983].
[a]Product Imports (SITC:5,6,7,8)/Total Imports(SITC:0-9).
[b]Product Imports (SITC:5,6,7,8)/Total Imports(excluding SITC:3).

abolition of unnecessary import restrictions on finished products is necessary. (As pointed out in Section II, the effective rate of protection on various products in Japan fell rapidly and a low ratio of finished product imports to the total due to tariff escalation may not be true any longer.[34]

Abstracting from the political nature of trade friction based on narrow national interests, distribution of economic gains can be seen as an important source of trade friction between Japan and other countries. Determination of distributive shares of different countries is always problematic but two factors could specially aggravate such conflicts. The first of these is the presence of imperfect markets such as monopolies or oligopolies, and the other, which is related to the first, is the presence of scale economies (cf. Chapter 10 of this book for a detailed discussion concerning this point). In this sense, it seems inevitable that oligopolistic and high technology industries are prone to economic friction. This point is discussed briefly below.[35]

One could easily cite a number of industries that have resulted in an inflow of monopoly rents from abroad at various stages in Japan's postwar industrial development.[36] As long as the suppliers do not act as price-takers, a shift in the competitive conditions between domestic firms and foreign firms would definitely result in a transfer of monopoly rents. This could result from a withdrawal of foreign producers from Japanese markets as much as from Japanese penetration of foreign markets. The transfer of monopoly rents reduces the overall surplus in the competing country's economy, causing a conflict of interest regarding the distribution of monopoly rents at the industry level as well as between nations.

The presence of strong scale economies is another factor that can aggravate trade friction. The industries in which R & D and learning effect are important can also be included in the same category, as discussed in Chapter 10, the Japanese IC industry being a case in point. Without delving in on the details of the analysis developed in Chapter 10, we may say that in the presence of scale merits the trade pattern of a country, with the economic welfare of the country depending on it, is determined by policy intervention and/or historical processes.[37] The charges of using "industrial targeting"[38] in the case of the IC industry in Japan, without commenting on its validity, are thus theoretically plausible. In the case of industries with scale economies and high economic benefits to the producer nations, the government can raise economic welfare by subsidizing the domestic producers in that industry. Since this rise in economic benefits to the subsidizing country is achieved at the cost of other countries, it raises the possibility of conflict over the share of the pie at firm as well as national levels. Policy support therefore becomes necessary for achieving an optimal marginal pricing principle in the context of industries with high learning effect and R & D. The criticism of Japanese policy to subsidize the IC and computer industries, in this light, is unwarranted. At the same time, if subsidies in one country are exceptionally large as compared to those in other countries, it can result in an inequitable distribution of gains from trade among countries. As trade in industries with scale merits is normally in a disequilibrium, different national interests need to be accommodated.

Notes

1. For example, see Tsusansho [1964], pp. 238–241.
2. Foreign exchange fund allocations (FA) and foreign exchange fund automatic allocations (AA), under the foreign exchange budget system (1949–1963), formed the core of import restrictions in the 1950s. They were replaced by the import quota (IQ) system and the automatic approval (AA) system in 1964 when Japan became an Article 8 country in the IMF. See Kojima and Komiya (1972) on these nontariff barriers.
3. Because foreign exchange allocations depended on export performance, it was termed a "link system." Most importantly, the foreign exchange disbursements for the import of raw materials were linked to the export performance of a commodity with an objective to promote exports, as will be discussed later.
4. The tariff rate imposed on competitive import goods with an express purpose of protecting domestic industry is termed the "nominal rate of protection" (NRP), while the increment in rewards to the primary factors of production or value added resulting from the imposition of tariff over its free trade value is termed the "effective rate of protection" (ERP). This distinction is important, as nominal tariffs would, if the raw materials and intermediate goods required in the production of the import competing commodities directly or indirectly are also covered by tariffs, overstate the rate of protection by the amount of tariffs on these imports. Since the degree of industrial protection is measured by the extent of distortion in allocation of resources as compared to that under free trade, it is the ERP, including the negative protective effect arising out of tariffs on intermediate imports, that is the economically useful concept.
5. Watanabe [1959], pp. 45–46.
6. The difference between the actual and the apparent rates of protection to the sectors involving higher levels of processing gradually vanished as the Japanese industries became competitive internationally and increased exports during the late 1960s.
7. For trade friction, see Section V.
8. See Chapter 12 for the automobile industry.
9. See Chapter 13 for the textile industry.
10. See Section IV for foreign exchange shortages.
11. See "Shihon no Jiyuka ni Tsuite" (Liberalization of Capital), the materials provided by Shihon Jiyuka Taisaku Tokubetsu Iinkai (Special Committee on Capital Liberalization) (formed 1967) in its first meeting (February 15, 1967). (The materials have been summarized in *Gaishi Donyu Nenkan* (Import of Foreign Capital Yearbook) [1967], pp. 6–7).
12. Cited from *Gaishi Donyu Nenkan* [1965], p. 11.
13. Cf. *Gaishi Donyu Nenkan* [1965]. For a counter argument, see Komiya (1975).
14. OECD (1967).

15. Adopted in 1956, the system fully liberalized purchase of a fixed amount of stock, not accompanied by foreign exchange transfers, by the United States and "other specified nationalities." The so-called "yen-based firms" established under the system were mostly 100% foreign capital companies like Coca Cola (1957), Pepsi Cola (1959), Esso-Standard (1961), Mobil (1961), Olivetti (1961), and Hoescht (1962). IBM was not a "yen-based company," but it had established a fully owned subsidiary in 1950. Cf. OECD (1967).

16. Texas Instruments applied for a license to establish a fully owned subsidiary to produce semiconductors, specially ICs, in 1964, but MITI refused to grant permission until 1967, in order to protect the Japanese electronic parts industry. Even this delayed approval was granted only if Texas Instruments agreed to (1) a 50–50 joint venture with a Japanese company; (2) disclosure of all the patents held by Texas Instruments; (3) production adjustment for a specified period after establishment. Cf. *Gaishi Donyu Nenkan* [1967], p. 3.

17. While holding technology import payments down to under $30,000 (Ministerial Ordnance concerning Control of Trade and Non-trade Transactions, 1963), MITI also widely publicized the type of technology desired. This was designed to get hold of advanced foreign technology in industries like chemicals, metallurgy, machinery, aircraft, electrical machinery, and the like, which formed the basis of the "advanced industrial structure," at as low a cost as possible. Cf. OECD (1967) and Krause and Sekiguchi [1976], p. 454.

18. For example, see Lindert and Kindleberger [1982], Caves [1982].

19. Cf. Caves [1982].

20. For monopoly rent, see Chapter 9 of this volume.

21. A rise in the degree of concentration has been actually observed in the developing countries receiving foreign investment. See Lall (1978) and Caves (1982).

22. For example, see *Tsusho Hakusho* (White Paper on International Trade) of the mid-fifties and Tsusansho (1980).

23. The belief that balance-of-payment deficits acted as a constraint on economic growth is clearly reflected in the financial stringency measures of 1957, 1961, and 1964. See Kosai and Ogino [1984], Chapter 2.

24. Nihon Ginko (Bank of Japan), *Honpo Keizai Tokei* (Economic Statistics of Japan) and *Keizai Tokei Nenpo* (Economic Statistics Annual).

25. Keizai Kikaucho [1972], p. 339.

26. Only the direct subsidies have been considered here. As for the role of the export promoting tax system including the effect of interest subsidies and other tax measures believed to have contributed indirectly to export promotion, see Chapter 5. The subsequent comparison with the Korean export subsidy ratios, which includes indirect subsidies as well, is not entirely satisfactory in this ssense. The conclusions, however, would not change much as the export subsidy ratio for Japan, including the indirect subsidies, was not exceptionally high in the rapid growth period.

27. C. Johnson [1982] notes: "the only industries in which we have seen export increases induce a production increment—instead of the other way round—are transistor radios and perhaps cameras," p. 230.

28. It is contended that the Japanese IC industry developed on the basis of demand for desk calculators.

29. The *ceteris paribus* assumption, more often than not, becomes quite important. In the case of countries such as Korea, Taiwan, and Singapore, which lack sufficiently large internal markets, export-led growth is the only way out. In the case of standardized

products, the interaction with consumers loses its importance and the export-led growth strategy may be effective.

30. In the presence of imperfectly competitive markets, export promotion policy can be justified on completely different grounds. Cf. Chapter 9 of this volume and Itoh [1984] for this point.

31. For a detailed analysis of the argument presented in this section, see Itoh [1984].

32. Bhagwati [1965] has made a similar point. For an economic analysis of voluntary export restraints and the trigger price mechanism, see Itoh [1984].

33. If the stagnating industries are more labor-intensive than the others, a policy enhancing interindustry factor movements could result in an overall rise in unemployment (cf. Neary [1982]). Mussa (1982) points out that policy intervention may be unnecessary if prices are flexible and people hold rational expectations, but these assumptions seldom hold in reality.

34. The lack of space forces us to leave out the discussion of the size of current-account surplus in Japanese balance-of-payments as a source of trade friction. See Komiya [1983] for details on this point.

35. Cf. Itoh [1984] on subsequent points.

36. Measurement of the size of monopoly rents in individual markets could be both interesting and useful. The following is the stance taken by MITI on color films during the Japan–U.S. trade negotiations as noted in Yanagida (1983).

"Mr. Avery, you have pointed out that liberalization could benefit Japanese consumers through lower prices as the U.S. holds a superiority in color films, but are you aware of the prices at which Kodak color film is being sold world over? It is costlier in Australia and cheaper in W. Germany as compared to its price in Japan. Why has a consumer to pay such different prices for the same film? . . . It is because in absence of competing firms in Australia it is being sold in Australia at a profit maximizing price. In the case of Japan, the 30% liberalization ratio coupled with the presence of competitors in Fuji and Sakura, has kept the prices a little lower. Strong competition in W. Germany makes it still cheaper there. Mr. Avery has been emphasizing "optimum production theory" but selling at maximum prices in the absence of a rival follows economic logic. Is the U.S. global enterprise not following such a strategy?"

37. Cf. Itoh (1984) for details.

38. See Semiconductor Industry Association, [1983].

CHAPTER 7

Technology Policy

AKIRA GOTO

Department of Economics
Seikei University
Tokyo, Japan

RYUHEI WAKASUGI

Department of Economics
Shinshu University
Matsumoto, Japan

I. Research and Development, Technological Change, and Economic Growth in Postwar Japan

Technological progress has been called the engine of growth. To use this somewhat overused metaphor, this engine seems to have worked in an excellent fashion in Japan. In a well-known study, Denison and Chung (1976) estimated that "advances in knowledge" accounted for 1.97% of the 8.8% growth in national income between 1953 and 1971, so that its contribution, including that of technological progress, to the Japanese economic growth was 22.3%.

It goes without saying that technological progress, far from being manna from heaven, requires various inputs and a proper environment. The factors leading to rapid technological progress and their contribution to rapid economic growth can be summarized in the following three points.[1]

The first of these points is the important role played by technology imports. Japan was shut off from technological developments in the West immediately before and during the Second World War, resulting in lower technological levels as compared to the West over a wide range of activities. According to Ohkawa and Rosovsky (1973), Japan suffered a dual technological gap in this era. The industries that developed just before and during the Second World War, like household electrical appliances, were nonexistent in the immediate postwar Japan, and the technological gap here was substantial. Even in the case of industries such as iron and steel and textiles, which had shown development in the prewar period, the wartime isolation resulted in Japanese technology lagging far behind the latest technology. In order to fill this dual gap, Japanese industry was engaged in importing technology already developed in the West. The contribution of technological change to economic growth under such circumstances would naturally be exceptionally high and the growth rate itself turned out to be very high.

The following two points, however, need careful attention while evaluating the role of imported technology. First, it is difficult to measure directly, the "size" of the role played by imported technology, but if the share of manufacturing production arising out of the use of imported technology to the total can be used as an indicator, it was around 10% in 1960.[2] Again, the share of foreign technology in equipment investment was about 15% at its peak in 1958. Whether these indicators are proper measures of the "size" of the role played by or the "degree of dependence" on imported technology is still open to argument. However, it must be emphasized that overestimation of this role may result in a lopsided understanding of Japanese technological progress. Second, there is a serious flaw in the simplistic logic in the argument that given a technological gap it is possible to raise the rate of growth through import of preexisting technology from abroad. According to this logic, a country should be able to grow faster the more backward it is. But among the backward countries that have actually employed, or are in the process of employing, imported technology, few have experienced high growth, and none has been able to match the Japanese achievement through an effective use of imported technology. The concept of "backwardness" does not provide a complete explanation of this process, and Kuznets' (1968) concept of "social capacity" to absorb and assimilate modern technology needs further research in this context. This paper is an attempt in this direction.

A second feature of Japanese technological progress has been the scale of research and development (R&D) effort undertaken indigenously. For example, R&D expenditures in real terms in 1942 were the same as in 1959.[3] In terms of percentage to national income, the Japanese R&D expenditures in 1959 were higher than those in France, slightly lower than in West Germany, but quite low when compared to the United States or United Kingdom. Vigorous R&D activity undertaken since before the War and the resultant high level of science and technology, besides making possible an efficient transfer of western technology, also laid foundations for creative R&D activity. The Japanese R&D activity has resurged since then and has, in terms of the inputs directed toward this activity in recent years, attained a level similar to or even higher than that of the western countries. For example, R&D expenditures stood at ¥5881.5 billion in 1982, 3.5 times that of 1965 (in real terms), higher than in the United Kingdom, West Germany, and France and surpassed only by the United

States in the capitalist world. With the number of research personnel at more than 30 thousand, Japan is second only to the United States. Thus we find a rapid expansion in the Japanese R&D activity with Japan attaining a level considerably higher than that of the major developed countries other than the United States.

The third aspect of Japanese technological progress relates to the content of R&D. In the major countries active in large-scale R&D, almost one-half of the R&D costs are borne by their governments. In contrast, only one-fourth of the Japanese R&D costs are borne by the government, while the rest comes from the private sector. Flow of research funds, besides the pattern of research cost burden, also affects the direction of research activity. The flow of research funds in Japan is vertical rather than horizontal. The public sector and the private sector are largely independent of each other, with only weak links between them. Most of the government R&D funds go to national or public research institutions and universities. In 1982, a meager 2% of the total private-sector research funds in Japan were provided by the government, the rest being raised by itself, while over 30% of the private-sector R&D costs in the United States were borne by the federal government.

The sources and flow of research funds being an important influence on the efficiency and direction of R&D, Japanese R&D became highly sensitive to market signals. The projects that could show immediate results in the market received greater importance, thereby accounting for the high contribution of technological progress to economic growth. On the other hand, it biased resource allocation against projects in which social returns outweighed private returns that were not reflected in market signals. Finally, the low intersectoral transfer of funds and the by and large self-financing of R&D in the private sector, while helpful in avoiding the costs of project selection and management accompanying R&D based on external funds, resulted in a rush for R&D in overlapping lines of research by a large number of firms.

In the above discussion, we have tried to put the issues involved in the R&D–technological progress–economic growth relationship in a proper perspective, and in what follows, we try to examine, in detail, the impact of the government policies aimed at the promotion of technological progress and the problems involved therein. The government's role in terms of its share in research funds, as pointed out earlier, was comparatively small, but as the government can affect the R&D activity and technological progress of a nation in various ways, the role calls for a more detailed analysis. In Section II, we seek the why (and why not) of the necessity for the government support of R&D and technological progress. Section

III focuses on the government policy for R&D, and Section IV discusses some implications of these policies.

II. Economic Rationale Underlying Government Support of R&D Activity

Before analyzing how the government influenced R&D and hence technological progress in practice, let us have a look at why government support of R&D activity is necessary. The R&D activity of a firm, just like its investment and sales promotion activities, is also guided by the profit motive. Why, then, are public support and assistance deemed necessary in the case of R&D? The argument for government support of R&D is usually based on the following three points.[4]

First, the government, as the sole supplier of such public goods and services as public health and sanitation, national defense, and so on is responsible for maintaining the quality and controlling costs of these public goods and services. Furthermore, on the demand side, the government is in a position to assess public wants. It is in order to fulfill this role and to help in technological materialization of public wants that the government assistance to R&D is considered necessary. Technology related to public health and national defense is representative of this category.

Second, it is contended that the government should foster R&D activity where social benefits outweigh private benefits. The logic underlying this reasoning, led by Arrow (1962), can be summarized as follows: Arrow views R&D as production of technological knowledge and information. The public-good characteristics of information makes it impossible for its producers to appropriate all the benefits entailing such production, thereby leading to an underinvestment of resources in R&D activity. Furthermore, R&D activity is bedeviled by uncertainty as to its costs, chances of success or failure, and time required for its fruition. Left to market forces, sufficient amounts of funds will not be invested in such activity, even if the R&D activity itself is highly desirable, unless there is a way to shift the risk completely. Finally, the indivisibilities and minimum optimum scale that characterize R&D activity imply exclusion of firms below a certain minimum size from this activity, resulting in underinvestment of resources. As allocation of resources to R&D falls short of the socially optimum level, government aid to R&D activity is deemed necessary.

A third area in which government support is considered to be justified is basic scientific research where positive externalities and low direct economic value of research leads to an underinvestment of resources.

These arguments, however, are controversial, and it has been argued that there could in fact be an over- rather than underallocation of resources in R&D. The issues involved are varied and only a brief summary of major points is presented in the subsequent discussion.

First, as against the argument that the government, as the sole supplier of public goods, should support R&D in order to keep the quality and cost of public goods at a proper level, there is a counter argument that there is no clearcut logical relationship between the maintenance of the quality and cost of public goods at a proper level and the government's obligation for R&D support. Even if the government is responsible for maintaining public health and sanitation, it does not necessarily justify government support of R&D in all inputs needed for producing these services. Firms would engage in R&D activity necessary for obtaining government's procurement orders and there is no convincing reason as to why this R&D should be generally supported by the government. As long as competition among the firms vying for the government's procurement orders promotes R&D and guarantees a reasonable quality and costs, government support of R&D in public goods-related industries is unnecessary.

Second, the market failure–underallocation of resources argument for compensatory government support of R&D has also been questioned. For example, Demsetz (1969) provides a thorough and convincing rebuttal of Arrow's (1962) argument. It is not possible to discuss the issue in detail here, but Demsetz contends that if information is not complete and there are positive transaction costs involved, it is not possible to judge the superiority or inferiority of government intervention in the event of market failure unless a proper analysis of all other possible alternative institutional arrangements is carried out. Government support to R&D is beset with a host of other well-known problems as well. The selection and supervision involved in deciding on the extent of support, the types of projects, and which firms are suitable for governmental support involves huge costs. According to Link (1977), Eads (1974), and others, political considerations such as vote buying get inadvertently interlinked with the distribution of public research funds. The widespread prevalence of market imperfections provides a convenient rationale for using government resources for personal gains. The market fails, but the government may also fail. Market failures thus do not necessarily justify government intervention.

Furthermore, resources to R&D may not be necessarily underallocated. If the leading inventor of a product or production technique as a result of R&D effort is in a position to reap rich dividends and the game is governed by competitive rules it might result in excessive investment of resources in R&D activity.[5] In the case of oligopolistic industries where nonprice competition is known to be pervasive, excessive R&D for trivial product differentiation may take place. Finally, knowledge and information producers could reap rich rewards by speculating on the basis of knowledge or information in their possession. The contention that producers of knowledge and information cannot fully realize the benefits accompanying such activity therefore is not necessarily true.[6]

The argument for government support of basic research seems to be relatively robust. But, usually it is difficult to delineate the three stages of R&D activity—basic, applied, and developmental—neatly; this is especially so in advanced technology industries. While acknowledging the need for government support of basic research, it may be pointed out that in the absence of any objective basis to determine the nature of research projects, government support may end up upholding research in areas arbitrarily designated as basic by the government or other public organizations.

As is clear from the above discussion, it is difficult to build up an unambiguous case for government support of R&D activity in general. The situation would differ with the type of R&D undertaken, competition among organizations undertaking R&D activity, institutional arrangements regarding industrial property rights, and so on. A debate over whether R&D activity would invite *a priori* an over- or underallocation of resources is bound to prove unproductive.

Measurement of the rate of return on R&D investment may perhaps provide some positive indications in this context and there have been some attempts to measure this rate in the United States and Japan. Including our results, presented in the appendix, all the studies show uniformly a very high rate of return. The persistently high rate of return on R&D investment may point to the need for additional transfer of resources into this activity. It is, however, important in this context, as pointed out above, to concentrate on the distribution of R&D resources over different types and areas of R&D rather than on the total amount of resources invested in R&D.

III. Policies Promoting Industrial Technology

The government policies affecting R&D activity, although many and varied, can be classified under two broad heads. First, there are policies that are directly targeted at R&D and technological progress and, second, there are policies that are meant primarily for achieving some other policy objectives but have a far-reaching impact on R&D and technological progress. The former set includes measures that support R&D activity, while the latter covers the macro policies like fiscal and monetary policies, antimonopoly policy, various types of regulations, and so on. Though we will concentrate primarily on the former set of policies, it does not imply in any way that the latter group of policies is unimportant. Technological progress demands a suitable environment and the policies included in the latter group have an important role in building an environment conducive to technological progress. We do not go into an analysis of this aspect below, not only because of space limitations, but also because of our subscription to Nelson's (1982a) optimistic view that an effective functioning of these policies in the area of their prime interest (e.g., proper functioning of the economy, maintaining competitive conditions, etc.) automatically generates an environment conducive to technological progress. Thus, in what follows, we concentrate on the technology policy in a narrow sense.[7]

Before analyzing the technology policy in its narrow interpretation, a brief discussion of some of the policies that were designed primarily for other purposes but were also effective as a tool of technology policy would not be out of place. The Foreign Capital and Foreign Exchange Control Laws are representative of this category. These laws were enacted basically to economize the use of persistently scarce foreign exchange but had a far-reaching impact on technology imports as well. Technology import licenses, using precious foreign exchange, were allowed preferentially to industries expected to contribute to heavy and chemical industrialization and attain comparative advantage as future export industries. Within the industries, the licenses were granted to the firms with a high promise of developing into foreign exchange earners as future exporters by embodying the imported technology in equipment investment.

Discriminatory treatment under these laws had a dual effect on technology imports. First, it had a restraining effect on technology imports, which is clear from the figures for average annual technology import agreements rising from a mere 103 per annum in 1950–1959, to 469 per year in 1960–1967 when the Foreign Capital Law was relaxed, to 1,061 in 1968, and 1,154 in 1969 when liberalization took effect. It is, however, also pointed out in a number of case studies that the restraining effect of the Foreign Capital Law was not very important, at least in the case of large firms above a certain minimum scale and technical level as these firms were in a position to get their desired technology imports, although with some delays.[8]

A check on royalty payments was another area in which these laws proved effective. The number of firms importing a given technology was restricted to a few either through "adjustments" amongst the Japanese firms or through the policy authorities' "guidance" to check a rise in payments that competition among the importing firms might have entailed.

Peck and Tamura (1976) found a general rise in royalty payments in the postliberalization period. Lynn (1982) points out that royalty payments on import of the oxidation process for steel production from Austria were held down to under 1 cent per ton for Japan through an agreement between MITI and the industry, while the U.S. firms paid up to 35 cents per ton for the import of the same technology.[9] The temporary restrictions on the number of firms importing a given technology within the framework of the Foreign Capital Law added to the bargaining power of the purchasers, enabling them to import technology at lower prices.

The tools of direct technology policy consisted of: (1) support of R&D in the form of subsidies, preferential tax measures, and the supply of low-interest funds through government financial institutions;[10] (2) setting up of national and public research institutions; (3) setting up of mining and manufacturing technology research associations; and finally, (4) the commendation system. We take these up one by one below.

A. Support of Research and Development Activity

Besides direct subsidies to R&D activity, reductions on and exemptions from tax payments under preferential tax measures, as well as reduction in interest burden due to low-interest loans extended by public financial institutions amounting to loan times the difference between the market rate of interest and that charged by the public financial institutions, can also be considered as subsidies in a broad sense. Table I presents time-series data for subsidies, in this broad sense, and private expenditures on R&D and technology imports. The figures reveal that while these subsidies accounted for over 5% of total research expenditure and technology import payments during the first half of the 1960s, a crude index of R&D input, the proportion fell to under 3% in the late 1970s. As for the composition of subsidies, preferential tax measures seem to have been more important in the 1960s, with direct subsidies (defined in narrow terms) replacing them in the 1970s.

1. Preferential Tax Measures

The preferential tax measures can be divided into two sets: those promoting investment in R&D and those promoting import of foreign technology. Items (i)–(iii) below represent the former while items (iv) and (v) fall in the latter category.

(i) *Special depreciation allowances on machinery for experimental research and development of new technology.* The former was adopted in 1952 and the latter in 1958. The systems allowed accelerated depreciation

TABLE I
Trends in R&D Subsidies (¥100 million)

Year	Subsidies[a]	Preferential Tax Measures[b]	Low-Interest Loans[c]	Total (A)	Research Funds plus Payments for Technology Imports	A/B (%)
1957	4	38	—	42	426	9.86
58	8	61	—	69	498	13.86
59	7	79	—	86	1,179	7.29
60	7	91	—	98	1,586	6.18
61	8	124	—	132	2,054	6.43
62	8	122	—	130	2,208	5.89
63	7	123	—	130	2,557	5.08
64	9	165	—	174	2,998	5.80
65	31	133	—	164	3,120	5.26
66	16	39	—	55	3,618	1.52
67	35	115	—	150	4,656	3.22
68	75	153	2	230	6,366	3.61
69	103	162	5	270	7,603	3.55
70	110	191	9	310	9,784	3.17
71	185	215	12	412	10,653	3.87
72	210	128	10	348	12,211	2.85
73	271	243	13	527	14,965	3.52
74	236	310	17	563	17,984	3.13
75	298	330	19	647	18,961	3.41
76	295	220	20	535	21,331	2.51
77	275	290	16	581	23,853	2.44
78	239	250	17	506	25,522	1.98
79	301	340	24	665	29,411	2.26
80	608	380	22	1010	35,190	2.87

[a]The total of research funds received from national and local public bodies including commissions; the data are from *Kagaku Gijutsu Kenkyu Chosa Hokoku* (Report on the Survey of Research and Development).

[b]The total of actual tax reductions resulting from various types of special tax measures related to R&D activity. The data are from the Tax System Council.

[c]Calculated as real subsidies on the basis of "indigenous technology development finance" by JDB as follows:

Real subsidy = balance of loans at year end × (1/12) [(monthly long-term prime rate) − (monthly interest rate on JDB loans)]

Loan balances since 1970 are actual figures, while for 1968 and 1969 the figures have been estimated using 1970 as a benchmark in the following manner:

Loan balance in the current year = actual loans in the period + loan balance at the end of the previous year.

and conferred special privileges in the form of allowing deferred payments on corporate taxes depending on the amount invested.

(ii) Tax deductions on experimental research expenditures. Instituted in 1966, this system allowed the firms to deduct a fixed proportion of their experimental research expenditures in the current year over and above the highest expenditures incurred in previous years (at present, 20% of the excess amount is deductible up to 10% of the firm's total corporate tax payments).

(iii) Special deductions on foreign technology transactions. The system, initiated in 1956, is still in force and allows the firms to include, in their expense account, a fixed proportion of payments received against supply of industrial property rights, know-hows, copyrights, and consulting services to clients abroad (the proportions are 28%, 8%, and 16%, respectively, at present up to 40% of the firm's income).

(iv) Reduction in withholding tax on fees for the use of important foreign technology. The system, adopted in 1953, was aimed at reducing withholding tax (10% in the beginning but raised to 15% later) on payments made to foreign corporations against import of technology. It was abolished in 1967 when a system of tax deductions on experimental research expenditures was adopted to promote development of indigenous technology.

(v) Tariff exemptions for import of important machinery. The system, set up in 1951, promoted import of foreign technology by allowing tariff exemptions on designated new or highly efficient industrial machines that were needed for Japanese economic development but could not be produced indigenously. The iron and steel industry had the largest number of designated products, followed by electric power generation equipment, paper, textiles, petroleum refining, and so on. The number of designated products fell after reaching a peak in 1954, and the system was reformulated in 1960 with the emphasis shifting from industrial development to anti-pollution measures.

Table II presents the amount of tax reduction, i.e., real subsidy, resulting from these special measures. The tax measures were instrumental in promoting R&D and technological progress in areas where the private sector would have entered eventually even in the absence of these measures rather than promoting specific R&D activity aimed at achieving predetermined policy objectives. These measures no doubt brought about rapid Japanese economic growth based on technological progress, but at the same time, research in selected fields where the government should have undertaken such R&D tended to be neglected.

Finally, Table II also reveals that, although promotion of technology imports played an important role in bridging the technological gap with

TABLE II
R&D Subsidies Emanating from Special Tax Measures[a] (¥100 million)

Fiscal Year	Grand Total	R&D Outlays				Import of Foreign Technology		
		Total	1	2	3	Total	4	5
1952	10	—	—	—	—	10	—	10
53	20	—	—	—	—	20	—	20
54	22	—	—	—	—	22	2	20
55	26	—	—	—	—	26	6	20
56	31	—	—	—	—	31	6	25
57	38	—	—	—	—	38	8	30
58	61	16	16	—	—	45	10	35
59	79	15	15	—	—	64	14	50
60	91	15	15	—	—	76	16	60
61	124	25	25	—	—	99	5	94
62	122	25	25	—	—	97	7	90
63	123	25	25	—	—	98	8	90
64	165	70	63	—	7	95	10	85
65	133	56	45	—	11	67	8	59
66	39	39	—	13	26	—	—	—
67	115	115	—	87	28	—	—	—
68	153	153	—	110	43	—	—	—
69	162	162	—	122	40	—	—	—
70	191	191	—	130	61	—	—	—
71	215	215	—	158	57	—	—	—
72	128	128	—	88	40	—	—	—
73	243	243	—	198	45	—	—	—
74	310	310	—	210	100	—	—	—
75	330	330	—	210	120	—	—	—
76	220	220	—	140	80	—	—	—
77	290	290	—	170	120	—	—	—
78	250	250	—	150	100	—	—	—
79	340	340	—	210	130	—	—	—
80	380	380	—	240	140	—	—	—

Source: Zeisei Chosakai [Tax System Council].

[a]The reductions in tax receipts resulting from special tax measures were treated as subsidy.

1. Special Depreciation on Machinery for Experimental Research and Commercialization of New Technology
2. Tax Deductions on Experimental Research Outlays
3. Special Deductions for Technology and other Foreign Transactions
4. Reduction in Withholding Tax in Respect to Use of Important Foreign Technology
5. Tariff Exemptions on Import of Important Machinery

the West in the immediate postwar period, the emphasis of public policy in the mid-1960s was already shifting to the promotion of indigenous R&D.

2. Subsidies and Research Contracts

The major items of the government subsidies and research contracts to firms for conducting R&D activity (in its narrow sense) can be enumerated as follows[11] (Table III).

*(i) Subsidies to R&D in important mining and manufacturing technology.*This was perhaps the most important subsidy for R&D before 1965, covering all mining and manufacturing. There was no policy discrimination by industry, as disbursements were approved on applications submitted by private firms in any industry. Its role diminished after 1965.

(ii) Research contracts on large-scale industrial technology R&D. The system, established in 1966, aimed at developing new technology and products in selected advanced technology fields by delegating R&D to the private sector. The research themes, though decided on by the government, reflected the needs of the private sector as well.

(iii) Subsidies for technological improvement. The system was adopted in 1967 to promote technological development in small- and medium-scale firms. The system is being effectively used by so-called "venture business" in recent years, despite the low ceiling on disbursements of ¥20 million per enterprise.

(iv) Subsidies to promote the development of computers and public transport equipment. These subsidies were instituted in 1972 and in 1968, respectively, to "protect and promote" and to "strengthen international competitiveness" of these industries.

(v) Research contracts and subsidies on R&D in energy technology. The system, adopted to promote R&D in energy technology after the oil shock of 1973, led to research in alternative energy sources.

(vi) Research contracts on next generation industrial basic technology. Initiated in 1981, the system selected and commissioned R&D on 12 themes in three areas—new materials, biotechnology, and new electronic devices. The reasons advanced for initiating such a system in industries like aviation and space, information processing, alternative energy sources, and bio-industry were long lead time, huge fund requirements, high risk, and the existence of the same type of projects in the western countries toward these areas.

The major target for R&D subsidies before 1965 was (i) above. The projects financed partly by these subsidies accounted for 15 to 40% of Japan's total research expenditures, resulting effectively in "pump-priming" of R&D activity in Japan. The system was applicable to all mining

TABLE III
Major Subsidies and Commissions to Private-Sector R&D (¥100 million)

1	2	3	4	5	6	7	8	9	10
1966	8	7	—			—	—	—	—
67	9	20	—			—	1	—	—
68	12	30	1			—	1	—	—
69	13	39	2			—	1	—	—
70	16	39	5			—	2	—	—
71	19	43	—			—	2	—	—
72	23	40	2			52	2	—	—
73	33	60	7			173	3	—	—
74	42	66	21			197	5	—	12
75	42	87	20			135	5	—	19
76	39	121	2			149	7	—	31
77	33	117	11			84	8	1	37
78	28	122	13			101	10	5	46
79	28	118	53		—	69	10	5	65
80	27	112	—	69	17	57	10	6	32
81	26	116	25	24	47	62	11	6	28
82	22	98	38	18	52	55	10	7	23

Source: Okurasho |Ministry of Finance|, *Hojokin Binran* (Handbook on Subsidies), various issues.

ªStated at ¥0.2 billion in 1955, ¥0.5 billion during 1956–60, ¥0.6 billion in 1961 and 1962, ¥0.7 billion in 1963 and ¥0.8 billion in 1964 and 1965.

1. Fiscal Year
2. Subsidies for R&D in Mining and Manufacturing Technologyª
3. Commissions for R&D in Large-Scale Industrial Technology
4. Commissions for R&D in Next Generation Basic Technology
5. Subsidies for Development of Public Transport Equipment
6. Subsidies for Developing Jet Engine for Passenger Aircraft
7. Subsidies for Promotion and Development of Computers
8. Subsidies for Technology Improvements
9. Subsidies for R&D in Energy Technology
10. Commissions for R&D in Energy Technology

and manufacturing industries and disbursements were granted upon application. Finally, since these subsidies were designed to meet a part of the firms' R&D costs, this system, just like the special tax measures, also accelerated R&D in areas where the private sector would have entered on its own instead of pursuing specific policy objectives in a selective fashion.

The importance of (i) gradually diminished after the mid-1960s, however, and the weight of other subsidies aimed at promotion of R&D in specific technologies and industries increased. Furthermore, the focus shifted to R&D in the technologically advanced industries like aircraft, computers, and alternative energy sources where both incentives and abilities for R&D were inadequate in the private sector.

3. Low-Interest Loans

The system was formulated to promote R&D by providing public funds at lower interest rates than the market rate. The reduction in interest payments because of interest differentials between the private and public financial institutions can serve as a conservative estimate of actual subsidies involved. The system was built on the loans provided by the Japan Development Bank and the Small Business Finance Corporation. The former began lending funds for "commercialization of new technology" in 1951 to which "heavy machinery development" financing was added in 1964. Financing of "commercialization of new machinery" was added in 1968 to complete the indigenous technology promotion finance system. The "financing for commercialization of new technology" was renamed "financing for development of new technology," bringing the experimental equipment also within its folds. The Small Business Finance Corporation also began lending for commercialization of indigenous technology to small- and medium-scale firms in 1970, and low-interest loans for experimental production of new machinery and its introduction on a commercial basis have also been provided.

These financing systems have basically promoted commercialization of the fruits of R&D rather than the R&D activity itself. But the process did strengthen incentives for R&D. The heavy and chemical industries, where investment was being actively undertaken, was the major beneficiary of these loans.

B. National and Public Research Institutes

Approximately half of the government research expenditures have gone to national, public, or private (nonprofit) research organizations or specially set up public corporations. These research organizations contributed in (1) carrying out basic research in areas closely related to industrial technology where universities were unable to help; (2) applied research in areas where testing the adaptability of the technology for industrial use required large-scale equipment; (3) helping in the transfer of technology to small- and medium-scale firms; (4) the development of antipollution technology, which was a public necessity and for which the private sector could not be relied on to conduct sufficient R&D and, (5) research concerning the development of standards and testing methods and norms.

Less than 20% of the research funds of these organizations have gone to basic research, while applied and development research have taken more than 40% each. This trend has only accelerated. Furthermore, these institutes maintain close ties with private firms and the kind of research undertaken at these institutes strongly reflects the needs of the private sector. The government has cooperated with and complemented private-sector R&D through these institutions instead of taking active leadership in conducting research in areas of public interest where markets could not be relied on to conduct such research. The collective research by the private sector, universities, and research institutes in the advanced fields of electronics, information processing, systems engineering, molecular engineering, and microbiotic engineering under the large-scale industrial technology R&D system is an obvious example. The complementarity of research being carried out in these institutes to that of the private-sector R&D is thus very clear.

A deeper look into the role of these organizations reveals that they complemented the private-sector R&D by providing the latter with information about the technical feasibility of particular types of technological development on the basis of their accumulated expertise in basic advanced research. The importance of this kind of information cannot be ignored in R&D. Further, these institutes formed the nucleus of a concerted research drive by the private sector and acted as a leader and arbiter among the firms as well, as will be discussed later in the context of Mining and Manufacturing Technology Research Associations. Finally, the institutes also complemented the private-sector R&D by testing and assessing its results.

The government R&D in specific mission-oriented areas was carried out through the establishment of special public corporations. In the case of nuclear power, the Japan Energy Research Institute and the Nuclear Fuel Corporation were established in 1956 (renamed the Power Reactor and Nuclear Fuel Development Corporation in 1967) to undertake R&D in areas ranging from technological development in the fields of nuclear power reactors, nuclear fuel, and reprocessing to their applications in accordance with the plan laid out by the Nuclear Power Commission. Similarly, the National Space Development Agency and the New Energy Development Organization were established for R&D in space development and energy fields, respectively.

These special corporations were set up as public corporations because public-sector R&D was considered more appropriate in these areas. Government investment in these bodies has been on the rise since 1970. The results of this R&D got percolated down to the private sector along with the active personnel exchanges that took place as the human resources for these institutions were drawn from the government, universities, and the private sector.

C. Mining and Manufacturing Technology Research Associations

The system, set up under the Mining and Manufacturing Technology Research Association Law, enacted in 1961, involved collective research by firms in specific areas. The research was conducted by pooling research workers and funds (in the form of grants rather than investments) into nonprofit Mining and Manufacturing Technology Research Associations. Besides the special depreciation allowances granted to the firms on funds thus contributed, preferential tax treatment was accorded to these associations. In all, 64 associations were established by 1983, out of which 45 are still functional.

Government support of collective research within a formal setup among a number of firms, as opposed to joint research by agreement among individual firms, was initiated in the United Kingdom in the form of Research Associations (RAs hereunder) from where it spread all over Europe.[12] RAs were set up at the industry level and received government subsidies. With some exceptions, these RAs were formed mainly in response to the technological problems faced by traditional industries consisting mainly of small and medium firms lacking the technological and financial ability to undertake R&D activity on their own.

As against this, Japanese research associations have been dominated by large firms and engaged in advanced technology research. The Japanese research associations have distinctive features in that, first, they were established to carry out research in specific areas and were dissolved as the objective was met (or if the theme lost its importance). Second, these associations were research-project-based rather than industry-based, permitting the firms to draw on a diversified technological base.

This system is, however, not always efficient and a large number of these associations met with only limited success. The most important drawback of this system lies in its impact on competition in R&D and in product markets. The two aspects, although intricately linked, are discussed separately for the sake of simplification.[13]

Since the fruit of collective research undertaken by research associations must be shared with other members, it could weaken R&D incentives of individual firms. In extreme cases, these associations could end up as R&D cartels[14] and thus impede technological progress. On the positive side, the research association system could minimize the negative effects arising out of overinvestment due to duplication of research in similar fields by a number of firms vying intensely for leadership in an industry as was discussed briefly in Section II.

In the context of research associations' impact on competition in product markets, one should be wary of the possibilities of collusion among the firms in the product markets as an extension of their association in R&D. In addition, such associations may put new entrants and nonmember firms in a disadvantageous competitive position.

An assessment of the impact of research associations on technological development in Japan is fraught with difficulties, but the following can be deduced from the discussion above. First, the system served as a focal organization to enable the individual firms to use resources of other organizations. Other organizations, here, imply government, national and public research institutes, other firms in the same industry, and suppliers of parts and equipment, while resources refer to research funds and research personnel. As for research funds, it was much easier for firms to obtain government subsidies for specific research projects in the name of a research association rather than for joint interfirm research. A large number of firms carried out their allotted share of the R&D project at their own companies even after organizing a research association. Had these firms undertaken the same research on their own, they might not have been able to avail themselves of government subsidies.[15] As for research personnel, in view of low labor mobility in Japan, including that of research personnel, the interaction among research personnel from national and public research institutes, other manufacturers within the industry, suppliers, and so on that took place under this system could have been important in its own way.

Second, research projects of these associations were mostly in the field of basic research or production of pilot experimental equipment where development of R&D competition would have been ruled out by the presence of extensive external economies. Hence, judging these associations in terms of their role in checking the flow of excessive investment of resources due to overlapping research by a large number of firms would be inappropriate. As collective R&D of the competitors in the form of research associations was confined to basic research and the production of pilot equipment in areas in which R&D competition would have led to under- rather than overinvestment of resources due to the presence of large externalities,[16] the research associations were effective in checking underinvestment rather than preventing overinvestment arising out of R&D competition with the help of government subsidies.

An association of firms for research purposes can easily expand into a competition-restricting collusion in the product markets, but in the case of Japan this effect seems to have been minimal due to the following reasons. First, as in the case of the VLSI Technology Research Association, the exposure to foreign competition restrained these associations from forming R&D cartels or restrict competition in product markets. Second, though collective research on comprehensive themes with wide coverage and requiring a long time span can, no doubt, result in restricting product-market competition, as pointed out in the guidelines of the Anti-Trust Law of the U.S. Department of Justice, research associations were confined to research on specific themes and were dissolved as the objectives were achieved. Therefore, opportunities for restricting product–market competition were few. Third, because the R&D activity was confined to basic research and production of pilot equipment, it left sufficient scope for the firms to exercise their individuality at the commercialization stage. Fourth, although the research was undertaken in the name of the association, the project was, more often than not, divided up among the member firms that carried out their share of the research at their own company's research facilities, reducing the possibilities of product-market collusion arising out of such interactions.

The research associations were effective in dealing with externalities accompanying R&D without restricting competition. The choice of a research project appropriate to the framework of research associations remains an important problem and an inappropriate choice may not only result in failure in meeting its objectives but may also bring the negative features associated with research associations into existence. The difficulty of effectively determining the suitability or unsuitability of particular research projects to this system beyond some general observations is perhaps the most severe problem to this system.

D. The Commendation System

Conferring commendations like the National Invention Merit Award or the Science and Technology Meritorious Services Medal served as incentives for research workers and firms to undertake R&D. Public recognition of new products or manufacturing processes that embody R&D is effective in giving them credibility, which puts the users' doubts regarding these products and production processes effectively to rest. This effect is specially important for small- and medium-sized firms. The commendations are also important in terms of the advertisement effect that they entail. According to one survey, the R&D incentives provided by the commendation system in the postcommercialization stage outweighed those of subsidies or tax preference measures and were lower only to those provided by the patent system.[17] The selection process for awards is no doubt problematic, but with the benefits of such a system being greater than the costs involved, the system merits careful attention.

IV. Conclusion

Technological progress played an important role in the rapid growth and structural change of the Japanese economy. It was pushed by vigorous technology imports and active R&D and pulled by rapid increases in demand, high rates of investment, and fierce competition among firms. The R&D activity was led by the private sector, with the government playing a supportive role. Various subsidies to R&D were of some substance up to the first half of 1960s, but in general, they were not very high. Policy intervention was mainly intended to support rather than replace the market mechanism. This resulted in promoting the kind of technological progress that was effective in bringing about rapid economic growth. The excessive emphasis that was placed on accelerating R&D in general in areas where the private sector would have eventually entered even in the absence of policy support, on the other hand, led to a neglect of R&D in areas needing policy support from the government, like those entailing high risks or where R&D was timeconsuming or where social returns exceeded private returns. The recent shift in policy goals from a general support of R&D to selective promotion of specific R&D projects draws attention from this point of view, but implementation of such a technology policy would perhaps have to face greater problems at this stage.

APPENDIX   Estimation of the Rate of Return on R&D Outlays

We attempt here to estimate the rate of return on R&D outlays. The specification of the model draws heavily on Terleckyj [1974] and Griliches [1980].

Let the production function be

$$Q = Ae^{\lambda t}L^{b}K^{1-b}R^{a} \tag{1}$$

where, Q is value added; A is constant; L is labor; K is capital except R; and, R is R&D capital (stock of technological knowledge, etc.).

Dividing (1) by $L^{b}K^{1-b}$

$$\frac{Q}{L^{b}K^{1-b}} = Ae^{\lambda t}R_{t}^{a} \tag{2}$$

The L.H.S. of equation (2) is nothing but total factor productivity (P). Differentiating with respect to time,

$$\dot{P}/P = \lambda + a\,(\dot{R}/R) \tag{3}$$

Since a is the elasticity of Q with respect to R, (3) can be rewritten as

$$\dot{P}/P = \lambda + a\,(\dot{R}/R) = \lambda + (dQ/dR)\,(R/Q)\,(\dot{R}/R) = \lambda + (dQ/dR)\,(\dot{R}/Q)$$

and hence,

$$\dot{P}/P = \lambda + vI$$

where, v is the marginal product of R&D capital (dQ/dR); I is the proportion of R&D outlay to total product (R/Q).

For actual measurement of the effect of government support of R&D, we used the following model:

$$\dot{P}/P = a + b_1\,(R_1/Y) + b_2\,[(R_2 + R_3)/Y] + u$$

where, R_1 is government R&D outlays going to the private sector; R_2 is payments for technology imports; R_3 is self-borne research outlays (private sector); and Y is value added.

The data sources are Sorifu (Prime Minister's Office) *Kagaku Gijutsu Kenkyu Chosa Hokoku* (Report on the Survey of Research and Development) for Rs; MITI's *Kogyo Tokei Hyo* (Census of Manufactures), industry volumes for Y; and unpublished estimates by Professor Masahiro Kuroda of Keio University for total factor productivity (we take this opportunity to thank him for his kind help).

The estimates were based on cross-sectional data by industry. The sample industries were foods, textiles, paper and pulp, publishing and printing, chemicals, petroleum and coal products, rubber, ceramics, iron and steel, nonferrous metals, metal products, machinery, electrical machinery, automobiles, other transport equipment, precision instruments, and miscellaneous manufacturing. Annual averages for 1976–1979 were taken for $\dot{P}/P;$ 1972–1975 averages were taken for R_1/Y and $(R_2 + R_3)/Y$ on an assumption that the time lag between R&D and its fruition is four years. The estimation result was as follows:

$$\dot{P}/P = -0.003 - 1.352(R_1/Y) + 0.393[(R_2 + R_3)/Y]$$

$$(0.469) \quad (0.259) \qquad (1.839)$$

$$R^2 = 0.196,\ F = 1.70$$

The coefficient of determination is low, presumably because productivity increases are dependent on variables other than R&D. The rate of return on the government R&D outlays is found to be negative, but the value is quite nonsignificant. The amount of government R&D outlays are only a fraction of the self-financed R&D outlays and payments for import of technology. It may be that the government research outlays are directed at basic research or research to meet other given public objectives so that their contribution in raising productivity may not be clearly reflected here. The coefficient of the self-financed research outlays and payments for the import of technology is positive and significant at the .05 level of significance. It shows that the rate of return on R&D outlays for technological progress by the private sector (self-generated research funds plus payments for technology imports) was fairly high at 39.3%.

Notes

1. For details see Peck and Goto [1981].
2. Based on Kogyo Gijutsu In [1964]. According to this source, even a 10% figure would be an overestimate of the "degree of dependence" as it includes items for which the Japanese firms had to enter formal import contracts, even though the technology was already known, in order to avoid infringement of licenses held by the foreign firms.
3. Kogyo Gijutsu In [1964].
4. Cf. Nelson [1982a], Link [1981], and Mansfield [1976].
5. Cf. Dasgupta and Stiglitz [1980a, 1980b], Loury [1979], Kamien and Schwarz [1982], and Barzel [1968].
6. Hirschleifer [1971].
7. Supply of technicians and technical education are important factors in the technological progress of a country. Although the discussion of technical education lies outside the scope of this study, its importance should not be lost sight of.
8. For example, cf. Uekusa and Nanbu [1973].
9. It may be pointed out in this context that actual steel production in Japan surpassed expected production by a large margin, which might also have contributed to the low royalty payments per ton.
10. Besides this, another possible alternative is credit guarantees by public institutions when firms borrow research funds from private financial institutions. In Japan, the Center for the Promotion of R&D Oriented Firms guarantees up to 80% of the obligations of small- and medium-sized firms engaged in R&D of new technology (the so-called venture businesses) borrowing R&D funds from financial institutions.
11. Subsidies and commission charges for contract research differ to the extent that, whereas the former are in the form of the government's support of private-sector activities that are properly in the private domain, the latter refer to the payments made to the private sector in lieu of engaging in activities that should have been undertaken by the government. When R&D is divided into three stages—basic research, applied research, and development research—the payments falling under the first stage are usually in the form of commissions and those under the second and the third categories are in the form of subsidies, but a clear demarcation of these stages is not possible. Furthermore, it is difficult to choose between undertaking R&D activity on a contract research basis or on a subsidy basis, as there are cases where the subsidy rate is 100% or the firms are throwing in their own funds for R&D, which is commissioned to them. It is only in the context of appropriation of the fruits of R&D that one can clearly distinguish between commissions and subsidies, since industrial property rights like patents are acquired by the government in the case of commissioned R&D activity.
12. For research associations in the United Kingdom, cf. Johnson [1971/72], and for those on the European continent, OECD [1965b].

13. When conceptualizing R&D as production of information, it is possible to treat it as any other good or service, but as our interest lies more in bringing out the major characteristics rather than generality of the discussion, we have treated these separately.
14. Quite well known is the case of collective research on exhaust control undertaken by the "big three" and AMC in the United States in which the research results had been proclaimed in line with those of the least advanced firm and thus came under questioning for the violation of the Sherman Act.
15. The VLSI research association has received ¥29.1 billion in subsidies.
16. For a discussion of externalities accompanying pilot plants and production of prototypes, see Weitzman et al. [1981].
17. Cf. Kikai Shinko Kyokai Keizai Kenkyusho [1981a].

CHAPTER 8

Industrial Policy and Technological Innovation[1]

Institute of Business Research
Hitotsubashi University
Tokyo, Japan

I. Introduction

The most appropriate way to look at Japanese industrial development since 1955 from the point of view of technological innovation and industrial policy is to divide the period into the following three phases.

The first phase corresponds to the decade of 1955 to 1964 following the postwar recovery. The plant-based industries producing basic materials such as iron and steel, chemicals, and electricity were the strategic industries[2] of this initial period of rapid growth. To realize economies of scale based on mass production technology was the major concern of the firms and industries. The discussions about industrial policy, therefore, also revolved around the weighing of the pros and cons related to organizational structures required for achieving these objectives (for example, the merger of firms).

The period from 1965 to 1973, just before the oil shock struck, forms the second phase. The automobile industry, the household electrical appliance industry, and other so-called assembly industries became the strategic industries in this period, and business strategy was geared to realize lower costs and better quality simultaneously through the learning process and development of organizational structures linking mass production and mass marketing. The industrial policy concern shifted gradually to distribution systems including wholesalers and retailers.

The period since the oil shock constitutes the third phase. The post-oil

INDUSTRIAL POLICY OF JAPAN   **205**   © Copyright 1988 by Academic Press Japan, Inc.
All rights of reproduction in any form reserved.

shock period is chosen as a separate period not because of any changes in industrial organization but because of the fact that a new pattern of Japanese technological innovation clearly emerged in this period. Moreover, such a development was directly relevant for a reorganization of the economy on the basis of modern high technology (for example, computerization of the iron and steel and chemical industries).

Industrial policy measures taken in the above three phases have been reviewed in Part I of this volume.[3] Following these, this chapter concentrates its attention on the rationale for government policy intervention in the process of technological innovation, and assesses the recent Japanese industrial policy related to high technology.

II. Characteristics of High Technology and Industrial Policy

A. High Technology Defined

High technology is normally defined as advanced technology requiring an intensive research and development effort. For example, in U.S. government publications and the like, the term *high technology* seems to have been used either as a generic term for information-and-communications technology covering semiconductors, computers, and communications or as a list of industries including pharmaceuticals, robotics, aircraft, biotechnology, space, optical fiber, computers (both hardware and software), semiconductors, and machinery components.[4] In Japan, microelectronics, biotechnology, and new materials (ceramics, amorphous, etc.) are normally included in high technology.[5]

A rigorous definition of the concept of high technology may not be a meaningful exercise to undertake. It suffices, for our purpose, to define high technology to be a technology that is R&D intensive[6] and "system oriented." The term *system oriented* here implies that individual elements of the technology are combined into a system and evaluated with respect to the function they fulfill within the whole system. In simpler terms, it is the package of technologies rather than individual technologies that is important. This restriction on the definition of high technology is necessary because of the following reason: R&D-intensive technologies can be those that are isolated and highly independent, as seen in specialized pharmaceuticals, but industrial policy is principally concerned with those high technologies that are strongly system-oriented as well as forming the basis of the new economic infrastructure.

B. The Development of High Technology

The development of a high technology, given the present technological conditions, is based on a continuous and cumulative process rather than on an abrupt breakthrough, and its commercialization is also an evolutionary process subject to natural selection in the market and organizations.

As has been proven by extensive research into the process of technological innovation conducted by Nelson and Winter (1982), Sahal (1981), and others in recent years, the system-oriented technology, as discussed above, can result only from a cumulative learning process as a system. Recent technological innovations, e.g., computers, clearly reveal that this process involves a large number of small innovations occurring over a wide range of time from the idea stage through the design to application stages. It is the accumulation of these small innovations that give rise to bigger breakthroughs.

The learning process as a system is what makes this accumulation effective. This learning process takes place in a comprehensive system encompassing a multitude of stages from improvement to creation, from basics to application, from design to testing, and from parts to assembly. This is because a proper interaction between stages and between parts, as well as informational feedbacks, forms a learning process that gives rise to cumulative innovations. This system, therefore, differs from the general linear model, from basic research to application and adoption, in that it is an evolutionary process that includes the iterative feedback process between different stages of research.

Furthermore, incremental innovations do not always imply improvements in existing technology. Efforts at commercialization of the fruits of research normally hit a bottleneck somewhere on the way, and most of the time, even when a pilot plant has succeeded, it is not easy to scale over this bottleneck. For example, in the case of voice recognition technology, even though machines that can recognize standardized voice patterns have already been developed, its application to capture actual voice patterns encompassing a wide variety of characteristics faces an impediment that cannot be overcome by piecemeal improvements and requires innovation based on some entirely new idea.

The process of technological innovation requires such a shift in ideas, even at the later stage of development, and the creation of a learning process that can deal with such a feedback process is most essential to technological innovation.

C. Characteristics of High Technology and Government Intervention

The characteristics of the developmental process of high technology as defined above not only provide us with the rationale for government intervention in high technology industries but also indicate the fundamental directions in which such intervention is necessary.

First, the high degree of R&D intensity that characterizes high technology raises the public-policy issue as to whether such research should be undertaken at the private or public sector level. As pointed out in Chapter 7 of the present volume, the available quantitative research on the rate of return on R&D outlays indicates the social rate of return in such activities to be generally significantly higher than the private rate of return. Thus, if this finding applies to R&D in high technology as well, it provides one reason as to why public funds should be invested here. Furthermore, even if we grant that the firms use their own resources to conduct such activity and are able to utilize the results for their own benefit, the theoretical part of such R&D, more often than not, becomes public knowledge. R&D, defined in abstract terms, is nothing but the production of information. So, the public-good characteristic of information always gives rise to public-policy issues.

Even if the existence of the problem as described above is taken for granted, it does not by itself constitute a case for the social desirability of supplementing investment in R&D of high technology with public funds. The case for public support is based on the argument that the presence of externalities leads to underinvestment. But there also is the overinvestment argument, as discussed in Chapter 7, pointing to a tendency for socially excessive investments in these fields even when these are left completely to the private sector.

Thus, supplementing the R&D activity publicly just on the basis of significant externalities that accompany it and its social return exceeding the private return would be hasty. It is necessary to consider the possibility of excessive private investments in some areas. Specifically, if we look at the "rush to invent" that has characterized the Japanese information and telecommunications industries recently, supplementing private-sector investments in R&D through public funds raises a number of pertinent questions. Our discussion above has already indicated that a macro approach to public intervention is inappropriate and since policies for R&D as well as technological development have differential impact on various sectors, a sectoral investigation becomes imperative.

Second, the emphasis on system orientation of technology, as it concerns itself with a technology set rather than component technologies, raises some issues concerning the "organization" around which such a set is built.

If we divide the process of technological development into three stages— basic research, applied research, and product development—it is normally believed that a high proportion of R&D in areas closer to basic research should be carried out in public institutes using public funds. This viewpoint, to some extent, is also applicable to R&D in high technology. Certain serious reservations, however, are necessary in order to link it up with the argument for the importance of publicly organized basic research. It is quite obvious that research involving fundamental principles and creativity requires an organizational framework different from that provided by the profit-oriented large firms, but the experience of using public organizational framework up to now does not affirm its suitability as an alternative organizational structure.

The available research in an industrial organization perspective indicates: (a) developmental research has been more successful when carried out by firms over a certain minimum size; but (b) new ideas and breakthroughs have sprouted predominantly in venture business firms inclined toward research and development or (especially in the case of the United States) in research institutes affiliated to universities. It is generally recognized that determining how to link (a) and (b) is the most important task now. It must be noted, however, that this research into industrial organization pertains mainly to the United States where universities are predominantly private. It is very difficult to envisage that the Japanese public organizations can effectively serve as a substitute for (b). Public intervention, in retrospect, tends to impede independent research. As will be discussed later, it is necessary to develop a new type of organizational structure in this field. The issue of public policy in this context is to compare the pros and cons of alternative organizational structures and help the formation of a system that would lead to creative R&D in the real sense of the word.

A third argument for the necessity of policy intervention in R&D is related to uncertainty accompanying R&D and the long period of research involved. The projects involving a high degree of uncertainty in the process of research with no guarantee of success and, in addition, requiring a long period of R&D do not easily lend themselves to R&D in the private sector, regardless of how important they may be from a national standpoint.

In this case as well, organization at the public level does not insure results. There is a strong possibility that research in public organizations may, in the absence of any alternative system and in the complete absence of competition, lead to an abuse of the bureaucratic system, resulting in the deprivation of research incentives.

In the context of the development of an organizational structure to deal with uncertainty, recent developments in organizational theory emphasize, following the basic principles of cybernetics, that the diversity of organizational structure is necessary to cope with a wide range of possibilities of uncertainty that exist. If the results of research are uncertain and it is necessary to gamble on a wide range of possibilities, the private and public organizational structures are equally necessary, as is their combination. If modern technology is highly characterized by system orientation, as was discussed while defining high technology, it is possible to build up a R&D strategy involving both the private and public organizational framework through an appropriate division of labor between them. Finally, it is necessary to keep in mind that, as technological innovations follow a path of spontaneous evolution under uncertainty, related organizational structures also evolve in a similar fashion.

III. An Evaluation of High Technology Policy in Japan

Based on the preliminaries discussed above, we embark in this section on an investigation into and an evaluation of the content of the Japanese government policy toward high technology. We begin by looking into the science and technology policy related to basic research, followed by a discussion of the problems directly related to industrial policy, then go on to discuss policy concerning the information industry, the area of immediate interest to us.

A. Science and Technology Policy

The Japanese science and technology policy can be divided into two streams, one carried out mainly under the Science and Technology Agency and the Ministry of Education in the fields related to basic research and the other in fields directly related to industry led by the Agency of Industrial Science and Technology of the MITI. A classification of the science and technology budget according to the above division gives the relative importance of the two, as depicted in Table I.

As is clear from the table, the science and technology budget accounted for 3% of the overall budget in Japan in 1979 and 1980, much smaller when compared to that in countries such as the United States (5.5%), France (5.8%), and the United Kingdom (3.6%), of which only about 15% was being used for industrial policy purposes, thereby indicating that the na-

TABLE I
Science and Technology Budget (¥100 million)

	1979		1980	
Basic research related	8,908	(77.4%)	9,772	(75.6%)
Science and Technology Agency	2,882		3,349	
Ministry of Education	6,026		6,423	
Industrial policy related	1,628	(14.1%)	2,135	(16.5%)
MITI	1,084		1,574	
Ministry of Agriculture and Forestry	538		561	
Others	972	(8.5%)	1,014	(7.9%)
TOTAL	11,508	(100.0%)	12,921	(100.0%)
Proportion of the Total Budget	3.0%		3.0%	

Source: Kagaku Gijutsu Cho (Science and Technology Agency), *Kagaku Gijutsu Hakusho (Science and Technology White Paper)*, various issues.

tional budget was not being specially directed toward industrial policy. As regards the proportion of research expenditures borne by the government, the role of government in R&D was much lower in Japan at 27% as compared to 35%–40% for the western governments, excluding defense expenditures. Nuclear power and space development accounted for an overwhelming proportion of the basic-research-related budget of the Science and Technology Agency and the Ministry of Education in Table I, and since the share of operating expenses has been on the rise within these research expenditures, the purely basic-research expenditures have been on the decline.

Table II presents the composition of R&D expenditures (both public and private) by the three types mentioned above. The share of basic research was 17.6% for Japan, higher than that for the United States, im-

TABLE II
Proportion of Basic, Applied, and Developmental Research Expenditures in Major Countries (%)

		Basic Research	Applied Research	Developmental Research
Japan	(1978)	17.6	24.9	57.5
United States	(1978)	12.8	22.7	64.5
United Kingdom	(1975)	16.1	25.4	58.5
France	(1977)	21.1	34.4	44.5
West Germany	(1977)	22.3	77.7	

Source: Kogyo Gijutsu In [1983a].

plying that basic research was not necessarily given low priority in Japan. (The proportion of basic research in the case of Japan has been on a decline, however, with the trend more pronounced in private-sector basic research, which fell to almost half of its level 10 years ago.)

The Japanese R&D expenditures grew gradually with the growth of the economy to a level of 2.96% of the national income, surpassing 2.65% for the United States; this R&D investment is high by international standards. The emphasis on applied and developmental research in Japan in the past is understandable if we look at the pattern of Japanese economic development up to now. From the point of view of science and technology policy, however, the proportion of basic research shows a downward trend, and if the nuclear power and space development expenditures are excluded, this becomes relatively sparse, indicating the possibility for policy-based improvement in allocation of research resources.

As discussed earlier, the simplistic arguments for focusing attention on basic research beg questions and, looking at the current status of such public organizations as universities in Japan, there is no guarantee that expected results would be realized simply by an increase in government budget allocations to basic research. Still, even if the emphasis is placed on applied and developmental research for industrial development, one can expect the need for basic research to grow, as feedback increases from nonbasic research. And as the pace of private-sector technological development hastens, the scope of basic research fields where the government should do supplemental research is also expected to expand. Since an evaluation of the science and technology policy itself is not our prime interest, we will refrain from discussing it further at this point, but it is clear that the Japanese R&D has been led by the private sector and the government's science and technology policy has played only a passive role in this context.

B. Large-Scale Projects

The industrial policy considerations were clearly reflected in the Japanese science and technology policy for the first time with the large-scale industrial technology R&D system—the so-called "large scale projects"—set up by the Agency of Industrial Science and Technology of the MITI. The government implemented this system by taking up the burden of providing the full amount of funds needed for the development of technology important from the point of view of the economy as a whole but which could not be undertaken in the private sector. This system was developed in order to compete with western technology and industry, which was believed to have resulted from the injection of a significant amount of national funds into the development of "leading technology" in industries such as electronics by the western countries since the mid-1960s through budgetary provisions for national defense, space, and nuclear power.

Table III, depicting the content of these investments, shows that about ¥ 30 billion were invested in high performance electronic computers and related fields in the earlier stages and about ¥ 120 billion were invested thereafter in other projects, including on-going projects. The scale of finances involved in these so-called large-scale projects, however, was relatively small and except for the jet engines for aircraft and pattern information processing projects, where overall R&D expenditure exceeded ¥ 100 million, most of the projects were below ¥ 50 million.

Looking at the large-scale projects in retrospect, it may be said that they laid the ground to the development of industrial technology under the guidance of the MITI. They were used as a beachhead by the government to determine the direction of the future course of technological development. Thus, energy-related projects within the large-scale projects were integrated, later, into the New Energy Development Plan and the

TABLE III
Large-Scale Industrial Technology R&D Projects (Large-Scale Projects)[a]

Project Name	Research Period	Total R&D Expenditure (100 million yen)
1. High performance computers	1966–71	100 (approx.)
2. Desulphurization technology	1966–71	26
3. New manufacturing processes for olefin, etc.	1967–72	11
4. Remote-control offshore deep-sea oil drilling rigs	1970–75	45
5. Desalination of sea water and utilization of by-products	1969–77	67
6. Electric automobiles	1971–77	57
7. Overall control technology for automobiles	1973–79	73
8. Pattern information processing	1971–80	220
9. Iron making by use of recycled hot gas	1973–77	137
10. Olefin manufacture from heavy oil	1975–81	199
11. Jet engines for aircraft	1971–81[b]	126
12. Technological system for recycling of resources	1973–82[b]	861

Source: Kogyo Gijutsu In [1983b].

[a]The projects listed are those that have already been completed. At present, eight projects, including High Speed Computer Systems, are under way.

[b]Covering two periods.

information-related projects led by the pattern information processing project with the Information Industry Policy, which will be taken up for a detailed discussion later.

C. Energy Development

Development of energy-related technology became an important and urgent problem after the oil shock, and the so-called "Sunshine Project" and "Moonlight Project" were conceived for the development of energy and energy conservation technology. Energy supply, once a constraint on the development of the Japanese economy, could again constrain growth, and the heavy dependence of the Japanese economy on energy imports became a weak spot in the international perspective. Under these circumstances, government assistance in the development of energy technology, especially the development of domestically produced energy, was more than socially justified.

The Sunshine Project was vigorously implemented, and judging from the *ex post* figures of government expenditures presented in Table IV, nuclear energy has received the highest importance. While being aware of the importance of developing solar and wind power as alternative energy sources, the project, as far as the end results show, did no more than accelerate the pace of nuclear energy development, which was already in progress. While placing high expectations on the development of renewable alternative energy, the government was not successful in promoting its development to a significant extent.

The low level spending for new energy sources simply reflects the fact

TABLE IV
Budgets for Research in Energy for Major Countries (million $)

	Japan	U.S.	West Germany	UK
Atomic energy	665(72.4%)	1,153(30.5%)	628(59.9%)	229(58.9%)
Nuclear energy (nonfast breeder)	531	399	422	72
Fast breeder reactor	134	754	206	157
New energy sources (solar, wind, ocean, biomass, geothermal)	39	624	46	19
Nuclear fusion	109	475	50	21
Others	106	1,531	324	120
Total	919	3,783	1,048	389

Source: Kagaku Gijutsu Cho (Science and Technology Agency), *Kagaku Gijutsu Hakusho (Science and Technology White Paper)*, 1981.

that the government attempted to utilize private-sector money by establishing the New Energy Development Organization. However, the reason for the unsuccessful result was that the government's concern for development of energy technology began and ended solely as a subsidy policy ignoring demand-side considerations such as efforts to build up demand for new energy. As discussed earlier, the government assistance for industrial technology has been most successful in cases in which the supply-side assistance has been supplemented effectively by assistance on the demand side in the form of government procurement and the like. In the case of the development of new energy (for example, solar power generation), what is important is to realize technological improvements and cost reductions in the process of trying to match actual production, however small, to the demand created by public and semi-public use for lighting roads, traffic control, schools, and hospitals, and rural areas and so on (Imai [1982b]). It is of utmost importance for technological development at the developmental stage to follow the learning process in which the information provided by the consumers is utilized for improving technology while continuing production on an experimental basis. On the side of organizations in charge of development, as revealed by the organizational theory, "being in motion" is important to provide the incentive for researchers and keep organizations vital.

Although this is not a proper place to discuss energy policy, we emphasize this aspect here in order to point out that a gradual development of the related organization through self-organizing, once the beachhead has been established, is necessary from the point of view of the government's technology policy, and the creation of demand for the technology concerned is one of the important factors that makes such development possible.

The industrial policy for technology development has been faced with a number of problems in the context of new energy as the petroleum demand and supply conditions have changed, and emergence of demand for new energy cannot be visualized in the near future. Although this has resulted from changes in external conditions, the emphasis of policy solely on supply-side assistance has also been responsible for magnifying the fluctuations. Furthermore, the necessity of a multisectoral organizational structure linking the public and the private sectors and the presence of organizational problems of a greater magnitude than what have been experienced elsewhere have also impeded the progress of new energy development. In contrast, the information industry, to be discussed below, was helped by favorable winds in the form of rapidly rising demand and, since a policy aligned to market trends was sufficient, it was able to produce results beyond all expectations. While this observation seems to be self-evident, it forms an important aspect in evaluating the Japanese industrial policy later.

D. Fostering the Information Industry

The information industry led by the computer industry, including both the hardware and software segments, forms the core of high technology industries. Since the 1970s, Japanese industrial policy has focused its attention on developing this industry as a strategic industry.

Looking at the course that this policy took in the context of hardware, we find it to have been steadfast in its fostering of Japanese computer makers through enacting various legislations, beginning with the Law on Temporary Measures for the Promotion of Electronics Industry (1957) through the Law on Temporary Measures for the Promotion of Specified Electronics Industries and Specified Machinery Industries (1971) to the Law on Temporary Measures for the Promotion of Specified Machinery and Information Industries (1978) aimed at promoting the computer industry. In the case of software, besides efforts to disseminate the concepts of "the information society" and of "the information industry" through reports by the Industrial Structure Council (mainly its Information Industry Committee), policies for the "promotion of education and training related to information processing" and the "development of information processing technology" were also adopted in order to build up the infrastructure for the information industry. Finally, a promotion policy for the narrowly defined information processing industry led by the software industry was also adopted.

The industrial policy toward the information industry did not stop with supply-side promotion in the form of technological assistance (mainly to the computer industry). It was also supplemented by demand-side policies, like the previously mentioned education and training programs and the introduction of computers into various government offices as they became more and more information oriented, in order to generate demand for computers. Moreover, this policy was quite comprehensive, and that is why it succeeded, in the sense that the concepts of the information society and the information industry, in a wider context, came to be linked to the policies for small- and medium-scale enterprises and regional development policies (for example, the promotion of the computerization plan of small- and medium-scale enterprises and the process of linking up with the "technopolis" project). But it must be noted that, for a growth industry, it is rather easy to accelerate its development by injecting some amount of funds into it and that, inasmuch as the industrial policy is an instrument for altering interindustry resource allocations, such a course would invariably involve sacrifices elsewhere in the economy. Moreover, it is important to investigate the equity consequences of pursuing such a policy. We evaluate the industrial policy related to the information processing industry hereunder by investigating these points one by one.

E. Phases of Industrial Development and the Computer Industry

Generally speaking, the content of the industrial policy differs according to the stage of development of an industry.

Let us consider a slightly extended version of the Abernathy (1978) model, which distinguishes three phases of development in an industry depending on the stage of technological innovation. As depicted in Table V, in Phase One when the industry has just started its development, the technology is still in a fluid state and innovations are primarily product innovations. The ideas (as well as necessary R&D) giving rise to these innovations can originate from a wide variety of sources, such as universities, venture businesses, R&D-intensive firms, research institutes affiliated with firms, and so on. As against this, in Phase Two, the technology becomes more "specific" as major designs get established through the process of natural selection in the competitive process during Phase One.

TABLE V
Phases of an Industry's Development and the Nature of Technology

		Phase 1	Phase 2	Phase 3
Nature of technology	Technology	Fluid	Specific	Refluidized
	Innovation	Product innovation	Process innovation	System innovation
	Sources of innovation	Diverse sources	Competition in production process	Integration
Related organization/ competition	Organizational linkage	Weak tie	Strong tie	Permeated
	Internal organization	Organic	Bureaucratic	Matrix type
	Organizational knowledge	Accumulation through search	Accumulation through learning	Reshuffling
	Competition	Competition among many	Competition among a few	Competition with alternative systems

This phase is characterized primarily by process innovations resulting from competition in manufacturing processes. Finally, in Phase Three, as the industry matures, the technology once again becomes fluid on account of stimulation provided by some new developments in technology and, as the technological base of the industry expands, system innovations are affected.

It is natural, given these three different phases of development of an industry, for industrial policy to have a different perspective in each of these phases.

As technological priorities are still unclear in Phase One and technological development is surrounded by a high degree of uncertainty, a number of justifications, as discussed earlier, could be provided for public assistance and intervention. Again, in Phase Three, new policies to facilitate technology transfers among industries and regions, as will be discussed later, become necessary to make the technology once again fluid. In the context of market failure arising out of external diseconomies, shifting from pollution to informational externalities, new industrial policies such as the recent new media policy also come into existence. In Phase Two, when technology becomes specific and innovations takes the form of partial improvisations accumulated through interfirm competition, it is difficult to find justification for an active industrial policy from the point of view of technological development. As the Japanese computer and IC industries have reached Phase Two, an international issue has arisen as to whether the industrial policy applied to these industries is a targeting policy directed at strategically protecting and promoting them.

F. Promotion of a Countervailing Power against IBM Dominance

The answer to the above charge is that the industry policy specific to these industries is intended to build up an indigenous countervailing power against IBM domination. As is well known, IBM was holding 70% of the world market for computers in 1970 and continues to corner 55% of the world market even now. Though it is questionable to measure IBM's market power simply on the basis of its large market share, it is difficult to denigrate the extent of IBM's control over international markets in the light of the fact that a system standard of the leading firm becomes a standard for the industry as a whole with respect to both hardware and software markets.

Ever since the report on the "Measures for Strengthening International Competitiveness of the Electronic Computers Industry" by the Electronics Industry Council was published in March 1966, an industrial policy to promote Japanese computer makers, in order to counter the IBM monopoly, has been followed. As discussed in Chapter 13, considering the computer industry as a strategic industry, this policy adopted strong measures of assistance to the industry in both the development of new models and marketing. Even though the need to counter the IBM monopolization was stressed, it cannot be justified on grounds of industrial organization policy. As has been discussed in the context of the effects of mergers on market competition, a merger among the second, third, and/or fourth ranked firms to counter the dominance of the top firm may increase the competition temporarily, but there is a possibility that, before long, the top and the merged second ranked firms could agree to collude, impairing competition.

However, a policy to foster Japanese computer makers, for a period just enough to allow them to accumulate enough technological and managerial resources to counter IBM, cannot be criticized in the light of the infant industry argument that has found recognition in the theory of international trade and in the theoretical discussion carried out in this volume. The policy was clearly successful as far as the Japanese industrial strategy of fostering strategic industries is concerned. Also, in terms of international industrial organization, the three Japanese makers and IBM are engaged in keen, albeit oligopolistic, competition for a 20% to 25% share of the Japanese markets as against the 50% plus share of IBM in the American and European markets. Had the Japanese firms not emerged on the international scene, it is possible that the recent technological progress, like the delicate improvements in inputting and outputting, may not have come about, and it is quite possible that the ambitious plans for the fifth-generation computers may also have not emerged. In this sense, the Japanese computer makers have played an innovative role in the international computer markets and the industrial policy that has given rise to this development may be favorably regarded.

G. Fostering the Semiconductor Industry

Still another policy that helped foster the information industry was the assistance provided to the semiconductor industry. Rather than delving into the details of this policy, it would be more appropriate to investigate the functioning of the VLSI Technology Research Association that has attracted international attention.[7] This VLSI Technology Research Association was established (under the Mining and Manufacturing Technology Research Associations Law) for a limited period of four years from 1976 to 1979 in order to conduct collective research to develop the technology needed to manufacture VLSIs, i.e., trying to place a memory of one megabit on a single chip, a technique that IBM was said to be in the process of developing at the time. In more concrete terms, this association was established by five firms, Fujitsu, Hitachi, Mitsubishi Electric Corporation, Nippon Electric Co. Ltd., and Toshiba, and the basic and joint research forming approximately 20% of the development themes were carried out at the Joint Research Institute, which was formed by a temporary staff of about 100 researchers who came from the five companies and the Electro-technical Laboratory of the MITI. The remaining 80% of the research was, effectively, carried out independently by the individual firms. The research themes were related to the technology for the manufacture of semiconductors, and six types of themes were selected and apportioned as depicted in Figure 8.1.

The total R&D expenditures during the four-year period amounted to ¥73.7 billion of which ¥29.1 billion, or 39.5%, came from the government in the form of subsidies.

The VLSI Technology Research Association was de facto dissolved in 1979 after meeting its objective within the initially allotted four-year period and now exists merely to administer some 1,000 patents that it holds. The association is using the profits being generated from its activities to repay the national treasury for the subsidies granted to it and is expected to complete these payments by the end of 1987. After this, the patents will revert back to the companies to which the inventors belonged.

There is a view, especially in the United States, that cooperative practices that ought to be forbidden in the spirit of antitrust legislation are permitted in Japan and that these practices are a source of Japanese superiority in high technology industries.[8] This argument, however, does not stand up to a deeper scrutiny of the facts.

First, one would have to consider the nature of the cooperative behavior induced by joint research among the participating firms and whether this

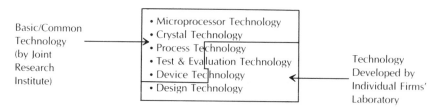

Fig. 8.1. Apportionment of research conducted by the VLSI Technology Research Association. From MITI, Agency of Industrial Science and Technology.

behavior could possibly lead to the elimination of competitors through the exercise of monopoly power or create impediments to competition through cartelization. Certainly, the participating firms were the major firms competing with one another in the VLSI and VLSI-using product markets, and if joint research could lead to cooperative behavior in the supply of VLSIs as well, it could generate the adverse effects of cartelization. It was not the VLSI itself but the equipment required to produce VLSI and the component technology necessary for this that were developed as the result of joint research. Such technologies should be seen as general input necessary for the manufacture of VLSIs, and actual VLSIs are manufactured by each firm using these technologies in different ways. The method of application, assembly of the manufacturing process, and management call for the know-how of the individual firms and this ensures the competitive characteristics of individual products. Thus, even though the general input technology was jointly developed, there is very little possibility that this leads to cartelization at the production and supply stage of VLSI.

Had this collective research been carried out by the firms producing and selling VLSI manufacturing equipment, there could have been a strong possibility of such a behavior to develop. No equipment manufacturer was a member of the joint research project, however; in fact, the collective research aimed at strengthening the basis of semiconductor manufacturing technology by supplying the technology to these makers.

Second, it is contended that if R&D itself is considered as an economic activity, the technology research association, since it expressly engaged in collective research and development, would contradict the principles of the Antimonopoly Law. This argument, however, is also not very persuasive. When subjected to economic analysis, it may be difficult to find positive factors associated with cartel formation that could give rise to social benefits in the case of the production of goods and services, but in the case of R&D to the extent that such collective behavior leads to the development of technology that would not have been otherwise developed, there are clear social benefits. Keeping in mind the approval of patent monopolies under the Antimonopoly Law from the reason that social benefits exceed social costs, it may also be appropriate to approve collective R&D to the extent that it does not interfere with the competitive process.

A third issue is related to the charges that firms were unfairly treated in implementing this industrial policy because the research association was limited to five firms with a significant amount of public funds injected in the project. Other firms, although willing to join, were excluded. Such discontent certainly existed to some extent.

If, however, the research association fails to produce results in the form of technological development, the investment of funds and human resources might be completely wasted. It is imperative for different firms involved in research to get together in a coherent organization with respect to the research at hand in order to make it successful. Since simply gathering together researchers may not necessarily lead to success, this becomes a crucial condition. It is extremely difficult to realize this condition and a large number of R&D associations or joint research projects fail on account of such difficulties. In the case of the VLSI Technology Research Association, (1) the overhanging threat of competition from IBM; (2) the concentration of a few firms whose researchers were already in close contact; and, (3) concentration on the basic research themes that provided strong incentives for cooperation were some special features that made the effective organization and management possible.

The existence of inequity in the treatment of various firms during such a process can be considered as a necessary evil for the production of social benefits. If such costs were very high, it would have been necessary to employ some alternative means within the industrial policy to deal with it, but since the process did not have any significant adverse effects on related firms, the costs might be considered to have been within acceptable limits.

H. Inductive Industrial Policy

We have analyzed the above industrial policy in the context of some Japanese high-tech industries. The content of the individual interventions by the Japanese government shows the scale of assistance to be relatively small. The contention by the MITI that "the Japanese industrial policy is based upon an indirect and inductive policy structure and hence is much softer policy as compared to the Western countries' policies towards industrial activity" seems to be particularly true in the case of the high technology industries. In order to evaluate the Japanese industrial policy, however, it is imperative to determine the content of such a "soft" policy.

In the case of the information industry, as discussed above, besides emphasizing the progressive information orientation of the economy through the Industrial Structure Council, efforts were made to build up a broad consensus in favor of such a choice. This consensus was developed through a close exchange of information with the related firms and then diffusing these ideas far and wide in the society.

This process could be developed, from the point of view of technological development, as follows. The first step is to select strategic areas with high innovation potential. As for the selection of the areas and the criteria for such a selection, the basic course is determined by taking into consideration the suggestions of specialists possessing "strong knowledge" (Nelson [1982b]) for putting the technology as well as future prospects of its economic impact into a proper perspective. Along with this, experts from the chosen industries and firms are mobilized to draw up a detailed scenario for the future. The results of these efforts are reflected in the reports of deliberation councils. Based on the understanding reached in these councils, assistance is provided to the necessary technological development activity to induce the industries to increase their R&D intensity. The potential for further technological development increases as the degree of R&D intensity increases, changing the expectations held by the private sector, inducing further investments in R&D activity, and building up a dynamism conducive to industrial development as such.

Although it is difficult to prove this process directly, we would like to illustrate these aspects through available case studies of industries and firms.

As for the computer industry, it is noted that the merging of digital technology for computers and telecommunications not only raised the potential for technological innovation but also opened up a wide area of developmental possibilities. But, for Nippon Electric Co., which had been aware of the importance of such developments for quite some time and was giving them due importance in its business strategy, the process of formulating and incorporating the C&C (Computer & Communication) strategy was not an easy task. In an interview conducted by us, the Chairman of Nippon Electric Co., Koji Kobayashi [1983] revealed that the development of the computer division as one of the main pillars of Nippon Electric was a rough process. In view of the fact that only a very few mainframe computer manufacturers have been able to survive in any country, it was not surprising to find periods when pessimism regarding the future of the computer division of Nippon Electric prevailed. It seems, if we look at the end results, that the bold investment decisions taken under the leadership of the then president Kobayashi (presently chairman) put the company on a developmental path supported by the two pillars of C & C. But one could easily discern behind such bold decisions the influence of the MITI's fostering of the computer makers. Not only publicly created demand and subsidies but also the creation of promising expectations of the business community regarding future opportunities in the information industry supported such investment decisions.

The Japanese semiconductor industry engaged in vigorous investment activity at a time when Japanese industry as a whole, following the second oil shock, was finding it difficult to anticipate its future and the VLSI Technology Research Association was still in the process of developing its production technology. The industry was able not only to perfect its production technology but also to establish itself. The industry has been evolving ever since on the basis of quality improvements resulting from firms' learning process and accumulation of innovations in the manufacturing process by leading medium-scale firms such as the DISCO, Shinkawa, and Takeda Riken Industries. As far as the factors that sustained investments during this critical period are concerned, the quantitative judgment about the future of the industry made by the government (MITI, mainly) and the government support (albeit small) in the form of shortening of the legally stipulated economic lives of the IC production equipment seem to have been at least one of the factors.

As an industry starts rolling on the tracks of self-development on the basis of a cycle of innovation potential→rise in R&D intensity→further rise in innovation potential,[9] the need for basic research develops anew and extra resources for conducting such research are also generated at the same time. The increases in R&D expenditures, especially on basic research, by the information- and communications-related firms in recent years have been particularly noticeable, and the major firms such as Hitachi, Nippon Electric, and Matsushita Communications are engaged in a number of basic research themes that have been of concern in the international academic circles as well. Such activity is expected to prepare the groundwork for the next stage of development and is expected to continue into new inducement policies for the next leap in the form of a MITI-led fifth-generation computer project.

I. Technology Transfer Policy

In general terms, the formation of the Japanese industrial system that formed the basis of the development of high technology in the decade since the oil shock could be described as follows.

First, as main designs for the production equipment got established, the major firms accumulated quality improvements and cost reductions based on their learning curve. We will refrain from delving into the content of this effect and an analysis of the characteristics of the Japanese firms that make such developments possible, as such an analysis has been undertaken elsewhere (Imai [1983]) and a number of such explanations have been proffered by other authors as well. In view of the fact that initial accumulation of production is decisively important for the competitive process based on the learning curve, it is quite obvious that the industrial policy, as discussed in the context of the information industry, had a positive effect.

Second, the technology and know-how developed in the major firms got diffused widely into the economy through ancillary and affiliated firms. Furthermore, these ancillary and affiliated firms as well as the users added up small innovations during this diffusion process, resulting in an "accumulation of small innovations."

Differentiating between diffusion and transfer of technology according to the accepted practice of defining the former as spontaneous transfer of technology and the latter as policy-directed transfer, it is clear that policy efforts for technology transfer are introduced at this second stage. Examples of such transfers are technology transfer through MITI's industrial testing laboratories or dissemination of education concerning information technology within the wide framework of the small- and medium-enterprise policy through programs for the promotion of technology transfers implemented by the Small Business Corporation. Recently, the wide technological base for the production of high technology has been growing in Japan using the dual mechanism of technology diffusion and transfer.

Third, the diffusion and transfer of technology have spilled over the industrial boundaries, giving rise to new combinations of technology across different industrial fields and, in turn, to vigorous new entry from widely differing fields.

As has been discussed earlier, the modern technological innovation is the result of cumulative learning process as a system and is generated by accumulating the knowledge and know-how derived from within the system.[10] The accumulation of knowledge and know-how related to industrial technology takes shape through feedbacks received from not only the firms that enter production on the basis of the technology in question but also from the machinery makers that engage in technological engineering to produce actual machinery and equipment as well as widespread information exchanges among the related firms. The formation of such a network as a single system gives rise to the capacity for continuous innovations. Hence, as the system grows in scale, possibilities for innovation through new technological combinations increase.

The size of the firm has been one of the controversial points in the discussion of efficiency of technological innovation since the celebrated work of Schumpeter. Interpreted in light of the above discussion, however, it seems that the size of the system involved in the learning process of technology development is more pertinent for the success of technological innovations. At the same time, the efficiency of the diffusion and transfer of technology within the system also needs to be taken into account.

The relatively favorable results, if any, shown by the Japanese firms in the new phase of technological innovation led by high technology are a function of the efficiency of the learning system in this sense and the speed of the spread of knowledge and transfer of information.

The "soft" industrial policy of the MITI in this sense has played a vital role in the creation of an industrial system as described above. The industrial base for technological development was strengthened by stimulating the markets through the mobilization, in parts, of the above noted measures such as the technological development policy, policies for technology transfers, regional development policies, small- and medium-enterprise policy, and the like. Needless to say, the policies for small and medium firms in the past have supported cartelization on the whole and have also administered subsidies on account of political pressures. These, however, are gradually shifting to self-help, and one can discern a transformation toward a new type of industrial policy aimed at the fostering of technology and technology transfer.[11]

IV. An Overall Evaluation

The Japanese industrial policy concentrated on the information industry in its broader sense, where high innovation potential and prospects for expansion in demand were expected, and induced a mechanism for development in the form of accumulation of small innovations, the cumulative learning process, and widespread diffusion and transfer of technology. The word *inducement* has a soft connotation and it might perhaps be described better as the appropriate initial kick urging the industry on the path to development. The policy could be considered to have been successful in the context of the manufacturing segment of the information-related industries as discussed earlier. The existence of segments where such a policy was ineffective is also quite obvious, with technological development in the chemical industry and computer software being some important examples.

To begin with, the innovations in the chemical industry are mostly science-based and are highly dependent on breakthroughs generated out of basic research and large-scale experiments rather than on the learning process based on accumulation of know-how. It is not to say that such areas do not require combinations of component technology, but the patent protected basic technology is dominated by comprehensive process technologies. As a result, there is a tendency for the learning system to narrow down to the interaction of some big firm and a particular research department of some university as opposed to such wider learning as develops in the machinery industry. The Japanese system in these areas thus cannot have a comparative advantage against the systems of the major international firms. In fact, the Japanese chemical industry is considered to lie outside the competitive sphere of technology development formed by the major international firms like Dupont and Bayer. There are certain areas such as fermentation technology where development is based on accumulation of know-how and Japanese firms are doing rather well in those areas. It is, however, difficult to deny that Japan has as yet failed to develop a system appropriate for science-based R&D, which represents the main current in fields such biotechnology. Moreover, there is no guarantee that the large number of R&D associations established to complement such research would succeed. It is rather difficult for these associations to meet the various conditions that the VLSI Technology Research Association was able to meet.

The production of software requires organizational principles that are totally different from those required in the case of the production of goods (for example, meritocracy rather than group consensus approach and task-oriented organization rather than hierarchical organization) necessitating totally different methods to foster its growth. It is not possible to go into details here due to space limitations (cf. Imai [1982a]), but it suffices to state that the policy approach in the production of software has to be completely different and the industrial policy up to now has had no impact on this aspect.

Seen in this light, Japanese industrial policy can be evaluated as having backed up market-based development in fields where success was obvious. One may find such an expression cynical, but such industrial policy could be considered to be a coherent policy from the point of view of technological development. As described earlier, technological development and innovation are governed by complex factors, and while there are certain fields that once set on the road to development would develop on their own, there are others where a vicious circle takes hold once they begin a decline and it is extremely difficult to put them back on the road to development. From the point of view of industrial policy, therefore, it is much more productive to cultivate those sectors that are capable of developing and absorbing resources employed in the areas headed for a decline.

Since industrial policy is a means by which the government complements the market mechanism, it is believed that industrial policy should subsidize the declining or the weak industries rather than fostering the growth industries. The effect of such policies, however, becomes questionable, at least to the extent that the particular characteristics of technological development, as noted above, are taken into account. Therefore, the fact that Japanese industrial policy, regardless of its intentions, resulted in the fostering of growth industries need not be criticized. This could also build up the capacity for adopting positive adjustment policies (PAP) in the context of declining industries. Japanese industrial development was based primarily on the market mechanism and industrial policy acted as a catalyst in accelerating this trend.

Notes

1. The author is grateful to Toshimasa Tsuruta, Masanori Yoshikai, and Tadashi Takashima for their detailed comments on the first draft of this chapter. Limitations of space forced us to shorten the presentation substantially as compared to the first draft and it has not been possible to answer all the questions raised, but additions, wherever necessary, have been made.

   As for industrial policy related to high technology, the author has presented papers at the Conference on Japanese Industrial Policy in Comparative Perspective held at New York from March 17–19, 1984, and the Conference of the High Technology Research Project at Stanford University, March 21–23, 1984. These papers, though overlapping in content with the present paper to some extent, develop the problems related to the technopolis policy, new media policy, and software policy not touched on in the present chapter. One of them was published as Imai [1986].
2. The strategic industry here refers to an industry that typifies the industrial society of its time in terms of technology and organization and leads the innovations at that time.
3. For the author's independent assessment of industrial development in Japan through these three phases, cf. Imai [1982c].
4. The example of the first set can be found in the Subcommittee on Trade of the Ways and Means, U.S. House of Representatives [1980], while the Working Group on High Technology Industries of the Cabinet Council on Commerce and Trade [1983] includes the latter set.
5. For example, Kikai Shinko Kyokai Keizai Kenkyusho [1983].
6. The top five industries in R&D intensity (R&D expenditures/sales) in Japan are:

Industry	R&D Intensity (R&D Expenditures/Sales)
Pharmaceutical industry	5.9
Telecommunications, electronics, and electrical measuring instruments	4.2
Electrical machinery and equipment	3.8
Precision instruments	3.5
Other chemical industries	3.0
Manufacturing Industries	1.9
All Industries	1.6

Source: Kogyo Gijutsu In (1983a).

7. For an analysis of the VLSI Technology Research Association from the point of view of industrial organization theory, see Sakakibara [1983].

8. The American view was discussed in Yamamura [1986].

9. A stimulating empirical analysis of this type of technological development is provided in Sahal [1981, 1983b].

10. The term *system* has been used until now, in this chapter, to imply a collection of elemental technologies and the use here in abstract terms is no different. But in more concrete terms, it represents an organizational link involved in the development of technology rather than the organization of just one firm or one university as a team. Again, by *accumulation*, we imply cumulation over time.

11. A coherent formulation of this is the new type of industrial policy, the so-called "Technopolis Plan." In broad abstract terms, the technopolis aims at creating a new socio-economic setup utilizing high technology. In order to utilize high technology within a society as well as in order to build up such a setup, a very wide range of research and development becomes necessary. The technopolis plan tries to integrate the R&D functions and the industrial functions, in this broad sense, closely with geographical dispersion.

PART III

Economic Theory of Industrial Policy

CHAPTER 9

Industrial Policy as a Corrective to Market Failures

MOTOSHIGE ITOH

Faculty of Economics
University of Tokyo
Tokyo, Japan

MASAHIRO OKUNO

Faculty of Economics
University of Tokyo
Tokyo, Japan

KAZUHARU KIYONO

Department of Economics
Gakushuin University
Tokyo, Japan

KOTARO SUZUMURA

Institute of Economic Research
Hitotsubashi University
Tokyo, Japan

I. Introduction

In postwar Japan, at least from the academic standpoint, the most commonly held view was that there was no positive role for industrial policy to play. The first reason for this was that there was initially no clear statement of what the goal of such policy was, and how tools other than the traditional ones of economic (fiscal and monetary) policy were to be used. This is because these issues were not made clear, even by the policymakers.[1] Second, it cannot be denied that an objective and theoretical analysis of such policy was hindered by the skeptical attitude of academic economists toward industrial policy, which was closely related to an image of such policy as being traditionally that of control and direct governmental regulation.[2]

In contrast to this, among Japanese and Western academic economists it seems that interest has recently been increasing in industrial policy—especially in Japanese industrial policy. The source of this is a sincere interest in increasing understanding of trade friction among the advanced countries and of development strategies for developing countries. To do this requires an unbiased analysis of the contributions of industrial policy to the postwar growth and development of the Japanese economy within the conceptual framework of economics. Our observations below arise from these same concerns.

In this and the following chapter, we classify various policies that comprised postwar Japanese industrial policy, and theoretically discuss whether or not in some sense these policies could have served to increase economic welfare. Our purpose then is to provide a standard against which the actual industrial policies of postwar Japan can be evaluated. We thus dispense with the previous negative presumption toward industrial policy, and analyze theoretically what industrial policy should consist of. We thus want to make it clear at the start that these two chapters, while seeking to deal with the real world as much as possible, do not have as their purpose the evaluation of actual industrial policies.

From the standpoint of economic theory, the definition of industrial policy is

> policy that attempts to achieve the national economic and noneconomic goals of a country by intervening in the allocation of resources among industries or sectors of the country, or in the (industrial) organization of an industry or sector.

Among such policies, the main objects of the following analysis are policies that can increase the level of economic welfare by intervening in an industry or sector of the economy where there is in some sense a market failure.

When the focus is limited to the postwar period, industrial policy that aimed at correcting market failures can generally be classed into three groups, excluding policies for adjustment in and assistance to declining industries, which are discussed separately in Chapter 14 of this book.

The first group of policies are those by which the government of a country sets out to deliberately create an industrial or trade structure that is thought desirable for economic development. Such policies are particularly meaningful when they are interventions in an "open" economy. When there is some sort of market failure in an industry, so that in the industry as a whole costs are declining, then through some means it is necessary to overcome the setup costs needed for the industry to establish itself. For this, policy intervention can influence the industrial structure, suggesting that the national economic welfare of the country or of other countries may be influenced in a positive or a negative fashion.[3]

The second group of policies consist of various measures that are used as policy interventions to alleviate market failures that arise in research and development and in the areas of information, risk, and externalities. In this case, in contradistinction to the first case, trade is of minimal importance, and it is adequate to analyze a country as if it were a closed economy.

The third group consists of policies by which the government tries to intervene directly in the industrial organization of a particular industry or sector. The main case in which such policy is meaningful is where the firms in an industry have market power because of scale economies or entry barriers.

The policy instruments used in industrial policy can next be classed into those that provide indirect incentives, those that regulate directly, and those that relate to information. Direct regulation consists of policies such as licensing and authorizing activities, rationing goods, controlling new entry, and forming cartels.[4] Such policies discriminate among individual firms in an industry and tend to create a vested interest in holding a license or position, so that in analyzing these policies, careful attention needs to be paid to side effects. In contrast, policies that provide indirect incentives include (1) policies that provide pecuniary incentives, such as taxes, subsidies, tariffs, and government loans, and (2) policies that change the variables of the environment in which an industry operates, such as trade restrictions and public investment. Finally, there are policies that relate to information, which serve to transmit information among industries or firms, or to provide a mechanism by which information can be transmitted. Government councils and the long-term "visions" of industrial structure, which are publicized by MITI, can be thought of as policy instruments falling into this last category.

In the following discussion, the side effects of industrial policies will not be directly addressed, but it is important not to forget the fact that, with the exception of temporary indirect incentive policies, industrial policies have a variety of economic and political side effects.[5] Again, in the following analysis, even if policy instruments are not always optimal, the focus has been limited to second-best measures that can be realistically implemented and that have relatively few side effects. Specifically, keeping in mind the various instruments of postwar industrial policy, the main focus of the analysis is on indirect incentive measures that do not discriminate among the constituent firms of an industry. In Chapter 10, in particular, the focus of the analysis of policy instruments will be on temporary indirect incentive measures. The placing of policies in terms of this limited range of policy instruments will be the focus of our analysis.

II. Research and Development and Learning by Doing

Research and development and learning by doing are linked to information, a good that is difficult to handle in market transactions, so that market failures are constantly occurring. An important point of dispute is what sort of (industrial) policy should be used for such market failures. Below, the argument will proceed by concentrating on three facets of R&D and learning by doing. The first is the public good aspect of technology, the second is that of the risk that accompanies R&D, and the third is economies of scale in R&D and learning by doing.[6]

The public good characteristics of technology occur because the consumption of technical knowledge is nonexclusive and collective. The technology developed by a firm, because of its nonexclusive and collective nature, can be utilized by other firms without additional cost. Because of this, unless the property rights of the technical knowledge that has been developed are guaranteed through patents or copyrights, the results of the development efforts of one firm readily spill over to other firms and become usable without cost. Since in this sense technology is not readily appropriable, the incentives for firms to undertake R&D are weakened, and as is generally true for public goods, this gives rise to a tendency for investment in R&D to remain at a lower level than is socially desirable. Therefore, to the extent that this is the case, it is desirable from the standpoint of resource allocation for the government to directly undertake R&D or to increase private incentives to undertake R&D by granting patents and copyrights so that the benefits of R&D can be retained by the firm. Nevertheless, because R&D is to some extent appropriable, in comparison to a pure public good, it must be noted that treating R&D strictly as a public good is not always proper.

First, in order to understand and copy specialized knowledge, it is necessary to have specialized knowledge and substantial resources, and requires a certain amount of time. In such cases, the spillover of R&D is effectively limited, and the party initially involved in the R&D can monopolize the resulting profits. In this the private incentives to undertake R&D are strengthened, and it is possible that in some cases from the standpoint of society there is overinvestment in R&D.[7] Thus it should be noted that policy intervention in or subsidization of R&D are not uniformly justified. In general, the locus for interventions and subsidies should be in basic research rather than in process innovations and other R&D that is closely linked to new product development and so would work to facilitate oligopolization in markets.

Again, in contrast to the case of a public good, the partial appropriability of R&D distorts the quality and direction of activity more than its level. This can be seen in the following example from Kreps and Spence [1983]. Let us assume that technology of types A and B can be developed. Assume also that the development cost of A-type technology is relatively low and that the technology can readily be appropriated by other firms, and the development cost of B-type technology is relatively great, but at the same time the technology is readily kept secret. In such a case, even though type-A R&D is socially desirable, because of the private incentives it can readily be conceived that a firm's investment will only be in type-B R&D. In other words, because the appropriability of a technology may be limited, the quality or direction of R&D is distorted. To resolve this problem, policies that provide nondiscriminatory pecuniary incentives to R&D in general are inadequate, and it is necessary for policy to provide subsidies for only specific types of R&D, for the government to itself undertake R&D or to sponsor R&D cooperatives, or otherwise to distinguish among types of R&D, or to directly intervene.

The second reason why, in a market, R&D does not take the desired form is because of risk. It is not possible to know ahead of time whether a technology can be successfully developed or the extent to which the technology that is developed will result in profits for its developer, and it is furthermore very difficult to obtain private insurance for such risk. Thus, by giving subsidies to R&D, the government can pool the private risk of firms so that the government in effect provides insurance to private firms. Hence, government subsidies for R&D can also be justified from this perspective. It should be noted, however, that if subsidies are being provided as a form of insurance, unless a portion of the profits from successful R&D are received by the government, this would result in a redistribution of income from general taxpayers to firms that undertake R&D.

Again, it must be noted that for subsidies to be justifiable as insurance, the risk accompanying R&D must be individual risk.[8] Individual risk is where the same sort of risk is independent among economic agents. In other words, where a number of firms are undertaking the same sort of R&D at the same time, the risk to an individual firm may be great, but if for the economy as a whole one such effort is successful, then social welfare will be improved. In such a case, social risk is less than individual risk, so that from the standpoint of society it is necessary, through policy intervention, for such risk to be borne. On the other hand, where only one firm is involved in a given type of R&D, individual and social risk are identical, so that in terms of risk there is no gap between private and social profitability, and there is no need to intervene.

There is one other reason why the risk of R&D leads to market failure.[9] To illustrate this point, let us consider two R&D projects that serve to reduce the unit production cost of a good. To simplify matters, we assume that the costs accompanying these two projects are identical. Below, initial unit cost is C, while project A will with certainty reduce unit cost by c. Project B, on the other hand, will lower unit cost by $2c$ with a probability of 1/2 and will utterly fail to lower unit cost with a probability of 1/2. In this case, where the demand curve is downward sloping, the increase in consumer surplus when the price is lowered from C to $C - 2c$ is more than double that of when the price is decreased from C to $C - c$. Then, the indirect social utility curve, which expresses the relation between the level of social welfare and the unit cost of the good, will as in Figure 9.1 be declining and concave. As a result, the expected level of welfare is greater under project B than project A. In other words, for cost-reducing R&D investments, projects with greater risk are socially desirable. However, because the developer of a technology cannot fully appropriate the consumer surplus, it is difficult privately to carry out high-risk R&D. This provides a place for intervention by the government. Now the above argument, because it assumes that the costs of the two R&D projects are identical, does not provide unqualified justification for interventions or subsidies simply because R&D investment in general lowers costs.

The third category of market failures of R&D and learning by doing is that of economies of scale. As in the above investment in cost-reducing R&D, or in investment in the development of new products, the greater part of investment in R&D comprises a fixed cost of production. Thus, as for instance in the case of investment to develop a new product, the greater the production of the new product, the lower the development costs of the product per unit of output. In this way, with the inclusion of the costs of the activities of a firm in developing new products, average production cost declines with output, resulting in economies of scale. Using the concept of a learning curve, we next illustrate the presence of scale economies in learning by doing.[10]

With the learning curve drawn in Figure 9.2, as cumulative output (the x axis) and consequently learning increase, there is a decrease in unit production cost (the y axis). With first-period production cost of C_0 and

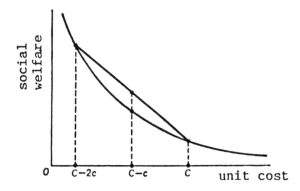

Fig. 9.1. Cost-reducing R&D investment and the level of social welfare.

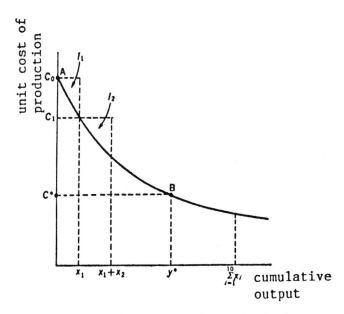

Fig. 9.2. The learning curve and economies of scale.

output of X_1, total first-period production cost is the area of the rectangle I_1. With this production, learning takes place, and in the next period, unit cost is lowered to C_1. If output in period 2 is X_2, then total production cost for that period is represented by the area of the rectangle I_2. If by the tenth period, production (as in the figure) is $\Sigma_{i=1}^{10} X_i$, then total cost, ignoring interest payments, will correspond to the area under the learning curve from 0 to $\Sigma_{i=1}^{10} X_i$. In such a case, with the increase in cumulative production, especially in the current period, long-run marginal and average costs decline, giving rise to scale economies.

When there are economies of scale, market failure can arise, as is discussed below, and there can arise the need to use (industrial) policy.

First, because of scale economies, there is a gap between private and social profitability. For example, assume that, with fixed cost in the form of development costs being great, there is no incentive from the standpoint of private profitability to undertake R&D. Even in such a case, if one considers that costs are lowered and consumer surplus increased, then it may be that it is socially desirable to undertake R&D. This being so, it is then necessary to use policy to increase the private returns to R&D and learning by doing through subsidy policies that provide pecuniary incentives for R&D and learning by doing or through policies that increase

demand in the industry. Additionally, as in the case of other industries
in which economies of scale exist, such as telephone and electric utilities,
it is also effective for the government to directly undertake R&D or to
form R&D cooperatives or at least to provide for the formation of such
cooperatives.

Second, when there are economies of scale, it becomes difficult to undertake policies that seek to maintain a competitive industrial organization.
This is because the attempt to maintain the presence of a large number
of firms in the industry becomes a barrier to gaining the benefits of scale
economies, while the attempt to force competitive price formation on firms
when their number is small enough to gain from scale economies removes
the incentives for firms to increase their efficiency. As a result, when an
oligopolistic industrial structure must be allowed, it is conceivable that a
second best policy consists of protecting or subsidizing such an industry
or upstream and downstream industries as a means of increasing the level
of national welfare. In other words, for industries in which R&D is important, private returns to R&D and production are increased, while if
related industries are protected or subsidized, then demand in the industry
and hence private returns are again increased. As a result, output in the
industry increases, and with economies of scale costs decrease, and international competitiveness increases.[11]

III. Exchanging and Transmitting Information

In this section, we consider the role of the government in gathering
information within the economy and transmitting that information to private economic agents or providing a forum for the exchange of information
among private parties in the economy. This role of the government as a
transmitter of information has been emphasized in terms of the concept
of indicative planning.[12] In current industrial policy in Japan, there is the
opinion that the most effective role of the government is as a transmitter
of information. A classic statement of this is the following evaluation of
industrial policy by Komiya:

> Regardless of the defects in the postwar Japanese industrial policy system, it cannot
> be denied that it served as an extremely effective means of gathering, exchanging and
> bringing about the transmission of information on industry. Government officials, people
> from industry and representatives from government financial institutions and the city
> banks gathered to discuss the problems then facing industry and to exchange information
> on new technologies and domestic and foreign markets. The people at the top level
> of the government, industry and financial institutions met in Councils and Committees,
> while those at a lower level met in their Subcommittees and in other less formal forums.
> Information on the various sections of industry is undoubtedly more plentiful and more

readily obtained in Japan than in most other countries. If the Japanese industrial system is thought of as a type of system for exchanging information, then apart from the consideration of the direct and indirect impact of the policy measures used in industrial policy, the industrial policy system may have been one of the most important elements supporting the rapid growth rate of Japanese industry.[13]

In order to examine this facet of industrial policy, it is useful to divide information into two categories. The first is information on the environment, and the second is information on the market. Environmental information consists of information about the values of the parameters, given by the environment, which are exogenous to the economy or agents within the economy, e.g., resource endowments, production technology, consumer preferences, and the environment narrowly defined. Market information, on the other hand, consists of information about the actions other economic agents are taking in markets.[14]

In an ideal world of perfectly competitive markets, environmental information is automatically transmitted through prices, and the allocation of resources that results thereby is Pareto optimal. In the real world, however, many markets are monopolistic or oligopolistic, and in such cases not all information can be transmitted by using only prices. It is then often the case that the most important information for a firm is about the parameters of the demand function and the quantity demanded rather than information about prices.[15] It is costly, however, to learn about these parameters. Thus economic agents only try to obtain such information when they expect the return to exceed the cost. And while *ex post* returns may exceed costs, it is possible that there will be no incentive to try to obtain such information.

One role of industrial policy in the face of incomplete information consists of the government aiding in the transmission of correct information to economic agents. If there are any positive aspects to the existence of the Industrial Structure Council or other government councils, committees, and commissions or the many economic plans, one such aspect may be found in the fact they transmitted essential information to economic actors. In other words, as touched on in the above conclusion of Komiya, through such institutions private economic actors may have been able to obtain information that they had not recognized as being important, or they may have been able to obtain information that, while recognized as being of value, they had not attempted to collect because of its cost.

A more important role for the government in serving as a forum for the exchange of information was undoubtedly in transmitting market information and in eliminating market uncertainty. Market uncertainty does not pose problems in perfectly competitive markets, where prices are flexible. In such markets, prices transmit all the information needed for an agent to choose optimal behavior, and there is no need to know what the choices of other economic agents will be. When one takes into consideration oligopolistically or monopolistically competitive markets, however, in order for firms to choose actions optimally, it is extremely important to predict what actions other firms will take, or what the response of other firms will be to one's own actions. When one takes into consideration this sort of interdependency among economic agents, there is a possibility that the elimination of market uncertainty shifts resource allocation of the economy as a whole in a desirable direction.

Through councils and similar forums, it is possible for the government to bring about the exchange of market information, and hence to reduce market uncertainty by repeatedly having firms exchange their investment, production, and pricing plans with those of other firms. In particular, the government has an important role to play when, because of the interdependency of oligopolistic firms, the actions undertaken on the basis of private incentives by individual firms may from the standpoint of the welfare of society as a whole result in too little production or too much investment. It must be noted, however, that aiding the transmission of information among the firms in a given industry tends to further collusive behavior among firms, as has apparently often been the case in contemporary Japan.[16]

An important related point on information problems is the "pump priming effect." This phenomenon refers to the following situation. The government lends money to an industry through (for example) the Japan Development Bank. Then private banks decide to lend money to the industry even though they had not previously done so. What remains for us to see is whether in fact this phenomenon ever occurred, and, if so, by what mechanism it occurred. Here we would merely like to indicate three possible means by which this might have occurred. The first relates to the transmission of information discussed above. Here, unlike the mere transmission of information, the government bears a real cost in the form of a loan, so that information that the government will grant favors to or protect an industry becomes more credible, and in this it becomes possible to "call forth" other loans. Second, if there are set-up costs in an industry, or capital markets are imperfect, it may be possible for the policy of a limited amount of government loans to substantially change the private profitability of the industry.[17] Third, there is the possibility that because of the internal decision-making organization of firms, the fact that the government has lent money to an industry may make it easier for private financial institutions to make an in-house decision to lend money to the industry. Our impression is that in current Japanese industrial policy this last aspect may be the most important.

IV. International Monopoly Power and Domestic Defenses

This section will briefly consider the welfare implications of policies undertaken by the government to protect domestic firms, where the industry has the following two special characteristics.

The first distinctive feature we have in mind is where in an industry there are economies of scale at the level of the individual firm, so that the organization of the industry is inherently oligopolistic. The main point we take up below is that, because of such economies of scale, it is typical that firms entering such an industry must in one lump invest in facilities that afterwards cannot readily be converted to other uses. The second special characteristic is that there are prior foreign entrants in the industry that have built a dominant oligopolistic or monopolistic position. Such firms, if they have no rivals, can earn monopoly rents, so that in terms of potential domestic entrants, foreign firms potentially may adopt a strategy that would frustrate at inception any plans to enter. The problem we set for ourselves is to make clear for such industries the welfare implications of protective policies toward domestic firms.[18]

For simplicity, we assume that the industry is initially monopolized by a foreign firm. Figure 9.3(b) illustrates the monopoly rent of the industry. In this figure, AR represents domestic demand, and MR the corresponding marginal revenue curve. The marginal cost curve of the monopolistic firm is MC_f and the profits of the monopolist are maximized when output Q_f^M is supplied at price P_f^M. In this monopolistic equilibrium, total social surplus is given by the area of the quadrilateral $ABDE$, and the area of triangle BCD represents the welfare loss due to monopoly. Now, of the total social surplus, consumers' surplus, which corresponds to the area of the triangle $P_f^M DE$, is retained domestically, but the monopoly rent corresponding to the area of the rectangle $ABDP_f^M$ as the monopoly rent of a foreign firm, flows abroad.

In such a situation, if in defense a domestic firm enters the industry, then the portion of total social surplus produced by this industry that is retained domestically increases, and so it is possible to improve domestic economic welfare by that extent. The problem is whether there are strategies that can achieve this.

Again, to simplify things, we assume that the output of the industry is homogeneous, and that there is only one potential domestic entrant. We must then consider the two-firm (duopoly) equilibrium in a market for a homogeneous good.

In Figure 9.3(a), the reaction curves of the foreign firm and the potential domestic entrant are drawn. The discontinuity arises in these curves because there are economies of scale in the industry, so that to the extent

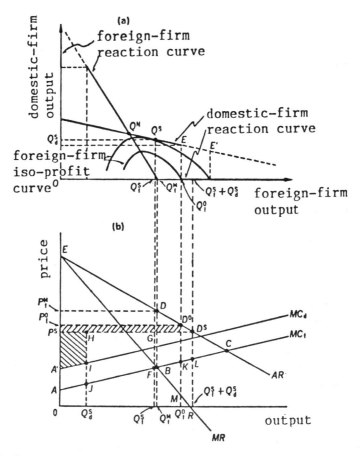

Fig. 9.3. Entrance-deterrence strategy and protection and nurturing policy.

that some minimum quantity of output cannot be guaranteed, the only prudent choice for the firm is not to enter the industry. For example, if in Figure 9.3 the foreign firm produces output greater than Q_f^o, the market available to the domestic firm is in the end too limited to support new entry, so that the reaction curve of the domestic firm for $Q_f \geq Q_f^o$ lies on the X-axis, and correspondingly, the same holds true for the foreign firm. Below we consider the case in which both reaction curves are downward-sloping, with absolute value of the slope greater than 1, and where for the relevant portion both firms have positive output. In this situation, the

Cournot–Nash equilibrium Q^N given by the intersection of these curves is stable.

Now it is difficult to imagine that the foreign firm, which as the original entrant has built a dominant position, will behave passively toward the domestic firm. Rather, when the domestic firm plans to enter, it is natural to assume that the foreign firm will adopt a strategy to frustrate the plan of the domestic firm. We then must consider the two-firm (duopoly) equilibrium in which the foreign firm is the leader and the domestic firm the follower.

In Figure 9.3(a), the convex curves are isoprofit curves of the foreign firm; the lower the curve, the greater the profit. Thus in this figure, given the domestic firms' reaction function, the Stackelberg equilibrium at which the foreign firm maximizes its profits is the point Q^s corresponding to foreign-firm output Q_f^s and domestic-firm output Q_d^s.

Assume now that the foreign firm is initially the only firm producing in the industry. If the domestic firm decides to enter and the foreign firm accedes to it, then the Stackelberg equilibrium arises.[19] The foreign firm, in the face of possible entry by the domestic firm, can, by choosing to produce Q_f^o, prevent entry. However, this sort of behavior to prevent entry may be an empty threat. Because if the domestic firm were to enter, the foreign firm might accept the domestic firm and produce Q_f^s, instead of Q_f^o. In Figure 9.3, though, we have drawn the curves so that the entry-deterring behavior of producing Q_f^o is a credible and not an empty threat.[20] This is because, assuming that the domestic firm chooses to enter, the foreign firm does not move to the Stackelberg equilibrium, because continuing to produce at Q_f^o results in greater profits. Thus in the situation depicted in this graph, the foreign firm will always try to prevent entry by the domestic firm, and because the threat is credible, the domestic firm will not be able to successfully enter.

In Figure 9.3(b), MC_f and MC_d represent the marginal cost curves of the foreign and domestic firms, respectively. In comparison to the monopolistic equilibrium at output Q_f^M and price P_f^M when there is no threat of entry by a domestic firm. If there is entry-deterring behavior the equilibrium is at output Q_f^o, and price P_f^o, with the important characteristic that $Q_f^o > Q_f^M$ and $P_f^o < P_f^M$. Because the equilibrium price is lower, consumers' surplus increases by the amount corresponding to the area of the quadrilateral $P_f^o D^o D P_f^M$, and as before, monopoly rent corresponding to the area of the quadrilateral $AKD^o P_f^o$ continues to flow abroad.

When there is a situation such as this, by undertaking measures to protect or foster the domestic firm, the government can bring about entry by the firm.

For example, by subsidizing fixed costs of the domestic firm, the point of discontinuity in the domestic firm's reaction curve may be moved to the right in Figure 9.3(a) from E to E'. Then, the foreign firm will have an incentive to choose the Stackelberg equilibrium Q^S, and will accede to the entry of the domestic firm, rather than taking entry-deterring behavior.[21] This sort of government policy will change the foreign firms' entry deterrence behavior from a credible to an empty threat. In the case depicted in Figure 9.3(b), $Q_f^S < Q_f^M < Q_f^S + Q_d^S$ so that total output in the industry is greater after the entry of the domestic firm, while the output of the foreign firm declines relative to what it was before entry. As a result, price declines to P^S, and domestic consumers' surplus increases by an amount corresponding to the area of the quadrilateral $P^S D^S D'' P_f^0$, while the domestic entrant earns gross profits corresponding to the area of the quadrilateral $A' IHP^S$. Pure social profits are then this gross profit less fixed costs and the amount of the subsidy. If the sum of the pure social profit and the increase in consumers' surplus is positive, then from the standpoint of national economic welfare, policies to protect and foster the domestic firm are justified.

Let us restate the essence of the above analysis. In an industry where a monopolist is able to exercise its market power to influence prices, the identity of the country to which the resulting monopoly rent accrues is of critical importance in determining the international distribution of income. When rents accrue to a foreign country, and the social costs that accompany the protective policies toward the domestic firm are sufficiently small, then from the standpoint of national economic welfare there is a possibility that policies that protect the domestic firm as a means of resisting the foreign monopolist are justifiable.

Now, what impact does the adoption of such domestic policies have on foreign economic welfare? First, the rents that accrue to the foreign country decline with certainty in comparison to when the foreign firm acts to deter entry. On the other hand, if the appearance of domestic countervening power lowers the price of the good in the foreign market, foreign consumers' surplus increases. In contrast to the theory of a retaliatory tariff, the policy considered in this section need not necessarily worsen economic welfare abroad. Of course, if in spite of this, the decrease in monopoly rents earned by the foreign firm is sufficiently great, then it is possible that foreign national economic welfare will be reduced. Furthermore, when approached in terms of the efficiency of resource allocation in the world as a whole, the fixed-cost burden that accompanies entry by the domestic firm, when combined with that of the foreign firm, leads to duplicate investment, so that it must be recognized that such policies could be inefficient.

Finally, we would like to list some qualifications that reflect on the nature of the arguments of this section.

First, if the protective policies toward the domestic firm undertaken by the government are only empty threats, then the welfare-improving effects argued for above will not appear. It is necessary for the government to show that it has the resolve to tear down the monopolistic position of the foreign firm through the actual payment of subsidies. Only through such credible threats can the government obtain an improvement in domestic welfare.

Two, in thinking about the economic development strategy of a country, it is often argued that foreign direct investment should be accepted as a way to utilize the capital and technology of foreign firms. If, however, the foreign firm achieves a monopolistic position in the domestic market, there is the possibility that through the repatriation of monopoly rents domestic economic welfare will be worsened. In such a case, it is desirable to regulate foreign direct investment to some extent and to seek to protect domestic industry.

Third, it is not easy to measure the extent to which in actual markets foreign monopolists are earning monopoly rents.[22] If, however, one wants to try to protect domestic firms for the reasons given in this section, it is not permissible to neglect the step of objectively evaluating the social costs that one is trying to eliminate through such policies. There is the danger that the reationale given here could be used as an excuse to justify policies for the protection of oligopolistic firms with their distortions to resource allocation, or otherwise serve as a justification when there is no other ready rationale.

Fourth, as has already been stated, there is the possibility that the protection of domestic firms will increase foreign consumers' surplus, but it is a certainty that the monopoly rents of foreign firms will decline. It is thus important not to forget that the nature of the policies considered in this section are such that domestic protection policies will inflict damage on foreign firms and can become a source of trade friction.[23]

V. Excess Competition, Entry Restriction, and Cartels

Finally, we would like to analyze from the standpoint of economic theory the implications of policies for directly intervening in the industrial organization internal to a given industry. What we have specifically in mind are entry restrictions for a given industry and guidance for forming cartels to coordinate production and facilities investment, for forming "recession" cartels, and for forming cartels to eliminate capacity. The guiding concept of industrial policy for coordination within an industry is the "elimination of excess competition." First we want to examine theoretically the concept of "excess" competition.

A. The Concept of Excess Competition

It is quite surprising that, despite the frequency with which the concept of excess competition is used in general discussions of industrial policy by the government, by business, and by journalists, until now there has been no common agreement on the economic meaning of the concept.[24] Among academic economists there is "a wide-spread belief that increasing competition will increase welfare,"[25] and from this perspective the phrasing that "competition" is "excessive" echoes of self-contradiction. On the other hand, one can make a strong claim that in general, that is, in the government, business circles, and journalism, there is a widespread belief that competition is evil. According to the understanding of those who believe this, in Japan since the end of the war cartels and government regulation have in fact been desirable. This welcoming of policy that restricts competition has been both wide-ranging and deeply rooted.[26]

But in reality, the relationship between competition and economic welfare is not as straightforward as the widespread belief in competition among economists would have one suppose. In fact, it is possible that measures taken to stimulate competition result in an inefficient equilibrium. To give an example of such a case, we analyze the relationship between competition and economic welfare in a concentrated, Cournot–Nash oligopoly in an industry with a homogeneous product.[27]

We assume that each firm in the industry we are analyzing behaves in a Cournot–Nash fashion. We also assume that the government can regulate entry into the industry, but cannot enforce for each firm marginal-cost pricing.[28] We refer to the number of firms that in this partial equilibrium model maximizes total social surplus (the sum of consumers' and producers' surplus) as the "second-best number of firms."[29] We refer to the number of firms operating in the industry in the long-run Cournot–Nash equilibrium, arrived at when firms can freely enter and exit, as the "equilibrium number of firms." The approach will then be to compare from the standpoint of national economic welfare the desirable number of firms (the second-best number of firms) and the number of firms operating in an industry arrived at naturally in the long run (the equilibrium number of firms). We can readily show that under relatively unrestrictive assumptions about firms' costs and demand in the industry, in this model one generally finds excess competition in the sense that the equilibrium number of firms exceeds the second-best number of firms.[30]

We argue that this straightforward result has a two-fold significance. First, when the number of firms in a Cournot–Nash oligopoly increases, the change does not always improve welfare, so that it serves to raise rational doubts about the myth that competition is always beneficial. Second, while it is in terms of a very specialized model of an oligopoly, we show that as a result of the autonomous entry and exit of private firms, there is the possibility of excessive entry relative to the second-best number of firms. Thus the model has a role in showing theoretically one situation in which the term excess competition is appropriate.

B. Coordination within an Industry and Excess Competition in Japan

In considering excess competition in relation to Japanese policies for coordination within an industry, there is one extremely important point on which we have so far deliberately not touched. This is that in Japan, excess competition is something that has arisen *after* industrial policy intervention. If this is true, then it is a crushing rebuttal to attempts to justify policy intervention for adjustment within industry in the name of eliminating excess competition.

In this direction, there are two different arguments with a common thread. The first is the "shelter from the storm" effect of industrial policy pointed out by Takafusa Nakamura [1969, 1978, 1981]. This is the claim that firms in an industry, in their competition for market share, invested more than their own capital permitted, thereby bringing about rapid growth of the industry as a whole because of their expectation that when at some point there arose excess production and firm profitability declined sharply, with industry facing a crisis, then "administrative guidance" would come to the rescue.[31]

The second point is that excess competition in investment in capacity is nothing other than the result of the government's efforts at some sort of quota allocation, as Komiya has repeatedly stressed.[32] According to this line of thought, excess competition in investment arises because, in industries in which plant capacity can be expressed in terms of a simple index, government permits are granted by allocating them in proportion to existing capacity and an incentive is given for firms to try to expand their capacity beyond the boundary of what would be thought appropriate in terms of market conditions.

It is difficult to prove or provide strong evidence for claims such as these. The insights, however, most certainly provide a very important perspective on the significance and results of industrial policy-type interventions in a market economy.

C. Theoretical Analysis of Policies for Forming Cartels

As a policy intervention for adjustments within an industry, in Japan there has often been administrative guidance for forming recession cartels, output or investment coordination cartels, and cartels for capacity scrapping. It is probably these cartel policies that have been the main basis for criticizing Japanese industrial policy. This is because cartel policy impedes the operation of the market mechanism and tends to end up protecting existing large firms, and in comparison with the many other policy instruments, it is exceedingly difficult to justify. It can probably be said that the negative image of industrial policy that has up to now been held is based on an understanding of cartel policy and administrative guidance as being the primary policy instrument.

We believe, however, that in terms of resource allocation a theoretical case can be made for investment coordination and capacity scrapping cartels or R&D cooperatives. Below, we examine the theoretical possibilities in the case of capacity scrapping cartels.

Let us consider here a declining industry, where currently capacity is redundant relative to expected demand, and where furthermore there is virtually no hope that excess capacity will in the future disappear. In addition, the industry is oligopolistic, where all firms are interdependent, and where firms act in cognizance thereto. To simplify the argument, we assume that the industry is a duopoly, that firms' profits coincide with total social surplus because, for instance, they are able to enforce perfect price discrimination, and finally, that it is not possible for institutional or ethical reasons, or because of their organization, for the two firms to merge.

Let us assume that these firms have only two possible strategies, (A) to abandon excess capacity or (M) to maintain it. If there is no policy intervention of any sort, then, for example, let the payoffs for the two firms be as indicated in Table I. These pairs of numbers represent, respectively, the payoffs of Firm 1 and Firm 2. Thus if Firm 1 follows strategy A, it abandons its capacity in the industry without any compensation, which results in a payoff of -2. If, on the other hand, firm 1 adopts strategy M, it earns a payoff of $+10$ when Firm 2 adopts strategy A and has a payoff of -1 when Firm 2 adopts strategy M. The parallel is true for Firm 2. In this case, neither firm on its own abandons capacity, regardless of the strategy adopted by the other firm, and so the strategy pair (M, M)

TABLE I
Payoff Matrix

Firm 1 \ Firm 2	A	M
A	(−2, −2)	(−2, 10)
M	(10, −2)	(−1, −1)

is a dominant equilibrium strategy.[33] Excess capacity in the industry will not be eliminated through private incentives.

Let us now assume that through policy intervention and administrative guidance a cartel is formed under the binding condition that the firm that remains in the industry will compensate the firm that exits for the scrapping of its facilities. The payoff matrix of the two firms will be as indicated in Table II. In this case, the two pairs of strategies (M, A) and (A, M) are each a Cournot–Nash equilibrium in that, given the strategy of the one firm, the other will have no motive to change its strategy. Among these two Cournot–Nash equilibria, Firm 1 will want to have (M, A) chosen (alternatively, Firm 2 would want (A, M) chosen), but when for some reason it is impossible for the two firms to merge, there is no way in which the impasse can be resolved. Whichever of these occurs, however, it will be more desirable from the standpoint of both firms than the inevitable equilibrium of (M, M) of Table I. The choice between these two equilibria must be made for some reason lying outside our story, such as differences in cost conditions of the two firms or administrative guidance by the government.

There are problems with the above model. The first problem is why total surplus increases from that of the oligopoly situation after a monopoly is formed as a result of strategy (M, A) or (A, M). A second, more fundamental problem is the following. When a firm abandons capacity, it has to bear the loss of sunk costs of 2. Even when both firms maintain their capacity, however, they face payoffs of only −1. In other words, when

TABLE II
Payoff Matrix

Firm 1 \ Firm 2	A	M
A	(−2, −2)	(0, 8)
M	(8, 0)	(−1, −1)

sunk costs are excluded, it is seen that the firms are earning positive profits, so that in fact there is no excess capacity.

In the case of investment in capacity or R&D, however, there is a source for excess competition on which we have not so far touched. For competition involving investment or technology, the firm that first builds capacity and captures the market or that first develops a technology and obtains a patent will gain an overwhelming advantage, so that firms that are in the least bit behind in this competition will only be able to secure meager profits. This sort of competition has some aspects of a rank-order tournament in time, where by using prices in a market mechanism, an optimal allocation of resources cannot be achieved.[34] In the case of capacity scrapping, the reason that these firms do not scrap capacity and exit from the industry is that, if the other firm goes bankrupt, the entire market becomes theirs and high profits can be earned.

To be specific, let us look at a two-period model where the discount rate is zero. When facilities are scrapped, payoffs in this period are -2 and next period 0, so that the total payoff over the two periods is -2. On the other hand, if the other firm scraps its capacity, both this period and next period a monopoly payoff of $+5$ is earned, giving a total payoff of $+10$. If both firms maintain their capacity, payoffs are -3.5 in the first period because of (excess) competition. As losses greater than sunk costs occur, one of the firms will go bankrupt because of this competition, so that in the next period only one firm will remain. In the next period, the bankrupt firm will earn profits of 0 and the remaining firm will earn monopoly profits of $+5$. Neither firm knows ahead of time which will go bankrupt, and we assume that each firm believes its probability of going bankrupt is 1/2. In this case, the expected profits of both firms consist of expected second-period profits of 2.5 less current-period losses of 3.5, giving total expected profits of -1, completing the payoff matrix given in Table I.

As a result, neither firm has an incentive to scrap capacity, and because the outcome of the rank-order tournament (consisting of which firm will in the end remain and which will go bankrupt) is unforeseeable, there is the possibility that excess competition will arise. In this case, some sort of government intervention, and in particular cartel policies, take on meaning.

There is now one more point relating to cartel policies. Unlike capacity scrapping cartels, for recession, output adjustment, and price cartels, the cartel agreement is readily broken through firms undertaking actions to increase their own profits. The incentive to do this is particularly strong when the number of members of the cartel is great, so that the effectiveness of the cartel will not be much affected even though a firm quits the cartel.

In fact, one can imagine that the incentive is greater, the greater the possibility that such a firm will be the only one to reap the benefits of the higher cartel price.[35] Thus, regardless of whether cartel policies themselves have meaning, to undertake such policies successfully requires that the industry be highly oligopolistic, and that the goal for which the cartel is formed is, as in the case of capacity scrapping, something that firms can readily monitor themselves or that otherwise makes it difficult to break the cartel.[36]

Notes

1. See the explicit discussion of this point by Kaizuka [1973] and Tsuruta [1982], pp. 278–9. For a representative attempt at justifying policy by those involved in policy formation, see Morozumi [1966] and Sangyo Seisaku Kenkyu Group [1984].
2. See Kaizuka [1973], p. 169, and Tsuruta [1982], p. 279.
3. Even when there is no market failure, it is always possible for a large country to exercise its monopoly power in international trade policy, influencing national welfare as is seen classically in optimal tariff theory. Optimal tariffs, however, are policies that seek to improve national welfare by income redistribution, so that the level of welfare of the world as a whole is necessarily reduced. In contrast, the cases that we want to examine are those where in the world as a whole there is inefficiency, so that there remains the possibility that the level of welfare of the world as a whole will be improved.
4. Below, "cartel policies" will refer to cases in which a policy arm of the government explicitly directs cartel behavior among the firms of an industry for adjusting price, output, or investment, or tacitly approves of such activities.
5. For a discussion of such points, see, for example, Chapter 18 of this book.
6. See also Chapters 7 and 8 of this book concerning the general problem of R&D, and especially the difficulties that arise from the public-good nature of technology.
7. For a more detailed analysis, see for example Barzel [1968], Loury [1979], and Lee and Wilde [1980].
8. For a discussion of the concept of individual risk, the relation of individual risk to insurance, and an analysis thereof, see Malinvaud [1972, 1978].
9. The following explanation is due principally to Dasgupta and Stiglitz [1980b].
10. For an analysis of the learning curve and its economic implications, see Spence [1981].
11. For a more detailed explication of the above points, see Sections II and III of Chapter 10 in this book.
12. The concept of indicative planning has been variously used by different writers and in different countries, and there is no consensus on the goal of such planning being the transmission and exchange of information, as we use it here. In this chapter, however, we use the concept to refer to the function of the government in transmitting and exchanging information.
13. Komiya [1975], p. 324.
14. This distinction corresponds to that between environmental and market uncertainty, which was introduced by Meade [1970] in his discussion of uncertainty. See also Hirshleifer [1971].
15. For this type of impact of information, see Chapter 10 on economies of scale and declining cost industries.

16. However, the role of the government as an institution for the transmission of information was not necessarily something that the government consciously sought. In fact, when the government sought to do this, it is not clear that its intentions were achieved in practice. The above argument is based on the assumption that private agents always supply accurate information, but when it is perceived that the government is collecting and transmitting information with the intent of changing the behavior of private agents, through intentional manipulation the providers of information may try to achieve the allocation fo resources that is most beneficial to themselves.

17. See Chapter 10 for a discussion of the set-up cost of an industry.

18. The following owes much to Brander and Spencer [1981], Dixit [1980], and Krugman [1983].

19. Dixit [1980] and Eaton and Lipsey [1981] show that this presumption is not that unrealistic.

20. The distinction between and application of the concepts of empty and credible threats is made clear in Shelling [1956]. For applications in the analysis of oligopoly, see Spencer and Brander [1983].

21. The same effect can be achieved by the payment of different types of subsidies. For example, a production subsidy increases the distance from the origin of the point of discontinuity in the domestic firm's reaction curve, meaning that the foreign firm's output at the point of discontinuity is increased, and at the same time, the subsidy shifts the curve as a whole outward. An import tariff shifts the foreign firm's reaction curve inward, while an import quota also bends it inward.

22. On this point, see Caves [1982] and Chapter 6 of this book.

23. From the perspective of capturing the monopoly rents split among oligopolistic firms that reside in different countries, the analysis of this section can be applied not only to the case of markets for a homogeneous good, but also to industrial policy in the face of competition in R&D. See Krugman [1983] and Spencer and Brander [1983] on this, including the application to export subsidy policies.

24. From the standpoint of standard economic analysis, representative sources that examine the various facets of this concept are Bain [1968], Chapter 12, Futatsugi [1974], Imai et al. [1972], pp. 248–256, Komiya [1975], pp. 314–315, Tsutomu Nakamura [1969], Takafusa Nakamura [1969], Scherer [1980] Chapters 7, 9, and 21, Stiglitz [1981], Suzumura and Kiyono [1987], Tachi et al. [1964], Part 2, and von Weizsäcker [1980a], [1980b]. See on the other hand Morozumi [1966], pp. 61–62, for the views of policy formulators. This Morozumi book is a compilation of internal studies done for the Industrial Policy Study Committee of MITI while Morozumi was Deputy Director-General of the MITI Enterprise Bureau.

25. This quote is from Stiglitz [1981], p. 184. Among economists who have been baptized as believers in neoclassical microeconomics, this sort of belief is undoubtedly widely held. For example, at the height of the "New Industrial Structure" debate, we find this quote expounding on the theory of workable competition, from Konishi [1967], p. 140.

    According to the claims of welfare economics, under perfect competition an optimal allocation of resources is achieved, and economic welfare is maximized. While it cannot be hoped that perfect competition can in reality be achieved, it can be expected that the greater the degree of competition, the more effectively resources will be allocated, the lower prices will be, and the closer production will be to the ideal level of output.

26. For example, see Imai et al. [1972], p. 255.

27. For the details of the following analysis see Suzumura and Kiyono [1987].

28. The empirical backing for this assumption is that, except for public enterprises and for firms that are members of cartels to which the Antimonopoly Law is not applicable, the Japanese government is in general not empowered to intervene in setting prices.
29. Here we use the term "second-best" because in our model the government authorities are unable to set prices optimally, that is, they are not able to force firms to set prices on the basis of marginal costs.
30. Here the term *excess competition* is defined to refer to the long-run equilibrium in an industry that is a concentrated oligopoly producing a homogeneous good. If only on this point, our understanding is close to that previously formulated by Kumagai [1970], pp. 45–49. In contrast to this, the "excessive competition," or "cut-throat competition," analyzed in Bain [1968] and Scherer [1980] refers to an unconcentrated industry in which there is ready entry, but where when excess capacity arises exit does not rapidly occur and in which labor mobility is low. It thus refers to the severe competition that arises during the course of adjustment to a new equilibrium in the industry. The concept of *excess competition* discussed in Chapter 3 of this book is similar to this concept.
31. T. Nakamura [1974], p. 62. See also T. Nakamura [1978], pp. 190–191. This theory of the role of industrial policy of Nakamura reminds us of the famous analogy of Schumpeter [1942], p. 88, that "a car with brakes of course is driven faster than one without."
32. Komiya [1975], Chapter 10. This line of thought can also be found in Imai et al. [1972], Chapter 13, Tachi et al. [1964], Part 2, Futatsugi [1974], p. 115, and Takafusa Nakamura [1969], pp. 331–332. See also Chapter 17 of this book.
33. A strategy is "dominant" when that strategy is an optimal action regardless of the actions of other firms. A "dominant strategy equilibrium" is one in which all firms adopt dominant strategies.
34. For an analysis of excess investment arising from this cause, see for example Barzel [1968], Loury [1979], and Dasgupta and Stiglitz [1980a].
35. For example, see Okuno, Postlewaite, and Roberts [1980].
36. For the problems of capacity scrapping in declining industries, see Chapters 13 and 14 of this book. In the latter, it is shown in detail that despite government intervention, capacity scrapping in the textile industry did not progress smoothly. From our analysis, the reason for this can be sought in the extremely large number of firms in the industry. In other words, when there are a large number of atomistic firms, it is extraordinarily difficult either to make agreements within the cartel binding in practice or to regulate the large number of "outsider" firms.

CHAPTER 10

Industry Promotion and Trade

MOTOSHIGE ITOH

Faculty of Economics
University of Tokyo
Tokyo, Japan

MASAHIRO OKUNO

Faculty of Economics
University of Tokyo
Tokyo, Japan

KAZUHARU KIYONO

Department of Economics
Gakushuin University
Tokyo, Japan

KOTARO SUZUMURA

Institute of Economic Research
Hitotsubashi University
Tokyo, Japan

I. Introduction

As a nation our land area is extremely limited . . . the populace of our nation cannot survive for a single day without imports to supplement domestic supplies of food and raw materials. In order to make possible these imports, our country must export to earn the funds to pay for imports. Our nation's economy is distinctive in depending on overseas production in that with our domestic land area we are not self-sufficient. Unless we depend on trade, both domestic production and employment must fall, and circular flows of the economy will decline to a low level, so that the standard of living will not be able to be maintained at a reasonable level.

As in the above quote, which opened the 1949 *White Paper on International Trade,* the concern of "modernizing the industrial structure"[1] was in the minds of the formulators of postwar Japanese industrial policy, so that, with gains from trade maximized, the Japanese economy could be rebuilt through trade. This can readily be seen in the content of the MITI Visions and the White Papers on International Trade, which from the 1950s and into the 1960s acclaimed first heavy and chemical industrialization and later high-technology industrialization.[2] There are probably many ways to go about defining the phrase "modernization of the industrial structure," but as will be detailed in the succeeding four sections, this referred to shifting the structure as much as possible to a group of industries in which it was easy to increase productivity, for which demand was forecast to expand in the future, and which had as a base high technology.

As was shown in Chapter 6 of this book, it can be claimed that Japan was able, perhaps serendipitously, to modernize its industrial structure. This change had as its source features unrelated to policy: the strong investment demand in the private economy, the rapid rate of technical progress, the large domestic market, and the abundant, capable labor force. As will be explained below, however, tariffs and the regulation of foreign direct investment also played an important role.[3] Furthermore, in each of the postwar periods, industries that were main foci of industrial policy or international trade policy played principal roles in the process of modernizing the Japanese industrial structure. Such industries included steel, shipbuilding, automobiles, petrochemicals, computers, and integrated circuits. The goal of this chapter is to analyze in simple models, from the standpoint of the domestic and world economies, the impact of the modernization of the industrial structure that these industrial policies sought.

Before starting our analysis, we would first like to give an overview of the theories relating to the mechanisms that might be thought to lie behind our models. In the classical Ricardian or Heckscher–Ohlin trade theory, the analysis is carried out taking industrial structure and technology as given. In such a world, each country gains from trade and in that sense is in a preconceived state of harmony. In the development of these theories, almost no importance is given to changes in the structure of the trade that accompanies changes in the industrial structure, and in most cases, this feature is altogether ignored.[4] The industrial structure of a country is, however, an important determinant of the gains it receives from trade. Changes in structure over time, and the direction of change, are furthermore readily influenced by policy interventions, chance historical events, and culture and institutions. Even for technology, much is not determined exogenously but is in large part the result of learning-by-doing, investment in R&D, and mutual interactions with the market. The level of technology and the industrial structure are thus not givens, and it is therefore necessary to analyze how the structure of trade and economic welfare are influenced by changes therein.

In an exchange economy, the gain (welfare) obtained by an economic actor through exchange depends on the initial endowment of the actor.[5] Even in international economics, the gains (welfare) an economy obtains through trade are greatly influenced by its industrial structure, which determines what goods can be exported and which must be imported. If the structure of industry and demand is such that goods can be exported for which foreign demand is strong, and goods that foreign countries can supply cheaply can be imported, then the economic welfare of the economy is higher. In this sense, the issue in analyzing industrial structure and trade is not simply the international allocation of resources and efficiency thereunder, but also is in great measure the distribution of the gains from trade among countries.

In orthodox trade theory, it cannot be said that the mechanism of the development of an industry or the relationship between industrial structure and the gains from trade have been adequately analyzed. For example, in the standard models of protection of an infant industry, the results generally hinge on the presence of dynamic externalities from learning by doing in the context of perfect competition and partial equilibrium analysis.[6] In such models, however, it is difficult to come to grips with features thought to be important in the development of Japanese industry, such as economies of scale that arise through the interaction of different industries. The purpose of this chapter is to analyze the effect of industrial development policies, by incorporating into the analysis features thought important in the case of Japan that have not been adequately examined in orthodox theory.

The chapter is organized as follows. In Section II, we will examine in a partial equilibrium model the role of policy interventions, and in particular policies protecting industry, looking at the social "setup" costs of developing an industry. When there are many declining-cost elements, and the (long-run) supply curve for an industry is decreasing, it will not be able to develop to maturity and be able to one day stand on its own through private incentives, even though it is capable of doing so once established. Social setup costs thus become for such an industry costs that hinder independence. When there exist social setup costs in fostering an industry, then some sort of policy intervention is required to firmly establish the industry. Here, from among various possible policies, we will primarily examine industrial development policies that are composed of import restrictions.[7]

Section III is a model of changes in the structure of trade when there is a declining-cost industry because of, for instance, economies of scale. In an industry in which declining costs are working strongly, trade arises through a mechanism totally unrelated to comparative advantage, and the interventions of industrial policy can substantially influence the pattern of trade. In considering Japanese industrial policy, the impact of policy under such economies of scale cannot be neglected.

As is made clear in the models presented in Sections II and III, the industrial structure of an economy is dependent in large part on policy interventions, the course of history, and cultural and institutional factors. Using a simple Ricardian model, Section IV analyzes how a country's industrial structure governs its gains from trade. Our main conclusion is that if the modernization of Japan's industrial structure is understood to mean the promotion of industrial diversification and the industries "on the margin," and in particular when it is aimed at an industrial structure centered around industries in which productivity can be readily increased, for which demand is foreseen as developing in the future, and which have a basis in high technology, then such modernization was effective in increasing Japan's gains from trade.

II. Setup Costs of Industry: Scale Economies, Learning by Doing, and Investment in R&D

In this section, we will consider economies of scale and declining-cost situations that arise from the setup costs of establishing an industry. One can conceive of many sources of declining costs, but those that are important in relation to the issue of fostering an industry can be divided into roughly three categories.

First, there is the textbook case of a declining-cost industry, driven by Marshallian externalities, in which the overall expansion of the industry brings an improvement in the technology and cost conditions of each firm. Specific examples are the automotive and household electrical goods industries, which were supported by a network of parts subcontractors. In these industries, with their development and the expansion of output, parts suppliers were built up and technology was transmitted, so that the costs of each firm declined.[8]

Second, there is the case that has been the main focus of traditional infant-industry arguments, where a dynamic process of learning by doing and the accumulation of experience and increased production know-how results in a decrease in costs. This dynamic externality is thought to have had a large impact in the integrated circuit, computer, and other high-technology industries. This type of externality seems to be a common feature of virtually all young industries and is probably both the most important and the most ubiquitous set-up cost. Despite this, in order to avoid the unnecessary complications of dynamic problems, we will keep our comments on it to a minimum.

Third, there is the case in which, for informational reasons, industries are not able to fully grasp the extent of demand. In terms of industries, one thinks here of those where, due to technology, there are economies of scale at the plant or the firm level, and where furthermore the output of the industry is used as an input by other industries, or where there are many other industries which supply the industry. The industry, in other words, comprises an important link in a hierarchy of industries. Using the terminology of Japanese industrial policy, these are "broadly based" industries, such as steel and petrochemicals, which require large-scale facilities. Because of economies of scale such industries are by necessity oligopolistic, and as is true for oligopolistic industries, prices by themselves do not transmit the information necessary for efficient allocation of resources. Thus it is often impossible to foresee how induced demand, or the supply of inputs, will change as the industry develops. In such a case, an entire industrial sector, composed of industries linked to the industry, tends to have set-up costs for the development of the sector as a whole.[9]

To make clear what we mean by the concept of the set-up costs for establishing an industry, let us consider by what mechanism we can guarantee optimal market transactions in the normal case in which there are no externalities and at the firm level there are increasing marginal costs. When costs are increasing, each producer's adjustment, which is optimal locally, leads automatically to global optimality. For example, if the marginal cost *(MC)* of a producer is less than the market price *(P)* of its good, then the producer will attempt to increase its output.[10] This sort of adjustment behavior by producers is also desirable for society as a whole, and eventually (when price and marginal cost reach equality) the socially optimal quantity of output will automatically be achieved. When, similarly, *MC > P,* then output is socially excessive, but it will also be adjusted autonomously by producers. In an economy in which costs are increasing in all industries, then the desirable structure of industry will be established without government intervention through the autonomous behavior of the private economy. Thus, the setup costs are zero for this industry, as there are no costs that hinder the establishment of the industry.

On the other hand, in an industry with declining costs, an optimal point will not be arrived at through local adjustments. Let us first explain this point for the case of Marshallian externalities.

In Figure 10.1 the curve *AC* is the average cost curve of the industry as a whole, or, alternatively, the long-run industry supply curve. (Here the average cost curve of the individual firm is always increasing, but as output in the industry as a whole increases, the curve shifts downward.) For instance, this cost curve is declining in part because as output increases, a network of parts subcontractors is built up and unit costs become lower. Here p^* is the international price of the good that the industry supplies, and *EF* is the export supply curve of the good from other countries. The foreign country export supply curve is horizontal because the home country is small.[11]

Let us assume that initially output is zero and that domestic demand of x_2 is supplied entirely by imports from abroad. If there is no intervention by the government, then home-country output in the industry will remain

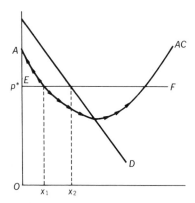

Fig. 10.1.   The average cost (AC) curve under Marshallian externalities.

at zero. This is because, with the marginal cost of each firm higher than the price, there is no incentive to increase output. In fact, as indicated by the arrows on the curve AC, when the output of the industry as a whole is below x_1, each producer will reduce its supply until the output of the industry as a whole becomes zero. If each producer could have a global view of the industry as a whole, and most producers worked in concert to increase their output, then it should be apparent that output greater than x_1 could be realized and adequate profits could be obtained. But individual producers are unable to see that far ahead and are furthermore unable to cooperate to achieve an output greater than x_1.

One conceivable method of establishing and developing such an industry is for the government to subsidize production. For example, if the amount represented by the length AE in Figure 10.1 is paid as a subsidy for each unit of output, production will thenceforth increase. If the costs of tax collection and the disbursement of subsidies are ignored, then this is an effective policy. But in practice, such social costs are quite substantial, so that direct subsidy policies are difficult to implement.

An alternative method is to temporarily restrict the supply of the good from abroad, using domestic demand as the driving force for developing the industry. For example, in Figure 10.1 the curve D is the economy's demand curve, so that if imports from abroad are temporarily halted, it becomes possible to pull the level of output of the economy above x_1. Once output greater than x_1 is realized, even if import restrictions are removed, the industry will be able to develop. Now in order for this method to be applicable, it is important to note that there must be substantial domestic demand. If the intersection of the demand curve and the foreign supply curve is to the left of x_1, then it will not be feasible to develop the industry through import restrictions.

In the case of Japan, the domestic market was sufficiently large, while because of the fiscal situation of Japan at that time, import restrictions were considerably more effective than subsidy policies. However, whether it was a policy of import restrictions or subsidies, domestic purchasers of the good were unable to avoid paying a high price, and there were also the distortions in resource allocation caused by taxation. Those who reaped the rewards of the development were the people connected with the industry and succeeding generations of consumers. One must therefore note that policies that protect declining-cost industries thus give rise to problems in allocation within and across generations.

Next, we want to analyze the case in which the products of the industry serve as intermediate inputs to other industries, looking at the cost curve for the entire industrial sector that contains the industry.[12] Steel and petrochemicals are such industries, where economies of scale operate at the firm (or factory) level. When economies of scale operate at the firm level, the industry is of necessity oligopolistic or monopolistic. Here, if another industry that produces final goods using the output of the industry as an intermediate input is protected, the scale and the number of firms in the final goods industry will increase, and the derived demand for the intermediate good will also increase. The output of each of the oligopolistic firms will increase because of this increase in derived demand, and there will also be new entry into the oligopoly. These new entrants will strengthen competition in the intermediate-good oligopoly, and if the increase in production of the individual firms through economies of scale lowers average costs, then the price of the intermediate good will also decline. As a result, the cost of the final good that is made using this intermediate input will decline as well, shifting the cost curves of the constituent industries further to the right. There will also be additional derived demand for the intermediate good. As a result, because of economies of scale in the intermediate-good industry, and the feedback effect operating back and forth across industries, the cost curve of the industrial sector as a whole that incorporates both the intermediate- and final-goods industries will in part decline, as depicted in Figure 10.1

In order to achieve these gains from scale economies within a market economy in which there is no government intervention, it is necessary for each firm in the intermediate-good industry to correctly foresee all the complicated changes arising in the process. Specifically, when a firm increases its output and lowers price, it must be able to correctly foresee, first, the process through which final and then derived demand are increased, next how such increases in derived demand occur in the case of other intermediate goods, and finally the process through which all of this decreases costs in the final-good industry. When one considers the cost incurred in collecting the information needed for correctly forecasting this (including estimating demand for the final-good industry and the extent to which costs can be decreased in other intermediate-goods industries), then when only private incentives are present, it is very difficult to bring into play economies of scale in the declining-cost sector. Therefore, as in the case of Marshallian externalities, it is necessary to utilize infant industry policies, which through temporary import restrictions redirect domestic demand.

The number of firms participating in an industry is extremely important as a determinant of performance in oligopolistic markets. When the number of firms is excessively small, price is probably close to the monopoly price, while when the number of firms is too large, no individual firm will be able to enjoy economies of scale. We want to note that, in the situation argued above, where an increase in derived demand lowers the price of the intermediate good, then not only was it necessary for each firm to have been able to bring into play economies of scale, but it was also essential for there to have been vigorous competition among firms. In the Japanese steel and petrochemical industries, or in the integrated circuit industry where learning by doing was important, there were 5 to 10 firms (a relatively large number) engaged in vigorous competition, which we believe underlay the good performance of these oligopolistic markets. In this the large size of the domestic Japanese market played a very important role.

III. Trade and Industrial Policy under Economies of Scale

When returns to scale are great, so that there is an industry in which costs decline, then trade can arise through a mechanism fundamentally different from that of comparative advantage. In this section, along with explaining this trade mechanism, we will make some observations on the role that industrial policy can play. Below we assume that Marshallian externalities are the source of the economies of scale. The same argument will, however, in general carry through when there are returns to scale in the normal sense or through learning by doing or R&D.

We can explain the basic mechanism of trade under economies of scale through a simple two-good model.[13] Let us consider an economy producing two goods with labor as the sole factor of production. For good 2 there are constant returns to scale, specifically, technology permits one unit of labor to always produce one unit. For good 1, we will assume that there are economies of scale because of Marshallian externalities. The curve AB in Figure 10.2 shows the production frontier. The frontier is convex to the origin because the greater the production of good 1, the lower the private marginal cost (the marginal rate of transformation) of good 1 measured in terms of good 2.[14] Because of the externality there are economies of scale, and if we assume that each firm is behaving as a perfectly competitive firm, then in the long run private marginal cost equals average cost. Let us assume that as a closed economy production is at point E. Then the relative price of good 2 measured by good 1 is expressed by the slope of the line AE. This is because the price of good 1 measured in terms of labor is always 1, while the price of good 2 is private marginal cost, which is equal to average cost; when measured in terms of labor, this is the amount of labor used in the production of good 2 (the length of the segment Ax_2^*) divided by x_1^*.

To simplify, let us assume both the home and the foreign country have identical production frontiers. This assumption avoids the unnecessary complication of introducing comparative advantage issues and is not critical for the following argument. What we need to note is that even though the production frontiers and demand patterns of the two countries are completely identical, because of the existence of economies of scale, trade can arise between the two countries. In Figure 10.3, ABC is the production frontier of this world, obtained by superimposing the home and foreign country production frontiers. At point A, both countries are specialized

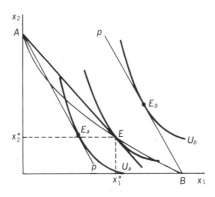

Fig. 10.2. Trade pattern and economic welfare under economies of scale.

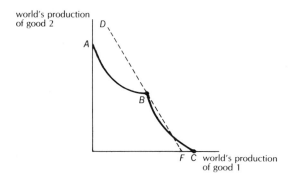

Fig. 10.3. The world's production frontier under economies of scale.

in the production of good 2, while in the segment *AB*, one country is specialized in the production of good 2, while the other country's production is not totally specialized. At point *B*, one country is specialized in good 1 and the other in good 2. For *BC*, one country is specialized in producing good 1 and the other is incompletely specialized. At point *C*, both countries are specialized in good 1.

The equilibrium point on this world production frontier depends on the shape of demand. Because of the particular shape that the production frontier assumes under economies of scale, however, the probability is high that under trade *B* will be the equilibrium point. (Equilibria lying on *AB* or *BC* are unstable, so that only the points *A*, *B*, and *C* are stable equilibria.) Assuming that point B represents the equilibrium under trade, one country is specialized in good 1 and the other in good 2. However, because the technologies of the two countries are identical, which country produces which is theoretically indeterminate. (The same is true when the technologies of the two countries differ as long as they do not differ by much.) Which country specializes in which good will be determined by factors that have so far been abstracted from our model. If, for instance, the source of the scale economies is learning by doing or R&D, the largest factor will be which country historically began to produce which good first.

At first glance, the national welfare of the two countries at point *B* would seem not to differ. The country that specializes in the production of good 1, however, will achieve greater welfare. This is because the international price at point *B* would conceivably be *DBF*.[15] Then, as is clear from Figure 10.2, even though both countries face the same relative price *p*, national welfare can differ substantially depending on the good in which the country is specialized. The country specializing in good 1 uses all its labor for producing this good, so that including rents, the wage is higher than in the other country.[16] When world demand for good 1 is larger (and hence the price of good 1 is higher), it is clear that the gains from specializing in good 1 are greater. Thus, when by chance a country is able to reap returns to scale because it initiated production first, the so-called first-mover situation, then through returns to scale the chance first-mover will have a comparative cost advantage, creating a barrier to entry to those who would later like to produce the good.

One other important factor for determining the pattern of trade when economies of scale are at work is policy intervention by the government. When which country specializes in which good cannot be determined on the basis of costs derived from technology, then policy intervention by the government can be extremely significant for determining the home country pattern of industry. At least from the home country standpoint, these policies to promote an industry are desirable when there are setup costs and when future demand is expected to rise. From the standpoint of the country that is the trading partner, however, the economic loss to it from the other country having such policies can be extremely high. Thus at issue when such government "leverage" is used in an industry is not simply costs versus benefits among producers in the industry, but, through changes in the structure of industry and trade in the two countries, gains and losses in national economic welfare of the two countries.

Regardless of whether Japan in fact followed "targeting" policies, as claimed by the United States and Europe, the recent U.S. criticism of Japanese targeting of the integrated circuit industry, as should be apparent from our argument thus far, reveals that in industries in which learning by doing and R&D play an important role in producing economies of scale, such criticism can easily arise. At the same time, as argued in the preceding chapter, one would presume that market failures readily occur where learning by doing and R&D are important, so that offhand government subsidies or other policy interventions in the industry cannot be rejected. The problem is when only one country uses extreme policy interventions, driving previously established industries in other countries out of the market, in other words, robbing other countries of benefits in order to obtain benefits for itself. Thus it is essential that there be international guidelines for the use of policy intervention toward learning by doing and R&D, and it is desirable that an international consensus be developed fostering an international division of labor where no one country monopolizes advantageous industries, and where foreign direct investment and industrial assistance are used to disperse production internationally.

IV. "Modernization" and Development of the Industry on the Margin

As seen in Section II, it is difficult for a declining-cost industry or sector to become established without temporary protection by the government. It is therefore possible through government policy for the industrial structure, and in particular, the structure of production to be controlled to some extent. Below then we will discuss which industry it would be profitable for a country to foster, given that the structure of production, that is, the supply conditions of a country, can be controlled by policy. In general, which industry should be promoted depends not only on the industry itself but also on the industrial structure of the country's economy as a whole together with the structure of demand in the world as a whole. Specifically, what determines a country's gains from international trade are the industries that on the margin are capable of exporting, or from which on the margin imports are possible. Below, to make this point clear, and to examine the impact of modernization of the industrial structure on economic welfare in Japan, we will analyze the relationship of gains from trade and industrial structure in the context of a simple Ricardian model.

A. The Model: Supply

Let us first examine the structure of production, that is, the supply side. To simplify the model, we will assume that the number of goods is infinite, and that these are indexed by a number n lying in the interval $[0,N]$. We assume only one factor of production, which we call "labor," and consider only two countries, the home and the foreign country. The technology for the production of each good in each country is represented by a given input requirement coefficient, i.e., by the quantity of the productive factor needed as an input to produce one unit of a good. We express the home and foreign labor input coefficient for producing good n by, respectively, a_n and a_n^*. In other words, all supply-side conditions, including the countries' technology levels and industrial structure, are completely summarized in a_n and a_n^*.

We denote the wage in terms of the home country currency by w and w^* for the home and foreign countries, respectively.[18] Now the following is a real model from which the monetary side has been abstracted, so that the only endogenous variable is the relative wage rate w/w^*, with the wage levels themselves otherwise unspecified. The pattern of trade under perfect

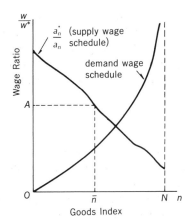

Fig. 10.4. Supply-wage and demand-wage schedules.

competition and free trade will then be determined as follows, with the country with a cost advantage being the exporter:

if $a_n w \leq a_n^* w^*$ the home country is the exporter,[19] and

if $a_n w > a_n^* w^*$ the foreign country is the exporter.

Under these conditions, goods for which a_n^*/a_n is greater than w/w^* will be home-country exports, and goods for which it is smaller will be home-country imports.

The declining curve a_n^*/a_n in Figure 10.4 represents this relationship, and will be referred to below as the supply-wage schedule. Here the curve is declining because goods have been indexed so that a_n^*/a_n is a declining function of n. Thus we have assumed that the smaller the value of n, the greater the home country's advantage. This wage-supply curve also expresses the relationship of the trade pattern of the two countries and the wage ratio w/w^*. For example, if the wage ratio is at point A on the vertical axis, then the goods indexed from 0 to $\bar{n}$ will be home-country exports, and those from $\bar{n}$ to N will be foreign-country exports. We will thus refer to $\bar{n}$ as the marginal good.

B. The Model: Demand

Next we set forth the demand side. The total labor supply of the home and foreign countries is fixed at L and L^*, so that income expressed in the currency of the home country will be wL and w^*L^* for, respectively, the home and the foreign countries. The crucial demand variable in our model is the expenditure ratio (the expenditure share) for each good, which we will express as δ_n and $\delta_n{}^*$ for, respectively, the home and the foreign countries. When all income is spent, the sum of the expenditure ratios (or, more precisely, their integral) equals 1, so that

$$\int_0^N \delta_n dn = \int_0^N \delta_n^* \, dn = 1$$

The expenditure ratio is in general a function of relative prices, but to simplify we assume that it is fixed (this is nothing more than the assumption of a Cobb–Douglas utility function).

Now, the boundary between exports and imports is the marginal good $\bar{n}$. Trade is balanced, so that the value of home-country imports must equal the value of foreign-country imports, or

$$\int_{\bar{n}}^N \delta_n \, dn \cdot wL = \int_0^n \delta_n^* \, dn \cdot w^* L^*$$

(The left side is home-country imports, and the right side is foreign-country imports.) Rearranging, we get

$$\frac{wL}{w^*L^*} = \int_0^{\bar{n}} \delta_n^* \, dn \bigg/ \int_{\bar{n}}^N \delta_n \, dn$$

or, equivalently,

$$\frac{w}{w^*} = \frac{\displaystyle\int_0^{\bar{n}} \delta_n^* \, dn}{\displaystyle\int_{\bar{n}}^N \delta_n \, dn} \cdot \frac{L^*}{L}$$

The increasing curve in Figure 10.4 represents the relationship between the relative wage w/w^* and the trade pattern (expressed by the marginal good, $\bar{n}$). Below, this curve is called the demand-wage schedule. The demand-wage schedule is always increasing because the greater the share of foreign expenditures on the home-country goods (or the smaller the share of home-country expenditures on imported goods), the higher the home-country relative wage ratio w/w^* and relative income ratio wL/w^*L^*.[20]

In our model, an increase in the home-country relative wage occurs through the increase in the range of home-country exports that accompanies an increase in the marginal good, $\bar{n}$, and a corresponding decrease in the range of imported goods. If the range of home-country exports increases, then to that extent the proportion of foreign-country expenditures on home-country goods will increase, and relative income will increase.[21] (More generally, income, or national factor income, is determined by the strength of demand for productive factors. Thus diversification of the range of home-country exports will expand demand, and the derived demand from this will increase demand for the home-country productive factor and raise home country income.)

C. The Model: Equilibrium

Equilibrium in trade between the two countries is given by the intersection of the supply-wage schedule, expressing the supply side, and the demand-wage schedule, expressing the demand side. In this model, the index $\bar{n}$ of the marginal good, expressing the trade pattern, and w/w^*, the relative wage, are determined by the parameters $\{a_n\}$ and $\{a_n{}^*\}$ expressing technology and industry structure, and $\{\delta_n\}$ and $\{\delta_n{}^*\}$ denoting demand.

D. "Technology Gaps": Industrial Development and Gains from Trade

We now introduce the concept of a "technology gap,"[22] so we can investigate the relationship between technology and gains from trade in the above model. In Figure 10.5, the curve A_1A_2 is the supply-wage schedule at the initial stage of industrial development of the home country. This

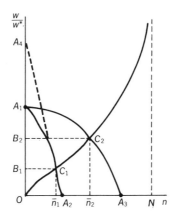

Fig. 10.5. Industrial development and change in the structure of trade.

crosses the horizontal axis at A_2 because, for goods with a greater index, the home country does not have the industry or technology to produce the goods. At this initial stage of development, the relative wage of the home country is extremely low (in the figure, OB_1), because with the undeveloped industrial structure of the home country, it is only able to absorb demand for goods with an expenditure ratio in $[0, \bar{n}_1]$. The lower the proportion of expenditures on these goods, the lower the height of the wage-demand curve in the interval $[0, \bar{n}_1]$ and the lower the relative wage w/w^*.

Let us now assume that the home country has been able to found a number of industries, so that relative to before, more industries are capable of production. The supply-wage schedule then shifts from A_1A_2 to A_1A_3. In other words, the industries producing the goods indexed on A_2A_3 have now been incorporated into the home country's technology and industrial structure. With the expansion of domestic industry, trade equilibrium shifts form C_1 to C_2, so that the goods indexed on $[\bar{n}_1 \ \bar{n}_2]$ are added to the range of home-country exports, thus the relative wage in the home country (both the relative wage and the wage in home-country currency) is increased in line with the demand-wage schedule, that is, by the amount of expenditure on these goods. This increase in the home-country relative wage following an increase in the range of home-country exports is by means of the mechanism explained in the subsection on demand above.

In the immediate postwar period, American GNP far surpassed that of other countries, and one of the main reasons for this can be found in the structure of world industry, which resembled that of Figure 10.5. In other words, America had an overwhelming lead in the automotive, steel, chemical, general and electrical machinery, and other industries, which accounted for a large proportion of demand. With an extremely high proportion of world expenditures for the products of these industries, the income level of America far exceeded that of other countries. Postwar Japanese economic development can be understood as a process of gradually overcoming the technology gap that existed at that time. Industries such as those listed above gradually came to be Japan's leading and export industries, and supported by the high proportion of expenditures for the goods these industries produced, the relative level of Japanese income rose, moving along the demand-wage schedule.[23] This sort of rise in relative income can theoretically occur as either an increase in the wage denominated in the home-country currency or as a decrease in the price of the foreign-country currency. During the period in which the exchange rate was maintained at ¥360 per U.S. dollar, the adjustment was borne chiefly by factor price changes denominated in the home-country currency, but since the 1970s part of the adjustment has occurred through movements in the exchange rate.

Besides this, there are other theoretically possible patterns of industrial development. The dotted line A_4A_2 in Figure 10.5 expresses an alternate pattern of industrial development. In other words, there could have been R&D or facilities investment in industries in which from the start Japan held a comparative advantage (the industries $[0, \bar{n}_1]$, which underlay the curve A_1A_2), so that the supply-wage schedule shifted from A_1A_2 to A_4A_2. If the Japanese economy (the home country in our model) developed in this fashion, then there would be almost no change in the structure of comparative advantage or in the relative wage. In the figure, this is indicated by there being absolutely no change in the equilibrium point C_1. In this case, there is a decline in the factor input coefficient for goods in the interval $[0, \bar{n}_1]$ in Japan (the home country), so that the only benefit received is a decline in the relative price of those goods (relative, that is, to other goods).[24]

In contrast to this, industrial development that expands the range of exportable goods of the home country by overcoming the technology gap shifts the equilibrium point along the demand-wage schedule (for example, from C_1 to C_2 in Figure 10.5). This shift increases the relative wage in the home country and brings not only the benefit of being able to consume cheaply the goods produced by the development of new industries, but through the rise in income (or an increase in the value of the yen), permits more goods to be imported than before—for example, the goods $[\bar{n}_2, \bar{n}_2]$ in the figure. Thus the pattern of industrial development followed by Japan was one that was in the pattern beneficial to the home country, raising the position of Japan in terms of relative income (which includes changes in the exchange rate).

On the other hand, when the home country's industries develop so as to overcome a technology gap, there is a dual impact on the foreign country. The first is a positive one in that, as a result of the development of home industry, goods whose production cost has been lowered can be imported at a lower price, while the second is a negative one, in that with the rise in home income, consumer prices rise. Let us explain this in terms of Figure 10.5. Assume that there has been development of home-country industries resulting in a shift in the supply-wage schedule from A_1A_2 to A_1A_3. As a result, the equilibrium shifts from C_1 to C_2, and the relative wage increases from B_1 to B_2. Then, the prices of the goods in the interval $[0, \bar{n}_1]$ rise, while the prices for goods in the interval $[\bar{n}_1, \bar{n}_2]$ fall in terms of foreign-country income. Which of these two occurrences has the greater impact depends on the extent to which the shift in the technology index

a_n is centered around the industries on the margin and the share that these industries on the margin have in total demand. The higher the expenditures are for industries on the margin, the greater the slope of the demand-wage schedule. If there is concentrated development of industries on the margin, for which the expenditure share is high, the chances increase that the result will be a sharp rise in the relative income of the home country, with losses to be born by the foreign country.

Whichever is the case, when a country is able to develop in a way that expands the range of its industries, then it is able to supply goods to the world at a lower price; at the same time, through trade this results in a redistribution of income among countries that is favorable to the country. With this change in international income distribution, this sort of development pattern can be extremely beneficial to the country. At the initial stage of Japanese industrial development, Japan was a small country so that the income redistribution effects of development were probably not very great. However, as Japanese exports came to include goods such as steel and automobiles, which account for a relatively large share of demand, the income redistribution effect among Japan and other countries became large. This, then, can be claimed as one source of trade friction.[25]

E. Industrial Development and Industrial Policy

Next we will examine the relationship between industrial development and industrial policy. The basic factors underlying Japanese industrial development were items such as private-sector economic vitality, an abundance of labor, and a high savings rate. The assistance given by industrial policy, however, cannot be ignored as a facet of this industrial development. Below we will take up three points we feel to be important.

First, there is the issue of the large setup costs that accompany the establishment of a new industry. As argued in the previous section, it is distinctly more difficult to establish a new industry than to further develop an existing one. The externalities stemming from the flow of transactions among industries and the important role of learning-by-doing at the initial stage, among other causes, give rise to tremendous setup costs in establishing an industry. When there are such setup costs, it is only through government intervention that the supply-wage schedule can be shifted. It cannot be denied that in the 1950s and 1960s the government, with its heavy-handed protection of domestic industry through trade policy, played an important role in assisting the establishment of a number of industries.[26] (It goes without saying that such industrial protection policies raised the domestic prices of imported goods, and so cannot be evaluated only from the standpoint of their impact on industrial development.)

Second, there is the issue of the gap between the benefits to society as a whole as opposed to the benefits to individual economic actors. A portion of the benefits from diversifying the range of home-country industries comes through changes in the exchange rate and an increase in income, which are induced by changes in the pattern of trade. This occurs in a macroeconomic fashion, and individual actors in the economy do not take this into account in their behavior.[27] For such reasons, using policy to move the direction of industrial development toward that of diversification can be evaluated favorably, especially from the standpoint of the home country.

Third, there is the issue of the direction of change of world demand. The pattern of world demand changes over time, with, for example, the expenditure share for goods with a high income elasticity of demand increasing as income increases. Another change has been the development of new markets and new goods. Upon examining postwar shifts in expenditure, it is clearly seen that a relatively large proportion is accounted for by new products, such as computers, large commercial jet airliners, integrated circuits, numerically controlled machine tools, supertankers, and household electrical goods. As these goods came onto the market and began to account for an increasing share of expenditures, the proportion of expenditures for other goods had to decline by an equivalent amount. Considering this in terms of Figure 10.5, the development of new products expanded the upper bound of goods N, with the demand-wage schedule shifting down and to the right, lowering the relative wage level. In order to respond appropriately to such long-run shifts in demand, it is necessary for the home country to always have the technology to produce new products. Since new products most often arise from industries with a high level of technology, it is necessary to have an industrial structure centered around industries incorporating high technology.

From the standpoint of an individual country, it is thus desirable to have an industrial structure centered around industries in which productivity can be readily increased, for which demand is foreseen as developing in the future, and that have a basis in high technology. If this sort of industrial structure is referred to as a "modern" industrial structure, then as long as the issue is the welfare of an individual country, that is, the possibility that foreign welfare will be lowered is ignored, then it can be said that policies seeking to modernize the industrial structure are desirable. It is difficult to judge whether MITI's efforts were meaningful in realizing a modern industrial structure, but as the points above have made clear, it is not right to totally discount the value of the MITI Visions and its call for modernizing the industrial structure.

F. Export Promotion and Import Restriction

Finally, in discussing the relationship of industrial policy and trade policy, let us touch the limitations of classical trade theory. In the standard trade models (and in particular in two-good models), it is assumed that which good is the import and which is the export is independent of the structure of tariffs and subsidies, so that export and import taxes and subsidies have the effect of only changing the quantity of exports or imports. In reality, however, there are many goods on the margin between those that are exported and those that are not traded, or between those that are not traded and those that are imported, so that if, for example, an export or production subsidy is provided for a good that is almost exportable, then that good may become an export. In this fashion, taxes and subsidies can have an impact by shifting the pattern of trade of goods on the margin. Subsidies for goods on the margin of exportables and tariffs on goods on the margin as importables increase the range of exportable goods and shrink the range of imported goods, respectively, raising the relative income of the home country and increasing national welfare.[28] This conclusion, and in particular the conclusion on the impact of export subsidies, contradicts the standard theory (e.g., Lerner [1936]), but this is due to the peculiar assumptions implicit in the standard models.

As is clear from the above discussion, however, this does not justify all export promotion policies. In order to evaluate actual export promotion policies, it is necessary to pay attention to the following. A policy of favoring all export industries with subsidies clearly reduces the utility of the home country, and in this the standard model is correct. Conversely, export subsidy policies that are focused on industries on the margin as exporters would seem in many cases to raise home country welfare.

Notes

1. For discussion of the meaning of the phrase "modernizing the industrial structure," see Chapter 7 of this book and Section III of this chapter.
2. See for example Tsusansho [1964], pp. 238–240.
3. There are many economies that have adopted industrial protection policies similar to those of Japan, but that have not achieved as high a growth rate. The significance of this point is that industrial protection policies are therefore at most only one of many bases of Japan's economic development.
4. An exception is the analysis of the impact of economic growth on the terms of trade.
5. This point becomes clear using the standard microeconomic box diagram analysis to

look at the relationship of initial endowments and the equilibrium exchange point to the level of welfare.

6. See Itoh et al. [1984] for a detailed discussion.
7. The focus of the analysis on import restricting policies is based on our understanding of these as having played the greatest role among Japanese industrial promotion policies. See also Chapter 6 on this point.
8. For details, see Young [1928] and Stigler [1951].
9. On the degree to which there were economies of scale in the Japanese steel and petrochemical industries, see Shinohara [1976].
10. This of course assumes the condition of perfect competition. When costs are declining, perfect competition will not occur.
11. In the case of a large country, there is the issue of the transfer of rents when the industry is already established abroad. To avoid introducing this issue into the model, we limit the analysis here to the case of a small country. For the case of a large country, see Section IV of this chapter and Chapter 9.
12. For a detailed presentation of the following argument, see Okuno [1984]. Note that investment in R&D and learning by doing also result in economies of scale. On this, see Chapter 9, Section II.
13. The following model is presented in detail in Ohyama [1982] and Williamson [1983]. See also Itoh et al. [1984]. The seminal work on trade under returns to scale is Negishi [1972].
14. In reality, economies of scale cease after production reaches a certain point, or decreasing returns for industry 2 dominate after a point, so costs as measured in terms of good 2 increase. In this regard, the model developed below analyzing economies of scale may not be realistic, but the results derived from this analysis are qualitatively the same as those derived from a more general model.
15. To be precise, when the price ratio is greater than the slope of the line joining AB and is less than that of the right-hand derivative of the production frontier at point B, then the equilibrium will be at B.
16. Wage rents arise because, even though production increases, economies of scale are assumed to be always present (see note 14) so that the equilibrium is a corner solution. There are, however, other sources of a first-mover advantage, which arise even when the equilibrium is an internal solution.
17. For a detailed mathematical explication of this section, see Itoh [1984]. Similar models are found in Dornbusch, Fischer, and Samuelson [1977] and Krugman [1979], [1982].
18. In fact, because the home and foreign countries have different currencies, it is also possible to develop a model that introduces the exchange rate. Itoh [1984] does this.
19. We have assumed that when this condition is an equality, the good becomes a home-country export. This is done to simplify the model and is not crucial to the following analysis.
20. The above formulae may be written in a slightly more general form, as follows:

value of home-country imports
   = (home-country average propensity to import) × (home-country income level)
   = value of foreign-country imports
   = (foreign-country average propensity to import) × (foreign-country income level).

Rewriting, we obtain:

$$\frac{\text{home income level}}{\text{foreign average propensity to import}} = \frac{\text{foreign income level}}{\text{home average propensity to import}}$$

21. In our model the goods are indexed one-dimensionally, but to make it more realistic, goods should be indexed by multiple dimensions to reflect many other characteristics. In this case, there will be a multiplicity of ways to increase the range of home-country export goods, but choosing to expand in the direction in which the proportion of foreign expenditures is highest will maximize the home-country level of income.
22. This argument is based on Krugman [1979].
23. In fact, during this period the demand side also changed greatly, which is important for understanding the modernization of Japanese industry. This is taken up in the following subsection.
24. To be precise, if the elasticity of substitution between the good whose relative price has declined and other goods is greater than 1, then home-country relative income will expand in proportion to magnitude of the elasticity.
25. On this point see Chapter 6 of this book and Itoh [1984].
26. See Chapter 6 of this book for specifics of the protective policies adopted by Japan.
27. The issue is of the same sort as that of optimal tariffs in international trade theory.
28. For details, see Itoh and Kiyono [1987] and Itoh [1984].

PART IV

Industrial Promotion Policy

CHAPTER 11

The Steel Industry

HIDEKI YAMAWAKI

International Management Institute
Berlin, Germany

I. Introduction

As is well known, after World War II the Japanese steel industry developed extremely rapidly, including improving its technology, especially from the 1950s through the early 1970s. During this period, raw steel output increased markedly, from 9.4 million tons in 1955 to 40 million tons in 1965 and 102 million tons in 1975. Domestic steel prices in general were declining from the late 1950s through the 1960s, and the export of steel products increased steadily throughout the 1960s and 1970s.

During the course of this period, the steel industry became a primary target of the government and the various ministries in their formulation and implementation of industrial policy. There was intervention in the industry through a variety of protective and promotion policies. In particular, the Ministry of International Trade and Industry (MITI) at the start of the period implemented a number of policies designed to encourage the strategic allocation of resources to the steel industry as the core of its so-called heavy and chemical industrialization policy. At the same time, MITI encouraged collusion among firms, with the intent of stabilizing investment, prices, and output. Later, MITI's position was to encourage an increase in the size of firms, with the goal of strengthening international competitiveness in the face of liberalization by Japan of trade and foreign direct investment.

In this chapter, we describe the specific measures through which these policies were implemented in the steel industry. At the same time, we will analyze and attempt to evaluate the impact these policies had on market structure and various facets of behavior, along with technical and allocative efficiency. After outlining in Section II the various measures im-

plemented with the goal of developing the steel industry and improving
its efficiency, we discuss in Section III interfirm coordination policies
undertaken by MITI. In Section IV, we analyze policies to encourage an
increase in the scale of firms.

II. The Development of the Steel Industry and Industrial Policy

From the early 1950s through the early 1960s, policies implemented in
the steel industry varied in their objective and strength. Basically they
were formulated with the goal of rationalizing and modernizing the industry, and of strengthening international competitiveness, reflecting the
underlying macroeconomic goals of growth in GNP, expansion of trade
and equilibrium in the balance of payments, and the achievement of full
employment.[1]

In the steel industry, the First Rationalization Plan was implemented
from 1951, based on the rationalization framework presented in the Report
[Toshin] of the Industrial Rationalization Council of MITI. With this plan
began the first significant new investment since the war. The distinctive
feature of this investment was that it was centered on the modernization
of rolling mills. Thus, of the total investment during 1951–1955 in ordinary
steel facilities, 13% was in smelting, 11% in steel production, and 50% in
milling (see Table I). The modernization of rolling facilities was realized
primarily through the conversion of former pullover rolling facilities into
strip mills, with approximately 60% of the new equipment being imported.
Alongside the importation of machinery, machine operating technology
also began to be introduced from abroad; the prime example of this was
the licensing in 1951 of strip-mill operation technology by Yawata and
Fuji Steel from the American firm, ARMCO.

With the implementation of the Second Rationalization Plan from 1956,

TABLE I
Investment in Steel under the Rationalization Plans [¥100 million, (%)]

	1st Plan (1951–55)	2nd Plan (1956–60)	3rd Plan (1961–65)
Pig Iron	162 (12.6)	973 (17.8)	1,373 (16.0)
Steel Production	137 (10.7)	535 (9.8)	790 (9.2)
Rolling Mills	641 (50.0)	2,631 (48.2)	3,555 (41.4)
Maintenance and Repairs	343 (26.7)	1,320 (24.2)	2,873 (33.4)
Total	1,282 (100.0)	5,459 (100.0)	8,592 (100.0)

Source: Nihon Tekko Renmei [1969], p. 305, Table 7, and p. 309, Table 8.

there was an emphasis on an expansion and increase in the scale of blast furnaces and LD converters and on constructing integrated production facilities, along with a continuation of the modernization of facilities from the First Plan period. During this period the share of investment in iron smelting in total investment rose to approximately 18%. During the First Plan, the only new blast furnace was the Chiba plant of Kawasaki Steel, but 11 new furnaces were completed by the end of FY 1960 (March 31, 1961) during the Second Plan. There was also an expansion in converters and strip mills, and as a result, production capacity in all sectors increased markedly over that of the First Period (see Figure 11.1). During the Second Period, the share of imported iron manufacturing equipment in total investment decreased to about 10%, but as shown in Table II, Class A foreign technology licenses doubled.

From 1960, investment took place under what is generally referred to as the Third Rationalization Plan, and together with the expansion of existing facilities, large-scale integrated facilities were constructed by each firm in the new coastal industrial zones; production capacity thus increased greatly (Figure 11.1). As a result, during the 1950s and 1960s unit production costs of ordinary (unfinished) steel products in the Japanese steel industry declined continuously (Table III). Similarly, the export ratio rose steadily, from an average of 16.1% during 1955–1959 to 18.0% during 1960–1964, to 24.6% during 1965–1969, to 28.2% during 1970–1974, and finally to 37.2% during 1975–1977 (see Table IV).

The nature of the Third Rationalization Plan was extremely different from that of the previous two plans. During the First Rationalization Plan, there was direct government regulation of the implementation of the investment plans, which were drawn up in accordance with the guidelines

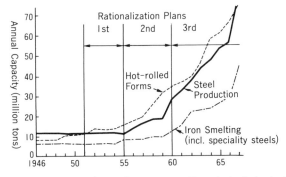

Fig. 11.1. Changes in capacity by product segment. Capacity includes both operating and idle facilities, but excludes facilities requiring repair or under construction. From Nihon Tekko Renmei [1969], p. 288.

TABLE II
Class A Foreign Technology Licenses[a] [number of cases (% of total cases)]

	1950–57	1958–65	1966–73
Pig Iron	1 (2.4)	5 (5.5)	16 (11.8)
Steel Production	4 (9.5)	15 (16.5)	22 (16.2)
Continuous Casting	2 (4.8)	4 (4.4)	23 (16.9)
Rolling Mills	12 (28.6)	25 (27.5)	35 (25.7)
Other Finishing Processes	23 (54.8)	42 (46.2)	40 (29.4)
Total	42 (100.0)	91 (100.0)	136 (100.0)

Sources: Nihon Tekko Renmei [1969], p. 387, Table 11, and Nihon Tekko Renmei [1981], p. 380, Table 5.
[a]Only licenses obtained directly by steel firms themselves are included.

TABLE III
Japanese Steel Unit Production Cost
Index[a] (ordinary steel, 1956 = 100)

Year	Unit Production Cost
1956	100.0
1957	111.2
1958	82.3
1959	75.1
1960	71.0
1961	76.4
1962	68.1
1963	65.9
1964	62.7
1965	63.7
1966	60.0
1967	58.0
1968	56.6
1969	58.4
1970	65.1
1971	67.8
1972	69.7
1973	84.3
1974	122.9
1975	132.9
1976	135.1

Source: U.S. Federal Trade Commission [1977], p. 113, Table 3–1.
[a]Material inputs + labor costs. See notes to Table VI.

TABLE IV
Steel Trade: Export and Import Shares (raw steel equivalents, %)

Year	Export Share[a]	Import Share[b]	Year	Export Share	Import Share
1950	15.0	0.07	1966	25.4	0.1
1954	18.9	1.7	1967	18.2	0.9
1955	24.5	1.2	1968	24.4	0.3
1956	14.6	3.0	1969	24.2	0.3
1957	10.0	12.3	1970	23.9	0.2
1958	18.3	2.0	1971	32.0	0.1
1959	13.3	2.7	1972	26.8	0.2
1960	14.2	1.6	1973	25.3	0.3
1961	11.3	1.6	1974	32.8	0.3
1962	19.1	1.1	1974	33.6	0.2
1963	22.8	0.3	1976	39.4	0.3
1964	22.5	0.2	1977	38.5	0.4
1965	30.9	0.1			

Source: Japan Iron and Steel Federation, Monthly Report of the Iron & Steel Statistics.
[a]Exports / Total Production.
[b]Imports / (Total Production + Imports − Exports).

of the Industrial Rationalization Council. While there were no deliberations by the Industrial Rationalization Council, during the Second Rationalization Plan investment was carried out with the guidance of and coordination by MITI under a Long-Term Facilities Plan that MITI compiled. In contrast to the previous two plans, however, with the Third Plan from 1960, the coordination of investment took place through autonomous coordination among firms.[2]

In order for direct intervention by MITI under the First and Second Rationalization Plans to be truly effective, that is, for the plans to be more than mere guidelines, it was essential that various laws (which were enacted at the commencement of the First Rationalization Plan) be kept in force to provide for such policies. The major measures included the following:[3]

1. the allocation through FILP (the Fiscal Investment and Loan Program) of funds for rationalization, and in particular for the financing of investment through Japan Development Bank (JDB) loans;

2. the provision of special depreciation allowances (a 50% increase over three years) for designated equipment through the 1951 revision of the Special Tax Measures Law;

3. the exemption from import tariffs of important industrial equipment through the 1951 revision of the Tariff Rate Law;

4. the provision of an increased first-year depreciation allowance to 50% of the purchase price of equipment and an exemption from property taxes through the enactment in March 1952 of the Enterprise Rationalization Promotion Law;

5. the establishment in 1953 of the system of special corporate income tax deductions for income from exports (abolished in March 1963);[4]

6. the establishment of the approval system for the licensing of foreign technology based on foreign exchange allocations under the 1950 Foreign Capital Law together with the allocation of licenses for other imports under the Foreign Exchange and Foreign Trade Control Law.

From 1951 the steel industry became eligible under the special depreciation allowance system, and key steel equipment was classified as designated equipment under the system. Together with the measures listed above, a revision of the depreciation schedule in 1961 reduced the statutory life of industrial equipment by an average of 20%, and there was a further reduction by an average of 15% in 1964, both of which were also important preferential tax measures. Finally, in order to encourage technical change, the Enterprise Rationalization Promotion Law recognized a special equiannual depreciation over three years for equipment for use in testing and research.

The goals of these individual measures, which certainly aimed at the protection and fostering of the steel industry, can be divided into (1) encouraging investment in the industry through the strategic supply of funds and tax reductions, (2) promoting technical change and exports through tax reduction provisions, (3) importing strategic technologies, and (4) protecting the industry from foreign competition.[5]

Of the total investment in the steel industry of ¥128.2 billion under the First Rationalization Plan, ¥17.2 billion (12%) was financed with JDB loans. In contrast, under the Second Rationalization Plan, JDB lending decreased relative to the first period to ¥9.5 billion or 1.5% of the total investment of ¥625.5 billion; the dependence on government financing thus declined in this period.[6] In its place, foreign loans were an important source of funds, centering on lending by the World Bank. The above indicates that the discretionary lending of government funds had an important influence on investment in the steel industry under the First Rationalization Plan. At the same time, the receipt of government loans served as a guarantee of the growth of an industry, and it must be noted that it thus "primed the pump" by indirectly encouraging private financial institutions to increase their allocation of loans to the industry.[7]

The long-run impact of special depreciation measures on investment in the steel industry has been made clear in Chapter 5 of this book. Table V gives the share of special depreciation allowances in fixed investment

TABLE V

Special Depreciation Allowances for Rationalization Investment of the Big 6 Firms (As Proportion of Fixed Investment and Depreciation, %)

Year	Special Allowances Fixed Investment	Special Allowances All Depreciation
1956	11.3	26.0
1957	11.5	37.8
1958	3.3	12.8
1959	20.2	50.0
1960	17.0	47.7
1961	6.4	21.7
1962	1.5	4.1
1963	2.5	4.0
1964	0.4	0.7
1965	2.6	4.0
1966	15.9	21.4
1967	4.8	8.7
Average, 1956–60 (Second Rationalization Plan)	12.7	34.9
Average, 1961–65 (Third Rationalization Plan)	2.7	6.9

Source: Nihon Tekko Renmei [1969], p. 490, Table 8, and p. 491, Table 9.

and total depreciation for the Big 6[8] steel producers. According to these figures, during the period of the Second Rationalization Plan (1956–1960), such allowances averaged 12.7% of investment and 34.9% of total depreciation, and these proportions were distinctly higher than during the Third Rationalization period (1961–1965). This shows that not only was the special depreciation system actively utilized under the Second Rationalization Plan, but also that the depreciation allowances were important as a source of investment financing. (The system of special depreciation allowances for rationalization equipment was eliminated in FY 1973.) In addition, the system of special deductions for income from exports, under which a set proportion of the receipts from export transactions could be excluded from income, was important in reducing taxes. For example, in the latter half of FY 1957 under the Second Rationalization Plan period, tax deductions under the system of deductions for income from exports for the major steel producers came to 11.8% of total income. This was the second greatest deduction, after the special depreciation allowance of 13.2%, giving an indication of the importance of the export income deductions.[9] This system was abolished in 1963, but was succeeded by an accelerated depreciation system for exports (abolished in 1972) and later by a tax-free reserve for the development of foreign markets. The first of these two systems recognized accelerated depreciation for exporting firms, while the latter allowed a set proportion of receipts from overseas transactions to be set aside in a reserve and later taken as a deduction from income. (From 1972, firms with a capitalization of over ¥1 billion were not permitted to use this reserve, and from 1977 its designation was changed to the Tax-free Reserve for the Development of Overseas Markets by Small and Medium Enterprises.) The role of this reserve system was great during the 1960s; at the end of FY 1970, the total in such reserves exceeded ¥10 billion.[10]

As outlined above, low-interest JDB loans together with reductions in corporate taxes through the special depreciation allowances for important rationalization machinery were actively utilized, in particular during the First and Second Rationalization Plan periods. These made it easier for firms to procure investment financing and clearly were one of the sources of the high investment rates realized during these periods.

Another policy that is thought to have influenced the development of the steel industry and contributed to improved efficiency was the approval system for foreign technology licenses based on the May 1950 Law Concerning Foreign Capital (hereafter, the Foreign Capital Law). This law decreed that in principle capital transactions with foreigners required the approval of the responsible minister. As a result, because the vast majority of the plans by private firms for licensing foreign technology required the payment of royalties, such licenses automatically required the approval of MITI. For the steel industry, based on the August 1950 Cabinet approval of the Outline of Measures for the Rationalization of the Steel Industry, the importation of foreign equipment and technology was given favorable treatment through preferential allocations in the foreign exchange budget. As a result, because of the preferential allocation of foreign exchange to the steel industry, the foreign technology licensing system helped to encourage the importation of technology.

Some of the more important cases during this period of active introduction of new technology were the operating technology for strip mills (1951), the basic oxygen conversion process (1956), and continuous casting technology (1954) (see Table II). These technologies provided an important base for the subsequent increase in efficiency in the industry. As has been discussed elsewhere,[11] in general the intervention of MITI in the royalty negotiations under the licensing system had the effect of keeping the amount of royalties paid by Japanese enterprises at a low level, especially until the mid-1960s. In these ways, the licensing system based on the Foreign Capital Law to some extent helped achieve the goal of the licensing of strategic foreign technologies during the early period of the industry's development. It is necessary to note, however, that the foreign technology licensing system also had the effect of regulating entry into individual product markets at any given point in time.

The Foreign Exchange and Foreign Trade Control Law (1949), which complemented the Foreign Capital Law, provided for a system for allocating foreign exchange for imports, thus functioning as a nontariff barrier to trade; this can be thought of as having an impact equivalent to that of a system for directly licensing imports. At the commodity level, from August 1950, pig iron imports were put on an FA ("funds allocation") basis for U.S. dollar settlement regions, and on an AFA ("automatic funds allocation") basis for non-dollar regions. For ordinary semifinished products and rolled steel, imports from the Pound Sterling region were on an AFA basis from August 1950 through September 1954 and an FA basis elsewhere, but from October 1954 imports from all regions were placed on an FA basis.[12]

Thus throughout the 1950s, FA classification under the foreign exchange allocation system was actively applied as an important means for restricting imports. With the June 1960 announcement of the Overall Plan for Trade and Capital Liberalization, however, its use was gradually eliminated, and from October 1960 for pig iron and June 1961 for ordinary semifinished products and rolled steel, application of the allocation system ceased.

With the 1951 revision of the tariff schedule, the tariff for raw steel was 15%, for ingots 12.5%, and for rolled steel 15%, which were high in comparison with the rates for the United States and the European Coal and Steel Community.[13] In the 1961 tariff revision, these rates were maintained, but with the conclusion of the Kennedy Round GATT negotiations in 1967, tariffs were reduced over the subsequent five years to 5.0% for pig iron, 6.25% for ingots, and 7.5% for rolled steel. Before the Kennedy Round, effective rates of protection are estimated to have been extremely high.[14]

To review the impact of the import restrictions that operated through the import allocation and tariff systems discussed above, let us examine changes in the share of imports. In general, throughout the postwar period, imports of steel products have been consistently at extremely low levels. As can be seen in Table IV, the import ratio in terms of raw steel content was 0.07% in 1950, 1.6% in 1960, and 0.2% in 1970, at a steady, very low level, so much so that it can be said there have been no imports of steel products in the postwar era.[15] In order to make the connection between the import ratio and import restrictions clearer, it is necessary to know what the changes were in the international competitive position of the Japanese steel industry. For this purpose, Table VI compares unit production costs for the United States and Japan.[16] In this table, cost estimates for hot- and cold-rolled steel include an estimate of fringe benefits as part of Japanese labor costs. As is clear from the table, production costs for

TABLE VI

Comparative Unit Production Costs: Japan and U.S.[a] (Japanese Unit Costs/American Unit Costs)[b]

Year	Ordinary Steel	Hot-Rolled Sheet[c]	Cold-Rolled Plate[c]	Year	Ordinary Steel	Hot-Rolled Sheet[c]	Cold-Rolled Plate[c]
1956	1.08	1.24	1.17	1967	0.59	0.76	0.73
1957	1.21	1.31	1.24	1968	0.57	0.74	0.71
1958	0.81	1.01	0.96	1969	0.56	0.72	0.69
1959	0.79	0.87	0.83	1970	0.57	0.75	0.72
1960	0.71	0.86	0.82	1971	0.56	0.70	0.68
1961	0.75	0.84	0.80	1972	0.54	0.68	0.67
1962	0.69	0.83	0.79	1973	0.63	0.75	0.74
1963	0.68	0.80	0.76	1974	0.68	0.83	0.82
1964	0.65	0.79	0.76	1975	0.59	0.75	0.75
1965	0.68	0.79	0.76	1976	0.55	0.69	0.69
1966	0.63	0.78	0.74				

Source: U.S. Federal Trade Commission [1977], p. 113, Table 3-1, for ordinary steel and Crandall [1981], p. 171, Table A-15, and p. 172, Table A-16, for sheet and plate.

[a]Production costs are materials plus labor, where the material inputs included are iron ore, scrap, coking coal, oil, electricity, and noncoking coal.

[b]These were originally stated in US$ per ton.

[c]Japanese labor costs include an estimate of fringe benefit costs.

steel in Japan were still high relative to U.S. costs in the 1950s, but from the beginning of the 1960s, Japanese production costs became lower than American costs, so that the comparative cost position of the United States and Japan was totally reversed. By the 1970s, unit rolled steel production costs in Japan were in general 70% or less of U.S. costs.

It has been shown above that although in the 1950s the international competitiveness of the Japanese steel industry was still inferior, imports were nevertheless minimal. This can be explained as being a result of the foreign exchange allocation system and the high level of tariffs described above. In other words, the nontariff barrier of foreign exchange allocations, together with tariff barriers, protected the Japanese steel industry from competition from imports, particularly in the 1950s.

In the 1960s, the Japanese steel industry became superior in terms of production costs to the steel industry in other countries, and taking into consideration transport costs for steel, the situation was such that high tariffs were unnecessary. Even after the conclusion of the Kennedy Round tariff reductions in 1972, the share of imports was still extremely low, and there was furthermore no apparent tendency for imports to increase.

We have examined above the industrial policy measures implemented from the 1950s through the mid-1960s, along with their impact. It is clear that industrial policy operated effectively in the early stages of the development of the steel industry. At the same time, it should not be overlooked that various factors relating to the market system were operating in a direction that would bring the same results.

With the splitting up of the old Nippon Steel in 1950 into Yawata Steel and Fuji Steel, market (seller) concentration in the steel industry moved to the level of intermediate oligopoly, and thereafter (until the late 1960s) with competition among the firms in the industry through investment and new entry, market concentration tended to decline (see Table VII). The long-term demand forecasts published by the government and the ma-

TABLE VII

Relative Changes in Market Concentration Indices (1955–1970; Initial year = 100)

		1955	1960	1965	1970
Steel Rails	Share of leading firm	100.0	77.6	61.6	82.8
	Share of leading 3 firms	100.0	98.8	99.1	99.7
	Herfindahl Index	—	—	100.0[a]	152.4
Tin Plates	Share of leading firm	100.0	90.9	81.7	99.2
	Share of leading 3 firms	—	100.0	100.1	109.7
	Herfindahl Index	—	100.0	93.6	122.4
Large Sections	Share of leading firm	100.0	39.3	50.4	79.8
	Share of leading 3 firms	100.0	65.6	70.8	86.2
	Herfindahl Index	—	100.0	108.2	182.0
Heavy Sheets	Share of leading firm	100.0	80.9	66.8	160.2
	Share of leading 3 firms	100.0	87.6	77.7	123.7
	Herfindahl Index	—	100.0	92.4	192.9
Wide Strips	Share of leading firm	100.0	91.9	41.9	68.0
	Share of leading 3 firms	—	100.0	72.2	89.9
	Herfindahl Index	—	100.0	56.5	91.9
Cold-rolled Wide Strips	Share of leading firm	100.0	75.5	43.5	65.0
	Share of leading 3 firms	—	100.0	58.4	84.7
	Herfindahl Index	—	100.0	42.8	76.5
Cold-rolled Sheets	Share of leading firm	100.0	56.6	39.9	71.6
	Share of leading 3 firms	100.0	71.6	53.8	81.4
	Herfindahl Index	—	100.0	66.8	123.4
Wire Rods	Share of leading firm	100.0	100.0	86.0	145.9
	Share of leading 3 firms	100.0	99.2	91.3	101.6
	Herfindahl Index	—	100.0	98.2	135.6
Pipes	Share of leading firm	100.0	69.8	70.1	64.0
	Share of leading 3 firms	100.0	80.4	84.3	83.6
	Herfindahl Index	—	100.0	99.4	86.1

Sources: Kosei Torihiki Iinkai [1975], Tekko Shinbun Sha (ed.), Tekko Nenkan [Steel Yearbook].

[a] For 1967.

croeconomic growth that was realized, together with the rapid growth of steel-using industries, made the steel makers feel confident (and at the same time optimistic) in their expectation that demand would continue to increase in the long run. In an industry in which concentration is that of a moderate oligopoly, its firms are only weakly motivated to maximize joint profit through use of their oligopolistic interdependence. Thus there is a strong possibility that the actions of one firm will simply be imitated or followed by other rival firms.[17] The rapid growth of the industry becomes a motive for each oligopolist to actively expand its capacity. Thus a market structure combining a moderate level of oligopoly and rapid macroeconomic growth can be important in encouraging rivalry by oligopolists through the expansion of capacity and competition for market share. Thus one can conclude that oligopolistic rivalry with this market structure, through capacity expansion, brought about the high rate of investment. This effect complemented that of the various industrial policies and increased in importance, especially after 1955, with the Second and Third Rationalization Plans. For an empirical analysis of this hypothesis about market concentration and investment, see Yamawaki [1984].

III. Intra-Industry Coordination and Industrial Policy

In the previous section we surveyed the industrial policies that were implemented from the 1950s through the middle of the 1960s. Parallel to these, MITI also undertook policy interventions to restrain competition. In other words, MITI, from the 1950s through the middle of the 1960s, intervened in the decision-making process of firms in price and quantity setting and investment with the goal of encouraging collusive behavior among firms. These interventions by the government were undertaken through administrative guidance that lacked the force of law. Below, in this section, we will examine the investment coordination and price and output coordination policies of MITI.

A. Investment Coordination

It has already been mentioned in the preceding section that from 1960 on, during the Third Rationalization Plan, firms were to undertake autonomous coordination among themselves. This began in December 1959 with the request by MITI that the steel industry implement appropriate long-term investment plans.

For investment coordination, the primary goal was to avoid excess capacity and the price competition that resulted. MITI obtained the individual investment plans of individual firms, which were aggregated by the Finance Committee of the Industrial Rationalization Council. The results were then compared with demand forecasts to calculate capacity utilization rates, and when it appeared necessary, requests were made for autonomous investment coordination. From 1967, the Steel Committee, established on the recommendation of the October 1966 Report *(Toshin)* of the Basic Steel Problems Subcommittee of the Industrial Structure Council, (1) drew up long-term and annual supply and demand forecasts, (2) drew up standards for investment coordination, (3) estimated capacity required in the long run and (4) calculated the new capacity on which construction would need to be begun in each year. The detailed allocation of investment among firms, based on the results of the Council studies, was to depend in the first instance on the autonomous coordination by firms themselves, and in instances in which coordination could not be obtained, decisions were to be made under the administrative guidance of MITI.[18]

The first case of autonomous coordination was the Working Committee meetings of the Japan Iron and Steel Federation, which began in February 1959 and lasted through March 1960, for investment to be completed by FY 1962. Initially MITI envisioned the start of construction in FY 1960 of two blast furnaces and one hot-strip mill, but the steel makers had in total plans for five blast furnaces. To reconcile this difference, then-President Inayama of Yawata Steel proposed that investment be coordinated on the basis of the market shares of individual firms over the previous 10 years, while Kawasaki Steel insisted that coordination be undertaken at the level of individual products and facilities. The final result was that three blast furnaces and two strip mills were approved, more than MITI had planned for. Come December 1960, however, three additional blast furnaces were approved: the Chiba plant of Kawasaki Steel, which under autonomous coordination was to be delayed; the Mizue plant of Nippon Kokan, which was to have been begun in 1961; and the Kure plant of a new entrant, Nisshin Steel.

Coordination in FY 1961 took place under the forecast that, come FY 1963, utilization of facilities for which construction was scheduled to begin in FY 1961 would be below 80%. Investment coordination was thus undertaken, with MITI negotiating separately with each firm. All the plans firms submitted, however, were approved, except those for cold strip and wire mills.

Coordination during FY 1962–1964, as in FY 1961, consisted of MITI presenting a coordination plan to the Working Group of the Japan Iron and Steel Federation, on the basis of which individual firms were to undertake autonomous coordination.[19] In FY 1965, however, coordination ran into difficulties, as it was decided on the one hand that no new rolling mills would be constructed during FY 1965 and FY 1966, while on the other hand all were agreed that for blast and converter furnaces, individual firms would be free to decide their own level of investment. In the co-ordination undertaken in November 1966, however, not only were all plans for rolling mill construction in FY 1967 approved, but the construction planned for FY 1966, which was to have been put on hold, was also approved. The result was the same as if each steel maker undertook investment based on its independent judgment.

At the time of coordination for FY 1967, MITI aggregated the investment plans of individual firms for blast furnaces to find that 18 new furnaces were being planned. While there was some minor adjustment in the actual start of construction, in the end not only was construction begun on all the facilities planned through FY 1971, but construction was also speeded up to begin by that year on three additional furnaces for which plans had not even been submitted in FY 1967.[20]

As can be seen above, in the end almost all the investment plans of the individual steel firms were approved. Furthermore, especially from 1967 on, construction was often advanced to a date earlier than had been in the plan, or facilities were built that were not even in the plan! It is thus clear that the goal of MITI of capacity coordination through collusion among firms by way of investment coordination was not achieved. Capacity coordination through administrative guidance, in terms of achievement of the administrative goals, was not effective, as has been pointed out by Miwa [1977] and Chapter 18 of this book.[21]

It was certainly true that capacity adjustment through administrative guidance *cum* industrial policy had insufficient administrative machinery and policy tools and lacked the requisite powers of compulsion to bring about collusive behavior among firms; they were insufficient to suppress the independent behavior of individual firms. But it should not be overlooked that these sorts of policy interventions in investment coordination worked against the carrying out of procompetitive policies by encouraging and giving explicit approval to collusion among firms.[22] What I want to point out is that during the process of autonomous investment coordination, each firm discussed its investment plans for each year many times with all the other firms, and it is patently obvious that information was exchanged, working to induce investment by individual firms and serving as a possible source of increased technical inefficiency in the industry. As observed by Imai [1976], even when investment coordination was unsuccessful and ended up as a mere exchange of information, it nevertheless served to reduce uncertainty. A reduction in uncertainty encourages investment and can increase excess capacity.

B. Price and Output Coordination

Decisions on pricing and output in the steel industry were also subject to government intervention. Direct controls on prices were abolished in July 1950, and accompanying the shift to market pricing, Yawata Steel established a quoted price system in contracts for future delivery, with the price to be set at cost plus an appropriate profit margin. Along with Yawata Steel, the firms that implemented this system at that time (for contracts for certain products where delivery was in two to three months) were the existing integrated steel producers, Fuji Steel and Nippon Kokan, together with the new entrants into integrated production of the 1950s, Kawasaki Steel, Sumitomo Metal Industries, and Kobe Steel. For products for which market concentration was low, however, the new entrants did not follow the quoted prices of the existing firms when market prices fell after June 1951, so that a gap arose between the quoted price and the sales price. With the recovery of the market in January 1955, the existing three firms reinstituted the quoted price system, but with the rise in market prices (and then their subsequent decline), the system proved difficult to maintain.[23] During this period, the products for which it was found difficult to apply the quoted price system comprised about 85% of ordinary steel products, so that the stability of prices became an issue between the steel makers and MITI. The list price system (*kokai hanbai sei*, literally, "open sales system") was adopted to resolve this problem.

During the 1958 recession, MITI sought a recovery in the market by using administrative guidance to request production cutbacks for plate, medium sections, bars, and other products. In order to increase the effectiveness of its requests for production cutbacks, MITI announced a "Summary of Steel Market Measures" in June 1958, and carried out administrative guidance toward the end of establishing the list-price system. The list-price system consisted of the following:[24]

1. On the basis of MITI production targets, each firm reported its expected sales for each month by product to MITI.

2. Each manufacturer was to sell its steel products at the same time at a fixed location, agreeing with wholesalers on the amounts to be purchased. Each firm was to carry out sales at the "list price" that it had previously reported to MITI.

3. After reaching agreement with its wholesalers, each manufacturer was to report by product the quantity contracted with each wholesaler and to publish its aggregate sales, together with amounts left unsold.

4. Manufacturers were to have a designated wholesaler for each product and were to make sales only through that wholesaler.

5. If there were unsold products, they were to be bought up by a sufficiently strong wholesaler at a predetermined price, and unsold amounts were to provide a basis for determining decreases in production for the following month.

6. The pricing of all products sold by wholesalers was to be the responsibility of the manufacturer, and when manufacturers violated their own list prices, MITI was to undertake administrative guidance accompanied by strong penalties; the same steps were to be taken for violations of production limits. A monitoring committee and a penalties committee were to be set up for this purpose.

7. Each manufacturer was to deliver to MITI a written promise by the president of the company that it would abide by an "Outline of Steel Market Measures" with this general content.

The list price system was applied initially to five products, plate (including medium sheet), small bars, medium bars, medium sections, and wire rods; from December 1959, thin sheets (both hot- and cold-rolled, and wide bands) were added. Initially 33 manufacturers participated.

In January 1959, increases in list prices occurred with the recovery in the economy, and in general a recovery in prices was seen. Concern arose about large increases in price for certain products, and in May 1959 MITI transformed the list-price system for the purpose of restraining prices (calling it the "strong economy" list-price system). In the "Summary of Steel Market Measures," MITI was empowered to issue a formal warning to firms whose prices were excessively high relative to what MITI judged appropriate that prices should be lowered, and at the same time, MITI was empowered to issue a formal warning that output should be increased when a firm's production or anticipated sales were excessively low.[25]

This "strong economy" list-price system shifted to a policy of price stabilization with the leveling off of the market in July 1960. The reporting of prices to MITI and the power of MITI to issue a warning to lower prices when they jumped remained the same as before, but MITI was now empowered to issue instructions that production should be coordinated when there were fears that prices would either drastically fall or rise.[26]

The impact of the implementation of the list-price system on steel prices varied to some extent with the product, but in general the market price closely followed the list price until 1962. However, from 1962, unlike before, the market price decreased substantially, and it is apparent that a gap arose between the list and the market price; as a representative example, prices for heavy sheets are given in Figure 11.2.

As a result, warnings to curtail output were issued from June 1962, and in addition list prices were lowered in July. These prices were termed "standard list prices," but it proved difficult to make them hold, and in

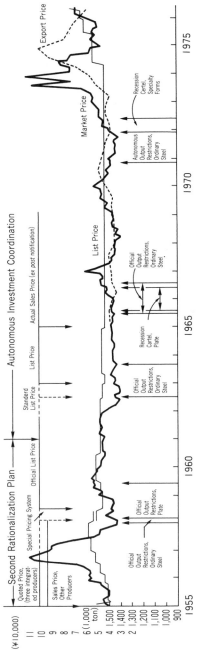

Fig. 11.2. Heavy sheet prices.

December 1962 a "maximum discount sales price" was set up by Yawata Steel, of which notification was given to MITI, which was separate from the list price. In January 1965 this price was again lowered to the "actual sales price"; a formal warning to curtail output of raw steel was issued in July 1965,[27] but while the market temporarily recovered, from 1967 on it again weakened.

It is clear from the above course of events that for the 10 years following the institution of the list-price system in 1958, the system continued in place even while its nature changed numerous times. When examined overall, as can be seen from the price movements in Figure 11.2, it ceased to function from 1962 on,[28] and with the notification by Yawata Steel to MITI of its "maximum discount sales price" in December 1962, the system effectively collapsed. In summary, output and price coordination by MITI through administrative guidance, in the form of the list-price system, was effective to some extent for 1958–1961 but was ineffective thereafter.

One reason pointed out in Chapter 18 for why list-price-system-type industrial policy was in general ineffective was the lack of active participation by MITI. As stated therein, the list price system, while instituted through the administrative guidance of MITI, had insufficient power and was backed by inadequate sanctions to enforce the coordination of price- and quantity-setting behavior among firms. There was insufficient agreement among firms participating in the cartel to implement sanctions or penalties for firms that violated the agreement, and in a cartel in which sanctions are weak, there is a strong probability of competitive price discounts by participating firms.[29] The direct reason why list prices could not be maintained in the steel industry was that (as suggested here) participating firms actively discounted prices, particularly during recessions.

The reasons that competitive price discounting arose from the late 1950s through the 1960s were that, first, as a result of competition through vigorous investment during this period, in economic slowdowns there was substantial excess capacity. In industries such as steel, where fixed costs are a high proportion of total costs, a decrease in capacity utilization brings about a rapid increase in unit fixed costs, which induces discounting. The price elasticity of demand that individual firms face is adjudged to be higher in the short run, so that discounting is expected to increase sales. The monitoring system put in place by the cartel was inadequate, and combined with the weak strength of and a general inability to impose sanctions, competitive discounting became rampant. Second, in this period concentration in the market for the various steel products in general was declining. Price setting in an oligopolistic industry is in general influenced by the extent to which individual firms recognize their mutual interdependence. In theory, when oligopolists act to achieve joint profit maximization, when other conditions are held constant, a decline in market concentration brings about a decline in the mark-up above production costs. Thus, when production costs are held constant, there is a positive correlation between market concentration and the optimal price set by firms. In the case of the steel industry, the fact that actual sales prices declined, gradually diverging from the inflexible list price, can to some extent be explained by this decrease in market concentration. For an empirical analysis of this hypothesis, see Yamawaki [1984].

One example of interfirm coordination policies undertaken by MITI in the steel industry in the 1960s was the issuing of official warnings to cut back the production of raw steel during 1962–1963 and 1965–1966. These warnings were used as part of administrative guidance for reducing the output of raw steel, the goal of which was to maintain the market price.[30] It is not clear what impact these warnings had on the recovery of the market. While there were differences among various products, as far as can be judged from Figure 11.2, in some cases there were mild recoveries in prices during periods when cutback warnings were in effect, but in other cases there was no discernible impact. Thus it can be said that such warnings were not very effective.

Thus far the discussion has been limited to investment coordination and the list-price system implemented through administrative guidance from the late 1950s through the 1960s, which aimed at setting up a system that would encourage the collusive behavior among firms as a means of coordinating investment, pricing, and output decisions. In terms of these goals, however, the policies were ineffective, except for the list price system during a limited period. While this administrative guidance (the nature of which was to restrict competition) may not in general have been effective in terms of these policy goals, it is again important to note that they may have had an indirect or secondary effect on the functioning of the market in the industry. Autonomous investment coordination may have induced greater investment by firms and hence been one source of excess investment. Similarly, the list-price system, functioning with some effectiveness for a limited period, made possible rigid pricing. By reducing price competition the latter also increased the importance of investment as a competitive tool for firms and hence also helped foster excess investment.

IV. The Yawata–Fuji Merger and Industrial Restructuring Policies

Trade liberalization was announced by the government in June 1960, in the "Outline of Plans to Liberalize Trade and Foreign Exchange." After the change from Article 14 to Article 8 membership in the IMF in April

1964 and the obtaining of membership in the OECD, the first round of capital liberalization was set for July 1967. In the steel industry, the use of foreign exchange allocations for imports of ordinary semifinished steel and rolled steel ceased in June 1961; in the first round of capital liberalization, steel was designated as a Class II industry (full liberalization), in which direct foreign investment would be permitted.

Direct foreign investment implied that foreign firms would be free to enter the domestic market, serving to increase competitive pressures in the domestic market. The increase of international competitive pressures that accompanied capital liberalization and the fears of the government and MITI that this would lead to the demise of domestic firms in foreign competition caused them to advocate reorganization of the industry with the aim of strengthening the overall international competitiveness of domestic firms.[31] The stance of MITI as an advocate of reorganization in the steel industry was made clear with the publication of the October 1966 Interim Report *(Toshin)* of the Basic Steel Problems Subcommittee of the Heavy Industry Committee of the Industrial Structure Council, "The Future of the Steel Industry." In this report the investment for modernization and the progress of large-scale mergers and combinations in the West was used as an example. The economies of large-scale facilities and the harm done by excess competition on international competitiveness were pointed out, and it was stated that there was a need for measures to build up the industry, coordinate investment, and stabilize prices. In the report, building up the industry meant the consolidation of separate management and investment organizations, held to be an efficacious means of encouraging the construction of state-of-the-art steel-making facilities, which would result in greater international competitiveness. In the report it was also viewed as important that a system be set up that would enable autonomous coordination among firms. For these reasons, the warning was sounded that consolidation through mergers, joint investment, and operating agreements was desirable.[32]

Such discussions were thus in the background at the time Yawata and Fuji Steel announced their intent to merge in May 1968. According to the merger agreement made public by the two firms, the reasons for the merger were (1) with the trend for the increasingly large size of facilities and slower growth in demand, it would prevent the inefficiency of duplicate investment stemming from their interfirm rivalry, (2) it would enhance their ability to undertake R&D, and in particular improve the effectiveness of such research, and (3) increased scale would serve to increase overall competitiveness through a strengthening of R&D capacity, financial strength, and the ability to raise funds.[33] The grounds given for the merger were thus that there were merits in a lessening of the number of firms and an increase in firm size. The reasons that Yawata and Fuji chose each other as a merger candidate were that, due to a similarity in the products of the two firms, there was duplication in production, distribution, research, and other facilities, and also that, because they had been at one time part of the same firm, there were personal ties, a common organizational structure, and other common features.

As is clear from the rationale provided for the merger of Yawata and Fuji Steel, it was a response to the increased international competitive pressures that accompanied capital liberalization and was in line with the recommendations of the report of the Basic Issues Subcommittee of the Industrial Structure Council. The Basic Issues Special Subcommittee of the Coordination Committee of the Council expressed support of the merger in its August 1968 report, ''Opinion on Reforming the Structure of Industry and Mergers.'' There is, however, no trace of preferential financing or tax measures to encourage the consolidation, which was advocated by the government and MITI in reports such as this, and it seems that there was no active intervention in the use by the government of its policy tools. In fact, it seems safe to say that the government did nothing beyond voicing a position of encouraging an increase in the size of firms and mergers. It is important, however, not to overlook that the stance taken by the government and MITI of supporting increases in the scale of firms and advocating mergers went against the implementation of procompetitive policies. It may well be that an increase in firm scale improved efficiency in the industry in the way the government had predicted. It is necessary, however, to note the potential for this at the same time to impede efficiency in resource allocation, another standard of market performance. It is this point that was at issue in the antitrust problems of the Yawata–Fuji merger.[34]

The market share of the new firm formed through the merger of Yawata and Fuji Steel was over 30% in semifinished products and the principal ordinary steel products. Since its market share would become relatively large compared to those of its rivals, the new firm would become a dominant firm, and the merger was thus taken under review by the Fair Trade Commission (FTC). In the end, the merger was approved in May 1969, when various conditions placed on the merger in the FTC report were accepted by both Yawata and Fuji Steel.

The birth of Nippon Steel in March 1970, the firm that resulted from this course of events, clearly had a direct impact on the structure of the steel market, as market concentration, which in general had been decreasing throughout the 1960s, was at once increased (see Table VII).[35] The influence of the Yawata–Fuji merger on price setting behavior in the steel market has been analyzed using econometric methods in Yamawaki

[1984]; here only a summary of the results of a counterfactual simulation will be presented. A simulation was carried out in order to estimate how endogenous decision variables such as price and capacity behaved when there was no merger in 1970. For the period following the merger (1971–1975), the estimated domestic price was in general lower than the actual price, while estimated export prices tended to be greater than the actual price. The impact of the merger on investment is not substantial, but in any event, the merger is observed to lower investment. Thus the Yawata–Fuji merger to some extent achieved a reduction in the investment competition, one of the initial goals, but at the same time it served to raise domestic prices and lower export prices.[36] It must be pointed out that at least in this instance, the encouragement given to reforming the industrial structure, as it was advocated by the government in its industrial restructuring policies, entailed a distortion of the market.

V. Conclusion

Throughout the late 1950s and the 1960s, a high rate of increase in productivity and a continual decline in unit production costs were achieved in the Japanese steel industry. In general, it was noted that the prices of steel products declined and exports increased. At the same time, it was pointed out that the postwar steel industry was one of the main targets of the industrial policies implemented by the government and the bureaucracy, and the variety of facets in which there was government intervention for protecting and fostering the industry were discussed. It can readily be concluded that the overall impact of postwar industrial policy for the steel industry was favorable, particularly in terms of improving overall efficiency in the industry.

Certainly a number of the measures implemented as part of industrial policy made it easier to finance investment, such as the use of government funds to provide financing through the JDB and the preferential tax treatment provided by the special depreciation allowances, the tax deduction for export income, and other items. Direct regulation, in the form of the explicit framework it provided for the implementation of the First and Second Rationalization Plans and the foreign technology licensing system, also contributed to lowering production costs by encouraging the modernization of facilities and the introduction of foreign technology. In addition, import restrictions operating through the foreign exchange allocation and tariff systems served to protect the domestic industry from the pressure of competition from imports. It can be safely concluded that these policies were effective in encouraging the development of the steel industry and improving the overall efficiency of the industry during the initial stage of its development, especially in the 1950s. It cannot be denied that this provided a base for the subsequent growth of the industry and contributed to the relatively high overall efficiency realized in the industry.

What I want to emphasize here, however, is that the development of the industry and the improvements in its efficiency from the late 1950s through the 1960s were the result of, in the first instance, the outworking of vigorous investment competition by the individual steel makers. This was a reflection of favorable expectations as to the growth of demand in a rapidly growing economy, in an industry where the market structure was one of a moderate degree of oligopoly. Combined with this was the active introduction of the latest technology from abroad in an effort to reduce costs. Without real competition among firms, such favorable market performance during this period could not have been expected.

While it can be held that the industrial policies mentioned above contributed directly and indirectly to the development and growth of the industry and its overall efficiency, it is also necessary to point out that the policies implemented by means of administrative guidance from the late 1950s through the 1960s—investment coordination, the list-price system, and warnings to curtail output—served to encourage collusion among firms, affecting a number of facets of their behavior. Such policies at the time undoubtedly increased the possibility of inefficient resource allocation and technical inefficiency.

Industrial restructuring policies were advanced with the aim of improving overall efficiency in the industry by strengthening international competitiveness and preventing excess investment; these policies encouraged an increase in the scale of firms and large-scale mergers, which drastically changed the market structure. While the government and MITI did not use their policy tools to intervene directly, the merger of Yawata and Fuji Steel which was carried out with the encouragement and explicit support of the government brought about a substantial increase in market concentration. The merger may well have been effective in restraining investment competition, as was claimed at the time by the Industrial Structure Council and by Yawata and Fuji and as was found in an econometric analysis carried out elsewhere by the author. At the same time it is necessary to note that the merger clearly made it easier to price discriminate between the domestic and export markets.

In examining the postwar industrial policies for the steel industry, in general the policies of the 1950s and early 1960s were formulated for the purpose of improving growth and overall efficiency in the industry and in protecting it from foreign competition. It can be concluded that these policies contributed to the achievement of these goals, but in subsequent periods policy often lacked an appropriate consideration of its impact on the efficient allocation of resources and the market structure. As a result, it may have reduced domestic economic welfare.

Notes

1. Ojimi [1972], pp. 11–18, and Tsusho Sangyo Gyosei Kenkyukai [1983], Vol. I, pp. 73–106 and p. 285.
2. Nihon Tekko Renmei [1969], p. 312.
3. Tsusho Sangyo Gyosei Kenkyukai [1983], Vol. I, pp. 85–96.
4. There were in addition a special depreciation system for the establishment of foreign offices (1954–1960), an export loss reserve fund (1954–1959), an extra tax allowance system for exports (1957–1967), a foreign transaction accelerated depreciation system (1961–1964), and other provisions. See Nihon Tekko Renmei [1969], pp. 506–512, and Tsusho Sangyo Gyosei Kenkyukai [1983], Vol. I, pp. 96–106.
5. See also Tsuruta [1982], pp. 46–51.
6. Nihon Tekko Renmei [1969], pp. 477–489.
7. Tsuruta [1982], p. 74.
8. The Big 6 were Fuji Steel, Yawata Steel, Nippon Kokan, Kawasaki Steel, Kobe Steel, and Sumitomo Metal Industries [translator's note].
9. Based on Table 3-9 of Tsuruta [1982], pp. 76–77.
10. Nihon Tekko Renmei [1981], pp. 506–507.
11. Peck and Tamura [1976], pp. 546–548.
12. Nihon Tekko Renmei [1969], p. 277.
13. Ibid., p. 283, Table 33.
14. According to the estimates of Yamazawa [1967], effective rates of protection were 24.4% for pig iron, 47.0% for steel ingots, and 35.1% for rolled steel.
15. The import ratio for 1957 was 12.3%, but this was due to emergency import measures undertaken by the government.
16. Cost is comprised of materials plus labor, while raw materials include iron ore, scrap, coal, oil, gas, and electricity.
17. Knickerbocker [1973] presents an analysis of the relationship between a recognition of mutual interdependence by oligopolists and their investment behavior. See also Esposito and Esposito [1974].
18. According to the October 1, 1966, interim report "The Future Status of the Steel Industry" of the Basic Steel Issues Subcommittee of the Heavy Industry Committee of the Industrial Structure Council found in Nihon Tekko Renmei [1969], pp. 831–837.
19. Nihon Tekko Renmei [1969], p. 314.
20. Nihon Tekko Renmei [1969], pp. 312–319, Kawasaki [1968], pp. 598–611, and Tekko Shinbun Sha [1975], Appendix pp. 8–14.
21. See also Tsuruta [1982], 791–793.
22. See also the understanding concluded in November 1966 between the FTC and MITI, "Sangyo no Kozokaizen no Suishin ni kansuru Dokusen Kinshiho no Unyo ni tsuite" (The Application of the Antitrust Law to the Use of Policies for the Reform of Structure of Industry) found in Tsusho Sangyo Gyosei Kenkyukai [1983], Vol. I, pp. 123–224.
23. Nihon Tekko Renmei [1959], pp. 587–590.
24. Tsusansho, "Tekko Shikyo Taisaku Yoko" (Outline of Policies to Deal with the Recession in Steel), June 20, 1958, and Kosei Torihiki Iinkai [1977], pp. 98–99.

25. Tsusansho, "Tekko Shikyo Taisaku Yoko" (Outline of Policies to Deal with the Recession in Steel), May 25, 1959.

26. Tsusansho, "Tekko Kakaku Antei Taisaku Yoko" (Outline of Policies to Stabilize Steel Prices), July 25, 1960.

27. The Steel Plate Recession Cartel was authorized from August 1965.

28. The price of ordinary wire rods was extremely stable. On the relationship of price and market structure, see Yamawaki [1977].

29. See for example Osborne [1976] on the theoretical basis of this argument.

30. Tsusansho, "Tekko Shikyo Taisaku ni tsuite" (On Policies to Deal with the Recession in Steel), July 25, 1960, and "Futsuko Atsuenyo Kokai no Gensan Sochi ni tsuite" (Measures to Reduce Production of Ordinary Steel Billets), July 26, 1965.

31. See Tsuruta [1982], pp. 115–158 for details.

32. According to the October 1, 1966, interim report "The Future Status of the Steel Industry" of the Basic Steel Issues Subcommittee of the Heavy Industry Committee of the Industrial Structure Council found in Nihon Tekko Renmei [1969], pp. 831–837.

33. Yawata Seitetsu and Fuji Seitetsu (Yawata Steel and Fuji Steel), "Gappei Shuisho" (Merger Agreement), May 1968.

34. See *Shukan Toyo Keizai* July 3, 1968 (Zokan), pp. 44–45 for the opinion of economists who took this stance.

35. See also Yamawaki [1977].

36. The model used consisted of seven structural equations and seven identities; each structural relationship was estimated using two-stage least squares. A dynamic simulation was made in which only the merger dummy in the equation determining market concentration was varied. For details, see Yamawaki [1984].

CHAPTER 12

The Automotive Industry

HIROMICHI MUTOH

Japan Economic Research Center
Tokyo, Japan

I. Introduction

The automotive industry is linked to a wide range of other industries, and the degree of its development is seen as a reflection of a country's level of industrialization. Looking at the structure of transactions in the auto industry in Japan in 1979, relative to output in the industry of ¥14.9 trillion (in 1975 prices), the industries that provided over ¥500 billion in inputs included cast and forged steel products, machinery (general), rubber products, financial and insurance services, and commerce, while steel milling, chemicals (other), ceramic and stone products, electrical equipment, and services provided over ¥100 billion each in inputs, thus incorporating a wide range of industrial fields. Among the 166 nations in existence, only 26 produce automobiles, and of the total output of 38.8 million vehicles in 1980 (of which 29.3 million were passenger vehicles), 90.5% were accounted for by the top ten countries: Japan, the United States, West Germany, France, U.S.S.R., Italy, Canada, the United Kingdom, Spain, and Brazil. That these countries are among those with the highest industrial level in the world goes without saying. As depicted in Figure 12.1, in 1979 Japanese automotive production for the first time surpassed that of the United States, and this was due in large part to the support given by the high level of technology in the iron and steel and machine tool industries, among the wide range of related industries.

The automotive industry was started after the end of World War II from a level of almost zero output. In September 1945, GHQ (the General Headquarters of the Occupation) gave permission for the production of trucks only, and in the following year output only came to 14,921 units. In 1982, production was roughly 10.73 million units, so that over a 36-

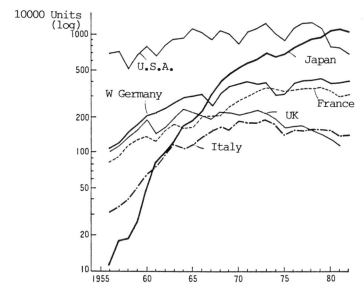

Fig. 12.1. Automotive production of leading countries. From Nihon Jidosha Kogyo Kai [Japan Automobile Manufacturers' Association], *Jidosha Tokei Nenpo* [Automotive Statistics Annual].

year period, production increased about 720 times, for an average annual growth rate of about 20%. Seven years elapsed from the time annual production surpassed the 100,000 unit level in 1956 until it exceeded the 1 million unit level in 1963, and the next 10-fold increase in production, to over 10 million units in 1980, required only 18 more years.

In what looks like a process of steady development, however, one cannot ignore the following turning points through which the industry passed:

1. *The Korean War (1950–1951).* With the establishment of the "Basic Automotive Industry Policy" in October 1948, the auto industry was eager to expand output, but the Dodge Line deflationary policies of 1949 led to large-scale firings. What saved the situation were Special Procurements by the U. N. Forces with the outbreak of the Korean War in June 1950, and the accumulation of capital at this time provided the basis for subsequent development.

2. *Trade Liberalization (1961 for commercial vehicles, 1965 for passenger vehicles).* From 1953, paralleling an increase in the output of cars made under licensing agreements with Western manufacturers, the output of purely domestic vehicles also increased rapidly. Toyota, Nissan, Isuzu, and Hino were the initial firms, and a later group consisting of Fuji Heavy

Industries, Toyo Kogyo (Mazda), Mitsubishi, and others entered into the passenger car field from the production of light 4-wheel vehicles. In 1958, when the government decided on the "Basic Guidelines for Trade and Foreign Exchange Liberalization," each firm strove to construct or expand facilities specializing in passenger vehicle production, and the mass production system was almost fully in place by the time of liberalization in 1965.

3. *Capital Liberalization (1971)*. While Japan became a member of the OECD in 1964, capital liberalization was decided on in the Japan–U.S. negotiations of August 1968, with implementation scheduled in October 1969 for October 1971 (actually put into effect in April 1971). Firms strengthened their ties to each other, not only with the merger of Nissan and Prince, and tie-ups between Toyota and Hino and Toyota and Daihatsu, but also by linking up with foreign firms, with ties forged between Mitsubishi and Chrysler, Isuzu and GM, and Toyo Kogyo (Mazda) and Ford.

4. *The Onset of Environmental Problems (circa 1970)*. Accompanying the rapid diffusion of automobiles, atmospheric pollution became a problem, and together with problems with defective vehicles, gave rise to a wave of reaction against automobiles. In August 1972 it became apparent the "Japanese Muskie Bill" would be enacted, and the auto industry was pressed to meet standards by the target year of 1975. The second-tier manufacturers, Honda, Suzuki, and Toyo Kogyo (Mazda) made great contributions to the development of emissions technology, and Japan met the strictest standards of any country in the world.

5. *Post-Oil Crisis (1973)*. The large-scale crude oil price hikes by OPEC raised concern throughout the world over fuel conservation. This increased the relative competitiveness of the Japanese auto industry, with its small cars and efforts to increase fuel efficiency. This was one element that made it possible for vehicle exports to surpass 2.5 million units from 1976 on.

6. *Auto Trade Friction (since 1980)*. The stagnation of the world economy accompanying the second oil crisis and the increase in fuel prices increased demand for Japanese vehicles, with their low fuel consumption and high performance, but it also had the side effect of producing management difficulties for foreign manufacturers and invited large-scale layoffs, becoming one cause of a rising protectionism. In response, the Japanese auto industry, based on intergovernmental negotiations, implemented voluntary export restraints and carried out direct foreign investment to initiate local production.

In this fashion, the events listed in (1) through (6) at times provided an opportunity for rapid advance, and at times were restraining factors, but at the same time one can also claim that they represented the transition in the stage of development of the industry from revival to maturity.

This chapter considers what sort of policy instruments were developed for the Japanese auto industry as it followed this development process and analyzes how these policies contributed to the development of the industry and to national economic welfare. Even when consideration is restricted to a range of selective policy measures, policies affecting the auto industry consisted of an extremely wide range of measures, including the building up of infrastructure (in particular, roads), the impact of commodity and import taxes, changes in conditions for finance, import restrictions, and policies to rescue specific firms. Furthermore, in Japan with a "vertical" government administration, this meant that policies affecting the auto industry involved not only MITI but also the Ministry of Construction and the Ministry of Transport. In other words, the industrial policies affecting automobiles were not simply the policies of MITI, but included a wide range of policies that need to be examined.[1]

This being said, it is impossible to treat these policies comprehensively in a limited number of pages. Thus, the consideration of the role of the government vis-a-vis the automotive industry will be limited to (1) the role of the government in putting in place the requirements for an industry, (2) the role of the government in protecting the industry, and (3) the role of the government as arbiter. Among such policies, we will limit our examination to, for (1), the construction of the road network and the setting of safety and emissions standards, for (2), various policies drawn up for the industry because it was designated a strategic industry, and for (3), the government's mediation in the U.S.–Japan auto negotiations. Section II will review the development of specific policies relating to (1) to (3) and Section III will evaluate the performance of policy. Finally, overall conclusions and remaining issues are allocated to Section IV.

II. The Development of Auto Industry Policies

A. The Road System, Emissions, and Safety

According to the Japanese Road Transport Law, an automobile is "a vehicle utilizing a motor, other than a bicycle equipped with a motor, which can be operated without depending on rails or electric lines." For automobiles to take root in society, nothing is more necessary than the construction of roads along which they can be operated. The 1953 Law on Temporary Measures Concerning Revenues for the Financing of Road

Construction (1) provided that from the standpoint of mapping out a long-term plan, from FY 1954 a Five-Year Road Construction Plan would be implemented and (2) provided for the appropriation of the gasoline tax as a stable, long-term revenue source. This philosophy was developed further in the FY 1958 Road Construction Emergency Measures Law, which has continued in effect through today. Table I presents planned expenditures and the proportion actually spent over the periods covered from the First Five-Year Road Construction Plan on.

Before 1973, the spread of automobiles exceeded that foreseen in the plans, and because of this, the government was pressed with the necessity of speeding up the construction of the road system. As a result, throughout the 1960s and 1970s, road construction comprised over 40% of all public works expenditures, and during the latter 1960s, when the pace at which automobiles spread was particularly rapid, it reached as high as 47%. During the same period, these expenditures came to 24.4% of all government construction (including related expenditures).[2] The gasoline, LPG, and other taxes specifically earmarked for road construction financed about two-thirds of the investment in roads, with the remainder being covered by general revenues, FILP investments, and local bonds.

Let us now turn to the issues of pollution and safety. In Japan, these issues surfaced circa 1970, and in both cases, the sequence of events followed almost the same pattern as with their occurrence in the United States.

First, for safety issues, there was in the case of Japan an ordinance on Safety Standards for Vehicles Used in Road Transport. Following partial revisions in 1968, 1969, and 1970, subsequent to the August 1972 Report of the Transport Technology Council, the First-Round Target for Ex-

TABLE I
Five-Year Road Construction Plans: Targets and Performance

Plan	Years (revised)*	Target Expenditures	Proportion of this Spent
First	1954–58 (1957)	¥0.26 trillion	70.0%
Second	1958–62 (1960)	¥1.00 trillion	52.5%
Third	1961–65 (1963)	¥2.10 trillion	59.6%
Fourth	1964–68 (1966)	¥4.10 trillion	53.4%
Fifth	1967–71 (1969)	¥6.60 trillion	52.5%
Sixth	1970–74 (1972)	¥10.35 trillion	60.1%
Seventh	1973–77 —	¥19.50 trillion	86.4%
Eighth	1978–82 —	¥28.50 trillion	98.9%

*The dates in parentheses are the years in which plans were revised and scaled up prior to completion.

tending and Strengthening Standards was set in June 1973 and the safety standards were again revised.

Emission controls, on the other hand, date to a 1966 regulatory "circular" of the Ministry of Transport, which applied only to gasoline vehicles and went no farther than to limit the carbon monoxide concentration in emissions to under 3%. When the Muskie Act (the Clean Air Act Amendment of 1970) saw the light of day in the United States, however, standards that conformed with those were adopted in Japan as well. In 1973 the regulation was changed from that of limiting the concentration of emissions to limiting their total mass, and standards were set in 1975 with the same targets as those in the Muskie Act. The limits were set based on measurements of emissions for 10 operating modes, which corresponded to the 10 driving condition patterns found in in-city driving. Emissions per kilometer were set at a maximum of 2.7 grams (average of 2.1 gms) for CO, 0.39 gms (0.25 gms) for HC, and 1.6 gms (1.2 gms) for NOx, and these were to be implemented for new model lines in April 1975, for existing model lines in December 1975, and for imported cars in April 1976. Finally, an attempt was made in 1976 to lower the 1975 ceiling for average NOx emissions to 0.25 gms, but due to auto industry demands this was postponed until 1978. Paralleling the setting of these standards was the provision of measures to promote compliance, with tax breaks[3] and subsidies for the development of an electric car.[4]

B. The Development of Protection and Promotion Policies[5]

Following World War II, the goals of direct government involvement with the auto industry shifted from military to economic objectives.[6] Opinion within the government, however, was divided over the status of the auto industry in September 1949, when the Industrial Rationalization resolution, which proposed establishing a system to guide industries so that they would fit in with the future industrial structure, was approved by the Cabinet. The debate in the government during 1949–1951 was between the Bank of Japan position of freely permitting auto imports and the MITI position of fostering the auto industry. During the debate, foreign exchange difficulties and the "Special Procurements" that arose in connection with the Korean War worked in favor of the protectionist stance, and the following guidelines were developed in the latter part of 1951 during talks between the auto industry and MITI.

1. Domestic manufacturers would be protected from direct investment by foreign firms and from imports of foreign vehicles.

2. Domestic manufacturers would be permitted to import foreign technology under favorable terms.

3. The government would provide financial assistance.

This basic policy stance was adhered to quite faithfully through 1969. For convenience, we will divide the protection and promotion policies that developed along the lines of this stance into protectionist policies, which suppressed the entry of foreign vehicles into the market, and promotion policies, which were taken to strengthen the international competitiveness of the industry.

First, protectionist policies were composed of four elements, (1) protective tariffs, (2) a commodity tax system favorable to domestic autos, (3) the restriction of imports using the allocation of foreign exchange, and (4) foreign exchange controls on foreign direct investment in Japan. Among these, tariffs, as can be seen in Figure 12.2, were highest through the 1960s for small passenger vehicles (those with a short wheelbase). This was favorable for domestic vehicles, most of which were small. In addition, commodity tax rates were adjusted so as to be unfavorable to large, imported vehicles; from April 1954 through March 1962, the tax rate on luxury passenger vehicles was 50%, on regular cars 40%, and on small cars 20%. The role of import restrictions carried out by means of the foreign exchange allocation system was also great. In 1952–1953, imports of small European cars rapidly increased, but from 1954, purchasers qualifying for allocations were limited to taxi companies and the media, resale was prohibited for a three-year period, and other measures were taken that severely restricted foreign vehicle imports. There was later a transition from currency allo-

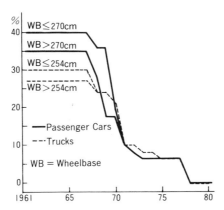

Fig. 12.2. Changes in automotive tariff rates. Derived from Nihon Kanzei Kyokai (Japan Tariff Association), *Jikko Kanzeirtsu Hyo* (Effective Tariff Rate Tables).

cations to quotas on the number of vehicles, but the quantity that could be imported was not effectively increased until after 1964. Finally, so severe were the foreign capital restrictions throughout the 1950s and 1960s that investment by foreign auto manufacturers did not even become an issue until Japan joined the OECD in 1964.

Corresponding to these protectionist policies were promotion policies, including (1) supplying low-interest rate loans through government financial institutions, (2) granting subsidies, (3) providing special depreciation allowances, (4) exempting necessary equipment from import tariffs, and (5) approving essential foreign technology. Among these, loans by the Japan Development Bank were particularly important, as indicated in Table II,

TABLE II
Automotive Investment and Japan Development Bank Lending

Year	Amount Lent (¥ million)	Fixed Investment (¥ million)	Loans as Share of Investment (%)	Purpose of Lending
1951	135	1,027	13.1	Truck and bus facilities
52	60	1,946	3.1	Truck and bus facilities
53	200	3,945	5.1	Truck and bus facilities and passenger car facilities
54	165	5,400	3.1	Domestic passenger car production
55	300	3,971	7.6	Domestic passenger car production and localization of production under foreign licenses
56	125	8,025	1.6	Parts manufacturers' facilities
1966	4,000	118,826	3.4	Mergers for minicar production
67	5,000	194,769	2.6	Mergers for minicar production and tie-ups for minicars
68	0	241,741	0.0	———
69	1,000	245,708	0.4	Tie-ups for minicar production
70	1,500	282,500	0.5	Tie-ups for minicar production
71	400	226,600	0.2	Tie-ups for minicar production

Sources: Tsusansho, *Shuyo Sanoyo no Setsubi Toshi Keikaku* (Fixed Investment Plans of Leading Industries), and Nihon Kaihatsu Ginko [1976].

with its loans during the period when the industry was being established coming to 4% of investment by the automotive industry. With the enactment in June 1956 of the Law on Temporary Measures for Promoting the Machinery Industries (Machine Industry Law), the automotive parts industry was selected as one of the 17 industries for promotion, and lending began by the Japan Development Bank to primary parts firms and by the Small Business Finance Corporation to secondary suppliers [firms that supplied the primary parts firms—*translator's note*]; the final-assembly industry was not, however, a direct target. For the designated industries, the goal of the Machine Industries Law was to set up a rational production system, to modernize facilities, promote exports, develop new technologies, and set overall raw materials policies. The law, which had a time limit of 5 years, was revised and extended in 1961 and again in 1966, and the list of designated industries was expanded to include automotive industry equipment and tooling, internal combustion engines, and industrial vehicles, along with automotive parts. Table III shows the amount of financing recommended over the 15 year period of this law; between the Japan Development Bank and the Small Business Finance Corporation, ¥34.8 billion was lent to 529 firms. Of total lending by the Japan Development Bank to designated machine industries, 32.1% went to the automotive parts industry during 1961–1965 and 54.2% during 1966–1974.

During 1951–1959, cumulative subsidies of ¥369 million were provided for projects contracted out to the Society of Automotive Engineers of Japan and the Midget Motor Manufacturers Association of Japan. For "rationalization" equipment designated under the Special Tax Measures Law, special depreciation allowances provided for 50% depreciation in the initial year, and for "important" machinery, a 50% increase in the amount for the first three years. In 1951 the automotive industry and in 1956 the automotive parts industry became industries designated under

TABLE III
Machine Industries Law Financing to the Auto Parts Industry

Law	Fiscal Year	Japan Development Bank		Small Business Finance Corporation		Total	
		Loans (¥ million)	No. Firms	Loans (¥ million)	No. Firms	Loans (¥ million)	No. Firms
First	1956–60	1,819	66	—	—	1,819	66
Second	1961–65	11,503	163	2,326	92	13,829	255
Third	1966–70	17,320	139	1,821	69	19,141	208
Total		30,642	368	4,147	161	34,789	529

Source: Nihon Kigyo Shinbun, [1982].

Article 6 of the Enterprise Rationalization Promotion Law. Import tariff exemptions were made available under special provisions of the Tariff Law and the Provisional Tariff Measures Law for "necessary" equipment, that is, for imports of machinery recognized as essential for the principal manufacturing processes, which were difficult to manufacture domestically. To overcome the quality and cost disadvantages that existed in the early 1950s, technology imports were approved, and despite the severe foreign exchange restrictions at the time, imports of knockdown vehicles were permitted for a limited period. Of the six applications made in accordance with these guidelines from October 1952, four were approved. These were for Nissan with Austin (U.K.) in November 1952, Isuzu with Rootes (U.K.) in March 1953, Hino with Renault (France) in March 1953, and Shin-Mitsubishi Heavy Industries with Willy's-Overland (U.S.) in September 1953.

Through these protection and promotion policies, the Japanese automotive industry steadily began to move away from its status as an infant industry. As a result, demands from foreign countries for trade liberalization began to strengthen, and in April 1961, trade in trucks and busses was liberalized. For passenger cars, liberalization was delayed until October 1964, due to the lag in production volume and performance. Two important policies that were adopted in the process of moving toward eventual liberalization were the 1955 "People's Car" concept and the 1961 "producer group" concept.

The People's Car concept aimed for the production of a popular, low-priced minicar, capable of being exported, with production concentrated in one firm. The initial specifications were that it should carry four passengers, be priced at ¥250,000, have an engine displacement of 350-500cc, have a curb weight of about 400 kg, and have a top speed of 100 km per hour. The producers' group concept was made public in May 1961 by the Industrial Finance Committee of the Industrial Rationalization Council. The concept envisioned producers being divided into groups of two to three firms each, with one group for "mass production" vehicles (passenger cars, with an output of 7,000 units per month), a second group for specialty vehicles (luxury and sports cars, with an output of 3,000 units per month), and a final group for minicars. In the end neither of these two plans saw the light of day.[7] Thereafter, however, these concepts were strongly reflected in the goals of later policies of expanding exports and establishing a mass production system.

In December 1962, the Passenger Car Policy Special Subcommittee of the Industrial Structure Advisory Council finalized a report on policies for the passenger car industry, and with its acceptance the passenger car industry was made eligible for "organizational development" loans from the Japan Development Bank from FY 1963. The amount of these loans is given in the lower panel of Table II, and the ¥11.5 billion lent over 1966–1971 went to Nissan with its leading role in mergers related to facilities for producing minicars, and to Hino, Daihatsu, and Fuji Heavy Industries, all of which were involved in tie-ups with either Nissan or Toyota. These clearly helped to establish a mass production system and provided explicit support for mergers and tie-ups, which worked to limit inefficient investment. In the case of the Nissan–Prince merger, the Minister of MITI at that time played a role in sounding out the two firms and acting as a conduit between the firms and their main banks (the Industrial Bank of Japan and Sumitomo Bank), showing that this merger was in line with MITI policy. Finally, the third Machine Industries Law took effect during that same time and provided for loans for the rationalization of the automotive parts industry, in preparation for capital liberalization. Organizational development lending and the above lending based on the Machine Industries Law both were halted with capital liberalization in April 1971. Protection and promotion of the auto industry effectively came to an end at that time.[8]

C. The Government as Mediator: U.S.–Japan Trade Friction

In the automotive industry the government was active as a mediator in the case of (1) conflicts with other industries, and in particular those with the steel industry over steel price hikes, and (2) friction with other countries. Because of space limitations, we will only take up the latter case.

Friction with foreign nations, and in particular the course of the negotiations in the U.S.–Japan auto dispute, have already been presented in detail by Ikema [1980], Destler and Sato [1982], Amaya [1982], and others. In the following discussion, we will thus examine the role played by the government as mediator, focusing on the agreement between the U.S. and Japan and its economic implications.

There were two overall phases to the government-level negotiations in the post-1979 U.S.–Japan auto disputes.

The first phase was during the Carter administration, with negotiations centering around two working-level conferences and the visit of United States Trade Representative Askew to Japan. There were three demands by the Americans at the time:

1. An easing of safety and other standards for exports of U.S. vehicles to Japan,
2. Elimination of the tariff on automotive parts, and

3. Construction in the United States of manufacturing facilities by the Japanese assemblers, and in particular, by Toyota and Nissan.

It goes without saying that one factor underlying these demands was the stagnation of the U.S. automotive industry. From a peak in 1977 of 9.21 million vehicles, U.S. automotive production fell to 9.18 million units in 1978, and 8.43 million units in 1979. Another factor was that, despite this, Japanese exports to the United States continued to increase. Japanese penetration in the U.S. new car market was 8.6% in 1975, but increased to 14.9% in 1979 (see Table IV). A third factor was the management crisis of Chrysler, the number three automotive firm in the United States. A loss of $200 million in 1978 expanded into a huge $1.1 billion loss in 1979, and the firm was driven to petitioning for financial assistance from the federal government.

A conclusion to the first phase of negotiations was arrived at on May 15, 1980, with an agreement between the two governments on the following points:

1. Encouragement by the Japanese government for Japanese auto manufacturers to invest in the United States,

2. Early feasibility studies by the Japanese government and Japanese parts manufacturers of the potential profitability of production in the United States,

3. A simplification of standards and licensing procedures in Japan,

4. Elimination by Japan of tariffs on automotive parts imports,

5. Promotion of the importation of automotive parts from the United States.

The U.S.–Japan trade dispute, however, was not resolved by means of these steps alone. The second phase consisted, after the inauguration of the Reagan administration, of negotiations between United States Trade Representative Brock and MITI. At that time the point of dispute became voluntary restraints by Japan on exports to the United States and seeking a way to do this that would not be in violation of U.S. antitrust laws.

The principal reason that the May 1980 agreement did not lead to an overall resolution of the dispute was increasing unemployment in the American auto industry. In August 1980 there were 250,000 workers in the United States on indefinite layoff, about one-third of the production workers. The United Automobile Workers (UAW) had already filed a petition requesting a finding by the International Trade Commission (ITC) of damage by imports, and the UAW sought the implementation of import restrictions. The finding of the ITC, however, was that Japanese cars were "innocent" of having caused damage, on the ground that the real cause

TABLE IV

Japanese Passenger Car Production and Trade (1,000 units)

Year	Production	Exports	Exports to U.S.	Imports	Imports from U.S.	New Registrations	Dependence on Exports	Market Penetration	
								U.S. in J	J in U.S.
1960	165	7	1	3.5	2.7	145	4.2%	1.9%	0.0%
1965	696	101	22	12.9	3.2	586	14.5	0.5	0.2
1970	3,179	726	233	19.1	5.3	2,379	22.8	0.2	2.8
1975	4,568	1,827	712	45.5	16.5	2,738	40.0	0.6	8.6
1976	5,028	2,539	1,051	40.4	13.8	2,449	50.5	0.6	10.8
1977	5,431	2,959	1,339	41.4	14.4	2,500	54.5	0.6	12.4
1978	5,976	3,042	1,409	54.5	13.3	2,857	50.9	0.5	12.9
1979	6,176	3,102	1,547	64.8	20.7	3,037	50.2	0.7	14.9
1980	7,038	3,947	1,819	46.3	10.5	2,854	56.1	0.4	20.8
1981	6,974	3,947	1,761	31.9	4.2	2,867	56.6	0.1	20.9
1982	6,881	3,770	1,692	35.3	3.1	3,038	54.8	0.1	21.8

Source: Nihon Jidosha Kogyo Kai (Japan Automobile Manufacturers' Association), *Jidosha Tokei Nenpo* (Automotive Statistics Annual).

of the blow that the U.S. automotive industry had received was the failure by management to respond to the shift in consumer preferences.

The issue had already become a political one, and the second phase negotiations led to the implementation of voluntary restraints on automotive exports to the United States. The six points of the agreement were roughly as follows:

1. Until March 1984, reporting and monitoring under the Japanese Foreign Exchange and Foreign Trade Control Law of automotive exports to the United States,

2. A voluntary restraint of exports in the first year (April 1981 to March 1982) of 1.68 million vehicles,

3. The quota for the second year would be increased by 16.5% of the expansion in the overall market,

4. The application of the Japanese export licensing system, if necessary,

5. The continuation of quotas for a third year would be decided on the basis of the situation in the U.S. market,

6. The measures would all expire as of March 1984.

It should go without saying that among these, (2), (3), and (5) related to the setting of the level of the restraints, while (1) and (4) were for the purpose of avoiding the application of U.S. antitrust legislation.

III. The Evaluation of the Government's Performance

A. The Evaluation of Infrastructure Policies

To what extent did the policies described in the previous section achieve their expected goals, and what was their impact on national economic welfare? First, for road development, despite the great contribution to the more efficient movement of goods and people, one can hardly claim that an acceptable level was achieved. One issue is the lag, by international standards, in the construction of expressways. As of FY 1981, Japanese expressways (national highways) totaled 3,010 km, a mere 76 meters per 1,000 vehicles. In contrast, in the United States, there are 557 meters per 1,000 vehicles, in West Germany, 299 meters; in France, 242 meters; and in the United Kingdom, 148 meters, so that the Japanese level is seen to be much lower. Another issue is extreme congestion. In the regions in which population is concentrated, about half of the improved roads are rated as congested, and even if plains and mountainous regions are included, 27.2% of the total road length has a congestion index of over 1.[9] Thus the construction of roads to support automobiles was not able to keep pace with the rapid advance of motorization. The rate of investment in roads, at roughly 2% of GNP, is the highest among the developed countries, but because historically the road network was inadequate, and because topography and high land prices tend to make construction expensive, the net effect is to strengthen the impression that the development of roads is still comparatively backward. Prior to World War II, West Germany already possessed about 2,100 km of Autobahns, and considering this, it probably would have been better to have made a bigger investment in roads at the start of the spread of automobiles in Japan. However, because in Japan the budget for investment in roads is linked to the targeted tax receipts, it was inadequate from the standpoint of providing for smooth transport, even though it has been excellent in providing a stable revenue source.

Second, regarding safety, I believe policies have produced quite favorable results. As can be seen in Table V, Japanese auto fatalities, at 3.1 per 10 thousand vehicles in 1980, were low in comparison to the level in other countries. Considering that the level had been by far the highest among these countries in the 1960s, this reflects a substantial improvement. Looking at the trend in fatalities per accident, the improvement also stands out, with the rate of 2.32 fatalities per 100 accidents in 1971 decreasing to 2.28 in 1975 and 1.84 in 1980. The recall program for defective autos, introduced in 1969 in connection with the automotive safety issue, is also functioning. There are about 20 to 30 notifications per year calling for the correction of defects, affecting a varying number of vehicles, ranging from a few 10,000's to over 1,000,000 vehicles, so one can evaluate the system favorably for bringing about the correction of defects when they come to light. Before the system was implemented, the auto industry had tried to repair defects in secret, fearing that reputation would be damaged, but in fact the program has led to forward-looking competition in publicizing and making an effort to recall defective vehicles.

TABLE V
Fatalities per 10,000 Vehicles

Country	1960	1965	1970	1975	1980
Japan	58	25	12.3	5.0	3.1
United States	5	6	5.1	3.5	3.3
United Kingdom	9	8	5.8	4.1	3.6
West Germany	—	16	13.2	7.8	5.3
France	11	10	7.6	7.5	5.8

Source: Sorifu [Prime Minister's Office], Kotsu Anzen Hakusho (White Paper on Transport Safety).

Third, regarding the prevention of pollution, the standards were achieved by 1978. In fact, rather than ending in a substantial rollback of standards as seen in the United States, Japan became the country that applied the strictest regulatory standards, and in recent years there has even been a plaint by European auto manufacturers who view the Japanese emission standards as constituting a nontariff trade barrier. Furthermore, among recent cases of filings of complaints and petitions over pollution, the proportion relating to air pollution has declined, while the proportion of auto-related cases dealing with noise and vibration has increased. At first glance this gives the impression that this was the result of government policies, but such a conclusion is premature. The first firms to meet the standards were second tier firms, Honda Motors, Suzuki Motors, and Mitsubishi Motors, so that one can see the contribution of the vigorous efforts of firms in the Japanese automotive industry and the severe competitive environment, in contrast to the lag in meeting standards in the United States and Europe, where an oligopolistic system had developed in the industry.[10] It also is interesting to note that the technical knowledge that accumulated in the course of the efforts by the Japanese firms to deal with emissions problems, together with the energy conservation efforts accompanying the first oil crisis, contributed to increased performance and cost competitiveness internationally.

B. The Evaluation of Protection and Promotion Policies

The Japanese automotive industry, which since 1979 has ranked first in the world in number of units produced, has increased its share of domestic value added in manufacturing from 3.1% in 1955 to 7.4% in 1980, and its share of manufacturing employment from 2.3% to 6.2%. Automobiles have increased from virtually zero to 17.9% of exports (or roughly 20%, if automotive parts are included), surpassing steel and ships. The aim of MITI of "nurturing international competitive strength and contributing to the modernization of the domestic economy" has been achieved beyond all expectations.

The impact of protection and promotion policies, however, should be judged on the basis of the extent to which they contributed to the achievement in the industry being considered of results that are desirable from the standpoint of the economic welfare of society as a whole. The issues that then must be considered are (1) the appropriateness of the industry as a target for protection/promotion and (2) the appropriateness of the government policies that were chosen and the way in which they were implemented.

Regarding point (1), in the immediate postwar period the foreign exchange rate was set at a relatively high value, so that Japan was troubled by trade imbalances, and it was not much of a mistake to target the automotive industry, in which the world demand elasticity for auto exports and domestic income elasticity of demand were high and where furthermore productivity increases could be anticipated. What must be noted, however, is that the automotive industry was not the only target for protection and promotion. Petrochemicals, the electronic industries, and other future growth industries were also included. But considering the lack of uniformity among industries and differences among countries in their level of development, one notes that protective and promotion policies are not a panacea for increasing industrialization. In the case of the Japanese automotive industry, there were not only the very favorable external factors of the rapid expansion in world demand and the trend of a relative decrease in gasoline prices up to the first oil crisis, but there were also the fierce competition among domestic manufacturers and the energetic efforts of the firms in the industry.[11]

Next, there are many issues relating to point (2), the selection and implementation of policies. As seen in the previous section, the policies that were adopted—high tariff rates, import restrictions, subsidy policies, and the People's Car concept—were almost all modeled after the policies taken in Europe during the 1910s through the 1930s. One issue of this approach is that the goal of the individual policies was left unclear. For example, there is no evidence of any comparison, in the process of policy implementation, of the differing impacts of establishing high tariffs, restricting imports, and providing subsidies to domestic firms.

With the establishment of the Japanese automotive industry, the rationalization efforts of the firms in the industry were of course crucial, but if the increasing share during 1951–1953 of European cars, which were able to overcome the tariff barrier despite its height, is noted, then the important role played by import restrictions policies cannot be ignored.

One further issue with protection and promotion policies was a lack of consistency in policy. For example, the promotion of mergers and tie-ups and financing for strengthening the organization of production and loans based on the Machine Industries Law were specific measures adopted as policies for promoting the industry. There were, in addition, the People's Car and the production group concepts lying in the background, as noted above. The progression of events conceived in the proposal for forming two giant firm groupings (keiretsu) was not, however, in fact seen. The development of two large groups, those of Toyota and Nissan, progressed quickly, but Mitsubishi, Toyo Kogyo (Mazda), Honda, and the other firms maintained their independence, as in the past.

In the history of the postwar reorganization of the industry, there were cases in which reorganization policies met with success, as in the merger of Nissan and Prince in August 1966 and the tie-ups of Toyota and Hino in December 1967 and Nissan and Fuji Heavy Industries in October 1968. There were, however, more cases of unsuccessful tie-ups, as in those between Isuzu and Fuji Heavy Industries in December 1966, between Isuzu, Fuji Heavy Industries, and Mitsubishi in December 1967, and between Nissan and Isuzu in March 1970. There also was movement that went against the initial intention of MITI to prevent any "landing" of foreign capital in Japan, with the tie-up between Mitsubishi and Chrysler in May 1969.[12] Tajima [1977] proposed the following three reasons why a relatively large number of auto manufacturers were able to exist in Japan:

(1) special features in the composition of model lines, as firms were able to accumulate profits in trucks, motorcycles and minicars, which were not in direct competition with products of the two giants in the industry,

(2) the rapid rate of increase in domestic demand, which provided much room for new entrants, and

(3) the protective policies of the government, which postponed the "landing" of foreign capital, strengthening the power of domestic manufacturers to compete.

In other words, when there is a rapid increase in demand behind heavy protective barriers, then with new entry occurring it is natural that exits and mergers fail to ensue. Toyota Jidosha Kogyo [1967], reflecting on price competition during 1959–1963, states that

Within the automotive industry of our nation, with the prospect of intense competition from the more advanced manufacturers in the U.S. and Europe just ahead, the decisive factor was above all the strengthening of operations. [As a young industry], we were particularly concerned lest the storm [of foreign competition] would break into the shelter provided by our "greenhouse."

The firms in the "greenhouse" avoided unnecessary price reductions, which gave rise to excess profits. In the long term these excess profits lowered the barrier to entry, making it possible for numerous firms to coexist. It is ironic that cooperation among domestic makers in fact worked to prevent increasing concentration in the industry.

C. The Influence of the Government as a Mediator

Here we will focus on two points relating to the results of the U.S.– Japan bilateral negotiations, (1) the extent to which the government could make commitments in agreements reached during negotiations, and (2) the extent to which the negotiations were tied to a resolution of the issues.

First, concerning (1), there were two viewpoints, as is well known. One is the understanding expressed in Ikema [1980], where the following claim was made regarding the demand by MITI at the time of the 1980 negotiations that Toyota and Nissan build plants in the United States: "Since the firms themselves were against setting up operations overseas, then if the government wants to encourage these firms to set up overseas operations, the government should give some sort of adequate guarantee in order that the firms advance abroad." In contrast to this, there was another stance, espoused by Amaya [1982]. This was expressed nicely in his noting that, "In a so-called free enterprise system, it is no exaggeration to state that the authority of management in making investment decisions is sacrosanct. Thus, to be frank, while MITI could attempt to convince the two firms, it was impossible for it to order them to [build plants in the United States]."

It is difficult to set forth definitive proof of the extent to which "administrative guidance" could be compulsive, but at least in the case of the postwar history of the automotive industry, there is no case in which MITI prevailed 100%. In February 15, 1983, Toyota and General Motors reached an agreement on setting up a joint venture to manufacture subcompacts in the United States, but these talks were undertaken following Toyota's judgment two years earlier that an agreement with Ford would not lead to anything. It is not the case, however, that MITI's opinions were totally ignored. Thus while there remained strong dissatisfaction with the export restraint quotas of 1981, in the end the firms were willing to live with the compromise. Undoubtedly the concern was with the extent of the reaction if there was a refusal to accept the intervention of the government.

If we consider what might have happened had the Japanese auto industry acted by ignoring the agreement by the government, then due to the circumstances described below, the probability would have been high that a much more protectionist reaction, such as the imposition of direct import restrictions, would have ensued. These circumstances were that (1) there had been a sharp difference in the rate of productivity increases between Japanese and U.S. manufacturers, and the indications were that this difference would become even greater,[13] (2) in terms of patent registrations, the number of patents held by Japan in other countries had begun to surpass that of the United States, indicating the increasing technological superiority of Japanese firms,[14] and (3) as seen in the estimates of Abernathy et al. [1980], the Automobile Panel [1982] and others, the per-unit cost advantage of Japanese cars was overwhelming (see Table VI). According to Gomez-Ibanez and Harrison [1982], the Abernathy estimate of a $1,650 cost advantage was too high, with a figure of $800 to $1,000 being more appropriate, but in any event Japanese cars were still far superior in terms of price competitiveness. Thus, while the voluntary export restraints were

TABLE VI
Cost Advantage: U.S.–Japan Comparison[a]

	Analysis A—Based on Aggregate Financial & Other Data			Analysis B Using Harbour & Assoc. Labor Data
	U.S. per Vehicle	Japanese per Vehicle	Japanese Advantage	
Materials	$2,575	$2,145	$ 430	$ 430
Labor Cost	2,800	880	1,920[d]	612
Japan Wage Difference				564[c]
Capital Charges	350	515	(135)	325
Warranty Cost				95
Selling and Administrative	425	560	(165)	(165)[b]
Transportation and Tariff	0	400	(400)	(400)[b]
Landed Cost Advantage	$6,150	$4,500	$1,650	$1,461.0

Source: Abernathy (1980).

[a]Figures are for the average vehicle within a comparable product mix; adjusted for vertical integration.

[b]Not considered in the Harbour & Assoc. analysis but added to offer comparable total cost comparisons.

[c]Categories pertinent to Harbour & Assoc. analysis only since this line item is incorporated in aggregate financial analysis.

[d]$955 attributable to wage rates; $965 attributable to productivity.

arrived at as a result of bilateral government negotiations, it should be realized that, to the extent there was a difference, the restraints were costly to American consumers.

Next, in terms of (2), the side effects of the negotiations must be noted. One side effect was that the bilateral negotiations did not stop with those between the United States and Japan, but spread to other geographical regions, so that in general they served to restrict free trade. For example, with the agreement between the United States and Japan, there was a fear that this would result in an increase in Japanese auto exports to Europe, so that weak voluntary restraints were agreed on in April 1981 with West Germany and with the Benelux countries. The same sort of arrangements also were made with Canada, with an agreement on voluntary restraints in May 1981. According to the U.S. Department of Transportation [1981], which carried out a study of trade restraints on automobiles in countries throughout the world, a majority of countries had adopted some sort of artificial restraints. The Japanese auto industry estimated that in 1982 exports from Japan faced restrictions in some 70% of the world market.

One further point relating to (2) is that the agreements that had been negotiated did not necessarily put a stop to further protectionist measures. In 1982 the House of Representatives of the U.S. Congress passed a local content bill (which failed in the Senate) incorporating severe measures that would require auto companies with annual sales in the United States of between 200,000 and 500,000 units to manufacture or procure 75% of their components in the United States by 1985. According to an estimate by Wharton Econometrics (WEFA [1983]), the impact of the bill, if enacted, would be to increase the price of automobiles by over 10% and to decrease aggregate employment by 1991 (an increase in the automotive industry by 58,000 workers and a decrease in other industries by 423,000 workers). While the bill is unlikely to become law, voluntary export restraints are likely to be maintained by the Japanese as a realistic compromise policy. (Negotiations in October 1983 resulted in continuing the voluntary export restraints, with the quota raised to 1.85 million units.)

From the above perspective, the role of the government as a mediator was effective in bringing a temporary calm to the strong trade-related friction. This is not, however, a long-term resolution to the disputes, and from the standpoint of maintaining a competitive environment on a worldwide scale, the issue still remains. One cannot overlook in the international agreements, as is evident in the policy systems of the countries included in Table VII, that they already incorporate substantial variations, such as the extent of national ownership. There also is the issue of how to narrow the gap in perceptions between the United States and Japan on safety standards and pollution controls, and the differences in the system of clerical procedures for imports.[15]

IV. Conclusion

Above, we have attempted to set forth and evaluate the course of various policies related to the automotive industry postwar, looking at their function in building up infrastructure, protecting the industry, and mediating internationally. The following three points broadly summarize the impact of industrial policy in these aspects:

First, the nature of policies relating to building infrastructure played a role in providing a base for industrial activity and at the same time linking the achievements of industry to national economic welfare. Evaluating policies from this standpoint, the construction of the road network contributed to the expansion of the market but was inadequate for expeditious transport. Safety and environmental policies have achieved a high level internationally, but this is due in large part to the competitive condition of the market and the efforts of firms.

TABLE VII

Summary of Automotive Sectoral Policies of Major Producing Countries

Roles of Government	USA	Japan	Germany	France	U.K.	Italy
Owner	NIL	NIL	40% of VW 5% of BMW	100% of Renault	99% of BL	100% of Alfa Romeo Indirect Share of Fiat
Underwriter						
General Subsidies	NIL	NIL	NIL	Major funding of Renault	Major funding of BL: Chrysler UK	Major funding of Alfa Romeo
General Credit	Significant loan guarantees for Chrysler	Major credit role by government banks	Negligible	Major funding for Renault and Peugeot-Citroen merger	Major funding of BL: Chrysler UK	Major funding of Alfa Romeo
Regional Programs	NIL	Negligible	Active in 1960s	Actively promoting investment in distressed regions	Actively promoting investment in distressed regions	Very actively promoting investment in the South
RSC Programs	Major programs underway	Some assistance	Major programs underway	Medium-scale programs	Small-scale programs	Negligible
Regulator						
Design/Safety	very extensive NHTSA standards	Extensive regulation	EEC directives; extensive safety and noise regulation	EEC directives; additional safety regulations	EEC directives; additional safety regulations	EEC directives; limited additional safety regulations
Emissions	Very extensive EPA regulation since 1970	Very extensive regulations	EEC regulations in force since late 1970s	EEC regulations in force since late 1970s	EEC regulations in force since late 1970s	EEC regulations in force since late 1970s

Fuel Economy	Mandated cafe standards since 1975	1979 standards: 6½% to 13% by 1985	Voluntary agreement between Government (1979)	Voluntary agreement between Industry & Government (1979)	Voluntary agreement between Industry & Government (1979)	Voluntary agreement between Industry & Government being finalized
Competition	Extensive antitrust oversight; FTC investigation	Competition law limits some activities	Cartel office regularly challenges price hikes but allows extensive cooperation	Cartel law exists; government promotes cooperation	Monopoly commission approved BL merger; PSA-Chrysler UK takeover	Cartel law exists; negligible impact on industry
Taxation	Auto sales & excise tax in state hands: lowest gas tax	Wt. & road tax auto commodity tax on car size: acquisition tax: moderate gas tax	Auto use tax on engine displacement; high gas tax	Road tax: auto tax on engine displacement; very high gas tax	Auto vat: moderate gas tax	Auto use tax on engine displacement; auto vat; very high gas tax
Trade	Low tariff; antidumping investigations; possible protection	No tariff; slow to eliminate non-tariff barriers	EEC tariff (11%)	EEC tariff; negotiated unofficial restrictions with Japan (3% of market)	EEC tariff; assisted in negotiating unofficial restrictions with Japan (11% of market)	EEC tariff; GATT exception limit Japanese exports to C2500 cars/year
Intermediary With other Automakers	NIL	Provides administrative guidance for industry	Plays significant consultative role	Provides direction; arranged Peugeot Citroen merger	Assisted in original BL merger (1968)	Negligible
With other Governments	Has presented industry views to EEC and Japan	Actively involved in trade questions	Occasionally represents industry in foreign markets/countries	Actively promotes industry in foreign markets/countries	Occasionally represents industry in foreign markets/countries	Occasionally represents industry in foreign markets/countries

Source: Mark B. Fuller and Malcolm S. Saulter, "Profile of the World-Wide Auto Industry," Harvard Business School, May 1980, modified by Transportation Systems Center.

Second, promotion policies were advanced with the recognition of the infant industry status of the Japanese automotive industry. It was not a great mistake in and of itself to have targeted it as an industry of the future, and with certain reservations, the initial import restrictions, the promotion of technology licensing, special depreciation allowances, and other policies did produce some positive results. Of course, there were also the rationalization efforts of the firms themselves, and these were able to function well because of the heavy initial protection. Policies after 1965, however, when the infant industry status had been overcome, unnecessarily served to delay liberalization and were not well accepted by the firms themselves.

Third, the interventions of the government as an international mediator occurred after the Japanese automotive industry had become a huge industry. While the criticism of the other developed countries provided an opportunity to engage in this, there was a sense in which the role could not be avoided, as failure to respond would certainly have led to even stronger protectionist policies. One cannot ignore, however, that the institutional rigidity relating to the complicated import procedures and safety standards provided an excuse to other countries, while the negotiations did not always result in a movement toward the elimination of protectionist policies.

On the other hand, while the above conclusions were reached, many issues yet remain. One is that there exist several important policy areas that could not be touched on in this chapter. Examples include the relationship among the manufacturers and the dealers from the standpoint of antitrust law, and the economic implications of the auto inspection system. Another is how to deal with the variances in policy that exist among different countries internationally. With the extent of the friction in trade, and the trend toward increasing local production, there will be henceforth an even greater need to clearly set forth standards for comparing the content of policies internationally.

Notes

1. On this point see Ueno [1978], Office of Technology Assessment [1981], and Lindbeck [1981].
2. See Chapter 5 of this book for an analysis from the standpoint of the FILP budget.
3. The following tax advantages were granted:

   For the 1975 standards: For vehicles in compliance in FY 1973 the automotive commodity tax would be reduced by one-fourth, and for April–September 1974 it would be lowered by one-eighth.

For the 1976 standards: For vehicles sold in FY 1975, complying in advance of the schedule, the commodity tax would be reduced by one-fourth and the transfer tax lowered from 5% to 3%.

For the 1978 standards: For vehicles sold in FY 1977, complying in advance of the schedule, the commodity tax would be lowered by ¥20,000 in FY 1977, and by ¥10,000 in April–August 1978, the transfer tax would be reduced by 0.25% in FY 1977 and 0.125% in April–August 1978, and the scheduled increase in automotive taxes would be waived.

4. See Chapter 8 of this book.
5. The analysis of this section is based on Ueno and Mutoh [1973].
6. The first automobile was produced in Japan in 1902, but the base for operations was weak, and in particular with the Great Kanto Earthquake in 1923, supply depended on Ford and GM. The 1936 Automotive Manufacturing Law, however, provided for subsidies to licensed domestic firms and a freeze on the scale of operations of the two U.S. firms. In 1939 Ford and GM left Japan, and automotive manufacturing developed, centered around three firms, Toyota, Nissan, and Diesel Automotive [later Isuzu]. Output in 1941 surpassed 40,000 units, and domestic manufacturers were well on their way to mass production; this record undoubtedly contributed to the postwar recovery. With the advent of the war, however, the focus of automotive production shifted to trucks, and then was depressed by increasing production of aircraft and ships. In the prewar period, then, the industry was strongly affected by controls with military objectives.
7. The concept of the People's Car seems to have been reflected in some of the models for the general market (the Toyota Publica and Nissan Sunny) and minicar models. For automobiles, however, where product differentiation is popular, the attempt was doomed from the start.
8. Prior to this, in June 1969 then-Vice Minister of MITI Kumagai had announced a change in the policy of reorganizing the auto industry.
9. The congestion index is defined as traffic volume divided by traffic capacity, where traffic capacity is the ability of the road to function in carrying traffic over a surveyed [reference] section.
10. See Ueno and Mutoh [1973] on the relationship of R&D and firm size. Uekusa [1978] provides details on the responses of firms to auto emission standards.
11. Kodama [1978] provides a quantitative analysis of the impact of government policy, comparing the actual levels with the hypothetical levels of the case in which there had been no intervention, and concludes that industrial policy contributed to achieving the desired goals. His method of determining the hypothetical levels, however, is rather subjective.
12. U.S. Dept. of Commerce [1972] and C. Johnson [1982] are more detailed on this point.
13. According to the Research Department of the Industrial Bank of Japan (Nihon Kogyo Ginko Chosabu [1982]), productivity (gross value added per employee) of the 10 Japanese automotive manufacturers increased 3.37 fold during 1966–1979, while that of the U.S. "Big Three" increased 1.59 times.
14. See OECD [1982].
15. In March 1983, the Ministry of Transport in its document on reforming the automotive standards and licensing systems indicated that it would actively work for the simplification of procedures and would participate in the Experts' Conference on Automotive Safety and Pollution of the United Nations European Economic Commission.

CHAPTER 13

The Computer Industry*

KOJI SHINJO

Faculty of Economics
Kobe University
Kobe, Japan

I. Introduction

The computer industry made its debut at the start of the 1950s in the United States, and supported by rapid technical progress and vigorous demand, it has evolved remarkably in the subsequent three decades. The computer industry forms the central nervous system of today's complex, modern economic society and has stimulated the development of related industries that encompass both hardware and software, such as the integrated circuit and information processing industries. It has come to hold an extremely important place as a leading industry in fostering a more information- and knowledge-intensive economy. Henceforth, further advances in semiconductor technology will lead to increasingly smaller, better performing, and less expensive computers, which will greatly increase the range of applications in, for example, FA (factory automation), OA (office automation) and HA (home automation). Together with the revolution in communications technology, it is anticipated that what may be called the "information revolution" will have a widespread impact on various facets of society and day-to-day living.

With this sort of strategic importance, in most countries the government has contemplated various policies to encourage the computer industry. In 1980, one single firm, IBM, accounted for 55.5% of the total value of

*I thank Prof. Tadashi Takashima of the University of Tsukuba and the other participants of the January 1984 Zushi Conference for their valuable comments. I also thank the staff of the library of the American Center in Osaka for their ready assistance in obtaining published sources and other materials.

installed mainframe computers worldwide; when other U.S. firms are added in, American firms account for 79.5% of the total, so that the market is distinctive in its domination by American companies. At the national level, IBM has over a 50% market share in almost every country; only in England and Ireland is the IBM share less, at 44.3% and 49.2%, respectively.[1] In other words, as is well known, the development of the computer industry has been led by IBM, with its superlative technical and product development ability, its adroit marketing strategies, and its customer service. It is thus no exaggeration to state that the history of the growth of IBM is itself the history of the development of the computer industry throughout the world.

This is true overall worldwide; yet while it has the largest share of any firm in the market, in Japan alone is the IBM share far less than its worldwide level, at 28.9% (1980 installed value). Even when the other American manufacturers are added in, their total at 38.2% is still less than half the market, an extremely unusual situation.[2] Looking at the electronic data processing sales (henceforth, EDP sales) of the Japanese mainframe computer manufacturers, since 1979, Fujitsu has taken away IBM's first place position, and the gap between them has been widening. The export ratio of the Japanese computer manufacturers has also been increasing, and according to Ministry of Finance customs clearance data, the export of computers (defined as central processing units, peripherals, and related equipment) has expanded very rapidly in recent years, and exports surpassed imports in 1981.[3]

A great deal of attention has been garnered overseas by the striking domestic and international development of the Japanese computer industry. In the United States, the source of this has been sought in the series of policies taken by the Japanese government (MITI) to protect and foster domestic manufacturers. The dominant point of view is that of sounding a warning about the advance of Japanese firms, backed up by their government, into overseas markets.[4]

In this chapter, the development process and current status of the Japanese computer industry will be clarified in Section II, the specific policies adopted by the government to protect and foster the industry will be examined in Section III, and an attempt will be made to evaluate the role of the government in fostering the computer industry in Section IV. As will be seen in Section III, policies to promote the computer industry had already been initiated in the 1950s, and were strengthened during the course of the 1960s. It was, however, not until the onset of the 1970s, and in particular after the first oil crisis, that the industry came to actually hold an important strategic place in the economy. In this sense, in taking up the computer industry, we can look at a specific example of the industrial policies of the period following the rapid growth era that aimed for building a knowledge-intensive industrial structure.

II. The Development and Current Status of the Computer Industry

First, we will in a very summary way look back on the development process of the Japanese computer industry and will try to grasp its current status. The main focus of our examination will be mainframe computers. As is well known, with the rapid progress of large-scale integrated circuit technology from the late 1970s, one began to see the appearance of a variety of new products in the computer industry, which until then had consisted almost entirely of mainframes, such as high-performance ("super") minicomputers and office, personal, and microcomputers; the computer industry is now in the process of shedding its old skin.[5] At present, however, mainframe computers, as before, continue to hold an overwhelmingly important place, and so we can understand why, in the direction of MITI policy, the emphasis has continually been placed on promoting a mainframe industry that can compete with IBM.

A. Mainframes: Number in Operation and New Installations

Table I gives data on the diffusion of mainframe computers in Japan[6] and also makes clear the rapid expansion of demand. As of the end of March 1983, there were 106,344 mainframes in operation, with a value of ¥4.7 trillion, which corresponds to 7.2% of computer facilities worldwide, second only to the 42.6% share of the United States.[7] Installations on a fiscal year basis were around 20,000 units in FY 1981, with a value of ¥1 trillion, representing a 15.1-fold increase over a 15 year period.

Table I gives the relative share in value of domestic and foreign computers,[8] and as is clear therein, during the 1950s and early 1960s foreign units held a predominant share in new installations, and until the mid-1960s foreign units maintained their superior position in terms of value. From the late 1960s, however, the situation was reversed, and in terms of both new installations and units in operation, domestic systems comprised the majority. Comparing the value (in terms of sales price) by type of unit, foreign systems were predominant among large-scale systems (those valued at over ¥250 million per installation), while as one progresses from medium to small and minicomputers, one can recognize a distinct trend of an increasing domestic share.[9]

TABLE I

Mainframe Computers: New Purchases and Systems in Operation

Fiscal Year	Purchases — Total: Domestic & Foreign Systems # of Systems	Value ¥ billion	Increase from Previous Year (%)	Proportion of Value* Of Domestic (%)	Of Foreign (%)	Systems in Operation — Total: Domestic & Foreign Systems # of Systems	Value ¥ billion	Increase from Previous Year (%)	Proportion of Value* Of Domestic (%)	Of Foreign (%)
1957	3	0.15	—	78.1	21.9					
1958	8	1.01	593.2	7.1	92.9					
1959	26	2.4	139.5	21.5	78.5					
1960	66	6.7	176.4	27.3	72.7					
1961	119	13.3	98.1	18.3	81.7					
1962	228	22.1	66.6	33.2	66.8					
1963	485	43.3	95.9	29.7	70.3					
1964	562	41.6	-3.8	42.8	57.2					
1965	636	51.5	23.7	52.2	47.8	1,455	130.0	—	31.9	68.1
1966	844	66.8	29.7	53.6	46.4	1,937	174.2	34.0	36.9	63.1
1967	1,162	108.6	62.6	47.2	52.8	2,606	224.8	29.0	45.1	54.9
1968	1,568	161.4	48.3	56.5	43.5	3,546	301.2	34.0	48.0	52.0
1969	2,135	212.4	31.6	57.5	42.5	4,869	441.2	46.5	51.4	48.6
1970	3,287	330.9	55.8	59.6	40.4	6,718	617.2	39.9	53.3	44.7
1971	4,244	350.1	5.8	58.8	41.2	9,482	891.2	44.4	55.3	46.7
1972	5,973	418.7	19.6	53.0	47.0	12,809	1,136.2	27.5	54.8	45.2
1973	7,978	528.3	26.2	51.4	48.6	17,255	1,373.3	20.9	53.5	46.5
1974	8,535	640.8	21.3	51.6	48.4	23,443	1,601.9	16.6	54.3	45.7
1975	6,903	614.0	-4.2	55.8	44.2	30,095	1,946.4	21.5	55.2	44.8
1976	7,533	731.5	19.1	56.7	43.3	35,305	2,258.3	16.0	56.9	43.1
1977	9,591	790.0	8.0	—	—	40,719	2,532.6	12.1	57.5	42.9
1978	13,043	798.3	1.0	—	—	48,132	2,820.7	11.4	—	—
1979	15,294	834.3	4.5	—	—	58,944	3,218.3	14.1	—	—
1980	18,373	970.3	16.3	—	—	72,108	3,623.9	12.6	—	—
1981	20,439	1009.8	4.1	—	—	88,223	4,164.7	14.9	—	—
1982	—	—	—	—	—	106,344	4,716.4	13.2	—	—

Source: JECC, *Konpyuta Noto,* each year.

* Not made public since 1977.

B. Installations by Manufacturer: Domestic Market Shares

The above JECC (Japan Electronic Computer Co.) and MITI surveys do not make public data on the market shares of individual firms, so here we will use the survey of computer installations[10] carried out every year by a specialty journal for the industry, *Konpyutopia*. Table II gives the market share of individual firms on an installed-value basis for the period from 1970 through 1982.[11] For 1982, the most recent year, the top share was that of IBM at 27.7%, followed by the three domestic firms of Fujitsu at 21.4%, Hitachi at 16.6%, and NEC at 14.4%. The proportion of domestic-to-foreign firms is 55.9% to 44.1%, so that here as well domestic computers surpass foreign ones.

Looking at changes after 1970, since the IBM share recorded its peak value of 33.2% in 1971 (which corresponded to the peak in shipments of the IBM System 360 series), it has declined little by little, and the shares of the above three domestic firms, together with that of Mitsubishi Electric, have all risen. The shares of the other foreign mainframe manufacturers have on the whole been stable, so that the total foreign share has shown a gradual declining trend from its 48.1% level of 1970. These foreign manufacturers include, among others, Nippon Univac/Oki Electric/Oki Univac, Burroughs, NCR Japan, Honeywell Japan, CDC Japan, DEC Japan, and Cray Research.

In Japan, in general, incentives have been given for the preferential adoption of domestic systems by the government, by government-affiliated institutions, and in the educational market.[12] This government procurement market (the "Buy Japan" market) in 1982 comprised about 18% of the entire market, and there domestic manufacturers maintained absolute superiority; the IBM share was a mere 3.5%, and the combined foreign firm share did not exceed 8.9%. Each of the four large domestic manufacturers depended on this government market for around 30% of their sales, so that one can see that they obtained a large benefit from this preferential market for domestic firms. Thus, in the "free" market, the IBM share is much greater, at 33.1%, far surpassing the 10% level of the domestic manufacturers. Even in this "free" market, however, the overall share of domestic systems is 48.1%, only slightly different from the 51.9% foreign firm share, and as a trend, the gap in shares has been narrowing.[13]

C. EDP Sales and Exports by Manufacturer

Our observations above on the Japanese computer market have been based on surveys among users of installed mainframe systems. Here we will take a slightly different tack, looking at sales and exports from the side of the manufacturers. We will consider the top 10 firms, composed

TABLE II

Market Share (Installed Value) for Mainframe Systems by Manufacturer (%)

Year	1970	71	72	73	74	75	76	77	78	79	80	81	82
IBM	31.9	33.2	29.9	30.8	29.8	29.6	29.5	29.0	28.0	27.8	28.7	27.6	27.7
Fujitsu	16.0	19.6	20.0	20.4	19.4	20.1	20.5	20.0	20.5	20.5	19.6	21.1	21.4
Hitachi	16.0	14.7	16.4	16.4	16.2	15.8	15.5	15.8	15.8	15.8	15.4	16.6	16.6
NEC	11.9	10.9	11.4	11.1	11.5	10.4	9.7	9.8	14.3	14.6	14.3	14.1	14.4
Nippon Univac	12.3	9.3	8.7	8.0	9.6	9.6	9.7	9.6	12.7	11.7	10.8	10.4	10.0
Toshiba	3.9	4.3	4.5	4.0	4.7	4.3	4.0	3.8	—	—	—	—	—
Oki Univac	2.9	2.7	2.7	2.6	2.5	3.3	3.9	3.8	—	—	—	—	—
Burroughs	2.5	2.4	2.2	2.4	2.4	2.8	3.1	3.8	3.8	4.3	4.3	4.1	3.8
NCR Japan	1.4	1.8	2.0	2.1	2.0	2.4	2.6	2.6	2.6	2.4	2.2	2.0	1.8
Mitsubishi Electric	1.1	1.1	1.4	1.4	1.3	1.1	0.9	1.0	1.5	2.2	3.2	3.0	3.5
Other Foreign Firms	—	—	0.8	0.8	0.7	0.6	0.6	0.8	0.8	0.8	1.5	1.1	0.8
Domestic Systems, Total Share	51.9	53.3	56.4	55.8	55.5	54.9	54.6	54.2	52.1	53.0	52.5	54.8	55.9
Foreign Systems, Total Share	48.1	46.7	43.6	44.2	44.5	45.1	45.4	45.8	47.9	47.0	47.5	45.2	44.1
Total	100.0	100.0	100.0	100.0	100.0	100.0	100.0	100.0	100.0	100.0	100.0	100.0	100.0

Source: Konpyutopia, each year, January issue.

of the 6 domestic ones of Hitachi, Fujitsu, NEC, Toshiba, Oki Electric, and Mitsubishi Electric and the top 4 foreign firms of IBM Japan, Nippon Univac, Burroughs, and NCR Japan. Table III gives the total EDP sales of these firms for 1976 through 1981.[14] According to this data, EDP sales of the top Japanese manufacturer, Fujitsu, surpassed those of IBM in 1979, and the difference has been increasing ever since. There is also a substantial gap between the sales of the top four and the bottom six firms. Furthermore, looking at the rate of growth over 1976–1981, the domestic firms have all grown by a factor of 2 to 3, with Toshiba at the bottom expanding only 1.6 times; in contrast IBM, the highest among the four foreign firms, grew only 1.56 times.

Table III also shows the share of EDP sales in total sales for each firm for their financial year 1981. The foreign firms all specialize 100% in EDP sales (excepting NCR, at 71.1%), while there is a wide spread of values for the domestic manufacturers, ranging from the 5% level for Mitsubishi Electric and Toshiba to 66.8% for Fujitsu. The significance of this, in other words, is that it points out a distinction of the domestic mainframe manufacturers, with their overall low dependence on EDP operations, so that even if EDP operations show a loss, it is possible to a certain extent to cover up such losses with profits from other operations. In fact, the second-tier domestic firms are at present said to be showing a loss on their EDP operations, and so that from the standpoint of profitability, the domestic manufacturers are quite inferior to the foreign firms. For example, comparing Fujitsu and IBM, in 1981, IBM Japan showed an after-tax profit of ¥39.19 billion, or a profit of 9.1% of sales, while the after-tax profit of Fujitsu was ¥18.45 billion, for a profit of a mere 3.2% of sales. This difference in profitability of course also affects the volume of funds that can be invested in R&D activities.[15]

Table III also shows the proportion of EDP exports for each firm. As a matter of course, IBM shows the highest proportion at 25.3%, but the four domestic firms excluding Mitsubishi and Toshiba have all reached the stage of exporting about 10% of their EDP sales, so that we can see they have achieved some measure of competitiveness internationally. For example, looking at the cumulative exports of each firm during 1976–1981, total exports for the four domestic firms were ¥442.7 billion, surpassing IBM at ¥360.0 billion; exports of Fujitsu alone have reached 60% of the IBM level.[16] It is necessary, however, to note that, along with their own brand products, a large amount of exports supplied on an OEM (original equipment manufacturer) basis are included. In other words, along with using their own marketing routes in their export activities, the Japanese manufacturers have actively sought to advance into overseas markets through sales and technology tie-ups with foreign firms, and it is believed

TABLE III

EDP Sales of the Top 10 Firms (¥100 million, %)*

Fiscal Year	1976	1977	1978	1979	1980	1981 (Share, %)	1981/1976 Sales	Degree of EDP Specialization (1981)	EDP Products: Proportion Exported (1981)
Total	10,543	11,571	12,640	13,965	16,092	19,726 (100)	1.87		
Fujitsu	② 2,396	② 2,745	② 3,030	① 3,268	① 3,821	① 4,484 (22.7)	1.87	66.8	12.9
IBM Japan	① 2,755	① 2,938	① 3,153	② 3,242	② 3,383	② 4,288 (21.7)	1.56	100.0	25.3
NEC	④ 1,140	④ 1,376	④ 1,669	④ 2,008	④ 2,404	③ 3,325 (16.9)	2.92	31.5	11.4
Hitachi	③ 1,420	③ 1,600	③ 1,900	③ 2,160	③ 2,500	④ 2,880 (14.6)	2.03	13.5	10.1
Oki Electric	⑦ 438	⑧ 444	⑥ 479	⑥ 628	⑥ 788	⑤ 1,091 (5.5)	2.50	50.9	11.6
Toshiba	⑥ 592	⑥ 591	⑨ 430	⑨ 504	⑤ 803	⑥ 950 (4.8)	1.60	5.4	8.0
Nippon Univac	⑤ 704	⑤ 678	⑤ 716	⑤ 736	⑦ 786	⑦ 909 (4.6)	1.29	100.0	2.0
Mitsubishi Electric	⑩ 320	⑨ 380	⑧ 450	⑧ 530	⑧ 620	⑧ 730 (3.7)	2.28	5.5	9.6
NCR Japan	⑧ 435	⑦ 450	⑦ 470	⑦ 546	⑨ 505	⑨ 573 (2.4)	1.32	71.1	0.1
Burroughs	⑨ 343	⑩ 369	⑩ 343	⑩ 343	⑩ 482	⑩ 496 (2.5)	1.45	100.0	1.9

Source: Konpyutopia, November 1982.
* The numbers in circles are the ranking in terms of sales. An underline indicates a change in the base for calculating EDP sales.

that in particular in the advanced regions, the United States and Europe, sales agreements (the supply of units and components on an OEM basis) have played an important role.[17]

III. The Computer Industry: Protection and Promotion Policies

In this section, we will look back on the policy formation process for the computer industry and will set forth how there has been policy involvement with the industry. The specific content of individual policy measures is summarized in Tables IV to VII, which appear later. We believe industrial policy for the computer industry, as in the following, can be divided roughly into three periods.[18]

A. The Initial Period of Fostering the Industry: 1951–1965

The first efforts to develop a computer in Japan go back to about 1952, when it is said that the University of Tokyo and Toshiba tried jointly to develop a vacuum tube model. This is virtually 10 years after the completion of ENIAC, the first electronic computer in 1946 in the United States.[19] In the 1950s, a number of other plans for developing a computer were also advanced, one of which was the joint development using the domestic parametron technology by the University of Tokyo and the Telecommunications Laboratory of NTT and KDD of the Musashino No. 1 computer, completed in 1953. There was also the development in the Electronics Laboratory of the Agency of Industrial Science and Technology of MITI of the Mark III in 1955 and the Mark IV in 1957.

We can therefore see that at that time Japan had already reached a high level of industrial technology, so as to be able to develop computers on its own, but at the same time the centers of development planning were the national research institutions rather than private firms. This fact determined the later trend for private firms to have an attitude of dependence on the government.

The results of technology development by the Agency of Industrial Science and Technology were made available to all domestic firms, and this formed the foundation for the development of commercial computers. During 1957–1959, NEC, Hitachi, Fujitsu, and Toshiba announced small-sized computers, and this was followed by the entry into the computer industry of Mitsubishi Electric, Oki Electric, and Matsushita Communication Industrial Company. During this same period, the importation of foreign computers such as Univac, IBM, and Bendix began.

In 1957, the first law relating to the computer industry, the Law on Temporary Measures for Promoting the Electronics Industry (the Electronics Industry Law) went into effect. The primary emphasis of this law was the household electrical goods industries. Its central focus was not the fostering of the computer industry,[20] but it did establish an Electronics Industry Division within the Heavy Industries Bureau of MITI (this later was reorganized into the Electronics Policy Division of the Machinery and Information Industries Bureau). This was important because the Electronics Industry Council was set up within the Division for the purpose of increasing understanding between the government and the computer manufacturers. This law became a pattern for later, similar laws and so will be briefly explained here. The coverage of the law was for electronic equipment, components, and materials, and was divided into three areas: Type I items, where it was in particular necessary to promote experimental research; Type II items, where it was in particular necessary to promote initial production or an increase in the scale of production; and Type III items, where it was in particular necessary to promote industrial rationalization. For each of these, for industries to be designated through Cabinet Orders, "promotion plans" were to be mapped out. Then, in specific, in line with these plans, subsidies for Type I items were to be given (Subsidies for R&D Expenditures for Important Technologies), special loans were to be provided for Type II items (from the Japan Development Bank), and Type III items, as well as being eligible for special loans, could also be designated under the Enterprise Rationalization Promotion Law, and hence be eligible for special depreciation allowances provided for in the Special Tax Measures Law.[21]

From the start computer hardware appeared under all three categories, and under the respective programs received R&D subsidies and Japan Development Bank financing, but direct subsidies were very small in amount (see Tables IV through VII). The most important element was not the financing itself, but rather that through this financing MITI indicated both inside and outside the government that computers were an important field to foster.

At the time, IBM held the basic patents for computer technology that were necessary for domestic manufacturers, and in 1960 the provision of patents was secured from IBM in return for a guarantee of being able to produce locally and to remit foreign exchange. IBM Japan began domestic shipments in 1964, and to be able to compete, each of the domestic manufacturers with the exception of Fujitsu signed technology licensing agreements one after another during 1961–1964 with the American rivals to IBM or set up joint ventures.[22]

For new computer installations around 1960, foreign machines were predominant, as was already seen in Table I, and a measure that was as a matter of course considered in this situation was for the government to protect domestic manufacturers through import restrictions by means of foreign exchange allocations and tariffs and through the regulation of the importation of technology and foreign capital. One other important measure for the protection of domestic manufacturers was the establishment of the Japan Electronic Computer Company (JECC). The dominant method of marketing computers was the rental system introduced by IBM, but under this system the recovery of costs took place over a long time and so required large amounts of financing. To ease this financing burden and to strengthen the marketing system of the domestic manufacturers, JECC was established in August 1961 through the joint investment of the seven domestic manufacturers. JECC then procured the financing for rentals, in place of the manufacturers themselves. For its financing of the purchase of domestic machines, JECC borrowed not only from the Japan Development Bank but also from the city banks and other private financial institutions, and capital increases by the shareholders (the manufacturers) and receipts of rental income were also allocated. As can be seen in the share of JECC purchases in total domestic machine purchases (see Table VI), JECC clearly played a large role in the subsequent development of the domestic manufacturers.[23]

The main project carried out in this period under the auspices of MITI was the FONTAC project. This was based on the Mining and Manufacturing R&D Associations Law, which went into effect in 1961, with an Electronic Computer R&D Association being established in September 1962 for the purpose of developing large-scale computers. Three firms participated—NEC, Fujitsu, and Oki Electric—and each firm received subsidies in its special area of competence from the Agency of Industrial Science and Technology for carrying out joint development. This project received subsidies totaling about ¥350 million and was completed in 1964 after a 2 year, 4 month development period, with each firm aiming to market a large-scale computer based on this technology. The FONTAC project served as the basic model for subsequent government–private joint development projects.

In the period through the early 1960s, the emphasis of government industrial policies was on the steel, chemical, automotive, and other heavy and chemical industries, and the computer industry had not become a key area of government concern, so that policy measures for encouraging it were modest overall, and the industry was still at an immature stage of development. On the other hand, the technical revolution in the American computer industry was progressing rapidly, with IBM announcing the System 360 series in 1964, and with them the third generation of computers,

TABLE IV

Subsidies to the Computer Industry*

1960	1965	1970	1975	1980	1983

(1) Subsidy for R&D based on the Electronic Industry Law and the Machinery and Electronic Industries Law (¥ 2.7 bn in 1957–72)
72

(2) Development of super high performance computer (¥ 10 bn) large scale project
71

(3) FONTAC subsidy (¥ .35 bn)
62 — 66

(4) Subsidy for Information Processing-Technology Agency (¥ 23.0 bn up to 1983)
71

(5) Development of pattern information processing system (¥ 22.0 bn) large scale project
71 — 80

(6) Subsidy for promotion of developing new types of computers (¥ 57.1 bn)
72 — 76

(7) Subsidy for promotion of developing computer peripherals (¥ 4.5 bn)
72 — 76

(8) Subsidy for R&D of ICs (¥ .35 bn)
73 — 74

(9) Subsidy for promotion of information processing industry (¥ 3.0 bn)
73 — 75

344

(10) Subsidy for computer rentals by chambers of commerce and industry (¥2.29 bn)
74 ⌐ 77

(11) Software production development program (¥6.62 bn)
76 ⌐ 81

(12) Subsidy for VLSI (¥29.1 bn)
77 ⌐ 80

(13) Subsidy for developing basic technologies for next generation computers (¥22.2 bn)
79 ⌐ 83

(14) | large scale project | Optical measurement and control system (¥18.0 bn, planned)
79 ⌐ 87

(15) | large scale project | High speed computer system for scientific and technological uses (¥23.0 bn, planned)
81 ⌐ 89

(16) Next-generation basic technology (¥25.0 bn, planned)
81 ⌐ 90

(17) R&D on 5th-generation computer (¥10.5 bn in 1982–84)
81 ⌐ 90

Source: JECC, *Konpyuta Noto*, each year.

*Large-scale projects are wholly subsidized. Other projects are subsidized about one-half. There are other important public R&D activities, including a special project on information processing technology conducted by the Electrotechnical Laboratory of the Agency of Industrial Science and Technology (¥8.0 bn in 1971–81) and R&D conducted by the NTT (Nippon Telephone and Telegraph Corporation) (¥88.5 bn in 1982).

345

TABLE V

Fiscal Investment and Loans for the Computer Industry*

1960	1965	1970	1975	1980	1983

(1) Loan based on the Electronic Industry Law (loan for computer industry—¥4.4 bn in 1966–71)

(2) JDB loan for software development (¥9.0 bn in 1970–73)
70

(3) JDB loan for promotion of on-line system
(4) JDB loan for promotion of data processing system (¥1.5 bn in 1972–73)
72

(5) Loan for structural improvement of computer industry (¥3.0 bn in 1972–73)
72   82

(6) Loan based on the Machinery and Electronic Industries Law (loan for computer industry—¥7.7 bn in (1972–77)
71   78

(7) Loan based on the Machinery and Information Processing Industries Law
78

(8) Debenture accepted by the Information-Technology Promotion Agency (¥116.3 bn up to 1982)
70

(9) JDB loan for JECC (¥523.5 bn up to 1982)
61

(10) Loan for safety measures for computer system
78   80

(11) JDB loan for promotion of manufacture of new computer types
83

Source: JECC, Konpyuta Noto, each year.
*Loan amounts cannot be ascertained for (2), (3), (4), and (5) from 1974 on and for (9) from 1978 on as they were lumped together with other JDB loans. For (9), see Table VI for more details. (8) is the amount of debentures issued by three long-term credit banks and accepted by the Information-Technology Promotion Agency based on funds of the Trust Fund Bureau of the Ministry of Finance.

TABLE VI
JECC Computer Purchases and Japan Development Bank Financing to JECC (¥100 million)

Fiscal Year	Computer Purchases	JDB Financing	JECC Purchases as a Proportion of All Purchases of Domestic Systems* (%)
1961	11	2	45.8
1962	32	8	43.8
1963	59	15	45.7
1964	117	25	65.7
1965	208	55	77.3
1966	269	70	74.8
1967	368	70	71.8
1968	666	90	73.0
1969	825	155	67.6
1970	922	215	46.7
1971	874	390	42.4
1972	892	150	40.0
1973	1,014	215	37.4
1974	1,244	325	40.1
1975	1,264	460	36.9
1976	1,341	470	32.3
1977	1,342	520	(30.0)
1978	1,305	560	(28.8)
1979	1,435	500	(30.3)
1980	1,777	480	(32.3)
1981	1,842	460	(32.2)

Source: Nihon Joho Shori Kaihatsu Kyokai, Konpyuta Hakusho, each year.
*The numbers in parentheses for FY 1977 on are estimates based on the proportion in FY 1976. JDB financing from FY 1978 on includes loans for structural reforms in the computer industry and the promotion of the information processing industry.

with integrated circuits forming the heart of the hardware, made their appearance. The conspicuous technological gap between foreign and domestic manufacturers was keenly felt. In 1964, the largest French computer manufacturer, Machines Bull, under the heavy burden of rental financing, was bought up by the American manufacturer, GE.

These two incidents brought about within Japan an understanding of the importance of computers and a recognition by the government and business leaders of the urgency in protecting and promoting domestic manufacturers in the face of dominance by the U.S. manufacturers, headed up by IBM. Within Japan at that time eight firms, including IBM Japan, were manufacturing computers, but the scale of the overall market was small and the level of specialization in computer-related activities of the

TABLE VII

Special Tax Measures for the Computer Industry

1961	1965	1970	1975	1980	1983

(1) Special depreciation for rationalization equipment based on the Enterprise Rationalization Promotion Law
(1) ———————————————————————— 71

(2) Tax exemption for important products
61 —— 66

(3) Electronic computer repurchase loss reserve (¥ 39.0 bn in 1972–81)
68 ——————————————————————————————

(4) Special depreciation of computers
70 —————————— 78

(5) Reduction of property tax on computers
71 ———————————————— 80

(6) Reserve for guaranteeing computer programs
72 —————————————————— 79

348

(7) Special depreciation for important compound machinery
78 └──┘

(8) Tax credit on purchasing computers
79 └─┘ 80

(9) Reserve for general-purpose software development
79 └──┘

Source: JECC, *Konpyuta Noto*, each year.

(1) First-year special depreciation of 50% of the purchase price of machinery and equipment.

(2) Corporate income tax is exempted on earnings accrued on computer equipment up to one-half of investment on such equipment.

(3) The reserve is tax exempt up to a certain proportion of sales of computers to JECC (10% at first, 15% in 1970–71, and 20% from 1972 on). The same measure applies to sales of computers to general rental firms from 1971 on.

(4) Special depreciation is allowed on computers purchased by users (first year, one-fifth to one-fourth in 1972–74).

(5) Property tax on computers purchased by users is reduced by one-third (one-fifth since 1976).

(6) As a measure for promoting the software industry, 2% of sales of computer programs is allowed to be added to the reserve (subsumed into (9) since 1979).

(7) Based on the Machinery and Information Industries Law, first-year special depreciation amounting to 13/100 of the purchase price of important compound machinery. In 1978, 3 computer-related machineries are included; in 1979, the on-line computer system is added.

(8) Investment tax credit amounting to 10% of the purchase price of equipment (including computers) purchased by small- and medium-scale firms for business conversion (not in excess of 20% of corporate income tax).

(9) 40% of revenue on general-purpose software is allowed to be added to the reserve.

It is not easy to estimate the amount of tax reduction in the computer industry due to these special tax measures. ¥ 39.0 bn for (3) is due to Wheeler et al. (1982), p. 100, but it is not clear how the figure is obtained.

domestic manufacturers was low. Considering the dominant position of IBM in the world market, the continuance of manufacture by domestic firms was itself considered doubtful.[24]

B. The Strengthening of Promotion Policies: Trade Liberalization, 1966–1975

With this situation before it, MITI consulted with the Electronics Industry Council on the direction for policies to promote the computer industry, and received its March 1966 *Report*, entitled "Policies for Strengthening the International Competitive Strength of the Electronic Computer Industry," which was of great significance in giving direction to the basic strategies for subsequent development of the computer industry. In it industrial promotion targets and a specific program were given. Among the targets were obtaining a superiority in technology independently and improving the market share of the domestic manufacturers and their profitability. Specific programs included the joint production of a large-scale computer, the strengthening of JECC, rationalization in the production of peripheral equipment, and the training of technical personnel. The budget necessary to implement each of these programs was also given, and from around 1966, subsidies for R&D expenses and Japan Development Bank financing began a large increase. This was expanded after 1971 into a response to trade liberalization.

One important program that had its origins in this report was the program, initiated in 1966, for large-scale projects. The first of these, the "Project for Developing an Ultra-High Performance Electronic Computer," was begun in the same year, with its goal being to surpass the IBM System 360 series, with the project itself being advanced centered around the Electronics Laboratory (now the Electrotechnical Laboratory) of the Agency of Industrial Science and Technology with private firms, academia, and the government cooperating.[25] Over ¥10 billion in subsidies were expended on this project, and it was concluded in August 1972, having largely achieved its goals. The next large-scale project, begun in 1971, was a 10-year ¥2.2 billion "Project for Developing Pattern Recognition Systems" aiming to develop a computer capable of processing voice, graphic, and other high-level information. Another important project during this period was the DIPS project of NTT, begun in 1968 with a budget of about ¥30 billion and the participation of three firms, NEC, Hitachi, and Fujitsu. These joint government–private projects are considered to have contributed to narrowing the technical gap relative to IBM on the hardware side.

In May 1970, the Information Promotion Law (the Law Concerning the Information-Technology Promotion Agency) was enacted,[26] with the goal of promoting the development of software, an aspect that was even more backward than hardware; there was, however, no change during this period in the emphasis of policy being on hardware. Then, in April 1971, with the termination of the Electronic Industry Promotion Law (the Law on Temporary Measures for the Promotion of the Electronic Industry), the Machinery and Electronic Industries Law (the Law on Temporary Measures for the Promotion of the Machinery Industries) was enacted, consolidating laws that had dealt with the electronics and the machinery industries separately. The promotion measures provided for under the new law followed the basic structure of the previous Electronic Industry Promotion Law.[27]

At the end of the 1960s, the computer industry was considered to have poor prospects for increasing its international competitiveness, despite government assistance, consisting as it did of six manufacturers producing similar machines competing in a small market that remained a fraction of the size of that of the United States. Furthermore, in 1970 IBM announced the System 370 series computers, whose basic hardware consisted of large-scale integrated circuits (LSIs), and domestic manufacturers were pressed to respond quickly. MITI held that the route through which domestic manufacturers could remain viable, given future trade and capital liberalization, was to seek economies of scale by forming groups of firms that would increase their scale of production by concentrating their production on a single computer model. MITI attempted to reorganize the industry in that direction, but facing a domestic market that continued to expand rapidly, a consensus could not readily be attained among the main competing manufacturers because of their sense of rivalry.

Trade and capital liberalization for computers had been delayed as much as possible in order to protect domestic manufacturers. With strong demands for liberalization by the United States, in June 1971, capital liberalization providing for up to 50% ownership in the production, marketing, and rental of electronic computers was announced, effective August 1974, along with trade liberalization in peripheral equipment (excluding memories and terminals), effective February 1972. The computer industry was thus finally faced with imminent liberalization.[28]

The period for liberalization having been decided, the response consisted of drawing up in November 1971 a modernization plan for electronic computers based on the Machinery and Electronic Industries Law. This consisted of two parts, a plan for experimental research and a plan for production rationalization. In this second part, specific targets were given for the performance, quality, and production costs of main processors, peripheral equipment, and terminals, with the issue being the ability to compete in terms of performance and price with the machines of foreign firms. The core of the first part, on the other hand, was the Subsidy Program for the Promotion of the Development of Computers and Related Equipment, which was set up in 1972. Four types of subsidies were set up under this program, one of which was the Subsidy for Promoting the Development of New Computer Models. This subsidy was to subsidize the development costs of a new series of machines to compete with the IBM System 370 series, and for this the domestic manufacturers were reorganized into three groups (Fujitsu and Hitachi, NEC and Toshiba, and Mitsubishi and Oki), which received about ¥57 billion for work on the development of new models during FY 1972–1976. Each group was as a result successful in developing new series in line with the liberalization schedule, with the announcement starting in 1974 by the Fujitsu–Hitachi group of the M series, followed by the ACOS series of the NEC–Toshiba group and the COSMO series of the Mitsubishi–Oki group, with complete lines of machines in these series by 1978.[29]

The emphasis of promotion policies during this period was a reduction in hardware manufacturing costs and the promotion of the development of new machines through the formation of groups of firms, but the extent to which this was economically rational hinges on the extent of economies of scale in the manufacture of computers and in R&D. For the production of central processors, the actual number of units produced is limited, and the reduction in costs with greater volume is considered minimal. Learning effects and the like operate for the manufacturing of components such as integrated circuits and for peripheral equipment, so that substantial economies of scale can be expected, while for the development of new models, large firms have a general advantage in staffing for R&D and in financing. It is dubious, however, that the MITI reorganization policies actually brought about greater concentration on the production side; the groups formed only to serve as conduits for the government subsidies. The effect of policy was thus, on the one hand, to assist the financing of R&D through the granting of subsidies, and on the other hand, worked to set a target for the development of new machines by fixing the timing of liberalization, serving to some extent to speed up their development period. In either case, the leading firms at least would have been capable of carrying on rapid development on their own without government assistance.

Fujitsu and Hitachi used the development of the M-series computers as an opportunity to take the route of compatibility with IBM, and as will be mentioned later, this decision later led to the IBM spy case, presumably because of the promotion policies during this period, which were concerned with the reduction of hardware costs rather than the development of software.

C. Post-Liberalization Policies: 1976 On

As of April 1, 1976, trade and capital were completely liberalized for all computer-related items, including software. By that time the development of systems competitive with IBM had been completed, so that there resulted almost no change in the market share in Japan of the domestic manufacturers.[30] With the rate of technical progress in computers being faster than anyone could imagine, however, the domestic manufacturers all had a sense of crisis, realizing that IBM would announce the 4th-generation FS series of computers, which utilize VLSIs (very large scale integrated circuits). At that time, a number of subsidy programs to promote the development of future-generation computers were begun; the one to garner the most attention was the VLSI project.[31] This was set up in 1976, with the goal of developing the technology for VLSIs required for the development of 4th-generation computers. For this, the domestic manufacturers were combined into two groups (Fujitsu, Hitachi, and Mitsubishi and NEC and Toshiba), and VLSI R&D Associations were set up. The Electrotechnical Laboratory of the Agency of Industrial Science and Technology and NTT also cooperated in this R&D program. The overall scale of the activities of the four-year project was ¥72 billion, of which ¥29.1 billion consisted of direct subsidies. Over 1,000 patents for the high-precision processes necessary for the manufacture of VLSIs and related items were issued, indicating some of the results achieved by the conclusion of the project.

In July 1978, at the expiry of the Machinery and Electronic Industries Law, the Machinery and Information Processing Industries Law was enacted with the aim of providing for the promotion of the industries that would be central in the future in bringing about the "knowledge-intensification" of the industrial structure. It represented another step in the progression of such laws in treating the electronic, machinery, and information processing industries as a unity. It was basically a continuation of the legal structure of the Machinery and Electronic Industries Law, imposing the obligation to draw up modernization plans for the promotion of better production technology and the rationalization of production. This law was distinctive in that the software industry was added to these modernization plans.[32]

Succeeding the VLSI Project was the program of subsidies related to the next generation of computers, the Project for Developing the Basic Technologies for the Next Generation of Computers, which aimed at developing the basic software (the operating system) and the technology for new peripheral equipment and terminals. This project sought to promote the development among other items of software technologies, in which Japan was lagging, and the technologies for processing the Japanese language. Two R&D Associations were established for this purpose under a five-year (1979–1983), ¥70 billion plan (¥22.2 billion of which was for subsidies). Another large-scale project initiated in 1979 was an eight-year, ¥18 billion plan for developing optical measurement and control systems.

In June 1981 the Information Industry Committee of the Industrial Structure Council issued a Report entitled "The Status and Policies for Information and Information Industries in the 1980's."[33] It showed a recognition that the information industries would have to bear a central role in promoting the "creativity- and knowledge-intensification" of the Japanese economy. It referred to the increased role of information in the 1980s as the "second information revolution," which was rapidly occurring in the areas of industry, society, and day-to-day life, and which would be essential to resolve the national issue of overcoming the limitations of natural resources in the 1980s. In particular, the computer industry was seen as the archetype of a resource- and energy-saving, knowledge-intensive industry. It was anticipated that the information industries would be the core of the leading industries that would pave the way for the onset of the twenty-first century due to the large technical spillovers into other industries.

In line with this vision of Japan as a technologically built-up country, a number of programs were advanced in computer technology areas, including a large-scale project for developing a high-speed computer system for problems in science and technology and the 5th-generation computer development program, which sought to move away from the importation of technology to creative, leading-edge R&D. Table IV lists these and other subsidy programs undertaken by the government for the computer industry, while Tables V and VI summarize policy measures related to the FILP budget, and Table VII lists tax measures.

IV. Evaluation of Promotion Policies for the Computer Industry

The policy goal during the course of MITI promotion of the computer industry was to protect the domestic market from domination by the foreign manufacturers headed by IBM by fostering domestic mainframe manufacturers who could compete against them. Judging from the recent share of domestic manufacturers in the mainframe market in Japan, it can be claimed that for now the goal has been met. For hardware in particular, the leading domestic manufacturers have grown to the point of today being able to compete against IBM. Thus the emphasis of policy at the present stage is, if anything, shifting from promoting the domestic industry to avoiding international trade friction, where in consideration of foreign relations the emphasis of policy is on fairness and transparency.

The current status of the computer industry in Japan is an extremely sharp contrast to that in Europe, where American manufacturers dominate the various national markets. Given this, it is natural that overseas a tendency has arisen to overrate the protection and promotion policies of the Japanese government as the true source of the development of the industry. In fact, as is clear from the previous section, a number of favorable measures not found in other industries were made available to the computer industry. Not only were financial and tax measures included in the policy menu, but there were also such assistance measures as the financing of rentals by JECC, the preferential government procurement of domestic equipment, and the joint government–private R&D projects. Next we will examine what influence these policy instruments had on the development of the computer industry, and how this influence should be evaluated.

First, it is necessary in considering the influence of industrial policy to take into account distinctive features in the demand and technology of the industry together with the environment in which the policy operates, so as to grasp the net impact of policy. The distinctive features of a computer as a product, then, are that it is a good that is highly technology-intensive, that performs with versatility in many applications, and that can be readily differentiated, or rather it is a good for which differentiation is the basic strategy of product development. Another feature is the extremely fast pace of technological change, with the consequent increase in cost performance giving rise to a rapid growth in demand. In the Japanese mainframe computer market, a vigorous oligopolistic competition in technical development and marketing has developed among seven firms—the six domestic manufacturers (seven through 1964, when Matsushita Communication Industrial Company exited from the industry) together with IBM—which has pushed strongly the development of the industry. In other words, it is the lively competition among firms, based on the market mechanism, that can be considered as the basic condition leading to the development of the industry. This does not imply, however, that industrial policy did not play an important role. I believe that the policies of the government to reserve a certain proportion of demand for domestic firms and to provide assistance in sales financing and R&D activities had a positive effect in permitting firms to maintain an aggressive management strategy by reducing the risk borne by firms in a situation

in which the future development of the industry was uncertain.[34] A point
that needs to be noted here is that because a computer is a product for
which an increased variety of types and product differentiation have developed, and for which the pace of technical advance has been very rapid,
even though through government guidance a joint research program was
set up in which firms were grouped together to develop basic technology,
this did not stifle competition in product development and marketing. This
point relating to the firmly established behavior patterns of Japanese firms
will be touched on again later.

The content of industrial policy itself changed greatly over time, so that
it is necessary to make a distinction between different periods in the importance of the impact of these policies. In other words, as the computer
industry developed and firms grew, the importance of policy declined as
a matter of course. In the case of the computer industry, the greatest
contribution was the protection given to domestic manufacturers from
imports and the regulation of technical licensing and foreign investment
in the 1950s and 1960s, when there was a conspicuous technical gap between the domestic and the foreign manufacturers. This is clearer if a
comparison is made with Europe.

The entry of IBM into the various European markets goes back to the
age of punchcard systems before World War II. IBM established a base
of operations, including the setting up of factories, very early on, so that
in the course of moving to computers at the end of the 1950s and in the
first half of the 1960s, IBM was able to capture a large proportion of these
markets in a short period of time.[35] In the case of IBM Japan, operations
were initiated in 1950 with 66 employees, based on the assets of Japan
Watson Business Machines Company, which had been confiscated during
the war as enemy assets. Although it thereafter began to grow rapidly, it
did not have an organization that was able to adequately respond to the
increase in demand as there was a shortage of sales engineers and software
technicians.[36] At the time, due to restrictions on the transfer of capital
and on the importation of products and accessories, the share of IBM
machines was restricted from expanding beyond a certain proportion of
the market. This, I believe, enabled domestic manufacturers to start up
their operations.

Again, for computers, another important industrial policy measure was
that the timing of trade and capital liberalization was particularly delayed.
In other words, during the intervening period domestic manufacturers were
enabled to improve their technical level to a considerable extent, and while
they vigorously opposed the decision to liberalize to the end, once the
timing of it had been fixed, each of the domestic manufacturers strengthened their product development efforts in line with that schedule. As a

result it can be considered that this had the impact of speeding up the development period and leading to the successful development of new machines.

Government assistance for the promotion of the computer industry had been considered from early on not only in Japan but also in the United States.[37] It can be noted that, in the case of Europe, the start of such efforts was somewhat delayed. In England, for example, the ACTP (Advanced Computer Technology Project) for subsidizing R&D began relatively early in 1963, but in France the first plan *Calcul* started in 1966, and in West Germany the first promotion plan began in 1967 when the first data processing program was initiated after the American manufacturers had already established their dominance of the market.[38] Something particular to computers is that, connected to the use of software, once it has been taken away, it is very difficult to recapture market share with incompatible machines. Thus one cannot help but consider the impact of policies promoting the computer industry in the European countries to have been limited because of this. This suggests that, if during the start-up period in Japan there had been no restrictions on imports or foreign capital, and that promotion policies had only been adopted in the mid-1960s, then there is a possibility that the computer industry today would look very different, with there being only one or two domestic manufacturers who, together with foreign manufacturers, comprised a harmonious oligopoly.

Underlying the rapid rate at which Japanese manufacturers were able to pursue the American firms, in contrast to those in Europe, was the fact that the home electronics industry was highly developed, with a great accumulation of electronics technology relating to semiconductors and integrated circuits, and that furthermore the industry had a very broad base.[39] In Japan, there were no large office equipment manufacturers, as there were in Europe and America, and it is thought that a large factor in the ability to keep up with the accelerating pace of technological progress in computers was that the major heavy electrical equipment and communications equipment manufacturers that entered the computer industry were diversified firms with strong technical resources and abundant financial strength. In particular, the Japanese computer manufacturers were at the same time major semiconductor manufacturers, and as a result, had the advantage of being able to mobilize the benefits of vertical integration in a direct way for the development of new chips for LSIs and VLSIs and the development of new machines.

In addition, IBM adopted the policy of pricing the same machine identically in all of its markets worldwide, adopting a pricing strategy for the System 360 and System 370 series machines that, for example, would provide a high rate of return on sales, on the order of 30% to 40%.[40] Japanese manufacturers, who lagged in terms of performance, were able to compete only by adopting a policy of price discounts, which for the time being disregarded profitability. This was only possible for large, diversified electronics manufacturers and communications equipment firms that could depend on government demand.

Furthermore, each of the computer manufacturers was a leading member of a business group composed of many firms, and the firms in the group considered it desirable, when it came to the introduction and utilization of computer-related high technology, to tie-up with the computer manufacturer in the same group. Thus each of these groups, in order to promote the development of a computer manufacturer within the group, was able to provide cooperation and assistance with the assurance of having a certain part of the market. This is also considered as part of the background underlying the intense competition that developed among these rival firms in the computer field.[41]

A distinctive feature of the policies for promoting the computer industry in Japan was the use of the joint government–private R&D projects.[42] In particular, the budget allocations for subsidies increased as one response to trade and capital liberalization from about 1971 on. The emphasis of policy thus shifted to assisting the R&D activities of firms, for which this system of joint government–private research served as a convenient receptacle. What should be the evaluation of the impact of these policies?

A comparison of the level of technology in the United States and Japan for large-scale mainframe computers was carried out in Kogyo Gijutsu In (Agency of Industrial Science and Technology) [1982]. Japanese products were superior in terms of processing speed and the size of the main memory, while the scope of operating system software had reached almost the same level. In terms of key technology, Japan in some areas was ahead in the production technology for chips, which was important for hardware, but the United States was ahead in the technology related to operating system software and systems design. Another survey was carried out by the same agency (Kogyo Gijutsu In [1983]) on the sources of these differences in technology and the factors influencing improvement in the level of technology. The factors listed as first in affecting the technology for producing the logic circuitry for large-scale mainframe computers were the competition in R&D among firms and their R&D efforts and quality control activities (TQC, QC). Next appeared the Technology R&D Associations, the subsidies for developing technology, and the research contracted out by the government to, for example, the large-scale projects. These were evaluated very favorably as a factor that contributed to increasing the level of technology.[43]

This was the evaluation of the technical people involved, but looking at the impact in terms of economics, one can consider there to be merit in effectively utilizing scarce technical abilities and research funding by concentrating them in carrying out joint research with predetermined goals for the R&D.[44] Most of the topics for technology development related to basic technology, and while there was cooperation in the development of such basic technology, the development of products and sales based on the results of this R&D were in fact carried out by each firm independently. This maintained effective competition in product markets. On the other hand, a demerit of this sort of system for joint research was that it was biased toward the development of hardware, and so there was inadequate development of systems technology that treated hardware and software together. This was in part because the government itself did not adequately recognize the importance of software, but it was also because the development of software is directly related to the product development strategies of firms. An important factor was that it was thus not suitable for such joint research.

Related to the above points, it is of course essential in evaluating the influence of industrial policy to make a judgment based on the overall costs and benefits to society. Japanese computer manufacturers have now achieved a relatively high technical level, even when viewed from an international perspective, and because the oligopolistic system of the industry is competitive, it can be judged to have realized a quite favorable market performance. If one considers in addition the diffusion of technology to other industries, then the role played by the computer industry today in improving national welfare is extremely large. As should be clear from the comments made thus far, the promotion policies of the government for the computer industry lessened in their urgency with the progressive development of the industry, but regarded overall, they must be considered one of the main factors in the development of the industry. In this sense, the point must first be made that from the standpoint of national welfare, industrial policy brought about certain benefits.

At the same time, each of the policy measures was in fact accompanied by substantial social costs. It goes without saying that the country had to bear the costs of tax and financing measures and of direct government subsidies. In addition the technical level of domestic machines was low and software was at an inadequate stage of development, so that making the use of domestic machines by the government for the most part a requirement, and restricting the import by the private sector of machines with better performance, made it impossible to realize the composition of computer systems that users desired. It was thus an impediment to national welfare in that it resulted in an inefficient use of resources. In particular, it is held that by guaranteeing a portion of demand in the form of the government market, domestic manufacturers were encouraged in their sales strategy to put off the development of software and to concentrate exclusively on marketing on the basis of hardware.[45]

As already indicated, government promotion policies underlay this neglect of software and bias toward hardware in the direction in which computers developed. The firms that followed this route most thoroughly were Fujitsu and Hitachi, with their IBM-compatible policy.[46]

The development of the IBM compatible business in the United States began in the late 1960s, when a market was formed by the appearance of peripherals that could be attached directly to IBM systems. Then in 1975 Amdahl began marketing a main processing unit that was fully compatible with IBM machines, and its success served as an impetus for successive entry by other compatible CPU (central processing unit) manufacturers, which today maintain a certain share of the market. A technical tie-up with Amdahl played an extremely important role in the development of the Fujitsu–Hitachi M-series computers, and this was decisive in setting the subsequent compatibility strategy of these two firms.[47]

Fujitsu and Hitachi, in other words, produced IBM compatible machines that could directly utilize the tremendous software assets that had accumulated through development by IBM, including the basic operating system as well as application programs. They sought, by using this and by selling systems at a lower price than IBM, to increase their market by taking away customers from IBM. This avoided the burden of software development costs, which had come to occupy a greater and greater share of the cost of an overall computer system, and allowed them to place their emphasis on the development of hardware technology.

To cope with this IBM-compatible business, IBM began to ship the System 303x series in 1978, and with the System 4300 series computers began to take the offensive with large price reductions, which was a tremendous blow to the PCM's (plug compatible manufacturers) in the United States. Then, in October 1981 the new system 3081K was announced, which was based on a design concept that differed radically from that previously in use. This not only sought a decisive shift from the design concepts in use since the System 360 series, but at the same time placed the operating system, which had in the past been made public, in the hardware on semiconductor chips, where it would not be easy to decipher. According to one explanation, IBM was seeking to drive under the Japanese PCMs, but in any event, what transpired in relation to the new 3081K operating system was the June 1982 IBM spy case involving Hitachi and Mitsubishi Electric.[48] The final resolution of this incident occurred in October 1983, with an out-of-court settlement of the civil action by Hitachi and IBM. Apart from this, it became known that a secret agreement had been made by Hitachi and by Fujitsu with IBM for the use of software, so that now a fixed fee had to be paid for the use of the basic software developed by IBM.[49]

What was unexpectedly brought into relief by the chain of events transpiring from the IBM spy incident to the software agreements was that, while at first glance the computer industry in Japan appears to have developed satisfactorily, it and the government promotion policies that supported it in fact conceal serious problems.

The payments by Fujitsu and Hitachi to IBM for the use of software will serve to immediately reduce the competitiveness of both firms, and it is impossible to foresee at present what structural changes will result in the Japanese computer industry in the long run from the dominance by IBM of software. Both Fujitsu and Hitachi now face the daunting task of somehow developing operating systems and other software more advanced than that of IBM, independent of IBM technology, in order to be able to compete with the dominance by IBM of software.

The government (MITI) is now also pressed to fundamentally reexamine the industrial promotion policies used thus far, and it is now considered an urgent task to consider shifting to an industrial policy based on a wider perspective, which will not only henceforth place an emphasis on independently developing software, but will shift from the previous stance of promoting domestic manufacturers that can compete with IBM to developing a system of joint development through international cooperation or of cross-licensing for the supply to other partners of superior technology.

Notes

1. The source of these numbers is a study by International Data Corporation (IDC) of the United States, cited in Nihon Joho Shori Kaihatsu Kyokai [1982].
2. This IDC study (note 1, *supra*) is thought to underestimate the share of foreign systems in the Japanese market. What constitutes the mainframe computer market, and whether the value of installed systems is an appropriate measure for firm share, will be touched on in note 11.
3. The ratio of exports to production has been definitely increasing in recent years, from 2.8% in 1971 to 6.0% in 1975 and 18.1% in 1981. It is necessary to note, however, that a substantial proportion are exports by IBM Japan. For mainframes only, imports are still substantially greater than exports. (Exports are from the *Tsukan Tokei* [Customs Clearance Statistics] and are for central processing units, peripherals, and related items. Domestic production is from the *Kikai Tokei Nenpo* [Machinery Statistics Annual].)
4. See, for example, U.S. Department of Commerce [1983a], [1983b] and Semiconductor Industry Association [1983], Preface, page v. This is also apparent in the hearings of the U.S. Congress and its committees.
5. A market survey of these new products, which have recently been growing extraordinarily rapidly, shows 1981 super minicomputer shipments (including anticipated shipments)

of ¥182.5 billion, up 18% from the previous year, small business system shipments (including anticipated shipments) were up 33.6% to ¥306.7 billion, while shipments of personal computers were up 2.6 times, to ¥107.0 billion. According to one American research report, the share of mainframe systems in total computer installations was anticipated to decline from the 69.4% of year-end 1981 to 41.5% five years later, in 1986. For details, see Chapters 2 and 5 of JECC, *Konpyuta Noto*, 1983.

6. This is from surveys carried out by JECC and by MITI. Computers included in the survey were (1) digital models, (2) with internal programming, (3) internal memory of over 2,000 bits, and which (4) carried out arithmetical functions using electronic logic. In terms of value, they ranged from ultra-large systems of over ¥500 million to very small systems of less than ¥10 million.

7. This is an estimate based on the IDC study cited in note 1 above, and *not* on MITI data.

8. The distinction here between foreign and domestic is whether over half of the shares are owned by Japanese. Thus the OUK system made by Oki Univac is a domestic system, while imports and domestic production by IBM Japan (System 360/20, System 360/40, System 370/155, IBM 4331, etc.) are foreign systems.

9. In these surveys, the proportion of foreign systems among large-scale systems in operation was 82.1% in 1966, 63.2% in 1970, and 57.0% in 1977. While still more than half, the share has nevertheless been declining.

10. This is not based on manufacturers' reports of purchases and orders but is based on published materials and interviews where the name of the actual user of the computer could be confirmed. Systems were limited to those with a purchase-price equivalent value of ¥30 million or more, thus covering about 70% of the systems in the above MITI survey. When there were price reductions or other price changes, these were also applied to existing installations of previous models. With its detailed description of the survey methodology, the *Konpyutopia* survey is thus considered highly reliable.

11. In connection with the U.S. Department of Justice antitrust suit against IBM, Fisher et al. [1983] concluded that the market share for mainframe systems calculated on the basis of installed value did not accurately represent the status of interfirm competition. The main points of their argument were (1) the performance of minicomputers and similar small machines had improved, so that they were substitutes for mainframes, (2) no distinction was made between sales and leases or rentals, and (3) systems purchased and leased out by independent leasing companies and others were still credited to the manufacturer. See Fisher et al. [1983], Chapters 3 and 4. These points can be considered as to a certain extent appropriate for the Japanese market as well, so that we will quote sales shares as well.

12. There was a Cabinet Resolution encouraging the use of domestic goods in September 1963, prior to trade liberalization. This resolution was rescinded overall in September 1972, but was still continued for electronic computers. A reform in government procurement practices was agreed on in a January 1978 Cabinet Resolution, and in the 1980 Tokyo Round of GATT, a treaty was signed agreeing that for purchases of more than a specified amount (SDR 150,000), government procurements would be made without distinction for domestic versus foreign. Thus in principle there is currently no discrimination, but there has nevertheless been no conspicuous change in market shares in government purchases.

13. This data is from the *Konpyutopia* survey cited above, and (ignoring discrepancies at the level of individual manufacturers) this corresponds well to the ratio of domestic and foreign systems obtained from industry-specific utilization data published by MITI. Such data is available only through 1977.

14. This is based on figures from corporate financial reports or data otherwise made public by firms, which are periodically published in *Konpyutopia*. In general, along with the different types of computer systems, even items such as terminals, OA (office automation) equipment, and software are included, so that there is not necessarily a uniform base for these totals. In this sense they only serve as a rough standard, but other than this, there is no source of information on EDP specialization at the firm level or on the proportion of EDP exports.

15. Looking at IBM (worldwide) for 1981, its sales of ¥6.7 trillion were 11.5 times those of Fujitsu, its after-tax profits of ¥760.8 billion were 41.2 times higher, and its R&D expenditures of ¥370.8 billion were 11.4 times greater (¥230 = US$ 1.00).

16. According to the *Konpyutopia* data, total EDP exports of IBM Japan and the six domestic firms for fiscal 1981 were ¥261.0 billion, and cumulative exports over their fiscal 1976–1981 were ¥802.7 billion. In comparison, customs clearance exports of computers (CPUs, peripherals, and related items) were ¥265.5 billion in 1981, and cumulative exports over 1976–1981 were ¥794.1 billion. Thus, the exports of the above seven firms would appear to account for almost all of Japanese computer exports, and the two sets of data correspond well. There is, however, no data on the composition by types of item available at the firm level.

17. Specifically, there are agreements between Fujitsu and ICL (U.K.), Siemens (West Germany), SECOINSA (Spain), and Amdahl (U.S.); between Hitachi and Olivetti (Italy), BASF (West Germany), and Itel (U.S., now NAS). NEC in general has exported under its own name, but according to recent press reports, it has reached agreements in principle to export the very large-scale ACOS System 1000 on an OEM basis to Honeywell (U.S.) and CII-HB (France). See *Nihon Keizai Shinbun* (Japan Economic Journal), March 28, 1984.

18. For descriptions of the course of development of the Japanese computer industry, see U. S. Department of Commerce [1972], Gresser [1980], Wheeler et al. [1982], and Takashima [1976], [1981]. Along with these sources, use was also made of the JECC, *Konpyuta Noto*, each year.

19. For an insider's report of the development of computers in Japan, see Minamizawa [1978].

20. The person who proposed and drafted the bill was not a MITI bureaucrat or a businessman, but was instead a division chief of the Electronics Experimental Laboratory of the Agency of Industrial Science and Technology. See Matsuo [1980].

21. In addition, output adjustment, R&D activity, materials purchasing, and other cartel activities were excluded from the application of the Antitrust Law.

22. See Takashima [1976] for details.

23. One aspect of the economic impact of the establishment of JECC was a reduction in interest costs through low-interest rate loans from the Japan Development Bank. (See also Chapter 5 of this book.) More important was that, in the 1960s, when the future development potential of the industry was uncertain, firms were able thereby to obtain financing for about 50% of the purchases of domestic systems (peaking at 77% in 1965). Japan Development Bank loans were for around 20% of computer purchases during this period, but it is also held that it was this back-up by the government that enabled the necessary amounts of funding to be borrowed from private financial institutions. Of course, the importance of JECC declined as computer manufacturers gained in financial strength. For example, from around 1970, Hitachi aimed at switching to renting on its own, and by the end of the 1970s made little use of JECC rentals. Currently the main firms that depend on JECC rentals are Fujitsu and NEC.

24. In September 1964, Matsushita Communication Industrial Company exited from the manufacture of mainframes.

25. Hitachi, NEC, and Fujitsu participated in the CPU part and Toshiba, Mitsubishi, Oki, and others on peripheral input–output devices.
26. For a description of this law and the content of the software promotion policies it incorporates, see JECC, *Konpyuta Noto*, 1971.
27. In the electronics industries, 6 industries were designated as Type II (start-up) industries, including integrated circuits, and 14 as Type III industries for rationalization, including electronic digital computers. See Tsusansho Jukogyo Kyoku [1971] for details.
28. Later, in April 1973, full capital liberalization was set for December 1975 for the manufacture, sale, and rental of computers, and for April 1976 for the information processing industry. During 1975 trade was to be fully liberalized for all items, including computer CPUs and integrated circuits, and all the liberalization plans were completed. Since September 1955, there had been a conventional tariff level of 15% on computers, although computers and input–output equipment over a certain value were exempted from tariffs until March 1963. From April 1972, the tariff was lowered by 10% to 13.5%. For details, see the annual volumes of JECC, *Konpyuta Noto*.
29. Compared to the IBM System 370 series, the new domestic systems (with a two-to-four-year lag) were faster (in terms of MIPS, million instructions per second) and combined with the low-price policy of the domestic manufacturers, they were able to compete with the IBM systems. See *Konpyutopia*, January 1976.
30. A conspicuous change since liberalization was that Burroughs and CDC Japan became 100% subsidiaries of their parent companies, while GE, Timeshare, and others entered the information processing fields.
31. The formal name was the "Program for Subsidizing the Costs of Promoting the Development of Large-scale Integrated Circuits for Use in the Next Generation of Electronic Computers." For a detailed description, see Chapter 6 of JECC, *Konpyuta Noto*, 1981, and (for an economic evaluation) Chapter 8 of this book.
32. See Tsusansho Kikai Joho Sangyo Kyoku [1979] for a detailed description of this law.
33. For a summary of the report, see Nihon Joho Shori Kaihatsu Kyokai [1982], Part 8, Appendix 1.
34. See Part II of this book for a discussion of under what conditions there exists a basis for the existence of industrial policy in an enterprise system based on the market mechanism.
35. For this period, see Kita [1978], Chapter 2.
36. On IBM Japan during this period, Aono [1977] claims:

   In 1958 there were 688 employees, and income during 1950–1960 increased by 1,500 times and during 1961–1965, by 6 times. . . . The operations of IBM Japan during this period consisted not so much of sales activity as, with the import quota being fixed, in the words of Chairman Inagaki, "of going around and apologizing to customers."

37. Katz and Phillips [1982] point out that all of the important developments in computer technology during 1945–1960 were the result of projects carried out with government assistance, including the appearance of the vacuum-tube computer, the discovery of the transistor, and the appearance of the second-generation transistor computer. With the development of the market after 1960, the role of the government became more indirect, and the importance of government programs diminished.
38. The history of the development of promotion policies for the computer industry in Europe is based upon JECC, *Konpyuta Noto*, 1981, Chapter 7.
39. Takeuchi [1973], p. 277.
40. For an analysis of the behavior of IBM, including pricing strategies, see Aono [1977] and Takashima [1976].

41. In the January 1975 issue of *Konpyutopia*, distinctive features in the utilization of computers by the firm groupings were surveyed. This study makes clear that Toshiba (Mitsui group) and Mitsubishi Electric (Mitsubishi group) did not have much influence with firms in their groups, while NEC (Sumitomo group), Fujitsu (Daiichi Kangin group), and Hitachi (Fuyo group) had a strong hold on the market of their groups.

42. Now, however, not only in Western Europe but also in the United States, there are many projects supported by the government for the development of high-technology items such as VLSIs, super computers, and 5th-generation computers. Such projects are thus not distinctive to Japan; see JECC, *Konpyuta Noto*, 1983, Chapter 6. For the role of the government in R&D, see Chapter 8 of this book.

43. Kogyo Gijitsu In (Agency of Industrial Science and Technology) [1982], [1983] used the survey method of selecting one technical person from each manufacturer and user in each product area for two rounds of questionnaires.

44. For this sort of merit to be obtained, it is essential that there be an exchange of useful information on technology among researchers belonging to different firms, and that research is organized so that government funding is distributed purposively and rationally. It can be said that the role of the government in this case was the forming of an effective research organization, in that without the participation of the government, that is, without subsidies, it was inconceivable that rival firms would participate in joint research. To examine the extent to which government subsidies were effective in lowering the R&D costs of firms, we can look, for example, at the case of Fujitsu, where during 1971–1980 total R&D expenditures were ¥196.4 billion in comparison to after-tax (current) profits of ¥92.9 billion. Thus, with an annual average of ¥20 billion in R&D financing, the weight of government subsidies was quite significant. (See Table IV.)

45. For software products in particular, there were many cases of defective products or products that did not perform as advertised. See Takashima [1976].

46. Mitsubishi Electric made it clear that a strategy of IBM compatibility had been adopted, although there was also a technical agreement between it and Sperry (U.S.).

47. For the development story of the M-series computers, see *Konpyutopia*, February 1975.

48. On the background to and course of events in the IBM spy incident, see Nano [1982] and *Konpyutopia* (ed.) [1982].

49. Currently (year-end 1983), the details of these agreements are not known, but according to press reports, in the case of Hitachi, along with approximately ¥10 billion for the use of software in the past, software payments will be about ¥6–7 billion a year for the next eight years, with total payments coming to more than ¥70 billion. See *Zaikai*, December 13, 1983.

PART V

Industrial Adjustment Policy

CHAPTER 14

Trade and Adjustment Assistance

SUEO SEKIGUCHI

Department of Economics
Seikei University
Tokyo, Japan

TOSHIHIRO HORIUCHI

Japan Economic Research Center
Tokyo, Japan

I. Introduction

Decline of an industry can come about as consumer tastes change, new substitutes are developed, or technological innovations take place, even in an economy completely cut off from the rest of the world. Adjustment assistance to declining industries has attracted great attention since the 1970s, however, due to the emergence of frictions among the nations on account of the impact of such policies on international trade flows.

In this chapter, therefore, we narrow the focus of our attention to those industries that declined as a result of import competition and were provided with adjustment assistance. Haberler [1950] attributed the adjustment problems of an economy with regard to interindustry allocation of resources because of a rise in imports to two factors: constraints on intersectoral factor mobility and inflexible factor prices. The latter was seen to result either from voluntary unemployment arising out of workers' work–leisure choices or from involuntary unemployment due to exercise of monopoly power by labor unions and the like. Import restrictions were justified as a means to stem a fall in national economic welfare if the consumption possibilities of the economy were contracted by involuntary unemployment even after income redistribution.

The adjustment assistance policies attracted closer attention as a realistic policy objective in the 1970s. Actual experiences and policy prescriptions of adjustment assistance have been discussed extensively at such conferences as the Pacific Trade Development Conference [PACTAD, 1973], Tripartite Economist Meeting [1973], OECD [1975, 1978, 1983b], and Trilateral Commission [1981].

Pure theory of adjustment assistance has been elaborated in the field of dynamic optimization. Lapan [1976], Neary [1982], and Mussa [1982] use dynamic optimization of adjustments in the presence of market distortions arising from factor price rigidity or lack of factor malleability. As will be pointed out later, however, there exists a large gap between the theory and practice, which needs to be filled up before any operational policy proposals can be chalked up given the constraints on the availability of information to the policy authorities.

This chapter is not intended to give case studies but to provide a comprehensive review of the Japanese industrial adjustment assistance policy since 1945. Section II defines the concept of adjustment assistance policy, and while analyzing the relationship between the policy goals and policy instruments using a two-commodity trade model, also develops on the actual adjustment process. The postwar Japanese industrial adjustment assistance policy is then reviewed in Section III using the framework developed in Section II. Finally, Section IV deals with the impact of the adjustment assistance policies on international trade and presents our understanding of the problem of adjusting divergent international interests.[1]

II. The Content of Adjustment Assistance Policy

A two-commodity trade model seems to be most appropriate in understanding the need for industrial adjustment assistance policies. For the sake of simplicity, let us consider the entry of a small country facing given international prices in international trade. Let us suppose that this country produced and consumed at point Q_0 (C_0) in the pre-trade situation in terms of Figure 14.1. With the beginning of trade, the price line shifts from p^0 to p^1. If the reallocation of resources was to be instantaneous, production would move to Q_1 on the long-run production frontier LL and consumption to C_1, enabling it to achieve a higher level of social welfare. In reality, since this would lead to a conflict of interests between the producers of commodity 1 and 2, transfer of income from the former to the latter using lump sum taxes and subsidies is required.

The industrial adjustment problem is rooted in the impossibility of instantaneous adjustment in production from Q_0 to Q_1. The less than complete output adjustment, and hence incomplete resource mobility, is the result of the following two factors: First, the factors of production, especially capital, are relatively immobile among sectors (even if the factors are mobile, the problem still remains when transfers are costly and take time). Second, factor price rigidities, especially of wages, hamper the required transfer of resources. These two factors can be differentiated in

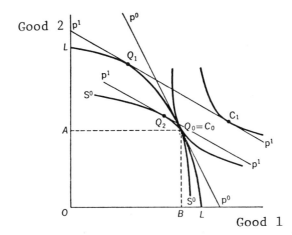

Fig. 14.1. Imperfect resource mobility and industrial adjustment.

terms of the above diagram as follows: If the factor mobility is incomplete, production would shift to point Q_2 on the S^0S^0 frontier in the short run. (If the factors are strictly immobile, S^0S^0 coincides with AQ_0B and Q_2 remains at Q_0.) If the prices are flexible, the factors of production would be fully employed. But if the prices are rigid, unemployment will result as the reduction in resources used in the industry affected adversely by changes in product prices (industry 1 in this instance) would not be completely absorbed in the industry affected favorably. In terms of Figure 14.1, this could be represented by a shift of the production point within the short run-production frontier.

If there are no market failures other than incomplete resource mobility and the private sector is fully aware of this less-than-complete resource mobility, government intervention is not called for. If the costs of resource transfer are also taken into account, the allocation of resources would be dynamically optimized. If, however, the expectations are not formed correctly (rationally) or if the social discount rate differs from the private discount rate, government intervention becomes necessary as was pointed out by Mussa [1982]. Obviously, the first-best policy in this context would be a policy that removes the causes of market failure (i.e., a policy to correct expectations or remove the factors leading to a deviation in the social and private discount rates or, in a nut shell, dissemination of information and technical training, etc.). Since these first-best policies lack applicability in the real world, often being unrealistic, industrial adjustment policy becomes necessary as a second-best policy in hastening the reallocation of productive resources through intervention in the dynamic adjustment process.

Sueo Sekiguchi and Toshihiro Horiuchi

As the presence of factor price rigidities constitutes a sort of market failure, it calls for intervention in itself. Measures like intervention in the process of price formation in product markets to neutralize price changes (exigency import restrictions, etc.), provisions for discriminatory use of subsidies to productive factors among sectors, and so on could help in preventing unemployment of resources and facilitating factor movements. Subsidies to contracting sectors reduce unemployment of resources in these sectors, thereby delaying resource transfers. Subsidies to expanding sectors hasten the pace of adjustment process (especially when resource transfers are hampered by sector specificity of the factors of production), but are not very effective in reducing unemployment in the short run. In the presence of these sorts of trade-offs, Lapan [1976] points out the desirability of choosing a higher unemployment rate in the initial phases the lower the social discount rate and the longer the plan period involved under such circumstances. That is to say, the optimal policy would be to keep the wage subsidies for maintaining employment in the initial period at a low level, concentrating on the expanding sectors, and to raise them afterwards.

Neary [1982] indicates another possible complication that could arise if factor prices are rigid. Rigidities in the prices of a single factor (wages, for example) would facilitate shift in the other factors (for example, capital). Now, if it is capital that is easy to shift, it would result in a large outflow of capital from the stagnating industry causing a steeper fall in employment of labor and a higher rate of unemployment in this industry. Under these circumstances, if wage-rate adjustment cannot be optimized, slowing down the reallocation of capital would become a second-best policy.[2]

III. The Japanese Adjustment Assistance Policies

An historical analysis of the postwar Japanese adjustment assistance policies is facilitated by dividing the period into the following three sub-periods: the period before the implementation of the Law on Temporary Measures for Stabilization of Specified Depressed Industries (Industry Stabilization Law) in 1978; the period of adjustment assistance when the above mentioned and other related measures were in force (1978–1983); and the period after the adjustment assistance laws were reformed in 1983.

A. The Period before the Implementation of the Industry Stabilization Law

The policies followed during this period were sector specific and ad hoc. A comprehensive discussion of the adjustment assistance policies during this period is facilitated by dividing them into short-term and long-term policies. Sulphur mining, coal mining, and textiles were the major target industries of the short-term policies, while the long-term policies aimed at protecting industries generally believed to be handicapped. The main beneficiaries of this set of policies were agriculture, the leather industry, and tiny retailers[3] (cf. Table I).

The decline of the coal mining industry became a matter of concern during the so-called energy revolution of the 1960s. The adjustment assistance policies in this sector were aimed at facilitating employment switch-overs by the workers and area development. As shifting the residents of coal mining regions to other areas was difficult both psychologically and economically, measures to lure new economic activities to these areas were adopted. Import restrictions, production subsidies and demand allocation measures were also implemented at the same time.[4] These measures were adopted under the provisions of the Law on Temporary Measures for Coal Mining Area Development [promulgated in November 1961] by the Coal Mining Area Development Agency [established 1962]. The Development Agency developed industrial-use land and offered it to the incoming enterprises with long-term loans. New industrial colonies with an area of 23.7 million m^2 (113 colonies) were established under this law, as well as its reformed and extended versions. Plans for development of about 15.86 million m^2 additional land are under way.[5]

The locally available employment opportunities for the workers laid off from the coal mines expanded as new industries were established in the region. Explicit measures to promote employment of workers laid off from the coal mines in the newly establishing firms were also resorted to. The enterprises with over 30% of their new work force coming from the pool of laid-off coal miners or their families were made eligible for preferential financing through the Area Development Agency.[6] The Law on Temporary Measures for Coal Mining Area Development was extended in May 1981 for another 10 years and presently holds an important position in the area development policy. Thus, when geographical mobility of labor poses problems, as compared to that of capital, the measures like those mentioned above are conducive to capital inflows into the declining areas by luring new firms. At present, this policy is serving the objectives of area development policy more than assisting the coal industry and hence can be treated as a long-term measure.

In contrast to the coal industry, adjustment assistance policies for the textile industry, especially in the initial phases, aimed at revitalizing the industry through subsidies instead of promoting resource transfer. The spinning, weaving, knitting, and textile printing sections of this industry were designated under the Law on Temporary Measures for the Structural Improvement of Specified Textile Industries (adopted in 1967), and pref-

TABLE I

Adjustments Undertaken by Major Industries

		1960	1965	1970	1975	1980	Notes
Textile[a]	Calendar Year						
	Production ('000 tons)	1,270.2	1,566.1	2,039.8	1,776.4	2,049.7	
	No. of Workers ('000 persons)	1,103.4	1,153.4	1,097.8	844.3	676.8	Regular workers at year end.
	Imports ('000 tons)	3.0	62.5	131.4	277.8		
Coal Mining[b]	Calendar Year	1960	1965	1970	1975	1980	Notes
	Domestic Production of Coal ('000 tons)	52,607	56,259	38,329	18,597	18,095	
	No. of Workers ('000 persons)	238,274	111,360	50,262	36,073	30,070	Regular workers at year end.
	Imports ('000 tons)	8,595	16,936	50,950	62,339	72,711	Actual amount arrived
Leather[c]	Calendar Year	1960	1965	1970	1975	1980	Notes
	Leather Production (tons)	83,535	137,419	147,952	188,987	184,238	
	No. of Workers ('000 persons)	22,708	31,401	31,202	35,845	32,212	Regular workers engaged in manufacture of leather, leather shoes, and leather goods for industrial use.
	Consumption of Imported Hides ('000 tons)	67,476	125,521	146,460	176,149	148,319	

Sulfur[d]	Calendar Year	1960	1965	1968	1970	1972
	Production ('000 tons)	248	213	261	103	17
	No. of Workers ('000 persons)	6,142	4,544	3,143	n.a	170
	Production through Petroleum Refining ('000 tons)	n.a	37	76	239	483

Citrus Fruits[e]	Calendar Year	1960	1965	1970	1975	1980
	Cultivated area ('000 ha.)	63.0	115.2	163.0	169.4	139.0
	No. of Cultivating Farms ('000)	210.0	n.a	371.0	353.4	302.3
	Amount of Harvested ('000 tons)	893.6	1,317.0	2,552.0	3,665.0	2,892.0
	Import of Grapefruit ('000 tons)	n.a	n.a	2.3	146.7	135.2
	Import of Lemon and Lime ('000 tons)	n.a	18.9	54.0	64.1	100.7

[a]Tsusansho (MITI), Sen'i Tokei Nenpo (Textile Statistics Yearbook), various issues.
[b]Tsusansho (MITI), Sekitan Kokusu Tokei Nenpo (Yearbook of Coal and Cokes Statistics) up to 1974 and Tsusansho (MITI), Enerugii Tokei Nenpo (Yearbook of Energy Statistics) after 1975.
[c]Tsusansho (MITI), Zakka Tokei Nenpo (Hikaku Hen) (Yearbook of General Merchandise Statistics) (volume on leather), various years.
[d]Sekiguchi (1975).
[e]Norin Suisansho (Ministry of Agriculture, Forestry and Fisheries), Norin Suisan Tokei (Agriculture, Forestry and Fisheries Statistics), various years.

erential financing of mergers and modernization of equipment was offered.[7] In 1974, on the expiry of the above law, a new Law on Temporary Measures for the Structural Improvement of Textile Industry was adopted. The law was extended further for a period of five years in 1979. The "specified textile industries" label was dropped and the necessity for a business switch-over was emphasized. At the same time, the need for safeguards and voluntary export restraints by the trading partners for orderly imports was also emphasized.[8]

B. The 1978–1983 Period

With the implementation of the Law on Temporary Measures for Stabilization of Specified Depressed Industries (Industry Stabilization Law), the Japanese adjustment assistance policies became less sector-specific and more function oriented. They are based on a set of four laws, consisting of (1) the Industry Stabilization Law, (2) Law on Temporary Measures for those Unemployed in Specified Depressed Industries, (3) Law on Temporary Measures for those Unemployed in Specified Regions, and (4) Law on Temporary Measures for Small and Medium Enterprises in Specified Depressed Regions, which were specially designed to assist employees and employers in specified depressed industries and regions. A brief summary of the policy tools of the above-mentioned laws is presented in Table II.

Law (1), the Industry Stabilization Law was aimed at suspension or scrapping of capacity in the industries specified under this law or by government ordinances.[9] The coverage of the other three laws was strongly influenced by that of the Industry Stabilization Law. Table III outlines the production adjustment and changes in exports and imports in the case of 14 industries specified under this law since 1977. Although all the industries suffered from an underutilization of capacity, the rate of capacity utilization rose during 1977–1981 for all but the aluminum refining industry primarily on account of a contraction in capacity.[10]

The policy under the law consisted of a Basic Stabilization Plan, a Trust Fund for Specified Depressed Industries, and guidance for joint actions by firms. The Basic Stabilization Plan, indicating the amount and time frame for capacity to be scrapped, was formulated by the relevant Ministry on the basis of recommendations made by the relevant advisory council. The Trust Fund financed the scrapping of capacity by supplying credit guarantees. Once the Stabilization Plan for an industry was approved, firms or groups of firms were eligible to use the Trust Fund. The aluminum refining industry, the open hearth and electric furnace industry, and some other industries did not make use of the Trust Fund at all. Recourse to joint action by firms was limited to cases in which the related ministry was convinced of the inability of individual firms to carry out the plan on their own. Formation of cartels, exempted from the application of the antimonopoly legislation, was allowed in these cases after proper consultations between the relevant ministry and the Fair Trade Commission.

As revealed in Table IV, the capacity scrapping targets were achieved in all the 14 industries, although the use of the Trust Fund and guidance for joint action varied from industry to industry. The industries in which joint actions were proposed and implemented, though small in number, invariably used the Trust Fund. Shipbuilding was the only industry among those in which joint action was not proposed that used the Trust Fund. For example, the aluminum industry, where actual curtailment in production (approximately 900 thousand tons as of July 1982) exceeded the target set in the initial plan of January 1979 (annual production capacity of 530 thousand tons), did not use the Trust Fund at all.[11]

The Trust Fund was authorized to issue credit guarantees of more than ¥100 billion, but only ¥23.2 billion worth of guarantees were actually provided by the fund (as of July 31, 1983) on a cumulative basis.[12] Credit guarantees provided by the Fund included loans for the payments of severance allowances to the workers laid off as a result of scrapping of capacity as well, and these payments accounted for ¥14.8 billion (or 64% of the cumulative guarantees).[13] The amount of public funds used for assisting capacity reduction through the Industry Stabilization Law was thus very limited.

Table V summarizes the policy measures under the other three laws. Although the designation of industries and areas under Laws (2) and (3) was guided mainly by designations made under Law (1), additions were made for the sake of employment adjustment. Subsidies in the form of payments of extended employment insurance[14] to laid-off workers and wage subsidies to the business owners under Laws (2) and (3) out of public funds amounted to ¥10.4 billion in fiscal 1982. As opposed to the credit guarantee system, these disbursements were transferred principally to laid-off workers. The scale of assistance provided out of public funds under these laws implemented by the Ministry of Labor was far bigger than the assistance provided through the credit guarantee scheme of the Trust Fund under the Industry Stabilization Law.

In order to limit the number of laid-off workers eligible for the assistance under Law (2), the firms going in for employment cuts exceeding a specific limit were required to submit reemployment assistance plans, and if the plan was approved the released workers were provided with special job-seeker-identity cards. A total of 103,200 cards were issued by November 30, 1982, with the workers laid off in the shipbuilding industry accounting

TABLE II

Industrial Adjustment Policy Measures: A Summary Table[a]

Name of the Law	Law (2)	Law (3)	Law (1)	Law (4)
Period Effective	Jan. 1978–June 1983	Nov. 1978–June 1983	May 1978–April 1983	Nov. 1978–June 1983
Information dissemination measures	Employment intermediation by Public Employment Stabilization Bureaus	Employment intermediation by Public Employment Stabilization Bureaus	Building up a Basic Stabilization Plan for Specified Depressed Industries taking into account the views of the related councils	No Specific Measures
Measures to raise capacity for change	Employment guidance and training seminars	Employment training and employment guidance	Repeated use of exigency import controls	Distress loans at a low interest rate (6.1%–6.6%) and financing of business switch-overs of specified small and medium firms
Measures to reduce the costs of carrying out interindustry transfer of resources — Affecting changes in the work place of the employees	The firms providing employment to specified unemployed job seeker seeking employment (those with specially issued job seeker identifications) were subsidized.	The firms employing laid-off workers, between age of 45 to 65, in specified depressed areas, were given subsidies for providing employment opportunities to specified job seekers	The Basic Stabilization Plan had to be formulated taking into account stabilization of employment as well	The implementation closely followed Law (3) (administered by Ministry of Labor)
Adjustments carried out by the firms	Employment adjustment subsidies in the form of layoff allowances, training costs, and wage subsidies for transferred workers	Employment adjustment subsidies in the form of layoff allowances, training costs, and wage subsidies for transferred workers	Credit guarantees by the Trust Fund for Specified Depressed Industries to firms in specified depressed industries and carrying out capacity adjustment in line with the Basic Stabilization Plan	Extending the period for reimbursement of loans incurred for financing equipment investments, preferential treatment in terms of credit guarantees, carrying over of losses and refunds on various taxes as special case, and accelerated depreciation

Measures to stabilize regional economies	Promoting employment of labor in public enterprises (with 40% absorption rates as target)[b]	Promoting employment of labor in public enterprises (with 40% absorption rate as target)[b]	The governors of the prefectures where scrapping of capacity could have severe negative impact on the local economy could make representations to the related ministry	Providing incentives to draw other enterprises to designated areas by providing subsidies for reallocation of factories
Temporary measures to compensate incomes	Extended payment of employment insurance (90 days for those over 40 and 60 days for those under 40)	Extended payment of employment insurance (90 days for those over 40 and 60 days for those under 40)	No special provision	The implementation closely followed Law (3) (Administered by Ministry of Labor)
Others	The industries designated under this Law were mainly from with those specified under Law (1); some discretion was, however, exercised by the Ministry of Labor	The Labor Minister selected specific areas out of areas designated by the government directive under Law (4)	Having designated the industries as specifically depressed, a Basic Stabilization Plan to promote a planned reduction of the excess capacity was set up. Joint action by firms was allowed, which was exempted from the application of the antimonopoly laws	Designation of specially depressed industries was followed by the designation of municipalities with a high concentration of such industries as specially depressed areas

Source: *Roppo Zenshu* (Compendium of Laws), 1982 edition, Vol. II (Tokyo: YuhiKaku).

[a]—Law (1) = The Industry Stabilization Law

Law (2) = Law on Temporary Measures for those Unemployed in Specified Depressed Industries

Law (3) = Law on Temporary Measures for those Unemployed in Specified Depressed Regions

Law (4) = Law on Temporary Measures for Small and Medium Enterprises in Specified Depressed Regions

[b]—See Section 14.3 of this chapter for "absorption rate."

TABLE III

Actual Conditions in the Industries Designated under the Industry Stabilization Law

Fiscal Year	Production ('000 tons; shipbuilding 10,000 gross tons) (Rate of capacity utilization %)					Imports ('000 tons; shipbuilding 10,000 gross tons) (Import ratio %)[b]					No. of workers (No. of firms)				
	1977	1978	1979	1980	1981	1977	1978	1979	1980	1981	1977	1978	1979	1980	1981
Open Hearth & Electric Furnaces	9,633 (62.7)	11,491 (84.5)	14,743 (89.8)	12,383 (81.0)	11,283 (80.0)	0 (—)	0 (—)	0 (—)	0 (—)	0 (—)	36,400 (69)	33,900 (65)	32,600 (62)	32,000 (61)	31,300 (59)
Aluminium Refining	1,188 (73.0)	1,023 (64.4)	1,043 (89.9)	1,038 (89.9)	665 (58.5)	472 (33.5)	756 (44.1)	678 (36.7)	862 (56.7)	1,062 (66.0)	7,642 (7)	6,535 (7)	6,038 (7)	5,503 (7)	4,344 (6)
Continuous Nylon Fibers	287.6 (78.9)	284.0 (95.7)	292.6 (98.6)	286.8 (92.9)	270.0 (88.5)	7.7 (4.1)	12.5 (5.9)	13.5 (5.6)	15.4 (6.7)	14.8 (7.2)	71,021 (6)	62,095 (6)	60,212 (6)	57,576 (6)	59,464 (6)
Discontinuous Acryl Fibers	341.4 (80.2)	351.3 (96.5)	334.6 (91.9)	325.7 (87.3)	327.1 (92.9)	10.2 (6.0)	52.1 (22.7)	49.8 (21.3)	29.4 (14.6)	25.0 (13.4)	45,270 (6)	39,607 (6)	38,793 (6)	38,475 (6)	39,408 (6)
Continuous Polyester	271.8 (76.9)	301.3 (96.0)	287.4 (89.0)	274.1 (81.7)	287.9 (86.2)	13.7 (8.4)	30.5 (15.8)	19.8 (10.7)	28.5 (16.0)	37.0 (19.4)	81,330 (8)	70,690 (8)	68,899 (9)	66,695 (9)	69,317 (9)
Discontinuous Polyester	297.4 (76.6)	321.5 (97.4)	318.2 (96.4)	317.8 (93.0)	321.1 (95.1)	17.3 (11.7)	38.2 (18.4)	31.2 (13.7)	27.1 (13.2)	24.8 (12.7)	66,217 (7)	56,959 (7)	55,433 (7)	53,320 (7)	55,841 (7)

Urea	1,972 (50.1)	2,135 (53.6)	2,033 (77.4)	1,555 (67.1)	1,311 (56.5)	1 (0.1)	3 (0.3)	3 (0.3)	4 (0.5)	10 (1.2)	417 (12)	355 (12)	332 (9)	299 (8)	300 (8)
Ammonia	2,810 (61.7)	2,869 (62.9)	2,832 (76.5)	2,306 (68.4)	2,102 (62.4)	0 (—)	0 (—)	0 (—)	0 (—)	0 (—)	1,057 (18)	1,002 (18)	865 (15)	793 (14)	790 (14)
Hydrous Phosphoric Acid	542 (58.0)	540 (69.1)	593 (75.8)	518 (68.1)	484 (63.6)	56 (9.8)	48 (7.9)	61 (9.4)	52 (9.4)	37 (7.2)	467 (21)	434 (16)	428 (16)	431 (16)	422 (16)
Cotton Spinning, etc.	883.9 (70.1)	982.0 (83.8)	1071.7 (94.1)	1030.0 (91.0)	946.4 (88.0)	111.7 (14.1)	227.5 (22.5)	235.4 (21.5)	201.3 (20.5)	220.9 (23.4)	71,996 (n.a)	67,474 (258)	65,656 (199)	61,132 (195)	61,100 (193)
Worsted Yarn Spinning	117.1 (64.3)	105.2 (62.5)	124.0 (85.0)	113.4 (80.3)	115.0 (83.0)	9.3 (8.3)	11.4 (11.6)	13.5 (11.6)	10.3 (10.0)	12.7 (11.8)	22,988 (142)	20,190 (125)	18,914 (123)	16,602 (119)	15,273 (109)
Ferro-Silicon	287 (55.4)	270 (52.1)	331 (80.3)	284 (68.9)	220 (63.6)	45 (13.7)	124 (30.5)	120 (27.2)	133 (32.0)	208 (47.8)	1,536 (16)	1,381 (13)	1,369 (13)	1,246 (11)	1,022 (10)
Cardboard	4,653 (62.9)	4,957 (65.7)	5,509 (88.4)	4,781 (75.2)	4,459 (68.8)	67 (1.5)	125 (2.5)	146 (2.6)	228 (4.8)	272 (5.9)	5,828 (88)	6,059 (84)	5,836 (77)	5,810 (77)	5,960 (77)
Shipbuilding[a]	943 (76.0)	492 (51.0)	450 (39.0)	659 (64.0)	862 (79.0)	0 (—)	0 (—)	0 (—)	0 (—)	0 (—)	164,000 (61)	137,000 (61)	120,000 (61)	113,000 (44)	114,000 (44)

Sources: *Kosei Torihiki Jiho* (Fair Trade Bulletin) No. 538 (Nov. 12, 1982); Kosei Torihiki Kyokai (1982).

[a]Shipbuilding firms with capacity of more than 5,000 gross tons.

[b]Imports/(Shipments + Imports − Exports).

TABLE IV

Capacity Scrapping under the Industry Stabilization Law ('000 tons/year)

Industries where Joint Actions Were Recommended[a]	Production Capacity before Scrapping	Capacity Targeted for Scrapping under the Plan	Cumulative Capacity Scrapped up to the End of 1981	Cumulative Credit Guarantees Provided by Trust Fund for Depressed Industries
Continuous Nylon Fibers	366.7	71.5	72.9	
Discontinuous Acryl Fibers	430.5	73.2	95.5	¥ 3 billion
Continuous Polyester Fibers	349.8	36.8	36.6	
Discontinuous Polyester Fibers	397.5	67.6	70.7	
Urea	3,985.0	1,790.0	1,670.0	¥ 2.7 billion
Ammonia	4,559.0	1,190.0	1,190.0	
Worsted Yarn Spinning	181.7	18.3	17.6	¥ 1.2 billion
Cardboard	7,549.0	1,147.0	1,083.0	¥ 2.1 billion

Industries Without Such Recommendations	Production Capacity before Scrapping	Capacity Targeted for Scrapping under the Plan	Cumulative Capacity Scrapped up to the End of 1981	Cumulative Credit Guarantees Provided by Trust Fund for Depressed Industries
Open Hearth and Electric Furnaces	20,790.0	2,850.0	2,720.0	Nil
Aluminum Refining	1,642.0	530.0	899.0	Nil
Shipbuilding (CGRT)	9,770.0	3,420.0	3,580.0	¥ 14.2 billion
Ferro-Silicon	487.0	100.0	100.0	Nil
Hydrous Phosphoric Acid	934.0	190.0	174.0	Nil
Cotton Spinning	1,204.0	67.1	52.3	Nil

Source: see Table III.

[a]The joint actions were carried out in all industries for which these were recommended. The synthetic fiber industry implemented the recommended cartelization in the initial plan, but such action was not recommended for this industry in the second plan.

for by far the highest number at over 40%, followed by the textile industry at over 30%.[15] Besides these measures, Laws (2) and (3) resorted to more conventional measures such as employment mediation, occupational training, and employment guidance as well through Public Employment Stabilization Bureaus. In order to provide preferential employment in public enterprises to the laid-off workers in the depressed areas, Law (3) stipulated that at least 40% of such employment should be from the pool of locally available laid-off workers (absorption system). The total number of man-days absorbed by the public enterprises stood at 2.58 million as of November 30, 1982.[16]

Law (4), promulgated to deal with the decline of specified areas, is addressed to the affected capital, as Law (3) aims at the affected labor. When a large number of small- and medium-scale firms in an area are dependent on a few large firms through subcontracting and other forms of relationships, the economic life of the residents of that locality is greatly affected by failures of these large firms. The above law was promulgated to mitigate the effects of such a disruption in the regional economic life. The small- and medium-scale firms found to fall within the terms of reference of this law could obtain distress loans at low interest (6.1% to 6.6%; the average bank loan rate during this period was 6.0% to 8.3%). The cumulative loans provided under this scheme stood at ¥42.7 billion at the end of fiscal 1981. In general, reallocation of capital within the region or capital inflow from other regions become the obvious policy alternatives if labor mobility across the regions is not smooth. This objective was achieved by Law (4) through financing of business switch-overs, increasing the limit for credit guarantees, providing for special reimbursements of income and corporate taxes and subsidies to lure firms into the area, and other such measures (regarding the scale of assistance, cf. Table V). The scale of assistance provided by this law out of the public funds, like that by Laws (2) and (3), was far greater than that under the Industry Stabilization Law.

It is clear from the above discussion that adjustment assistance policy in this period had a much wider applicability, as it was directed at facilitating capital and labor mobility as well as supporting the foundations of the local public finances. It is here that the policies in this period differ from those in the earlier period. Formally, the Industry Stabilization Law was supposed to be the main legislation, but in terms of the actual scale of assistance out of the public finances, the assistance provided through its three subordinate laws was much larger than that provided through the principal law. Attainment of capacity adjustment targets set up in the Basic Stabilization Plan can perhaps be attributed to the interactive functioning of voluntary adjustments carried out by the private firms pursuing maximum profits, the policy toward large-scale firms, and policies designed for labor and small firms.

TABLE V

Scale of Employment Adjustment Assistance and Measures Related to Specified Areas[a]

Items	Law (2)	Law (3)	Law (4)
Major policy guidelines and the implementation process	When the scale of employment adjustment of a firm in an industry designated as a depressed industry exceeded a certain level, the firm had to formulate a reemployment assistance plan. The firm where over 30 workers were to be laid-off in a single month or when the total of laid-off and transferred workers exceeded 100, the employer was required to set up a plan and then get it approved by the director of the Public Employment Stabilization Office. The employers and the workers where the plan was approved were then eligible for special measures.	Laid-off workers residing in the Labor Ministry designated depressed areas and the business firm owners within such areas were automatically made eligible for special treatment under the law	This Law attempted to deal with the dislocation of regional economies due to closure of some of the large enterprises in an area with high dependence on such firms due to the presence of some form of subcontracting or other dependency relationships on account of adverse business conditions. In order to avail of the special measures under this law, a firm within the specified depressed area had to get the approval of the head of the municipality
	Cumulative number of cases for which the plan was approved up to end of November 1982 stood at	The number of individuals receiving extended employment insurance granted on a case-by-	Seven industries and 32 areas (35 Municipalities) were designated under this law by September 1982.

The scale of policy measures: nonpecuniary	6,600 (the proportion of obligatory plans being 10%) and those of reemployment cases at 68,200. The number of specific job-seeker identifications issues was 103,200, while training was provided to 10,760. Forty industries were designated as depressed industries	case basis averaged 4,941 per month on a cumulative basis up to the end of November 1982. The number of man-days absorbed in the public enterprises during the same period amounted to 2,580,000 persons. Forty-four areas were designated as recessionary areas.	Further additions were also made. A total of 5,060 small and medium firms were given approval under this law by the end of fiscal 1981.
The scale of policy measures: pecuniary	¥ 10.4 billion in conjunction with the provisions of Law (3). The two laws were discontinued in July 1983 and replaced by Employment Stabilization in Specified Industries and Areas Law with the budgetary provisions expanding to ¥ 15.8 billion	A total of ¥ 3.6 billion were disbursed by November 1982 in the form of employment adjustment assistance and ¥ 0.2 billion in the form of subsidies for employment generation for specified job seekers (the payments made because of employment generation for old workers under the predecessor law, however, amounted to ¥ 8.3 bn up to the end of fiscal 1981).	Up to the end of fiscal 1981, ¥ 42.7 billion were provided as exigency loans, ¥ 0.17 billion for financing business change, ¥ 18.6 billion by the way of raising the limits of the credit guarantees, ¥ 2.4 billion in terms of special reimbursement of income and corporate taxes, and ¥ 1.5 billion for luring firms into specified regions.

aFor full names see Table II.

C. 1983 and After

The Industry Stabilization Law expired at the end of April 1983 and was replaced by the Law on Temporary Measures for the Structural Improvement of Specified Industries (The Structural Improvement Law), which had a five-year limit. Basic Structural Improvement Plans, similar in nature to the erstwhile Basic Stabilization Plans, were drawn up for industries designated under the Law or by government ordinances by the ministry concerned,[17] covering, besides capacity adjustments, business cooperation including concentration and mergers among the firms as well as investments in new equipment and research and development. The Trust Fund for Specified Industries, which replaced the Trust Fund for Depressed Industries, offered credit guarantees for the extended coverage of the new law. Besides the credit guarantees, other measures such as various types of subsidies (mainly for R&D) and preferential tax treatment were also introduced under the new law.[18] As far as the designation of industries targeted for policy either under the law or by government ordinances and the provisions for guidance in joint actions by the firms are concerned, the new legislation retained the essence of its predecessor.

Following the shift to the Structural Improvement Law, Laws (2) and (3) were also replaced in July 1983 by the Law on Special Measures Concerning the Stabilization of Employment in Specified Depressed Industries and in Specified Depressed Regions. Provisions for prevention of unemployment, i.e., providing adjustment assistance before the workers were laid off so as to stabilize employment, were newly added under this law. The designation of industries and areas was also made more flexible. A part of the wages of the workers for whom training programs were set up by the employer before the workers were laid off was subsidized for the period of such training (the subsidy rate was two-thirds (three-fourths in the case of small and medium enterprises) for a period of six months). If a worker got employed through the mediation of his erstwhile employer, a wage subsidy (equivalent to one-fourth of the wage (one-third in the case of small and medium firms for a one-year period) was provided to the old employer as a part of the wages of such employees.

Finally, Law (4) was also replaced in July 1983 (by the Law on Temporary Measures for Dealing with Regions Related to Specified Depressed Industries). Development of new fields of business by the firms received high priority under this legislation, and new assistance measures such as subsidies and loans for development of new markets and new technology for nurturing human resources necessary for such purposes were also adopted. These subsidies are disbursed by the Small and Medium Enterprise Cooperatives of the area in accordance with the action program sanctioned by the governor of the locality. The central and the prefectural governments share equally the burden of subsidies, with ¥10 million as the upper total limit. Firms, with approval from the governor, can also avail themselves of low-interest loans from the Small Business Finance Corporation under the extended provisions of this law.[19]

D. A Tentative Evaluation

The Japanese adjustment assistance policy until 1978 was basically ad hoc in nature tackling sectoral problems as they arose. It included assistance for modernization of equipment and concentrated efforts at rejuvenation of particular activities.

With the adoption of the Industry Stabilization Law and related adjustment assistance legislations, the scope of the adjustment assistance policy widened, making it more general in nature. The policy included measures directed at businesses and capital [Laws (1) and (4)] and at labor [Laws (2) and (3)]. Both were locality-specific. Although the Industry Stabilization Law is credited for its significant role within the adjustment assistance policies, it is seen that in terms of the actual assistance provided by the government out of public funds, the measures related to labor and localities outstripped the assistance under this law proper.

How can the Japanese adjustment assistance policy be evaluated within the theoretical framework provided in Section II of this chapter? The evaluation of assistance measures aimed at reallocation of labor is relatively straightforward. The extended employment insurance payments do not, by themselves, promote job changes, but subsidies for the reemployment of designated workers could have been effective in lowering frictional unemployment. Besides the policy measures, reallocation of labor to firms within a business group, a practice that is being increasingly made use of in recent years, may also have affected labor mobility significantly.[20]

The policy measures subsidizing new investment in designated areas are not directed merely at businesses and capital but also promote job changes by opening up new employment opportunities in the area. If the firms established under these schemes can eventually stand on their own without the help of the subsidies, these area-related policies [Laws (3) and (4)] could be credited with the promotion of industrial adjustment.

On the other hand, how far were the adjustment assistance policies directed at businesses and capital, especially the policy toward large-scale enterprises under the Industry Stabilization Law, successful in meeting their objectives? As pointed out earlier, the actual assistance provided by the government out of the public funds was quite small. A large proportion of the industries designated under the Industry Stabilization Law did recover their rate of capacity utilization through capacity reduction with a minimal use of the credit guarantees intended for financing the scrapping of capacity. Though the industries implemented almost similar measures to achieve this objectives, they differed in their use of credit guarantees.

The effects of other measures such as the "guiding joint actions" by firms for affecting capacity and production adjustments are also ambiguous. It was seen in Table IV that the difference in the recovery of the rate of capacity utilization between the industries making use of guidance for joint actions and those that did not was hardly significant.[21] We believe that neither the pecuniary incentives nor the administrative guidance ("guidance for joint actions" here) policies aimed at capital and management of the large firms had any substantial impact.

Finally, let us have a look at the import-restricting measures designed to smooth fluctuations in product prices. Japan did not frequently resort to price intervention with the intention of slowing down the speed of price adjustment, as wage rigidities were not so pronounced. Import restrictions on raw silk and silk fabrics and the Tariff Allocation Scheme on aluminum ingot imports can be cited as examples of such a policy, but other areas by and large remained relatively free from explicit controls. The extent to which the above mentioned joint actions resulted in curbing imports in the presence of industrial groups is not very clear at the present juncture.

A new adjustment assistance policy subsidizing research and development activity undertaken to promote business switch-overs has been introduced since 1983, but it is too early to judge the impact of this policy. It is perhaps safe to argue, however, that the policy framework has increasingly begun to emphasize promotion of industrial adjustment.

IV. Conclusion

The discussion in the previous sections has concentrated on the evaluation of the adjustment assistance policies from the point of view of national economic welfare. The exigency import restrictions, subsidies for domestic restructuring, or subsidies aimed at maintaining the status quo, on the other hand, have a profound impact on trade flows. In this sense, the adjustment assistance policies result in eruption of trade friction among nations. Let us conclude this chapter with a discussion of the adjustments in international conflicts of interests.

To begin with, a broad outline of the adjustment assistance policies followed by some of the major countries may be helpful. In the case of the United States, the Trade Reform Act of 1974 dictates the conditions under which assistance is to be provided to the firms, workers, and communities, as well as conditions governing exigency import restrictions. These measures are far less sector-specific than the Japanese policies, but the similarities between the Japanese and the American policies have been on the rise since the 1962 legislation.[22]

Though a generalized discussion of adjustment assistance policies followed by the West European nations is difficult, the earliest of these can be traced back to the Rome Agreement (1957), which specified adjustment assistance, and to the establishment of the European Social Fund for assistance to workers undergoing job changes.[23] Although we will not delve into the actual policy measures undertaken and their effectiveness, piecing together the fragmentary information provided by OECD [1971, 1975, 1978] reveals that the coal, textile, and shipbuilding industries were targeted for sector-specific adjustment assistance and assistance directed at affecting labor force shifts, and specific regions also formed a common strand of the policies in the European countries. The use of exigency import controls based on multilateral agreements and demands for voluntary export restraints are well known facts.

On the other hand, if we look at frictions generated by the impact of adjustment assistance on trade, we find conflicts among closely competing producers to be most predominant. In the absence of international transfers of income, the distribution of producers' and consumers' surpluses among the four interest groups over the two countries cannot be carried out to the satisfaction of all parties.[24] The main objective of adjustment assistance policies, on the other hand, having dealt with the adjustment of domestic conflict of interests, shifts to the pursuit of interests based on international division of labor in line with long-run comparative advantage.

The optimum adjustment assistance policy, both from the point of view of the national as well as international economy, would be the one that removes distortions that give rise to adjustment costs. In this sense, the policies intended to raise labor mobility (employment introductions and arbitration, subsidies for training and relocation, etc.) being adopted by individual countries are quite rational. Accelerated depreciation and subsidies for the dismantling and reinstallation of capital would also be effective in line with the above argument, although it would certainly depend on the degree to which the adjustment costs involved in shifting capital between its uses exceeds the costs of the dismantling, transfer, and international reallocation of capital.

In the short run, however, when the factor market distortions have to be taken as given because of the presence of labor unions and various other factors, wage and capital subsidies, directed at maintaining the status quo, become a necessity. Since such intervention reduces the exports of foreign countries to a level lower than what would prevail in the absence of such intervention, it creates dissatisfaction among those countries. On the whole, however, the fall in the welfare level concomitant with such intervention is smaller than under import restrictions, and trade distortion is small as well.[25] This, therefore, qualifies as a second-best policy.

One cannot rule out the possibility of resorting to exigency import restrictions to the extent that foreign trade leads to a reduction in domestic production. Article 19 of the GATT lays down the rules for dealing with such situations conditional on (1) the nondiscriminatory nature of such import restrictions, and (2) provisions for compensating the exporting nations. The voluntary export restraints (VER) have been increasingly used in the recent years to get around these severe conditions.[26] Finally, resorting to discriminatory exigency import controls is being increasingly advocated in the West mainly by the European countries.

VER or selective import restrictions tend to be welcomed by other potential exporting nations, which are exempt from these discriminatory trade measures, on account of their favorable impact on export opportunities. In a country that adopts VER as well, its oligopolistic producers prefer VER to tariffs and import quotas because VER are expected to restrict competition in an agreeable manner at home. For these reasons, VER and selective import restrictions are likely to be politically acceptable. These policy responses, however, are not really appropriate to the policy target of domestic industrial adjustment assistance. It is because supplies tend to expand from countries other than the one that accepts import restrictions. Indeed, VER when applied to a particular country exert immediate influence upon other countries. To meet the objective of domestic industrial adjustment, it suffices to adopt nondiscrimanatory exigency import restrictions on the product under consideration.

The provisions for compensation as provided for in Article 19 of the GATT to check the use of import restrictions are understandable as a rule and may perhaps be sufficient if exigency import controls with a limited time frame to help economic adjustment assistance are allowed for.

Notes

1. Kyonosuke Sasaki (Small and Medium Enterprise Agency), Hideya Nakano (Employment Policy Division of the Ministry of Labor), Kuniaki Date (Trust Fund for Specified Depressed Industries) were kind enough to provide us with the materials used in the present chapter. Incisive comments by Masao Baba, Konosuke Odaka, Yoshiyasu Ono, Masu Uekusa, Akira Goto, and other participants in the Zushi Conference were also very helpful. Finally, we also benefited from suggestions made by the editors of

the book. While expressing our deep gratitude to all these people, the authors take full responsibility for the shortcomings that still remain.

2. Neary [1982] does not clearly enumerate the policy measures that could be resorted to for such a slowdown. For example, intervention in product prices through exigency import restrictions could be one such measure. The sources of subsidies, on the other hand, are assumed to be raised through a lump sum tax.

3. Protection policy is not the main theme of this paper. Those interested in the details are referred to Sekiguchi and Horiuchi [1981].

4. The producers of thermal power were required to use a given quantity of coal. Besides, the prices of petroleum, an alternate source of fuel were also raised. Cf. Sekiguchi [1975].

5. Cf. Shigen Enerugii Cho (Agency of Natural Resources and Energy) [1980a, 1980b]. The measure had an employment effect on a total of 90,000 workers by the end of fiscal 1979, of which 43,000 were the workers laid off from coal mines.

6. The measures undertaken, in principle, provided for 40% of the total loans at 7.7% (after May 1980), to be redeemed within 10 years after a deferment period of 3 years. See note 5 for the source.

7. The Small Business Corporation loans carried an interest rate of 2.6%, with a 10-year redemption period after deferment for 2 years and were applicable to 70% of the requirements. The amount of loans stood at ¥142 billion, including those by the Japan Development Bank (Nihon Kagaku Sen' i Kyokai [1981]).

8. Cf. Tsusansho Seikatsu Sangyo Kyoku [1977] and Chapter 15 of the present volume.

9. In addition to promotion of capacity adjustments from the point of view of scrapping of excess capacity, installation of new equipment and renovation of the existing equipment were also limited or completely forbidden.

10. See Kosei Torihiki Kyokai [1982].

11. The tariff allocation scheme was introduced on the import of aluminum ingots in the 1978 tariff revision and continued up to 1981 with some revision. The difference between the primary tariff (5.5%) and the secondary tariff (9%) was given to the Aluminum Industry Structural Improvement Promotion Committee and was utilized in the structural improvement of the aluminum refining industry. Furthermore, the Committee also provided interest subsidies on borrowings up to the full book value of the equipment scrapped at a rate of 6.1% in 1979 and 5.1% in 1980. The capacity frozen also received preferential treatment. A system of tariff exemptions on imports of aluminum ingots by aluminum refiners was adopted in 1982 (for a period of three years). The amount of imports exempted from tariffs were limited to those covered by the capacity adjustment plan of the industry under the Industry Stabilization Law (the amount exempted from the tariffs in 1982 equaled the amount under the adjustment plan at 393,000 tons). The imports covered by the tariff exemption system encompassed all kinds of aluminum. Besides this, measures like refunding a part of tariffs on imports of crude oil used as a raw material in the ammonium industry, one of the industries designated under the Industry Stabilization Law, were also adopted to reduce the tax burden in 1978 and were still in force during 1983 after a number of changes. Cf. Nihon Kanzei Kyokai (Japan Tariff Association), *Kanzei Kaisei no Subete (All About Tariff Revision)*, various issues, and Chapter 15 of this book.

12. While the credit guarantees for the purpose of facilitating capacity adjustments can be divided into three types based on their content, the largest proportion went to individual firms for their capacity adjustments. As credit guarantees by the Trust Fund lowered the costs of screening by the private financial institutions, the rate of interest on borrowings could have been lower than what would have been obtained in the absence of such guarantees.

13. The Trust Fund provided credit guarantees at the time of bank debenture issues (underwritten by the Ministry of Finance Trust Fund Bureau) of three long-term credit banks in 1978–1979. The funds raised were used in preferential financing of payments of severance allowances.

14. The "employment" insurance corresponds to the unemployment insurance in other countries (Editor).

15. Cf. Rodosho Koyo Seisaku Ka [1983a, 1983b].

16. Law (2) also resorted to the absorption system, but the totals are calculated on the basis of Law (3). The absorption system has been taken recourse by schemes other than these laws but no scheme has treated a specific segment of laid-off workers preferentially.

17. As far as the designated industries are concerned, the most important change was to drop the shipbuilding industry and include the petrochemical industry.

18. As regards preferential tax measures, one could cite special measures related to losses carried over under the corporate tax law, special depreciation schemes for newly installed equipment, and measures to reduce corporate taxes and registration fees for newly established corporations. The subsidies fall into three categories—subsidies for the construction of thermal power generation plants based on coal to promote switchovers in fuel use (¥2.2 billion in fiscal 1983), subsidies on developmental costs of petroleum substituting energy technology to promote technological development (¥2.31 billion in fiscal 1983), and subsidies to the research and development costs of industrial revitalization technology (¥460 million in fiscal 1983).

19. The upper limit on loans was raised from ¥210 million to ¥300 million and the preferential loans carried a 7.3% rate of interest (the normal rate of interest was 8.1%), which was to be raised to 7.8% from the fourth year onward.

20. According to the Ministry of Labor's followup survey on employment, reemployment of workers was largely within the same or related sectors, perhaps because of constraints on the technical skills of the workers (Rodosho Koyo Seisaku Ka [1983b]). If wage subsidies for the job-switching within a sector continued for a long time, these would no longer be effective in facilitating reallocation of the work force.

21. Chapter 10 of this book demonstrates that cartel practices are helpful to the oligopolistic firms in avoiding the prisoner's dilemma resulting from the conditions of entry and exit. Though it is difficult to guess whether the industry is in the cyclical downswing phase or on the road to secular stagnation, an early exit by a firm expecting long-term stagnation, as implied in the discussion carried out above, must be advantageous. A detailed discussion of the differing aspects of interfirm conflict of interests in industries taking recourse to joint actions and those where no such action was resorted to as well as how to carry on the cooperative game, and soon have not been dealt with at this stage due to a lack of information.

22. For a detailed discussion of the changes taking place between the 1962 Legislation and the 1974 Legislation, cf. Frank [1975], on which this chapter depends exclusively. For a comparative evaluation of the Japanese and U.S. policies, see Wheeler, Janow, and Pepper [1982].

23. See Ohlin [1975] for details. Discussion regarding how these stipulations were implemented is, however, lacking.

24. OECD [1978, 1983b] and Diebold [1980] favor an "active adjustment policy" for raising welfare in the long run. The discussion, however, becomes ambiguous when it comes to sectoral conflict of interests among nations. The OECD guidelines therefore provide no more than a general policy frame.

25. We assume here that the producers and exporters are in no position to hold monopoly power.

26. Komiya [1972] and Bergsten [1975] are some earlier works on VER. Takacs [1978] carries a detailed discussion of equality of tariffs and VER, while Itoh and Ono [1982] deals with the problem in the context of monopolistic competition and analyzes the price setting behavior and the changes in the profits of oligopolistic producers.

27. In order to deal with unfair competition among producers of specific countries, some other provision within GATT could be resorted to. The use of VER as a measure against specific monopolists is hardly evident in the case of adjustment assistance. Kanemitsu [1981] comes close to our viewpoint but differs to the extent that it advocates selective import restrictions with stiff supervisory conditions in order to provide GATT rules with effectiveness.

CHAPTER 15

The Textile Industry[1]

IPPEI YAMAZAWA

Department of Economics
Hitotsubashi University
Tokyo, Japan

I. Introduction

The textile industry possesses a complex structure with 150,000 establishments engaged in various phases of production from raw materials to final products (and a further 200,000 wholesalers and retailers are engaged in its distribution). The industry has continued to receive adjustment assistance for over 30 years since the end of World War II and has naturally been the target of severe criticism not only from without but from within as well. The Japanese adjustment policies, however, in their adherence to the free trade system, despite competitive pressures from the products of developing countries both in export as well as import markets, stand in sharp contrast to the policies, especially import restrictions, adopted by the Western countries. It was perhaps this adherence to the free trade system that fueled the impressive structural change by maintaining internal and external competitive pressures.

An analysis of the mechanism by which the complicated industrial structure of the Japanese textile industry adapted to the changing internal and external competitive conditions and the role played by the domestic adjustment assistance along with the commercial policy is imperative for an evaluation of the Japanese textile policy. This, therefore, forms the central theme of the present chapter. Production and manufacturing stages of thread production (cf. Fig 15.1) are of prime concern to us, while the production of synthetic yarn receives a secondary treatment.

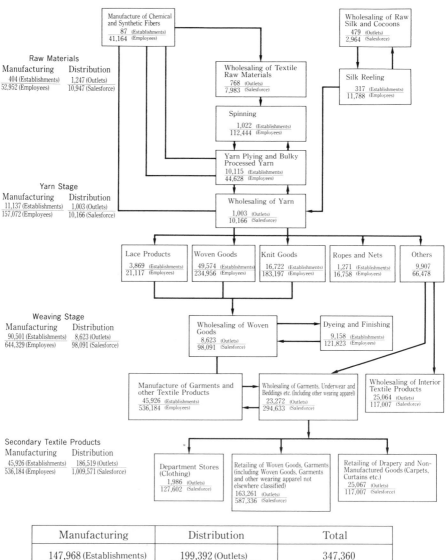

Fig. 15.1.   An overview of the manufacturing and distribution network of the textile industry by stages of production (1980). Prepared by Tsusansho Seikatsu Songyokyokj (MITI, Consumer Goods Industries Bureau) from *Census of Manufactures*, 1980, and *Census of Commerce*, 1979.

II. The Japanese Textile Industry—An Overview

A. Industrial Structure

The share of the textile industry in Japanese manufacturing has been declining for the past quarter century. Between 1965 and 1980, its share in manufacturing employment fell from 17.3% to 12.7%, in value of shipments from 11.7% to 5.7%, and in value added from 11.3% to 6.5%. The proportion of textile products in total exports fell from 18.7% to 4.7% in the same period. Despite this, the industry in 1980 still employed 1.39 million workers in its production and processing stages alone and, if the workers in its distribution network are also included, the figure rises to 2.52 million.

Figure 15.1 provides a general picture of the production, processing, and distribution network of the industry by the stages of production from raw materials to spinning, weaving, and secondary products. Raw materials and spinning form the upstream stage, weaving the midstream stage, and textile products the downstream stage. Table I depicts changes in the value of shipments and value added by stage of production during the 1970s.

TABLE I

Composition of Value of Shipments and Value Added in Textile Industry by Stage of Production (¥100 mn, %)

	Value of Shipments			Value Added		
	1970	1975	1980	1970	1975	1980
Upstream Segment	14,099	24,638	31,602	8,396	5,807	8,594
	(37.0)	(26.2)	(25.7)	(36.0)	(17.4)	(18.4)
Chemical Fibers Industry	7,802	7,662	11,457	4,387	1,719	2,758
	(12.7)	(8.1)	(9.3)	(18.8)	(5.2)	(5.9)
Spinning Industry	11,071	12,093	14,869	3,014	2,795	4,225
	(18.1)	(12.9)	(12.1)	(12.9)	(8.4)	(9.1)
Midstream Segment	16,107	47,597	60,908	11,044	18,205	24,143
	(47.3)	(50.6)	(49.6)	(47.4)	(54.6)	(51.8)
Weaving Industry	11,867	17,127	20,935	4,232	6,113	8,298
	(19.4)	(18.2)	(17.1)	918.2)	(18.3)	(18.6)
Knitting Industry	7,040	12,299	16,501	2,475	4,322	6,080
	(11.5)	(13.1)	(13.4)	(10.6)	(13.0)	(13.0)
Dyeing and Finishing Industry	5,299	10,151	12,043	2,616	4,948	5,627
	(8.6)	(10.8)	(9.8)	(11.2)	(14.8)	(12.1)
Downstream Segment	4,410	21,802	30,268	3,855	9,336	13,893
	(15.6)	(23.2)	(24.7)	(16.5)	(28.0)	(29.8)
Textile Manufacturing	34,616	94,037	122,778	23,294	33,347	46,631
	(100.0)	(100.0)	(100.0)	(100.0)	(100.0)	(100.0)

Source: Tsusansho, Kogyo Tokei Hyo (Census of Manufactures).

The business strategies of the large- and medium-scale firms engaged in spinning and synthetic textiles in the upstream stage, though contributing only 15% of value added as of 1980, have had a great effect on the structural changes in this industry.

The midstream phase of production accounts for 52% of total value added in the industry. It is characterized by a large number of small- and medium-scale firms, as revealed by the number of workers per establishment (cf. Table I), and forms the basis of the so-called "production centers" type of division of labor spread over different localities all over the country. The number of firms in these production centers varies from a score to over a thousand, but a large proportion of these firms are, in fact, small and tiny firms in a subcontracting relationship with a few major firms, local trading companies, or upstream firms, depending on those for the supply of yarns, sale of products, and financing. Many of them do commissioned work on weaving machines they own. Other firms that are engaged in closely related fields, like thread twisting, dyeing, and finishing, participate so as to form a system of organic division of labor. There are 62 (government designated) production centers for cotton and spun rayon fiber weaving (including synthetic discontinuous fiber textiles) and 19 for silk and rayon textiles (mainly chemical and synthetic continuous fiber textiles) in the country as a whole.

Apparel production has shown a substantial increase in recent years. A few major bulk producers of underwear and outdoor clothes have shown a steep rate of growth. They subcontract work to many tiny sewing firms, while themselves concentrating on product planning and sales aspects. The production centers specializing in traditional products such as shirts and hosiery are dominated by a large number of small and medium scale firms. There are relatively weak ties between the apparel producers in the downstream segment and the producers in the upstream and midstream segments.

The peculiarities of the structure of the Japanese textile industry can be found in the coexistence of large-scale firms and a large number of small- and medium-scale firms and the manner in which these are integrated in a complex distribution network. A proper understanding of these peculiarities is a necessary precondition to a discussion of structural adjustment in the textile industry.

B. Deterioration in International Competitiveness

A proper understanding of the problem of industrial adjustment in the Japanese textile industry requires a closer look at the world trends, especially textile production and trade in East and Southeast Asia.[2] During the early 1950s, Japan was the only country producing and exporting modern textiles in the whole East and Southeast Asian region. Taiwan and Hong Kong began developing a modern textile industry in the early 1950s and Korea in the mid-1950s, but, apart from Hong Kong, Taiwan and Korea both lacked exportable surplus until the 1960s. Since the cotton industry of the ASEAN countries was also relatively underdeveloped at the time, Southeast Asia was a major export market for Japanese cotton products in the 1950s.

The ASEAN countries achieved import substitution in cotton products at a rapid pace during the 1960s. The Japanese firms, responding favorably to these countries' policies of actively inviting foreign direct investment, shifted from exports to local production and thereby helped in hastening the pace of import substitution. Exports of cotton products from Hong Kong, Taiwan, and Korea were also replacing Japanese products in the U.S. market at the same time. Thus, the Japanese exports to the U.S. market were replaced by exports of the East Asian nations and those to the ASEAN market by indigenous production (although a large proportion of this production emanated in the joint ventures between Japanese and local firms). Finally, protectionist measures undertaken by the Western countries also reduced Japanese exports. This represents the first phase of industrial adjustment in the Japanese textile industry.

The ASEAN countries began producing synthetic fibers and textiles during the late 1960s, and by the early 1970s these countries had not only completed import substitution at a fast pace but had begun exporting as well. Export of synthetic fibers and textiles from the ASEAN countries flourished during the latter half of the 1970s. Having achieved sufficient competitive power the ASEAN exports, led by products from East Asia, extended their markets to Europe and the Middle East and began penetrating Japanese markets. The Japanese textile industry lost its competitive edge as wage costs rose following the development of labor scarcity in the process of rapid growth up to the early 1970s and the repeated appreciation of the yen in 1971, 1973, and 1978. Imports of textiles, mainly of low quality products, rose rapidly. The Japanese textile industry was thus forced to compete with the products from other Asian nations in the domestic market. This is the second phase of industrial adjustment in Japanese textile industry.

Table II presents the export/production and import/domestic demand ratios[3] for all textile products. The export/production ratio, although fluctuating, declined while the import/domestic demand ratio is seen to have risen sharply since the end of the 1960s. Raw materials preceding the yarn stage are not included in these ratios. Although exports still surpass imports, the difference is expected to fall with time.

TABLE II
Capacity Scrapped to the Present

	Total Cost of the Program				No. of Looms Scrapped						Spinning		
	Total	Borne by the Industry	Subsidies	Loans	Total	Cotton & Staple Fibers	Silk & Rayon	Wool	Jute	Towel	Spindles ('000)	Knit Goods	Others
Old Textile Law (1956–63)	2,768	1,186	1,582	—	79,882	48,927	30,955	—	—	—	—	—	—
New Textile Law (1964–66)	961	—	—	961	—	—	—	—	—	—	—	—	—
Measures to Deal with Structural Depression (1966)	294	160	134	—	2,814	2,265	549	—	—	—	—	—	—
Structural Improvement of Specified Textile Industries Law (1967–73)	5,606	1,803	1,803	2,000	35,836	22,117	13,719	—	—	—	1,120	—	—
Special Measures for Textile Industry (Controls on Exports to U.S.) (1971–73)	183,094	2,441	48,920	131,733	86,533	58,053	21,624	5,684	400	772	1,049	13,358	69,679
Law Concerning Unregistered Looms (1974–78)	5,487	5,487	0	0	38,615	17,698	11,813	6,535	307	2,262	—	—	—
Structural Improvement of Textile Industry Law (1979–84)	—	—	—	—	—	—	—	—	—	—	—	—	—
Financing by Small Business Promotion Corporation (1977–81)	179,900	7,100	0	172,800	108,743	56,059	42,341	10,343	—	—	2,821	22,638	91,421
Total	378,100	18,177	52,439	307,494	352,423	205,119	121,001	22,562	707	3,034	4,990	35,996	161,100

Source: MITI Consumer Goods Industries Bureau.

C. Changes in Industrial Structure and Adaptation by Firms

It is clear that the Japanese textile industry began to suffer from a comparative disadvantage because of the labor shortage, the rise in labor costs, and the catching-up achieved by the newly industrializing countries. This, however, far from being a smooth process, has been accompanied by pronounced structural changes following the changing conditions of demand and supply. The *Textile Demand and Supply Tables* reveal an upward trend in domestic demand as well as production until the early 1970s. Since then, per capita consumption of textiles leveled off at 13–14 kg, but its composition continued to change. Synthetic fibers increased their share of total production from 44.1% in 1970 to 58.0% in 1981 while that of continuous fiber fabrics rose from 29.9% to 39.3% and that of ready-made clothing from 46.0% to 76.4%. Although growth in demand has lagged in quantitative terms, qualitative diversification has led to a pattern similar to that of the developed countries.

The structural changes mentioned above came about as a result of the medium- and long-term measures undertaken by the Japanese textile firms in response to changing conditions of internal and external demand. The measures resorted to by the Japanese firms to meet the challenge of changing conditions can be classified as follows: (1) modernization of equipment and technological improvement; (2) product switching; (3) strengthening of vertical ties, mergers, and business tie-ups; (4) overseas investment and development of other forms of international division of labor; and, (5) business switch-overs and closures.

The need for measure (1), modernization of equipment, arose because a large proportion of equipment in the midstream segment of the industry was of prewar vintage. The technological change facilitated modernization further and lowered per-unit costs of production by economizing on labor requirements, increasing automation, and raising the speed of the production process. The doubling of the operating speed of ring-frame machines, introduction of open-end spinning machines, automatic transfer between individual operations, diffusion of various types of shuttleless looms, and computer control of the weaving and sewing operations are some noteworthy examples of such changes. Widespread use of high tensile standardized synthetic yarn also contributed in this direction.

Measure (2) on the list was effective in circumventing competition with the products from the less developed countries by promoting differentiation and the upgrading of products. The increasing use of high-count thread and processed textiles in the postwar period and a shift in markets to that for exports to developed countries and domestic demand were the results of such measures. Development of new specialty synthetic threads like

the high twisted yarn and weight-reduced finish and invention of dyeing
and weaving processes suited to these can also be encompassed within
this category. The export boom in differentiated polyester filament in the
1979–1981 period can be attributed to the latter.

Measures (1) and (2) are not mutually exclusive. A combination of the
two using microelectronic technology is expected to raise efficiency in
the production of a large variety of products in small lots. The automated
sewing research and development project of the Ministry of International
Trade and Industry (1983–) has also concentrated its efforts at eliciting a
quick response to changing fashions rather than on realization of economies
of bulk production. These technological improvements, while raising capital intensity of production as well as productivity, have also resulted in
a severe reduction in employment.[4]

As for vertical integration [Measure (3)], producers of synthetic continuous fibers formed business groups with weaving and dyeing firms,
which use their yarn to secure the sales outlets as well as to preserve
their differentiated technology. The spinners of discontinuous fiber yarn
have also, in recent years, diversified into textiles by integrating the high
value-added weaving stage. The late 1960s, on the other hand, saw mergers
among large spinning companies and the organization of small and medium
spinners into groups by large spinners, and finally, during the 1970s, joint
sales companies established by large spinners in collaboration with synthetic fiber producers came into vogue.[5]

Locating factories in developing countries with low labor costs or col-
laborating with local firms in the area of sales planning and technology
without capital investments under item (4) shifted the source of supply to
underdeveloped countries. Relocation of production in low-wage developing countries was imperative as, unlike in the United States and Europe,
Japan did not allow labor immigration even after the Japanese economy
turned into a labor-scarce economy in the 1960s. Overseas investment,
resorted to on a wide front since the mid-1960s, was a significant way of
adaptation for the Japanese textile industry and contributed to, as discussed earlier, the catching-up achieved by the neighboring Asian countries. The latter method is being widely used in Hong Kong, South Korea,
and China in the case of clothing. Initially, cloth was exported from Japan
and tailored on a commission, but in recent years planned imports of
clothing using cloth produced locally or in third countries have increased
substantially.

The above measures undertaken in the face of changing conditions of
demand and supply in domestic and international markets were responses
geared to the principles of market mechanism and did not require any
policy support so long as individual firms were willing to carry out the

measures themselves. Not all firms, however, were in a position to choose and implement such measures. Producers of chemical and synthetic fibers and large spinning firms in the upstream segment of the industry resorted to all of the measures, (1) to (4), and also to the diversification measures of (5) above to such an extent that their nontextile activities now account for over a quarter of their sales.[6] Likewise, manufacturers-cum-wholesalers of apparel have also been able to carry out (1) to (4) as domestic demand expanded. But the small- and medium-scale firms, forming an overwhelming proportion of the spinning, weaving, and apparel operations, could carry out (1) and (2) partially, but were in no position to resort to (3) and (4) on their own, while opportunities for entering other businesses (5) were also far limited. Finally, for a very large number of tiny firms in the mid- and downstream segments of the industry, who lacked the capacity to raise funds and had low technological capabilities to innovate, all four alternatives were closed. They often shut down in a recession when they could not break even. The only job opportunities open to them, as long as they stayed in their locality, were restricted to agriculture or manual labor.[7]

The government policy on the textile industry has concentrated primarily on assisting the small and medium firms in the mid- and downstream segments of the industry in adopting the measures mentioned above. Access to capital markets, disadvantages in technological development, region orientation, and employment problems faced by the small and medium firms formed the basis of such a policy. Since the sudden changes in competitive conditions were invariably linked to foreign policy considerations, implementation of domestic adjustment policies was hampered to a certain extent.[8]

III. Export Controls and Domestic Adjustment Assistance

A. Changes in Exports and Textile Industry Policy

The export of cotton products was resumed in 1947, and from 1951 to 1969 Japan was the world's largest exporter of cotton products. The ratio of exports of cotton products started to decline after peaking in 1965. The industry, experiencing three-to-four-year cyclical fluctuations, was subjected to a series of textile industry policy measures.

Adjustments in production and capacity were first resorted to in 1952 when the exports fell off by about 20% in the aftermath of the Korean war boom. The cotton spinning industry carried out the required curtailment in operations from March 1952 to May 1953 and spinning machines, equivalent to 20% of capacity, were withdrawn (sealed off). Foreign exchange allocations to spinning firms for purchase of raw cotton were used as a means to enforce curtailment of operations and noncompliant firms were punished by a reduction in their allocations.[9] For firms engaged in weaving and other operations down the line, where raw cotton allocations could not be employed, the Law on Temporary Measures Concerning the Stabilization of Small and Medium Enterprises (1952), which became a permanent law as the Small and Medium Enterprises Stabilization Law in 1953, was used to control production and capacity by introducing a system of registration of weaving and knitting machines.

Anticipating liberalization of raw cotton imports (April 1961), a registration system for spinning machines also was adopted under the Law on Temporary Measures for Textile Industry Equipment (Old Textile Law) in 1956. In addition, a purchase-and-scrap program for eliminating "surplus looms" also came into force under this Law. The law aimed, simultaneously, at (1) modernization of equipment, upgrading and diversification of products, and strenthening of export competitiveness by promoting synthetic fibers; and (2) affecting production and capacity adjustments to avoid excess competition and to maintain reasonable export prices. Despite a call for abandoning these controls and leaving the firms to their own machinations to build up competitiveness, the textile policy continued using both (1) and (2) judiciously.[10]

Synthetic yarn was exempted from controls under the Law on Temporary Measures for Textile Industry Equipment and Related Equipment (New Textile Law) enacted in 1964. To make capacity adjustments effective, a scrap-and-build principle was adopted, which allowed the installation of one new machine for every two machines scrapped. Besides, Japan Development Bank (JDB) loans and special depreciation allowances were also used to assist efforts on rationalization and modernization of equipment. Scrapping of excess capacity, modernization of equipment, and bringing the firms to an optimum scale, conceived of as means to overcome the structural depression in 1965, formed three main pillars of the Law on Temporary Measures for the Structural Improvement of Specified Textile Industries of 1967.

The purchase-and-scrap program to deal with excess capacity, which made use of government finances, was introduced not only for weaving but was extended to spinning machinery as well during this period. The scale of these measures was increased three-fold under the Temporary Special Measures for the Textile Industry (cf. Section 3.2) to control exports to the United States and were thus accepted as a normal means for management of excess capacity (see Table II).[11] This method to scrap excess capacity was resorted to again under the joint scrapping program

(1976–1981) of the Law on Business Conversion of Small and Medium Enterprises.

As for modernization of equipment, a Structural Improvement Program was started to promote modernization of equipment in the mid- and downstream segments of the industry. After being extended for a period of two years, this program was replaced by the New Structural Improvement Program under the Law on Temporary Measures Related to Structural Improvement of Textile Industry. We will discuss capacity adjustments and the Structural Improvement Program in detail at a later stage as the two important pillars of the textile industry policy.[12]

B. The After-Effects of Japan–U.S. Textile Friction

Japan began exporting cotton products using high count yarn, processed fabric, and ready-made clothes to circumvent the catching-up by its neighboring countries, thus raising the proportion of exports to industrialized nations of Europe and America. These exports encountered import restrictions in the developed country markets as early as the 1950s. The voluntary restraints on exports to the United States during 1957–1961 were followed by adoption of Short-Term Cotton Textile Arrangement (STA, 1961) in the wake of election promises made by President Kennedy and continued into the Long-Term Textile Arrangement (LTA, 1962–1974) (see Table III). This framework of controls limited the increase in exports from 235 million square yards in 1957 to 476 million square yards in 1973, a 2.02-fold rise (4.1% average annual rate of growth). Exports to Europe were also restricted under the residual import restriction clause of GATT and the use of Article 35 to discriminate against Japan during the 1950s and then by bilateral agreements under the LTA after 1962.[13]

President Nixon also proposed import restrictions on woolen and synthetic products from Japan and three Far-Eastern countries (Korea, Taiwan, and Hong Kong) as one of his election promises in 1969. Since the textile industry was prosperous in the United States at that time, the Japanese textile industry, using "no restrictions in unaffected areas"[14] as a slogan, stiffly opposed the restrictions by establishing the Japan Textile Industry Federation (January 1970), which led to the development of a severe "Japan–U.S. wrangle" that continued for three years.[15] The dispute was finally settled, along with the return of Okinawa Islands, in a political compromise between Japanese and U.S. leaders, and a "Japan–U.S. Government to Government Agreement" (October 1971) on case-by-case restrictions on 18 fabric and clothing products was worked out. The Japan Textile Industry Federation alleged that the government forsook the industry without further efforts to pursuade the industry to extend its pro-

TABLE III

The Progress of Structural Improvement Programs

	1967	1968	1969	1970	1971	1972	1973	1974	1975	1976	1977	1978	1979	1980	1981	Total
1. Cost of Structural Improvement under Structural Improvement of Specified Textile Industries Law	(10,143)	(14,156)	(22,793)	(29,700)	(31,083)	(19,263)	(32,690)									(159,828)
(1) Specified Weaving Industry (Cotton, Staple Fiber, Silk, and Rayon)	10,143	14,156	19,758	22,504	21,563	12,922	28,800									129,846
(a) Financing by SBPC[a]	7,100	10,043	13,831	15,752	15,094	8,600	20,153									90,573
(b) Equipment Leased (Value)	7,495	12,935	16,808	20,422	19,162	11,063	24,989									112,874
(c) Lease Ratio (b/(i))(%)	(73.9)	(91.4)	(85.1)	(90.7)	(88.8)	(85.6)	(86.8)									(86.9)
(d) Associations Engaged (No.)	(28)	(36)	(38)	(40)	(40)	(35)	(39)									(41)
Proportion of Investment under the Structural Improvement of Specified Textile Industries Law to Total Investment in Cotton, Staple Fiber, Silk, and Rayon Industries (%)	32.0	43.3	47.2	36.9	37.0	25.6	44.8									No. of Assocns.
(ii) Knit Goods Manufacturing			2,446	5,939	7,325	3,816	2,262									21,808
(a) Financing by SBPC			1,704	4,155	5,095	2,663	1,541									15,158
(b) Firms Engaged (No.)			(26)	(50)	(57)	(38)	(21)									(64) No. of big firms

406

(iii) Specified Dyeing Industry	569	1,257	2,195	2,525	1,628												8,174
(a) Financing by SBPC	398	875	1,536	1,768	1,045												5,622
(b) Firms Engaged (No.)	(2)	(5)	(5)	(5)	(4)												(8)
2. Cost of Structural Improvement under Structural Improvement of Textile Industry Law						(6,898)	(12,710)	(7,391)	(5,245)	(2,586)	(6,470)	5,705					(47,005) No. of firms
(a) Financing by SBPC						4,515	7,797	4,336	2,627	1,464	4,042	3,589					28,370
(b) Equipment Leased (Value)						1,750	2,047	1,502	1,330	1,453	4,168	3,419					15,669
(c) Lease Ratio (b/(i))(%)						(25.4)	(16.1)	(20.3)	(50.0)	(56.2)	(64.4)	(60.0)					(33.3)
(d) Groups Engaged (No.)						(30)	(57)	(60)	(62)	(19)	(26)	(30)					(94) No. of groups
Subtotal (1 + 2)	10,143	14,156	22,793	29,700	31,083	19,263	32,690	6,898	12,710	7,391	5,245	2,686	6,470	5,705			206,833
Proportion of Investments under the Structural Improvement of Textile Industry Law to Total Investments in the Industries Where it Was Applicable (%)								4.8	7.1	4.3	3.8	1.6					
3. Financing by the Japan Development Bank (Finance Base)	(650)	(4,690)	(2,730)	(4,455)	(5,285)	(2,830)	(8,390)	(1,330)									(30,360)
(a) Specified Spinning Industry	650	4,690	2,530	3,425	4,245	1,730	6,525	430									24,225
(b) Specified Dyeing Industry			200	1,030	1,040	1,100	1,865	900									6,135
Total	10,793	18,846	25,623	24,155	36,368	22,093	41,080	1,330	6,898	12,710	7,391	5,245	2,586	6,470	5,705		237,193

Source: MITI Consumer Goods Industry Bureau.
"Small Business Promotion Corporation.

407

posal of all-round voluntary export restraints (June 1971). It asked the government to chalk up compensatory relief measures for the industry.[16]

The Government to Government Agreement was implemented in the form of allotment of export quotas to individual exporters under the Trade Control Ordinance, but in practice the local trade and industry associations were in charge of adjustments in shipments from individual producers under the Law Concerning the Organization of the Small and Medium Enterprise Organizations.[17] In the meantime, the government also instituted relief measures (Temporary Special Measures for the Textile Industry, amounting to ¥ 183 billion, cf. Table II) by way of purchasing and scrapping capacity (various kinds of looms, knitting machines, textile printing machines, sewing presses, and spinning machines of small and medium spinners) of the producers closing down or introducing production cuts and also provided low-interest, long-term loans through the government financial institutions specializing in small enterprises. Conflicting opinions within the government, one opposing the measures claiming that "there was no precedent of compensating businesses following negotiations with foreign countries" and the other emphasizing the "need for a more active policy in the form of a Structural Improvement Program," came to the fore.[18] In practice, however, for a large number of firms, the purchase-and-scrap program was implemented by the local associations that supervised the actual implementation of this program, by uniform allocations to the firms. As revealed in the implementation process of these measures, it is no wonder that the textile firms interpreted the Temporary Special Measures for the Textile Industry as compensation for export restraints.

The three Far-Eastern countries also implemented similar agreements and the system expanded into a Multi-Fiber Arrangement (MFA) in 1974, drawing a large variety of textile products into its fold. Almost all the developed countries and major textile exporting developing countries participated in this arrangement. The importing countries worked out bilateral agreements with the individual exporting countries and set up quota restrictions on a product-by-product basis. Accepting the need for progressive liberalization of textile trade and promotion of economic development in the developing countries in principle, the MFA had originally allowed for an annual increase of 6% in quotas for individual products. In practice, however, the rise in import quotas was restricted to 1% per year and the controls stiffened as the arrangement extended into MFA 2 (1978–1982) and MFA 3 (1983–1987), respectively. The MFA has provided the United States, the EC, and other European countries with effective controls to insulate the domestic industry against the effects of rising imports of textile products. Japan is the only developed country not resorting to import controls under MFA provisions while entering into bilateral agreements with the United States and Canada as an exporting country.

C. Capacity Adjustment

Capacity registration and the purchase-and-scrap program to deal with excess capacity form two important pillars of the capacity adjustment policy.

The capacity registration system required registration of capacity presently held, limited the number of product varieties produced, and restricted the use of existing nonregistered capacity and the installation of new capacity. This measure was employed for the spinning industry only under the Old and New Textile Laws, while the measure has been in force for the weaving industry for the past 30 years under the provisions of the Small and Medium Enterprises Stabilization Law and the Law on the Organization of Small and Medium Enterprise Organizations. This measure was also resorted to in industries other than the textile industry but was gradually discontinued. Of the 11 industries in which this measure is still in force, 10 are related to the textile industry.

Scrapping of excess capacity was introduced in the case of looms under the Old Textile Law and was extended to the whole of the textile industry, including spinning, under the Law on Temporary Measures for Structural Improvement of Textile Industry. The government finances were used to purchase and scrap the excess, which was calculated with reference to the demand and supply projections prepared by the government in collaboration with the industry. The financing of major large- and medium-scale spinning firms was carried out through the LTCB (Long-Term Credit Bank) and JDB (at around 8% rate of interest), while subsidies and low-interest loans to small and medium firms were provided through the Small Business Promotion Corporation.[19] Table II reveals that the scrapping-of-capacity program of the government had cost a total of ¥380 billion by 1981 and 350 thousand looms and 5 million spindles of spinning machines (including thread plying machines) were scrapped. This amounted to scrapping of one-third of the number of looms and two-fifths of the spindles existing in 1966.

The use of the capacity registration system, controls on building up new capacity under the scrap-and-build program, and the purchase-and-scrap strategy were expected to solve the problem of excess capacity, but the problem still persists. Some of the factors responsible for such a situation are as follows: (1) The conversion factor used for exchanging old and new looms was too small, leading to a rise in the real productive capacity as the scrap-and-build program progressed. (2) The old-style looms, which were not subject to registration, escaped the controls and were utilized during business upswings. Measures to register a large part of these un-registered looms were adopted in 1973.[20]

Finally, the biggest stumbling block was (3) the recourse by the firms to unscrupulous practices in terms of neglect of voluntary scrapping of capacity without compensation as registration papers became an asset in the process of repeated application of purchase and scrap measures. These registrations were used as collateral for obtaining bank loans to renovate equipment or were transferred at a premium. The premium on registration certificates appeared during the large-scale purchases under the Temporary Special Measures for the Textile Industry during 1971–1973, fluctuated with the changing business environment in the textile industry, and rose sharply in 1977 when the joint scrapping was undertaken on funds supplied by the Small Business Promotion Corporation.

The registration system has attracted severe criticism from without as well as within the industry, and the number of believers in the ability of this system to redress the problems that it was supposed to deal with, i.e., capacity adjustment, has dwindled. It was alleged that the obsolete machinery that would have been discarded by the firms on their own in-itiative was being held on to in the hope of getting it approved as surplus machinery to be scrapped under the purchase-and-scrap program. There is, however, a strong demand for continuation of the registration system and raising the conversion factor from the mid- and downstream firms in textile centers. This is due to the fact that (1) the registration system has been contributing to the systematic organization of the textile centers through the associations, and (2) it is expected to play a role in carrying out adjustments while preventing the entry by large firms. In the case of spinning machines in the upstream segment, 480,000 excess spindles were voluntarily scrapped under the Law on Temporary Measures for the Sta-bilization of Specified Depressed Industries.[21]

D. Structural Improvement Program

The Structural Improvement Program has usually been justified as a form of "assistance to small and medium firms lacking fund raising and business management capabilities in their efforts to adjust to sudden changes in the business environment." The term is believed to have come from the "Structural Readjustment" theory developed by the OECD Spe-cial Committee on Textiles and implemented by the United Kingdom and France.[22]

To date, Japan has formulated two Structural Improvement Programs.

These are the Old Structural Improvement Program (1967–1973) under the Law on Temporary Measures for Structural Improvement of Specified Textile Industry and the New Structural Improvement Program (1975–1981) under the Law on Temporary Measures for the Structural Improvement of Textile Industry.

The Old Structural Improvement Program, emphasizing the need for strengthening international competitiveness, concentrated on overall modernization of equipment in textile centers as a whole and worked in the direction of increasing firm size through concentration (mergers). The business associations in "production centers" formulated plans for scrapping worn-out machinery and for the automation and installation of modern equipment under the guidance of the prefectural government. The associations allocated the plan targets to individual firms on the basis of requests received and capability of the firms to implement the program, and the firms with approval were provided with loans for the Improvement Program by the Small Business Promotion Corporation (70% of the needed finances at 2.6% rate of interest to be redeemed in 10 years after allowing for two years of deferment).

How can one evaluate the impact of the Old Structural Improvement Program? The program has come under severe criticism for its failure to meet its objectives in terms of either the reduction in equipment and number of firms or the increase in scale and improvement of business environment for the remaining firms.[23] These criticisms are, however, based on averages for the weaving industry as a whole and include the large number of small and tiny firms that did not participate in the Structural Improvement Program. If we restrict ourselves to firms participating in the Structural Improvement Program, we find a significant rise in the rate of automation as well as labor productivity. Thus it may be possible to conclude that the Old Structural Improvement Program did contribute to the nurturing of a group of efficient firms.[24]

The loans provided by the Corporation were subject to the same arrangement under the New Structural Improvement Program, though the policy emphasis shifted to increasing knowledge-intensity and promoting cooperation among firms engaged in different activities within the same textile centers. The firms were encouraged to form groups strengthening vertical ties and assistance was provided for setting up Product Development Centers and other joint facilities. In contrast to the modernization of mechanical equipment, the main focus of the Old Structural Improvement Program, the New Structural Improvement Program concentrated on promoting modernization in the organization of the textile centers to raise their efficiency.

The rate of utilization, however, was quite low for the New Structural

Improvement Program as revealed in Table III, due supposedly to difficulties encountered in availing the provisions of this program. It is pointed out that (1) the obligation to set up Product Development Centers was not necessarily coducive to its use; (2) the nucleus around which the firms could group themselves was lacking as the local trading firms were excluded initially; and (3) joint functioning was not compatible with development of new products and technological improvements that require a certain amount of trade secrecy. The measures for increasing knowledge-intensity and strengthening ties among firms pursuing different activities are basically dictated by the market mechanism as discussed earlier in Section II, C, and application of such measures to assist small and medium enterprises lacking the ability to undertake them on their own is therefore justified. Since these measures impinge on the foundations of business practices, there is a limit to what the government can accomplish in this area.[25]

Besides the above mentioned measures, interest-free loans (to firms with less than 100 workers, up to 50% of the fund requirements with an upper limit of ¥15 million) and leasing of equipment (to firms with less than 20 workers) were also provided under the Law on Aiding Small and Medium Enterprises with Funds for Modernization (1956–); loans for business switch-overs and closures (at 7.3% to 7.8% rate of interest, redeemable over five years with an upper limit of ¥27 million) were provided under the Law on Temporary Measures for the Business Conversion of Small and Medium Enterprises (1978–). All these measures were carried out under the policy framework for small and medium firms, but the textile firms were, by far, the biggest group benefiting from these measures.[26]

IV. Import Policy and Competitive Pressures

A. Increase in Imports and Reduction in Tariffs

As revealed in Figure 15.2, Japan started importing textile products toward the end of 1960s. Import of garments accounted for over half of these (54% in 1982), followed by that of cloth (20%) and yarn (15%). The four neighboring countries—Korea, China, Taiwan, and Hong Kong—supplied 62% to 66% (1976–1982) of these imports. Falling competitive power of the Japanese textile industry in low-quality standardized textile products and repeated appreciation of the Japanese yen on three occasions in the 1970s were major factors contributing to this trend. Adoption of import liberalization measures during the same period was also responsible to some extent.

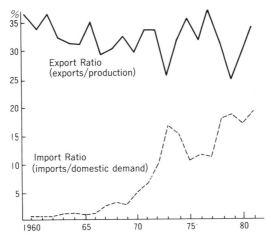

Fig. 15.2. Trends in textile export and import ratio (quantity base). From Tsusansho (MITI), *Sen'i Jukyu Hyo* (Textile Demand-Supply Tables).

The Japanese import duties on textile products were scaled down as a part of the trade liberalization policy for manufactures beginning with the Kennedy Round (KR) through to the Tokyo Round (TR). (See Figure 15.3.) The import duties on textile products in the developed countries, which were substantially high to begin with, came down and ranged rather widely between 5% to 25% in Japan and EC and between 5% to 45% in the United States following the KR. This range was expected to be narrowed down to 5% to 15% for Japan and EC and 5% to 20% for the United States by the end of the TR in 1987. Japan, however, undertook a unilateral cut in its tariff rates in 1972 and thus achieved the targets set for the post-TR period at a much earlier date and presently has the lowest import duties on textile products in the world.[27]

In addition, the Generalized Scheme of Preferences (GSP) was adopted in 1971, which benefited mostly Korea, Taiwan, and Hong Kong. It is also true that the reduction in preferential tariffs on textile products, which would normally have been brought down to zero, were reduced only to half the level, proclaiming textile imports as "items of extreme importance," and in a number of instances, preferential tariffs were instituted on an item-to-item basis. An import rush occurs at the beginning of each fiscal year in April in order to take advantage of the preferential system thereby heralding import expansion into Japan. The Japanese import liberalization measures stand out against the United States, which excluded items covered by the Multi-Fiber Arrangement (MFA) from the GSP right

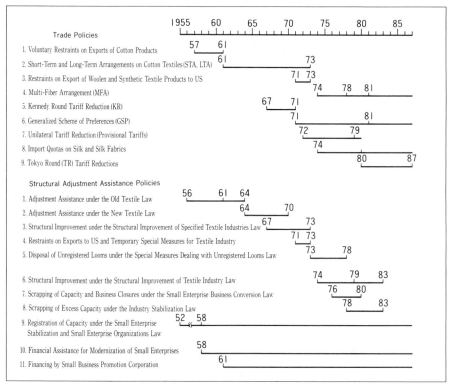

Fig. 15.3. Chronology of trade and structural adjustment assistance policies in textile industry. From Tsusansho (1979).

from the beginning and the EC, which also ran for the cover of MFA for all practical purposes in 1982.[28]

B. Demand for Import Restrictions

The import spurt of 1973–1974 was an abnormal departure from the long-term trend in import growth. There was a manifold increase in imports in the wake of the worldwide commodity boom prior to the oil crisis because of an exceptionally high level of speculative demand at distribution stages induced by the boom. A large number of importers rushed to secure supply sources in various countries and suffered heavy losses on piled-up inventories as a result, which also accounts for their cautious approach to import expansion in the aftermath.

Following this spurt in imports, demand for import restrictions emerged for the first time in Japan. The Japan Textile Industry Federation (cf. Section III, B) set up a committee to deal with imports in May 1973 to make all-out efforts to get import restrictions instituted at various levels. First, the government was asked to implement MFA provisions and introduce import restrictions, including bilateral agreements in respect to the nine items for which the import increase was very steep. Second, the importers and import associations were asked to meet periodically to restrain inorderly imports. Finally, the exporters in Korea and Taiwan were requested, at the industry level, to implement voluntary export restraints. The rise in imports from 1978 onwards was spurred on by the appreciation of the yen, which rose to its peak value in 1978, but remained within the limits of the long-run growth trend. The demand for import restrictions escalated as imports rose steadily.

The rise in imports of cotton yarn and cotton cloth has been most remarkable in recent years. The imports of technologically simple and standardized 20-count yarn during January to September 1982 amounted to 48.1% of the total domestic production, a 2.33-fold rise over the same period in the preceding year. The Japan Spinners' Association petitioned that antidumping duties be imposed on imports of cotton yarn from Korea and countervailing duties on cotton yarn from Pakistan. Repression of domestic prices because of imports of low-priced yarn from these countries was advanced as the main reason. The plea against Korea was withdrawn (June 1983) following the announcement of voluntary export restraints by the Korean Spinners Association, and the inquiry into the imports from Pakistan was dropped (February 1984) as the Pakistan government agreed to withdraw subsidies to the industry.

The Japan Weavers' Association,[29] on the other hand, has been opposed to the rising trend in imports as such and has taken every opportunity to warn against imports of cotton cloth from China. The demand for import controls from manufacturers of garments has been, as compared to Europe and the United States, on a low key as the Japanese apparel makers and wholesalers have followed a carefully designed plan for the import of low-priced products that form a major proportion of garment imports, and China has quickly emerged as an overseas base for garment making in recent years.

The main arguments for import restrictions can be summarized as follows.[30] (1) A sudden spurt in imports hampers domestic efforts at production adjustment and scrapping of capacity and renders voluntary switch-overs to other products or industries difficult by throwing the markets into a disarray. (2) The use of MFA in the European and American countries could lead to a rush to unrestricted Japanese markets, thereby deepening the confusion. (3) A sudden rise in imports of some textile products would not only destroy the domestic industries in direct competition but also could impair linkage effects, thereby stagnating other textile industries where Japan still holds a comparative advantage.

The first of these arguments is close to the "exigency import controls" argument justifying such controls for avoiding excessive adjustment costs that could result from a sudden rise in imports[31] and is taken note of in Article 19 of the GATT. The second and third arguments call for preventive controls and Article 19 of the GATT is inapplicable here. Besides, there are complicated conflicts of interests among textile industries linked to one another through input–output relationships. For example, controls on imports of cotton yarn, as demanded by the spinning industry, would raise its domestic price, which would invite stiff opposition from the weaving industry and would necessitate similar import controls in that industry as well. It is highly probable that such import controls would not stop at restricting imports of specific products but would spread to the whole range of textile products.

C. Import Surveillance and Administrative Guidance

The sum and substance of the government response to the textile industry's call for import restrictions is documented in the Textile Industry Council's "Recommendations of 1976" (December 1976). In the light of the experience of a surge in imports during 1973–1974, it emphasized the "importance of grasping the trends in domestic demand, imports and price movements as early as possible so as to maintain a proper balance in demand and supply" and recommended provisions for (1) a system of import surveillance, (2) administrative guidance to importers, (3) an appeal to the foreign suppliers, at the private level, for orderly exporting, and (4) implementation of temporary import restriction measures approved under GATT if a sharp spurt in imports based on unfair trade threatened to damage the domestic producers seriously.

Of the above, (1) has been implemented for major items since 1976 and (2) has been resorted to in the case of cotton yarn since 1981. As for (3), the Japan Spinners' Association has been meeting periodically with their counterparts in Korea and Pakistan, while the Japan Cotton Weavers' Association has been in close contact with the producers' organization in China. We have already mentioned the institution of inquiries into dumping of yarn and unfair trade practices in Japanese markets, an example of (4). Furthermore, a recent report on textile policy (November 1983, discussed later) does not exclude the possibility of resorting to import restrictions under MFA, but the authorities have been cautious in putting these measures into practice.

Measures (1) to (3) are preventive in nature and are inadequate to block a rise in imports. It has been contended that since Japan resorts to import restrictions through the above-mentioned measures, it need not take recourse to the more open measures under MFA, but as shown hereunder, this belief is contrary to the available evidence.[32]

1. Import Surveillance System

The Japan Textile Importers' Association conducts a monthly questionnaire survey of 597 importers (210 association members and the rest nonmembers with a certain minimum import performance), on behalf of the Ministry of International Trade and Industry, regarding import contracts signed within the reporting month for delivery within 3 to 6 months (totals by type of commodity). These responses are collected by the Association by the 10th of the following month and the compiled information is fed back to the respondents by the 20th. This was supposed to disseminate information regarding the overall import trends to individual importers and prevent "unguided imports."

This survey covers 80% of the total imports. Although the responses are requested in the name of the Director of MITI Consumer Goods Industries Bureau, respondents are not too eager to comply with this voluntary survey because the feedbacks they receive are the only incentive. So, the association has to keep on urging the firms for responses to keep the rate of coverage high.

2. Administrative Guidance

The International Trade Division of the MITI Consumer Goods Industries Bureau, on the other hand, collects information from a score of importers regarding their current import agreements every 10 days in the case of specific commodities whose imports have risen significantly. If the imports are found to exceed the estimates made by the Textile Industry Council by a significant margin, the Division contacts by telephone a dozen top importers of the Cotton Yarn Council of the Japan Textile Importers' Association to express its concerns regarding the rising trend in imports and requests them to refrain from entering into speculative import agreements. The Division, however, refrains from mentioning specific figures for import reduction. The Division cannot ask the importers to cancel their contracts, but it does request them to delay the deliveries and refrain from entering into new contracts. The monetary and personnel costs involved in telephonic contacts limits the number of firms that can be included and hence the effectiveness of administrative guidance. Such administrative guidance may be useful in the case of import of cotton yarn where the imports are concentrated in the hands of a small number of large importers, but it is difficult to implement in product categories with a wide range of varieties and where the number of importers is large.

The effectiveness of administrative guidance is limited because of the small number of firms targeted for guidance. Table IV shows cotton yarn imports by members and nonmembers compiled by the Textile Importers' Association from invoice statistics (imports actually cleared at the customs). The imports of cotton yarn rose by 190% in 1977–1978 and 20% in 1978–1979. It is clear that whereas imports by the member firms rose only marginally in both the years, imports by the nonmember firms increased substantially both in terms of the number of importers as well as quantity. It seems that administrative guidance was successful in restraining imports by the member firms but could not reach the nonmember firms. Since the number of weaving firms using imported cotton yarn was limited, entry of new firms into the distribution network may have been relatively difficult. This suggests that either the nonmember importers were somehow linked with big member firms or that the member firms were importing in the name of dummy nonmember firms.

It may be possible to prevent the recurrence of an import surge "unrelated to actual demand" such that as happened in 1973–1974[33] by disseminating reliable information about current import trends and providing administrative guidance to specific importers. The textile imports can be kept in order in this sense. Administrative guidance, however, affects only a small number of importers and does so without any legal coercion;

TABLE IV
Imports of Cotton Yarn by Association Members and Nonmembers

	Total Imports (Bales)	Members		Nonmembers
		%[a]	Number of Importers	Number of Importers
1975	146,521	88.0	54	13
1976	218,903	92.2	33	59
1977	148,241	83.6	28	56
1978	436,594	53.6	31	124
1979	520,462	45.7	37	143
1980	363,877	55.2	26	97
1981	394,995	53.7	32	94
1982	596,672[b]	—	—	—

Source: Nihon Sen'i Yunyu Kumiai (Japan Textiles Importers' Association), *Zuhyo de Miru Sen'i Hin Yunyu no Suii* (Textile Imports in Figures), 1977–81 issues.
[a]Percent of total value of imports.
[b]Preliminary.

therefore, it has only a limited effect on controlling overall growth in imports. As is clear from the above analysis, administrative guidance is unable to keep imports from growing when imports follow actual demand under the influence of market forces. Administrative guidance, therefore, is no match for the import restrictions practiced by the American and European nations under the MFA. However, as the actual functioning of the system is unclear except to those who are directly involved, it is easily misunderstood.

V. Conclusion

The above discussion can be summarized as follows. First, the Japanese textile industry has undergone significant structural changes in response to changes in internal and external environment during the past three decades. Measures to reduce labor input, the use of synthetic raw materials, product differentiation, and the opening up of new markets were actively undertaken as domestic labor costs rose, the value of the yen appreciated, and competition was intensified with the products from developing countries.

Second, competitive pressure in the domestic and foreign markets was the main force inducing individual firms to carry out adjustments actively. This began with competition against the products from developing countries in foreign markets spreading to competition with imports in the domestic market and finally to competition among domestically produced goods. It also reflected the deteriorating conditions in export markets as voluntary restraints on exports to the European and American markets and import liberalization policies were adopted. In this regard, it differed from the European and American countries, which resorted to import restrictions under the MFA.

Finally, on the other hand, small and medium firms in the midstream section of this industry have continued to receive substantial domestic adjustment assistance, but a part of it was, as discussed earlier, in the form of compensation for the adverse effects of the commercial policy.[34] Scrapping of excess capacity under the capacity registration system and measures taken under the Structural Improvement Programs have been major tools of the adjustment policy. While the latter may be credited for a contribution to structural adjustment through subsidization of modernization of equipment, the former tended to delay voluntary scrapping of capacity and business switch-overs.

Today, the Japanese textile policy is standing at crossroads of change. In anticipation of the expiry of the Textile Law in June 1984, the joint proposal, "Textile Industry in a New Era," announced d in October 1983 by the Textile Industry Council and the Textile Industry Division of the Industrial Structure Council spells out three areas of prime importance for the revitalization of the Japanese textile industry.

1. Development of an advanced, knowledge-intensive industry based on technological change and inventiveness.

2. Development of a system industry taking full advantage of the comprehensive inter-relationships existing in the industry.

3. Internationalization of the industry within the framework of an international division of labor.

In 1974, when the Law on Temporary Measures on the Structural Improvement of Textile Industry came into force, the first import rush peaked and consequently the industry attempted to invigorate itself primarily on the basis of domestic demand. Now, the industry attempts to revitalize itself and move on to promoting exports, guided by the advance of electronics and other related machinery industries and the 1980–1981 export boom in synthetic continuous fiber fabrics. Furthermore, the government has been called on to dismantle the subsidized scrapping of excess capacity and Structural Improvement Programs under the administrative reform, and the industry itself has demanded that domestic adjustment assistance be replaced by import restrictions. This is a complete turnabout of the existing textile policy in Japan, but such a course would, in fact, as the discussion in this chapter shows, result only in delaying the process of domestic adjustment.

There seems to be a strong resistance to any changes in the existing policy. The new proposal, while reiterating the need for abolishing the registration system, a proposal that was announced under the "1976 Recommendations," makes no concrete suggestions as to how long the system would be retained.

Although left out of the above discussion, the Raw Silk and Sugar Prices Stabilization Corporation intervened in the purchase and sale of domestic raw silk to maintain the market prices of silk within a specific range (¥14,000 per kg. at present) in order to preserve the incomes of domestic sericulturists under the Silk Thread Price Stabilization Law. Besides, an exclusive system for import of raw silk was adopted under which imports of cheap foreign silk (¥7,000 to ¥8,000 per kg) were prohibited to all but the Corporation. On the other hand, bilateral agreements with China and South Korea limit the imports of silk fabrics quantitatively. The rise in the prices of silk products in the wake of domestic price support and import restrictions resulted in a declining demand, and a huge amount of inventory of surplus silk accumulated with the Corporation. Even with these measures, the production of raw silk and woven silk has been falling, and the business environment has worsened. This serves as a good example of how excessive protective measures can result in the preservation of economic irrationality and the contraction of the industry as a whole.

Expansion in domestic demand or exports can no longer be expected, even in the case of cotton and synthetic fiber, with a wide variety of uses and possibilities for product differentiation. As product differentiation, upgrading, and the introduction of innovated mechanical equipment proceed under the conditions of quantitatively limited demand, it may not be possible to avoid the switch-overs and closures of some of the inefficient firms and the unemployment of older workers.[35] The pressures generated by import competition are but only one of the factors behind industrial change. A shift in the emphasis of domestic adjustment assistance policy from capacity adjustment to business switch-overs and closures and measures to deal with laid-off workers while maintaining domestic and foreign competitive pressures seems to be highly desirable.

Notes

1. The data used in the present study were made available by the Consumer Goods Industries Bureau of the Ministry of International Trade and Industry and the Japan Textile Importers' Association. We also benefited from the comments on an earlier draft by Kikutaro Takizawa (Nagoya University) and Masayuki Yoshioka (Teijin Co.). The penetrating comments from the participants in Zushi Conference, especially Masao Baba, Konosuke Odaka, Sueo Sekiguchi, and Toshimasa Tsuruta, were appreciated. Suggestions by the editors of this volume also proved helpful. While we are deeply indebted to all those who contributed directly or indirectly in the preparation of this study, the author alone is responsible for any shortcomings that still remain.

2. See Yamazawa [1981a] for details of the "catching-up" process in the neighboring Asian Nations.

3. The *Textile Demand and Supply Tables* are prepared by the Demand-Supply Estimation Division of the Textile Industry Council and provide information on all textile products weighted in terms of yarn. That is to say, textile raw materials like cotton, wool, and chemical and synthetic fibers are excluded. For the composition of imports by commodity and country refer to Section 3.1.

4. For recent technological improvements in the textile industry, cf. Yamazawa [1983].

5. For example, consider the merger of Toyobo and Kurehabo in April 1966 and of Nippon Rayon and Nichibo into Unitika in October 1969. The number of spinning firms declined from 139 in 1961 to 84 in 1977. Cf. Nihon Boseki Kyokai [1979].

6. "An Analysis of Mid-year Settlement of Accounts of Synthetic Fiber Makers and Large Spinners", *Nihon Sen' i Shinbum* (Japan Textile News), November 25–December 29, 1982.

7. One cannot, however, neglect the importance of tiny firms. Plants with one to three workers (with 10 looms on the average) formed 51% of the total number of cotton and spun rayon weaving establishments, accounting for 6% of total value of shipments

(Census of Manufactures, 1979). For an example, see Yamazawa [1981b]. Furthermore, very few of these firms participated in the Structural Improvement Programs discussed later.

8. For the theoretical underpinnings of the policy toward small- and medium-scale firms, see Chapter 20 of the present volume. The reason for adopting a specific policy toward those firms in the textile industry, in contrast to those in other industries, lies in the fact that no effective policy could be formulated without taking into account their mutual relationships with large firms in the upstream segment of the industry. On the other hand, it also functioned as a policy for declining industries by bearing a part of the adjustment costs of industries with deteriorating comparative advantage through public funds, as discussed in Section II, A.

9. See Nihon Boseki Kyokai [1982], Chapter 4, Section 3. The raw cotton allocation system was also employed to control an increase in spinning capacity under the Occupation administration, but as allocations under this system were based on the capacity held by individual firms, it generated intense competition among the firms to increase capacity.

10. See Nihon Boseki Kyokai [1979], Chapter 1, for the statement of Kiyoshi Tsuchiya in 1961 in the Textile Industry Council and assertions made by some influential firms like Nisshin Spinning

11. As discussed later (cf. Section II, C.), excess capacity was designated only after determining the registered capacity and demand-supply estimates; the theoretical justification for the use of policy measures to scrap is not very clear.

12. The Structural Improvement Program would include capacity adjustment as well if defined in a broader sense, but we stick to the narrower definition of the concept in this chapter.

13. Cf. Nihon Boseki Kyokai [1982], Chapter 3, Section 5.

14. Nihon Sen' i Sangyo Renmei (Japan Textile Industry Federation) "Declaration of Voluntary Restrictions on Exports to America," June 1971, as reported in Nihon Boseki Kyokai [1979].

15. From the title of Destler, Fukui, and Sato [1979].

16. The Japanese Textile Industry Federation filed a petition (later retracted) against the illegality of the Government-to-Government Agreement. The details of Japan–U.S. textile confrontation and its political analysis can be found in Destler et al. [1979] and Chapter 3 of Ohtake [1979]. Also, cf. Nihon Boseki Kyokai [1979].

17. The controls on individual items under the Government-to-Government Agreement were put into operation by setting up quotas of export licenses under the Trade Control Ordinance and of shipment adjustments under the Small and Medium Business Enterprise Organizations Law. In practice, the latter measure was resorted to in the main. Difficulties faced in the implementation of adjustments, however, led to removal of woven goods in 1976 and knit goods in 1981. Cloth and cottonwear were the only remaining categories implementing this system in 1983. The export association supervised export restraints (allocation of quotas and reallocation of used and unused quotas, etc.) for woven goods and knitwear in accordance with Article 11 of the Export–Import Transaction Law.

18. Ohtake [1979], p. 126.

19. Item 8 in Table II, in effect, amounts to subsidy as the business associations disbursed 45% of the funds received from the Small Business Promotion Corporation with the remainder invested and to be repaid later (4 year grace period and 16-year maturity).

20. The Law on Special Measures for Unregistered Looms came into force through the efforts of legislators from four political parties, the Liberal Democratic Party, the Socialist Party, the Democratic Socialist Party, and the Komei Party. Of the 160,000

      unregistered looms (a large number of these is assumed to have been held by very small weavers) three-fourths were allowed to be registered unconditionally, and of the remaining one-fourth, registration was allowed if desired on payment of a registration fee, and whatever remained unregistered were purchased and scrapped.

21. Nihon Boseki Kyokai [1982] Part 3, Section 3.

22. See Nihon Boseki Kyokai [1979], p. 87. Initially, "structural improvement" was referred to as "structural adjustment," a direct translation of the term from the English.

23. Yonezawa [1981].

24. The data on fixed assets *(K)*, annual increments in fixed assets *(I)*, value added *(Y)*, and number of workers *(N)*, are taken for textile industries at the JSIC 3–4 digit level from *Census of Manufactures*. It is seen that the investment ratio *(I/Y)* peaked at 15%–29% in 1970–1971, while labor productivity is seen to have risen 2 to 2.5 times during 1967–1973. For the spread of automated looms, see Yamazawa [1981b].

25. In 1980, investment financing amounted to ¥4 billion and leasing of equipment to ¥3 billion, one-tenth of the respective totals. Of the 116 industries covered under the Business Conversion Law, 24 were textile industries. (Chusho Kigyo Cho [1982]).

26. According to a questionnaire survey regarding investments by small and medium weavers (September 1982), self-financing accounted for 12%, borrowings from financial institutions for 43%, and policy finance for 39% of the total investments made, indicating that the financing by regional trading companies and yarn makers was minimal. Furthermore, 75% of the respondents expressed a lack of desire to invest in the near future (1–2 years) on account of unclear trends in demand and no assurances for funds for commissions. Policy financing no doubt constituted a major fraction of investment funds, but the role of individual decision making is also quite apparent. The above is based on unpublished materials from the Textile Industry Council.

27. Yamazawa [1980] pp. 448–450.

28. Yamazawa [1980] pp. 450–452.

29. The full name is Japan Cotton and Staple Fiber Weavers' Association.

30. For a discussion of textile import restrictions see Emoto [1974], Hirai [1978–79], and Nihon Boseki Kyokai [1982].

31. Refer to Chapter 14, Section II of the present volume.

32. For example, Keesing and Wolf [1980]. Our analysis of the import surveillance system and administrative guidance depends heavily on the questionnaire survey by the Textiles Importers' Association.

33. At this time imports were carried out with no buyers lined up for purchase of imported yarn; consequently, distributors' inventories piled up.

34. There seems to have been no attempt at coordinated implementation of the capacity adjustment and structural improvement plans under various textile laws and the textile-related commercial policy being resorted to at the same time. However, since the commercial policy was determined and implemented on the basis of exogenous considerations while the indigenously determined policies had sufficient room for manipulation, the latter was also used to supplement the former in quite a few instances.

35. The proportion of young female workers was traditionally high in the textile industry and as these workers were lured into other industries during the phase of rapid growth, a shortage of job seekers in this industry became a problem. The older male workers, on the other hand, were primarily owners of small and tiny businesses of their own and the policy measures for the small and medium firms did help this segment. Business closures and business switch-overs within this group are expected to rise in the future.

CHAPTER 16

The Shipbuilding Industry

YOSHIE YONEZAWA[1]

Department of Economics
Aoyama Gakuin University
Tokyo, Japan

I. Introduction

The characteristics of the development process of the Japanese ship-building industry[2] are clearly brought out in Table I. While the problems faced by the Japanese shipbuilding industry during the 1960 to 1980 period are brought in a clear relief, it also defines the scope of the present study.

In terms of orders received, the demand for ships grew rapidly between 1960 to 1973 despite a few minor setbacks in between. The situation, how-ever, changed drastically with the first oil shock in 1973. The demand for ships dipped suddenly in 1974 to bring it down to 30% of the 1973 level and further down to 10% in 1978, a level close to what prevailed around 1961. Thus, the demand expansion that had taken a dozen years to build up vanished in a matter of just five years.

The share of the Japanese shipbuilding industry in world orders for ships grew from 24% (1960) to 64% (1966), well over 50% in the first half of 1960s, whereafter it fluctuated in damped oscillations converging to the 50% level. Exports accounted for the most part of production during this period, while imports were almost nil. No other major shipbuilding nation had experienced such a structure of export–import dependency.

This trend is clear in terms of completions as well, although in a some-what smoother form. The fall in share in terms of completions, however, was steeper during 1975 to 1978. Korea and other countries came up strongly during this period and the earnings position of the domestic ship-building industry deteriorated even further. These fluctuations in share foreshadowed the internal and external predicament in which the Japanese shipbuilding industry was placed.

TABLE I

Development of the Japanese Shipbuilding Industry

	Orders Received		Completions		Foreign Dependence[a]		Production				Profit Differential[c] (Manufacturing = 100)		Wage Differential[d] (Manufacturing = 100)	
	Amount (1973 = 100)	Share (%)	Amount (1975 = 100)	Share (%)	Export Dependence (%)	Import Dependence (%)	Keels Laid (1974 = 100)	Number of Persons Engaged (1975 = 100)	Amount of Capital (1976 = 100)[b]	Berth, Construction Dock Capacity (1975 = 100)	Shipbuilding[e]	Automobiles[f]	Shipbuilding[e]	Automobiles[f]
1960	2.7	23.9	10.8	21.9	—	—	8.7	63.1	—	—	—	—	191.1	167.4
1961	8.6	34.4	10.2	21.3	—	—	11.8	67.1	—	—	—	—	178.3	158.6
1962	5.8	34.6	12.2	25.3	—	—	10.4	64.3	12.8	—	70.3	128.7	184.5	162.8
1963	13.0	39.2	13.4	25.1	—	—	16.1	64.5	15.0	—	95.8	171.0	175.4	161.0
1964	17.5	48.4	22.1	38.7	66.6	0.0	23.0	67.9	16.7	40.5	125.4	178.4	174.4	146.2
1965	20.9	49.5	28.8	41.5	52.8	0.0	28.8	72.6	20.5	50.7	123.6	167.8	175.9	148.1
1966	31.8	63.7	38.2	46.0	59.7	0.0	35.8	71.0	23.8	60.1	121.1	166.3	167.8	149.1
1967	26.4	42.2	42.5	47.6	60.9	0.0	42.6	77.8	26.9	58.2	98.6	183.9	170.1	142.2
1968	26.5	36.5	49.1	50.0	61.1	0.0	43.4	80.3	29.8	61.8	104.2	206.1	167.0	137.0
1969	34.5	40.8	54.0	48.9	60.4	0.0	50.9	76.8	31.6	64.0	91.1	164.3	161.0	137.2
1970	52.4	47.0	59.4	48.1	60.7	0.0	53.7	82.4	39.0	84.5	97.6	132.7	157.1	141.5
1971	45.3	53.6	65.5	45.6	54.9	0.0	62.6	86.8	46.9	89.9	139.5	108.8	155.4	139.1
1972	52.0	61.5	75.7	48.1	58.5	0.0	65.6	95.1	56.7	95.3	136.0	123.5	164.6	145.0
1973	100.0	48.0	86.8	48.5	69.6	0.0	78.8	96.6	70.1	97.9	128.4	125.4	156.0	143.9
1974	28.1	38.7	99.4	50.4	83.1	0.0	100.0	98.3	66.9	100.0	123.2	94.4	151.0	134.8
1975	19.5	49.1	100.0	49.7	82.0	0.0	65.7	100.0	82.0	99.8	102.3	116.3	149.3	146.4
1976	21.3	56.3	93.3	46.8	78.8	0.0	47.2	90.1	100.0	99.8	87.8	172.6	150.7	147.7
1977	17.2	52.4	68.9	42.5	83.8	0.0	34.7	82.0	97.9	99.5	84.2	189.7	151.7	145.8
1978	10.4	44.3	37.1	34.7	76.9	0.0	17.7	66.4	86.7	99.5	31.2	164.7	163.1	153.3
1979	23.7	49.0	27.6	32.9	60.0	0.0	22.8	48.8	65.0	99.5	9.8	147.8	147.7	159.0
1980	28.6	52.4	35.9	46.5	55.1	0.0	36.8	48.0	60.1	65.0	62.8	125.8	124.6	159.5

Sources: Nihon Senpaku Yshutsu Kumiai [Japan Ship Exporters' Association], Zosen Kankei Tokei Shiryo [Statistical Materials Related to Shipbuilding Industry, International and Domestic Volumes]; Tsusansho [MITI], Kogyo Tokei Hyo [Census of Manufactures, Industry Volumes]; and Nihon Ginko [Bank of Japan], Keizai Tokei Nenpo [Economic Statistics Annual].

a As a percentage of launchings and completions.
b The value of tangible fixed assets (beginning of year), by the price index of investment goods.
c The profit rate is the ratio of (value added–cash earnings) to the value of tangible fixed assets.
d Wages of annual cash earnings per person engaged.
e JSIC 3641 (Shipbuilding and Repairs Industry).
f JSIC 3611 (Manufacture of Automobiles).

How did the firms respond to such a reversal in their business environment and how far were they successful in meeting their objective? Trends in production (starts), employment (persons engaged), and investment (amount of capital) clearly reflect the time profile of these responses. Production peaked in 1974, followed a year later by a peak in employment, which in turn was followed by an investment peak with a one year lag. Since then, falling production has led rapid adjustments in employment and investment.

The differences in characteristics of the Japanese shipbuilding industry during the 1960s and the 1970s can be vividly captured by designating the former as the decade of rising international competitiveness and the latter as the period of industrial adjustment. Let us look at the extent to which it was successful. Table I reveals the wages of workers engaged in shipbuilding to be over 50% higher than the average for manufacturing workers.[3] As the wages in other industries also rose sharply during this period, the advantage gradually disappeared. Since 1979, wages in this industry have been lower than those of automobile workers. In contrast, the profit rate in this industry surpassed the manufacturing average only twice, 1964–1966 and 1972–1975. The decline in the rate of profit during 1975–1980 was beyond anything expected of the "world's topmost shipbuilding industry."

Attainment of international competitiveness followed by the success of industrial adjustment, as detailed above, tends to give an impression that industrial policy played an important role and was effective in the development of the Japanese shipbuilding industry. But how far can one agree with such an evaluation of industrial policy in this industry? The present chapter adopts the following approach to answer this querry. Section II presents the environment and structure within which the industrial policy in the Japanese shipbuilding industry was implemented. This is followed in Section III by a discussion of "planned shipbuilding" and "deferred-payment exports," two main pillars of the postwar industrial policy in shipping and shipbuilding, as well as their significance for the shipbuilding industry, while adjustment assistance policies adopted in the latter half of the 1970s are outlined in Section IV. Finally, Section V statistically analyzes the effects of these policies and draws implications therefrom.

II. The Policy Environment and Structure of the Shipbuilding Industry

In this section we investigate the environment in which the shipbuilding industrial policy, believed to have affected the development process of the Japanese shipbuilding industry directly and indirectly as discussed above, was implemented by looking into its structure and its legal and financial basis.

A. The Structure of the Shipbuilding Industrial Policy

To begin with, the government could intervene in the shipbuilding industry using (1) direct controls such as the licensing system, or indirect controls such as financial and tax incentives. The latter could be affected by giving (2) direct subsidies to the shipbuilding industry or by (3) providing assistance to domestic and foreign shipping firms, thereby raising the demand schedule facing the domestic shipbuilding industry.

The measures related to (2) above were as follows: the Export Earnings Special Tax Deduction System (ordinary deductions 1953–1964; accelerated deductions 1953–1960),[4] the Tariff Reimbursement System (1965–1972),[5] and the Exports-Based Accelerated Depreciation System (1961–1971).[6] These measures were the major policy tools resorted to for promoting exports. Furthermore, the Special Depreciation Scheme (1957–1975)[7] was adopted for promoting investment activity.

Besides these measures for promoting investment and exports, the tariff measures aimed at protection of the domestic shipbuilding industry through import restrictions cannot be ignored. The basic tariff, in force in 1964, was a flat rate of 15% on all ships (CCCN classification 8901). It is believed that the prices of Japanese ships were higher than those for British and West German ships by 10% to 15% around 1950 because of 20% to 40% higher prices of domestically produced steel.[8] In this light, a 15% tariff was considered sufficient to effectively protect the domestic industry. This tariff was reduced to 9% to 10.5% in 1970 after the Kennedy Round of Negotiations, but a complete abolition came about only in 1975.

The much-talked-about shipbuilding policy that has been followed until now has been characterized by direct controls within the framework of various shipbuilding laws as well as indirect financial assistance via the domestic and foreign shipping firms. These items are discussed below.

B. Legal Underpinnings of the Shipbuilding Policy

The Japanese shipbuilding industry is under the supervision of the Shipbuilding Bureau of the Ministry of Transport. The Bureau enacted 32 legislations up to 1982, which provided a legal basis for various measures adopted in the context of this industry.[9] Among these legislations, three, i.e., the Shipbuilding Law (1950–   ), the Temporary Law on Regulation of Shipbuilding (1953–   ), and the Law on Temporary Measures for Rationalization of Production of Small and Medium Sized Ships (1959–1964,

1964–1966), which was later continued as Law Concerning the Production and Operation of Small Ships (1966–   ), were directed solely at the shipbuilding industry.

The shipbuilding industry also took advantage, as need arose, of various permanent legislations like the Small and Medium Scale Enterprises Organizations Law (1957–   ), and the Small and Medium Enterprise Modernization Promotion Law (1963–   ), as well as time-bound legislations forming the core of such industrial adjustment assistance policy as the Law on Temporary Measures for Business Conversion of Small and Medium Enterprises (1976–1986), the Law on Temporary Measures for Stabilization of Specified Depressed Industries (1978–1983), the Law on Temporary Measures for Small and Medium Enterprises in Specified Depressed Regions (1978–1983), and the Law on Temporary Measures for Assisting Small and Medium Enterprises to Cope with Yen Appreciation (1978–1980).[10]

The Shipbuilding Division of the Industrial Council of the OECD, existing since 1963, in the wake of international conflict of interests in the shipbuilding industry, provided a forum for policy adjustments among major shipbuilding countries and a number of agreements were concluded.[11]

An outline of the three major laws related to the shipbuilding industry forming the core of the shipbuilding policy referred to above is presented below.[12]

1. The Shipbuilding Law

Objectives: (i)   Improving shipbuilding technology
                (ii)   Smooth functioning of the shipbuilding industry

Instruments: (i)   Restriction of new entry

A. *Licensing by Minister of Transport* of construction, transfer, or leasing of building berths, docks, or equipment for manufacturing or repairing ships equipped with slipway berths, which are capable of manufacturing or repairing steel vessels of more than 500 gross tons or more than 50 meters long.

B. *Reporting to Minister of Transport* of engagement in manufacturing or repairing of steel vessels, manufacturing or repairing of nonsteel vessels of more than 20 gross tons or more than 15 meters long, or manufacturing of marine engines of more than 30 shaft horsepower or of marine boilers of more than 150 square meters in heating area.[13]

                (ii)   Regulation of equipment

Licensing by Minister of Transport of construction, addition, or expansion of building berths, docks, or slipway berths necessary for manufacturing or repairing vessels.

(iii)   Dictation of business improvement

A. *Advice by Minister of Transport* to licensed or reporting shipbuilders to improve their business operations or to rationalize their business costs.

B. *Advice by Minister of Transport* to licensed or reporting shipbuilders to introduce new technologies, to modernize their facilities, and to adopt other means of technological improvements.

2. Temporary Law on Regulation of Shipbuilding

Objectives: (i)   Temporary regulation of shipbuilding
                 (ii) Healthy development of Japanese international shipping

Instruments: Quantitative restriction

Prior licensing by Minister of Transport of such construction or important remodelling as prescribed by the government ordinances of steel vessels of more than 500 gross tons or more than 90 meters long and of the structure prescribed in the Safety of Vessels Law, which can be classified as far-faring or near-faring vessels.

3. Law on Production of Small-Sized Ships

Objectives: (i)   Maintaining appropriate levels of shipbuilding production technology for building small-sized ships
                 (ii) Healthy development of the industry engaged in building small-sized ships
                 (iii) Improving the quality of small-sized ships

Instruments: (i)   Restriction of new entry

A. *Registration at Ministry of Transport* by small-scale ship builders of the categories of ships and the place of establishments.

B. *Reporting to Minister of Transport* of the inauguration of business.

(ii)   Regulation of equipment

Maintenance of the technological levels of specially-designated equipment to be used in business at standard prescribed by Ministerial ordinance.

C. Official Financial Base of the Shipbuilding Policy

Financial assistance through government financial institutions such as the JDB (Japan Development Bank) and the EIBJ (Export-Import Bank of Japan) under the planned shipbuilding and deferred payments on ships systems formed the core of the Japanese shipping and shipbuilding industry policies. The domestic shipping firms approved as competent ship owners by the government[14] were eligible for allocations under the "planned shipbuilding" system for which finances were provided by the JDB. The foreign shipping firms fulfilling certain minimum requirements[15] could benefit from the EIBJ financing of deferred payments. The shipbuilding loans and loans for deferred payments in Table II represent the financing under the planned shipbuilding and deferred payments on ships schemes, respectively. While leaving the discussion of the implications that such financing had for the shipbuilding industry to the next section, we will try to evaluate the importance of the huge injections of public funds for the government and the shipping industry.

The proportion of JDB loans to domestic shipping firms, including funds for building ships on a yearly basis, stood at 21% of the total JDB loans in 1961. Despite some setbacks in between, this proportion had risen to 45% by 1965. Thereafter, it began declining, gradually falling to 31% in 1970, 10% in 1975, and finally to around 3% in 1977 and 1978. The ratio recovered somewhat to go up to 13% in 1980. This clearly shows that the shipping industry held a very large share of the JDB loans during the first half of the 1960s. Reflecting these shifts in the JDB loans, the weight of JDB financing in the total outstanding debt of the shipping industry also rose perceptibly from 45% in 1961 to 60% in 1969, falling gradually thereafter to around 30% level in 1980.[16]

In comparison, if we look at the weight of financing for ships in the total financing of the EIBJ, we find it rising from 45% in 1960 to a peak of 58% in 1964 from where it fell off gradually to 45% in 1970, 8% in 1975, and around 2% in 1978 and 1979, rising marginally once again to 8% in 1980. This trend can also be discerned in stock terms as the share of the financing for ships in the outstanding loans of the EIBJ was only 5% in 1980 as against 37% in 1960, 44% in 1965, and 46% at the peak (1966–1969).[17]

In the light of the above discussion, the policy environment and structure in the Japanese shipping and shipbuilding industries seems to have, at

TABLE II
Working of the Shipbuilding Policy

| | JDB Financing | | | | | EIBJ Financing | | | | Proportion of Deferred Payment Ships to Total Export of Ships (%)[b] | (Proportion of Shipbuilding Finances + Deferred Payment Financing) to Total Value Added (%) | (Planned Shipbuilding + Deferred Payments Ships) to Total Ships Authorized to be Built |
	Finances for Requisitioning Ships (¥100 mn)	Proportion (%)	Period (Years)	Interest Differential (%)[a]	Proportion of Planned Shipbuilding to Total Domestic Ships (%)[b]	Financing of Deferred Payments (¥100 mn)	Proportion (%)	Period (Years)	Interest Differential (%)[a]			
1960	133	50–80	13	68.6	22.3	395	70→80	8	42.2	—	52.3	—
1961	223	50–80	13	53.4	35.5	422	80	8	42.7	78.2	53.2	58.1
1962	182	50–70	13	43.1	55.6	504	80	8	43.1	76.5	51.7	69.7
1963	261	70–80	13	43.9	62.3	784	80	8	43.9	84.0	83.5	79.8
1964	553	70–80	13	44.4	67.0	1,156	80	8	44.4	83.0	96.3	77.0
1965	850	70–80	13	44.9	76.9	1,059	80	8	44.9	89.0	92.8	85.2
1966	911	70–80	13	46.0	75.4	1,334	80	8	46.0	85.6	98.8	83.1
1967	871	70–80	13	47.3	67.0	1,466	80→70	8	47.3→50.2	93.0	85.9	83.9
1968	980	70–80	13	47.6	67.8	1,339	70	8	53.6	95.2	71.5	85.9
1969	970	63–66.5	13	65.9	69.8	1,791	70	8	56.9	98.3	84.6	88.2
1970	1,072	63–66.5	13	65.0	65.3	2,096	70→60	8	59.1	89.0	75.7	83.2
1971	1,154	52–61.75	13	64.9–68.4	49.6	2,108	60→55	8	59.0→81.1	43.6	58.5	46.7
1972	1,358	52–61.75	13	68.5–72.2	60.7	2,108	55	8	85.6	12.9	51.2	20.8
1973	854	52–61.75	13	67.2–70.8	25.7	1,515	55	8	83.9→86.7	15.7	25.3	17.5
1974	968	52–61.75	13	67.7–76.9	43.7	971	55	8→7	81.8→92.2	29.6	17.0	35.1
1975	743	60–70	13	84.1–89.7	21.2	716	55	7	89.2	58.1	13.9	51.2
1976	232	60–70	13	83.2	10.3	2,287	55→45	7	88.8	64.3	21.8	54.1
1977	281	60–70	13	76.9–88.8	20.6	1,653	45	7	94.7	46.8	17.1	40.2
1978	210	65–75	13	78.4–84.2	23.6	330	45→55	7	103.6	12.5	8.0	17.0
1979	1,022	65–75	13	32.6–59.6	56.7	188	55	7	102.3	20.6	31.4	30.2
1980	1,823	65–75	13	54.9–65.3	64.5	629	55	7	97.7	47.2	35.9	52.2

Sources: Nihon Senshu Kyokai [Japan Shipowners' Association], *Kaiun Tokei Yoran* [Handbook of Shipping Statistics]; Nihon Senpaku Yushutsu Kumiai [Japan Ship Exporters' Association], *Zosen Kankei Tokei Shiryo* [Statistical Materials Related to Shipbuilding Industry] (Domestic and International Volumes); Nihon Ginko [Bank of Japan], *Keizai Tokei Nenpo* [Economic Statistics Annual], Tsusansho [MITI], *Kogyo Tokei Hyo* [Census of Manufactures, Industry Volumes].

[a] Ratio of interest rate charged on the financing to that on domestic long-term loans; – represents the maximum and minimum on terms that varied with the type of ship; → indicates that the terms were changed in between.

[b] In terms of weight.

least formally, strong features of both direct controls through the licensing system built up around the Shipbuilding Law as well as of an industry receiving public funds for investment through a Planned Shipbuilding scheme at the core.

Under what circumstances could such a system be justified? The following four explanations could be advanced for such an intervention. First, it could be justified in terms of the objective of attaining political and economic security for Japan. Second, it could be explained as the historical legacy of the prewar and war periods. Third, it could also be attributed to institutional and administrative factors. Finally, it could be explained with reference to the peculiarities of the production process and the market for the shipbuilding industry.

The last of these explanations tries to provide an economic justification for the government intervention. It is pointed out that production, investment, and management in the shipbuilding industry is highly unstable as reflecting speculative shifts in demand for the shipping industry. Under favorable business conditions the number of new entrants rises steeply giving rise to what is termed as excess competition in the industry while bankruptcy and unemployment are pervasive during a downturn. The industry, therefore, is inherently problematic. Still another economic explanation is in terms of substantial economies of scale associated with this industry and is based on the observation that the postwar Japanese shipbuilding industry has been predominated by large-scale production as witnessed from a remarkable increase in the size of ships after World War II. The Shipbuilders' Association of Japan, on the other hand, tends to denigrate the presence of any economies of scale in the shipbuilding industry. Yoshihiro Kobayashi's findings also uphold this view by pointing out that entry barriers to the shipbuilding industry were never very high.[18] If this view is accepted, the market for and the production process in the shipbuilding industry could not be substantially different from any other capital or investment goods industries nor could the instability and excess competition arising out of business cycles be any different in this industry. In this light, the economic reasoning for an especially high degree of policy intervention in this industry, as contrasted to the others, falls through.

What about the remaining three noneconomic factors? The shipping and shipbuilding industries were protected and promoted by the government in the prewar period under the "wealthy nation and strong military" slogan and, during the Second World War, these industries were brought under complete government and navy control because of their importance in munitions production. This structure, however, was dismantled during the Occupation period following Japan's defeat in the War.

Later, a shift in the U.S. policy toward communism led to a shift in the Occupation policy to support economic independence of Japan. As a result, not only was Japan able to avoid paying indemnities in the form of ships and shipbuilding facilities, a part of the war indemnities demanded from Japan, but the necessity of replenishing the Japanese merchant fleet and shipbuilding capacity to the prewar levels also became an accepted goal. One of the policy formulations translating this intention into practice was the adoption of a planned shipbuilding scheme through investment of scarce national funds. As a consequence, "the authority of the Ministry of Transport, the ministry in charge, in the guidance and direction of the shipping and shipbuilding industries strengthened."[19]

Looking at this historical process, it is clear that the Ministry of Transport's intervention in the shipbuilding industry through the use of the licensing system was justified on grounds of the huge amounts of public funds invested rather than as a legacy of war-time controls. The Ministry of Transport was expected to effectively supervise the recipients of public funds as a representative of the public. If this was the case, the grounds for justifying the intervention on the strength of administrative and institutional factors disappeared in the 1970s as is to be discussed in the following section.

It was primarily Japan's unique security consciousness that accounts for the maintenance of the present structure of Japanese shipping and shipbuilding policies through time. That is to say, the security of Japan, with its peculiar geopolitical situation (an island country poor in natural resources) and economic structure (export or perish), is highly dependent on the availability of a certain level of ships and sailors and the possibility of requisitioning ships domestically that can be controlled by the government in times of emergency. Amiable relationships between the shipping industry, the shipbuilding industry, and the government during normal times could therefore be effective in ensuring concerted action during an emergency.

It has been a widely held view that the shipping and shipbuilding policies based on the licensing system were valid in order to meet such objectives. The rapidly changing Japanese and international political and economic structures and interrelationships, however, point toward the ineffectuality of the security principle and the policies that had been used to achieve such objectives. It is in this context that the validity of the received explanation of the Japanese shipping and shipbuilding policies has been challenged.

III. The Essence of the JDB and the EIBJ Finances

In this section we examine statistical evidence to investigate the significance of financial assistance provided under the planned shipbuilding and deferred payments for ships schemes for the Japanese shipbuilding industry.

A. Assistance to Domestic Shipping Firms

A large proportion of the finances needed for purchase of ships by the shipowners approved under the planned shipbuilding scheme were provided by the JDB and private banks at more favorable terms than those prevalent for market loans. That is, the government and private banks provided funds for shipbuilding and interest subsidies simultaneously. The shipowner, using these funds, would place an order with a shipbuilding firm that had the lowest price for ships. Although there were no institutional constraints prohibiting the placement of orders with foreign firms, the orders for the ships being financing under the allocation system were, in principle, placed with domestic shipbuilders as a matter of custom. Thus, to the extent that planned shipbuilding allocations were implemented, it materialized as demand for the indigenous shipbuilders.

What was the size of subsidy content of the JDB loans to the shipping industry? There is no way in which one can specify this and hence it is extremely difficult to estimate the proportion that flowed into the shipbuilding industry. If we look at shifts in the terms and conditions of JDB loans (amount of shipbuilding cost, percent financed by JDB, loan period, interest rate) (see Table II), i.e., the minimum amount of information on financial assistance, we find that although the length of the loan period does not change, other terms and conditions changed over time providing some indications about shifts in the policy stance. In broad terms, the assistance is found to have been strengthened during the 1960s, while in the 1970s it took a back seat. Toward the end of the 1970s, however, there was a turnaround and assistance was strengthened once again. These shifts in terms and conditions of loans, as will be pointed out later, reflect a shift in the policy stance from assistance aimed at strengthening international competitiveness of the Japanese shipping and shipbuilding industries in the 1960s to that for providing industrial adjustment assistance toward the end of the 1970s.

Table II presents the trends in the ratio of planned ships to total domestic ships and the ratio of interest rates on shipbuilding loans and those on domestic long-term loans. It is clear from this that 70% of the total domestic demand for ships in the early 1960s arose out of the planned shipbuilding scheme. The interest rates on loans during the same period were less than half the market rate of interest. Though showing some twists and turns, the weight of planned shipbuilding declined thereafter and the differential with the market rate of interest also vanished. The trend, however, reversed in 1975 and financing of planned shipbuilding rose once again.

B. Subsidies to Foreign Shipping Firms

The terms and conditions attached to the loans to finance deferred payments on ships ordered by foreign shipping firms from Japanese shipbuilding firms were constrained after 1965 by the Understanding on Credit for Ship Exports implemented by the Shipbuilding Division of the Industrial Council of the OECD. Japan began complying to this "understanding" from 1969 onward. In general, as will be shown later, the terms and conditions accompanying these loans became stiffer.

Although loans for financing deferred payments were provided by the EIBJ and the private banks acting in concert, we will narrow the focus of our attention to the EIBJ finances only as an indicator of government assitance. The degree to which Japanese financing through EIBJ is attractive to foreign shipping firms depends on the opportunities for profitable fund raising outside of Japan. In order to estimate this rigorously, it would be necessary to obtain and analyze data on terms and conditions of financing obtaining in major countries, which lies outside the scope of this study. We limit ourselves here to tracing the trends in the proportion of ships built on deferred payments basis in total export of ships and the ratio of the interest rate on loans to finance deferred payments to that on long-term loans in the domestic market.

Let us go back to Table II to confirm this point. It is seen from the figures that most of the exports of ships during the 1960s were financed by means of deferred payments. Particularly, toward the end of the 1960s, ship exports were almost wholly covered under the deferred payments system. There, however, was a sharp reversal in 1972 and this proportion fell to 10%. Thereafter, it showed large fluctuations as the proportion rose to 50% in 1975 and 1976 and then fell back once again to 10%. Looking at the interest rates charged on loans for deferred payments, the advantage is found to be visibly smaller in the 1970s as compared to the 1960s, and by the end of the period, differential with the market rate of interest vanished. Entering the 1970s, the terms and conditions of EIBJ financing were no longer attractive for the foreign shipping firms.

C. Assistance to the Shipbuilding Industry through Both Routes

What were the implications of the assistance provided through the above mentioned dual routes for the Japanese shipbuilding industry? There are two indices for this. The first of these is given by the proportion of the JDB and EIBJ loans in the total value added in the shipbuilding industry on the assumption that the full amount of these loans, decided on in that year, flowed out into the shipbuilding industry in the same year. The other index is given by the proportion of planned ships and ships with deferred payments to the total tonnage of ships approved to be built. A glance at the first of these indices in Table II reveals that the scale of financing was as high as 90% during 1964, 1965, and 1966. In terms of the latter index as well, it is seen that the JDB and EIBJ finances were linked with over 80% of the total ships built in the second half of the 1960s. It is clear that the Japanese shipbuilding industry in the 1960s was highly affected by the shipbuilding policy in terms of finances as well as amount of work. In the 1970s, however, this feature was quickly lost.

IV. The Working of Industrial Adjustment Assistance Policy[20]

While the world demand for ships fell off steeply after the first oil shock, new shipbuilding countries also surfaced. As the Japanese shipbuilding industry was losing international competitiveness, a wide range of industrial adjustment measures were resorted to in the latter half of the 1970s. Although the process of industrial adjustment progressed in the manner discussed at the beginning of this chapter, we will concentrate, in the following discussion, on the process of operations curtailments and capacity adjustments believed to have influenced the massive industrial adjustment that took place in the shipbuilding industry.

A. Operations Curtailments

The index of demand for ships in terms of orders received fell from 100 in 1973 to 20 in 1975 and to 10 in 1978. The number of keels laid also declined at the same time. Following this, employment adjustments beginning with the laying off of subcontractual workers started, but no changes were discernible in terms of berths and docks, the core of shipbuilding capacity, until 1979. As a direct consequence, the profit position in the shipbuilding industry deteriorated sharply in 1978–1979 (see Table I). Why did the capacity adjustments lag behind? One of the factors responsible for such a state of affairs was the existence of the operations adjustment to be discussed below.

The Ministry of Transport recommended curtailment of operations by major firms, as depicted in Table III, on the basis of Article 7 of the Shipbuilding Law, in November 1976. Operation time was used as the basis for curtailments in the initial recommendations, but there remained a possibility that the intended reduction in production might not materialize if

TABLE III
Curtailment of Operations

Capacity of Shipbuilding Facilities	Annual Tonnage Built (launches) (10,000 gross tons)	No. of Firms	Prescribed Operations Time as a Proportion of Operations Time in the Base Year[a] (%)			Prescribed Operating Tonnage as a Proportion of Operating Tonnage in Base Year[b] (%)		
			1977	1978	1979	1979	1980	1981
10,000 gross tons and above	100–	7	67	63	55	43	34	45
	10–100	17	76	70	66	45	45	60
	0–10	16[c]	82	75	70	49	49	65
5,000 gross tons and above	2–	7	—	85	63	—	—	—
		av. for all firms	(70)	(70)	(63)	(39)	(39)	(51)

Source: Un'yusho [Ministry of Transport], Un'yu Hakusho [Transport White Paper].
[a]Base year is set as the year with highest operating time during 1973–1975.
[b]Base year is the year with highest operating tonnage during 1973–1975.
[c]As a result of capacity adjustments in 1979, 11 firms since 1980.

the firms increased the intensity of work. Besides, the prescribed curtailments were far more gradual as compared to the fall in demand. The basis of curtailment in operations was, therefore, shifted to production tonnage (Compensated Gross Registered tonnage) in December 1978, taking recourse, thereby, to rather direct controls while increasing the intensity of curtailments as well.

The Fair Trade Commission pointed out that the Ministry of Transport's recommendations might possibly infringe on the Antimonopoly Law, but as depression in the shipbuilding industry deepened, it also came around to the view that the recommendations should be placed in the context of a depression cartel beyond the jurisdiction of the Antimonopoly Law. The Ministry of Transport thereby advocated formation of a depression cartel in the industry (meaning Shipbuilders' Association of Japan and the Cooperative Association of Japan Shipbuilders'), and the industry responded to these efforts.

The depression cartel was to be allowed for a period of two years, 1979 and 1980, with curtailments in line with those presented in Table III, and firms could enter or exit the cartel at will. There were dissensions with the cartel within the industry, and the shipping industry also raised its voice in opposition. For example, small shipbuilders complained that the allocation of curtailment of operations was favorable to the large firms; some large firms expressed dissatisfaction that, since 1973, 1974, and 1975 were set as the base years, it put at a disadvantage the firms that installed new capacity and started operations later. Furthermore, as the collective behavior to control production and restrict competition could put an upward pressure on prices, the shipping industry (Japanese Shipowners' Association) complained to the Fair Trade Commission as regards the inappropriateness of the cartel. Despite this, an extension of the depression cartel until the end of fiscal 1981 was granted in April 1980.

B. Capacity Adjustments[21]

Despite the implementation of short-term measures like employment adjustments and curtailments of operations with the help of the depression cartel, the profit position of the shipbuilding firms did not improve.

Under these circumstances, the Ministry of Transport used its power under the Shipbuilding Law to refuse approval to new constructions and extensions of berths and docks with over 5,000 gross ton capacity and allowed new constructions below this size only on the condition that the construction did not lead to a rise in number. It was these strict controls that account for the lack of fluctuations in number and capacity of berths and docks over 1976 to 1978 as revealed in Table I. Introduction of government funds and formulation of an adjustment assistance plan for the industry, which was designated under the Industry Stabilization Law in 1978, brought about immediate capacity adjustments.

The policy measures undertaken under this law, a part and parcel of the industrial adjustment assistance policy in the shipbuilding industry, can be itemized as follows:

Legal Backing: The Law on Specified Shipbuilding Stabilization Association (adopted on October 18, 1978).

Details of Implementation: Purchase of equipment and land of specified shipbuilding firms (shipbuilding firms using shipbuilding equipment of over 5,000 ton capacity) in line with the basic stabilization plan (cf. Table IV) set up under the Industry Stabilization Law on the recommendations made by the Shipping and Shipbuilding Rationalization Council.

Implementing Authority: Specified Shipbuilding Stabilization Association (established December 12, 1978).

Method of Implementation: The above association bought the equipment and land from the specified shipbuilding firms, scrapping the former and selling off the latter or transferring them if need arose.

Method for Raising Funds: Total capital ¥2.05 billion (government ¥1 billion, private ¥1.05 billion); funds for purchases, ¥96 billion (borrowed from the JDB and private banks).

Method of Reimbursement of Borrowings: Funds for purchase of land were reimbursed out of the sales proceeds of land. The burden of reimbursement of funds used for purchase of equipment was passed on to the remaining firms, with a redemption period of 10 years.

The passing on of the burden to the remaining firms was the basic distinguishing characteristic of the adjustment assistance policy. This method allowed sharing of the burden of adjustment costs of the inefficient firms in the shipbuilding industry by the government and efficient firms (remaining firms). In practice, the association collected the funds required for redemption of its debt incurred for purchase of equipment through the contributions made by the remaing firms to the association. These contributions were raised by the remaining firms by putting aside a fixed proportion of the price of orders or contracted ships (1/1,000 of the ship price in 1979, 1.5/1,000 in 1980, and 2/1,000 in 1981 and 1982).

The Ministry of Transport asked the firms to submit capacity scrapping programs by October 1979. The process closely followed the Basic Stabilization Plan as depicted in Table IV. The ministry found that structural improvement (industrial adjustment) in the Japanese shipbuilding industry progressed as a result.

The method of raising the funds necessary for meeting costs of capacity reductions (the mainstay of industrial adjustment) within the industry through the remaining firms was quite unique. This is because the consequences of inefficiency in a capitalist system are supposed to be borne, in principle, by the firm concerned. It is true that the inefficient firms have to undertake capacity adjustment but the fact that the efficient firms have to set apart a portion of their earnings for this purpose implies an increased burden for the remaining firms that would, in the long run, lower the efficiency in the industry as a whole. This method, thus, contradicts the basic objective of the shipbuilding policy. The strategy was chosen, despite this contradiction, by giving preference to the shipbuilding industry's wishes for "equitable sharing of burden" that emphasized institutional behavior rather than the economic and business principles.[22] Formulation of the above mentioned industrial adjustment assistance policy could not have been envisaged without it.

V. An Analysis of the Impact of the Shipbuilding Policy and Its Implications

How did the shipbuilding policy, discussed in Sections III and IV, affect the rise in the international competitiveness of the Japanese shipbuilding

TABLE IV

Capacity Adjustment (Capacity Scrapped in Designated Shipbuilding Industry: By Size of the Firm)

| | Basic Stabilization Plan | | | Actual Scrapped Capacity | | | | |
| | Capacity before Scrapping | | Tonnage Targeted for Scrapping | Reduction in Number | Capacity Scrapped[f] | Achievement Ratio[g] | Post-Scrapping Capacity | |
Class	No.	10000 CGRT[h]	10000 CGRT[h]	No.	10000 CGRT[h]		No.	10000 CGRT[h]
7 Large firms[a] (40%)[e]	55	569	228	25	225	99	30	343
17 Medium sized firms[b] (30%)	38	289	87	10	103	(100) 119	28	205
16 Medium sized firms[c] (27%)	23	79	21	9	25	(98) 119	14	45
21 Other firms[d] (15%)	22	40	6	6	5	(78) 81	16	26
Total [average: 35%]	138	977	342	50	358	(99) 105	88	619

Source: Un'yusho [Ministry of Transport], Un'yu Hakusho [Transport White Paper], 1980.

[a] Those equipped for building over 10,000 gross ton ships and producing over 1,000,000 gross tons (launching base) annually.

[b] Those equipped for building over 10,000 gross ton ships and producing over 100,000 gross tons but less than 1,000,000 gross tons (launching base) annually.

[c] Those equipped for building over 10,000 gross ton ships with annual production less than 100,000 gross tons (launching base).

[d] Those equipped for building over 5,000 gross ton ships but not included above.

[e] Figures within parentheses represent targets for capacity scrapping.

[f] Capacity scrapped is the reduction in capacity and re-adjustments within the group between building up new capacity under 5,000 gross tons and capacity scrapping using the number of ships to be scrapped as the base.

[g] Figures within ( ) exclude 9 firms related to purchases by the association.

[h] CGRT = Compensated Gross Registered Tonnage.

TABLE V
Estimation of the Orders Received Function

Explanatory Variable	[1]	t-statistics	[2]	t-statistics	[3]	t-statistics	[4]	t-statistics
Constant	-42.995	-1.515	-45.944	-1.730	50.668	0.895	25.769	0.532
m	3.558	4.315	3.552	4.614	4.650	4.154	4.407	4.680
$PX/\overline{PX}$	-5.386	-1.804	-5.489	-1.967	-6.102	-1.806	-6.295	-2.226
k_{-1}	-3.052	-4.530	-2.695	-4.695	-3.061	-3.515	-3.277	-4.466
$i1$					-0.282	-0.513	-0.262	-0.567
$c1$					-0.417	-1.324	-0.697	-2.421
$i2$					-0.721	-1.028	-0.850	-0.588
$c2$					-0.423	-1.152	-0.107	-0.321
dum			-13.733	-1.791			-24.376	-2.393
$\overline{R}^2$	0.611		0.661		0.617		0.732	
D.W.	2.604		2.644		2.809		2.875	
Sample Period	1962-80		1962-80		1962-80		1962-80	

Sources: Nihon Senpaku Yushutsu Kumiai [Japan Ship Exporters' Association], *Zosen Kankei Tokei Shiryo* [Statistical Materials Related to Shipbuilding Industry, Domestic and International Volumes]; Nihon Ginko [Bank of Japan], *Gaikoku Keizai Tokei Nenpo* [Foreign Economic Statistics Annual]; *Keizai Tokei Nenpo* [Economic Statistics Annual]; Un'yusho [Ministry of Transport], *Zosen Tokei Yoran* [Handbook of Shipbuilding Statistics]; Nihon Senshu Kyokai [Japan Shipowners' Association], *Kaiun Tokei Yoran* [Handbook of Shipping Statistics]; Okurasho [Ministry of Finance], *Gaikoku Boeki Gaikyo* [Trade of Japan]; IMF, *International Financial Statistics.*

Explained Variable—O: Orders received for new Japanese ships from all over the world.

Explanatory Variables—m: the world index of mining and manufacturing production, PX: export ship price of Japan, $\overline{PX}$: ship price except for Japan, k_{-1}: shipping tonnage in the world in the previous year, $i1$: ratio of interest on shipbuilding financing to interest rate on domestic long-term loans, $c1$: planned shipbuilding to total domestic ships ratio, $i2$: interest rates charged for financing deferred payments to that on domestic long-term loans, $c2$: deferred payment ships to exports of ships, ratio, dum: dummy variable, (dum = 1 for 1974–77, dum = 0 otherwise)

$\overline{R}^2$—Coefficient of determination adjusted for degrees of freedom

D.W.—Durbin-Watson ratio.

industry during the 1960s and its industrial adjustment process during the 1970s?

Kobayashi (1973) attributes the rise of Japanese shipbuilding to the top position in the world to (1) the fact that this industry is characteristic of the semi-advanced stage of industrialization; (2) the existence and potentialities of high technological levels and capacity accumulated in the prewar period; (3) the existence of sufficient demand to absorb the rising supply; (4) the provision of export credits; and (5) the availability of an adaptable work force. Scrutinizing the loans for financing of deferred payments provided by the EIBJ from 1950–1971, he further points out that "export financing had a far-reaching impact upon expanding Japanese exports. Though the effect of assistance policies for domestic or exportable ships cannot be measured precisely, it is quite obvious that these acted as a propellant for the development of the Japanese shipbuilding industry."

As seen earlier, the development of the Japanese shipbuilding industry was quite remarkable. At the same time, the industry was believed to have gotten strong bolstering from the shipbuilding policy in the first half of the 1960s. The development of the Japanese shipbuilding industry and shipbuilding policy in the 1960s attracted the following type of comments from European shipbuilders: "the Japanese shipbuilders' success has been mainly the result of governmental assistance, not owing to their skills and fair salesmanship alone."[23]

The industry itself summed up the industrial adjustment in the 1970s by pointing out that

> among the factors responsible for the recovery of the Japanese shipbuilding industry from the dire situation. . . . this time . . . the strengthening of planned shipbuilding through the revival of the interest subsidy system implemented over a three-year period from 1979 was directly responsible . . . and this was . . . a set pattern of planned shipbuilding scheme's contribution to pull the shipbuilding industry out of a depression as and when required.[24]

To begin with, those related to policy formulation or to the industry that has been able to avoid losses due to the existence of the policy cannot be expected to denigrate the propriety of such a policy, and it is rare to find a champion of the industry who would accept that the domestic shipbuilding industry was internationally uncompetitive. Even if the pronouncements made by the respective representatives are discounted, did the shipbuilding policy measures, such as the planned shipbuilding scheme, exports on deferred payments basis, curtailments of operations, and capacity adjustment, not have considerable effects? The answer to this question, as revealed by a comparison of the development process of the shipbuilding policy and that of the shipbuilding industry as discussed in the earlier sections, seems to be in the affirmative. The above mentioned statements are based on such an intuitive reasoning.

How far is this impressionistic evaluation appropriate? To answer this question, we have attempted a regression analysis to determine how significant was the effect of changes in the indices of policy assistance, as discussed in Sections III and IV, on demand and investment in the Japanese shipbuilding industry.

A. Effect of Policy on Demand

As seen before, the Japanese shipbuilding industry was able to corner the highest share in the international market by securing orders at a rate surpassing that for the world industry as a whole. In what way did the JDB and EIBJ finances contribute to the success of the Japanese shipbuilding industry? Let us consider this question in the light of the results of the regression analysis presented in Table V.

What could be the factors underlying a decision by the domestic and foreign shipping firms to place orders with the Japanese shipbuilding firms? In Table V, the index of world (including Japan) mining and manufacturing production (m), the relative price of Japanese ships to that of the rest of the world ($PX/\overline{PX}$), and shipping tonnage of the world as a whole in the previous year (k_{-1}) represent the economic variables, the indices of JDB assistance ($i1,c1$) and EIBJ assistance ($i2,c2$) the policy variables, and a dummy variable (dum) the shift parameter to capture the changes in behavior of the shipping firms following the first oil shock.

For a shipping firm, its demand for ships represents investment behavior of a sort. There are a number of models explaining investment behavior of a firm (industry), and the choice of a particular model is dependent on the purpose of analysis. The demand for the product of the industry in question, the rate of return on investment, the rate of profit, and the capital stock can be considered as the universal factors influencing investment behavior in general.[25] Of these, the first three raise investment while the last reduces it. Of the variables mentioned in the previous paragraph, m represents the size of demand as it is one of the factors that impinge on the world demand for Japanese ships, and since $PX/\overline{PX}$, ($i1,c1$), and ($i2,c2$) affect the rate of return and the profit rate, these can be taken as proxy variables for profitability. It goes without saying that k_{-1} is the capital stock variable.

Keeping the above in mind, let us have a look at the results in Table V. Equations (1) and (2) take only the economic variables into account. The signs are all as expected, but the significance of the relative price variable is suspect. Equations (3) and (4), on the other hand, try to measure the policy effects. From the way the variables are defined, we expect the coefficients of $i1$ and $i2$ to be negative while those for $c1$ and $c2$ to be positive. The signs of the first two are as expected, but those for the latter are contrary to the expectation. These wrong signs, however, seem to be proper once we look at them in the light of the process of utilization of these funds. That is to say, policy assistance is not required when internal and external demand for ships is flourishing during an upswing and hence the planned shipbuilding and deferred payments systems are unnecessary.

From the point of view of the analysis here as well as the coefficient of determination, equation (4) seems to be of most interest. The estimates reveal that changes in economic conditions and the oil shock were the most important influences on the trend in orders received by the Japanese shipbuilding industry and, barring planned shipbuilding, no other policy variable seems to have had any significant impact. The shipping and shipbuilding industries were targeted for assistance in almost all of the major shipbuilding nations and it is quite possible that the effect of the policy assistance measures undertaken by different countries might have been more or less canceled out. The results of our analysis that finds the effect of the JDB and the EIBJ financing to be negligible are perhaps a reflection of such conditions.[26]

B. Effect of Policy on Investment (Investment Adjustments)

Let us now have a look at the impact of policy on investment in the Japanese shipbuilding industry, which established itself through a proper handling of its orders under such prevailing pricing conditions. As in the case of estimation of the orders-received function, equations (1) and (2) in Table VI estimate the impact of economic variables only, while equations (3) and (4) try to bring out the effect of policy measures as well. The economic variables considered here are keels laid ($b1$), the rate of profit (g), and the value of tangible fixed assets in the previous year (rk_{-1}), while the index of financial assistance in value terms, $V1$ and the index of assistance in terms of production tonnage, $V2$, reflect the policy variables. Dummy variables (op) and (ep) capture the effect of curtailment in operations and capacity adjustments, respectively. The variable dum, as in the orders received function, is used to capture the effect of the oil shock.

How do these variables correspond to the four determinants of investment behavior (demand, yield, rate of profits, and capital stock)? Variables $b1$ and $V2$ correspond to demand, g and $V1$ to yield or rate of profit, and rk_{-1} to capital stock. The dummy variables can be considered to have dampening impact on investment.

Let us look at the estimates presented in Table VI. All the estimates in equations (1) and (2) have proper signs except that the stock and oil

TABLE VI
Estimation of the Investment Function

Explanatory Variable	[1]	t-statistics	[2]	t-statistics	[3]	t-statistics	[4]	t-statistics
Constant	−654.901	−2.340	−736.609	−2.811	−429.815	−0.769	−214.021	−0.422
$b1$	20.271	6.276	22.962	6.924	22.774	4.302	21.998	4.679
g	8.256	3.090	7.031	2.753	9.277	3.295	8.104	3.161
rk_{-1}	−0.046	−1.529	−0.012	−0.347	−0.141	−1.281	−0.062	−0.586
$V1_{-1}$					−15.953	−2.198	−13.559	−2.081
$V2_{-2}$					13.868	2.574	8.135	1.451
op					−63.359	−0.125	−273.184	−0.591
ep					205.520	0.589	−98.450	−0.285
dum			−389.569	−1.853			−517.436	−1.942
$\bar{R}^2$	0.755		0.791		0.803		0.846	
D.W.	1.757		1.578		2.316		2.324	
Sample Period	1963–80		1963–80		1963–80		1963–80	

Sources: Tsusansho [MITI], Kogyo Tokei Hyo [Census of Manufactures, Industry and Enterprise Volumes], plus those cited in Table V.

Explained Variable—f/pf: investment funds utilized in real terms (f: investment funds; pf: investment goods price index).

Explanatory Variables—$b1$: Keels Laid, g: rate of profit = [value added—cash earnings]/value of tangible fixed assets (beginning of year), rk_{-1}: real value of the tangible fixed assets in the previous year (beginning of year), $V1_{-1}$: (shipbuilding financing + deferred payment financing) in the previous year/value added, $v2_{-2}$: (planned shipbuilding + deferred payment ships) year before last/ships authorized to be built, op: dummy (operations adjustment: $op = 1$ for 1977–80, zero otherwise), ep: dummy variable (capacity adjustments: $ep = 1$ in 1979–80, zero otherwise), the rest is the same as in Table V.

shock dummy variables do not seem to have a significant effect. This indicates that the speed of investment adjustments was higher than expected.

What was the impact of policy? Equation (4) seems to be most appropriate for answering this question in terms of signs as well as coefficient of determination. The signs of estimates for operations curtailment (op) and capacity curtailment (ep) indicate that these factors had a dampening effect on investment as expected, but the estimates are not significant. How did $V1$ and $V2$ affect investment? The variable $V1$ impinges on investment with a one-year lag, while $V2$ has a two-year lag reflecting the time profiles of policy implementation and the production process. Furthermore, by definition, a rise in these indices is believed to result in higher investment and a positive sign for both is naturally expected. The sign for $V1_{-1}$, however, turned out to be negative. Even this result seems plausible in the light of the content and implementation of the financing of the deferred payments system. That is, the loans for financing deferred payments have to be assigned to the working capital of the shipbuilding firms.[27] Then, by definition of working capital, the value added is reduced (implying by definition, a shortage of working capital), the rate of profit (g) is lowered, and shipbuilders' business and financial conditions deteriorate. Under such conditions, an increase in loans for financing of deferred payments leads to a rise in $V1$. While such a reinterpretation of the reversed sign is possible, the estimates for $V1_{-1}$ and $V2_{-2}$ cannot be considered significant by any standard.

The implications of the above analysis can be summarized as follows: (1) It is difficult to accept the proposition that the JDB and EIBJ financing had a significant role to play in improving the international competitive power of the Japanese shipbuilding industry (expansion in orders); (2) The positive and the negative effects of the JDB and EIBJ finances in the development of the shipbuilding industry (expanding investment) canceled each other out; (3) The progress of capacity adjustments was affected mainly by the shipbuilding firms' response to changes in economic and business environment and the depression cartel and the Industry Stabilization Law played only a secondary role. This conclusion is therefore contradictory to the impressionistic evaluation of the shipbuilding policy put forward at the beginning of this section.

The conclusions of our analysis indicate that the received view of the Japanese shipbuilding policy within Japan as well as abroad has been a sort of "illusion" or perhaps a "myth." The conclusions of this chapter, however, should also be taken with a grain of salt on account of the limitations inherent in the analytical approach adopted here.

Notes

1. The author is indebted to Masu Uekusa, Konosuke Odaka, and Keijiro Ohtsuka for their useful comments as well as Yasutoyo Shouda of the Japan Economic Research Center for helping out with the statistical analysis.
2. The shipbuilding industry, for the purposes of this study, corresponds broadly to JSIC (Japanese Standard Industrial Classification) 3641 (Manufacture and Repair of Steel Vessels). Needless to say, not all data used in this study are strictly for this JSIC industry.
3. In making wage comparisons, it is important to adjust for working hours and worker attributes. Here, in Table I annual wage differentials are compared on the presumption that the critical income variable entering in workers' decisions on change of employment is their annual income.
4. This system was set up under the Law on Special Tax Measures. The ordinary deductions allowed for either 50% of export income (raised to 80% in 1955) or 5% of the total value of exports, whichever was smaller, while the rest was subject to corporate tax. This system came under fire in the GATT in November 1960 and was withdrawn in March 1964. The accelerated deductions on the other hand allow for a deduction of 7.5% of the difference between the value of exports in the current business year and those in the base year from total income.
5. The system, under which 0.06% of the export price of the ship was reimbursed, made use of the Tax Reimbursement Scheme Related to Raw Materials used for the Production of Export Cargo under the Ordinance to Revise a Part of the Fixed Tariff Enforcement Ordinance.
6. This system allowed accelerated depreciation at a rate 50% above the normal depreciation in case the amount of exports exceeded those in the base year and the export/production ratio exceeded that in the base year.
7. For the details of this system and estimates of amount of depreciation, cf. Chapter 5 of the present volume.
8. See Nihon Zosen Kogyo Kai [1980], p. 179. For tariff rates, see Nihon Kanzei Kyokai (Japan Tariff Association) *Jikko Kanzei Ritsu Hyo* (Effective Tariff Rates Table).
9. As listed in "Names of the Laws under the Sole or Joint Jurisdiction of the Shipbuilding Bureau of the Ministry of Transport and the Legislations Related to the Exercise of the Jurisdiction," in Un'yusho (Ministry of Transport), *Zosen Tokei Yoran* (Handbook of Shipbuilding Statistics), 1982.
10. See Chapter 14 of this volume for details of such industrial adjustment assistance policies. For the author's view of the industrial adjustment policy, cf. Yonezawa [1979]. Nihon Zosen Shinko Zaidan (Japan Foundation for Shipbuilding) [1983] points out that the shipbuilding industry rarely made use of various adjustment assistance policies directed at small- and medium-scale enterprises as revealed by the records of their use. This would seem quite natural if we take note of the fact that smaller ships were demanded during the 1970s, following which berths and docks also shrunk in size.
11. The following were the three major agreements: (1) "An 'Understanding' on Credits for Ship Exports," (2) "A 'General Agreement' on a Gradual Removal of Impediments in the Way of Fair Competition in the Shipbuilding Industry," and (3) "General Directive in the Shipbuilding Policy."
12. Cf. Ueno [1978].
13. Whether the act of reporting constitutes controls or not is a controversial question. The effect differs depending on whether it is done ex-ante or ex-post. But as far as the act entails psychological and administrative costs, it may have some dampening effect.

14. One of the conditions for approval was that cargo for the next 10 years be guaranteed for the ship being built. This condition was relaxed to some extent in view of the sluggish shipping markets in recent years.
15. The main conditions were to mortgage the ship built, to have a backup guarantee from a first-rate bank, and the like.
16. Cf. Nihon Senpaku Yushutsu Kyokai (Japan Ship Exporters' Association), *Zosen Kankei Tokei Shiryo* (Statistical Materials Related to Shipbuilding) (Domestic), and Chapter 5 in the present volume.
17. See Nihon Senshu Kyokai (Japan Shipowners' Association), *Kaiun Tokei Yoran* (Handbook of Shipping Statistics), Un'yusho (Ministry of Transport), *Zosen Tokei Yoran* (Handbook of Shipbuilding Statistics), and Chapter 5 of this volume.
18. Nihon Zosen Kogyo Kai [1980], p. 244, and Kobayashi [1973], p. 199.
19. Nihon Zosen Kogyo Kai [1980], p. 24.
20. Discussion in this section is based on Ministry of Transport's *Un'yu Hakusho* (Transport White Paper), Nihon Zosen Shinko Zaidan [1983], and May 16, June 26, August 2, and November 9, 1979, issues of *Nihon Keizai Shimbun*.
21. The shipbuilding capacity encompasses a wide range of equipment, such as berths, docks, transportation equipment, hull construction equipment, electric power sources, shipbuilding equipment (diesel equipment, etc.), ancillary equipment, and others. We use the term capacity here to refer to berths and docks.
22. Nihon Zosen Shinko Zaidan [1983] p. 49.
23. Katayama [1970], p. 18.
24. Cited from the preface of Nihon Zosen Shinko Zaidan [1983].
25. Cf. Allen [1967], pp. 57–58.
26. Cf. Denton, et al. [1975], pp. 188–191, OECD [1976], and Nihon Senshu Kyokai (Japan Shipowners' Association), *Kaiun Tokei Yoran* (Handbook of Shipping Statistics).
27. The deferred payment loans could be used, in principle, only as working capital (payments for raw materials, labor, interest, and the like) for the shipyards. Cf. Nihon Zosen Kogyo Kai [1980], p. 186.

CHAPTER 17

Aluminum Refining Industry

NAOKI TANAKA

Independent Economist
Tokyo, Japan

The aluminum refining industry typifies the industries that, having attained the ability to meet practically the whole of the domestic demand, have been forced to make way for international division of labor through reduction in capacity as internationalization of the Japanese economy has progressed. This chapter briefly discusses the environment in which the aluminum refining industry developed and follows up with a discussion of the firms' adjustments as stagnation set in. We also trace the policy intervention, categorizing it by period and by type of measures. Finally, having looked at the interrelationship between the policy goals and policy intervention, we present a comprehensive evaluation of the industrial policy framework in the case of the aluminum refining industry. Although the aluminum refining industry is expected, in the final analysis, to follow the coal industry on the road to stagnation, this chapter attempts an empirical verification of the theoretical basis of the role of industrial policy.

I. Aluminum Refining Industry and Its Environment

A. The Deepening Crises

After peaking at 96,000 tons in July 1980, the monthly production of the aluminum refining industry showed an uninterrupted decline up to the beginning of 1983, stabilizing at 22,000 tons per month thereafter. In contrast, monthly imports rose from 70,000 tons in 1980 to over 100,000 tons in 1983. The aluminum ingot, often called "canned electricity," has been losing ground in Japan following the sharp rise in energy prices after the

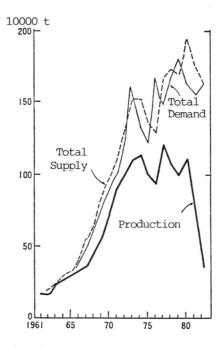

Fig. 17.1. Demand and supply of new aluminum ingot. From *Shigen Tokei Geppo* (Resources Statistics Monthly).

second oil shock. According to one of the producers, "engaging in aluminum refining in Japan is like growing sugarcane in Hokkaido."

Figure 17.1 presents long-term trends in the demand and supply of new ingot (as distinct from reprocessed ingot). The difference between the supply line and the production line represents imports. The imports are seen to have risen from the early 1970s, but a radical change is observed after the second oil shock. As electricity production depends heavily on petroleum in Japan (cf. Table I), the Japanese aluminum industry has been wholly uncompetitive internationally in terms of per-unit electricity cost (see Figure 17.2). The Kanbara plant of Nippon Light Metals (depending on self-generated hydroelectric power) and the Miike plant of Mitsui Aluminum (based on a mixture of powdered coal and crude oil) were the only two plants in Japan in a position to provide any competition to the imported ingot. As revealed in Figure 17.3, the relative increase in the share of the Kanbara and Miike plants came about after the second oil shock.

Figure 17.4 presents the market prices for new ingot. The domestic prices closely reflect the prices in the international markets. Price fluc-

TABLE I

Sources of Energy for Aluminum Refining in Major Countries (%)

Energy Source	Japan	US	Canada	W. Germany	UK	France	Switzerland	Italy	Norway
Petroleum	76	5	—	6	—	23	4	62	—
Hydroelectricity	11	36	100	9	10	26	80	23	100
Coal	13	40	—	65	33	11	—	—	—
Natural gas	—	15	—	—	—	33	—	15	—
Nuclear power	—	—	—	20	57	7	16	—	—
Total	100	100	100	100	100	100	100	100	100

Source: Predictions for 1980 on the basis of OECD [1976] data. For Japan, actual figures as of December 1980 (Japan Aluminum Federation).

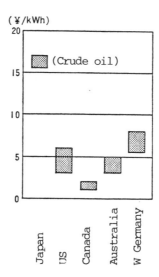

Fig. 17.2. International differences in per unit electricity cost in aluminum refining. From Japan Aluminum Federation.

tuations in recent years are shown in more detail in Figure 17.5. Producers' price quotations apparently exerted little influence in both domestic and world markets. One finds some indications of recovery since the beginning of 1983, but it is primarily the result of a sharp business recovery in the United States and completion of inventory adjustments. This recovery in international markets is still insufficient for the survival of the Japanese industry. The Japanese industry, as yet, does not satisfy the necessary conditions for a production recovery.

In examining the industrial policy for the aluminum industry, it is important to take note of the ingot buyers' view of the conditions prevailing in the industry. Let us have a bird's eye view of the post 1970s era, which encompasses a significant change.

B. Characteristics of Industrial Organization

Of the processes of Bauxite mining, production of alumina, electrolysis of alumina ore, production of aluminum, and rolling and processing, the aluminum refining industry comprises the production of alumina and its electrolysis. Until now, the Japanese refining industry has stayed away

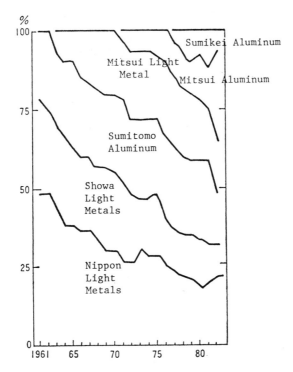

Fig. 17.3. Change in production share of new aluminum ingot. From *Keikinzoku Kogyo Shimbunsha* (Light Metal News), *Nikkan Keikinzoku* (Light Metals Daily).

from bauxite mining as well as rolling and processing. In contrast, the giant integrated aluminum firms in the Western countries have gone in for a vertical integration of these activities. Separation of the refining and the rolling and processing segments is a distinguishing feature of the organization of the Japanese aluminum industry.

The Japanese aluminum industry doubled its refining capacity in the 1970s. The annual capacity for producing aluminum ingot rose sharply from 800,000 tons in 1970 to 1,640,000 tons in 1978. A major factor contributing to such a sudden rise in refining capacity was a misreading of the economic environment by the Japanese firms. As discussed earlier, the sudden jump in the energy prices resulting in higher costs of refining was a decisive factor in putting the Japanese industry at a price disadvantage in relation to the imported ingot.

Another factor causing the ingot refining capacity to rise sharply was

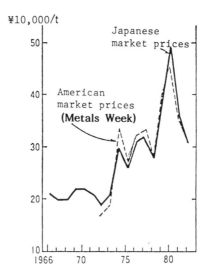

Fig. 17.4. Changes in prices of new aluminum ingot. For Japan, from *Tekko Shimbun* (Iron and Steel News); for the United States, from *Metals Week*.

the separation of the refining and the rolling and processing segments of the industry, a problem related to the organizational structure of the industry. The consumers of ingot, the big rolling firms, tried in vain to enter the refining stage, while the erstwhile refiners concentrated their efforts on building up additional capacity as a defensive measure. The barriers to entry in the aluminum refining industry have never been very high.[1] One of the reasons for the excess refining capacity in the 1970s, thus, has been the historical separation between the refining and the rolling and processing stages, with refining given preference in terms of earnings for a long time.

Why did the refining industry not integrate the rolling and processing stages? As to be discussed later, the rolling and processing segments were characterized by severe competition and hence the firms specializing in refining did no more than build up group relationships with the firms in these fields. Entry into the refining stage, on the other hand, was highly desired by the rolling and processing firms. A typical example is the confrontation between Sumitomo Chemicals and Sumitomo Light Metals, which resulted in the establishment of Sumikei Aluminum Industries[2] as a new entrant into the refining business. The new company, established in February 1973, began production in 1977 at its Sakata plant in Yamagata Prefecture, with an annual production capacity of 99,000 tons, but the

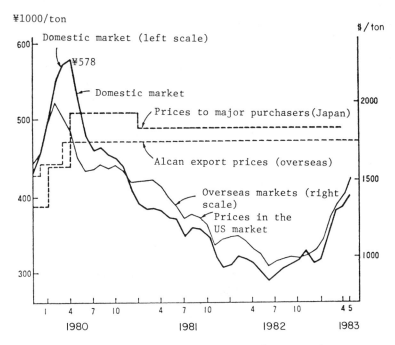

¥1000/ton

\$/ton

Domestic market (left scale)

¥578

Domestic market

Prices to major purchasers (Japan)

Alcan export prices (overseas)

Overseas markets (right
scale)

Prices in the
US market

2000

1500

1000

600

500

400

300

1   4   7   10   4   7   10   4   7   10   4 5

1980   1981   1982   1983

Fig. 17.5.   Aluminum ore prices. From Japan Aluminum Federation.

company had to fold up operations in May 1982. It was anticipated that
the relationship between the specialized refiners and the rolling and processing firms that were purchasers of refined ingot from the former would
change into a competitive one in the 1970s and, to a certain extent, this
anticipation was realized. The oil crises complicated this process of rapid
expansion in refining capacity.

It is only after the oil shock that first attempts at integrating the rolling
and processing stages, led by Nippon Light Metals, began in order to
rescue the industry. This was followed by a gradual pullout by various
firms from the refining business. The policy intervention by the government
was expected to smooth out the changes started by the firms. In practice,
however, the industrial policy toward the aluminum industry resulted in
maintenance of refining capacity. This divergence needs to be set right.

C. Collapse of the International Oligopolistic System

The 1970s saw structural shifts in the international supply of aluminum
ingot. Prior to this, the aluminum industry was characterized by inter-

national oligopolies. Six companies, Alcan of Canada; Alcoa, Reynolds Metals, and Kaiser Aluminum of America; P'echiney of France; and Alswiss of Switzerland were supplying an overwhelming share of the new ingot, as much as 80% of the total in the non-Communist world in 1960–1970. The share, however, has come down to 40% in recent years as a result of the entry of developing countries like Bahrain, Egypt, and Venezuela into aluminum refining. Furthermore, a third of the capacity, primarily in the developing countries, is in the hands of the public sector.

A decisive shift in the supply structure came about with the beginning of transactions in aluminum ingot on the London Metals Exchange (LME) in 1978. The market price of aluminum fluctuated every day and the industry became market-sensitive. The breakup of the strangle hold of the international oligopolies was instrumental in bringing this industry on to the market just like copper, lead, and zinc. The export prices set by Alcan, holding an overwhelming export capacity among the six major companies, had been influential in the formation of international prices. In the 1970s the supply structure began to change, the aluminum price came to be determined in the London Metals Exchange, and the Alcan export prices ceased to have an impact on world prices from the middle of 1980 as is revealed in Figure 17.5. Finally, a 23-month futures market for aluminum ingot came to be established at the New York Commodity Exchange (COMMEX) on December 8, 1983. Thus, aluminum ingot is fast becoming a speculative commodity.

As market conditions changed, the six major concerns also begun to behave differently. For example, Alcan capitalized fully on its superior cost conditions and sustained an 80% rate of utilization even during a recession. Expansion of market share, thus, continued to guide the firm's behavior despite the depressed business conditions—a drastically different behavior pattern from heretofore observed. Such a shift in supply pattern would obviously affect the buyer's perceptions as well. Given the fact that the aluminum ingot price is market-sensitive internationally and changes in the domestic market just as in the international market (Figure 17.4), it is difficult to justify the maintenance of domestic aluminum refining capacity on grounds of "guaranteeing economic security" and as a bargaining chip in international negotiations.

D. Competition among the Users

The demand for aluminum ingot rose sharply during the period of rapid growth. The demand for aluminum sash and aluminum doors in the construction industry contributed tremendously in this direction. Severe competition in construction materials business, especially for aluminum sash, influenced the aluminum refining industry as well. As revealed in Figure 17.3, which depicts the shares of the firms, it was easy for the new entrants like Mitsubishi Light Metals (Mitsubishi Chemicals at that time) and Mitsui Aluminum to get a share in the market precisely due to the fact that the quickly rising demand for aluminum ingot because of severe competitive conditions in the construction materials industry provided them with an opportunity to get a firm foothold through price concessions. The effectiveness of price cuts continues to hold sway in the industry even now. As long as the competition in the user industries persists, a shift to cheaper supply of imported ingot is but natural. Figure 17.1 shows that the rate of growth in production fell short of the rate of growth in demand from the late 1960s to the early 1970s. This is accounted for by, among other things, conservative demand outlook of the refining firms and their attempt at raising an already high rate of capacity utilization. It may be pointed out here that the aluminum refining firms were highly conscious of their internationally high electricity costs and were wary of a decline in their profits concomitant on a lower rate of capacity utilization. Rationing of ingot during the period of stringent demand and supply conditions of aluminum ingot was resorted to and Nippon Light Metals was nicknamed the "MITI in Ginza" (the business district in Tokyo where the Company's headquarters were located).

The postwar aluminum industry in Japan began with three firms, Nippon Light Metals, Showa Denko, and Sumitomo Chemicals. Entry by Mitsubishi Chemicals in 1963 and Mitsui Aluminum in 1968 raised the number to five. The desire of the aluminum ingot users to get cheaper supplies of the ingot to improve their competitive position helped the new entrants to raise their share of the market quickly. The ¥ 360/$ rate of exchange collapsed in 1971 raising the proportion of imported ingot as the yen appreciated and, as depicted in Figure 17.4, the market for aluminum ingot also fell through. Thus the aluminum ingot buyers were raising their dependency on imported ingot even before the advent of the oil crisis. The changing business environment for the domestic refining industry was therefore a reflection of the disposition of the buyers.

The major rolling firms, specializing primarily in sheets, found it impossible to continue to purchase high-priced ingot from the domestic refiners, given the severity of international competition they faced. To rolling and tertiary processing firms, a rise in the price of aluminum products would imply a disadvantageous competitive position vis-a-vis the competing goods like steel and plastic products. The high rate of growth in demand for aluminum products in the past was based upon substitution of the competing materials. Purchase of high priced ingot by the rolling and tertiary processing firms would have been suicidal. It was natural, therefore, for them to shift to cheaper imports. As the market for the ingot became predominantly a buyers' market, production of ingot in Japan declined. Since 1983, imports account for over 80% of the domestic demand for the ingot.

II. Policy toward the Aluminum Refining Industry

A. Policy Backdrop

As far as MITI's policies toward individual industries are concerned, the aluminum refining industry remained in the periphery. The *Twenty Years of MITI*, published in 1969 by MITI (Tsusansho (1969)), did not mention any policy concerns whatsoever with respect to the aluminum refining industry. The Investment Finance Committee of the Industrial Structure Council had been undertaking investment planning in major industries since 1958, but aluminum refining and rolling was included in the list as the 16th industry only in 1969. Until then it was the Fair Trade Commission that had shown some interest in the aluminum industry. The stickiness in aluminum ingot prices was a topic discussed by the Anti-monopoly Consultative Group[4] in its December 1969 meeting.[5]

The lack of policy concern in the aluminum industry is also evident from the fact that it became the top batter in the efforts for trade liberalization. Trade liberalization began in June 1961 and the aluminum industry was considered to be the most internationally competitive industry as far as basic metals were concerned. Nippon Light Metals held more than a 50% share of the market at that time and the fact that Alcan held 50% of its equity[6] also seems to have affected MITI's policy interest in this industry.

Let us have a look at the attitude of the MITI toward the aluminum industry before the oil crisis. For this the "Investment Plans for Major Industries—Its Present Position and Problems" published by MITI at the beginning of every fiscal year is perhaps the most appropriate source.[7]

The greatest concern of the aluminum refining industry, as revealed in the 1973 edition brought out in July 1973, just before the first oil shock was with the further reduction in import prices of aluminum ingot in the new floating exchange-rate regime, reduction in domestic producer prices, and increasing ingot imports. At the same time, the electrolytic segment of the industry was adding on new capacity, which was expected to reach 1,650,000 tons by 1975.[8] The question of overseas location, an important consideration while making investment decisions, was also considered. Thus,

> Considering the plethora of problems like environmental pollution, electric supply, currency problems, resource development, and agreements with resource abundant countries, the aluminum refining industry needs to take stock of the situation for its long-term future development, including overseas location in an international perspective, at an early date.

The 1974 edition of July 1974 expected the demand-supply situation to be stringent given the rampant inflationary expectations following the oil shock. A special section on considerations regarding adjustment in the investment plans points out that "the refining capacity is necessary for the maintenance of medium-term demand-supply balance and in view of the fact that all the projects are already under way, no adjustment would be resorted to."

The 1975 edition, brought out in May 1975, refers to the sharp reduction in capacity utilization in the industry and also touches on the government guidance of the ingot price. It also mentions the price freeze of March 1974, the assessment for the proposed price increase in July 1974, the rapid build-up of inventory after that, and the fall in the effective price due to price differentials with imports. It concludes by pointing out that the Aluminum Industry Committee of the Industrial Structure Council was deliberating on the long-term prospects of the industry and would be coming out with its recommendations in the near future. It was at this time that MITI finally put its hands into industrial policy for the aluminum refining industry.

B. The 1977 and 1978 Reports of the Industrial Structure Council

The aluminum refining industry posted a big loss during the 1976 recession as a result of a sharp rise in electricity charges and a large slip in demand. A few firms called for the voluntary retirement of employees. They became conscious of the fact that the recession was structural rather than cyclical. Thus, an aluminum industry committee was set-up within the Industrial Structure Council to deliberate on the long-run "vision" for the period 1975–1985. The preliminary report was submitted on August 12, 1975. At the same time short-run policy intervention was also resorted to. The 1976 edition of the *Investment Plans for Major Industries* carries the following comment:

> Measures like publishing guidelines (anticipated demand) for facilitating voluntary production cuts by the producers with a view to adjusting excessive inventories and appeals to the major importers and consumers for self restraints on ingot imports have been undertaken in the face of the prevailing demand-supply situation.

The term *guidelines* refers to the half yearly demand estimates prepared by MITI since January 1976. These estimates served as a reference point for the production cuts carried out by individual refining firms, which amounted to 40% during this period. Although the inventories in the hands of the producers at the end of March 1976 were still at a high level of 350,000 tons, these were down by as much as 70,000 tons as compared to the level at the end of December 1975. The MITI guidance, in effect, acted as a production control cartel.

Let us have a look at the thinking presented in the preliminary report of 1975. It called for a cautious build-up of refining capacity using crude based thermal power and an active pursuit of shifting the industry to overseas locations. The report estimated the demand for aluminum ingot at 2,130,000 tons for 1980 and 3,100,000 tons for 1985. No mention was made, however, of the division of the supply between domestic and imported sources. In any case, the report set the stage for the implementing of industrial policy by establishing an Aluminum Industry Committee within the Industrial Structure Council.

Emergency stockpiling of aluminum ingot was also resorted to during this period. On August 31, 1976, 9,570 tons were bought up, followed by a purchase of another 12,440 tons on June 30, 1978. Purchase prices were guaranteed by the government and interest subsidies were provided out of the General Budget appropriations. These emergency stocks were sold off on July 31, 1979, when the prices turned up sharply and thus were handy in demand-supply as well as price adjustments during the abnormal period.

The aluminum refining industry chalked up big deficits in 1975 and 1976. The three chemical companies, Sumitomo Chemicals, Showa Denko, and Mitsubishi Chemicals, which had been engaged in aluminum refining as a secondary activity, separated out their aluminum divisions to form independent companies specializing in aluminum refining. This clearly reflects the belief of the refiners as to the noncyclical nature of the recession. This began a process of rationalization in the aluminum industry.

The Aluminum Industry Committee of the Industrial Structure Council began to investigate what to do with the industry. A meeting was held on November 24, 1977, to announce its interim report, which recommended a reduction in annual productive capacity from 1,640,000 tons to 1,250,000 tons. Need for incentives for promoting capacity adjustment was felt and a tariff allocation scheme was adopted for this purpose. The scheme called for (1) introducing tariff allocations for 387,000 tons of imported ingot, equivalent to the amount of capacity frozen, (2) reducing this (primary) tariff from 9% to 5.5% and using 3.25% of the 3.5% difference between the primary and the secondary tariff (9%) to provide interest subsidies against freezing of capacity through the Aluminum Industry Structural Improvement Promotion Committee and giving the remaining 0.25% to importers as handling charges.

This system was devised to lighten the burden of the firms introducing capacity reductions in the form of interest subsidies on loans equivalent to the book value of the capacity scrapped. The tariff allocation system began on an experimental basis for one year in 1978 with a revision of a part of the Law on Interim Tariff Measures. The Aluminum Industry Structural Improvement Promotion Committee was able to collect ¥2.54 billion from the importers of aluminum ingot in the form of contributions in the first round. Of this amount, ¥1.588 billion were distributed to the firms that introduced capacity freeze as structural improvement funds, which may be interpreted as a form of interest subsidies.

In view of the continuing slide of the aluminum refining industry even after the interim report of November 1977, a new report was announced on October 23, 1978. The tariff allocation system was extended for another year, and the primary tariff was lowered to 4.5%. The difference between this primary tariff and the 9% secondary tariff was passed on to the Aluminum Industry Structural Improvement Committee as structural improvement funds to be distributed over 1979 and 1980. Further scrapping of capacity was undertaken to reduce the scale of domestic production to 1.1 million tons.

The industry was designated as a depressed industry under the Law on Temporary Measures for the Stabilization of Specified Depressed Industries on May 15, 1978, and a Basic Stabilization Plan was chalked out under which 298,400 tons of capacity was to be put out of commission and another 186,000 tons were earmarked for scrapping. This Basic Stabilization Plan was implemented beginning April 1979 and the refining capacity was reduced from 1.64 million tons to 1.11 million tons.

The international market for aluminum soared in 1979 and the domestic price also recovered from ¥305,000 per ton at the beginning of 1979 to ¥508,000 per ton by April 1980, thereby turning the aluminum firms' business accounts into the black. But the industry once again went into a deeper recession from mid-1980, forcing the closure of Mitsubishi Light Metals' Naoetsu plant (annual production 160,000 tons) in September 1981, Sumitomo Aluminum's Isoura plant (annual production 79,000 tons) in March 1982, and Showa Light Metals' Oomachi plant (annual production 18,000 tons) (Cf. Table II).

The Aluminum Industry Committee of the Industrial Structure Council reconvened in April 1981 to deliberate on the future prospects of the aluminum industry.

TABLE II
Capacity Scrapped and Residual Capacity in Various Firms [Uts (1,000 tons)]

Item	Peak Load (A)	Residual Capacity as of June 1983 (B)	Tax Exempt Allocations in 1982 (C)	B/A (%)
Nippon light metals				
Kanbara	95	64		
Niigata	148	0		
Tomakomai	134	72		
Total	377	136	90.7	36.1
Showa light metals				
Kitakata	29	17		
Oomachi	43	0		
Chiba	170	58		
Total	242	75	91.2	31.0
Sumitomo aluminum				
Nagoya	53	0		
Isoura	79	0		
Toyama	177	82		
Toyo	99	99		
Total	408	181	101.0	44.4
Mitsubishi light metals				
Naoetsu	160	0		
Sakaide	192	77		
Total	352	77	80.8	21.9
Mitsui aluminum: Miike	164	144	29.3	87.8
Sumikei: Sakata	99	99	0	100
Grand total	1,642	712	393	

Source: Prepared from *LM Tsushin,* May 11, 1982.

C. The 1981 Report of the Industrial Structure Council

The Aluminum Industry Committee of the Industrial Structure Council presented its report on the future of the aluminum industry after the second oil shock on October 9, 1981. Despite reductions in the domestic refining capacity and measures for structural improvement such as the introduction of the tariff allocation system following the 1977 and 1978 reports, which was implemented with the view of improving within the next five years the competitive position of the industry faced with a severe depression after the first oil shock, the business conditions for the aluminum industry only worsened calling for a new review of the refining industry.

The 1981 report, though admitting the necessity for a further cut in the domestic refining capacity down from 1.11 million tons, came to the conclusion that at least 700,000 tons of domestic capacity was indispensable. (The basis of this recommendation is to be discussed later.) A target year of 1975 was set up for achievement of this objective. Tariff exemptions on ingot imports by the refining industry up to the extent of capacity scrapped were introduced along with changes in the tariff allocation system. Under this system the firms engaging in refining, at however small scale, could get a complete tariff exemption on their ingot imports up to the amount of scrapped capacity until the end of 1984. The amount of capacity to be scrapped was decided within the framework of the Basic Stabilization Plan prepared under the Industry Stabilization Law and exemption from the 9% tariff on imports equivalent to the amount of scrapped capacity was to be allowed for three years, 1982–1984.

Measures such as the efficient use of collective thermal power stations and the provision of subsidies and Development Bank Loans for shifting the energy for these collective thermal power stations to coal or other energy sources have also been considered for reducing the electricity costs in the industry. Futhermore, as the refiners were facing severe business problems due to accumulation of huge inventories in 1982, the Metal Mining Agency of Japan engaged in emergency purchase of a part of these inventories through the Metal Mining Products Stockpiling Program. Purchases worth ¥20 billion in November 1982 and ¥23 billion in March 1983 were made. The stockpile was to be kept for three years.

III. An Evaluation of the Policy toward the Aluminum Refining Industry

A. Evaluation as a Structural Adjustment Measure

The 1981 report of the Aluminum Industry Committee of the Industrial Structure Council states that the domestic aluminum refining industry has the following six contributions to make:

1. Stabilizing the supply of aluminum ingot,
2. Maintaining bargaining power,
3. Insuring economical supplies of high-quality ingot for which it is difficult for imports to substitute,
4. Maintaining a technological base,
5. Providing a driving force behind overseas development projects,
6. Contributing to the related industries and regional economies.

Justification of policy intervention in the aluminum refining industry on the basis of the above six points implies that this industry was not considered a stagnating industry like the coal industry. The Aluminum Industry Committee of the Industrial Structure Council could take either of the followng two ways for policy intervention in the aluminum refining industry. First, it could, leaving the development of the industry to international division of labor and adopt an industrial adjustment policy to smooth out the process of industrial change. Second, it could list the reasons as to why the industry could not be left to the workings of international division of labor and continue to pay additional costs for maintaining productive capacity.

The 1981 report, when it found 700,000-ton capacity to be "reasonable domestic refining capacity" in order to maintain a stable supply of the ingot, indicated its adherence to the latter of the two approaches mentioned above. The debate over the placement of the aluminum refining industry within the international division of labor, given the high electricity costs, has continued for over 20 years.[9] A shift to complete reliance on international division of labor as the basis of policy formulation was strongly opposed in view of the huge refining capacity that had been built up. The individual refiners, however, were concerned more with either a continued existence or complete withdrawal rather than with "stable supply" principle.

Sumikei Aluminum decided to close down by refraining from applying for tariff exemption on ingot imports, the very base of the rescue policy for the aluminum refining industry. The remaining five refining companies were allocated 393,000 tons (see Table II). The withdrawal of Mitsubishi Light Metals from the industry is also quite obvious. It closed down it Naoetsu plant without waiting for the 1981 report of the Industrial Structure Council and was left with only the Sakaide plant. The Oomachi plant of Schowa Light Metals also closed its doors and the remaining Kitakata and Chiba plants are also in the process of being shut down. The company is now expected to become an importer of ingot. Showa Light Metals entered into capital participation of CRA Co. of Australia in April 1981 and began receiving its ingot supplies form Comalco, a subsidiary of CRA, under a long-term contract.

Sumitomo Aluminum and Mitsui Aluminum also cannot be expected to survive no refining business alone. The Kanbara plant of Nippon Light Metals was also expected to be scrapped as it superannuated, and closure of the Tomakomai plant is highly probable unless the switch-over to coal proves profitable. A changeover to rolling and processing business is the strategy to be followed. Looked at from this viewpoint, it would have perhaps been better if the policy intervention had aimed at facilitating withdrawals rather than justifying maintenance of refining capacity. It is difficult, even for an insider of the industry concerned, to clearly discern the extent of cyclical influences when the industry is subject to structural and cyclical factors at the same time. Under the conditions of uncertainty, time in itself can be a solution. Allowing the firms some time to find a solution on their own could be beneficial from the point of view of the overall economy even when positive adjustment policy is to be followed.

Sudden changes in relative prices and brisk pace of technological progress give rise to significant shifts in estimates of future demand as well as international competitive power. The Japanese aluminum refining industry provides a typical example of such shifts. Except for a few industries, Japanese industry has been operated on a principle that it should foster all-round development encompassing all stages from basic materials to processing and assembly. As a means to overcome the resource constraints, industrial complexes and collective thermal power stations were created in aluminum refining and petrochemicals. A large number of developing countries, however, are on the road to industrialization on the strength of their advantage in resource availability. In the interdependent international economy based on the international division of labor, the presumption that all industries should grow in the Japanese economy has to be discarded. This is precisely the problem faced by the Japanese aluminum refining and petrochemical firms.

The future adjustment assistance policy, while giving due respect to the autonomy of the firms, would have to devise ways and means for their withdrawal from industries that have lost comparative advantage with a minimum of friction. The report of the Industrial Structure Council should have accepted this fact as it is. Adoption of a time-bound tariff allocation system as a positive structural adjustment measure, in this light, seems to be an ingenious idea. Tariff exemption to the five firms was of the order of ¥400,000 × 400,000 tons × 0.09 or ¥14.4 billion per year. Its continuation for three years in 1982–1984 would imply a ¥43.2 billion rescue package for the five firms involved. The cumulative losses of the aluminum refining industry were ¥93.3 billion at the end of 1981 an ¥132 billion at the end of 1982 and would have been much higher in the absence of the rescue package. The rescue package, amounting to over 2% of the total sales of the industry in 1982, seems to be reasonable if interpreted as adjustment assistance for the withdrawing firms. In terms of the declared necessity for maintaining 700,000 tons of refining capacity to achieve "ability to stabilize supplies" and "attain bargaining power," however, the policy was a failure, as the production levels fell below 300,000 tons with no sign of recovery in sight. No discontent over loss of "ability to stabilize supplies" or "attainment of bargaining power" has been expressed. The market participants seem to have a high degree of confidence in the international divison of labor determined within the framework of an open economy.

The Japanese aluminum industry is inevitably moving toward rolling operations as its main business, and consequently the focus of policy intervention has to shift. As the Japanese aluminum rolling firms strengthen ties with foreign firms, the scope of domestic industrial policy is being sharply narrowed down. Foreign refiners are aiming at furthering their supplies of ingot to the Japanese market through business tie-ups and long-term contracts with an eye on the high rate of growth of the Japanese market. The era for an industrial policy based on the presumption that the receiving country is invariably at a disadvantage seems to be over.

B. Adjustments in Industrial and Firm Level Profits

There was one particular area in which the refining firms were not able to get their demands met by the Aluminum Industry Committee of the Industrial Structure Council. This was their plea for setting up a system of special rebates on electricity charges for the refining industry. MITI does not appear to have given a proper consideration to this proposal. Nothing is more at variance with the basic principles of the post-oil-shock economic policy of Japan than preferential treatment of energy-intensive industries. Due to this, the refining industry's demand for special electricity rates was considered presumptuous.

The aluminum refining industry attempted to get the time-bound measures prolonged as far as possible. The need for reformulation of a part of the Law on Interim Tariff Measures, including the tariff allocation system and tariff exemptions, was stressed on the Diet toward the end of every fiscal year. When this was achieved, the emphasis shifted, for the first half of the fiscal year, to try for concessions on electricity charges. In the second half of the year, once again, efforts were renewed on getting the time-bound legislation extended. In this sense, there was a built-in momentum for the continuation of protection even in the case of time-bound measures. Taking for granted the premise that the industry would give precedence to its own interests, implementation of the policy becomes a matter of concern for all those involved in the making of an industrial policy.

One of the objectives that the report of the Industrial Structure Council considered worthy to strive for was building up a unified understanding between the policy authorities and the firm groups in the future. The formation of the Aluminum Blast Furnace Process Research Association is a typical example of such an approach.

The 1981 report of the Aluminum Industry Committee of the Industrial Structure Council clearly points out the need for vigorous efforts at developing the blast furnace process as a means to recover international competitiveness through technological development. The blast furnace process, though similar to blast furnace iron making, requires temperatures as high as 2,000 to 2,200° C as compared to 1,000 to 1,600° C in the case of iron. Furthermore, as the product is an alloy of aluminum, silicon, and iron, the production of pure aluminum requires refractory refining process. Research and development in this area was being carried out at home by the Mitsui group and the National Chemical Laboratory for Industry of the Agency of Industrial Science and Technology, and abroad by Alcoa. The Japan Aluminum Production Technology Research Center, established in August 1982, built on the research done by the Mitsui group. The Center began experimental research at the Oomuta factory of the Mitsui Metallurgical Works in 1982 with ¥200 million in research commissions from the Aluminum Industry Structural Improvement Promotion Committee and has been successful in improving the fluidity of by-product slag, preventing shutdowns necessitated by the emission of volatile substances in the furnace, and raising the rate of aluminum recovery through the use of lead in the refining process.

The government budget for 1983 funneled subsidies in this direction and an Aluminum Production Technology Research Association was established in March of the same year by the five aluminum refining firms along with Kobe Steel Works and Ishikawajima Harima Heavy Industries, which inherited the research work being carried out by the Research Center. Having set up a bench scale blast furnace with an outlay of ¥514 million in 1983, research for the next pilot plant is already under way.

It is believed that, because of the degree of complexity, the development of furnace building materials capable of withstanding temperatures of over 2000° C and the recovery and use of carbon monoxide emitted as a by-product would require over a decade to be realized even with the cooperation of iron and steel producers in related industries. The aluminum refiners, except Mitsui Aluminum, were reluctant to contribute to the development of a new blast furnace process but were forced to join the Technology Research Association as they could not ignore the guidelines set by the Industrial Structure Council. In the final analysis, the refining firms could not simply kick whichever part of the Industrial Structure Council's report they did not like.

Notes

1. Echigo [1973] finds the entry barriers to be low on the basis of an analysis of economies of scale, electric power, raw materials (bauxite), technology, minimum funds required, and sales network.
2. Sumitomo Light Metals was established as a spin-off from the Sumitomo Metal Industries and engaged in rolling operations with aluminum ingot supplied by Sumitomo Chemicals. While formulating a plan to build up a new rolling factory at Sakata, it decided to begin refining ingot on its own. As a result, Sumikei Aluminum was established with 40% of the funds coming from Sumitomo Light Metals, 30% from Sumitomo Chemicals, and the rest from other Sumitomo group firms. *The History of Sumitomo Chemical Industries Limited* [1981], p. 670 presents the following picture of the process involved.

   Despite the fact that coordinations within the Sumitomo group have been smooth till now, entry of two firms in refining business not only goes against the one-firm-one-business tradition of the group but also would result in an overlapping of investment and hence is undesirable. The beginning of operations from October 1975 under these circumstances was believed to upset the order maintained in the aluminum refining industry by the existing firms like this firm (Sumitomo Chemicals), Mitsubishi Chemicals and Nippon Light Metals, which had delayed all plans of capacity expansion so as to maintain demand-supply balance in the industry. They tried to persuade Sumitomo Light Metals to give up the undertaking. It, however, adamant. No agreement was reached and the negotiations remained deadlocked. The whole industry was looking forward to a solution of the problem. However, the firm suddenly asked the then Minister of Trade and Industry, (Kakuei) Tanaka, to mediate.

3. The flourishing investment demand by the firms during the period of rapid growth resulted in the supply capacity of the basic materials industries like the steel and petrochemicals to grow at a rate over and above that of demand. The aluminum refining industry, in contrast, showed an exactly opposite trend. The suppressed investment behavior of the refining firms during the period of rapid growth was a major factor behind the attempts by major rolling firms to enter refining business during the 1970s. Though Sumitomo Light Metals was the only firm successful in diversifying into refining from rolling operations, Furukawa Aluminum and Kobe Steel were also seriously considering entering.
4. The Anti-Monopoly Consultative Group was set up by the Fair Trade Commission as it felt disturbed about the increased merger activity in Japanese industry in anticipation of capital liberalization. The group was to study the changes occurring in market structure and competitive conditions and to formulate a future course for the antimonopoly policy. It consisted of 21 persons representing academia, the press, industry, consumer organizations, and small-business organizations. The first meeting was held in November 1968. The results of its deliberations were published in *Kanri Kakaku [Administered Prices]* [1970].
5. Imai [1976], Chapter 3, presents a framework for analyzing this problem.
6. The San Francisco Peace Treaty came into effect in April 1952. An application for approval of capital participation under the Foreign Capital Law was made to the Foreign Capital Council on April 8, 1952. Nippon Light Metals was the first case of foreign capital participation in the post-independence period. Its company history (Nippon Light Metals [1959]) lists up a host of merits related to foreign capital participation, including those

in the field of funds, technology, and raw materials. It received wide attention as a multifaceted agreement including equity, loans, and technological assistance.

7. This publication was brought out by Tsusansho Kigyokyoku (MITI Enterprises Bureau) up to 1973 and Tsusansho Sangyo Seisakukyoku (MITI Industrial Policy Bureau) since then. It carries a brief summary of the trends in demand-supply, prices, business, investment, and investment funds by industry.

8. Since it was postponed a number of times, the capacity rose to 1,640,000 tons only in 1978.

9. Mr. Kitagawa, former Director of the Nippon Light Metals Research Institute, states that at the time of the setting up of the Industrial Structure Council within MITI on October 1961, the Council spared some amount of time for a deliberation of the view against the aluminum refining industry. Thus:

At a time when trade in aluminum has been liberalized and it is possible to procure the ingot freely given the international excess supply, there seems to be no necessity for increasing domestic production of high cost ingott. Importing cheap ingot and concentrating on the development of processing industries not only is suited to the domestic conditions in our country but is also dictated by the international division of labor in the framework of an open economy. (Kitagawa [1983]).

PART VI

Industrial Organization and Industrial Policy

CHAPTER 18

Coordination Within Industry: Output, Price, and Investment

Faculty of Economics
University of Tokyo
Tokyo, Japan

I. Introduction

Evaluating the impact of a specific policy is not easy, no matter what its form. In most cases, as with taxes, subsidies, low-interest financing, and tariffs, it is clear what the policy function was (what was performed in the name of policy, namely, what instruments the policy employed and how the policy was operated). It is, however, extremely difficult to estimate the impact of a policy, i.e., to discern what condition would have resulted if the policy had not been undertaken, or if the form or extent of the policy had been different.

In the case of the focus of discussion in this chapter, coordination within industry of output, price, or investment (hereafter, "intraindustry coordination" or simply "coordination"),[1] it is neither clear what the policy function was, nor what was done in the name of policy. As an obvious consequence, there is almost no information available to try to understand what the impact of such actions was, so that the attempt to evaluate the effects of policy meets here with even greater difficulties.[2]

The specific reasons why it is difficult to distinguish the impact of policy may be illustrated here by referring to the example of the list price system (*koukai hanbai seido*, literally open [public] sale system) in the steel industry to be discussed in Section III:

1. If, as those involved at the time claimed, the use of depression cartels was to be avoided, even though they were permissible under the Antimonopoly Law, the policy of production (and price) coordination through

the list-price system was used as a substitute. This consisted merely of a cosmetic change.

2. It is necessary to judge on the basis of specific facts what the influence of the government (that is, MITI) was on the output of individual firms under the list-price system. The content of policy cannot be understood simply from the fact that the list-price system was implemented, or that the government took the lead in having it implemented (although, in fact, that does not seem to have been the case). Furthermore, even if MITI indicated specific targets that it officially warned the industry association or individual firms to respect, it is still not possible to know the actual content of the policy.

An evaluation of the impact of a policy presupposes a knowledge of the real significance of government participation [action]. Because the use of such policies varied across time and by industry, one must be cautious about overgeneralizing the conclusions of this chapter. My opinion is that most of the studies publicized to date do not clearly specify the boundaries of what they mean by policy, so that there is a tendency to overestimate the role and impact of the government.[3]

While there has recently been some change, intraindustry coordination, the focus of discussion of this chapter, has all along been considered as part of the core of industrial policy.[4] Furthermore, the continual dispute over the suitability of specific coordination policies and what was the desirable relationship between such policies and antitrust policy has been one of the most prolific debates over postwar industrial policy.[5] It is also the case that the content of coordination *cum* industrial policy varied quite substantially from era to era and industry to industry. Again, it is true that "while the content of policy was widely reported at the time in newspapers in a fragmentary fashion, an overall picture of the system of "industrial policy" was almost never clearly presented, and there were many things which remained virtually unknown to people in general (including scholars)."[6]

Therefore it is necessary to work on developing a methodology which can lead to some general conclusions about the effectiveness of coordination *cum* industrial policy.

In this chapter, keeping in mind the goal of deriving some general conclusions, the main focus of analysis will be the steel industry during the rapid growth era. For comparison, we will also take up the petroleum refining industry during roughly the same period. This selection was made for the following reasons:

1. The steel industry during this period was representative of the in-

dustries in which a list-price system and capacity coordination were utilized, so that it can be regarded as a model case.

2. In discussions of the appropriateness of industrial policy (especially from the standpoint of policy on competition) the industry was also consistently a focus, so that information can be obtained comparatively easily.

3. The steel industry was a main target of industrial policy throughout the postwar period and was provided in particular with favorable tax and other treatment. The government, however, did not hold the same sort of strong powers over the industry as it did in the case of such industries as petroleum refining and petrochemicals (detailed in Section V). The industry is thus held to be close to the archetypical case of industrial policy carried out by means of administrative guidance.

4. During this period of progressive trade liberalization, the government lost its hold over industry stemming from the ability to allocate import licenses, it is also the period when the Antimonopoly Law was least influential. Because of these two elements, we can observe industrial policy carried out by means of administrative guidance in its purest form.

5. In order for the government to be able to effectively participate in making intraindustry coordination function meaningfully, one would presume that the industry would need to meet the criteria below. These are the same criteria that make it possible to form a strong cartel. The steel industry met all of these.

(a) The number of firms must be small,
(b) the product must be undifferentiated,
(c) production capacity must be readily expressed as a simple index, such as tons per month, and
(d) the industry association must have a long tradition of carrying on a wide range of activities, with intraindustry coordination carried out either by the association or through the association by the government.

6. As stated in the opening paragraph of Section V, the findings derived from analyzing the steel industry prove useful in judging the situation in other industries.

Preliminary observations are made in Section II, while Sections III and IV, respectively, consist of case studies of the list-price system and investment coordination in the steel industry. For comparison with the conclusions drawn in these sections, Section V takes up output coordination in the petroleum refining industry. Section VI examines the secondary effects of intraindustry coordination, and Section VII presents overall conclusions.

II. Preliminary Observations

The debate still continues today among specialists on administrative law as to when government interventions require a basis in law, and in particular in which situations a legal basis is required for administrative guidance.[7] Intraindustry coordination *cum* industrial policy, however, has almost without exception been carried out by means of administrative guidance for which there was no direct legal basis, and apparently without regard for the existence of this legal debate. For this reason, the "guidance" proffered has not been made public, and only limited records of it remain, so in most cases there is no way for outsiders to know what the content of the administrative guidance was.[8]

It is necessary to note that there are severe limits to the admissible range in which output, prices, or the level of investment can fall if they are taken as policy targets in MITI's administrative guidance given to individual firms or an industry association.

When administrative guidance is adhered to, or where firms follow such guidance, then the "quantity" chosen will be within the range of the policy function, so that the guidance and the actions of firms coincide. This needs indicate nothing more than that those doing the "guiding" are avoiding a situation in which those being guided will refuse the guidance, that is, choose a "quantity" outside the range of the policy function. And in the normal case, there was indeed prior negotiation between those doing the "guiding" and those being "guided" on the permissible range of options and the particular choice that should be made within that range.

When the government has "power" because of, for example, its authority as the grantor of a variety of licenses, then this can be used as a lever to increase the operating range of policy. Even in this case, however, the use of such leverage has generally been held as undesirable, so that there are severe limitations to using such power.[9]

Before undertaking the discussion of specific cases in the following sections, we will look at an example of output coordination that is thought of as the most representative case of coordination. The main source quoted is a collection of documents compiled by the Administrative Management Agency. The example taken up below consists of reports from both the government and industry in connection with supply/demand forecasts drawn up for output coordination in the synthetic fiber industry.

The system is explained as: "a supply/demand forecasting method [which] is a method of output coordination wherein the government indicates a production target, and firms . . . . each draw up their production plans with this target as a base, and then submit these to the government."[10]

The government in its report claimed that:

looking at the actual results, the target given by the government and the plans drawn
up by firms did not differ by that much, so that this method proved effective. [This
was because] . . . at the stage of drawing up the supply/demand forecast, discussions
were held with the Supply–Demand Council of the industry association [and because]
firms themselves were also intent on reducing production, as excess production would
lead to their own demise.[11]

Such explanations are inadequate when, as here, we have the aim of evaluating the effectiveness of policy.

Assuming that the above explanation of the reason "there was not much
difference" is valid, then there can be no presumption that there would
have been much difference in the behavior of firms or of the industry as
a whole had the government not acted. Thus there is no reason to believe
the evaluation that "this method proved effective." Regardless of whether
there was in fact not much difference, it is above all necessary to make
clear on the basis of facts what the role of the government was, of how
the government acted when they were different, and the process by which
it saw to it that there was not much difference.

Contact between the government (*genkyoku*) and firms in an industry
in the case of administrative guidance was normally carried out through
the industry association.

From the standpoint of the industry. . . . the main function of the industry association
was to convince the *genkyoku*. . . . to adopt favorable policies. From the standpoint
of the *genkyoku*, the function of the industry association and the firms of which it was
comprised was to cooperate with the *genkyoku* in carrying out industrial policy, and
to bring into line firms which were not well behaved or which voiced contrary opinions.[12]

The report of the government here states that "the management association
played an extremely important role in carrying out the administrative
guidance of MITI."[13]

There is no detailed statement of the purpose of "output adjustment"
in the report. The government was not acting in its policy role with some
clear goal of its own, but was, rather attempting to prevent what was
thought of as excess production and excess competition by most firms
and the government. It seems that both firms and the government held
such goals as axiomatic. The definition of these conditions, however, was
not always made clear, and so one cannot presume that there was a consensus among the firms involved, or among firms and the government.
Furthermore, there is no reason to presume that this had always to be
the primary goal.[14]

In the reporting of the government side, the first point raised in the
evaluation of administrative guidance was that "it cannot be implemented

when there is no agreement or acquiescence by the other party," while from the side of the industry, the primary merit of administrative guidance was that "the government was effective as a fair and authoritative mediator," giving a frank view of the role of the government in output coordination. If one adds to this the statement by the government that the primary "point about which administrators must take care . . . is to never cause balance to be lost in the overall situation," the following picture of the government role can be drawn.[15]

A role for the government in output adjustment arises when there is a difference in intentions among firms, so that if matters are left to themselves there can be the presumption that the situation will deteriorate into excess production. Even in this case, there is no guarantee that the government will always be successful in fulfilling its role of a fair and authoritative mediator and be able to work on firms to obtain their acquiescence and agreement. In order to be successful, a minimum condition is to "never cause balance to be lost in the overall situation." The government does not have much of a free hand in carrying out the above role.

The report claims that firms acceded to administrative guidance, and argues why that was the case, but one must note that this is with "guidance" of the nature depicted above.

III. The Steel List-Price System

The list-price system in the steel industry is held up as an archetype of "output adjustment" and "price adjustment." Drawing from a history of antitrust policy, the outline of the system was as follows:[16]

1. On the basis of MITI production targets, each firm reported its expected sales for each month by product to MITI.

2. Each manufacturer was to sell its steel products at the same time at a fixed location, agreeing with wholesalers on the amounts to be purchased. Each firm was to carry out sales at the "list price" that it had previously reported to MITI.

3. After reaching agreement with its wholesalers, each manufacturer was to report by product the quantity contracted with each wholesaler and to publish its aggregate sales, together with amounts left unsold.

4. Manufacturers were to have a designated wholesaler for each product and were to make sales only through that wholesaler.

5. If there were unsold products, then they were to be bought up by a sufficiently strong wholesaler at a predetermined price, and unsold

amounts were to provide a basis for determining decreases in production for the following month.

6. MITI would take appropriate steps against manufacturers who went against MITI guidance as to production limits and appropriate pricing.

7. Each manufacturer was to deliver to MITI a written promise by the president of the company that it would abide by an "Outline of Steel Market Measures" with this general content. For monitoring purposes, a designated monitoring committee was also to be established.

This list-price system has been referred to as both a "steel pricing system"[17] and an "administrative guidance cartel."[18] For our purpose of taking up this industrial policy as an archetypical case and trying to evaluate the extent of its effectiveness, the above description is inadequate. It is necessary to carefully weigh what actual government action (here, the policies of the *genkyoku,* MITI) consisted of, and what the government's influence was. The above explanation gives the impression that MITI had a controlling voice or something close to it, and that it had a strong impact as a policy organ. Our conclusion, however, is totally at variance with this.

There are many items that need to be questioned to arrive at a clear understanding of the reality of the list-price system, but for our purposes the following two are particularly important:

1. Who determined the specific content of the production limits and appropriate prices to be administered by MITI and how were they determined?

2. What was the content of the steps in the "appropriate steps MITI will take against manufacturers that violated" these limits? Were such steps ever used in practice?

Let us first look at query (1). The period in which the list-price system was said to have functioned was not very long (from June 1958 to December 1962), but even during this period the system was modified many times. The "Outline of Steel Market Measures" referred to in item (7) above seems to have been circulated to the industry association (the Japan Iron and Steel Federation) on July 25, 1960. According to the *de facto* leader of the list-price system, the Chairman of the General Affairs Committee of the Federation, Yoshihiro Inayama, "if this system is adopted, then unlike in the past, we can be confident that we can actually count on achieving stable steel prices."[19] Thus, with this, the list-price system would become a much stronger set of measures for output and price coordination.

The method was one of "at base self-coordination," where MITI would devise "ceiling and floor prices" and would use administrative guidance toward any firm that went over the ceiling in its submitted price list, suggesting that it not be exceeded, and would similarly offer guidance that "if prices are less than the floor, it is permissible to adjust output." The ceiling price was to be "the price currently listed by manufacturers," while the floor price was to be that price "less ¥2,000 – ¥4,000," but "if the production cost has risen or fallen markedly, then the ceiling and floor prices are to be adjusted immediately." Furthermore, "when the list price was to be maintained, or the subcommittee was to carry out an adjustment in production, then when the figures were filed with MITI, it would in turn transmit the production target to each firm. We would have to submit a written promise that we would in all cases adhere to the quantity."[20]

If in addition the following quote is considered, then the answer to our first query should be clear. "Until now production adjustment has not been permitted, but this time production adjustment will be openly permitted, if the listed price falls below the floor price. . . . We have thus been able to some extent to realize the steel price measures which we had desired in the past."[21]

The production limits and appropriate prices to be administered by MITI were not in fact decided by MITI on the basis of some sort of standard, but were determined by the manufacturers (who were to be "guided"!) *prior* to any actual "guidance" incorporating floor price restrictions. At least from this standpoint, it cannot be held that MITI played any active policy role.

If there was some sort of policy role for MITI, it would have been to prevent the appearance of manufacturers who did not adhere to the "production limits or appropriate prices," or to actively intervene to change such behavior when it appeared. From this standpoint we can now answer query (2); the reality of the appropriate steps that MITI would take against manufacturers that violated MITI guidance was made clear in 1962.

When looked at from the standpoint of output and price coordination, the real function of the list-price system would be called into play only when the growth in demand slowed or was expected to slow, so that excess capacity arose or was predicted to arise. The start of the list-price system coincided with the starting point of the "Iwato Boom," June 1958, and the economy continued to expand extremely rapidly until July 1961, when with an increase in the discount rate a period of tight money commenced. The phrase "investment calling forth more investment" became the catch phrase of this growth period, and the rate of increase in demand for steel products far surpassed that foreseen even by optimists.

Initially, the system was invented as an alternative to a recession cartel;[22]

helped by the situation of expanding domestic demand and the steel strike in the United States, the system "achieved its goals with great success."[23] The situation changed drastically, however, with the onset of tight money.

In mid-1961, in the market for sheet steel, where there continued to be rapid expansion of capacity, prices fell substantially below list prices, giving rise to discontent. Again, "the steel market was facing its greatest crisis since the institution of the list-price system, and in December, prices for steel plate, which had thus far held to the list price, fell below it, and from then on the situation became serious, with no hint of recovery."[24]

Then, during the July–September quarter, there was an attempt to revive the market, which was strengthened from October. These attempts, however, had no discernible impact; the list-price system had effectively collapsed, and a request was made for permission to form that which had been avoided all along, a recession cartel. What calls for our attention is the functioning of the list-price system during this progression.

What is notable throughout this progression is the plaintive wailing that measures whose implementation had been promised were not being implemented. These complaints became obvious from the end of 1961,[25] but the following is a particularly straightforward statement of the reasons why the series of market measures had failed.

> I think many points can be raised concerning the reason for failure of the market measures which have been drawn up with so much effort by the individual manufacturers. In fact, while it is embarrassing for me to say this, I think one of the most important reasons is that the measures which were supposed to be implemented were not put into effect according to plan.[26]

There is absolutely no indication that MITI made any active attempt to correct this situation.

With the passage of time, market conditions worsened, and a series of market measures were taken while "one should say that the list price system . . . is not so much on the verge of falling apart as having already collapsed."[27] The first of these was in the July–September quarter, when steel ingot production was to be reduced by 20% from the level of the third quarter of the previous year, with "open hearth furnaces being sealed on the 17th and 18th of July." The second was that all the production of the manufacturers other than the 10 blast furnace firms was to be bought up by wholesalers.[28] In addition to these two pillars of the policy, on-site inspectors were to be sent.

In the April 24th report of the List Price Committee, there is the statement that "MITI engaged in administrative guidance to see that there was strict adherence to the targets for steel plate and shapes production, and retroactive to January, the Output Reduction Monitoring Committee began to monitor the output of each factory."[29] It was only in July, however, that it was reported that "from the 23rd on-site inspectors have been sent to each factory, to monitor the reduction of production of plate and all types of steel shapes."[30]

The judgment was rendered at the end of October that, due to the market measures "it appeared at one time, from the end of June through the beginning of July, that the market was recovering, but thereafter the market failed to pick up at all, and recently efforts to undersell at very low prices have become rampant."[31]

In all this the following two points should be noted. First, there is no trace to indicate that MITI was an active participant in the process of continually debating and implementing market measures.[32] Second, as noted for the reduction in ingot production, "there was the fear that, when it came to reducing ingot production, monitoring would be very easy, and with each manufacturer considering its own interests, nothing has to this date been done."[33] I believe this statement is symbolic of the nature of the list-price system, but what is important for our purposes is that even in this there is no evidence of MITI taking an active hand. The list-price system was not applied to all products, and there were also outsiders who did not participate. There is no evidence that MITI took an active hand even in changing this situation. In other words, not only was there no effective policy for strengthening output and price coordination, there is no evidence that the government even attempted an active role in this direction.[34]

It was stated that MITI would take appropriate action against manufacturers that violated the system, but in spite of there having been a stream of violations (by, in fact, all manufacturers), there is no evidence that any action was ever taken, nor even any evidence of suggestions that action be taken.

As a result of the above review, we are led to the conclusion that the government did not play a role or have a substantial direct influence on output and price coordination within the framework of the list-price system. In evaluating intraindustry coordination *cum* industrial policy, our conclusion must be that it was ineffective in the case of the list-price system in the steel industry.

IV. The Coordination of Investment in the Steel Industry

The situation describing the role and effect of government action in connection with the list-price system holds even more clearly in the case of investment coordination in the steel industry. In this, the government not only took no active role (there was nothing that could be called policy), the various items referred to by investment coordination did not have in any direct way a clear impact on the investment behavior of the firms that were involved.[35]

The beginning of investment coordination was in December 1959, when MITI requested that the industry coordinate on its own the implementation of the long-term capacity plan. Formally, the goal was for the industry to draw up a long-term investment plan for approval by the Industrial Finance Committee of the Industry Rationalization Council. Each firm in principle was to discuss and report by the end of the fiscal year (the end of March) for the coming fiscal year on the "coordination" of investment, which meant principally the timing of the start of construction of new blast furnaces; often this was not done until the fiscal year had begun.

In the history of investment coordination, the two years where it foundered most were FY 1960 and FY 1965. For our purposes, it is sufficient merely to examine the views of those involved on the outcome.[36]

In FY 1960, the outcome was that coordination was left by the wayside. At the year-end meeting of the List Price Committee, the evaluation by Chairman Inayama of the General Affairs Committee of the Steel Federation was that "at the beginning of the fiscal year autonomous coordination failed miserably, for while somehow or other the appearance was maintained, the reality was exposed in that manufacturers did not in fact coordinate their efforts in the least."[37]

For coordination in FY 1965, at the start of the coordination procedure MITI advised that it would be best in principle to cease all new investment, calling for a one-year moratorium. Opposition was strong, however, especially by Sumitomo Metal Industries, which was in the process of building its Wakayama Steel Mill. The final conclusion, reached in July, was that for the two years of FY 1965 and FY 1966, firms were free to initiate new construction.[38]

Let us conclude with the comments of one observer of the FY 1967 coordination process, Mr. Tokunaga,[39] which can be viewed as an evaluation of the entire history of investment coordination:

> The final outcome of the FY 1967 steel industry investment coordination, the result of roughly a half year's discussion, was that in effect each firm's plans would be approved in full, for both steel making and milling facilities. This was virtually the same outcome as that of the autonomous coordination which took place in FY 1965 and 1966, so that it can be seen how difficult it was if only those involved tried to coordinate on their own to achieve that which would be seen as desirable from the standpoint of the national economy.[40]

V. Output Coordination in Petroleum Refining

As has been seen thus far, at least in the case of the steel industry during the rapid growth era, we do not believe that the government was actively involved in intraindustry coordination, whether it was of output, prices, or investment, nor do we feel that it had any notable influence.

The goal of this section is to attempt a generalization of our evaluation of intraindustry coordination *cum* industrial policy, by examining or inferring the situation in other industries, with the case of the steel industry as a base for comparison.

The reasons why the steel industry during the rapid growth era was chosen as the main focus of analysis have already been set forth in Section I. Here we want to be reminded of the fifth of those reasons, which was that for intraindustry coordination to be effective an industry had to meet four conditions, and the steel industry met all of these conditions. Considering at the same time both this and the conclusions reached in the previous section, the following reasoning is not that forced.

Of the four conditions (a) through (d), if any one of them is not met, then even more than in the case of the steel industry, successful coordination is unlikely. In this case, the role that the government could play will be even more limited, and in such an industry it is inconceivable that government participation will be more positive and have greater influence. Most industries would be thought to fall into this category.

The next point is to ask, when these four conditions have been met, what additional conditions must at the same time be fulfilled in order for coordination *cum* industrial policy to be evaluated as having been different from that of the steel industry. While such conditions cannot be comprehensively examined, probably no one would dispute that the representative situation is one in which, for at least one of output, price, and investment coordination, the government is expected to do the coordination and has been given power to do so. Here we will take up petroleum refining under the Petroleum Industry Law as a typical case in which these conditions are met, and we will examine what intraindustry coordination consisted of, and in what way the government was active in this, keeping the case of the steel industry in mind for comparison.

From 1962 petroleum refining fell under the Petroleum Industry Law, and "the industry had the striking distinction" that there was strong government intervention in output, pricing, and investment. The course of enactment and implementation of the law teaches us many things, as the law was intended to allow "to the minimum extent required coordination of the activities of firms in the industry, as with the liberalization of petroleum imports it is expected that the petroleum market will be in dis-array."[41]

The first point to be noted is that, in the process of enactment of the Petroleum Industry Law, there was strong criticism of direct intervention by the government. Initially, in the "Summary of the Petroleum Industry Bill" made public in December 1961, "there was a strong outcry because of its overly strong control coloration," so that the Petroleum Industry Bill submitted to the Diet in March of the next year had been substantially revised.[42] In the debate in the Commerce and Industry Committee of the House of Representatives, Director-General Kawade of the MITI Mining Bureau testified concerning the drawing up of petroleum supply plans under Section 3 of the Bill:

> The petroleum supply plan will be a guide for the activity of firms, but it is possible that the sum of individual firm production plans will substantially exceed the overall plan target. However, we are not thinking of automatically notifying each firm of the excess and asking them to reduce output accordingly.[43]

He also testified (concerning Section 15 of the Bill) that the notification of standard prices "will be done to appeal to the social responsibility of firms as a psychological measure, and will not be legally binding."[44] Finally, on the permit for [new] facilities (Section 7), which in the later implementation of the law would be used as the strongest lever for achieving conformance with MITI's intentions, he testified that "they will be licensed in accordance with the law, and we are saying that we will issue a license whenever [these] three basic conditions are met. We think it is unfair to use this as a means to obtain revenge for some unrelated matter" a famous statement expressing the essence of administrative guidance.[45]

The actual implementation of the law was at variance with the explanation of the aim of the bill. This testimony, however, provides a frank indication of the situation that government intervention faced at that time, when direct intervention by the government in the actions of individual firms was strongly criticized. This gives us an understanding of the strong restrictions placed on MITI policy.[46]

The second point we want to note is that, at least formally, the method of output adjustment in the industry, even under the Petroleum Industry Law, barely differed from that of the steel industry. MITI requested the cooperation of the Demand Specialists Committee of the Petroleum Association of Japan in January and February of each year, to draw up the "Demand Outlook," which formed the basis for the Petroleum Supply and Demand Plan, which in turn underlay the Petroleum Supply Plan required under Section 3 of the Petroleum Industry Law.[47] According to the Fair Trade Commission "the Petroleum Supply Plan . . . only indicates the planned volumes which MITI feels desirable for the country as a whole, and does not indicate production levels for each individual petroleum refiner."[48]

For example, for the publication of the Petroleum Supply Plan for the second half of FY 1962, the first plan following the enactment of the Petroleum Industry Law, MITI had each firm submit its plans for the second half of FY 1962 to the Petroleum Association of Japan as a way of probing the direction the industry was taking. This was done prior to the registration of production plans by the refiners, which was required by the Law. The total amount of crude oil required, however, was 25% more than that of the Supply Plan, so after consulting with the Petroleum Council, a request for output coordination was made to the Petroleum Association of Japan.[49]

The third item to be noted is that under the industry law for this industry the content of government participation differed from that in other industries when its requests to the industry association for output coordination did not succeed. In the case of this industry, "in order to obtain 'voluntary' cooperation through 'autonomous' discussion among industry members, MITI in fact had to use forceful guidance or direct intervention. Such administrative guidance functioned successfully because in the background MITI held power to license investment and to issue a formal request for a change in production plans."[50]

At the time of the above coordination for the second half of FY 1962, "there was disagreement among those in the industry on the standard for coordination, and developing it was not easy. At that point MITI through administrative guidance pushed for autonomous coordination, obtained the approval of the Petroleum Association of Japan for a standard, and pressed for output coordination on this basis."[51] It is doubtful that this could have been done without the power described above.

For the second half of FY 1963, the previous standard was maintained: "Idemitsu Kosan and Daikyo Oil, which had expressed displeasure with output coordination from the start, opposed carrying it out, but under strong guidance from MITI the Petroleum Association of Japan . . . decided upon output coordination. In response, Idemitsu Kosan:

> was unhappy because it would not be able to adequately utilize its [newly completed] facilities, and so it did not go along with output coordination and instead went ahead with its own production plans. It did not respond to the efforts of the Petroleum Association to persuade it to conform, and on November 12th gave notice that it was quitting the Petroleum Association.[52]

This is the so-called Idemitsu Incident. MITI officials and the Chairman of the Petroleum Council tried to persuade Idemitsu to cooperate in output coordination, but Idemitsu refused. Then, in January, "Idemitsu finally began to move when MITI indicated that it had decided to issue a formal warning as provided for by the Petroleum Industry Law." In a meeting on January 25th between the Minister of MITI, the Chairman of the Petroleum Council, and the President of Idemitsu, it was decided to adopt a compromise plan that took into account some of Idemitsu's demands, such as that in the future output coordination would cease,[53] and that for January through September 1964 a new standard would be adopted that provided for greater output by Idemitsu. To this Idemitsu acceded.

The fourth point we wish to note is that, as can be seen above, even when the government had "power," it was not a simple matter to make output coordination function effectively or to maintain the system.

The fifth item we want to note is that output coordination took place with "strong guidance and direct intervention" by MITI, while at the same time, even though standard prices were posted "in order to improve the market for petroleum products," these efforts were successful neither in improving nor in maintaining market conditions.[54] A straightforward description of the situation at this time comes from an interview—itself unusual—on April 1, 1964, with Minister Hajime Fukuda of MITI.

> The most regrettable thing is that, even though for example output coordination is being carried out under administrative guidance as part of the implementation of the Petroleum Industry Law, there has been much haggling and posturing among the firms, and there is a lack of any semblance of cooperation in seeking stability for the petroleum industry as a whole. This has led to delays in and violations of output coordination, and I believe has resulted in the loss of the anticipated benefits. At this time I am strongly demanding a change in heart by each member of the industry, to cooperate as one in eliminating the excess competition which stems from an excessive concern with market share. I am calling for renewed resolve in adhering strictly to output coordination and posted prices, so that the petroleum industry will carry out its social responsibilities in full.[55]

If the real impact of output coordination in the petroleum refining industry is viewed as far surpassing that in the case of steel, then the most important factor must be the additional one of the presence of "power" stemming tfrom the Petroleum Industry Law. Since it has been quite unusual for an industry to have such a law, the petroleum industry was indeed "strikingly distinct."

Let us now list again the information relevant here for generalizing our [initial] evaluation to intraindustry coordination in general, the aim of this section.

1. Whether it related to output, prices, or investment, there was severe criticism of government intervention in the activities of individual firms.

2. Even when the government was provided with strong "powers," "autonomous coordination" was normally chosen as the basic approach.

3. Only when "autonomous" coordination did not function well did government participation commence. In order for such participation to be influential, some sort of power was needed for leverage. Furthermore, there had to be a consensus that the use of such power toward the object of the government's participation was proper.

4. In order for government participation to achieve its goals, active cooperation by the relevant firms was essential, and so it was necessary to set forth the principles underlying the government's actions and obtain the agreement of firms to these principles. In this sense, the room for discretion by the government in its use of "power" was not wide.

5. Even when the government used its power to participate in coordination, it was not easy to actually attain its goals.

In jointly considering the conclusions of our discussion above on output coordination in the petroleum refining industry, the results of the discussion of the steel industry in the preceding sections and the conclusion of the first half of this section, that "in the majority of industries . . . the government was neither an active participant in coordination, nor had great influence," we are led without forcing matters to the following generalization about how intraindustry coordination in its various forms should be evaluated: Intraindustry coordination in the form of coordination of output, pricing or investment has been consistently held to be an important part of industrial policy. However, in fact the government almost never was an active participant as part of its policy, or had through its participation a clear, direct impact on industry.[56]

VI. Secondary Effects

In the previous section, the conclusion was qualified by the word *direct*. This is because the conclusion does not take into account that when, as happens in either output, price, or investment coordination, a situation continues in which there are regular meetings and the exchange of all sorts of information with the government and among rival firms, then it can be presumed that there are important influences on the behavior of firms. If one requires that evaluating the impact of coordination *cum* industrial policy encompass such influences, then the impact was not small, and the government can perhaps be regarded as an active participant in that its presence gave rise to the necessity of holding meetings.[57] This influence took many forms, but one can suspect that in almost no case was this foreseen by even the responsible government officials. The two main points to be noted are as follows.

First, in the history of intraindustry coordination, one can often think of firms that spoke out against coordination.[58] When, however, there is a lengthy history of industry association activity, where "coordination" has served as a forum for meetings over time with rival firms along with the government, then it would of course require resolve to speak out against coordination, and to face servere criticism by rival firms and government officials of any firms making plans public that would result in coordination becoming more difficult. Thus one might presume that the actions of each firm would be heavily influenced by coordination. One might think that the extent of such influence would increase with the length of time over which there had been coordination and the degree to which it had taken root.[59]

When rival firms confer regularly, and exchange their opinions on the direction markets are currently moving, on future demand expectations, and on future capacity and the like, and discuss the necessary responses, then one need hardly stress again that this will influence the behavior of each firm, and hence influence supply and demand conditions in the industry as a whole.

Second, when rival firms confer with each other or with the government on a regular basis, the information exchanged is not limited that specifically to intraindustry coordination. One can thus find the following very favorable evaluation:

> The issues with which industry is currently faced are jointly examined, and information is exchanged on new technologies and domestic and foreign markets . . . [so that] it cannot be denied that [these fora] have been an extremely effective measure for collecting and exchanging and transmitting information about industry . . . [In sum] if one thinks of this as a system for the exchange of information, then . . . it may well have been one important cause underlying the high growth rate of postwar Japanese industry.[60]

The above effects or influences should perhaps be treated as by-products or side effects, but to the extent that they are emphasized, then it is likely that a difference of opinion will arise regarding the evaluation of intraindustry coordination.[61]

The attitude of people in general to this sort of industry association activity and to the relationship between the government and business stems in great part from the tradition since the Meiji Restoration of a strong central government and to the influence of the wide-ranging economic controls that were present during and immediately after World War II.[62] Accordingly, even in intraindustry coordination *cum* industrial policy had taken a different form or not occurred at all, there must have been effects such as mentioned above. It is for this reason that such effects are not taken up as positive features of intraindustry coordination *cum* industrial policy in this chapter.

VII. Policy Evaluation and Related Points

Our conclusions when intraindustry coordination is analyzed as a form of industrial policy are as follows.

It is claimed that intraindustry coordination *cum* industrial policy was used in many industries. In almost all cases, however, government participation had almost no discernible impact, no matter what standard of evaluation is used. At base, then, our overall evaluation is that as policy it was ineffective. There are two important observations related to this.

First, the exceptional case of the petroleum refining industry, where the government was given strong powers, provided useful material for the anticipated conclusion that in such a case it was significantly more feasible to carry out intraindustry coordination *cum* industrial policy. But with the above conclusion that in the petroleum refining case intraindustry coordination was not always effective, it is said that to the policy guidelines (put into place after the Petroleum Industry Law was implemented) "were added [to the effect] that there should be consideration given to small and medium sized private firms independent of foreign capital, which expressed in a direct way the exceptional nature of the industry law . . . . so that claims for consistency as industrial policy are extremely dubious."[63]

Second, What should we learn from the lively debate that developed over the appropriateness of the goals of industrial policy, and particularly of intraindustry coordination? The elimination of excess competition, "the strengthening of international competitiveness, the promotion of exports, the improvement of the balance of payments, the development and modernization of the domestic industrial structure," obtaining a stable supply of basic natural resources, and other "extremely generalized slogans" were all stressed as goals or justifications of industrial policy. However, the nature of these was such that "for each industry and *genkyoku*, what was important was that, in short, favorable measures be provided to the industry. If something was useful in persuading the relevant parties, it would be used as needed with the addition as appropriate of any reason or excuse."[64]

If attention is paid to this, then it can readily be understood why there was no resolution to the debate over the appropriateness of goals, and why the same debate was repeated time and again. As the "goal" was to "persuade the relevant parties," then it need not be presumed that there was any consensus among firms or an industry and the *genkyoku*. It is possible that there was not even any coordination of actual opinions as to the goals.

Notes

1. It is necessary to explain why the term *intraindustry coordination (sangyo nai chosei)*, which is hardly ever used, is employed in this chapter. In the literature on postwar Japanese industrial policy, the terms *output coordination, price coordination*, and *capacity (investment) coordination* appear frequently. These are applied to an extremely wide range of industries, and it seems that such policies are often thought of as being the model of industrial policy, or at least a representative form. I am applying to these as a whole the term *intraindustry coordination* and am analyzing them together in this chapter for three reasons. First, these all are often closely linked in practice and can be observed to play complementary roles. Second, all of them have the common characteristic that they seek to coordinate the mutual interests of the firms that comprise an industry. Third, though to a varying extent, there is a common feature in that the government often participates in a variety of ways, although its role may not be obvious and it may often participate for some particular purpose.

   Thus in this chapter intraindustry coordination is used as a general term for the various patterns referred to as output, price, and capacity investment coordination. Whether or not each of these fits into this mold can be judged for each of the cases described in the following analysis. Instead of intraindustry coordination, the phrase *intraindustry coordination policies* could be used, but this analysis as a whole, and in particular Section II, should serve as an explanation of why this has not been done.

2. For example, Tsuruta [1982], p. 186, states concerning the petrochemical industry that "when there is government intervention based on legal powers of compulsion, then the performance of the industrial organization helps directly in evaluating the effectiveness of the government intervention." However, it is not easy, for example, to judge the effectiveness of medical treatment by the course of a patient's illness following hospitalization, because a patient's demise may not imply that there were faults in his or her treatment. Hence this sort of reasoning cannot be thought appropriate. Even though there may be "legal powers of compulsion," they do not extend to all facets of a firm's behavior, and it is wrong to think that there are no restrictions on the use of this power. Again, policy is not able to handle all the factors that affect the "performance of the industrial organization." For example, when it became possible to procure low-cost oil, it was inconceivable that some policy response could have been used to forestall a worsening of performance in the coal industry.

3. For example, the merger of Yahata Steel and Fuji Steel, which gave birth to Nippon Steel, is often used as a representative example of policies to promote largeness and mergers. If, however, this is seen as being the result of (industrial) policy, and it is claimed that this is representative of industrial policy, then it is necessary to make clear what the policy function was, in what way the policy operated, and what the benefits were from bringing about a merger.

4. Recently there has been heightened interest in "industrial policy," but it should be noted that this has been focused on policies toward high-technology industries, or what are often called targeting policies.

5. Representative are the New Industrial Structure and Special Industries Law debates of 1962–1963 and the debate arising from the 1968 merger of Yahata Steel and Fuji Steel.
6. Komiya [1975], p. 308.
7. See, for example, Harada [1983].
8. Because in Japan (Kyogoku [1983], p. 347) "the basic unit of the bureaucracy in allocating responsibility is the division in the main ministry with jurisdiction [over the industry]. . . . For matters within a given jurisdiction, each division of the ministry by itself personifies the Japanese government." Even for senior officials in a ministry, or for officials who belong to different divisions or enter the division at a later date, it is impossible to know in detail the content of administrative guidance.
9. Details of the argument are presented for the petroleum refining industry in Section V.
10. Gyosei Kanricho [1981], p. 105.
11. Ibid.
12. Komiya [1975], p. 311.
13. Gyosei Kanricho [1981], p. 107.
14. Ibid, pp. 105 and 109. This situation reflects the nature of output coordination and the role of the government therein. Section VII also touches on this point.
15. Ibid, pp. 110 and 113.
16. Kosei Torihiki Iinkai [1977], p. 99.
17. Imai [1976], p. 154.
18. Uekusa [1982], p. 209.
19. Shin Nippon Seitetsu [1970], p. 205. This volume is a compilation of the main sections of the *Eigyo Junpo* (Ten-Day Operations Report) for the years 1959–1962. I expect that there will be objections to using this source as the primary material for judging the actual functioning of the list-price system. I feel though that this material is relevant for the following three reasons: First, this firm was always regarded as the leader of the industry, and was furthermore a continually enthusiastic leader of the list-price system. Second, these materials were drawn up for firms with which they had a long-term business relationship, so that one would imagine them to be frank. Third, this period was referred to as one in which the Antitrust Law was in hibernation, and so one would presume that the opinions expressed in it are not biased by the existence of the Antitrust Law or any concern with public opinion in support of the law.
20. Ibid, pp. 206–207.
21. Ibid, p. 207. This statement is from a summary explanation by Inayama at the July 26th meeting of the Public Sale ("list price") Committee. See page 215 for the evaluation of the system by trading firms/wholesalers and steel consumers. See page 69 for the determination of prices before the change in the system.
22. Mr. Inayama, then Managing Director of Yahata Steel, stated at the January 20, 1959, Futures Committee meeting that "although there is such a thing as a recession cartel, the fact of the matter is that we are carrying out the list price system under administrative guidance, without bothering to request approval of a recession cartel." (Ibid, p. 26)
23. Ibid, p. 26.
24. Ibid, p. 433, for April 20, 1962.
25. For example, ibid, p. 358 (November 25), p. 396 (January 21) and p. 423 (March 27).
26. This is a portion of the statement by Mr. Abe, Director of the Sales Division of Yahata Steel, at the October 24, 1962, meeting of the Futures Committee.
27. This is a portion of the statement by Mr. Inayama at the Public Sale ("list price") Committee meeting of May 25, 1962.
28. Concerning the aim of this, Mr. Inayama, the Chairman of the General Affairs Committee, stated that:

If this is done, then because it is accompanied by financing for the full quantity of the products, there is of course no need to discount heavily. Until now, it was feared that the method of buying up unsold steel would lead to under-the-counter sales and the sales of many cheap products, along with it being very difficult to monitor. From now on, however, if all steel, including secondary products, are bought up by a specified trading firm/wholesaler, then not a single item will leave the factory. (ibid, p. 448)

29. Ibid, p. 435.
30. Ibid, p. 469.
31. Ibid, p. 503. In this period, the "proportional decrease in ingot production will be increased by 5 percentage points . . . and at the same time the product-specific output reduction system will be strengthened . . . with heavy and medium plate output to be cut by 40% from the base level of January of this year." Ibid, p. 491.
32. The monitoring system consisted of "industry members sending people to each other to monitor production." (Ibid., p. 518)
33. Ibid, p. 448.
34. In Section II, recall that it was stated that "furthermore, there is no reason to presume that this must always be made the primary goal." Here we do not consider the issue of whether MITI considered this to be desirable, or whether it had that sort of power.
35. For the details of this sort of argument, see Miwa [1977].
36. For an analysis that includes the details of these events, see Miwa [1977], pp. 50 and 56, the relevant sections.
37. Shin Nippon Seitetsu [1970], p. 239.
38. In contrast to this sort of view, I would expect that some would mention that the Sumitomo Metals Incident arose over the way in which output coordination was handled in 1965, but I do not feel it is relevant. There was a time lapse between the decisions on capacity investment coordination and the occurrence of the Sumitomo Metals Incident (see Miwa [1977], p. 50), and even the closing off of the allocation of import licenses for bunker coal was not sufficient to force output coordination (ibid, p. 54). In view of how we saw industrial policy to be carried out in Section II, the Sumitomo Metals Incident is an example of the failure of industrial policy, and this incident sheds light not on what the government could do, but can rather be viewed as useful in judging what the government could not do.
39. Hisatsugu Tokunaga was at the time a Managing Director of Fuji Steel and was a former Administrative Vice-minister of MITI.
40. Tokunaga [1967], p. 58.
41. Tanaka [1980], pp. 19 and 28.
42. Ibid, p. 23. For the details of this, see pp. 22–23.
43. Ibid, p. 29. This is according to Section 10 of the Petroleum Industry Law.
44. Ibid.
45. Ibid, p. 29. This standard is set forth in Section 6 of the Law.
46. Later, in the summer of 1962, the Industrial Structure Committee made known its basic line of thinking on the New Industrial Structure, which was the successor to the proposed Special Industries Law (Law on Temporary Measures for the Promotion of Specified Industries). It should be noted that there were two main points in the criticism by industry of the Special Industries Law. First, it was feared that the restrictions on the freedom of industrial activity that the law would impose would open the way to a system of bureaucratic control. Second, it was feared that, if anything, the setting of promotion standards in line with bureaucratic-type thinking and restrictions on firm

activities would lead to a weakening of competitive strength. This draws from Tsuruta [1976], pp. 442–443.
47. Kosei Torihiki Iinkai (Fair Trade Commission) [1983], p. 205. See note 48 below on this source.
48. Ibid, p. 210. This source is a compilation of the series of Tokyo High Court decisions during 1980–1981 on the so-called Petroleum Cartel Case. This is used here because it includes the September 26, 1980, decision on the Petroleum Association of Japan and two others in the Output Coordination Case.
49. Ibid, p. 212.
50. Ibid, p. 211.
51. Ibid, p. 211. On page 212 it is stated that this standard "was based on a composite index, with weights of one-third each of the market share of fuel oil sales, the share of all imported oil processed for domestic consumption and the current share in total average capacity."
52. Ibid, pp. 213–214.
53. It ceased in the second half of FY 1966. Ibid, p. 217.
54. This was done from November 1962 through February 1966.
55. Ibid, pp. 216.
56. It is necessary to note that this is different from the criticism of intraindustry coordination from the standpoint of emphasizing procompetition policies.
57. It is undoubtedly wrong to assume, however, that without government participation in this fashion, such meetings would not have been held or continued. To claim this would be to overrate the effectiveness of policy.
58. For example, in the 1960s there were Idemitsu Kosan, Nisshin Spinning, and Sumitomo Metal Industries and more recently Tokyo Steel Mfg.
59. The report of the government discussed in Section II states that one of the reasons that firms followed administrative guidance was because "Japanese firms are organized into associations industry by industry, and it is difficult for them to act as outsiders. Larger firms in particular are strongly aware that they comprise an industry, and dislike threatening their own foundation by upsetting the order within their industry." (Gyosei Kanricho [1981], p. 107).
60. Komiya [1975], p. 324.
61. In particular, the situation described in point (1), particularly in the second paragraph, had a deleterious effect on the maintenance and furthering of competition, and so this can serve as a basis for judging that "coordination" itself is undesirable.
62. See Komiya [1975], pp. 327–328.
63. Tanaka [1980], p. 34.
64. Komiya [1975], p. 322.

CHAPTER 19

Mergers and Reorganizations

AKIRA IWASAKI

Department of Economics
Konan University
Kobe, Japan

I. Introduction

The merger and reorganization policy has been a powerful tool of the postwar Japanese industrial policy and has been considered indispensable for industrial restructuring and adjustments. Its implications, however, differ according to the degree of development of the national economy and the type of industries or firms targeted for reorganization. One cannot expect the impact of reorganization in the context of infant industries, while with potentially extensive scale merits, faced with a small domestic market and lacking international competitiveness due to extremely small size of the firms, to be the same as in the context of mature or stagnating industries that are in the process of losing their international competitiveness following a change in their economic environment. This study focuses attention primarily on the mergers and reorganizations carried out since the late 1950s to the early 1970s. This choice is based not only on the expectation that the merger and reorganization policy could have had a far-reaching impact as a large number of major industries, at least in the first half of this period, were still in their infancy but also due to the fact that industrial policy is believed to have played an important role during this period.

Section II below presents the background of mergers and reorganizations implemented during the 1960s, along with the perceptions of the policy authorities that promoted them. Section III discusses the trends and peculiarities of the mergers and reorganizations carried out along with a discussion of the merger and reorganization policy. Section IV, then, follows up with an investigation into the economic impact of the merger and reorganization policy, while Section V rounds up the discussion by evaluating the role of the merger and reorganization policy as a tool of industrial policy as well as its future direction.

II. Background of the Merger and Reorganization Policy and Awareness of the Policymakers

A. Background of the Merger and Reorganization Policy

Japan was experiencing major changes during the late 1950s and the early 1960s. The European countries had recovered the convertibility of their currencies toward the end of the 1950s and had already started the process of exchange liberalization. Japan, while participating in forums like GATT and IMF espousing the doctrine of free, nondiscriminating, and multilateral trade, was in an anomalous situation as it continued with its import and exchange restrictions. Furthermore, Japanese exports during this period grew at a rate twice as high as the rate of growth in world trade, while the United States was faced with unprecedented deficits in its international balance of payments.

In the context of these objective conditions, and especially as a result of the U.S. pressure, the Japanese government prepared in 1960 a "framework for a trade and exchange liberalization plan" for the 1960s that determined the pace and sequence of the liberalization policy as well as measures to deal with the new situation arising out of such liberalization. Although the liberalization policy was a part of an international trend, it also entailed strong apprehensions. Despite the fact that the firms had grown in size, only a limited number of these firms in a very few industries, such as steel and general electrical machinery, could come up to international standards. The underdeveloped capital markets kept Japanese firms dependent on borrowing from financial institutions and these firms lacked overall strength. Exchange-rate adjustments were a taboo at that time, and measures to strengthen the competitive power of the Japanese firms were considered imperative. It seems that the policy authorities were convinced of the effectiveness of the merger and reorganization policy in this context.

B. Perception of the Authorities

The model for the desired form of the industrial policy in the era of liberalization, as put forward by the policy authorities, can be found in the 1963 report on the "New Industrial System" by the Industrial Structure

Advisory Committee of the Ministry of International Trade and Industry (MITI).

According to this report, the size of the Japanese firms at that time was exceedingly small in terms of the scale of production and business and was inappropriate in an era of increasingly large-scale technology characteristic of technological innovations over the postwar period. The existence of a large number of exceedingly small-scale firms gave rise to excess competition in terms of prices, product improvements, investment, and R&D, and it was believed that if nothing was done to curb such excess competition, the firms would be unable not only to avoid a decline in their rate of capacity utilization and worsening of profit position but also to attain competitive power against foreign firms. Besides benefiting consumers via bringing down costs through an expansion of the scale of firms entailing economies of scale, deliberate restraints on excessive free competition by promoting mergers, business tie-ups, and collective behavior among the firms were also deemed necessary to help these firms acquire international competitiveness.

The Draft Law on Temporary Measures for the Promotion of Specified Industries, drafted on the basis of such a perception, which had deep intonations of bureaucratic controls, failed to be adopted in face of stiff opposition from the private sector and domestic political conditions. Such understanding, however, took form in individual legislations such as in the Petroleum Industry Law, capacity coordinations in industries such as steel and textiles through administrative guidance, government-enforced concentration in the shipping industry, and the like.

It is interesting to note that such thinking persisted among those related with formulation of industrial policy in the government for a long time. For example, the basic content of the "Industrial Structure Improvement and Mergers among Firms—A Viewpoint," presented by the Special Committee on Basic Issues set up by the Coordination Division of the Industrial Structure Council in 1968 when the balance of payments was no longer a constraint on aggregate economic management and the scale as well as international competitiveness of the firms had also been sufficiently strengthened, was hardly any different from that presented in the 1963 report on "New Industrial System." That is to say, the new report insisted that conditions in most Japanese industries, as they were characterized by exceedingly small and excessively numerous firms, were inappropriate in an era of competition, opened up by the process of capital liberalization, based on the overall strength of the firms in technological development, fund raising, market development, and business management. Development of an oligopolistic structure led by foreign firms was feared in the absence of an overall strengthening of the Japanese firms by increasing their size through formation of groups, collectivization, and mergers. The fears of development of domestically controlled oligopolies as the result of such a concentration of indigenous firms, on the other hand, were heavily discounted in the light of the high growth potential of Japanese industry, the rapidity of technological progress, the intensification of international competition, and the firms' penchant for growth under the separation between ownership and management.[1]

Noting the internationalization of the Japanese economy, the industry circles also viewed the necessity for mergers and reorganizations in similar light as the government. The larger the firm the more was its behavior affected by its concerns about internationalization. The financial institutions that exercised an overwhelming power over the funds raised by the firms were also encouraging industrial reorganization.[2]

While the argument for industrial reorganization was getting widespread support, academic economists were becoming increasingly critical of the merger and reorganization policy, especially toward the large-scale mergers in the late 1960s. The firms that were able to attain higher productivity levels on the basis of the postwar technological progress had not only been able to garner international competitiveness at the fixed exchange rate of ¥360 to a dollar but had also grown to a size that was in no way inferior, at least, to that of the European firms. They felt that any further attempts at mergers and reorganizations could lead to unnecessary oligopolization of the markets and could result in the establishment of an oligopolistic structure by the indigenous firms.

III. State of Mergers and Reorganizations

A. The Scale of Mergers and Reorganizations

Industrial reorganizations may take a wide range of forms from small-scale business tie-ups to mergers, but it is difficult to cover all these on the basis of the published available data. It is possible, however, to get hold of the published materials of the Fair Trade Commission regarding mergers and acquisitions that have been covered under a reporting system in force since 1950.

The trends in mergers and acquisitions come out clearly in Table I presenting quinquennial averages by size of reorganization. The number of mergers, the most important means of reorganization, rose steeply in the 1960s and kept on rising until the first half of the 1970s. There were two cycles, the first peaked in 1963 with the number of mergers rising to over 1,000, and the second peaked between 1968 to 1973 with the number of

TABLE I
Average Annual Scale of Mergers and Reorganizations (capital, ¥ bn)

	Less than 0.1	0.1–1	1–5	5–10	10 and more	Total
(a) Number of Merger Cases Reported by Amount of Capital (Annual Average)						
Fiscal 1950–54	339	19	2	0	0	361
1955–59	351	24	7	1	0	382
1960–64	607	88	18	3	5	721
1965–69	845	114	22	3	5	989
1970–74	884	182	28	3	9	1,106
1975–79	725	176	27	4	4	936
1980–82	768	205	31	5	6	1,015
(b) Number of Acquisition Cases Reported by Amount of Capital (Annual Average)						
Fiscal 1950–54	138	19	5	1	0	162
1955–59	110	29	11	0	0	150
1960–64	137	33	13	1	1	183
1965–69	232	52	12	2	4	302
1970–74	315	77	25	7	11	435
1975–79	415	95	32	4	14	558
1980–82	570	127	33	8	17	755

Source: Kosei Torihiki Iinkai [Fair Trade Commission] [1983]; Kosei Torihiki Kyokai [1982] pp. 305–306. The row entries may not add up to the total due to rounding off.

cases exceeding 1,000 once again. As far as the argument for mergers and reorganizations is concerned, the need for concentration was emphasized for large firms in the heavy industry sector, which was still in its infancy. It is true, from a glance at the number of merger cases by capital class, that the mergers of firms in the capital class of over ¥5 billion or over ¥10 billion were on the rise up to the early 1970s. But if we take into account the rate of inflation and an all-round increase in the size of the firm, the mergers of large firms were most spectacular in the first half of the 1960s.

Acquisitions, on the other hand, have been continuously on the rise since the 1960s, and the number of acquisition cases by large firms has also been increasing with time.

The drastic nature of a merger or acquisition, although the most thorough method of reorganization, sometimes leads to a choice of milder methods of combination. In such cases, the controlling firm may engage in taking up directorships in or capital participation with its controlling firm. The Fair Trade Commission has conducted an inquiry into the latter. As shown in Table II, the stock ownership by the large Japanese companies rose

TABLE II
Equity Ownership and Number of Related Firms in 100 Largest Nonfinancial Firms

	Amount of Capital (¥ bn)	Value of Shares Owned (¥ bn)	Value of Shares Owned / Total Capital (%)	Number of Related Firms Equity Share (%)			
				10–24	25–49	Over 50	Total
1960	1,032	324	31.4	1,042	857	1,576	3,475
1970	3,453	1,916	54.1	1,731	3,063	2,818	7,612
1970/ 1960	3.43	5.91	1.72	1.66	3.57	1.79	2.19

Source: Kosei Torihiki Iinkai, [1971], pp. 148–149.

steeply in the decade of the 1960s when the merger and reorganization policy was being vigorously pursued, and accounted for 50% of the total paid-in capital. As these figures would include the stock sharing by loyal stockholders in a bid to avoid any takeover moves, a direct relationship between the rise in equity holdings and reorganization may be erroneous. However, the rise in the number of related firms whose management could be influenced on the basis of equity holdings suggests that there was a steep rise in the use of combinations among firms, a milder way of reorganization as compared to mergers. Notably, the number of related firms subject to management control through minority control of over 25% of the equity without recourse to majority control by holding over 50% of the shares has increased rapidly.

B. Morphology of Mergers and Relationships among Merging Firms

If strengthening of the international competitiveness of Japanese firms was the ultimate aim of the merger and reorganization policy, the morphology of the mergers and reorganization, along with their scale, also becomes quite important. In order to reap economies of scale resulting from large-scale production and business, as espoused steadfastly by the policy authorities, it would be necessary to carry out either a horizontal integration of firms in the same lines of business or a vertical integration among firms intricately linked by technology or sales relationships.

In Japan, data throwing light on the morphology of mergers is not available for earlier years. Among the major mergers that absorbed assets of over ¥1 billion in the latter half of the 1960s, horizontal mergers were overwhelming at 50%, followed by conglomerate mergers at between 30% to 50%, while vertical mergers were at a very low level. The conglomerate mergers were mostly for product expansion or territory expansion and only 10% to 20% of the total was accounted for by pure conglomerate mergers.[3]

In terms of the number of firms disappearing as a result of mergers in the beginning of the 1970s, conglomerate mergers accounted for the highest proportion, in the neighborhood of 50%, and the proportion has been increasing gradually. The horizontal mergers followed with a 25% to 30% share. In terms of total assets of the disappearing firms, the horizontal mergers continued to dominate other forms of mergers, accounting for 50% to 80% of the total, while the share of pure conglomerate mergers was no more than a mere 10%.[4]

The horizontal mergers, at least as far as major mergers are concerned, have been quite important during the decades of the 1960s and the 1970s. Horizontal mergers in the heavy industry sector where economies of scale are most prominent were quite compatible with the objectives of the reorganization policy. One should not forget, however, that such mergers could, at the same time, infringe on the Antimonopoly Law.

Another feature that attracts attention, along with the morphology of mergers, is the relationships among the merging firms. There are business groups in Japan, either tracing back to the old *zaibatsu* or built up around the major city banks. A classification of the major mergers in the postwar period in relation to business groups uncovers some interesting facts.[5]

Classifying 63 major merger cases between 1953–1973, mergers between firms belonging to the same group were found to account for 33 cases, over half the number. This was followed by 15 cases of mergers between firms not belonging to any of the groups and only 14 cases of mergers between firms belonging to some group and those without any group affiliations. Finally, there was only a single merger in which the participating firms belonged to different groups. This was the merger between the Osaka Shosen and Mitsui Senpaku, two shipping companies that merged, contrary to all expectations, in the wake of concentration efforts in the shipping industry strongly promoted by the government in the mid-1960s.

The major reorganizations through mergers in Japan have been predominantly among firms related to one another in terms of personnel or capital, such as those in a parent–subsidiary relationship before the merger, or firms within the same group (especially those that had been split under the Law on Prevention of Concentration of Excessive Economic Power), and the merger and reorganization targets have been carefully chosen.

C. The Role of Merger and Reorganization Policy

Let us have a look at the extent to which industrial policy influenced the merger and reorganization decisions in the private sector. The promotion of mergers, groupings, business tie-ups, and collective investments that lay at the heart of the policy authorities' repeated proclamations were intended basically to improve the industrial structure. Interestingly enough, this was also an idea put forward as one of the objects in the New Socio-Economic Development Plan of 1970. The only way to understand the actual reorganization policy adopted is to look at specific cases. In what follows, we identify four types of reorganization policies depending on the effectiveness of policy measures and the economic environment.

The first type of reorganization is the reorganization policy called on as a means to deal with the effects of trade liberalization in the automobile industry. The MITI, in 1961, came out with a plan to concentrate the automobile industry into three groups specializing in mass-produced automobiles, specialty automobiles, and mini automobiles, respectively, keeping in mind the smallness of the domestic market and extensive economies of scale involved in production. The automobile firms, although of relatively small scale, were earning high profits and the automobile industry had just reached the threshold of growth. The late entrants were surprised by the three-group plan and, contrary to MITI expectations, entered the potentially high growth passenger car industry one after the other. The 1962 Draft Law for the Promotion of the Automobile Industry was intended to promote mass production of a small variety of automobiles by a small number of firms by taking recourse to checks on new entry, limiting new models, priority channeling of public funds, and restructuring the industry, but since the policy authorities failed to consider the environment that enabled the automobile industry to sustain rapid growth with high profits, even though under government protection, the bill never saw the light of day. On the contrary, it resulted in the new entry of a large number of firms.

The second type of reorganization is represented by the mergers in the banking industry since 1964. The Ministry of Finance (MOF) had adopted a policy of nonapproval of bank mergers in the postwar period except when a bank was to be rescued from serious business adversity. In the mid-1960s, however, following the progress of reorganization in the nonfinancial sector, the MOF made a sudden turnabout in financial administration, calling for efficiency of the financial markets and modernization of financial institutions. This led to mergers of city banks such as those creating the Daiichi Kangyo Bank and the Taiyo Kobe Bank. While there is no doubt that permitting these merged banks to rearrange branches after a merger was an effective policy measure, the announcement of a clear policy change by the Ministry of Finance helped in furthering the already present potentiality for reorganization.

The third type of reorganization is the reorganization enforced under government leadership, typified by concentration efforts undertaken in the shipping industry in 1964 through the use of stringent policy measures and which would not have been adopted by the private sector on its own. The policy measures were to exempt the whole amount of interest on Japan Development Bank (JDB) loans and one-half of interest on loans from private banking institutions and to give interest subsidies amounting to 4 and 6 percentage points on JDB and private banking loans for future shipbuilding, respectively, provided that the shipping industry would form groups centered on merged firms so as to push on with rationalization efforts. The reorganization policy was able to produce some intended results, despite some vicissitudes, as the shipping firms reorganized themselves into six groups. Subsequently, the Japanese shipping industry began losing its international competitiveness as the developing countries emerged in the arena of shipping and the necessity for further reorganization was advocated. One may conclude from this observation that the 1964 reorganization of the shipping industry was not sufficiently successful, but it would be hasty to reach a conclusion that the reorganization policy as such was a failure in view of the problems related to social controls for navigational safety and economic controls on shipping routes.

Finally, the fourth type of reorganization policy is the setting of minimum capacity new standards as in the petrochemical industry in which the government set up 300,000 ton scale as the standard for new ethylene facilities in 1967, with the view to strengthening international competitiveness and reorganizing the industry. On the strength of its licensing authority on the construction of ethylene plants, the MITI went in for ethylene plants of over 300,000 ton capacity when 100,000 ton plants were the norm in 1965–1967. Building a plant with an annual capacity of 300,000 tons was a daring step to take under the Japanese conditions of 1967, and hence it was expected that small, weak firms would withdraw from the industry. As it turned out, however, the reorganization policy was not able to achieve the desired effects, as the late entrants did not withdraw from the industry and, contrary to the expectations held by the government and the industry, there developed a mad rush of applications for new capacity. The government landed into such a predicament due to its failure to have a proper grasp of the perceptions of firms' as regards the growth potential of the petrochemical industry as well as their behavioral patterns.

IV. Economic Impact of Mergers and Reorganizations

A. Rationalization of Facilities and Increase in Firm Size

The basic intention behind the implementation of the reorganization policy by the policy authorities was presumably strengthening of the firms through expanded scales of production and business in potential growth industries affected by trade and capital liberalization, leading eventually to raising national economic welfare. The scale of the steel and petrochemical industries showed an impressive increase during the era of rapid growth, which is sometimes also referred to as the age of "giganticization."

Let us look at the giganticization phenomenon in various manufacturing industries by following the trends in share of large-scale plants employing over 1,000 workers. Table III shows a somewhat unexpected result. That is, the share of large-scale plants employing over 1,000 workers, with the sole exception of the general machinery industry, remained constant or declined marginally during the 1960s when the argument for industrial reorganization was at its zenith and giganticization of plants in a few industries was being observed with interest. It is interesting to note that small-scale plants were able to maintain or even increase their share notwithstanding the strong advocacy of large-scale production that was prev-

TABLE III
Share of Large-Scale Plants[a] in the Total Value of Shipments by Industry

	1955	1960	1965	1970	1975
Food and kindred products	2.8	4.3	4.5	3.1	2.5
Textiles	15.7	15.0	13.5	11.2	2.7
Paper and pulp	22.2	20.7	18.1	15.3	15.2
Publishing and printing	25.8	26.8	23.0	24.3	21.9
Chemicals	41.0	39.1	36.9	36.2	29.0
Rubber products	31.8	43.0	45.4	40.6	40.0
Ceramics	12.8	12.6	12.9	11.2	8.5
Iron and steel	57.3	56.2	55.4	57.3	59.4
Nonferrous metals	43.5	44.1	36.4	38.3	30.3
Metal products	2.3	1.9	3.8	3.9	2.4
General machinery	13.6	27.5	29.7	32.3	30.7
Electrical machinery	40.2	60.2	51.5	52.2	44.7
Transport machinery	59.8	68.0	70.3	68.5	67.0
Precision instruments	18.1	28.7	31.6	28.4	26.0

Source: Tsusho Tokei Kyokai [1982b].
[a]Plants with 1,000 or more workers.

alent during those times and following which some industries carried out impressive investments in huge plants.

Expansion of the scale of business also became a preoccupation of industrial policy and, specially since the 1960s, large mergers giving rise to Mitsubishi Heavy Industries, as the top Japanese company, and Nippon Steel Corporation were backed by MITI. According to the *Fortune* Magazine, whereas 13 Japanese firms were ranked among the top 100 firms in the world, excluding the U.S. firms, in the early 1960s, about 20 Japanese companies have come to be ranked in the list since the 1970s. The large-scale Japanese firms have grown at a fast pace by international standards and a part of it has been the result of reorganization.

The results of a survey on aggregate concentration trends conducted by the Fair Trade Commission capture interfirm scale differentials in the large domestic firms.[6] The capital concentration ratio in the top 100 firms in the nonfinancial sector fell continuously from 39.4% in 1964 to 33% in 1970 and 25% in 1980. This does not imply that the impact of the reorganization activity on the scale differentials among large firms was small. According to a Markov process analysis of changes in the scale distribution of large firms during the 1960s, mergers during this period brought about exceptionally large changes in the scale structure.[7] There were, however, many new entries, while middle level firms grew in this rapid growth environment, thereby checking a rise in the position of the large firms.

B. Improvements in Efficiency

How far did the increase in the scale of production and business brought about by the merger and reorganization policy contribute to an improvement in efficiency? Any evaluation of the merger and reorganization policy has to depend, in the final analysis, on the findings related to this question. An improvement in efficiency can be expressed in terms of various indicators of economic activity, but the trends in firms' profit rate is perhaps the most comprehensive indicator. Since changes in the degree of market control by the firms and the business environment in which they operate may be reflected in the movements in their rates of profit just before and after the merger and reorganization, a careful separation of the effect of efficiency improvements alone is required.

There are a number of existing studies that have tried to analyze the movements in the rates of profit just before and after merger and reorganization. Of the 14 major mergers during the 1957–1966 period leading to formation of firms with total capital amounting to over ¥1 billion, the cases in which the rate of net profits on sales improved and those where it deteriorated were exactly half at seven each, and it is not possible to draw any clear-cut conclusion as to the effect of mergers on efficiency.[8]

As for 44 major cases of mergers between 1964–1975,[9] a comparison for three years before and after the merger shows no case of improved rates of profit, but a comparison extended for a five year period before and after the merger reveals such cases. In particular, for the 18 large-scale mergers, about two-thirds show an improvement in the rate of profit. In view of policy authorities' enthusiasm on the reorganization policy, it is interesting to note that the mergers of firms with poor performance or of those in depressed industries ended up with results not coming up to original expectations.

The Japanese studies on this subject cannot be considered sufficient, and no firm conclusions regarding the improvements in the rate of profits reflecting improved efficiency as a result of mergers are yet available. It may, however, be possible to say that the efficiency improvement effect of mergers is not as pronounced as claimed by the supporters of mergers and reorganizations.

C. The Possibility of Market Control through Mergers and Reorganizations

The merger and reorganization policy is believed to aim at raising efficiency by increasing the scale of production and business. But, at the

TABLE IV
Trends in Industrial Concentration

Concentration Ratio	No. of Industries	1950	1955	1960	1965	1970	1974	1980
Top 3 firms	43	100.0	93.5	91.5				
	170			100.0	97.8	104.0		
	163				100.0	102.9	103.8	
	394						100.0	100.5
Top 10 firms	43	100.0	96.4	95.5				
	170			100.0	100.4	102.8		
	161				100.0	101.2	101.5	
	394						100.0	100.9
Herfindahl Index	170			100.0	96.8	110.1		
	163				100.0	107.6	110.6	
	394						100.0	100.7

Sources: Uekusa [1982], p. 29; Senoo, [1983], p. 107.

same time, it may also result in restricting competition in the market through increased market control. There are sufficient grounds for such a development in the case of Japan, where over half the large-scale mergers have been horizontal mergers.

As revealed in Table IV, the market concentration ratio (to be precise, production concentration ratio) fell steadily up to the mid-1960s followed by a rise until the beginning of the 1970s, whereafter it has been relatively stable. Mergers and reorganizations are also expected to have influenced these trends in the concentration ratio. The trends in the concentration ratio during the 1960s, when merger and reorganization activity was particularly brisk, have been explained as follows:[10]

1961–1965:

$$\Delta CR_3 = 1.107 - \underset{(2.39)}{0.061ER} - \underset{(2.30)}{0.0037GD} + \underset{(1.76)}{0.0761MD}, \qquad \bar{R}^2 = 0.196$$

1965–1972:

$$\Delta CR_3 = 1.149 - \underset{(1.30)}{0.0436ER} - \underset{(3.03)}{0.0064GD} + \underset{(3.32)}{0.129MD}, \qquad \bar{R}^2 = 0.171$$

where,

ΔCR_3 = changes in the top-three-firm concentration ratio,
ER = rate of entry,
GD = rate of growth in shipments of the industry,
MD = dummy variable for horizontal mergers

The merger activity is clearly seen to raise the concentration ratio, especially in the latter half of the 1960s, but the effect is found to be unexpectedly small at 0.1 to 0.2 points over a five year period.

As the top-three-firm concentration ratio does not accurately capture the differentials by firm size, and since the instantaneous and long-term effects of mergers are not separated, the above regression results underestimate the effects of mergers. Although 22 major cases of mergers during the 1957–1966 period were spread over 33 commodities, for six of these commodities the premerger top firm absorbed other firms, while for another 24 commodities the firms resulting from the mergers came to be ranked among the top three.[11] The instantaneous effect of mergers on market concentration, therefore, may not be as small.

Improved efficiency and elimination of competitors through mergers, if successful, give rise to the long-term effect of raising market concentration. In Japan, however, the long-term effect of mergers has generally worked in the opposite direction. For example, of the 38 major cases of mergers in 1963–1975, a rise in share of the merged firms of over 1 percentage point was observed in 5 cases only. On the contrary, a fall in the share by over 1 percentage points after merger was observed in 11 cases, while the remaining 22 cases showed virtually no change in terms of share.[12]

Even in the case of the historically most controversial merger of Yahata Steel and Fuji Steel in 1970, the merger had no permanent positive effect on market concentration. With respect to the concentration in pig iron and crude steel, the following regressions are obtained for 1960–1980:

$$\text{Pig Iron: } H_t = 1597 + 1842D - 17.11t - 35.67D_t,$$
$$\phantom{\text{Pig Iron: } H_t =} (26.65) \quad (14.33) \quad (0.65) \quad (1.07)$$

$$\overline{R}^2 = 0.95, \qquad \text{D.W.} = 1.75$$

$$\text{Crude Steel: } H_t = 1112 + 1278\,D + 42.61\,t - 115.7\,D_t,$$
$$\phantom{\text{Crude Steel: } H_t =} (29.14) \quad (15.80) \quad (2.62) \quad (5.67)$$

$$\overline{R}^2 = 0.96, \qquad \text{D.W.} = 1.98$$

where, H_t = Herfindahl Index; D = dummy variable taking value 1 after the merger, and t = year, (0 for 1969, just before the year of merger). That is to say, there is no evidence that market concentration showed a rising trend in the Japanese steel industry after the Yahata–Fuji Steel merger. On the contrary, market concentration tended to fall, more clearly in the case of crude steel. It may be said that the Japanese market system was equipped with an automatic adjustment mechanism to erode the basis of a strong monopoly even if a merger led to the establishment of one. It may take several decades, however, for such a mechanism to work itself out. Therefore one cannot be too sanguine about the formation of market control as a by-product of the merger and reorganization policy.

V. An Evaluation of the Merger and Reorganization Policy

The present chapter investigated the mergers and reorganizations from the late 1950s to the early 1970s primarily in industries with high growth potential. The firms succeeded, on the whole, in expanding their scale of production and business. Normally, with only few exceptions, the intentions of the firms for reorganization did materialize and the government's reorganization policy also promoted it. Leaving aside the cases in which the government resorted to stringent policy measures, however, reorganization at the industry level did not always proceed in accordance with the guidelines laid down by the government, as it depended, to a large extent, on whether or not private firms were favorably inclined toward reorganization.

The mergers and reorganizations definitely led to an increase in the scale of production and business. A large number of relatively small-scale plants, however, continued to exist in various industries and in some cases even increased their market shares because of the rapid growth in domestic and overseas markets that enabled small firms to survive. Furthermore, there is no conclusive evidence that the merged firms improved efficiency substantially and raised their rates of return as compared to other firms. Looked at in this light, it is doubtful how firmly the government's industrial reorganization policy was based on objective conditions and whether or not effective policy measures were resorted to in its implementation.

Again, in the context of the Antimonopoly Law, the policy authorities seem to have underplayed the importance of competition-promoting factors such as growth in markets and intensification of international competition. Since the mid-1960s, when reorganization efforts were enforced, a stop was placed to the fall in market concentration and a significant positive relationship began to appear between market concentration and industry average rates of return. Now that the reorganization policy is being applied to mature industries faced with stagnating domestic and overseas markets, a careful reevaluation is required as regards its appropriateness and effectiveness as a policy measure.

Notes

1. The asymmetry in the policymakers' treatment of domestic and foreign oligopolies must have been due partly to the vigorous takeover activity by the U.S. firms in the European markets and partly to their judgment that foreign firms were beyond the purview of administrative guidance.
2. Tsusansho Kigyo Kyoku (MITI Enterprise Bureau) [1970] carries an interesting inquiry into the attitudes of those related to the mergers, the clients and the related banks, for 219 mergers that took place within the jurisdiction of the MITI during 1963–1967.
3. Kosei Torihiki Iinkai [1971] pp. 72–73.
4. Ikeda and Doi [1980] p. 21.
5. Okumura [1976] places importance on this point in his analysis.
6. Senoo [1983]. Results may differ slightly depending on how the firm size is measured.
7. Iwasaki [1972].
8. See Baba [1974], pp. 55–56.
9. See Ikeda and Doi [1980] pp. 119–121.
10. Uekusa [1982], p. 42.
11. Kosei Torihiki Iinkai [1969], p. 107.
12. Ikeda and Doi [1980], p. 88.

CHAPTER 20

Small and Medium Enterprises[1]

TAKASHI YOKOKURA

Department of Economics
Musashi University
Tokyo, Japan

I. Introduction

In Japan there are a vast number of small and medium enterprises (henceforth, "SMEs") in a wide range of fields, especially in manufacturing, wholesale and retail trade, and services.[2] This phenomenon is by no means peculiar to the Japanese economy, but the weight of SMEs in output and employment is high, and there are furthermore differentials in wages and productivity in SMEs relative to large enterprises. Because of this, in the postwar period fostering the "modernization" of SMEs became a task, and a wide range of multifaceted policies were developed.

Industrial policy was in general focused on particular industries, but in contrast SME policy was distinctive in that its target was a group of firms of a specific scale. In this chapter, the basis on which SME policy was seen as necessary and the role it fulfilled will be discussed in combination with examining trends in SMEs in the post-World War II era.

II. SME Policies as Industrial Policy

A. SMEs in Japan: Background

Table I presents data on nonprimary sector SMEs on an establishment basis, as a proportion of all establishments.[3] In 1981, SMEs comprised 99.4% of all establishments and accounted for 81.4% of employment. SMEs in three sectors, manufacturing, wholesale and retail trade (distribution), and services, accounted for 83.6% of SME establishments and 75.6% of

Table I
Small and Medium Establishments* and Employment by Industry

		Number of SMEs (thousands)			Persons Engaged in SMEs (thousands)		
		Number	Percent of All Establishments in Industry	Percent of Nonprimary Sector Total	Number	Percent of All Employment in Industry	Percent of Nonprimary Sector Total
Manufacturing	1957	541	99.4	15.6	5,475	73.5	33.7
	63	616	99.4	15.9	7,247	69.6	33.3
	69	733	99.4	15.9	8,680	69.0	31.7
	75	809	99.5	15.1	8,929	70.5	28.3
	81	868	99.5	13.9	9,551	74.3	25.7
Wholesale & retail trade	1957	1,804	99.8	52.2	5,635	94.4	34.7
	63	1,956	99.7	50.3	7,336	91.9	33.7
	69	2,287	99.6	49.5	9,010	86.9	32.9
	75	2,623	99.6	49.0	10,703	86.8	33.9
	81	3,011	99.5	48.3	12,978	87.4	34.9
Services	1957	773	99.4	22.3	2,318	88.8	14.2
	63	843	99.3	21.7	2,861	81.4	13.1
	69	973	98.9	21.0	3,664	74.5	13.4
	75	1,120	98.7	20.9	4,361	71.1	13.8
	81	1,335	98.5	21.4	5,580	69.2	15.0
Construction	1957	176	99.9	5.0	1,097	88.3	6.7
	63	240	99.8	6.2	1,886	86.4	8.7
	69	345	99.8	7.5	2,931	89.3	10.7
	75	447	99.9	8.3	3,866	92.9	12.3
	81	550	99.9	8.8	4,714	95.3	12.7

Real estate	1957	23	100.0	0.6	60	98.3	0.3
	63	80	99.9	2.1	175	96.9	0.8
	69	127	100.0	2.7	294	95.7	1.1
	75	177	100.0	3.3	454	97.6	1.4
	81	238	100.0	3.8	610	97.6	1.6
Transportation & communications	1957	67	100.0	1.9	799	82.3	4.9
	63	76	99.3	2.0	1,184	78.8	5.4
	69	84	99.3	1.8	1,549	81.9	5.7
	75	105	99.5	2.0	1,751	85.6	5.6
	81	133	99.6	2.1	2,083	88.8	5.6
Nonprimary sector total	1957	3,452	99.7	100.0	16,222	82.8	100.0
	63	3,886	99.6	100.0	21,763	79.9	100.0
	69	4,624	99.4	100.0	27,414	78.3	100.0
	75	5,358	99.4	100.0	31,530	79.5	100.0
	81	6,230	99.4	100.0	37,206	81.4	100.0

Source: Sorifu [Prime Minister's Office], Jigyosho Tokei Chosa Hokoku [Census of Establishments].
*Establishments with less than 300 workers (less than 100 workers in whosesale trade and less than 50 workers in retail trade and services).

employment, so that the great weight of these sectors is apparent. Looking at the number of establishments, the share of SMEs has not changed much, but in terms of employment, there was a change from a decreasing to an increasing trend in the share, with 1969 as the turning point, so that in recent years the share of SMEs has been if anything increasing. However, while the weight of SMEs in distribution, in services, and in construction and real estate has been increasing, the weight in manufacturing has been continuously declining.

If we look in more detail at shifts within manufacturing, distribution, and services, then the following is observed. The share of SMEs in manufacturing shipments declined during 1955–1960,[4] and after increasing in 1960–1965, continued to increase in the 1970s. The change in the late 1950s and early 1960s was due to shifts in the structure of final demand. Thus the expansion of private investment and the relative decline of personal consumption expenditures in the late 1950s worked to lower the share of light industry (which accounted for most SMEs), while the increase in personal consumption expenditures in the early 1960s worked to increase the share.[5] In the 1970s, machinery and other processed goods industries expanded tremendously, but there was also an increasing trend for SMEs in the processed goods industries, showing that SMEs were able to adapt to changes in the industrial structure.[6]

In retailing, small and medium scale retailers[7] accounted for 99.6% of all retail outlets, 88.4% of retailing employment, and 79.9% of retail sales. Within this, very small retailers (those with four or fewer workers) accounted for 84.1% of retail outlets, 47.9% of retail employment, and 32.8% of retail sales in 1982. Reflecting changes in the structure of consumer expenditures and consumer purchasing behavior, variations can be seen at a more disaggregated level, but overall the share in retail sales of small- and medium-scale retailers has been declining, and the decline has been especially great for very small retailers.[8]

In services, with the increase in demand there has been a marked increase in the number of establishments and of employment.[9] In 1981, SMEs accounted for about 70% of employment, but as can be seen in Table I, this share has been declining. This is due to the demand for personal services, such as laundries, hair dressers, and public baths, which account for many SMEs having expanded less rapidly than the demand for business services such as leasing and information services, where large firms predominate.[10]

Thus, while varying sectoral changes can be seen for SMEs, the number of such firms continues to increase, and their share in the number of firms and in employment is maintained.

B. The Basis for SME Policy

SME policy differs from other types of industrial policy in using firm size as a criterion instead of being directed at specific industries. Policies toward SMEs as a whole are necessary where policy intervention is effective in dealing with problems that stem from a difference in firm size, and where furthermore such policies using size as a criterion are more effective than those with an industry-specific approach.

The relationship between SMEs and large firms can be divided into two general classes, (1) those in which the firms are competitors, selling or buying in the same market, and (2) those in which one group is the seller and the other the purchaser. The issues that arise from these relationships are as follows. In the first case, when both are sellers, and SMEs and large firms are competitors, then it becomes an issue in particular where large firms are entering a field in which SMEs predominate. When both are purchasers, in procuring labor (people), financing (money), technology (information), and raw materials (goods), SMEs are at a relative disadvantage. In the second case of transactions between SMEs and larger firms, large firms are able to dominate in the market as sellers or buyers.

The issue that SMEs face is that of imperfection in the markets for people, money, goods, and information, as these work to the relative disadvantage of SMEs. In other words, if one looks at the labor market, then there are dual markets, one for larger firms and one for SMEs, with extremely limited movement of labor between them. One aspect of this is that, compared to large firms, SMEs are able to use low-wage labor, which if anything works to their advantage. SMEs are at a disadvantage, however, when it comes to skilled labor (human resource) formation. In large firms, skilled labor can be developed through training within the firm (OJT, on-the-job-training), which is effective because most workers remain with the firm as long-term employees. In contrast, workers in SMEs are less likely to stay with the firm than those in large firms,[11] and this characteristic becomes stronger the smaller the firm, which inhibits the formation of skilled labor.[12] With imperfect labor markets, there arises a differential between large firms and SMEs in the ability to carry out human resource formation.

In obtaining financing, there are institutional limitations on SMEs raising funds through stock and bond issues, and even when borrowing from financial institutions, there is a difference in the cost of lending due to the scale of the transactions, so that the interest rate for SMEs is high compared to that for large firms. Furthermore, from the standpoint of reduction by financial institutions of the risk of transactions (especially for long-term funds), banks prefer to maintain ongoing transactions with particular large firms. This preference over borrowers by financial institutions is strengthened even further under conditions of tight markets for funds. Capital markets are imperfect due to institutional restrictions, and funds markets are imperfect due to economies of scale and the presence of uncertainty in transactions. These factors make for difficulties for SMEs in obtaining funds (especially long-term funds) and cause uncertainty (especially in making financing difficult to obtain in periods of tight money). It also makes borrowing terms less favorable for SMEs, all making for firm size differentials in raising funds.[13]

Imperfections in product markets, when SMEs and large firms coexist in the same industry, make it possible for SMEs to hold their own ground through product differentiation and other means,[14] but it cannot be denied that the marketing and purchasing power of large firms works to the disadvantage of SMEs when they sell or buy from each other. When large firms have market power and sell to SMEs at high prices, then SMEs face high purchase and low sales prices. Furthermore, in transactions of small- and medium-scale manufacturers with department stores, large supermarkets, trading firms, and wholesalers, as well as subcontracting relationships between large and small manufacturers, it is also possible that the large firm is able to use its market power as a purchaser. The imperfection introduced into product markets due to the market power of large firms works to the disadvantage of SMEs in their transactions.

For transactions in information as well, it is difficult to begin with to standardize the quality or content of information. Even if the quality of the information is readily apparent to the seller, this may not be the case for the buyer. Because of this sort of imperfection in the market for information, firms tend to produce and use information internally rather than procure it from outside. While technology or the information produced by market research organizations may be procured, internal firm resources are invested in the R&D for product and production technology development and the collection of information on the market environment. Due to economies of scale and the limitations of their human resources and financing, this works as a disadvantage for SMEs in internalizing the production of information.

The basis for policies that focus on SMEs is thus to alleviate these imperfections in the markets for people, money, goods, and information. Such policies thus include subsidies for the formation of human resources, special provisions for financing, and the provision of information. Furthermore, the difficulties of SMEs in obtaining and building up management resources make it difficult for them to respond to rapid changes in their environment, and so policy is claimed as necessary as one link in intraindustry coordination[15] when the friction in such adjustment is great. The use of subsidies for SMEs to change their line of business was a response to the necessity of SMEs to change under the impact of structural recessions due to, for example, the dollar shock and the appreciation of the yen and the rapid increase in imports from LDCs. Again, for the disadvantages in transactions with large firms, policies can be sought that regulate the market power of large firms and that increase the countervailing power of SMEs by creating SME organizations. The regulation in antitrust policies of the abuse by large firms of their superior position (unfair transactions) and the exclusion of organizations such as SME cooperatives from the jurisdiction of the Antitrust Law are such measures.

These bases for SME policies consist of policies trying to correct disadvantages arising from market imperfections, but the following must also be added. First, there are also cases that work to the advantage of SMEs. These include diseconomies that arise in large organizations, fields in which economies of scale do not operate strongly, and areas in which the market is finely segmented due to product differentiation. Second, it is difficult to quantify the extent to which market imperfections create disadvantages. In particular, it is even more difficult to judge whether their extent is such as to require policy intervention. Third, the degree to which market imperfections impose a disadvantage changes as the relevant markets change in character. This suggests that the content (emphasis) of SME policies will need in turn to be adjusted.

III. History and Content of SME Policies

A. The History of Small Business Policies

The content of SME policies has responded to changes in the environment and the accompanying policy concerns. From the end of World War II through the present, we can divide this history into three periods: (1) from the end of the war through the middle of the 1950s, (2) from the mid-1950s through the 1960s, and (3) from the 1970s on. Roughly stated, in the first period passive and protective policies were developed to "save" SMEs, which were held to be "weak." In the second period more "active" modernization policies were developed for modernizing facilities and "consolidating" (increasing the scale of) firms, centered on manufacturing. In the third period, there has been, on the one hand, an emphasis on building up "soft" management resources for advancing "knowledge-intensity" in SMEs, while, on the other hand, there have been industrial adjustment policies such as assisting firms to change their line of business.

In this latter period, a change in the viewpoint toward SMEs can be seen, with them being evaluated in a positive fashion as representing a seedbed of vitality.

Through the mid-1950s, the main elements of SME policy were financial and SME organization policies. Financial policies toward SMEs, which faced difficulties in obtaining financing, consisted principally of establishing government financial institutions that specialized in SME financing and building up supplemental credit institutions.[16] Thus the People's Finance Corporation was established in 1949 to provide loans for very small enterprises, while the Small Business Finance Corporation was set up in 1953 to provide loan long-term funds. Funds from the FILP budget were channeled into these new government financial institutions in addition to the Shoko Chukin Bank (the Central Bank of Commercial and Industrial Cooperatives), which had been in existence since 1936.[17] A credit guarantee program was set up under the Credit Guarantee Corporation Law (1953) to strengthen the provision of credit for SMEs, guaranteeing borrowings from private financial institutions, and the Credit Insurance Program was also established (1950) to guarantee the liabilities of the credit guarantee associations.

In terms of organization policies, the Small and Medium Enterprises Cooperative Association Law (1949) was enacted in response to the postwar democratization movement, furthering cooperative activities in associations, without the strong economic control coloration of the wartime associations. The point to be noted about organization policies during this period is that stability for SMEs was sought through measures that restricted competition. For this the Small and Medium Enterprises Stabilization Law was enacted in 1952, which provided for activities to be regulated (that is, cartels formed) by SME associations. This law, reflecting the demands of SMEs in the textile and other industries during the recession that followed the Korean War, was drawn up and enacted at the initiative of the Diet [rather than the bureaucracy—*translators note*].[18] The philosophy during this period of "stabilizing" SMEs through policies that restricted competition was also reflected in the enactment of the Department Store Law (1956) and the Law on Special Measures for the Adjustment of Retail Business (1959), which restricted the activities of department stores and cooperative stores in retailing.

Policies in the 1960s changed from "passive" to "active" ones that sought the modernization of facilities and increases in the scale of firms. In the mid-1950s, attention was focused on differentials in wages and productivity between SMEs and large firms, which were seen as reflecting the dual structure of the Japanese economy.[19] In the latter half of the 1950s investment by larger firms increased the demand for labor, causing wages to rise, which put pressure on SMEs, which had depended on low-wage labor to increase their productivity through investment in facilities and other means. The need to increase international competitive strength with the liberalization of trade at the start of the 1960s made it even more necessary to do this. The SME modernization policies that got fully underway in the 1960s were a policy response to this necessity. From the mid-1950s, policies for the modernization of facilities were reflected in the Facilities Modernization Capital Lending Program (1954) and the Law on Financing and Other Measures for Aiding Small and Medium Enterprises (1956), which permitted the central government to provide grants to the prefectural governments for loans for facilities financing. Apart from the textile and machinery industries, which were treated separately,[20] the modernization of facilities in other industries was also systematically promoted by the Small and Medium Enterprise Modernization Promotion Law (1963). Under this, financing and tax measures were provided in a more systematic and organized fashion than in the past for the modernization of facilities and the consolidation of firms (the increase in the scale of firms), under plans drawn up on an industry-by-industry basis. Finally, the fundamental direction for SME policies, and the measures therefor necessary, were systematically set forth in the Small and Medium Enterprise Basic Law (1963), based on which the Small and Medium Enterprise Guidance Law, the Law on Financing for the Modernization of Small and Medium Enterprises, and the Small Business Investment Company Incorporation Law (all 1963) were successively enacted.[21]

While in the 1960s the emphasis was on the modernization of the facilities of individual firms, in the 1970s policies for structural improvement were propounded for the modernization of entire industries, emphasizing the development of new products and new technologies, the fostering of human resources, and other measures promoting an increase in "knowledge-intensity." Several revisions to the Small and Medium Enterprise Modernization Promotion Law reflected this change.[22] For structural improvement, the Japan Small Business Promotion Corporation (1967) was established to provide one body for the counseling and financing of SMEs.

In the 1970s, there were changes in the economic environment that had a great impact on the affected SMEs. These included the dollar shock, the appreciation of the yen, and decreased competitiveness relative to the products of developing countries. To help SMEs respond to this, an industrial adjustment policy was adopted that promoted changes in SMEs line of business.[23] On the other hand, with movement by large firms to enter the domain of SMEs, policies restricting competition were adopted, with a series of laws restraining such entry enacted. These were the Large Retailer Law (the Law Concerning the Adjustment of Retail Activities by

Large-Scale Retail Stores, 1973) and the Industry Opportunity Law (the Law on Securing Business Opportunities for Small and Medium Enterprises by Adjusting the Business Activities of Large Enterprises, 1977).

B. The Content of Small Business Policies

Small business policies have a quite varied content, as can be seen from the overview of their history. The following discussion sorts out these policies in terms of their focus and their instruments.

Policies can first be divided into those that focus on SMEs as a whole (general or basic policies), and those that focus on particular groups of SMEs (particularistic policies).

General policies have the goal of supporting the existence of SMEs by alleviating their disadvantages due to failures in the markets for people, money, goods, and information. Such policies include labor policies, which support the development of skills policies through occupational training and other programs; financial policies, such as the provision of financing through the specialized government small business financial institutions and the credit guarantee program; policies for maintaining appropriate interfirm transactions, such as the regulation of abuses by large firms of their market power and the organization of SMEs; and consulting and guidance policies, which provide information on technology, markets, and management. Particularistic policies include those that focus on a specific industry, such as industry-specific modernization policies and industrial adjustment policies for structurally depressed industries, and those that focus on a specific type of firm, such as very small firms or subcontractors. Particularistic policies are a response to the policy topics (specific policy goals) of the moment, complementing the general policies.

Policy instruments include a large variety of measures, such as financial, tax, subsidy, and regulatory measures, the provision of information, and preferential government procurement. On the finanical side, low-cost funds are provided, through allocations in the General and the FILP Budgets to the government small business finance institutions and the Japan Small Business Corporation. Alongside general measures to reduce the tax burden of unicorporated enterprises and medium and small corporations, a special depreciation system for facilities modernization and other measures have been taken to provide subsidies through the tax system for specific policy goals. Direct subsidies have been given to local public bodies and SME associations for financing and consulting activities. Regulation has been used as a policy instrument toward abuses by large firms of their market power and their encroachment on sectors dominated by SMEs and for stabilization activities (cartels) by SME associations. The provision of information has included the drawing up of industry-specific modernization plans and Visions, along with providing information on technology, markets, and management. Demand-side policies have been used to ensure the procurement of SME products through national and local government purchasing; the Public Procurement Law (the Law on Ensuring the Receipt of Orders from the Government and Other Public Agencies by Small and Medium Enterprises, 1966) is designed to permit SMEs to obtain such orders.

TABLE II
Small Business Policy Budget and Other Statistics

Fiscal Year	1960	1965	1970	1975	1980
General budget (¥ million)					
1. Promotion of SME modernization	1,475	5,141	3,710	5,467	8,147
2. Institutions for SME modernization	—	7,060	26,278	50,183	92,034
3. SME consulting activities	711	2,431	6,043	21,976	40,387
	(403)	(1,743)	(4,081)	(16,894)	(31,247)
4. Financing measures	—	8,000	11,750	43,931	90,300
		(—)	(—)	(16,531)	(18,400)
Total (including misc. items)	2,581	21,793	50,318	127,815	243,475
FILP investments (¥ 100 million)					
5. Small Business Finance Corporation	315	1,043	2,263	5,830	15,265
6. People's Finance Corporation	290	868	2,364	6,217	15,066
7. Shoko Chukin Bank	30	134	122	473	723
8. Japan Small Business Corporation	—	—	204	422	164
Total (including misc. items)	744	2,045	5,523	14,505	34,004
Share of government financing in total SME financing (%)					
9. Fixed capital	29.0	19.5	17.9	21.7	20.1
10. Working capital	5.2	6.2	6.6	10.2	10.3
Total financing (9 + 10)	8.7	8.8	9.3	12.8	12.6

Sources: Budget Statistics are from Okurasho [Ministry of Finance], *Kuni no Yosan* [The National Budget], and loan statistics are from Nihon Ginko [Bank of Japan], *Keizai Tokei Geppo* [Monthly Economic Statistics].

(1) is for assistance for facilities modernization, promotion of subcontractors, and modernization of SMEs in commerce and services; (2) is for investments in and subsidies for the Japan Small Business Corporation; (3) is for assistance for small enterprise counseling, for consulting and internship programs, for technical consulting and subsidies for promoting R&D, and for organizational policies; (4) is for investments, subsidies and loans to the three government small busines financial institutions, loans to the Credit Insurance Corporation, and loan guarantees; For (3), the figures in parentheses indicate amounts for small enterprise programs and for (4), amounts for the program for financing small enterprise management reform; Financial shares are as of year end for the outstanding balance of all the loans to SMEs by all financial institutions.

As outlined above, the goals and instruments of small business policy are quite varied, but as can be seen in Table II, the amount of government funds provided for these in 1980 was ¥243.5 billion, or only about 0.6% of the overall budget. In contrast, in the same year FILP investments came to ¥3.4 trillion, or about 19% of the total FILP budget. Within the general budget, the allotment for SME modernization measures comprised 41% of the total, financial measures 30%,[24] and small enterprise measures 20%,[25] making up over 90% of the total budget for SME measures in 1980.

The general budget allocation for modernization measures consists of investments and subsidies for the financing activities of the Japan Small Business Corporation, and when combined with investments in and subsidies given to the government SME financial institutions, it accounts for about three-fourths of the entire budget. Judging from this and from the size of FILP investments, it is clear that within SME policy, financial instruments play a great role.[26]

If, however, one compares the amount and content of the budget for SME policies with that of agriculture and fisheries, the other sector that along with SMEs has been labeled "pre-modern," then the following differential can be observed. Subsidies for agriculture, forestry, and fisheries in the 1980 General Budget came to ¥1.9 trillion (including funds for land improvement and other activities to improve the infrastructure), while 1980 FILP investments came to ¥890 billion. In contrast, 1980 General Budget subsidies for SME policies came to ¥61 billion, while 1980 FILP investments came to ¥3.4 trillion. In contrast to the huge subsidies expended on agriculture, those for SMEs are small, and the dependence is on FILP investments.

IV. The Subcontracting System

A. The Subcontracting System: Description

Of SMEs in the manufacturing sector, 65% act as subcontractors.[27] As per Table III, the number of SMEs that act as subcontractors has been increasing since 1966, and the proportion of SMEs that are subcontractors has also been rising. Of SME subcontractors, 80% are very small firms (less than 10 workers). The smaller the firm size, the higher the proportion of subcontractors, and the higher the proportion of firms that specialize as subcontractors, that is, with a high dependence on subcontracting transactions. By industry, subcontractors are numerous in the machine industries (metal products, general machinery, electrical machinery, transport machinery, and precision machinery) and the textile industries

TABLE III
SME Subcontractors

	Number of SME Subcontractors[a] (hundreds)	% of SMEs That Are Subcontractors	% of SMEs That Specialize in Subcontracting[b]
Manufacturing			
1966	2,996	53.3	—
1971	3,552	58.7	—
1976	3,734	60.7	81.3
1981	4,654	65.5	82.4
Manufacturing, by firm size (number of persons engaged, 1981)			
1–9	3,856	67.8	84.4
10–99	752	56.4	73.5
100–299	46	54.8	66.7
By industry			
Food processing	135	17.5	38.1
Textiles	836	84.9	94.2
Apparel and other textile products	409	86.6	91.0
Wood and wood products	188	47.8	65.4
Furniture and fixtures	215	51.3	69.6
Pulp, paper, and paper products	83	51.6	72.6
Publishing and printing	272	59.0	62.5
Chemicals	18	38.5	53.6
Petroleum and coal products	2	38.9	62.8
Rubber products	55	71.8	86.9
Leather, leather products, and furs	86	68.8	91.8
Ceramics and stone products	107	36.6	71.5
Iron and steel	59	72.0	73.1
Nonferrous metals	47	73.6	79.5
Metal products	675	78.6	79.7
Machinery (general)	524	84.1	84.0
Electrical machinery	273	85.3	88.6
Transport machinery	188	87.7	89.7
Precision machinery	98	80.9	88.2
Other manufacturing	389	62.2	78.4

Source: Chusho Kigyo Cho [Small and Medium Enterprise Agency], *Kogyo Jittai Kihon Chosa Hokoku Sho [Basic Survey of Manufactures].*
[a]Firms with less than 300 workers that engage in subcontracting.
[b]Those where 80% or more of their sales are of subcontracted products.

(textiles, apparel). In these industries, the dependence by large firms on purchases from subcontractors is also high.[28]

The production system (the division of labor) using subcontractors is called the subcontracting system. The widespread presence of this subcontracting system is one of the peculiarities of Japanese industrial organization. The special features of this subcontracting system are (1) while on occasion there is a reorganization of subcontractors, the transactions between the "parent" firm and the subcontractor are continuing and long-term, and (2) is it a hierarchial structure. Regarding item (1), the continuing nature of subcontracting transactions is suggested by the fact that in one survey, over the preceding five years, the proportion of firms that had had a change in their "parent" firm (the largest firm with which they had transactions) was a mere 16%, and the larger the size of the parent firm, the lower this proportion.[29] The loan by a parent firm to its subcontractors of equipment, the granting to them of technical guidance and financial assistance, and the carrying out by subcontractors of investment in coordination with parent firm production plans all presuppose this sort of continuing, long-term subcontracting.

Looking with respect to (2) at the archetypical case of subcontracting in the automotive industry, the automotive manufacturer and its affiliated and independent parts suppliers and the subcontractors of these firms form a pyramidal structure. Primary subcontractors are subcontractors for finished parts, while most secondary and lower level subcontractors are carrying out stamping, machining, or forging processes. The huge size of the system is indicated by the number of subcontractors for one automotive manufacturer, which had 168 primary, 4,700 secondary, and 31,600 tertiary subcontractors.[30] This hierarchical structure of the subcontracting system, while indicating the great extent of the division of labor, also indicates that at the bottom of the structure there are a tremendous number of very small firms.

B. The Subcontracting System: Evaluation

The utilization by the parent firm of continuing, long-term subcontracting permits it on the one hand to avoid the demerits from having to fix in place the management resources required for inhouse manufacturing, and brings with it the merits of being able to obtain a stable supply of purchased goods of the necessary quality, timing, and quantity.[31] Subcontractors also foresee the merit in the long run of being able to have a stable business and to obtain guidance and assistance from the parent firm. Subcontracting is long-term and continual when subcontractors are able to have specialized technology, know-how, and facilities, and are able to respond to demands by the parent for quality, timeliness, and price. This situation is reflected in a survey in which the reason most frequently given by parent firms for using subcontractors is "to use the specialized technology and production facilities of subcontractors," while the vast majority of parent firms had in the past, and would in the future, emphasize "quality and precision."[32]

On the other hand, subcontractors that are unable to respond to parent firm demands are "discarded" by their parent. This is the reorganization of subcontractors through being weeded out, by the consolidation of orders, and by synthesizing several parts into a single unit. In the subcontracting system, there are a great number of subcontractors who have no way to market a product other than to a particular buyer, and whose production and technology have been meshed in with the production system of a particular purchaser, so that there is the possibility that they will be in a disadvantageous position in transactions.[33] Policies to regulate transactions where a parent firm can utilize its "dominant position in a transaction" to "unfairly impose unprofitable conditions" are a response to this feature. The 1956 Law on the Prevention of Delay in the Payment of Subcontracting Charges and Related Matters, aimed at preventing delays in payments to subcontractors, is one such policy.[34] The results of surveys of trends in subcontracting indicate that the number of subcontractors has been increasing where "the determination of the prices of orders strongly reflects the position of subcontractors" and where the 'parent' firm from the start indicated [to subcontractors] its procurement schedule," so that a movement to improved subcontracting transactions can be seen.[35]

Competition among parent firms develops into competition among groups of firms including subcontractors. This makes for stringent parent firm demands on subcontractors, and at the same time increases competition among subcontractors. The pressure of this competition increases the merit (efficiency) of a division of labor and specialization among subcontractors. If the performance of subcontractors is even briefly analyzed, it will be seen that it is not the case that this has brought on a long-term decline in the profitability of subcontractors.

Table IV presents a comparison of the profitability of SMEs and large firms in transport machinery (excluding shipbuilding) and electric machinery, in which the subcontracting system is widely observed. In the transport machinery industry, there is a differential in the profitability of SMEs and large firms, and the fluctuation over time in SME profitability is great. These trends, however, cannot always be found in the electric machinery industry. Furthermore, the relatively high profitability of large firms in transport machinery is due to the nature of the final market and other features besides subcontracting. Thus one cannot directly draw the conclusion that large firms are able to utilize their purchasing power in

TABLE IV
SME^a and Large Firm^b Profitability, Selected Industries: Operating Profits/Total Capital (%)

Fiscal Year	Transport Machinery		Electrical Machinery		All Manufacturing	
	SMEs	Large Firms	SMEs	Large Firms	SMEs	Large Firms
1975	3.4	3.8	1.0	2.8	2.4	0.1
1976	2.7	7.1	6.2	5.5	3.6	2.9
1977	5.9	7.3	4.8	5.7	3.8	3.1
1978	3.6	7.6	5.0	6.0	3.9	4.0
1979	6.0	8.4	6.0	7.7	5.5	5.4
1980	6.0	8.1	5.7	7.8	5.1	5.1

Source: Okurasho [Ministry of Finance], *Hojin Kigyo Tokei Nenpo [Incorporated Enterprise Statistics Annual]*.
^{a}Firms with capitalization of less than ¥100 million
^{b}Firms with capitalization greater than ¥100 million.

subcontracting. Finally, the profitability of these SMEs is at a level higher than average profitability for manufacturing as a whole.[36]

Two factors were at work in the development of the subcontracting system in the Japanese machine industries. These were that, with the expansion of output from the mid-1950s, large firms responded by developing subcontractors, increasing their outside orders for parts, while new entry into subcontracting continued with, for example, employees in SMEs leaving to start their own firms.[37] Later parent firms began to consolidate orders and switch to ordering multipurpose units, to require delivery in fixed quantities at precise times (in the early 1960s), and to adopt a "key subcontractor" system (in the latter 1960s), in which "key" subcontractors were picked out with other subcontractors being regrouped underneath them for the key firms to supervise. Subcontractors were able to respond to these changes in subcontracting and purchasing management. The effectiveness of the competitive mechanism within the subcontracting system was important in establishing it as an efficient system for the division of labor, but at the same time, the guidance and assistance given by parent firms to their subcontractors (in particular the transfer of technology to them) and the role played by the government policies for the modernization of subcontractors cannot be ignored. Among policies for the modernization of subcontractors, a large role was played by subsidies for modernizing facilities based on the 1956 Law on Temporary Measures for Promoting the Machinery Industries, aimed at the machinery industries in which subcontracting was widespread.[38]

V. Small Business Policies: Evaluation

A. Evaluation of SME Modernization Policies

The Small and Medium Enterprise Modernization Promotion Law was the basis on which small business policy was developed in the 1960s and early 1970s. The essence of this policy was that guidelines were drawn up through the development of industry-specific modernization plans, and financial and tax measures were used along the lines indicated therein for the modernization of SME facilities and the achieving of an "appropriate" scale for firms and production. Financial assistance policies consisted of a special lending program of low-interest loans provided for financing facilities modernization through the Small Business Finance Corporation and the People's Finance Corporation, while tax measures consisted of implementing an accelerated depreciation system for facilities.[39]

The goal of modernization policies was, in response to the rise in wages, to aim for an increase in the capital intensity (the capital–labor ratio) of SMEs as a way to increase labor productivity. The result of modernization policies under the Modernization Promotion Law can be evaluated by asking to what extent this goal was realized.[40] Table V presents changes in the capital–labor ratio and labor productivity for the industries designated under the Modernization Promotion Law. From the latter 1960s through the early 1970s, the increase in these for the designated industries was slightly higher or the same as that for SMEs as a whole, with none of the differences significant, and if anything the variance among different industries was higher. Thus, while this shows that there were designated industries where labor productivity was increased through the modernization of facilities (mechanization) and through mass production, it also shows that there were designated industries in which such changes were small.

If the modernization of facilities and mass production would be effective only where "there was a technical innovation which made mechanization and mass production profitable, and where in addition an expansion in demand was foreseen that would be sufficient to utilize the resulting expansion in the scale of production,"[41] then it is difficult to conceive of all the designated industries as meeting these criteria.[42] Modernization policies in the 1960s sought to increase labor productivity in SMEs through facilities modernization and mass production, but it is not the case that this was effective in all industries.[43] As can be seen in the fact that policies under the Modernization Promotion Law were to foster modernization in an industry-specific fashion, the conception was one of "selective" policies

TABLE V

Changes in Productivity and Capital Intensity for Manufacturing Industries Designated under the Modernization Promotion Law (10,000 Yen)

	Labor Productivity[a]				Capital Labor Ratio[b]	
	1965	1970	1975	Increase, 1965–1970	Increase, 1970–1975	Increase, 1965–1970	Increase, 1970–1975
SMEs in all manufacturing	75.3	159.5	302.4	2.118	1.895	1.739	2.175
SMEs in designated industries[c]	88.4	184.1	350.2	2.082	1.958	1.816	2.159
(Average standard deviation)	(39.6)	(86.7)	(159.8)	(0.272)	(0.452)	(0.389)	(0.326)

Source: Tsusansho [MITI], *Kogyo Tokeihyo* [*Census of Manufactures*].
[a] Value added per worker.
[b] Fixed assets per worker.
[c] The 64 industries designated during the 5 years 1963–1967.

that would emphasize the peculiarities of specific industries. In actuality, however, as is obvious from the fact that to date over 200 industries have become designated industries,[44] these policies were indiscriminate, consisting of giving something to everyone, thereby weakening the effectiveness of modernization policies.

B. Overall Evaluation of Small Business Policies

As noted in the description in Section III, B of small business policies from the 1960s on, the emphasis has been placed on assisting the adaptation of SMEs to changes in the industrial structure. Small business policy was part of overall social policy from before World War II through the 1950s, but the nature of small business policy has now changed to that of being one facet of industrial policy.[45] For small business policy as industrial policy, there has been the criticism that the policies were indiscriminate.[46] Certainly from the standpoint of the focus of policy, there were of course general policies aimed at SMEs as a whole, but even for particularistic policies aimed at specific industries or classes of firms, as was seen in the case of industries designated under the Modernization Promotion Law, it is difficult to claim that there was such a focus in practice. In terms of policy instruments, a variety of tools such as financial, tax, and subsidy measures, regulation, the provision of information, and priority in procurement were utilized. There is some tendency for an indiscriminate application of policy to be found in areas other than small business policy, but it is especially evident in the case of small business policy because the following mechanism was at work. Specifically, because of the number of SMEs and their dominant weight in employment, together with the situation that SMEs have come to be viewed as "weaklings," it has always been necessary for almost all of the political parties to proclaim the expansion of small business policy as one of their key policies. On the other hand, the arms of the government (the ministries and agencies) that draw up policy have responded by actively drafting small business measures (which can be expected to meet the approval of all political parties) because they generally have a favorable impact in increasing the drafters' budgets and authority.

This mechanism for indiscriminate policy interferes with forming and implementing policy based on an analysis of whether it is necessary or would be effective in assisting SMEs to adapt to their environment by their needs for people, goods, money, or information, or in deciding, with the tremendous diversity that exists in the accumulation of management resources and conditions in given industries, which types of firms or industries should be the focus of policy. It is difficult to deny that the indiscriminate nature of policy has weakened the impact (effectiveness) of policy.

This conspicuous trend for indiscriminate use does not always mean that there resulted a growth of protective policies that defend the inefficient, marginal firm. Indeed, the negative effect of preserving marginal firms has probably been very small. First, competition restraining policies, which would restrict competition in SME sectors, have not had that much weight, and second, with FILP investment as the primary policy instrument, direct subsidies have had a relatively minor weight. These two features of policy tools have made it possible to maintain competition in SME sectors. This is quite different from the case of agricultural policy.

As part of small business policy, some measures were used to restrict competition, such as the recognition of cartels under the SME Organization Law (the Law Concerning the Organization of Small and Medium Enterprise Organizations, 1957) and restrictions on entry by large firms into specific SME markets in retailing and elsewhere. When the actual workings of these policies are examined, cartels under the SME Organization Law increased yearly through the early 1960s, when modernization policies began in earnest, and thereafter decreased rapidly, so that at the end of 1983 there were cartels organized in only 19 (for the most part narrowly defined) industries.[47] A turnabout in competition-restricting policies from the latter 1960s can thus be noted. This is also reflected in a policy stance of restraint in the use of competition-restricting policies, with positive industrial adjustment policies such as assisting firms to change industries being used when, from the 1970s, imports increased rapidly in SME dominated industries.

It has already been mentioned that loans for SMEs and SME organizations (such as cooperatives) from the FILP budget were used heavily as a policy instrument. Financing policies carried out through the government SME financial institutions assisted SMEs in general in obtaining financing (a general policy) and were also used as an instrument for realizing individual policy goals by assisting specific types of SMEs in obtaining financing (a particularistic policy). Such financing by government SME financial institutions constituted about 10% of loans to SMEs (see Table II), so it seems to have contributed to the ability of SMEs to obtain financing.[48] This does not imply, however, that such government financing served to protect marginal firms.

In the case of financing, it differed from a direct subsidy in that firms had to repay the principal and pay interest, while the market mechanism was utilized so that financing was not provided to firms without the ability to repay. While direct subsidies were also used as part of small business policy, the weight of this relative to the use of the FILP budget for financing was quite small.

It is probably safe to state the following as an overall evaluation of small business policy. It was difficult to avoid entirely the indiscriminate use of such policies, both because of the many ways in which market imperfections worked to the disadvantage of SMEs and because of the operation of political-economic factors in the formation and implementation of policy. It cannot be denied that this indiscriminate use weakened the effectiveness of policy. The primary role of financing, operating through the market mechanism, rather than the use of competition-restricting measures and direct subsidies as policy instruments, served to put a stop on the use of small business policy as a protective policy. In this, there is a sharp contrast to agricultural policies, with their use of import restrictions and direct subsidies.[49]

VI. Conclusion

Let us here summarize the preceding analysis.

1. While the industries in which SMEs are numerous have shifted, the share of SMEs in employment and the total number of firms have if anything increased in recent years.

2. Small business policy serves to alleviate the disadvantages to SMEs of imperfections in the markets for people, goods, money, and information.

3. Until the 1950s small business policy comprised one facet of overall social policy, consisting of financial and cartel policies. In the 1960s, policies for assisting in the modernization of SME facilities formed one facet of industrial policy. In the 1970s and 1980s, modernization policies emphasized human resources (people) and technology (information) and industrial adjustment policies consisting of measures such as assistance for firms to change their line of business.

4. Small business policy tended to be indiscriminate in the focus of policy and the use of policy instruments. This was in part because of the great variety of disadvantages faced by SMEs, but this indiscriminate use was also due to the operation of political-economic mechanisms.

5. It cannot be denied that the impact (effectiveness) of policy was weakened due to the indiscriminate use of small business policy, such as was seen in the designation of industries under the Modernization Promotion Law.

6. In small business policy, the primarily use was of financing, operating through the market mechanism, rather than of competition restricting measures and direct subsidies. Despite the indiscriminate nature of policy, this served to put a stop to the use of small business policy as protective policy. There is a sharp contrast in this to agricultural policies, which depended on the use of import restrictions and direct subsidies.

7. The subcontracting system, observed widely in manufacturing, is not something unique to Japan, but it is distinctive in the hierarchical structure that encompasses a vast number of firms from the parent firm down to minuscule subcontractors at the bottom, and in that the subcontracting relationship among firms is long-term and continuous. Competition among parent firms, through the mechanism of inducing competition among the groups of firms that includes these subcontractors, has spurred the formation of an efficient subcontracting system.

Notes

1. I would like to thank conference participants, especially Masao Baba (Kyoto University), Konosuke Odaka (Hitotsubashi University), Yoshiyasu Ono (Osaka University), and Sueo Sekiguchi (Osaka University) for valuable comments and suggestions they gave me in the process of writing this chapter.
2. The term *small and medium enterprises* will be used herein, unless otherwise noted, as it is defined in the Small and Medium Enterprise Basic Law.

Translator's Note: Under this law, SMEs are defined as:

(a) For manufacturing enterprises, those with less than 300 workers or a capitalization of less than ¥100 million. Of these, small enterprises are those with less than 20 workers.
(b) For wholesale enterprises, those with fewer than 100 workers or a capitalization of less than ¥30 million. Of these, small enterprises are those with less than 5 workers.
(c) For retail/service enterprises, those with fewer than 50 workers or a capitalization of less than ¥10 million. Of these, small enterprises are those with less than 5 workers.

In establishment statistics, employment is the criterion. Note that workers are regular workers, and that the capitalization criteria ceilings have been increased several times; the ones above are the current ones. The term *very small enterprises* is also used, with a variety of definitions. In manufacturing, it generally refers to enterprises with fewer than 5 (in some contexts, 10) workers. In the wholesale/retail sector and services, very small enterprises are those with fewer than 2 workers.
3. Statistics on an establishment basis differ from those on an enterprise basis. The SME share tends to be overstated in the former as it includes SMEs of larger, multi-establishment firms. Such statistics are used because of data limitations.
4. According to the *Census of Manufacturers,* the share of SME shipments on an establishment basis (the value of shipments of establishments with less than 300 workers as a share of total manufacturing shipments) was

1955	1960	1965	1970	1975	1980
54.6%	47.9%	49.9%	48.9%	51.3%	52.0%

5. Over the period 1955–1965, the value of shipments of light manufacturing industry increased 1.84 times, while that of heavy industry increased 2.92 times. In contrast, during 1960–1965 the order was reversed, with the value increasing, respectively, 1.95 and 1.91 times. This change, reflecting changes in the structure of final demand, affected the share of SME shipments, 68% of which in 1955 were in light industries. Industries are classified as follows, with all data from the *Census of Manufactures*.

Light Industries:

Materials industries:

food products; textiles; wood and wood products; pulp, paper, and paper products; rubber products; ceramic and stone products.

Processed goods industries:

apparel and other textile products; furniture and fixtures; publishing and printing; leather and leather products; and other manufacturing goods.

Heavy Industries:

Materials industries:

chemicals; petroleum and coal products; iron and steel; nonferrous metals.

Processed goods industries:

metal products; machinery (general); electrical machinery; transport machinery; precision machinery.

6. During 1965–1980, the value of shipments of processed goods industries increased 8.4 times (of which SME shipments increased 8.7 times), while materials industry shipments increased 6.5 times (SME, 6.9 times). The proportion of shipments accounted for by SMEs in processed goods industries rose from 39.5% in 1965 to 45.5% in 1980. This change in the composition of shipments reflects the shift in the industrial structure from light to heavy industry and from materials to processed goods industries, to which SMEs responded, as these figures indicate. The changes in the composition of SME shipments in more detail are as follows.

	1955	1965	1980
Light Industry (share, %)	67.7	60.7	53.7
Of which, materials:	(56.7)	(45.6)	(37.4)
Heavy Industry, processed goods:	16.3	24.4	29.0

7. Retail stores with 50 or fewer workers. The figures in the text are all from Tsusansho, *Shogyo Tokeihyo [Census of Commerce]*.
8. The share of small and medium and very small retail outlet sales in total sales have continually declined, as can be seen in the following. All figures are from Tsusansho, *Shogyo Tokeihyo [Census of Commerce]*.

Year	1956	1960	1966	1972	1979	1982
SM Retailer Share (%)	90.5	86.9	82.3	80.4	79.2	79.9
Of which, Very Small Retailer Share	53.3	47.0	40.8	33.9	33.5	32.8

9. Employment increased by 1.89 times during 1957–1969 and 1.64 times during 1969–1981, greater than the increase in total nonprimary sector employment of, respectively, 1.79 times and 1.31 times. (Data is from the *Census of Establishments.*)

10. During 1969–1981, employment increased 1.15 times for laundries, barbers, hair dressers, and public baths, of which 96.2% were SMEs in 1981. In contrast, employment increased by 2.76 times in information services, marketing research and advertising, where large-scale establishments comprise over half of the industry. (Data is from the *Census of Establishments.*)

11. That labor mobility is much greater in SMEs than in large firms is reflected in the differential in the tenure of employment. In 1981 the average tenure for large firms with over 1,000 workers was 14.9 years, while for SMEs with 10 to 99 workers it was 9.9 years. Similarly, the proportion of workers with over 10 years tenure was 69% for large firms and 38% for SMEs. (Data are from Rodosho [Ministry of Labor]. *Basic Survey of Wage Structure*).

12. See Koike [1981] on skill formation and the disadvantageous conditions SMEs face.

13. Looking, for example, at financing to and borrowing conditions of manufacturing firms as of the end of 1981, one finds that for firms with 19 or fewer workers, only 25.4% of outstanding borrowings were from regular banks, while 28.9% of outstanding borrowings were from the government institutions specializing in small business finance, from other government financial institutions or from local public bodies. For firms with 20 to 299 workers, 22.2% of outstanding borrowings were from the government small business financial institutions, and for firms with 300 or more workers, 75.8% of borrowings were from regular banks. Similarly, the effective interest burden (interest and discounts paid net of interest received on deposits, divided by outstanding borrowings and discounts net of deposits) for firms with less than 300 workers was 12.4%, while that for firms with 300 or more workers was 12.1%. (Data are from Chusho Kigyocho and Tsusansho, *Kogyo Jittai Kihon Chosa* [Basic Survey of Manufactures].)

14. In industries in which large firms and SMEs coexist, large firms turn out mass-produced and brand-name goods, while SMEs, seeking to maintain their own niche, turn out a large number of small-lot products and nonbranded goods, adapting by producing goods with a limited demand or geared for a specific customer.

15. See Chapter 14 of this book.

16. Around the time of the establishment of the government financial institutions, private small business financial institutions were also being built up. Credit cooperatives (*shinyo kumiai*) [similar to pre-deregulation credit unions in the United States—*translator's note*] were set up under the 1949 Law on Small and Medium Enterprise and Other Cooperative Associations, credit associations (*shinyo kinko*) [small business banks—*translator's note*] were set up under the 1951 Credit Bank Law, and mutual loan and savings banks (*sogo ginko*) were set up under the 1951 Mutual Bank Law.

17. As of the end of 1957 the share of the three government small business banks in the outstanding borrowings of SMEs (firms capitalized at less than ¥10 million and unincorporated enterprises) was 8.7% and the share of financing of facilities (fixed) investment was 32.5%, indicating the great importance of these banks as a source of long-term funds. Data are from Nihon Ginko [Bank of Japan], *Keizai Tokei Geppo (Monthly Economic Statistics)*.

18. Along with financial measures, controls imposed by SME associations were the pillars of pre-World War II small business policy. Price and other cartels could be approved under the Small and Medium Enterprise Stabilization Law when "due to competition exceeding normal bounds, it is feared that the operating conditions of SMEs will become unstable." The number of cartels increased through the end of the 1960s.

19. The dual structure debate noted that in the Japanese economy there coexisted a "modern sector" mainly composed of large firms, and a "non-modern sector" comprised of agriculture and SMEs, with there continuing to be a substantial differential in wages and productivity between the two sectors. See Kawaguchi et al. [1962].

20. In 1956 the Law on Temporary Measures for Textile Industry Equipment and the Law on Temporary Measures for the Promoting of the Machinery Industry were enacted. See Chapter 15 of this book on the former and Chapter 2 on the latter.

21. The Enterprise Consulting Program was expanded under the Small and Medium Enterprise Guidance Law, the establishment of joint facilities and the construction of industrial parks was promoted by the Law on Financing and Other Measures for Aiding Small and Medium Enterprise Modernization, and the provision of financing for increases in capitalization was the object of the Small Business Investment Company Incorporation Law.

22. In the Second Revision (1969) to the Small and Medium Enterprise Modernization Promotion Law provision was made for a Structural Improvement for designated industries. In the Third Revision (1973) provision was made for a new Structural Improvement Program, with the emphasis on developing "soft" management resources such as the development of new products and technologies and of human resources. In the Fourth Revision (1975) provision was made for programs for structural adjustment to include enterprises in industries linked to the designated industries and for adjustment through firms switching their line of business to growing industries.

23. Measures providing financing and tax breaks for firms to change their line of business are based on the 1976 Law on Temporary Measures for Line-of-Business Conversion by Small and Medium Enterprises, the 1978 Law on Temporary Measures for Small and Medium Enterprises in Specific Depressed Regions, and the 1979 Law on Temporary Measures for Regional Small and Medium Enterprises.

24. This is the share of the budget for financing measures, excluding the budget for the Program for Financing Management Reform by Small Enterprises.

25. From 1960 counseling and consulting (for management reform or general operations) were provided through Commerce and Industry Associations and Chambers of Commerce and Industry for small enterprises (those with 20 or fewer regular workers, or in commerce and services, with 5 or fewer workers). In 1973 the Program for Financing Management Reform was set up to provide unsecured and low-interest rate financing to very small enterprises (enterprises with 5 or fewer workers, or in commerce and services, with 2 or fewer workers).

26. Looking at special tax measures, tax receipts were reduced (1) by ¥38 billion (FY 1980) by tax exemptions for small enterprise owner-operators' compensation, on the "blue form" tax return, (2) by ¥53 billion (FY 1980) for special depreciation allowances for facilities modernization, and (3) by ¥5 billion in FY 1979 for an allowance for provisions for bad credits. (Data are from Chusho Kigyocho, *Chusho Kigyo Taisaku Yosan-To Ichiran* [Budget Summary].)

27. Subcontracting firms are those firms that receive orders from firms larger than themselves in size (parent firms) to manufacture or otherwise process parts or other items for use in the products of the parent. Transactions between a parent and a subcontractor differ from market transactions for standardized products in that the parent provides spec-

ifications as to quality, function, form, design, or other features, and there is also a difference in the size of the firms acting as sellers and purchasers.

28. In 1976 the dependence of large firms (firms with 300 or more workers) on procurements as a proportion of sales was 32.9% for transport machinery, 31.6% for precision machinery, 20.2% for machinery (general), and 25.6% for apparel and other textile products (according to Chusho Kigyo Cho and Tsusansho).

29. This means subcontracting by smaller scale firms is more unstable (Chusho Kigyo Cho [1977]).

30. Kikai Shinko Kyokai Keizai Kenkyujo [1981b].

31. The subcontracting system is evaluated as an intermediate form (an intermediate organization) between use of the market (market purchases) and use of organization (in-house manufacturing), or as a form of quasi-integration. See Imai et al. [1982], Tsutomu Nakamura [1983], and Imai [1982].

32. Chusho Kigyo Cho [1980].

33. Market power of the purchaser is emphasized by Uekusa [1982], Sato [1976], Shinohara [1976], and Caves and Uekusa [1976].

34. In FY 1980, of 75,130 establishments surveyed, 5,625 parent establishments were reported in possible violation, but because of the many facets of subcontracting transactions that are considered (such as the method of payment, price, and delivery conditions), and the interactions among them, it is very difficult to judge whether a specific transaction is "unfair."

35. Chusho Kigyo Cho [1981].

36. This indicates that the profitability of SME subcontractors in these two industries was not below the normal rate of return. Because of the presence of industry-specific factors, however, taking the average profitability in manufacturing to be the normal rate of return is not without problems.

37. On the formation and development of the subcontracting system see Sato [1983], and for the machinery industries in particular see Odaka [1978].

38. Odaka [1983] notes that for the automotive parts industry, technical assistance by the automotive assemblers played an important role, and financing under the Machinery Industries Law made investment in facilities easier. See also Chapter 2 of this book for an evaluation of the Machinery Industries Law. As a policy for the modernization of subcontractors, there is also the 1970 Law on the Promotion of Subcontracting Small and Medium Enterprises, which provides for developing facilities and joint operations in industries with a high dependence on SME subcontractors. This law is distinctive in that it aims to promote the modernization of the group of subcontractors (including those in other industries) of designated parent firms. Through 1983 it has been applied in only 11 cases.

39. In terms of the "appropriate scale" of firms and production, there was the provision of low-interest rate financing needed for mergers, joint activities, and the formation of associations through the Program of Loans for Financing Modernization of the Japan Small Business Promotion Corporation, together with tax measures such as a lowering of the corporation tax in the case of mergers.

40. This method of evaluation is not without problems. See Chapter 18 of this book for details.

41. S. Nakamura et al. [1981], p. 204.

42. There are cases where mechanization and mass production led to the bankruptcy of SMEs. The "modernization bankruptcies," which surfaced at the time of the 1965 recession, are an example of this and were due to excess competition (an increase in capacity coupled with a decline in demand).

43. For example, in the fabric industry, structural reform activities for facilities modernization were effective in increasing labor productivity. See Chapter 15 of this book.

44. These are industries designated during the 1963–1980 period. A few nonmanufacturing industries were also included, but of the total of 300 to 350 4-digit industries in manufacturing that are dominated by SMEs (those where SMEs accounted for 70% or more of shipments), over one-half appear to have been "designated."

45. This does not mean that a social policy facet was entirely lacking. The special financing and consulting programs provided for very small firms in general are more in the nature of social policy.

46. For example, Shinohara [1973].

47. Of these, 14 were textile industries. See Chapter 15 of this book on investment coordination in the textile industries under the Small and Medium Enterprise Organizations Law.

48. With conditions in financial markets easing, there has been a debate on whether government financing for SMEs is necessary. See Miyake [1980] and Yamashita [1977].

49. On subsidies and related issues in agricultural policy, see Imamura [1978].

CHAPTER 21

Conclusion

MASAO BABA[†]

Institute of Economic Research
Kyoto University
Kyoto, Japan

KEN'ICHI IMAI

Institute of Business Research
Hitotsubashi University
Tokyo, Japan

MASAHIRO OKUNO

Faculty of Economics
University of Tokyo
Tokyo, Japan

KOTARO SUZUMURA

Institute of Economic Research
Hitotsubashi University
Tokyo, Japan

I. General Comments I (Masao Baba)

Numerous points of course deserve comment in the essays in this book, which analyze many facets of postwar Japanese industrial policy. Here, however, I will limit myself to voicing some thoughts on the foundations of industrial policy. According to Ryutaro Komiya, in the introduction of this book, those who have analyzed and studied Japanese industrial policy can be divided into the "prehistoric" generation and the "younger" generation. In terms of age, I clearly fit into the prehistoric group, but I write these comments as a researcher whom I trust, on the basis of methodology, would be labeled as belonging to the younger generation.

There is the term *to map out (sakutei) the industrial structure* that often appears in statements and discussions relating to economic planning and industrial policy. It seems that most people use this term without thinking very deeply about it. But what really gets my ire is that they are nonchalant about using the term. Looking in a dictionary, I find that *sakutei* is defined as "to draw up a plan and determine its details." But in an economic society consisting of a free enterprise system, the structure of industry should be formed through, and should change as a result of, the cumulative impact of the free decisions and actions of private firms. It is not something that, under one or another banner, the government should try to change.[1]

[†]Deceased October 27, 1986.

In postwar Japan, the goal of industrial policy has been held to be the modernization of the industrial structure, which in practice meant first "heavy and chemical industrialization," and later "knowledge-intensification." It seems that this may now become "making industry high-tech." When the conception of such an industrial structure is set forth, several standards have been considered by policymakers in the mapping out of the industrial structure. For the fostering of "heavy and chemical industrialization," this was the idea of combining the standards of a high income elasticity of demand and a rapid rate of increase in productivity. For "knowledge-intensification," the concepts of "population congestion and environmental considerations" and "work conditions" were added.

This line of thought regarding standards was, as far as I know, first propounded by Miyohei Shinohara [1960], and was reformulated in the *Report (Toshin)* of the Industrial Structure Advisory Committee (now the Industrial Structure Council) released in November 1963. The standards for mapping out the industrial structure were stated as follows:

> The rate of increase of demand is not uniform among all industries. In some industries, demand increases more rapidly than the growth rate of income; in other industries, demand increases at a pace slower than that of income. This is due in part to differences in the income elasticity of final demand. Because there are differences in the income elasticity of demand for different industries, the structure of domestic demand and the structure of trade both change in the long run. Thus, if we specialize in income-elastic products, then to that extent we can also anticipate a rapid growth of exports, which is desirable from the standpoint of economic growth . . . [however] . . . While specialization in products with a high income elasticity is a necessary condition for increasing the growth rate of exports, it is not sufficient. In order for goods with a high income elasticity to in fact be exported, it is necessary to have sufficient competitive strength internationally. Competitive strength must be guaranteed by increasing productivity.

The so-called heavy and chemical industries are typically thought of as industries that simultaneously meet these two criteria. However, as also noted in the *Report*:

> The heavy and chemical industries to which "heavy and chemical industrialization" refer are, *theoretically, not the heavy and chemical industries as a whole.* The term "heavy and chemical industries" is used as a symbolic expression of the industries which meet the income elasticity and productivity increase standards, and in this sense the "heavy and chemical" industries not only can include what is normally thought of as light industry, but may also exclude industries normally thought of as heavy industries. (The emphasis is mine.)

What, then, in specific *are* the "heavy and chemical" industries in the above sense? While there was the qualification noted in the above quote, there was almost no attempt to measure or investigate its empirical significance. Thus, with this inadequate analysis, the term "heavy and chemical industrialization'' served not merely as a symbolic slogan, but became a goal in and of itself and often had the effect of giving rise to policies which developed in a direction which placed their overall emphasis on the heavy and chemical industries as a whole.

Maintaining such doubts, as part of the reference materials for one study group I carried out a calculation by industry of income elasticity and the rate of productivity increase.[2]

For income elasticity, I deflated the value of shipments for industries in the *Census of Manufactures* by the industry-specific wholesale price indices (1960 weights) published by the Bank of Japan, and did a least squares regression of this in log-linear form against real gross national product (from the *Annual Report on National Income Statistics*). I used 1955–1965 as the period for the estimation. For the rate of productivity increase, I again used the *Census of Manufactures*, with the same sample period, calculating the average annual (compound) rate of increase in labor productivity (value added per worker).[3]

Other things could have been taken into account to make the analysis more precise, such as calculating the elasticity of exports relative to world income, or taking into account the pronounced differences in the rate of industry growth in the first and second halves of the sample period. The results are extremely interesting, however, even if one looks only at the results of this analysis at the 2-digit industry level. The eight industries that met the two criteria—that is, their income elasticity and their rate of productivity increase both exceeded the average for manufacturing as a whole—were apparel and accessories, furniture and fixtures, chemicals, petroleum and coal products, metal products, general machinery, transport equipment, and "other" manufacturing. Two of what are clearly thought of as light industries were by these two standards high on the list, while what are clearly thought of as representative heavy industries such as iron and steel, nonferrous metals, and electrical equipment were unable to pass these two criteria together, to my considerable surprise. I also carried out the same calculations using 4-digit industry data, and when industries were more narrowly defined the results were much more complex than in the case of the 2-digit industry analysis. I can still remember my bewilderment as to how empirically to define the "heavy and chemical" industries.

Today, of course, "heavy and chemical industrialization" is no longer the goal of industrial policy. I believe, however, that the line of thought incorporating the twin standards for mapping out the industrial structure of high income elasticity and a rapid rate of productivity increase form an undercurrent to Japanese industrial policy which even today is hard to exclude.

There is as well another criticism of these two standards due to Kenichi Miyazawa [1974], according to whom the essence of the issue is that both standards "should be viewed from the standpoint of dynamic comparative advantage, and if the price system under the given institutional framework is appropriate, then they will naturally be achieved under that system."[4] I concur entirely with this criticism. And if this is so, then the emphasis of Japanese industrial policy should above all have been to eliminate as thoroughly as possible government interventions that mitigated against the fair and free operation of the price mechanism and that restricted competition.

It is, however, difficult to state that this was in fact the case and to claim it was so is either a falsehood or an exaggeration. I can support this claim in many ways, but recent examples could be given from the enactment and operation of the Industrial Stabilization Law and the Structural Improvement Law.

Among Westerners misunderstanding and misinterpretation of Japanese industrial policy has been commonplace, but (thankfully!) I think that compared to one time, the degree of understanding has recently shown tremendous improvement. Here I would like to call attention to the references cited in Chapter 4 of this book of Trezise, Hadley, Patrick, and others. I would also like to refer readers to the report of the U.S. International Trade Commission (USITC [1983]), which analyzed Japanese industrial targeting policies and their impact on American industry, and the OECD report on the "transparency" of industrial adjustment policies (OECD [1983a]). In the OECD report, it is stated that "and during the 1970's Japanese industrial policy became less interventionist," (p. 139), while the USITC report, based on quite detailed research and analysis, concluded that, in comparison with "extremely aggressive policies" prior to the mid-1960s, direct government intervention in markets decreased substantially thereafter. I can safely say that this conclusion corresponds closely to our own interpretation.

However, while the USITC report, for example, shows what could be considered a favorable understanding of small business cartels, rationalization cartels, and export and import cartels, I want to call attention to the severely critical stance it adopts toward cartels designated under the Industrial Stabilization Law and the Structural Improvement Law. The exclusion of designated industries from the domain of the Antitrust Law has been an important part of industrial policy, but I feel this needs to be more critically regarded, particularly in terms of the operations and impact of cartels, and especially in the impact of restrictions on competitive imports.

II. General Comments II (Ken'ichi Imai)

A. Point 1

In this book, there has been a detailed analysis using the methodology of economics of the content of Japanese industrial policy, based on the analytic definition in the introduction of industrial policy as "policy interventions in response to market failures."

From the perspective of an economist this is a natural definition, and I myself wrote Chapter 8 of this book from such a stance, but there is still a substantial gap to be crossed in going from this sort of definition to an actual analysis of industrial policies. In the introduction three issues were also noted:

> (1) What sort of conditions will be recognized as constituting market failures? (2) What sort of policy measures are appropriate in response to the various types of market failure? (3) It is also true that policy measures may fail. How are policy failures to be dealt with?

Almost any evaluation of industrial policy can be made, depending on how these questions are answered.

For example, let us consider what the standard types of market failure are. Imai et al. [1972], which has come to be regarded as a standard textbook on price theory, deals mainly with such issues. In it, market failures are divided into four classes: (1) declining costs, (2) externalities, (3) public goods, and (4) dynamic issues and uncertainty. We may put these together as follows: when costs decline due to economies of scale, where there are positive or negative environmental externalities, where anyone can in principle appropriate the output of (for example) R&D activities, and when intertemporal resource allocation is undertaken under uncertain conditions, then market failures are likely to arise and some sort of policy response becomes necessary. If policymakers were to read this sentence with current industrial activities in mind, then they would naturally believe that market failures are commonplace at critical points for most industries and so industrial policy must be brought to the forefront so as to alleviate these failures.

It goes without saying that the real issue here is what alternative form resource allocation must assume when the market fails. The mechanism that traditionally arises is that of government, with the alternative method of resource allocation consisting of planning. We are then faced with the classical problem of the market versus planning. The market fails, but planning also fails. Thus the issue becomes that of choosing a method of resource allocation through a comparison of the relative extent of the failures of these two. The experiences of individual countries in the postwar period show that the failures of "strong" plans that replaced the market have far surpassed the failures of the market itself, so that which is the better has been obvious to all. The choice then is between the market and "weak" plans, which expresses the idea that, while depending primarily on private-sector vitality, the government will when necessary undertake policies to rectify matters. Analytically, what such weak-form plans consist of, and how in practice they should be evaluated in contrast to market failures, has been the central issue that each essay in this book has taken up in examining the situation in its respective industry.

To comment critically, if one asks whether an analytic framework adequate to carrying out such an analysis has been clearly set forth in this book, then the answer must be negative. To rephrase this, while in economics to date considerable light has been shed on the nature of resource allocation in markets, when it comes to the issue of resource allocation in alternatives to the market, there has been almost no study of the nature of such alternatives or of the principles of resource allocation therein. My first point will consist of elaborating on this issue.

First, what arises in response to market failures is not restricted to the limited mechanism of government, but is "organization" in general. As Kenneth Arrow stated, "organizations are a means of achieving the benefits of collective action in situations in which the price system fails."[5] More precisely, firms, labor unions, universities, and the government are all organizations, and these carry out resource allocation in areas in which the price mechanism or the market cannot function appropriately. Hence, if industrial policy is an instrument to be used in response to market failure, then the principles of resource allocation in these organizations must also be taken into account, and the two alternative modes of resource allocation, the market and organization, must be clearly taken up. The methodology of considering whether industrial policy should be used through a comparison of the relative merits of these two modes must be brought more to the fore. One framework for this sort of approach is provided by Oliver Williamson in his *Markets and Hierarchies*,[6] while I together with H. Itami have developed this further, proposing the framework of the "mutual infiltration of markets and organizations."[7] Here is neither the place to go into the details of this nor to question the effectiveness of this approach to the problem, but in reading through this entire book I could not help gaining the impression that the viewpoint of the analysis is a partial one, and that this is probably because this issue that I have been discussing was not brought to the fore.

Certainly in the theoretical portion of this book methods of supplementing resource allocation in the market were analyzed with the case of specific market failures in mind, and a framework for analysis was set forth. That analysis surpassed the level of preceding work. The analysis, however, was not extended to the point of considering by what sort of mechanism this would be done, nor were the organizational principles under which it would be carried out considered. Hence, the questions are still totally unanswered as to the extent to which alternative mechanisms used in the face of market failure can succeed, or of the likelihood with which they will fail. The only answer given is that resource allocation can be improved. But this is only a point of departure for the analysis of industrial policy. Examples (such as petroleum refining) in which the organizational response adopted in an attempt to overcome market failure itself failed are not uncommon, and under the combined failures of both market and organization the industry totally lost its ability to reform itself. On the other hand, as seen in the case of some types of R&D, there are clearly cases where organizational responses were successful. If this is the case, then with the initial presumption that organizational responses will succeed, or at least will not be a complete failure, it then becomes meaningful to propose it as an alternative method of resource allocation in the face of market failure. However, since in the theoretical portion of this book these conditions were left unspecified, and only the possibilities for there being an improvement in resource allocation were analyzed, to borrow a phrase used by one of the participants at the conference, one was left with the impression of being "infatuated" with industrial policy.

On the other hand, those in this book who undertook empirical analyses, and in particular most of the authors of general essays, held a negative stance toward organizational responses, so that even if the market failed to a greater or lesser extent, they held it was desirable to emphasize the market mechanism. While noting that Japanese industry operated under the pressure of government interventions, most also took the stance that the economy developed because at base it still operated under the market mechanism. It seems that most of these people, while keeping market failures in mind, evaluated the market favorably for its dynamism. Phrased more positively, their view is that the efficiency of the market mechanism is played out at its fullest in its dynamic aspects. I, too, am one such person. At present, however, this statement cannot be demonstrated theoretically. In fact, as I stated previously, in a textbook analysis dynamics and uncertainty are if anything thought of as representing cases of market failure. Why is it that what is thought of in a textbook world as market failure in the real world proves a success? Or, rather, why do those who analyze the economy adopt the stance that the efficiency of the market can to some extent be relied on in a dynamic context? For example, in the Uekusa chapter, there is the extremely dry reference to "dynamic economic development based on the market mechanism." What was not questioned in this was the reason why the market is able (or was able) to transcend failures of the market in its dynamic aspects. Unfortunately, I am left with the strong impression that this point of concern has not been adequately treated. Below I would like to continue with my own comments on this point.

B. Point 2

If one is to hold that resource allocation in the market can be dynamically efficient, then a necessary condition must be that firms, the organizations that operate in the market, must be innovators in the broad sense, and the entrepreneurs and managers who act as decision makers in firms must despite uncertainty take on risk and resolutely carry out investment decisions. This gives rise to a cumulative diffusion of such innovations and investment into other parts of the market. As a result of this cumulative process, the market will function such that those firms that are suitably adapted to their socioeconomic environment will grow, while firms that are unsuited will decline. When this process of natural selection works, the economy's overall performance will be improved, and one will be able to state that the market has carried out an efficient allocation of resources in this dynamic form.

In the theoretical framework for economic analysis developed to date, however, entrepreneurs and managers do not enter explicitly into the analysis. Because firms' actions are assumed to be undertaken to maximize profits under given conditions, who it is that makes decisions is irrelevant. It goes without saying that, unlike more comprehensive models that take reality into account, formal models that attempt an understanding of the heart of basic mechanism of the economy fasten around their theoretical core a protective belt that facilitates a response to reality. To bring entrepreneurs and managers inside this belt, however, is an unconvincing exercise—it is about as effective as trying to graft bamboo onto a tree. Recently, Nelson and Winter of Yale, who label themselves neo-Schumpeterians, have proposed an "evolutionary model" that attempts to formalize the Schumpeterian model of innovation.[8] I feel that more attention ought to be devoted to this approach and due regard given to it in Japan. It is at least possible to incorporate entrepreneurs and managers in their model, which emphasizes search activities alongside of the routine activities of the firm.

I believe that in reality it is extremely important in analyzing postwar industrial policy to consider the "indicative" policies engaged in by MITI and others and the impact they had on the investment decisions of leading firms. Of course, these moved away from the rather strong forms taken initially, e.g., import license allocation, to weak forms that are merely projections of the future. For example, in the case of the iron and steel industry, what prompted Kawasaki steel to take its decision to invest in the construction of an up-to-date, large-scale integrated steel mill in Chiba was clearly the entrepreneurial spirit of its president at the time, Yataro Nishiyama. The entrepreneurial spirit, however, was not manna from heaven, but I believe was something refined in the tense relations that ensued from the opposition of financial circles and the concerned government ministries. I think that there was at the core of investment decisions formed in this way what J. Hirschmeier has referred to as "the optimism of the entrepreneur" in believing in his ultimate success. But I think it was also because of expectations Kawasaki Steel formed about the future prospects of the steel industry—not aggressive, but firmly held—differing from those that had been formed by MITI and the leading firms of Yahata and Fuji Steel. It hardly needs stating that there is no way to conclusively back up this interpretation, and I will leave it in the hands of Seiichiro Yonekura and other business historians.[9] But what I want to point out in this comment is that if there is no forceful explanation as to why the market was successful in its dynamic aspects, then one cannot help but feel that the analysis is hollow and empty.

Related to this, in the book there are often references to the "role of the government in serving as a forum for the provision of information," and I wonder but what it might not be possible to place this in a more positive fashion in the framework of the evolutionary approach. Certainly I greatly appreciate the fact that the issue of exchanging information is emphasized, and that its essence is further developed in the theoretical portion of the book. This analysis, however, is still a long way from the insight or hypothesis of Komiya that "if one regards the Japanese industrial system as one type of system for the exchange of information . . . then this industrial system may be one of the most important elements which supported the rapid growth of postwar Japanese industry." I think this distance can to some extent be lessened in the following way. The heart of the issue is that the exchange of information gives rise to synergies. In the case of investment decisions, the process of exchanging information removes uncertainty that arises when each party has to read what the other is up to. When a certain number of firms undertake investment and a threshold value is exceeded, then all firms undertake investment *en masse*, thereby triggering the cumulative process in the industry as a whole. The concept of synergism lies at the core of the evolutionary approach, and while there are references to empirical work in biology where

efficiency rapidly increases through interactions once some threshold value
is exceeded, it is also true that in many empirical studies in economics
the rate of increase in the efficiency in an industry is S-shaped against
cumulative total output. The learning curve in which costs decrease with
cumulative output is the reverse side of this issue. The industry develops
when the cumulative process including this sort of synergism begins to
operate. My understanding of industrial policy is that it provides Myrdal's
"initial kick"[10] to start the process. The provision of a forum for the exchange of information is an instrument to give an appropriate direction
to this initial kick.

This explanation seems to depend so much on synergism, which is after
all a borrowed concept. However, synergy, to use economic vocabulary,
is nothing but a positive externality. In the market such external effects
are not taken into account in the economic calculations of individual
agents. For example, private firms in the market in their investment decisions do not take the externality into account. Then there is a market
failure in this sense, and they do not invest enough. It may perhaps be
due to this externality, however, that investment was so active in Japan
that the phrase "investment calling forth investment" was used. If that
is the case, then one can obtain the opposite of the normal explanation,
that it was because of the presence of this externality, which is regarded
as a source of market failure, that the market in Japan has proven successful thus far. This book began with an explanation of market failure,
but I feel it is necessary to directly address the question of why the market
was successful. In the process I think it is possible to point out one important issue that this book has improperly ignored. This is the issue that,
while they are being affected by positive externalities, the firm itself, or
more precisely entrepreneurs, managers, and employees, learn and change.
In the process of exchanging information, people learn and grow. It is
quite natural that the synergism of evolutionary theory takes into account
this point, but there is a difference in this from the concept of a positive
externality. In the chapters of this book the terms *learning* and *learning
effects* almost never appear, which I cannot help but find strange. Reflecting on the postwar era, there has been a development of industry that
no one foresaw, with people managing through trial and error to arrive
at their present situation. It is certainly important to coolly sort this out
after the fact through the analytic eyes of social scientists. But can one
in fact explain what happened without emphasizing studying, learning-
by-doing, and similar concepts? I cannot avoid the feeling that the cool
eye of analysis has missed something important on the wayside. Both
firms and the government really studied, learning a lot and changing.
Economists have also carried out tremendous academic studies and have

raised the level of theory, but I think one must say that they have been lacking in the innovative attitude that learns from reality and ultimately changes through a trial and error process. The above is my own personal criticism, and I can only hope that I have not been overly severe.

III. Conclusion[11] (Masahiro Okuno and Kotaro Suzumura)

In previous studies of industrial policy, there was not always agreement as to the meaning or content of the concept of "industrial policy" on which the studies focused. Undoubtedly the main reason for this, as touched on in the Introduction and in Part I of this book, can be found in the fact that the content of the policies that were adopted and the aim of these policies in each of the postwar eras changed greatly over time.

As analyzed in detail in the three studies that comprise Part I of this book, the history of industrial policy can, roughly speaking, be divided into three eras. The first era was the reconstruction period from the end of the war through the beginning of the rapid growth. Industrial policy during this period was distinguished by economic management through bureaucratic controls, which were strongly colored by the remaining dregs of the wartime controlled economy. Specifically, while there was some variation depending on the subperiod, there were policy directions along the lines of a planned economy, such as the priority production system and industrial rationalization plans, which sought their goals through the discriminatory use of policy instruments, such as direct interventions in the form of price controls and foreign exchange allocation, along with the provision of low-interest loans through public financial institutions and the use of special tax measures. A great many bureaucrat-dominated policies were adopted (Chapter 2).

In contrast, the rapid growth era through about 1970 can probably be said to be an era of conflict between policymakers and firms. The government attempted to maintain the policy framework of bureaucrat-dominated controlled-economy type industrial policies, which had already lost much of their effectiveness by the end of the reconstruction era. Firms sought economic management based on the entrepreneurial spirit of firms and relying on the market mechanism. In this period, due to rapid growth of the economy, industry advanced rapidly, and the previous policy framework collapsed. The government, while having lost much of the powers that had permitted many of its interventions, continued trying to intervene directly through so-called "administrative guidance" and other measures centered around the *genkyoku*. In particular, under the banner of industrial restructuring and industrial rationalization, policies were taken in response to issues arising from trade and capital liberalization; as part of these a variety of intraindustry coordination policies were attempted. It must be noted, however, that in only a small number of industries was the responsible arm of the government able to completely realize its aims (Chapter 3).[12]

The rapid growth era began to show signs of ending from around 1970, and with the oil shock the Japanese economy entered a new phase. The philosophy of the policymakers of the government (and MITI in particular) also appears to have changed greatly from around this time. The organizational reform of 1970, when there was a transformation from the previous pattern of a vertical structure centered around the *genkyoku* to a horizontal structure focusing on policy coordination, symbolized that bureaucrats themselves from around the end of the 1960s had begun to sense the limitations of bureaucrat-dominated direct control policies. The main industrial policies of this era were for encouraging "technology" and "knowledge" and for assisting adjustment in declining industries; at least at the level of slogans, there were also energy and pollution policies. This indicates that within the bureaucracy itself there grew the recognition in this era that industrial policy ought to function not so much to replace the price mechanism as to supplement it (Chapter 4 and the Introduction).

Thus, as the content and intent of industrial policy changed substantially during each postwar period, it is not possible to carry out an appropriate evaluation without making clear the definition of what is meant by "industrial policy." Most of the previous criticisms of industrial policy seem to implicitly conceive of the mainstream or typical form of industrial policy as consisting of intraindustry coordination policies designed to foster oligopoly, such as industrial restructuring and rationalization policies, under the guidance of the bureaucracy. In contrast, those analysts who were to a greater or lesser extent appreciative of industrial policy emphasized its facet of supplementing the price mechanism and tended to view industrial policy very broadly.

In this project, even though the same term *industrial policy* is used, we have tried to define industrial policy based on a framework of standard economic theory, in an attempt to avoid the unnecessary confusion that arises from in fact having in the background different images of "policy." This is done in detail in the Introduction and in Chapter 9, but to quickly summarize, our use of *industrial policy* is to refer to the totality of policies that use some sort of policy instrument to intervene in the allocation of resources among industries or sectors, centering on manufacturing, or to intervene in the industrial organization within a given industry by trying to influence the level of activity of private firms. From this perspective, typical examples of policies include those that use administrative guidance for industrial restructuring or rationalization, that tax imports, or subsidize exports, and includes the use of special tax measures and low-interest loans provided through public financial institutions. We also thereby understand such policies to include those relating to roads, ports, and other infrastructure, the various Visions published by the government, and the presence of bodies such as the government councils.

Based on the above historical evolution and the definition of industrial policy, how then should we evaluate Japanese industrial policy? The first point we should make is that of the role of industrial policy in the rapid growth of postwar Japan. All the participants in this project recognize that, excluding the brief period immediately after the end of the war, the foundation of rapid growth was competition operating through the price mechanism and a flourishing entrepreneurial spirit. In opposition to the "Japan, Inc." thesis, it can even be said that the course of the history of industrial policy in the principal postwar periods (in particular the 1950s and the 1960s) has often been that the initiative and vitality of the private sector undermined the plans of the government authorities to try to utilize direct intervention in the nature of "controls."

Saying this does not mean that there were not industrial policy measures that should be favorably evaluated for their role in supplementing the price mechanism. There has been close to a consensus among the participants in this joint project that examples of policies that should be evaluated favorably include the use of trade restrictions to protect and nurture domestic industry, and the various mechanisms that functioned to effectively transmit information valuable for the activities of private enterprises through bodies such as the Industrial Structure Council and the use of other government councils and committees, and through long-term plans and the Vision policies. Below we will summarize the conclusions of this book on these two areas of policy.

First, policies for the protection of domestic industries through trade restrictions can be divided into roughly two groups. As discussed in detail in Part III of this book, one of these was infant industry policies, designed to protect and foster industries that (because of setup costs) would not be able to establish themselves without government intervention. The other was policies designed to foster countervailing power in the face of a foreign monopolist or oligopoly.

There are countless examples of the former type of policies; Chapter 6 verifies that machine tools, automobiles, and many other industries were established through tariffs and other trade restrictions (see also Chapters 11, 12, and 16). Passive policies under trade liberalization to impede liberalization in marginal industries are also concluded to have been effective, in the sense of providing leeway for such industries to become established.

What is considered important in this context is that, despite the building of barriers to competition from abroad through trade restrictions, there were multiple firms acting as competitors domestically. The history of the protection of domestic firms in postwar Japan indicates the important fact that trade restrictions will be more effective in developing countries, the greater is the extent to which the domestic market is supported by multiple firms, where in addition an environment has been created in which firms can effectively compete. As has already been stated, one important facet of the government authorities in Japan was that their interventions acted in the direction of eliminating competition among a multiplicity of firms. In this sense we must note the reservation that trade restrictions were effective not so much because of the success of the government in achieving its aims as because of the strong vitality of private firms.

The archetypical example of policy to foster countervailing power against a foreign monopolist is that of the computer industry, treated in Chapter 13. It can probably be said that policies to protect and foster the film, integrated circuit, and other industries were also to some extent economically successful. Because such policies tend to give rise to international tensions among the developed countries, however, we believe that in this sense problems still remain (Chapter 6).

Second, while it is extraordinarily difficult to provide a quantitative evaluation, we feel that a relatively effective element in Japanese industrial policy has been the mechanism for collecting, processing, and transmitting information through the various councils, Vision policies, and the drawing up and publication of economic plans. It could be said that these were only a necessary political instrument for drawing up and putting into law other policy instruments. Nevertheless, individual firms were thereby able to obtain projections through these councils of the future of other industries and firms, at least after the fact, and on the basis of that were themselves able to form clearer projections of the future. Again, through the many government plans, firms were able to understand the government projections for the future of the economy and what future policies might be. We believe that this was effective in that it supplemented the price mechanism, and in particular its informational limitations (Chapter 9).

Chapter 5 provides a quantitative analysis of the main policies considered important in changing the distribution of resources among industries: FILP investments, special tax measures, and low-interest loans by public financial institutions. What is made clear there was that, except for a limited period and for certain industries, industrial policy consisting of such pecuniary incentives was, at least quantitatively, not effective enough to cause one to look twice. In comparison to the subsidies and loans to agriculture, forestry, and fisheries, the resources directed into the manufacturing sector were rather limited. Nevertheless, for certain industries and in certain time periods, one cannot ignore the role played by such pecuniary incentives. Of these, those felt to be particularly important were loans to the iron and steel industry during the reconstruction era, subsidies to the merchant marine and shipbuilding such that shipbuilding was able to capture a 50% share of the world market, investments in roads, ports, and other infrastructure, which provided an environment suitable for the development of many industries, not the least of them being the automotive industry, and finally, assistance for small and medium enterprises (see also Chapters 11, 12, 16, and 19 on these). While these subsidies or special tax measures provided leverage for intervention in the carrying out of policies, as indicated in Chapter 20, they differed from subsidies to agriculture in that they were not booty to be selfishly garnered, but consisted of subsidies that were granted according to specified rules for low-interest lending or the utilization of tax measures. From the standpoint of the equity of policy, and from the small distortions that resulted in the price mechanism, these can be regarded favorably. Now one can also conceive of there having been supply-side effects in that investment was speeded up through the provision of special depreciation allowances, as well as other tax measures and low-interest loans. The attempt to make clear empirically this impact in Chapter 16 and elsewhere, however, cannot be said to have been successful.

Industrial policies providing pecuniary incentives were also the primary policy instruments used for R&D. As stated in detail in Chapters 7 and 8, however, the amounts of government subsidies for R&D were in postwar Japan quite small and had only a marginal impact on the private incentives for firms for R&D. The government R&D policies worthy of favorable evaluation were, rather, those policies that operated in an informational or organizational aspect, which are typified by the cooperative R&D ventures in computers, integrated circuits, and other industries.

Adjustment in and assistance to declining industries that had lost their comparative advantage due to the oil crisis became one of the primary goals of industrial policy after 1970. Part V of this book consists of an overview of such policies. In Japan, many adjustment and assistance policies have been relatively successful, such as the trade policies in the textile industry and the use of the market mechanism in the aluminum industry. They are also distinctive in their many-faceted approach, including labor and regional policies. As stressed in Chapter 12, these policies, along with direct interventions such as recession cartels and the buying up of excess capacity, bring on many economic, political, and administrative distortions. In contrast to these, the various measures for reallocating labor from declining industries, along with regional policies,

are considered effective when coupled with Japanese employment practices (Chapter 14).

Finally, we must touch on the classic industrial policies of direct government regulation as in industrial restructuring and rationalization policies. Chapter 18 treats the promotion of joint activity, in the coordination
of output, prices, and investment, along with recession cartels, where
administrative guidance was the main policy instrument, while Chapter
19 treats merger and restructuring policies. As stated in the Introduction,
the guiding principle for such intraindustry coordination policies was a
constant reference to the need to eliminate excess competition. As shown
in Chapter 9, however, the concept of *excess competition,* which has in
the past been criticized, is not without theoretical justification. Nevertheless, there is a consensus among the participants in this project that
the use of excess competition as an excuse for direct intervention policies
should not be accepted, because it causes a multitude of distortions in
the operation of the price mechanism. Furthermore, our evaluation of
whether such direct intervention policies have been effective in achieving
the original goals of these policies cannot but be extremely negative
(Chapter 18).

The above has presented our overall evaluation of the topics taken up
in this book, but below we would like to comment on a number of issues
that were not treated in the book. First of all, we must offer some explanation for why petrochemicals, petroleum refining, and other industries
that were principal targets of industrial policy were not treated in this
book. When we surveyed the existing literature at the beginning of this
project, we found that there were already a number of works of high academic repute that dealt with the significance and evaluation of industrial
policy in these industries.[13] This was the main reason for not including
them as industries to be focused on in this project; we were selective
because our aim was that the results of this project should complement
existing work. When it came time to draw together the results of the project
in the form of this book, we felt that the issues that might arise from failing
to treat these classical industries as main objects of our analysis were in
fact made sufficiently clear. For those readers who have an interest in
these, we recommend that the works referenced above be read together
with this book. In any case, in this book the petroleum refining industry
is nevertheless touched on in Chapter 18, as are the petrochemical and
the machine tool industries in Chapter 3.

In the carrying out of postwar industrial policy, the tension between
industrial policy and antitrust policy was very important, and in evaluating
industrial policy, the issues of industrial policy as seen from the perspective
of competitive policy cannot be ignored. It was not, however, possible

in this book to treat these issues except for passing comments in Part I and Part VI. From both the standpoint of pure theory and of economic policy, these issues require much further study, and we hope that this book will provide an impetus to the furthering of such research.

It seems that much of the recent interest in industrial policy has arisen in connection with international friction relating to trade and economic policy. Since the purpose of this book was to carry out a rigorous analysis of postwar Japanese industrial policy from the standpoint of economic theory, we did not take up the issues of such international friction. We hope rather that this book provides a start for much new research in economics and political science on this issue.

In the course of summarizing this project, we could not help but realize the number of points at which we did not take up issues that called for examination, or which in the initial planning stages we failed to consider, but which in the looking back over the results of the project we realized represented points of view that should have been incorporated. We feel that the results of the project that we have incorporated in this book nevertheless are for now the best synthesis of what we know at the present time about Japanese industrial policy. We hope that this book will serve as a base for the development of much further research.

Notes

1. Baba [1975] sets forth this line of thought in greater detail.
2. Baba [1967].
3. The data for 1955 are for gross value added in establishments with 4 or more workers, while for 1965 the figures are for net value added in establishments with 100 or more workers. Thus there are somewhat different coverage and different conceptions of value added, but due to data limitations it was not possible to make adjustments for this.
4. According to Miyazawa [1974], population congestion and environmental standards and work standards deal with "market failures and distributional issues," and so there is no theoretical link between these and the income elasticity and productivity improvement standards with which they are grouped. "Rather, what is of decisive importance is that these are conflicting [standards], and tacking on these additional standards serves only to sweep under the rug this unresolved issue."
5. Arrow [1974], p. 33.
6. Williamson [1975].
7. Imai and Itami [1985].
8. Nelson and Winter [1982].
9. Yonekura [1983].
10. Myrdal [1957].
11. As per the course of events set forth in the Preface, this book presents the results of a joint project of two years' duration. During the course of editing, we attempted to

coordinate the viewpoints among the different essays and to impose a minimum unity of style. It cannot, however, be said that there was unity of opinion among the participants on all points, and in particular in the evaluation of the various individual industrial policy measures there remain mild differences of opinion. Thus we want to clearly indicate that we alone are in the end responsible for the following comments summarizing the results of this joint project and the issues that remain unresolved.

12. As exceptions we can mention industries such as petroleum refining and shipbuilding.
13. Regarding petroleum refining see, for example, Imai [1969] and Tanaka [1980], and for petrochemicals see S. Nakamura et al. [1971] and Kano [1979].

References

Abernathy, W. J. (1978). *The Productivity Dilemma*. Baltimore: Johns Hopkins Univ. Press.

Abernathy, W. J., J. E. Harbour, and J. M. Henn (1980). *Productivity and Comparative Cost Advantages; in the U.S. and Japanese Auto Industries*, Report to the U.S. Department of Transportation.

Allen, R. G. D. (1967). *Macro-Economic Theory*. London: Macmillan.

Amaya, Naohiro (1982). *Nihon Kabushiki Kaisha, Nokosareta Sentaku [Japan, Incorporated: Remaining Option]*. Tokyo: PHP.

Aono, Tadao (1977). *IBM no Hikari to Kage [Light and Shadow of IBM]*, new edition. Tokyo: Nihon Keizai Shinbun Sha.

Arisawa, Hiromi (1948). *Infureshon to Shakaika [Inflation and Socialization]*. Tokyo: Nippon Hyoron Sha.

Arisawa, Hiromi (1953). *Saigunbi no Keizaigaku [Economics of Rearmament]*. Tokyo: University of Tokyo Press.

Arisawa, Hiromi (1957). *Gakumon to Shiso to Ningen to [Study, Thought, and Human]*. Tokyo: Mainichi Shinbun Sha.

Arisawa, Hiromi and Shuzo Inaba, eds. (1966). *Shiryo Sengo Nijunenshi [20-Year Postwar History: Materials]*, vol. 2. Tokyo: Nippon Hyoron Sha.

Arrow, K. J. (1962). "Economic Welfare and the Allocation of Resources of Invention," Nelson, R. R. ed., *The Rate and Direction of Inventive Activity*. Princeton: Princeton Univ. Press.

Arrow, K. J. (1974). *The Limits of Organization*. New York: Norton.

Automobile Panel, Committee on Technology and International Economic and Trade Issues of the Office of the Foreign Secretary, National Academy of Engineering and the Commission on Engineering and Technical Systems, National Research Council (1982). *The Competitive Status of the U.S. Auto Industry: A Study of the Influence of Technology in Determining International Competitive Advantage*. Washington, D.C.: National Academic Press.

Baba, Masao (1967). *Sangyobetsu Shotoku Danseichi Keisoku Kekka [Estimates of Income Elasticities by Industry]*. Osaka: Osaka Chamber of Commerce and Industry, mimeographed.

Baba, Masao (1974). *Han Dokusen no Keizaigaku [Economics of Anti-Monopoly]*. Tokyo: Chikuma Shobo.

Baba, Masao (1975). *Sangyo Kozo no Henka o Kangaeru [Thoughts on Changing Industrial Structure]*, Japan Economic Research Center, series No. 13. Tokyo: Japan Economic Research Center.

Baba, Masao (1983). *Ekonomisuto no Shiten [Viewpoints of an Economist]*. Tokyo: Chikuma Shobo.

559

Bain, J. S. (1968). *Industrial Organization*, 2nd ed. New York: John Wiley & Sons, Inc.

Barzel, Y. (1968). "Optimal Timing of Innovations," *Review of Economics and Statistics*, 50 (August), 348–355.

Bergsten, C. F., ed. (1975). *Toward a New World Trade Policy: The Maidenhead Papers*. Lexington, MA: Lexington Books.

Bhagwati, J. N. (1965). "On the Equivalence of Tariffs and Quotas," R. E. Baldwin et al., *Trade, Growth and the Balance of Payments*. Chicago: Rand McNally.

Bhagwati, J. N., ed. (1982). *Import Competition and Response*. Chicago: Univ. Chicago Press.

Brander, J. and B. Spencer (1981). "Tariffs and the Extraction of Foreign Monopoly Rents under Potential Entry," *Canadian Journal of Economics* 14 (August), 371–389.

Bresciani-Turroni, C. (1937). *The Economy of Inflation. A Study of Currency Depreciation in Postwar Germany*. London: Allen and Unwin.

Bruno, M. and J. Sachs (1981). "Supply versus Demand Approaches to the Problem of Stagflation," H. Giersch, ed., *Macroeconomic Policies for Growth and Stability: An European Perspective*. Tübingen: J. C. B. Mohr.

The Cabinet Council on Commerce and Trade (1983). *An Assessment of U.S. Competitiveness in High Technology Industries*. A Study prepared for the Working Group on High-Technology Industries of the Cabinet Council on Commerce and Trade.

Caves, R. E. (1982). *Multinational Enterprise and Economic Analysis*. Cambridge: Cambridge Univ. Press.

Caves, R. E. and M. Uekusa (1976). *Industrial Organization in Japan*. Washington, D.C.: The Brookings Institution.

Chusho Kigyo Cho [Small and Medium Enterprise Agency, MITI] (1980, 1981). *Chusho Kigyo Hakusho [White Paper on Small and Medium Enterprises]*, 1980 ed., 1981 ed. Tokyo: Government Printing Office.

——— (1982). *Chusho Kigyo Shisaku no Aramashi [Outline of Small Business Measures]*. Tokyo: Chusho Kigyo Cho.

Clark, J. M. (1940). "Toward a Concept of Workable Competition," *American Economic Review*, 30 (June), 241–256.

Dasgupta, P. and J. Stiglitz (1980a). "Uncertainty, Industrial Structure and the Speed of R&D," *Bell Journal of Economics*, 11 (Spring), 1–28.

Dasgupta, P. and J. Stiglitz (1980b). "Industrial Structure and the Nature of Innovative Activity," *Economic Journal*, 90 (June), 266–293.

Demsetz, H. (1969). "Information and Efficiency: Another Viewpoint," *Journal of Law and Economics*, 12 (April), 1–22.

Denison, E. F. and W. K. Chung (1976). *How Japanese Economy Grew So Fast*, Washington, D.C.: The Brookings Institution.

Denton, G., S. O'Cleireacain and S. Ash (1975). *Trade Effects of Public Subsidies to Private Enterprise*, London: Macmillan, for the Trade Policy Research Center.

Destler, I. M., H. Fukui, and H. Sato (1979). *The Textile Wrangle: Conflict in Japanese-American Relations, 1969–1971*, Ithaca, NY: Cornell Univ. Press.

Destler, I. M. and H. Sato (1982). *Coping with U.S.-Japanese Economic Conflicts*, Lexington, MA: Lexington Books, 1982.

Diebold, W., Jr. (1980). *Industrial Policy as an International Issue*. New York: McGraw-Hill.

Dixit, A. (1980). "The Role of Investment in Entry Deterrence," *Economic Journal*, 90 (March), 95–106.

Dokusen Kinshi Konwakai [Anti-Monopoly Consultative Group] (1970). *Kanri Kakaku [Administered Prices]*. Tokyo: Government Printing Office.

Dornbusch, R., S. Fischer and P. A. Samuelson (1977). "Comparative Advantage, Trade and Payments in a Ricardian Model with a Continuum of Goods,'' *American Economic Review*, 67 (December), 823–839.

Eads, G. (1974). ''U.S. Government Support for Civilian Technology: Economic Theory versus Political Practice,'' *Research Policy*, 3, 2–16.

Eaton, C. and R. Lipsey (1981). ''Capital, Commitment, and Entry Equilibrium,'' *Bell Journal of Economics*, 12 (Autumn), 593–604.

Echigo, Kazunori (1973). ''Aruminium'' [Aluminum], Kumagai, H., ed., *Nihon no Sangyo Soshiki [Industrial Organization in Japan]*, vol. II, Tokyo: Chuo Koron Sha.

Economict, Henshubu, ed. (1977). *Sengo Sangyoshi eno Shogen [Testimonies to Postwar Industrial History]*, Tokyo: Mainichi Shinbun Sha.

Emoto, Haruhiko (1974). ''Yu'nyu Seigen Mondai o Kangaeru—Nihon Sen'i Sangyo eno Teigen'' [''Thoughts on Import Restrictions: A Proposal to Japan's Textile Industry''], *Kasen Geppo [Monthly on Synthetic Fibers]*, No. 319 (November).

Esposito, L. and F. F. Esposito (1974). ''Excess Capacity and Market Structure,'' *Review of Economics and Statistics*, 56 (May), 188–194.

Fisher, F. M., J. J. McGowan and J. E. Greenwood (1983). *Folded, Spindled and Mutilated: Economic Analysis and U.S. v IBM*, Cambridge, MA: MIT Press.

Frank, C. Jr (1975). ''Trade Adjustment Assistance in the United States,'' OECD (1975).

Futatsugi, Yusaku (1974). ''Kato Kyoso no Mekanizum'' [''The Mechanism of Excess Competition''], Shinohara and Baba, 105–120.

Gomez-Ibanez, J. A. and D. Harrison, Jr. (1982). ''Imports and the Future of U.S. Automobile Industry,'' *American Economic Review*, 72 (May), 319–323.

Gresser, J. (1980). ''High Technology and Japanese Industrial Policy: A Strategy for U.S. Policymakers,'' Subcommittee on Trade of the Committee on Ways and Means, U.S. House of Representatives. Washington, D.C.: U.S. Government Printing Office, October.

Griliches, Z. (1980). ''Returns to Research and Development Expenditures in the Private Sector,'' J. W. Kendrick and B. N. Vaccara, eds., *New Developments in Productivity Measurement and Analysis*. Chicago: Univ. of Chicago Press.

Gruber, W. H. and D. G. Marquis (1969). *Factors in the Transfer of Technology*. Cambridge, MA: MIT Press.

Gyllenhammar, P. G. (1977). *People at Work*. Reading, MA: Addison-Wesley.

Gyosei Kanricho [Administrative Management Agency] (1981). *Gyosei Shido ni kansuru Chosa Kenkyo Hokokusho [Study Report on Administrative Guidance]*. Tokyo: Gyosei Kanricho.

Haberler, G. (1950). ''Some Problems in the Pure Theory of International Trade,'' *Economic Journal*, 60 (June), 223–240.

Hadley, E. M. (1983). ''The Secret of Japanese Success,'' *Challenge* (May–June), 4–10.

Harada, Naohiko (1983). ''Gyosei Shido—Ho no Shihai to Nihonteki Gyosei Taishitsu'' [''Administrative Guidance: Judicial Control and Characteristics of Japan's Administration''], *Jurisuto*, No. 29.

Hayashi, Shintaro (1967). ''Sangyo Saihensei no Hitsuyosei to Susumekata'' [''The Necessity of Industrial Reorganization and How to Carry it On''], *Ekonomisuto*, April 20.

Hayashi, Yujiro, ed. (1957). *Nihon no Keizai Keikaku [Japan's Economic Planning]*. Tokyo: Toyo Keizai Shinpo Sha.

Hayek, F. A. (1931). *Price and Production*. London: Routledge and Kegan Paul.

Hirai, Toko (1978–79). ''Shinko Kogyokoku kara no Sen'i Seihin Yunyu Zodai no Eikyo'' [''Impact of Increasing Imports of Textile Products from NICs''], *Kanzei Chosa Geppo [Tariff Study Monthly]*, 32.

Hirshleifer, J. (1971). ''The Private and Social Value of Information and the Reward to Inventive Activity,'' *American Economic Review*, 61 (September), 561–574.

Houthakker, H. S. and S. P. Magee (1969). "Income and Price Elasticities in World Trade," *Review of Economics and Statistics*, 51 (May), 111–125.

Ikeda, Katsuhiko and Noriyuki Doi (1980). *Kigyo Gappei no Bunseki [Analysis of Business Mergers]*. Tokyo: Chuo Keizai Sha.

Ikema, Makoto (1980). "Nichibei Boeki Masatsu—Jidosha no Baai" ["U.S.–Japan Trade Frictions: the Case of Automobiles"], *Kikan Gendai Keizai [Contemporary Economy]*, No. 39 (Summer), 35–49.

Imai, Ken'ichi (1969). "Sekiyu Seisei" ["Petroleum Refining"]. Niida and Ono, 159–200.

Imai, Ken'ichi (1976). *Gendai Sangyo Soshiki [Modern Industrial Organization]*. Tokyo: Iwanami Shoten.

Imai, Ken'ichi (1982a). "Software Shijo no Keisei Katei to Software Kigyo no Senryaku" ["The Process of Formation of the Software Market and Strategy of Software Firms"], *Business Review*, 30 (September).

Imai, Ken'ichi (1982b). "Shin Enerugi Kaihatsu no Senryaku to Soshiki Ron" ["Strategy of New Energy Development and Theory of Organization"], Discussion Paper No. 103, Institute of Business Research, Hitotsubashi University.

Imai, Ken'ichi (1982c). "Japan's Changing Industrial Structure and United States–Japan Industrial Relations," K. Yamamura, ed., *Policy and Trade Issues of the Japanese Economy*. Seattle: Univ. of Washington Press, 47–75.

Imai, Ken'ichi (1983). *Nihon no Sangyo Shakai—Shinka to Henkaku no Dotei* [Japan's Industrial Society: Paths of Evolutionary Change]. Tokyo: Chikuma Shobo.

Imai, Ken'ichi (1986). "Japan's Industrial Policy for High Technology Industry," Hugh Patrick, ed., *Japan's High Technology Industries: Lessons and Limitations of Industrial Policy*. Seattle: Univ. of Washington Press, 137–169.

Imai, Ken'ichi, and Hiroyuki Itami (1985). "Mutual Infiltration of Organization and Market—Japan's Firm and Market in Comparison with the U.S.," *International Journal of Industrial Organization*, 5 (Spring).

Imai, Ken'ichi, Hiroyuki Itami, and Kazuo Koike (1982). *Naibu Soshiki no Keizaigaku* [Economics of Internal Organization]. Tokyo: Toyo Keizai Shinpo Sha.

Imai, Ken'ichi, Hirofumi Uzawa, Ryutaro Komiya, Takashi Negishi, and Yasusuke Murakami (1972). *Kakaku Riron [Price Theory]*, III. Tokyo: Iwanami Shoten.

Imamura, Naraomi (1978). *Hojokin to Nogyo Noson [Subsidies and Farming-Firms]* Tokyo: Ieno Hikari Kyokai.

Inaba, Shuzo and Tetsuo Sakane, eds. (1967). *Shihon Jiyuka to Dokusen Kinshiho [Capital Liberalization and Anti-Trust Law]*. Tokyo: Shiseido.

Itoh, Motoshige (1984). "Boeki Masatsu to Seisakuteki Taio" ["Trade Frictions and Policy Responses"], *Kanzei Chosa Jiho [Tariff Study Journal]* (Tariff Bureau, Ministry of Finance), 35.

Itoh, Motoshige, and Kazuharu Kiyono (1987). "Welfare-Enhancing Export Subsidies," *Journal of Political Economy*, 95 (February), 115–137.

Itoh, Motoshige, Kazuharu Kiyono, Masahiro Okuno, and Kotaro Suzumura (1984). "Sangyo Seisaku no Keizai Bunseki" ["Economic Analysis of Industrial Policy"] (1), *Kikan Gendai Keizai [Contemporary Economy]*, No. 58 (Summer), 73–90.

Itoh, Motoshige, and Yoshiyasu Ono (1982). "Tariffs, Quotas and Market Structure," *Quarterly Journal of Economics*, 97 (May), 295–305.

Itoh, Motoshige, and Yoshiyasu Ono (1984). "Tariffs vs. Quotas under Duopoly of Heterogeneous Goods," mimeographed.

Iwasaki, Akira (1972). "Big Business no Kyosoteki Kozo" ["Competitive Structure of Big Business"], *Keizai Hyoron*, 21 (June), 128–150.

Japan Machine-Tool Builder's Association (1968). *Kosaku Kikai Nyuusu [Machine Tool News]* No. 58.

References

563

—— (1969). *Kosaku Kikai Nyuusu [Machine Tool News]* No. 65.
—— (1971). *Kosaku Kikai Nyuusu [Machine Tool News]* No. 75.
Johnson, C. (1982). *MITI and the Japanese Miracle—The Growth of Industrial Policy 1925–1975*. Stanford: Stanford Univ. Press.
Johnson, P. S. (1971/72). "The Role of Co-operative Research in British Industry," *Research Policy,* 1 332–350.
Kaizuka, Keimei (1973). *Keizai Seisaku no Kadai [Problems of Economic Policy]*. Tokyo: Univ. of Tokyo Press.
Kamien, M. I. and N. Schwartz (1982). *Market Structure and Innovation*. Cambridge: Cambridge Univ. Press.
Kanamori, Hisao, ed. (1970). *Boeki to Kokusai Shushi [Trade and Balance of Payments]*. Tokyo: Nihon Keizai Shinbun Sha.
Kanemitsu, Hidero (1981). "Senshinkoku no Boeki Seigen to Sangyo Chosei" ["Trade Restrictions and Industrial Adjustment of Advanced Countries"], S. Sekiguchi, ed., *Nihon no Sangyo Chosei [Japan's Industrial Adjustment]*, Tokyo: Nihon Keizai Shinbun Sha.
Kano, Yoshikazu (1979). "Sekiyu Kagaku Sangyo Kenkyu" ["Study of Petrochemical Industry"]. *Kokumin Keizai,* No. 141 (April).
Katayama, Nobu (1970). *Nihon no Zosen Kogyo [Japanese Shipbuilding Industry]*. Tokyo: Nihon Kogyo Shuppan Sha.
Katz, B. G. and A. Phillips (1982). "The Computer Industry," R. R. Nelson, ed., *Government and Technical Progress, A Cross-Industry Analysis*. New York: Perganon Press.
Katzenstein, P. J., ed. (1978). *Between Power and Plenty*. Madison, Wisc.: Univ. of Wisconsin Press.
Kawaguchi, Hiroshi et al. (1962). *Nihon Keizai no Kiso Kozo [The Basic Structure of the Japanese Economy]*. Tokyo: Shunjusha.
Kawasaki, Tsutomu (1968). *Sengo Tekkogyo Ron [Postwar Steel Industry]*. Tokyo: Tekko Shinbun Sha.
Keesing, D. B. and M. Wolf (1980). *Textile Quotas Against Developing Countries*. London: Trade Policy Research Center.
Keizai Kikakucho [Economic Planning Agency] (1953). *Keizai Hakusho [Annual Report on the Japanese Economy]*, 1953 edition. Tokyo: Government Printing Office.
—— (1958). *Showa 31 Nendo no Kokumin Shotoku [National Income of 1956]*. Tokyo: Government Printing Office.
—— (1961). *Kokumin Shotoku Baizo Keikaku [National Income Doubling Plan]*. Tokyo: Government Printing Office.
—— (1972). *Keizai Hakusho [Annual Report on the Japanese Economy]*, 1972 edition. Tokyo: Government Printing Office.
—— (1976a). *Kokumin Shotoku Tokei Nenpo [Annual Report on National Income Statistics]*, 1976 edition. Tokyo: Government Printing Office.
—— (1976b). *Gendai Nihon Keizai no Tenkai [Evolution of the Contemporary Japanese Economy]*. Tokyo: Government Printing Office.
—— (1982). *Keizai Hakusho [Annual Report on the Japanese Economy]*, 1982 edition. Tokyo: Government Printing Office.
—— Keizai Kenkyusho [Institute of Economic Research] (1962). *Shihon Sutokku to Keizai Seicho [Capital Stock and Economic Research]*. Tokyo: Government Printing Office.
——, Chosakyoku [Research Bureau] (1972). *Shiryo Keizai Hakusho 25 Nen [25 Years' Economic White Papers: A Compendium]*. Tokyo: Nihon Keizai Shinbun Sha.
Kikai Shinko Kyokai Keizai Kenkyusho [Economic Research Institute, Japan Society for the Promotion of the Machine Industry] (1981a). *Gijutsu Kakushin to Tokkyo Seido [Technological Innovation and the Patent System]*. Tokyo: Gijutsu Shinko Kyokai.

────── (1981b). *Jidosha Sangyo ni okeru Kokusai Bungyo no Shinten to Shitauke Kigyo [International Division of Labor and Subcontracting Firms in the Automobile Industry]*. Tokyo: Kikai Shinko Kyokai.

────── (1983). *High Technology Sangyo ni okeru Management no Kokusai Hikaku [International Comparison of Management in High-Technology Industries]*. Tokyo: Kikai Shinko Kyokai.

Kita, Masamitsu (1978). *IBM no Chosen—Computer Teikoku IBM no Uchimaku [The Challenge of IBM: Inside Story of IBM the Computer Empire]*. Tokyo: Kyoritsu Shuppan.

Kitagawa, Jiro (1983). "Sengo Aruminium Seirengyo no Ayumi" ["Postwar Development of the Aluminum Refining Industry"], *Aruminium [Aluminum]*, May.

Knickerbocker, F. T. (1973). *Oligopolistic Reaction and Multinational Enterprise*. Boston: Division of Research, Graduate School of Business Administration, Harvard University.

Kobayashi, Koji (1983). " 'C&C' Senryaku no Keisei to Tenbo" ["Formation and Review of C&C Strategy"]. *Business Review*, 31 (August).

Kobayashi, Yoshihiro (1973). "Zosen" ["Shipbuilding"], Kumagai (1973a), 183–234.

Kodama, Fumio (1978). "A Framework of Retrospective Analysis of Industrial Policy Based on Dynamic System Theory of Development," Institute for Policy Science Research Report, Saitama University, July.

Kogyo Gijutsu In [Agency of Industrial Science and Technology, MITI] (1964). *Gijutsu Kakushin to Nihon no Kogyo [Technological Innovations and Japanese Industry]*. Tokyo: Nikkan Kogyo Shinbun Sha.

──────, Somubu Gijutsuchosaka [Technology Research and Information Division, General Coordination Department], ed. (1982). *Wagakuni Sangyo Gijutsu no Kokusai Hikaku—Shuyo 43-seihin Bunya no Teiryo Hyoka [Japan's Industrial Technology Internationally Compared: Quantitative Evaluation in 43 Major Product Areas]*. Tokyo: Tsusho Sangyo Chosakai, August.

────── (1983a). *Wagakuni no Kenkyu Kaihatsu Katsudo Shuyo Shihyo no Doko [Movements of Major Indicators of R&D Activity in Japan]*, revised.

──────, Kenkyu Kaihatsukan Shitsu [Office of Development Programs], (1983b). "Ogata Projects" ["Large Scale Projects"], *58 Nendo Shuppan News [1983 Publications News]*.

Koike, Kazuo (1981). *Chusho Kigyo no Jukuren [Skills in Small Business]*. Tokyo: Dobunkan.

Kojima, Kiyoshi and Ryutaro Komiya, eds. (1972). *Nihon no Hikanzei Shoheki [Japan's Nontariff Barriers]*. Tokyo: Japan Economic Research Center.

Komiya, Ryutaro (1967). "Shihon Jiyuka no Keizaigaku" [Economics of Capital Liberalization], *Ekonomisuto*, July 25.

Komiya, Ryutaro (1972). "Yushutsu Jiyu Kisei" ["Voluntary Export Restraints"], in Kojima and Komiya (1972).

Komiya, Ryutaro (1975a). *Gendai Nihon Keizai Kenkyu [Studies of Contemporary Japanese Economy]*. Tokyo: Univ. of Tokyo Press.

Komiya, Ryutaro (1975b). "Planning in Japan," M. Bornstein, ed., *Economic Planning: East and West*. Cambridge, MA: Ballinger.

Komiya, Ryutaro (1983). "Nichibei Keizai Kankei no Chosei Kadai—Boeki Masatsu no Keizai Bunseki" ["Adjustment Problems of U.S.–Japan Economic Relations, An Economic Analysis of Trade Frictions"]. Tokyo: Nihon Kokusai Mondai Kenkyusho [Japan Institute of International Research].

Komiya, Ryutaro and Akihiro Amano (1972). *Kokusai Keizaigaku [International Economics]*. Tokyo: Iwanami Shoten.

Komiya, Ryutaro, and Kazuo Yasui (1983). "Japan's Macroeconomic Performance Since the First Oil Crisis: Review and Appraisal." Discussion Paper 83-F-8, Faculty of Economics, University of Tokyo, August.

Komiya, Ryutaro and Miyako Suda (1983). *Gendai Kokusai Kin'yu Ron [Modern International Finance]*, 2 vols. Tokyo: Nihon Keizai Shinbun Sha.

Konishi, Tadao (1967). *Handokusen Seisaku to Yuko Kyoso [Anti-Monopoly Policy and Workable Competition]*. Tokyo: Yuhikaku.

Konpyutopia, Henshubu (1982). *IBM Supai Jiken no Zenbo—Nichibei Konpyuta Senso no Butai Ura [All About the IBM Spy Case]*. Tokyo: Computer Age Co.

Kosai, Yutaka (1981). *Kodo Seicho no Jidai—Gendai Nihon Keizaishi Noto [The Age of Rapid Growth—Notes on Contemporary Economic History of Japan]*. Tokyo: Nippon Hyoron Sha.

Kosai, Yutaka, and Yoshitaro Ogino (1984). *The Contemporary Japanese Economy*. London: Macmillan.

Kosei Torihiki Iinkai [Fair Trade Commission] (1969). *Nihon no Sangyo Shuchu—Showa 38–41 Nen [Japan's Industrial Concentration, 1963–66]*. Tokyo: Toyo Keisai Shinpo Sha.

—— (1971). *Nihon no Kigyo Shuchu [Japan's Enterprise Concentration]*. Tokyo: Government Printing Office.

—— (1975). "Shuyo Sangyo ni okeru Ruiseki Seisan Shuchudo to Herfindahl Shisu no Suii" ["Changes in the Cumulative Concentration Ratio and the Herfindahl Index in Major Industries"], Tokyo: Secretariat of the Fair Trade Commission, July.

—— (1977). *Dokusen Kinshi Seisaku 30-nen Shi [30-Year History Anti-Trust Policy]*. Tokyo: Secretariat of the Fair Trade Commission.

—— (1983). *Kosei Torihiki Iinkai Shinketsu Shu (28), Sekiyu Karuteru Jiken Kankei Tokyo Kosai Hanketsu [Decisions of the Fair Trade Commission (28): Tokyo High Court Decisions on the Petroleum Cartel Case]*. Tokyo: Fair Trade Commission.

——, Keizai Chosa Kenkyukai [Economic Research Group] (1982). "Teiseicho Keizai ka no Sangyo Chosei to Kyoso Seisaku" ["Industrial Adjustment and Competition Policy under Low Economic Growth"], November.

Kosei Torihiki Kyokai [Fair Trade Association], ed. (1982). "Keizai Chosakai Hokoku— Teiseicho Keizai ka no Sangyo Chosei to Kyoso Seisaku—Tokuni iwayuru Kozo Fukyo Sangyo Mondai ni tsuite" ["Economic Research Group Report on Industrial Adjustment and Competition Policy under Low Economic Growth," especially in connection with so-called structurally depressed industries], Tokyo: Fair Trade Association.

Koyama, Shigeki (1966). "Kigyokan Kyoso to Kin'yu" ["Interfirm Competition and Finance"], Kanamori, H., ed., *Keizai Seicho to Kigyo Kin'yu [Economic Growth and Business Finance]*. Tokyo: Shunjusha.

Krause, L. B. and S. Sekiguchi (1976). "Japan and the World Economy," Patrick and Rosovsky (1976), 384–458.

Kreps, D. M. and A. M. Spence (1983). "Models of Spillovers in R & D," mimeo.

Krugman, P. (1979). "A Model of Innovation, Technology Transfer and the World Distribution of Income," *Journal of Political Economy*, 87 (April), 253–266.

Krugman, P. (1982). "Trade in Differentiated Products and the Political Economy of Trade Liberalization," J. N. Bhagwati, ed., *Import Competition and Response*. Chicago: Univ. of Chicago Press, 197–208.

Krugman, P. (1983). "New Theories of Trade Among Industrial Countries," *American Economic Review*, 73 (May), 343–348.

Kumagai, Hisao, ed. (1973a, 1973b, 1976). *Nihon no Sangyo Soshiki [Japan's Industrial Organization]*, vol. 1 (1973a), 2 (1973b), 3 (1976). Tokyo: Chuo Koron Sha.

Kumon, Hiroshi, Yoshiji Okamoto, and Yoneo Taniguchi (1983). *Zusetsu Zaisei Toyushi, Shouwa 58 Nen Han [Government Fiscal Program Illustrated, 1983]*. Tokyo: Toyo Keizai Shinpo Sha.

Kuznets, S. (1968). "Notes on Japan's Economic Growth," L. R. Klein and K. Ohkawa, eds., *Economic Growth: The Japanese Experience Since the Meiji Era.* Homewood, IL: Richard D. Irwin, 385–422.

Kyogoku, Jun'ichi (1983). *Nihon no Seiji [Japan's Politics].* Tokyo: Univ. of Tokyo Press.

Lall, S. (1978). "Transnationals, Domestic Enterprises, and Industrial Structure in Host LDCs: A Survey," *Oxford Economic Papers,* 30 (July), 217–248.

Lapan, H. E. (1976). "International Trade, Factor Market Distortions, and the Optimal Dynamic Subsidy," *American Economic Review,* 66 (June), 335–346.

Layton, C. (1968). *Trans-Atlantic Investments.* Bonlogne-sur-Seine: The Atlantic Institute.

Lee, T. and L. Wilde (1980). "Market Structure and Innovation: A Reformulation," *Quarterly Journal of Economics,* 94 (March), 429–436.

Lerner, A. P. (1936). "The Symmetry Between Import and Export Taxes," *Economica,* 3 (August), 306–313.

Lindbeck, A. (1981). "Industrial Policy as an Issue in the Economic Environment," *World Economy,* 4 (December), 391–406.

Linder, S. B. (1961). *An Essay on Trade and Transformation.* Stockholm: Almqvist and Wicksell.

Lindert, P. H. and C. P. Kindleberger (1982). *International Economics.* Homewood, IL: Richard D. Irwin.

Link, A. N. (1977). "On the Efficiency of Federal R&D Spending: A Public Choice Approach," *Public Choice,* 31 (Fall), 129–133.

Link, A. N. (1981). *Research and Development Activity in U.S. Manufacturing.* New York: Prageer.

Lipton, D. (1981). "Factor Cost and Economic Growth in Japan," chapter 4 in *Investment and Growth in Open Economies: Some Simulation Studies,* Ph.D. Dissertation, Harvard University.

Loury, G. C. (1979). "Market Structure and Innovation," *Quarterly Journal of Economics,* 93 (August), 395–410.

Lynn, H. L. (1982). *How Japan Innovates.* Boulder: Westview.

Machlup, M. (1962). *The Production and Distribution of Knowledge in the United States.* Princeton: Princeton Univ. Press.

Malinvaud, E. (1972). "The Allocation of Individual Risks in Large Markets," *Journal of Economic Theory,* 4 (April), 312–328.

Malinvaud, E. (1978). *Leçon des Theories Microeconomique,* 4th ed. Paris: Dunod.

Mansfield, E. (1968). *The Economics of Technological Change.* New York: Norton.

Mansfield, E. (1976). "Federal Support of R&D Activities in the Private Sector," Joint Economic Committee, 94th Congress, *Priorities and Efficiency in Federal Research and Development.* Washington, D.C.: Government Printing Office.

Matsuo, Hiroshi (1980). "Nichibei Handotai Sangyo 30-nen (15), Denshinho Seitei to Nichibei no Josei" ["30 Years of the Semi-Conductor Industry in Japan and the U.S. (15): Enactment of the Electronic Industry Law and the Situations in Japan and the U.S."], *Konpyutopia,* August.

Meade, M. E. (1970). *The Theory of Indicative Planning.* Manchester: The Manchester Univ. Press.

Minamizawa, Yoshiro (1978). *Nihon Konpyuta Hattatsu Shi [History of the Japanese Computer Industry].* Tokyo: Nihon Keizai Shinbun Sha.

Miwa, Yoshiro (1959). "Jidosha Jakuden Sangyo ni okeru Senmon Seisan no Shinko" ["Progress of Specialized Production in the Automobile Industry and the Light Electrical Machinery Industry"], *Gekkan Chusho Kigyo [Small Business Monthly],* October.

Miwa, Yoshiro (1977). "Tekkogyo no Setsubi Toshi Chosei no Keizaiteki Kiketsu" ["Economic Consequences of Investment Adjustment in the Steel Industry''], *Keizaigaku Ronshu* (Shinshu Univ.), No. 11 (March).

Miwa, Yoshiro (1979). '' 'Fukyo Karutel,' 'Kyozo Fukyo Ho' to Jiju Kyoso ni tsuite'' [''Recession Cartels,'' ''Depressed Industry Law'' and Free Competition], *Sango Nenpo* (Kokumin Keizai Kenkyu Kyokai).

Miyake, Takeo (1980). ''Chusho Kigyo Kin'yu Seisaku no Hyoka'' [Evaluation of Small Business Finance Policy], K. Ara et al, *Sengo Keizai Seisaku Ron no Soten [Postwar Controversies in Theory of Economic Policy]*. Tokyo: Keiso Shobo.

Miyazaki, Yoshikazu (1966). *Sengo Nihon no Keizai Kiko* [The Economic Mechanism of Postwar Japan]. Tokyo: Shin Hyoron Sha.

Miyazawa, Ken'ichi (1974). ''Sangyo Seisaku no Rinen to Shijo Kiko'' [''The Ideal of Industrial Policy and the Market Mechanism''], *Shukan Toyo Keizai Rinji Zokan*, No. 29 (June 18), 35–43.

Morozumi, Yoshihiko (1966). *Sango Seisaku no Riron [Theory of Industrial Policy]*. Tokyo: Nihon Keizai Shinbun Sha.

Morozumi, Yoshihiko, Yoshito Chigusa, et al. (1963). *Sangyo Taisei no Sai Hensei [Reorganization of the Industrial System]*. Tokyo: Shunjusha.

Murakami, Yasusuke (1982). ''Sengo Nihon no Keizai System'' [''The Economic System of Postwar Japan''], *Ekonomisuto*, June 14.

Murakami, Yasusuke (1984). *Shin Chukan Taishu no Jidai [The Age of the New Middle Mass]*. Tokyo: Chuo Koron Sha.

Mussa, M. (1982). ''Government Policy and the Adjustment Process,'' Bhagwati, 73–120.

Myrdal, G. (1957). *Economic Theory and Under Developed Regions*. London: Gerald Duckworth & Co.

Nakai, Shozo (1961). *Jiyuka no Boeki to Gaikoku Kawase [Trade under Liberalization and Foreign Exchange]*. Tokyo: Seki Shoin Shinsha.

Nakamura, Hideichiro, Hajime Yamashita and Kimihiro Masamura, eds. (1971). *Gendai no Kagaku Kogyo—Kozo to Dotai [Modern Chemical Industry: Structure and Dynamics]*. Tokyo: Toyo Keizai Shinpo Sha.

Nakamura, Hideichiro, Shigeo Akiya et al. (1981). *Gendai Chusho Kigyo Shi [History of Modern Small Business]*. Tokyo: Nihon Keizai Shinbun Sha.

Nakamura, Takafusa (1969). ''Sengo no Sangyo Seisaku'' [''Postwar Industrial Policy''], Niida and Ono, 303–315.

Nakamura, Takafusa (1970). ''Jiyuka to Nichibei Kankei'' [''Liberalization and Japan–U.S. Relations''], Kanamori.

Nakamura, Takafusa (1974). ''Nihon ni okeru Sangyo Seisaku no Tokushoku to Hyoka'' [''Features and Evaluation of Japan's Industrial Policy''], *Toyo Keizai Rinji Zokan* (Special Issue on Industrial Policy), No. 3810 (June 18, 1974), 58–64.

Nakamura, Takafusa (1978). *Nihon Keizai—Sono Seicho to Kouzo [Japanese Economy: Its Growth and Structure]*. Tokyo: Univ. of Tokyo Press.

Nakamura, Takafusa (1981). *The Postwar Japanese Economy, Its Development and Structure*. Tokyo: Univ. of Tokyo Press.

Nakamura, Tsutomu (1969). ''Kato Kyoso ni tsuite'' [''Excessive Competition''], *Keizai Kenkyu*, 20 (July), 269–273.

Nakamura, Tsutomu (1983). *Chusho Kigyo to Daikigyo [Small Business and Big Business]*. Tokyo: Toyo Keizai Shinpo Sha.

Nakayama, Ichiro (1953). *Nihon Keizai no Kao [The Face of the Japanese Economy]*. Tokyo: Nippon Hyoron Sha.

Namiki, Nobuyoshi (1973). ''Kigyokan Kyoso to Seisaku Kainyu'' [''Interfirm Competition and Policy Intervention'']. Shinohara and Baba, 35–51.

Nano, Hiko (1982). *Nichibei Konpyuta Senso—IBM Sangyo Supai Jiken no Teiryu [U.S.–Japan Computer War: Undercurrent of the IBM Spy Case]*. Tokyo: Nihon Keizai Shinbun Sha.

Neary, J. P. (1982). "Intersectoral Capital Mobility, Wage Stickiness, and the Case for Adjustment Assistance," Bhagwati, 39–67.

Negishi, Takashi (1972). *General Equilibrium Theory and International Trade*. Amsterdam: North Holland.

Nelson, R. R., ed. (1982a). *Government and Technical Progress*. New York: Perganon.

Nelson, R. R. (1982b). "The Role of Knowledge in R&D Efficiency," *Quarterly Journal of Economics*, 97 (August), 453–470.

Nelson, R. R., J. P. Merton, and E. D. Kalachek (1967). *Technology, Economic Growth and Public Policy*. Santa Monica, CA: The Rand Corp.

Nelson, R. R. and S. G. Winter (1982). *An Evolutionary Theory of Economic Change*. Cambridge, MA: Belknap Press.

Nihon Boseki Kyokai [Japan Spinners' Association], ed. (1979). *Zoku Sengo Boseki Shi [Postwar History of Spinning, Continued]*. Tokyo: Nihon Boseki Kyokai.

——— (1982). *Wagakuni no Sen'ihin Yunyu Mondai o Kangaete [On Japan's Textile Imports]*. Tokyo: Nihon Boseki Kyokai.

Nihon Ginko [Bank of Japan] (1981). *Bukka Shisu Nempo [Price Index Annual]*.

Nihon Joho Shori Kaihatsu Kyokai [Japan Information Processing Development Center] (1982). *Konpyuta Hakusho* [White Paper on Computer]. Tokyo: Nihon Joho Shori Kaihatsu Kyokai.

Nihon Kagaku Sen'i Kyokai [Japan Chemical Fibers Association], ed. (1981). *Kasen Handbook, 1982 [Chemical Fibers Handbook, 1982]*. Tokyo: Nihon Kagaku Sen'i Kyokai Kasen Geppo Kankokai.

Nihon Kaihatsu Ginko [Japan Development Bank] (1963). *Nihon Kaihatsu Ginko 10-nen Shi [Ten-Year History of the Japan Development Bank]*. Tokyo: Nihon Kaihatsu Ginko.

——— (1976). *Nihon Kaihatsu Ginko 25-nen Shi [25-Year History of the Japan Development Bank]*. Tokyo: Nihon Kaihatsu Ginko.

——— (1982, 1983, 1984). *Nihon Kaihatsu Ginko no Genjo [The Present State of the Japan Development Bank]*. Tokyo: Nihon Kaihatsu Ginko.

Nihon Kanzei Kyokai [Japan Tariff Association]. *Boeki Gaikyo [Trade of Japan]*. (1983). *Boeki Nenkan [Trade Yearbook]*.

Nihon Keikinzoku [Japan Light Metals] (1959). *Nihon Keikinzoku 20-nen Shi [20-Year History of Japan Light Metals]*. Tokyo: Nihon Keikinzoku.

Nihon Keizai Kenkyu Senta [Japan Economic Research Center] (1979). *Sekai Keizai no Kozo—Data Base [The Structure of the World Economy: Data Base]*. Tokyo: Japan Economic Research Center.

Nihon Kikai Yushutsu Kumiai [Japan Machinery Exporters' Association] (1982). "Plant Yushutsu Finance Kiso Chosa Iinkai Chosa Hokoku" ["Report of the Committee on Plant Finance Basic Study"], June.

Nihon Kogyo Ginko [Industrial Bank of Japan] (1957). *Nihon Kogyo Ginko 50-nen Shi [50-Year History of the Industrial Bank of Japan]*. Tokyo: Nihon Kogyo Ginko.

——— (1981). *Kogin Chosa [Industrial Bank Survey]*, No. 207.

——— Chosabu [Research Department] (1982). *Nihon Sangyo no Shin Tenkai [New Development of Japanese Industry]*. Tokyo: Nihon Keizai Shinbun Sha.

Nihon Tekko Remmei [Japan Iron and Steel Federation] (1959). *Sengo Tekko Shi [Postwar History of Iron and Steel]*. Tokyo: Nihon Tekko Remmei.

——— (1969). *Tekko 10-nen Shi Showa 33 nen-42 nen [10-Year History of Iron and Steel, 1958–67]*. Tokyo: Nihon Tekko Remmei.

——— (1981). *Tekko 10-nen Shi Showa 43 nen–52 nen [10-Year History of Iron and Steel, 1968–77]*. Tokyo: Nihon Tekko Remmei.

Nihon Tokei Kenkyusho [Japan Statistical Institute] (1956). *Shihon Chikuseki to Kakaku Kozo [Capital Accumulation and Price Structure]*. Tokyo: Nihon Tokei Kenkyusho.

Nihon Zosen Kogyo Kai [Shipbuilders' Association of Japan] (1980). *Nihon Zosen Kogyo Kai 30-nen Shi [30-Year History of the Shipbuilders' Association of Japan]*. Tokyo: Nihon Zosen Kogyo Kai.

Nihon Zosen Shinko Zaidan [Japan Foundation for Shipbuilding Advancement] (1983). *Zosen Fukyo no Kiroku—Daiichiji Sekiyu Kiki ni Taioshite [Record of the Shipbuilding Depression: Coping with the First Oil Shock]*. Tokyo: Nihon Zosen Shinko Zaidan.

Niida, Hiroshi and Akira Ono, eds. (1969). *Nihon no Sangyo Soshiki [Japan's Industrial Organization]*. Tokyo: Iwanmai Shoten.

Nomura Sogo Kenkyusho [Nomura Research Institute] (1983). *Wagakuni Yushutsunyu Kozo no Tokushoku to Boeki Masatsu ni kansuru Chosa [A Study of Salient Features of the Structure of Japanese Exports and Imports and Trade Frictions]*. Tokyo: Nomura Sogo Kenkyusho.

Odaka, Konosuke (1978). "Shitaukesei Kikai Kogyo Ron Josetsu" ["Some Observations on the Role of Subcontracting Firms in the Development of Machinery Industry"], *Keizai Kenkyu*, 29 (July), 243–250.

Odaka, Konosuke (1983). "Jidosha Buhin Kogyo no Hatten to Teitai" ["The Growth and Stagnation of the Automobile Components Industry"], *Keizai Kenkyu*, 34 (October), 337–359.

OECD (1965). *Industrial Research Associations in France, Belgium and Germany*. Paris: OECD.

——— (1967). *Enquiry into the Regulations and Conditions Covering Certain International Capital Movements in Japan*. Paris: OECD.

——— (1971). *The Industrial Policies of 14 Member Countries*. Paris: OECD.

——— (1972). *The Industrial Policy of Japan*. Paris: OECD.

——— (1975). *Adjustment for Trade: Studies on Industrial Adjustment Problems and Policies*. Paris: OECD.

——— (1976). *Measures of Assistance to Shipbuilding*. Paris: OECD.

——— (1978). *Selected Industrial Policy Instruments: Objectives and Scope*. Paris: OECD.

——— (1981). *International Investment and Multinational Enterprises: Recent International Investment Trends*. Paris: OECD.

——— (1982). *Long-Term Perspectives of the World Automobile Industry*. Paris: OECD.

——— (1983a). *Transparency for Positive Adjustment: Identification and Evaluating Government Intervention*. Paris: OECD.

——— (1983b). *Positive Adjustment Policies: Managing Structural Change*. Paris: OECD.

——— (1983c). *Long-Term Perspectives of the World Automobile Industry*. Paris: OECD.

Office of Technology Assessment (1981). "U.S. Industrial Competitiveness, A Comparison of Steel, Electronics, and Automobiles," July.

Ogura, Seiritsu and Naoyuki Yoshino (1985). "Tokubetsu Shokyaku, Zaisei Toyushi to Nihon no Sangyo Kozo" ["Impacts of Accelerated Depreciation and Government Loan Programs on Japanese Industrial Structure"], *Keizai Kenkyu*, 36 (April), 110–120.

Ohkawa, K. and H. Rosovsky (1973). *Japanese Economic Growth*. Stanford: Stanford Univ. Press.

Ohkita, Saburo (1961). *Kokumin Shotoku Baizou Keikaku no Kaisetsu [Exposition of the National Income Doubling Plan]*. Tokyo: Nihon Keizai Shinbun Sha.

Ohlin, G. (1975). "Adjustment Assistance in Sweden," in OECD.

Ohno, Taiichi (1978). *Toyota Seisan Hoshiki [Toyota Production Method]*. Tokyo: Diamond Publishing Co.

Ohtake, Hideo (1979). *Gendai Nihon no Seiji Kenryoku, Keizai Kenryoku [Political Power and Economic Power in Contemporary Japan]*. Tokyo: San'ichi Shobo.

Ohyama, Michihiro (1982). "Gekika suru Kokusai Boeki Masatsu" ["Intensifying Trade Frictions"]. *Kikan Gendai Keizai*, No. 48 (Summer), 6–20.

Ojimi, Yoshihisa (1972). "Basic Philosophy and Objectives of Japanese Industrial Policy," in OECD, 11–31.

Oka, Shigeo (1964). *Sengo Nihon no Kanzei Seisaku [Postwar Japanese Tariff Policy]*. Tokyo: Nippon Hyoron Sha.

Okumura, Hiroshi (1976). *Nihon no Rokudai Kigyo Shudan [Big Six Business Groups of Japan]*. Tokyo: Diamond Publishing Co.

Okuno, Masahiro (1984). "Scale Economies, Oligopolistic Competition and Effects of Industrial Policies," mimeo.

Okuno, M., A. Postlewaite, and J. Roberts (1980). "Oligopoly and Competition in Large Markets," *American Economic Review*, 70 (March), 22–31.

Okurasho [Ministry of Finance], "Shuyo Sangyo ni okeru Toshi Koka no Bunseki" ["Analysis of Impacts of Investment in Major Industries"], *Zaisei Kin'yu Tokei Geppo*, No. 53.

———, Zaiseishi Shitsu [Office of Fiscal History Study] (1976, 1981, 1982). *Showa Zaisei Shi—Shusen kara Kowa made [Showa History of Public Finance, From War's End to Peace Treaty]*. Tokyo: Toyo Keizai Shinpo Sha, vol. 3 (1976), vol. 17 (1981), and vol. 18 (1982).

Osborne, D. K. (1976). "Cartel Problems," *American Economic Review*, 66 (December), 835–844.

PACTAD (1973). *Structural Adjustments in Asian-Pacific Trade*, 2 vols, ed. by K. Kojima, The Fifth PACTAD Report. Tokyo: Japan Economic Research Center.

Patrick, H. (1983). "Japanese Industrial Policy and Its Relevance for United States Industrial Policy," prepared statement before the Joint Economic Committee, U.S. Congress, July 13.

Peck, M. J. and A. Goto (1981). "Technology and Economic Growth: The Case of Japan," *Research Policy*, 10, 222–243.

Peck, M. J. and S. Tamura (1976), "Technology," H. Patrick and H. Rosovsky (1976), 525–585.

Penrose, E. T. (1959). *The Theory of the Growth of the Firm*. Oxford: Basil Blackwell.

Rodosho Koyo Seisaku Ka [Employment Policy Division, Ministry] (1983a). "Tokutei Fukyo Gyoshu Rishokusha no Saishushoku to no Jittai" ["State of Reemployment etc. of Those Laid Off Workers in Specified Depressed Industries"], *Shokugyo Antei Koho [Bulletin of Employment Security]*, vol. 34, no. 18.

——— (1983b). "Fukyo Gyoshu, Chiiki Koyo Antei Ho no Gaiyo" ["Summary of the Depressed Industry-Region Employment Security Law"], *Shokugyo Antei Koho [Bulletin of Employment Security]*, vol. 34, no. 18.

Sachs, J. (1981). "The Current Account and Macroeconomic Adjustment in the 1970s," *Brookings Papers on Economic Activity*, 201–282.

Sachs, J. and D. Lipton (1981). "The Supply Approach to Oil Shocks and the Slowdown in Japanese Economic Growth," Japanese translation in *Shukan Toyo Keizai Rinji Zokan*, No. 57 (July 10), 124–135.

Sahal, D. (1981). *Patterns of Technological Innovation*. Reading, MA: Addison-Wesley.

Sahal, D. (1983). "Invention, Innovation and Economic Evolution," *Technological Forecasting and Social Change*.

Sakakibara, Kinoyori (1983). "From Imitation to Innovation: The Very Large Scale Integrated

(VLSI) Semiconductor Project in Japan,'' Working Paper, MIT Sloan School of Management.

Sangyo Kenkyu Jo (1979). *Sengo Wagakuni Kogyo no Choki Doko Bunseki [Long-Term Trends of Postwar Japanese Manufacturing]*, March 1979.

Sangyo Kozo Chosa Kai [Industrial Structure Advisory Committee] (1963). "Toshin—Sangyo Kozo Seisaku no Hoko to Kadai'' ["Report on Direction and Tasks of Industrial Structure Policy"], November 29.

———— (1964). *Nihon no Sangyo Kozo [Japan's Industrial Structure]*. 5 vols. Tokyo: Tsusho Sangyo Kenkyusha.

Sangyo Seisaku Kenkyu Gruupu (1984). "Nihon no Sangyo Seisaku'' ["Industrial Policy in Japan"], *Nihon Keizai Shinbun*, October–November.

Sato, Yoshio (1976). *Kasen Taisei to Chusho Kigyo [Oligopoly System and Small Business]*. Tokyo: Yuhikaku.

Sato, Yoshio (1983). "Shitaukesei'' ["Subcontracting System"], in Uekusa (1983).

Scherer, F. M. (1980). *Industrial Market Structure and Economic Performance*, 2nd ed. Chicago: Rand McNally.

Schumpeter, J. A. (1942). *Capitalism, Socialism and Democracy*. London: Allen & Unwin.

Sekiguchi, Sueo (1975). "Industrial Adjustment Policies in Japan (1),'' in OECD (1975).

Sekiguchi, Sueo, and Toshihiro Horiuchi (1981). "Foreign Trade and Industrial Policies, A Review of Japanese Experiences," Discussion Paper No. 46, Japan Economic Research Center.

Semiconductor Industry Association (1983). "The Effect of Government Targeting on World Semiconductor Competition: A Case History of Japanese Industrial Strategy and Its Costs for America."

Senoo, Akira, ed. (1983). *Gendai Nihon no Sangyo Shuchu, 1971–1980 [Industrial Concentration of Japan, 1971–80]*, Tokyo: Nihon Keizai Shinbun Sha.

Shelling, T. C. (1956). "An Essay on Bargaining,'' *American Economic Review*, 46 (June), 281–306.

Shigen Enerugi Cho [Agency of Natural Resources and Energy, MITI] (1980a). *Santan Chiiki Shinko Taisaku no Gaiyo [Outline of Promotion Measures Taken in Coal Mining Areas]*. Tokyo: Shigen Enerugi Cho.

———— (1980b). *Santan Chiiki no Genjo [Present State of Coal Mining Areas]*. Tokyo: Shigen Enerugi Cho.

Shimomura, Osamu (1971). *Keizai Taikoku Nihon no Sentaku [Options for Japan the Economic Superpower]*. Tokyo: Toyo Keizai Shinpo Sha.

Shin Nippon Seitetsu [Nippon Steel Corporation] (1970). *Soshu Eigyo Junpo 2—Shikyo Hen II [Ten-Day Report on Operations 2—Market Conditions II]*. Tokyo: Nippon Steel Co.

Shinohara, Miyohei (1960). "Sangyo Kozo to Toshi Haibun'' ["Industrial Structure and Investment Allocation"], *Keizai Kenkyu*, 8 (October), 314–321.

Shinohara, Miyohei (1973). "Chusho Kigyo Seisaku'' ["Small Business Policy"], Shinohara and Baba (1973), 109–124.

Shinohara, Miyohei (1976). *Sangyo Kozo Ron [Industrial Structure]*. Tokyo: Chikuma Shobo.

Shinohara, Miyohei and Masao Baba, eds. (1973). *Sangyo Seisaku [Industrial Policy]*, vol. 3 of *Gendai Sangyo Ron [Modern Industry]*. Tokyo: Chikuma Shobo.

Shinohara, Miyohei and Masao Baba, eds. (1974). Sangyo Soshiki [Industrial Organization], Vol. 2 of *Gendai Sangyo Ron [Modern Industry]*. Tokyo: Chikuma Shobo.

Shouda, Yasutoyo (1982). "Effective Rates of Protection in Japan,'' *Nihon Keizai Kenkyu*. No. 11 (March).

Spence, M. (1981). "The Learning Curve and Competition,'' *Bell Journal of Economics*, 12 (Spring), 49–70.

Spencer, B. and J. Brander (1983). "International R&D Rivalry and Industrial Strategy," *Review of Economic Studies*, 50 (October), 707–722.

Stigler, G. J. (1951). "The Division of Labor is Limited by the Extent of the Market," *Journal of Political Economy*, 59 (June), 185–193.

Stiglitz, J. E. (1981). "Potential Competition May Reduce Welfare," *American Economic Review*, 71 (May), 184–189.

Subcommittee on Trade of the Ways and Means, U.S. House of Representatives (1980). "High Technology and Japanese Industrial Policy: A Strategy for U.S. Policy Makers."

Sumitomo Kagaku [Sumitomo Chemicals] (1981). *Sumitomo Kagaku Kogyo Kabushiki Kaisha Shi [History of Sumito Chemical Company]*, Tokyo: Sumitomo Kagaku.

Suzumura, Kotaro, and Kazuharu Kiyono (1987). "Entry Barriers and Economic Welfare," *Review of Economic Studies*, 54 (January), 157–167.

Tachi, Ryuichiro et al. (1983). "Koteki Kin'yu to Minkan Kin'yu no Arikata ni tsuite" ["What Public Financing and Private Financing Ought to Be"], *Kin'yu (Zenkoku Ginko Kyokai Rengo)*, No. 446 (November).

Tachi, Ryuichiro and Ryutaro Komiya (1964). *Keizai Seisaku no Riron [Theory of Economic Policy]*. Tokyo: Keiso Shobo.

Tachi, Ryuichiro, Ryutaro Komiya, and Hiroshi Niida (1964). *Nihon no Bukka Mondai [Price Problems of Japan]*. Tokyo: Toyo Keizai Shinpo Sha.

Tajima, Toshihiro (1977). "Jidosha Sangyo Saihensei no Yukue" ["Where to the Reorganization of the Automobile Industry"], N. Namiki, ed., *Nihon no Jidosha Sangyo [Japan's Automobile Industry]*. Tokyo: Nihon Keizai Shinbun Sha.

Takacs, W. E. (1978). "The Nonequivalence of Tariffs, Import Quotas, and Voluntary Export Restraints," *Journal of International Economics*, 8 (November), 565–573.

Takashima, Tadashi (1976). "Konpyuta" [Computer]. Kumagai, 1–73.

Takashima, Tadashi (1981). "Wagakuni Konpyuta Sangyo no Hatten to Gijutsu Kakushin" ["Development and Technological Innovation of Japan's Computer Industry"], *Keizai Hendo to Gijutsu Kakushin [Economic Change and Technological Innovation]*. Tokyo: Zeimu Keiri Kyokai, 1981.

Takeuchi, Hiroshi (1973). *Gendai no Sangyo, Denki Kikai Kogyo [Modern Industry: Electrical Machinery Industry]*, rev. ed. Tokyo: Toyo Keizai Shinpo Sha.

Tanabe, Toshihiko, ed. (1983). *Zusetsu, Nihon no Sangyo [Japanese Industry Illustrated]*. Tokyo: Zaisei Shoho Sha.

Tanaka, Naoki (1980). "Sangyo Seisaku no Minaoshi to Gyosei Kaikaku" ["Reexamination of Industrial Policy and Administrative Reform" *Keizai Hyoron*, November.

Tekko Shinbun Sha, ed. (1975). "Sengo Nihon Tekkogyo no Ayumi (Saikin 20-nen Shoshi)" ["Short History of Latest 20 Years of the Iron and Steel Industry"], *Tekko Nenkan [Yearbook of Iron and Steel]*, 1974 ed. Tokyo: Tekko Shinbun Sha.

Terleckyj, N. E. (1974). "Effects of R&D on the Productivity Growth of Industries: An Exploratory Study," National Planning Association (Washington, D.C.).

Tokunaga, Hisatsugu (1967). "Jishu Chosei o Saikento subeshi" ["We Ought to Reexamine Self-Coordination"], *Shukan Toyo Keizai*, July 22.

Toyo Keizai (1968). *Shukan Toyo Keizai Rinji Zokan*, Special Issue on Business Mergers, July 3.

Toyota Jidosha Kogyo [Toyota Motors] (1958). *Toyota Jidosha Kogyo 20-nen Shi [20-Year History of Toyota Motors]*. Nagoya: Toyota Jidosha Kogyo.

——— (1967). *Toyota Jidosha 30-nen Shi [30-Year History of Toyota Motors]*. Nagoya: Toyota Jidosha Kogyo.

Trezise, P. H. (1983). "Industrial Policy is Not the Major Reason for Japan's Success," *The Brookings Review*, 1 (Spring), 13–18.

Trilateral Commission (1981). *Task Force Reports*, 15–19. New York: New York Univ. Press.

Tripartite Economist Meeting (1973). *World Trade and Domestic Adjustment*. Washington, D.C.: The Brookings Institution.

Tsuruta, Toshimasa (1976). "Jiyuka Taisaku no Konran" ["Confusions in Liberalization Measures"], H. Arisawa, ed., *Showa Keizai Shi [Showa Economic History]*. Tokyo: Nihon Keizai Shinbun Sha.

Tsuruta, Toshimasa (1978–79). "Chusho Kigyo Karuteru ni kansuru Jissho Kenkyu" ["An Empirical Study of Small-Business Cartels"], *Kokumin Keizai* (Kokumin keizai Kenkyu Kyokai), No. 139–140.

Tsuruta, Toshimasa (1982). *Sengo Nihon no Sangyo Seisaku [Postwar Industrial Policy of Japan]*. Tokyo: Nihon Keizai Shinbun Sha.

Tsusansho (abbreviation of Tsusho Sangyo Sho [Ministry of International Trade and Industry]) (1949). *Tsusan Hakusho [White Paper on International Trade]*, 1949 edition. Tokyo: Government Printing Office.

——— (1957). *Sangyo Gorika Hakusho [White Paper on Industrial Rationalization]*. Tokyo: Nikkan Kogyo Shinbun Sha.

——— (1964). *Tsusan Hakusho [White Paper on International Trade]*, 1964 ed. Tokyo: Government Printing Office.

——— (1969). *Tsusho Sangyo Sho 20-nen Shi [20-Year History of the Ministry of International Trade and Industry]*. Tokyo: Tsusho Sangyo Chosakai.

——— (1972). *Shoko Seisakushi [History of Industry and Commerce Policy]*, vol. 10, *Sangyo Gorika 2 [Industrial Rationalization 2]*. Tokyo: Tsusho Sangyo Chosakai.

——— (1975). *Tsusho Sangyo Gyosei Shihanseiki no Ayumi [A Quarter Century of MITI Administration]*. Tokyo: Tsusho Sangyo Chosakai.

——— (1979). *Tsusho Sangyo Sho 30-nen Shi [30-Year History of the Ministry of International Trade and Industry]*. Tokyo: Tsusho Sangyo Chosakai.

——— (1980). *Nihon no Boeki Seisaku [Trade Policy of Japan]*. Tokyo.

——— (1982). *Tsusho Hakusho [White Paper on International Trade]*, 1982 ed. Tokyo: Government Printing Office.

———, Jukogyo Kyoku [Heavy Industry Bureau] (1956). *Kikai Kogyo Shinko no Hoto [Ways to Promote Machine Industry]*. Tokyo: Tsusho Sangyo Chosakai.

———, ——— (1971). *70-nendai no Denshi Kikai Kogyo—Kidenho no Kaisetsu [Electronics and Machinery Industries in the 1970s, Notes on the Electronics and Machinery Industries Law]*. Tokyo: Tsusho Sangyo Chosakai.

———, Kigyo Kyoku [Enterprise Bureau] (1952). *Kigyo Gorika no Sho Mondai [Problems of Enterprise Rationalization]*. Tokyo: Sangyo Kagaku Kyokai.

———, ——— (1970). *Kigyo Gappei no Bunseki [An Analysis of Business Mergers]*. Tokyo: Government Printing Office.

———, Kikai Joho Sangyo Kyoku [Machinery and Information Industries Bureau] (1979). *Kijoho no Kaisetsu [Notes on the Machinery and Information Industries Law]*. Tokyo: Tsusho Sangyo Chosakai.

———, Sabisu Sangyo Kenkyukai [Service Industry Study Group], ed. (1979). *Sabisu Sangyo no Genjo to Kadai [Present State and Problems of Service Industries]*. Tokyo: Tsusan Seisaku Koho Sha.

———, Sangyo Kozo Shingikai [Industry Structure Council] (1971). *70-nendai no Tsusho Sangyo Seisaku [MITI Policy for the 1970s]*. Tokyo: MITI.

———, ——— (1974). *Sangyo Kozo no Choki Bijon [Long-Term Vision of Industrial Structure]*. Tokyo: MITI.

———, ——— (1980). *80-nendai no Tsusho Sangyo Seisaku Bijon [Vision for MITI Policy for the 1980s]*. Tokyo: Tsusho Sangyo Chosakai.

————, Sangyo Seisaku Kyoku [Industrial Policy Bureau] (1978). *Kozo Fukyo Ho no Kaisetsu [Notes on the Structurally Depressed Industries Law]*. Tokyo: Tsusho Sangyo Chosakai.

————, Seikatsu Sangyo Kyoku [Consumer Goods Industries Bureau] and Sen'i Kogyo Kozo Kaizen Jigyo Kyokai [Textile Industry Rationalization Agency], eds. (1977). *Atarashii Sen'i Sangyo no Arikata [What the New Textile Industry Ought to Be]*. Tokyo: Tsusho Sangyo Chosakai.

Tsusho Sangyo Gyosei Kenkyukai [MITI Administration Study Group] (1983). *Gendai Gyosei Zenshu, Tsusho Sangyo (1) (2) [Contemporary Administration:* MITI (1) (2)]. Tokyo: Gyosei.

Tsusho Tokei Kyokai [MITI Statistics Association] (1982). *Sengo no Kogyo Tokei Hyo [Postwar Census of Manufactures]*, vol. 2. Tokyo: Tsuho Tokei Kyokai.

Uekusa, Masu (1978). "Haigasu Kisei Taisaku Sha no Kaihatsu oyobi Seisan no Kosuto" ["Development and Production Costs of Gas Emission Control Cars"], December.

Uekusa, Masu (1982). *Sangyo Soshiki Ron [Theory of Industrial Organization]*. Tokyo: Chikuma Shobo.

Uekusa, Masu, ed. (1983). *Nihon Sangyo no Seidoteki Tokucho to Boeki Masatsu [Institutional Characteristics of Japanese Industry and Trade Frictions]*. Tokyo: Sekai keizai Kenkyu Kyokai.

Uekusa, Masu and Tsuruhiko Nanbu (1973). "Gosei Sen'i" ["Synthetic Fibers"]. in Kumagai (1973b), 149–218.

Ueno, Hiroya (1978). *Nihon no Keizai Seido [Economic Institutions of Japan]*. Tokyo: Nihon Keizai Shinbun Sha.

Ueno, Hiroya (1980). "The Conception and Evaluation of Japanese Industrial Policy" K. Sato, ed., *Industry and Business in Japan*. Armonk, NY: M. E. Sharpe, 375–434.

Ueno, Hiroya, and Hiromichi Mutoh (1973). "Jidosha Sangyo" ["Automobile Industry"], in Kumagai (1973a), 119–181.

Uno, K. (1983). "Input–Output Tables in Japan, 1951–80," Statistical Data Bank Project, Institute of Socio-economic Planning, Univ. of Tsukuba.

U.S. Department of Commerce (1972). *Japan: The Government-Business Relationship, A Guide for the American Businessman*. Washington, D.C.: Government Printing Office.

———— (1983a). *Japanese Industrial Policies and the Development of High-Technology Industries: Computers and Aircraft*, prepared by International Trade Administration, Department of Commerce, February.

———— (1983b). *An Assessment of U.S. Competitiveness in High Technology Industries*, prepared by International Trade Administration, Department of Commerce, February.

U.S. Department of Transportation (1981). "The U.S. Automobile Industry, 1980: Report to the President from the Secretary of Transportation," July.

U.S. Federal Trade Commission (1977). "The United States Steel Industry and its International Rivals: Trends and Facts Determining International Competitiveness," FTC Staff Report, Bureau of Economics, Washington, D.C.: Government Printing Office.

U.S. International Trade Commission (1983). "Foreign Industrial Targeting and Its Effects on U.S. Industries, Phase I: Japan," Report to the Subcommittee on Trade, Committee on Ways and Means, U.S. House of Representatives on Investigation No. 332-162. USITC Publication 1437.

Vernon, R. (1966). "International Investment and International Trade in the Product Cycle," *Quarterly Journal of Economics*, 80 (May), 190–207.

von Weizsäcker, C. C. (1980a). "A Welfare Analysis of Barriers to Entry," *Bell Journal of Economics*, 11 (Autumn), 399–420.

von Weizsäcker, C. C. (1980b). *Barriers to Entry: A Theoretical Treatment*. Berlin: Springer Verlag.

Watanabe, Fukutaro (1969). "Sangyo Kozo to Kanzei Taikei" ["Industrial Structure and Tariff System"], Niida and Ono, 28–48.

WEFA (Wharton Econometric Forecasting Associates) (1983). *Impact of Local Content Legislation on U.S. and World Economies*.

Weitzman, M. L., W. Newey, and M. Rabin (1981). "Sequential R&D Strategy for Synfuels," *Bell Journal of Economics*, 12 (Autumn), 574–590.

Wheeler, J. W., M. E. Janow, and T. Pepper (1982). *Japanese Industrial Development Policies in the 1980s: Implications for U.S. Trade and Investment*, Hudson Institute Research Report HI-3470-RR. New York: Hudson Institute.

Williamson, J. (1983). *The Open Economy and the World Economy*. New York: Basic Books.

Williamson, O. (1975). Markets and Hierarchies: Analysis and Antitrust Implications. New York: Free Press.

Yamamura, Kozo (1986). "Joint Research and Antitrust: Japanese vs. American Strategies," Hugh Patrick, ed., *Japan's High Technology Industries: Lessons and Limitations of Industrial Policy*. Seattle: Univ. of Washington Press, 171–209.

Yamashita, Kunio (1977). "Chusho Kigyo Kin'yu no Hoko to Seisaku" ["Direction and Policy of Small Business Finance"], Seiichi Kato et al., *Keizai Seisaku to Chusho Kigyo [Economic Policy and Small Business]*. Tokyo: Doyukan.

Yamawaki, Hideki (1977). "Tekkogyo ni okeru Kakaku Kettei Kodo Henka" ["Changes in Price-Setting Behavior in the Iron and Steel Industry"], *ESP*, June.

Yamawaki, H. (1984). "Market Structure, Capacity Expansion and Pricing: A Model Applied to the Japanese Iron and Steel Industry," *International Journal of Industrial Organization*, 2 (March), 29–62.

Yamazawa, Ippei (1967). "Kanzei Kozo to Sangyo Hogo" ["Tariff Structure and Industrial Protection"], *Sekai Keizai Hyoron*, June.

Yamazawa, I. (1980). "Increasing Imports and Structural Adjustment of the Japanese Textile Industry," *The Developing Economies*, 8.

Yamazawa, I. (1981a). "Trade and Industrial Adjustment in the Asia-Pacific Region," H. Kitamura, I. Yamazawa and Y. Eguchi, *Prospects for Closer Economic Cooperation in the Asia-Pacific Area*. Tokyo: The Asian Club.

Yamazawa, Ippei (1981b). "Sen'i Sangyo no Kozo Chosei to Yunyu Seisaku" ["Structural Adjustment of the Textile Industry and Import Policy"], *Kasen Geppo [Chemical Fibers Monthly]*, No. 399 (July).

Yamazawa, I. (1983). "Renewal of Textile Industry in Developed Countries and World Textile Trade," *Hitotsubashi Journal of Economics*, 24 (June), 25–41.

Yanagida, Kunio (1981). *Nihon no Gyakuten shita Hi [The Day Japan Caught Up]*. Tokyo: Kodansha.

Yanagida, Kunio (1983). *Nihon wa Moete iruka [Is Japan Burning?]*. Tokyo: Bungei Shunju Sha.

Yasuba, Yasukichi (1970). "Yen Kiriage to Bukka" ["Revaluation of the Yen and Prices"], *Boeki to Kanzei [Trade and Tariffs]*, June.

Yonekura, Seiichiro (1983). "Sengo Nihon Tekkogyo ni okeru Kawasaki Seitetsu no Kakushinsei" ["Innovative Behavior of Kawasaki Steel in Post-War Japanese Industry"], *Hitotsubashi Ronso*, 90 (March), 69–92.

Yonezawa, Y. (1979). "The System of Industrial Adjustment Policies for Trade in Japan," Discussion Paper No. 35, Japan Economic Research Center, December.

Yonezawa, Y. (1980). "Adjustment in Japanese Shipbuilding Industry and Government Shipbuilding Policy," Discussion Paper No. 37, Japan Economic Research Center, January.

Yonezawa, Yoshie (1981). "Sen'i Sangyo Chosei Mondai to Sen'i Seisaku" ["Adjustment

Problems of the Textile Industry and Textile Policy], *Kasen Geppo [Chemical Fibers Monthly]*, No. 399 (July).

Yoshitomi, Masaru (1977). *Gendai Nihon Keizai Ron [Contemporary Japanese Economy]*. Tokyo: Toyo Keizai Shinpo Sha.

Yoshitomi, Masaru (1981). *Nihon Keizai—Sekai Keizai no Arata na Kiki to Nihon [Japanese Economy: A New Crisis of the World Economy and Japan]*. Tokyo: Toyo Keizai Shinpo Sha.

Young, A. A. (1928). "Increasing Returns and Economic Progress," *Economic Journal*, 38 (December), 327–542.

Zeisei Chosakai [Tax System Council] (1963, 1972). *Zeisei Chosakai Kankei Shiryo Shu [Reference Materials Concerning Tax System Council]*. Tokyo: Tax System Council.

Author Index

Subject Index